THE OVERSEER STATE

In this compelling work, Sascha Auerbach offers a bold new historical interpretation of late-stage slavery, its long-term legacies and its entanglement with the development of the modern state. In the wake of abolition, from the Caribbean to southern Africa to Southeast Asia, a fusion of government authority and private industry replaced the iron chains of slavery with equally powerful fetters of law and regulation. This "overseer state" helped move, often through deceptive and coercive methods, millions of Indian and Chinese indentured laborers across Britain's imperial possessions. With a perspective that ranges from Parliament to the plantation, the book brings to light the fascinating and terrifying history of the world's first truly global labor system, those who struggled under its heavy yoke and the bitter legacies left in its wake.

SASCHA AUERBACH is an associate professor of history at the University of Nottingham and a former Fulbright Scholar and Leverhulme Trust Fellow. He is the author of *Armed with Sword and Scales* (2022) and *Race, Law and "the Chinese Puzzle" in Imperial Britain* (2009).

Critical Perspectives on Empire

Critical Perspectives on Empire is a major series of ambitious, cross-disciplinary works in the emerging field of critical imperial studies. Books in the series explore the connections, exchanges and mediations at the heart of national and global histories, the contributions of local as well as metropolitan knowledge, and the flows of people, ideas and identities facilitated by colonial contact. To that end, the series not only offers a space for outstanding scholars working at the intersection of several disciplines to bring to wider attention the impact of their work; it also takes a leading role in reconfiguring contemporary historical and critical knowledge, of the past and of ourselves.

A full list of titles published in the series can be found at:
www.cambridge.org/cpempire

THE OVERSEER STATE

Slavery, Indenture and Governance in the British Empire, 1812–1916

SASCHA AUERBACH
University of Nottingham

CAMBRIDGE
UNIVERSITY PRESS

CAMBRIDGE
UNIVERSITY PRESS

Shaftesbury Road, Cambridge CB2 8EA, United Kingdom

One Liberty Plaza, 20th Floor, New York, NY 10006, USA

477 Williamstown Road, Port Melbourne, VIC 3207, Australia

314–321, 3rd Floor, Plot 3, Splendor Forum, Jasola District Centre,
New Delhi – 110025, India

103 Penang Road, #05–06/07, Visioncrest Commercial, Singapore 238467

Cambridge University Press is part of Cambridge University Press & Assessment,
a department of the University of Cambridge.

We share the University's mission to contribute to society through the pursuit of
education, learning and research at the highest international levels of excellence.

www.cambridge.org
Information on this title: www.cambridge.org/9781009315791

DOI: 10.1017/9781009315777

When citing this work, please include a reference to the DOI 10.1017/9781009315777

First published 2025

A catalogue record for this publication is available from the British Library.

Library of Congress Cataloging-in-Publication Data
Names: Auerbach, Sascha, author.
Title: The overseer state : slavery, indenture and governance in the British Empire,
1812–1916 / Sascha Auerbach.
Description: Cambridge, United Kingdom ; New York, NY: Cambridge University Press,
2024. | Series: Critical perspectives on empire | Includes bibliographical references and index.
Identifiers: LCCN 2024019835 | ISBN 9781009315791 (hardback) | ISBN 9781009315760
(paperback) | ISBN 9781009315777 (ebook)
Subjects: LCSH: Forced labor – Great Britain – Colonies – History – 19th century. |
Indentured servants – Great Britain – Colonies – History – 19th century. | Slavery – Great
Britain – Colonies – History – 19th century. | Labor policy – Great Britain – Colonies –
History – 19th century. | Great Britain – Colonies – Histor – 19th century.
Classification: LCC HD4875.G7 A94 2024 | DDC 331.11/730941–dc23/eng/20240627
LC record available at https://lccn.loc.gov/2024019835

ISBN 978-1-009-31579-1 Hardback

For my dearest *gufo*, MC Hannah Richter, RB.
Before you, "I was lonely as a tunnel. The birds flew from me. And night invaded me with her powerful army."

The magistrate must keep court here and give us our rights.

—Attributed to an indentured Indian worker of plantation Devonshire Castle, Essequibo, British Guiana, shortly before five of his colleagues were shot to death by police constables (testimony of Madaree, court interpreter, October 10, 1872)

CONTENTS

MAPS AND TABLES

Maps

Tables

PLANTATIONS

Annandale	Demerara (see Chapter 2)
Anna Regina	Essequibo (see Chapter 3)
Belle Alliance	Essequibo (see Chapter 3)
Better Hope	Demerara (see Chapter 2)
Devonshire Castle	Essequibo (see Chapter 5)
Friends	Berbice (see Chapter 2)
La Belle Alliance	Demerara (see Chapter 2)
La Penitence	Demerara (see Chapter 2)
Leonora	Demerara (see Chapters 5 and 7)
L'Espérance	Berbice (see Chapter 2)
New Forest	Berbice (see Chapter 2)
Plegt Ankar	Berbice (see Chapter 2)
Portushope	Demerara (see Chapter 1)
Profit	Demerara (see Chapter 2)
Prospect	Demerara (see Chapter 2)
Resolution	Berbice (see Chapter 2)
Rose Hall	Berbice (see Chapter 5)
Scotland	Berbice (see Chapter 2)

Malaysia

Prye Estates	Penang (see Chapter 6)

PREFACE

More than a few friends and colleagues have commented on how rapidly this book was produced. I wish I could make claims to such efficient productivity, but it has been more than a decade in the making. Its completion was possible only due to the continued vibrancy of the global network of historians who soldier on in the face of declining enthusiasm for humanities research in both government and university administrations. Those who insist that only research of immediate and concrete practical impact should be supported would be wise to heed the words of Oscar Wilde that "we can forgive a man for making a useful thing as long as he does not admire it." We must counter, even more forcefully, the insistence by prominent figures in the UK and the US that engagement with the national past can only be celebratory. Strongest of all must be our adamant rejection of the persistent delusion that, in the words of former Tory Home Secretary Suella Braverman, "the defining feature of [the UK's] relationship with slavery is not that we practiced it, but that we led the way in abolishing it."[1] Given that Great Britain enthusiastically supported slavery and the slave trade for more than two centuries, and that its legacies remain present in our economy, culture and society two centuries after its abolition, this is not a matter of drawing lines in a politically expedient culture war, but merely a question of doing good history. Neither the archival record nor math have any inherent ideology. Abolition and emancipation, as I hope *The Overseer State* demonstrates, may have ended one system of racialized labor exploitation, but they also signaled the beginning of another in which the British government was even more thoroughly entangled and for which it must be held even more accountable by posterity. The history of both of those systems, enslavement and indenture, continues to haunt the world today. The effort to explore and understand them, and all who suffered under their yoke, is work that is both useful and necessary, whether or not one admires it.

[1] David Wilcock , *"Suella Braverman Says White People Should Not Feel 'Collective Guilt' over Slavery as Maneuvering Home Secretary Uses Speech to Challenge Rishi Sunak on Immigration – and Jokes Keir Starmer Could Be the First 'Female Prime Minister,'" Mail Online, May 15,* 2023. https://bit.ly/3Tz7dsX.

ACKNOWLEDGMENTS

Coming to the end of my third book project, I am reminded more than ever of the immense debt owed to the tireless work of my colleagues around the globe, and to the generations of our predecessors who paved the way for the scholarship we conduct today. What has struck me especially in recent years is how often the most insightful and productive historians are also the most self-effacing and most willing to offer their assistance with no expectation of recompense. It is to them that I offer my most profound gratitude for their intellectual generosity and for continuing to advance our knowledge of the human past, one hopeful record request at a time.

Global in scope as this work was, it was made possible only by support from a variety of sources. These include the Canadian Social Sciences and Humanities Research Council, the Leverhulme Trust, the University of Nottingham, the University of Northern British Columbia, King's College London, University College London (UCL) and the National University of Singapore (NUS). The initial stages of the work were funded by a Fulbright fellowship from the US–UK Fulbright Commission. Support from the Isaac Menessah Meyer Fellowship at NUS and from UCL's Institute for Advanced Studies allowed its continuance. The book was completed under the auspices of a Leverhulme Trust Research Fellowship.

The archival research was conducted with the aid of the excellent staff at the National Archives of Mauritius, the National Archives of Malaysia, the National Archives of Trinidad and the National Library and National Archives of Singapore. I imagine that my requests for information on labor statistics one moment and gambling prosecutions the next caused some confusion, and I appreciate your patience throughout. The staff at the University of Nottingham libraries have provided invaluable assistance to my work for over a decade now, and the staff at the British Library and the National Archives for twice that span. I may have cut the fabric and sewn the suit, but it was the kind professionals in all of these institutions, many of whom are formidable scholars in their own right, who provided the cloth. A number of different venues generously (and, no doubt, to their eternal regret) offered forums for presentation of the work-in-progress. These included Cambridge University, Columbia University, the University of Dundee, the NUS, the

University of Sydney, the Institute of Historical Research (London), the International Islamic University of Malaysia, Leeds University, Nottingham University, the University of Warsaw, the Wissenchaftskolleg zu Berlin (Institute for Advanced Study), UCL's Institute of Advanced Studies (several times), the University of Melbourne, McMaster University and the University of North Carolina – Chapel Hill (also more than once, thank you!).

This is the second time that I have had the pleasure to work with the editors and staff at Cambridge University Press, and I cannot thank them enough for their courtesy, dedication and professionalism. Michael Watson and the external referees offered invaluable advice. Mathilde Grimaldi, as always, did terrific work on the maps. Throughout the project, I also had the chance to collaborate once again with Cecelia Cancellero on our new book series, "The Histories of Slavery and its Global Legacies," cofounded with Juanita de Barros. Lori Hearford and Geethanjali Rangaraj were aces during the final processes of proof-reading, editing, and typesetting. Although this volume was not published under its auspices, the conversations with them and with the potential authors for it were a constant source of inspiration and insight.

My colleagues in the profession, at Nottingham and elsewhere, were always willing to help, advise and encourage. Special thanks to Ana Lucia Araujo, Joerg Arnold, Nick Baron, Dean Blackburn, Antoinette Burton, Porscha Fermanis, Catherine Hall, David Lambert, David Laven, Lynn Hollen Lees, Andrea Major, Amanda Nettelbeck, and Susan Pennybacker for their excellent professional counsel and support. Conversations with the three PhD students whom I helped supervise to completion during the course of this project – Matthew Kidd, Freddie Stephenson, and Liz Egan – were always enlightening for me, if not necessarily for them. My friends, even those that are not (luckily) academics, had to endure endless discussions of the project, which they always bore with good humor and, astonishingly, repaid with more substantive fare. I am especially grateful to Cennydd Bowles, Colin Burns, Carl Collins, Mark Condos, Paul Deslandes, Aaron Fichtelberg, and Anna Greenwood. The hoops crews at Seymour Place and the Kensington Leisure Centre did their part, usually by providing camaraderie and a welcome break from my labors, and occasionally by injuring me so severely that I could do nothing *except* sit at my desk and write. The extended Auerbach-Crosby clan in Los Angeles, New York and Gil also contributed by repeatedly asking what I was writing now, and admirably feigning interest in my response. As punishment for maintaining this façade, they will now have complimentary copies of yet another book that they will be required to pretend they have read. A quiz will follow shortly. To my mother, Rita Crosby Auerbach, and my father, Norbert Theo Allen-Auerbach, although you both closed your last books some time ago, I write with you always on my mind and in my heart. What are we historians if not the keepers of memory? The memories of you I keep most dearly of all.

Did my son, George, actually aid in the production of this volume? He certainly provided a distraction, sometimes welcome, sometimes infuriating, but always amusing. He was also, in large part, the motivation. In the difficult times to come, the skills of a historian may be of little use beyond chronicling the immense challenges laid at the feet of your generation by the greed and myopia of my own. But, perhaps in some small way, charting the long history of racial injustice will help foster a more just world for you to inhabit.

Last and most, all my love and gratitude to my brilliant partner and collaborator, Dr. Hannah Richter, to whom this book is dedicated and without whom it would not have been written at all (or at least would have been substantially worse and taken exponentially longer). However many days and pages we have together, it will never be enough.

Nottingham and London, 2023

Introduction

Paper Chains for Iron Chains

> The obligations of the slave are enforced by violence . . . while the obligations of the indentured labourer, like those of the free labourer, are only to be enforced by law, and his rights he is invited and encouraged to defend.
>
> *Report of the Commissioners Appointed to Enquire into the Treatment of Immigrants in British Guiana*, British Parliamentary Papers, 1871

> To his slave workers from Africa the symbol of Massa's power was the whip, liberally applied; records exist showing that 200 lashes were not infrequent and a tremendous howl was raised by Massa when British law tried to step in and limit punishment to 39 lashes under supervision. To his contract workers from India the symbol of Massa's power was the jail. Massa's slogan was: the Indian worker is to be found either in the field or in the hospital or in jail.
>
> Eric Williams, "Massa Day Done," 1961

> In the face of today's global migration crisis, yesterday's laws are simply not fit for purpose . . . this government must act decisively. Must act with determination. Must act with compassion.
>
> Suella Braverman, Home Secretary of the UK, Speech on the Illegal Immigration Bill, March 7, 2023

The statements excerpted above offer three different views on the character of global migration and the British state's involvement in it.[1] They were offered at crucial intervals, the first a little less than seventy years after the slave trade and a little less than forty years after slavery itself were both outlawed in the British Empire;[2] the second on the eve of Jamaica and Trinidad and Tobago achieving their formal independence from Great Britain; and the third amidst what the Tory government has described as an "invasion" of migrants from Continental Europe in the wake of Brexit. The oldest, from a parliamentary commission examining the "treatment of immigrants" in British Guiana in 1871, favorably compares indenture, a system of state-regulated and state-sponsored labor

[1] The expression that forms the title for this chapter comes from Cheddi Jagan, *Forbidden Freedom. The Story of British Guiana* (1954; repr. Georgetown: Hansib, 1994), 16.
[2] C.393, vol. xx, 588.

migration, with its predecessor, slavery. In contrast to slavery, the commissioners asserted, a system enforced by violence and one that Britain had discarded a half-century previously, indenture was governed by laws that guaranteed the rights of workers against abuse. The second statement is from the pioneering Trinidadian historian Eric Williams. Williams asserted that this same labor system, far from protecting immigrant workers, had been no more than a sinister merging of the state's authority with the established power of plantation-owners. The latter remained in the exploitative and abusive position of "massa," even if they now wielded their unjust authority over indentured Indian laborers rather than over African-Caribbean slaves. In the final passage, (now former) Tory Home Secretary Suella Braverman insists that the state is morally obligated to intervene in the process of migration, and that its laws must be continually strengthened if it is to do this effectively. Taken together, these statements demonstrate both how long the state's role in overseeing migration has been a crucial issue of debate and how intensely relevant it remains today. But whereas the first two passages explicitly acknowledge this history, the final one stubbornly denies it. Global migration, Braverman implies, is a "crisis" that was not of the state's making but rather one thrust upon it and to which it must respond "decisively" and with "determination," albeit tempered with "compassion."[3] Then, as now, those who administer a system of immigration control often maintained through coercion and violence garb it in the moral camouflage of paternalism and just governance. The death of a few (thousand) unfortunates in these circumstances is regrettable but unavoidable, and hardly the fault of those only seeking to enforce eminently sensible regulations.

The anchoring of the colonial state's power in its role as the overseer of migration and labor governance, how those who fell under its authority adapted to it, and what the social, legal, economic, and cultural consequences of this were across the breadth of Britain's Crown-ruled, southern hemisphere colonies in the nineteenth century are the subjects of this book. To understand the significance of this "overseer-state," we must first recognize that the vast majority of those under the yoke of colonial rule in these regions were not of British or European descent.[4] They consisted, instead, of tens of millions of Indians, African-Caribbeans, Africans, Chinese, and an array of other peoples from the Global South. The economic value of this sprawling imperial edifice depended upon the diverse range of commodities produced and subsequently exchanged across the oceans. Among the most valuable of these, and forming key elements in Britain's continued domination of global trade, were sugar and

[3] UK Government, "Home Secretary Statement on the Illegal Immigration Bill," March 7, 2023, www.gov.uk/government/speeches/home-secretary-statement-on-the-illegal-immigration-bill.

[4] Seeley defined India, by contrast, as a mere "dependency."

tin, both of which are examined in this volume. One resource, however, far outstripped these in importance, as it constituted the necessary precursor for them and for much of the diverse range of other imperial commodities. It was the resource most closely controlled by colonial officials and most carefully scrutinized by their superiors in London. It was also the one that cost colonial governments the most, in both financial and political capital, to organize and regulate. That resource was labor.[5]

Control of labor, Indian and Chinese labor in particular, in Britain's southern hemisphere plantation and mining colonies, an archipelago that stretched from the Caribbean to South Africa to Malaysia, was not only the wellspring of the empire's trade income; it also became the keystone of colonial governance legally, politically, and culturally in the nineteenth century. The capacity for governing the working populace in these regions, in the view of colonial administrators, was both the most essential characteristic of white Britons and the most glaring inadequacy of their colonial subjects in the Caribbean, Africa, and Asia.[6] In the minds of administrators across the imperial system, the workers of the empire, much like those of Britain itself, *had* to be ruled both for the economic and social survival of the imperial system and for their own good. How this came to be so was a direct result of the kind of empire Britain sought to fashion for itself, both in structure and in ideology. The state apparatus that resulted, however, was not the product of official effort alone. It was a dynamic, adaptable, and contested entity, shaped by the ruled as well as by the rulers. And when it was formally dismantled at the beginning of the twentieth century, its apparent demise owed much to the gnawing, low-level resistance that it had prompted since its origins in late-stage slavery.

Looking through the lens of imperial labor organization, we can see that, post-1815, imperial administrators, colonial officials, and colonial landholders found themselves confronting three remarkable changes resulting from the interrelation of Britain's imperial expansion and the abolition of the slave trade in 1806–7. The majority of territory seized or otherwise acquired during the Napoleonic period lay in the tropical zones, where the primary revenue would come from either agriculture or resource extraction. In order for both the older and the newer British colonies to produce revenue, a central concern of administrators and colonial landowners alike, a significantly expanded labor force was necessary. Subsequent to 1834 and emancipation, however, the pool of available labor provided by enslaved Africans, formerly classified as

[5] For an overview of the historiography on networks (of people, capital, commodities, information, etc.) as a fundamental aspect of the British Empire, see Tony Ballantyne, "The Changing Shape of the Modern British Empire and Its Historiography," *The Historical Journal* 53, no. 2 (June 2010), 442.

[6] Jack Jin Gary Lee, "Plural Society and the Colonial State: English Law and the Making of Crown Colony Government in the Straits Settlements," *Asian Journal of Law and Society* 2 (2015), 230.

property and therefore under private control, consisted instead of Crown subjects whose status was the purview of the state. As a consequence, the colonial state apparatus, which had played a key role in maintaining the slave trade but a tertiary one in governing slave labor, became the keystone to organizing, managing, and disciplining the colonial workforce. This amplification of the state's role in labor management accompanied the rising importance of supplying and managing that labor throughout the empire. Whereas the majority of plantation agriculture in the pre-Napoleonic British Empire had taken place in the Caribbean with labor performed by enslaved Africans, the plantation–mining complex that developed in the wake of the Napoleonic Wars was global in scale. It would require close collaboration between state and private interests to meet its voracious demand for a subordinated workforce.

The intersection of rising labor demand, the conversion of a regional enslaved labor force to a global labor force of "free" Crown subjects, the perceived need (in the name of social order and moral obligation) to firmly govern that workforce, and the rapid expansion of the empire through the addition of Crown colonies in the southern hemisphere provided the impetus behind the creation of an "overseer-state."[7] This entity was composed of laws, institutions, officials, processes, and guiding concepts all focused on the governance of African, Indian, and Asian laborers across the empire. The overseer-state was, like colonialism, simultaneously a political, economic, cultural, and social project and one that shaped the relationship between these elements in colonial societies. The overseer-state did not just comprise the concrete structures of colonial labor systems, such as policies and laws, it shaped what labor meant in the colonial context; its processes were not merely expressions of state authority, they defined its limits and offered avenues for its negotiation and contestation; its operation was not only a response to wider concepts of race, it generated and disseminated them. And the complex interactions produced by the shift from private authority to state authority as the paramount overseer of labor systems affected both the concrete experiences *of* employers and laborers and their identities *as* laborers and employers, individually and collectively.

The authority of the state over the movement and activity of workers, which constituted the anchor of colonial power across Britain's archipelago of Crown-ruled, tropical plantation and mining colonies, was ubiquitous and highly asymmetrical. But it was never complete and uncontested. Colonial

[7] Here, I am using "overseer" differently from how Vijava Teelok has; he interprets the term as supervision rather than direct interference. Like Teelok, I look at how the state, much like plantation overseers, was becoming increasingly entangled in the direct control and regulation of labor in the colonies. See Vijava Teelok, *Bitter Sugar: Sugar and Slavery in 19th Century Mauritius* (Moka: Mahatma Gandhi Institute, 1998).

authority more broadly – here defined as the ability to shape both the conceptual and the concrete aspects of the relationship between racialized designations of ruler and ruled – was always uneven across the empire, and the overseer-state was no exception to this.[8] Its strength of expression was directly proportional to the perceived necessity of any given cohort's economic and social contribution as labor and inversely proportional to their perceived inclusion in the dominant schema of imperial culture. Put another way, the authority of the overseer-state was expressed with greatest force against those whose labor was considered most essential, but whose willingness to contribute that labor and respect that authority without strong state oversight was thought to be most unlikely and whose potential threat to the social, economic, and political dominance of white colonists was seen to be most severe.

This formulation of the overseer-state may, at first glance, appear to harken back to the interdependence between imperialism and capitalism articulated so prominently by J. A. Hobson and other Marxist-inflected scholars in the early twentieth century. But the assertion here is that the overseer-state's power was not harnessed solely, or even primarily, in service of economic need.[9] The mechanisms of state labor oversight deployed across the nineteenth century in Britain's plantation and mining colonies in the Caribbean, southern Africa, the Indian Ocean, and Southeast Asia, while serving the needs of employers, often as not contradicted market forces, were highly inefficient, and required vast expenditures of state capital and energy to sustain. In contradiction to the expressed principles of liberalism and free-market trade, an extensive and expensive new bureaucracy had to be erected solely for the purpose of labor management. For these new institutions and officials of colonial governance, which rapidly overtook private property-owners as the paramount authority colonial labor relations, the goal was always a particular vision of *control* and *order* more than it was economic need as defined by employers.[10] The

[8] On the unevenness of British imperial authority in the modern era, see Antoinette Burton, *The Trouble with Empire: Challenges to Modern British Imperialism* (Oxford: Oxford University Press, 2015), especially 1–23.

[9] For a recent assessment of this approach and its persistence to the present day, see Mark Harvey, "Slavery, Indenture and the Development of British Industrial Capitalism," *History Workshop Journal* 88 (Autumn 2019), 66–88. More recently, the concept of "racial capitalism," the process by which racial identity is employed (against the will of groups or individuals) as a means of deriving social and economic value, has gained popularity as a lens for viewing slavery, indenture, and other means of coerced labor extraction with racial overtones. See Nancy Leong, "Racial Capitalism," *Harvard Law Review* 126, no. 8 (June 2013), 2151–226; Jodi Melamed, "Racial Capitalism," *Critical Ethnic Studies* 1, no. 1 (Spring 2015), 76–85. For its application in the British colonial context, see Jonathan Saha, "Racial Capitalism and Peasant Insurgency in Colonial Myanmar," *History Workshop Journal* 94 (Autumn 2022), 42–60.

[10] On the long intellectual tradition, in liberal political discourse, of advocating more despotic forms of governance in the colonial context, see Uday S. Mehta, "Liberal

continued political, cultural, and social subordination of the largely non-white workforce ultimately superseded the demands of the balance sheet, even if the rising expense of governance kept the latter as an ever-present concern.

This preeminent need for a highly racialized vision of order and control, articulated explicitly by all those involved in the management of colonial labor systems from the Caribbean to Southeast Asia, had been a prominent element of plantation slavery. During its final decades, the process of reform and "amelioration" saw this need become a paramount concern of state agents and institutions.[11] To maintain a firm hold over the plantation workforce, the British colonial system in the post-Napoleonic period, ostensibly liberal in ideology, decentralized in structure, and increasingly market-based in operation, borrowed unabashedly from the centralized and statist apparatus of its Continental antecedents.[12] The shared assumption by European colonizers that maintaining stern authority over a multiracial workforce in the post-emancipation Caribbean was thoroughly embedded in broader articulations of race and colonial power. This has an important historiographical, as well as historical, dimension – the centrality of state-regulated labor control in anchoring colonial authority more broadly has, for the most part, been taken as a given in previous scholarship.[13] As a result of this enculturation of labor control across the periods of slavery, emancipation, and post-emancipation free labor, the ways in which the state itself was transformed have remained largely unexamined. So, too, has how integral were the responses of all those involved in that transformation. When studies move across this chronology

Strategies of Exclusion," in Frederick Cooper and Ann Laura Stoler, eds., *Tensions of Empire: Colonial Cultures in a Bourgeois World* (Berkeley: University of California Press, 1997), 56–86.

11 O. Nigel Bolland, "Systems of Domination after Slavery: The Control of Land and Labor in the British West Indies after 1838," *Comparative Studies in Society and History* 23, no. 4 (October 1981), 592.

12 On the circulation and sharing of regulations concerning slavery between Spain and the Americas, and between Spanish, French, and British colonies in the latter, see Alejandro de la Fuente and Ariela J. Gross, *Becoming Free, Becoming Black: Race, Freedom, and Law in Cuba, Virginia, and Louisiana* (Cambridge: Cambridge University Press, 2020), 18.

13 In this, such studies have followed the precedent set by the two most influential works on emancipation and indenture in the British imperial context, Thomas Holt's *The Problem of Freedom: Race, Labor, and Politics in Jamaica and Britain, 1832–1938* (Baltimore, MD: Johns Hopkins University Press, 1992) and Hugh Tinker's, *A New System of Slavery: The Export of Indian Labour Overseas, 1830–1920* (London: Oxford University Press, 1974). On the key role of law and governance in the expression of imperial power, see Lauren Benton, "Colonial Law and Cultural Difference: Jurisdictional Politics and the Formation of the Colonial State," *Comparative Studies in Society and History* 41, no. 3 (1999), 563–88; Elizabeth Kolsky, "Codification and the Rule of Colonial Difference: Criminal Procedure in British India," *Law and History Review*, 23, no. 3 (Fall 2005), 631–83.

and engage late-stage slavery and indenture in the same analytical frame, which is rare, they tend to draw rhetorical connections between the former and the latter, much as contemporary critics did, but not concrete ones vis-à-vis the state.[14] Equally overlooked has been both how the processes and dynamics of state labor oversight linked the disparate locales of the British Empire together and how their structural precedents borrowed from Spanish, French, and Dutch colonial rule in the Caribbean and from Chinese enterprise in Southeast Asia.

In scholarly discussions of the contrast between the increasingly centralized authority of Crown colonies in the Caribbean, Africa, and Asia and, in contrast, the tendency toward independence and self-government in white-settler colonies, this commonality is often overlooked. The general growth in the state apparatus, which could be found in nineteenth-century Britain as well, confounds the simple racialized division between British officials' faith in the alleged moral capacity of white Europeans to adopt the principles and practices of liberal, rational governance and their *lack* of faith that Africans and Asians possessed the same capacity.[15] Albeit arising from a very different set of political circumstances, a common concern in the metropole and the empire was to what extent both the working population and those who wielded economic power and political influence locally could be trusted to accord with administrators' visions of public order and economic and social progress. The implementation of regulations on economic and social activity, along with the institutional infrastructure to enforce them, developed in inverse proportion to that level of trust.[16] It is therefore no accident that the apparatus of state plantation discipline expanded in the former slave colonies in tandem with the expansion of the criminal justice system in Britain itself. A key difference was that the increasing political mobilization of the working class in Britain largely prevented the direct criminalization of labor discipline, while in the Crown

[14] Such is the case in the excellent work by Madhavi Kale, *Fragments of Empire: Capital, Slavery, and Indian Indentured Labor in the British Caribbean* (Philadelphia, PA: University of Philadelphia Press, 1998). Some scholars, Richard B. Allen most prominent among them, have argued vehemently for the distinct historical character of indenture, and for a critical decoupling of its study from that of slavery (the "Tinkerian paradigm"). Richard B. Allen, "Reconceptualizing the 'New System of Slavery,'" *Man in India* 92, no. 2 (2012), 225–7.

[15] On the views of British officials vis-à-vis the incapacity of Africans and Asians for liberal self-governance, see Holt, *The Problem of Freedom*, xix–xxii; Karuna Mantena, *Alibis of Empire: Henry Maine and the Ends of Liberal Imperialism* (Princeton, NJ: Princeton University Press, 2010), 6–7.

[16] On liberal self-governance in Britain, see Martin Wiener, *Reconstructing the Criminal: Culture, Law and Policy in England, 1830–1914* (Cambridge: Cambridge University Press, 1990), 11; Patrick Joyce, *The Rule of Freedom: Liberalism and the Modern City* (London: Verso, 2003), 14–15; and Patrick Joyce, *The State of Freedom: A Social History of the British State since 1800* (Cambridge: Cambridge University Press, 2013), 4–6.

colonies of the southern hemisphere, the fusion of criminal justice and labor regulation, in the face of a largely disfranchised African and Indian laboring cohort, proceeded unchecked.[17]

With the interrelationship of race, labor, imperialism, and the state as its focus, this study recasts the history of labor governance in Britain's Crown-ruled tropical colonies in a manner that demonstrates its relevance for a wider scope of historical study. It shows how late-stage slavery and its successor, indenture, played a crucial role in the development of the modern state and in the construction of race and race relations. The oversight of these labor systems, I argue, catalyzed new functions and new types of authority for the state, introducing methods of monitoring, regulating, and discipline that were shared across the empire and persisted well after the "second abolition" of indenture in 1916–20.[18] The state's involvement in governing workers also helped to define the economic, legal, social, and cultural dimensions of labor and labor rights, and to set the boundaries of colonial state authority. The expansion of the state's role in labor matters impacted the use of violence and its moral justifications in colonial governance, shaped evolving definitions of individuals and individual agency in liberal ideology, and even motivated anti-colonial activism. These state-sponsored and state-regulated institutions altered the nature and understanding of racial categories in the empire, particularly as they were applied to labor, and reconfigured relations between different cultural groups. They did so not only for the groups from which laborers themselves were drawn but for the myriad other cohorts found in colonies where slavery and indenture were commonly practiced. Ultimately, I argue, labor governance became, in many regions, the central pillar of colonial rule.[19]

Most concretely, the empire-wide implementation of ameliorated slavery and indenture fused the interests and authority of private landowners and other investors in Britain's global plantation–mining complex with the institutions and operations of the colonial state. This alloying was apparent at multiple levels, from the state's underwriting of labor recruitment and transportation costs to the harmonization of indentured labor policy across

[17] The deployment of the newly reorganized apparatus of policing and judicial discipline against workers deemed disruptive, to deal with mass demonstrations and to discipline the social behavior of the working class more generally, on the other hand, also increased rapidly across the nineteenth century. Sascha Auerbach, *Armed with Sword and Scales: Law, Culture, and Local Courtrooms in London, 1860–1914* (Cambridge: Cambridge University Press, 2021), 141–74.

[18] In 1917, indentured recruitment was outlawed, but it was not until 1920 that all contractual obligations remaining from the indenture system were finally abrogated. Radica Mahase, "'Plenty a Dem Run Away': Resistance by Indian Indentured Labourers in Trinidad, 1870–1920," *Labor History* 49, no. 4 (2008), 465.

[19] On the interrelationship of land and labor control, see Bolland, "Systems of Domination after Slavery," 616–17.

multiple colonies to the symbiosis of criminal justice and plantation labor management. The policies and practices of the resulting overseer-state provoked a wide-ranging debate over individual rights, and it helped define the limits of those rights across Britain's imperial edifice. The new duties and responsibilities of the colonial state vis-à-vis labor and laborers also prompted a reevaluation of the moral and legal limits of coercion and violence in colonial governance. They granted extended life to coercive paternalism, usually in the guise of protection, public order, and public health. This particularly insidious brand of conservative, hegemonic authority had suffered a serious setback during the long abolition campaign, when liberal ideals of freedom and rights had been deployed in tandem with the concept of universal humanity to successfully attack slavery on moral, legal, and political grounds.[20] As the master was forced to share authority with the magistrate, colonial labor governance lent new vitality to old methods of control while introducing novel forms of discipline as well. The treadmill worked in tandem with the lash and the stocks, the workhouse and the prison replaced the plantation dungeon, and the district hospital took the place of the estate sick-house.[21]

The overseer-state became ubiquitous, but it was never omnipotent. Far from an efficient and consistent edifice, it was characterized by constant contestation and fracture. Its own representatives were often at odds with one another, it was riven by contradictory impulses, and it was increasingly on the defensive as the nineteenth century wore on. Those who wielded state authority were faced with a nearly impossible task of simultaneously controlling a vast, diverse, and sometimes disruptive labor force, legitimizing a harsh regime of daily punishment and the violent suppression of sporadic demonstrations, and reconciling these coercive processes with the public discourse of moral colonization and just rule. Thus, while the overseer-state's processes continually reinforced a racialized system of labor control, they also provided

[20] All paternalism has an element of coercion. I mean here that it is *legally* coercive (or even punitive) and explicitly disciplinary. On the coercive aspects of paternalism in the colonial context, see Amanda Nettlebeck, *Indigenous Rights and Colonial Subjecthood: Protection and Reform in the Nineteenth-Century British Empire* (Cambridge: Cambridge University Press, 2021), 1–3. For a recent discussion of the relationship between race, legal institutions, and the discourse of law in the Caribbean, see Juanita de Barros, "The Death of Molly Shultz: Race, Magic, and the Law in the Post-Slavery Caribbean," *Journal of Social History* 55, no. 2 (2021), 345–73.

[21] Eric Williams eloquently laid out how, with the changeover from slavery to Indian indenture in the Caribbean, "the whip, liberally applied" was replaced by the jail as the primary means by which the power of "the Massa" was exerted over plantation workers. Eric Williams, "Massa Day Done (Public Lecture at Woodford Square, 22 March 1961)," *Callalloo* 20, no. 4, Eric Williams and the Postcolonial Caribbean: A Special Issue (Autumn 1997), 726. See also Jane Lydon, "A Secret Longing for a Trade in Human Flesh: The Decline of British Slavery and the Making of the Settler Colonies," *History Workshop Journal* 90 (Autumn 2020), 189–210.

the means of criticizing and challenging that system.[22] In a wider sense, the state's entanglement with colonial labor organization epitomized many of the inherent contradictions of imperial governance and its ideological adjuncts. The most significant of these contradictions was that while British colonial governance was defended by its advocates as a mechanism for bringing social order, economic progress, and cultural uplift, it often sowed social disorder, sustained economic exploitation, and tore asunder families and communities.[23] What has been less apparent, and what this study engages throughout, is how frequently and effectively those at the sharp end of colonial rule were able to recognize and exploit these weaknesses. Enslaved men and women and indentured laborers alike proved adept at pitting the state's own tools against it, maneuvering its different elements into conflict, and employing the language of rights and justice that allegedly composed its moral foundation to instead critique its practices and contest its authority.[24] Ultimately, these efforts provided the grist with which anti-colonial activists successfully challenged indenture, the keystone of the overseer-state, on ethical and legal grounds, hastening its demise.[25]

In the fraught history of the overseer-state's century-long trajectory, one of the key failures of Britain's imperial project is also brought into sharper focus. The end of slavery and the expansion of Britain's imperial system of agriculture and resource extraction across the southern hemisphere thrust the state, often reluctantly, into the role of monitoring and maintaining the first commodified, global labor market. It was a task for which it was singularly ill-equipped; the economic operation and the political culture of the overseer-state were an uneasy fit with the underlying moral and legal principles that formed the explicit basis of nineteenth-century imperial administration.[26] The incompatibility between, on the one hand, the ostensible commitment to moral

[22] The last comes as no surprise since the colonial state's ability to co-opt and redefine such challenges as reinforcements of its own justification and authority has been very much a part of the historical narrative of empire.

[23] Alan Lester, Kate Boehme, and Peter Mitchell, *Ruling the World: Freedom, Civilisation and Liberalism in the Nineteenth-Century British Empire* (Cambridge: Cambridge University Press, 2021), 9–10; Caroline Elkins, *Legacy of Violence: A History of the British Empire* (London: Bodley Head, 2022), 10–13.

[24] Though, as was the case with female industrial workers in Britain, in the empire, paternalistic efforts to protect colonial workers against exploitation by colonial employers reaffirmed the former's subordinate status and amplified their inability to engage structures of law and governance on any but the most disadvantageous terms. Louise A. Tilly, "Women, Women's History, and the Industrial Revolution," *Social Research* 61, no. 1 (Spring 1994), 124–5.

[25] Mahase, "Plenty a Dem Run Away," 467; Sunil Amrith, "Indians Overseas? Governing Tamil Migration to Malaya, 1870–1941," *Past & Present* 208 (August 2010), 15.

[26] Duncan Bell, *Reordering Empire: Essays on Liberalism and Empire* (Princeton, NJ: Princeton University Press, 2019), 107.

colonization, the task of safeguarding its subjects' rights, the prevalent discourse of "rule of law," and the promotion of free labor and, on the other, the violations of all of these principles through the state's involvement in indenture and other forms of coerced labor proved increasingly untenable as the decades wore on.[27] Far from encouraging free labor or preserving rights, at multiple levels of operation, from local magistrates to the Colonial Office, the overseer-state constructed a hierarchy of racial difference. It also produced a public record of the abuses endemic to colonial labor systems for which the state could be held accountable both morally and legally by reformers and critics.

This discordance between practice and principle, despite repeated attempts to reconcile them through a malleable racial discourse, was a constant source of tension and a perennial generator of instability. The legal system facilitated the daily deployment of intimidation, coercion, and violence as mechanisms of labor control. The camouflaging of these mechanisms under the rubric of labor law strengthened the hand of plantation management and local judicial authorities by criminalizing workers' attempts to avoid or resist such regulations. It also justified the violent suppression of collective resistance or mass demonstrations, branding their participants criminals and even rebels. But the self-same legal system that shackled workers to their employers also precluded the latter and their judicial allies from deploying the full panoply of authoritarian control measures. As critics of the system, and sometimes the laborers themselves, were quick to point out, workers in the post-emancipation empire remained legally entitled to the rights and protections due to all Crown subjects. The stark racial inequalities promoted by the system prompted a steady stream of moral censure and legal challenges from humanitarians, antislavery campaigners, judicial contrarians, and Indian activists that grew in volume across the decades preceding the First World War. Although workers could be, and often were, beaten, jailed, and even killed, the records of these events provided powerful leverage for the critics of these systems, even as they provoked ever more determined adaptation, contestation, and defiance by those entangled within it.

Like their analogs in metropolitan Britain, state processes in the tropical Crown colonies were sites of contest over the organization of labor and the concepts that shaped official and public discussions of it. Most notable among these concepts were race, order, justice, and freedom. These contests both shaped and were shaped by the dynamics of authority (legal and cultural) of various iterations of government and by the dynamics of agency. Such processes

[27] On the origins, development, and contradictions of humanitarianism in the colonial context, see Alan Lester and Fae Dussart, *Colonization and the Origins of Humanitarian Governance: Protecting Aborigines Across the Nineteenth-Century British Empire* (Cambridge: Cambridge University Press, 2014) and Zoë Laidlaw, *Protecting the Empire's Humanity: Thomas Hodgkin and British Colonial Activism 1830–1870* (Cambridge: Cambridge University Press, 2021).

worked in complex, contested, and sometimes contradictory ways. New laws on labor discipline could enhance the power of plantation owners over their workforce, be they enslaved African slaves or indentured Indian and Chinese workers. But the arenas in which these laws were adjudicated and enforced could provide avenues of resistance for the latter, or elevate an individual laborer's grievance into a topic of fierce public debate in the British Parliament.

Just as these contests were entangled with colonial authority, the means by which historians access and portray those contests are also embedded in dynamics of power.[28] This is in part because the expansion of the state's remit over colonial labor was accompanied by its expansion as a mechanism for generating the records of colonial rule.[29] The state thus operated both as an apparatus of labor governance and as an apparatus of archive-creation about labor, workers, law, morality, justice, and a host of other related concepts and topics.[30] Primarily, this apparatus generated information that, while masquerading as neutral, ultimately served to justify its own authority. But the colonial state was anything but a monolithic entity. It was internally fractured and faced constant challenges, internal and external, both concrete and conceptual.[31] This was particularly true of the issues of labor, race, law, and migration. Metropolitan officials, colonial administrators, local magistrates, and a host of other actors continually struggled to reconcile coercive measures with their ostensible commitment to liberal ideals such as free labor, just rule, and moral governance. Workers themselves also articulated their own visions of rights, freedom, justice, and morality even as they sought to engage the state on their own terms and integrate its newfound powers into their lives.

With these dynamics in mind, a key goal of *The Overseer State* is to unpack the wider significance of workers' responses to late-stage slavery, indenture, and, in Southeast Asia, large-scale contract labor. Moving beyond a binary of

[28] As Ann Laura Stoler maintains, colonial archives are "both transparencies on which power relations were inscribed and intricate technologies of rule in themselves." Ann Laura Stoler, "Colonial Archives and the Arts of Governance," *Archival Science* 2 (2002), 87.

[29] On the state as an archive-making apparatus, see Ann Laura Stoler, *Along the Archival Grain: Epistemic Anxieties and Colonial Common Sense* (Princeton, NJ: Princeton University Press, 2010).

[30] The classic treatise on the methodological issues posed by employing "ruling-class" documents to understand the history of workers is Dipesh Chakrabarty's "Conditions for Knowledge of Working-Class Conditions: Employers, Government and the Jute Workers of Calcutta, 1890–1940," in Ranajit Guha and Gayatri Chakravorty Spivak, eds., *Selected Subaltern Studies* (Oxford: Oxford University Press, 1988), 179–230.

[31] Scholars looking at the political economy of indenture have similarly tended to focus on the relatively smooth transition of colonial labor, financial, and governance systems from slavery to indenture and argue, quite rightly, that the colonial plantation systems remained dependent on unfree labor in one form or another throughout the nineteenth century. See Sunanda Sen, "Indentured Labour from India in the Age of Empire," *Social Scientist* 44, no. 1/2 (January–February 2016), 35–74.

coercion and resistance and examining the complexities of the engagement of slaves, apprentices, indentured laborers, and contract laborers with state agents and institutions opens up important new interpretive opportunities.[32] Most importantly, exploring workers' encounters with the state, which ranged from judicial grievances to demands for rights and justice to open defiance of official authority, reveals the wider significance of their actions in the context of labor organization and governance across the British Empire. The confinement, in current scholarship, of workers' contestations to merely local importance, as a window into changing social and economic roles, or as a failure of reform, is understandable.[33] Such contestations appeared to lack coherent ideology, and this apparent absence has encouraged the divorce of indentured labor from the established historical understandings of workers' evolution as an organized political force in the imperial context.[34] Labour history rarely incorporates the vast cohorts of Indian, Chinese, and other groups who were employed via indenture and contract-labor, and includes only enslaved and free Africans to the extent that they were developing distinct political identities, most typically along Marxist lines.[35] Likewise, the historiography that

[32] Some of these methodological issues are summarized in Natasha Lightfoot, *Troubling Freedom: Antigua and the Aftermath of British Emancipation* (Durham, NC: Duke University Press, 2015), 13. See also Prabhu P. Mohapatra, "Eurocentrism, Forced Labour, and Global Migration: A Critical Assessment," *International Review of Social History* 52, no. 1 (2007), 110–15.

[33] This was characteristic of Hugh Tinker's approach; he argued that indentured workers thought mostly "in terms of immediate objectives" (Tinker, *A New System of Slavery*, 226), an interpretation that has continued to color scholarly approaches to workers' responses even as the concept of "immediate objectives" itself has been more thoroughly politicized by James C. Scott, among others. As examples of the former approach, see Maurits S. Hassankhan, Brij. V. Lal, and Doug Munro, *Resistance and Indian Indenture Experience* (New Delhi: Manohar, 2014); Goolam Vahed, "Power and Resistance: Indentured Labour in Colonial Natal, 1860–1911," *Man in India* 92, no. 2 (April 2012), 315.

[34] The vast majority of this has focused on the creation of a "white labor" identity in the white-settler colonies of Australia, New Zealand, Canada, and South Africa. In the process, Chinese and Indian labor more commonly served as a foil for this identity. Jonathan Hyslop, "The Imperial Working Class Makes Itself 'White': White Labourism in Britain, Australia, and South Africa before the First World War," *Historical Sociology* 12, no. 4 (December 1999), 398–421; Marilyn Lake and Henry Reynolds, *Drawing the Global Colour Line: White Men's Countries and the International Challenge of Racial Equality* (Cambridge: Cambridge University Press, 2008); Duncan Money and Danelle van Zyl-Hermann, "Revisiting White Labourism: New Debates on Working-Class Whiteness in Twentieth-Century Southern Africa," *International Review of Social History* 66, no. 3 (December 2021), 469–91.

[35] See Kevin D. Smith "A Fragmented Freedom: The Historiography of Emancipation and Its Aftermath in the British West Indies," *Slavery & Abolition* 16, no. 1 (1995), 101–30; Henderson Carter, *Labour Pains: Resistance and Protest in Barbados, 1838–1904* (Kingston: Ian Randle, 2012).

examines workers' resistance to colonialism has tended to overlook engagement with legal institutions and the state, given the latter's thorough entanglement with the mechanisms of plantation discipline. To what extent these acts can be considered "resistance" as historians most commonly define it in relation to colonialism and authority, and to colonial labor systems in particular, is certainly debatable.[36] And given the relatively narrow definition of resistance often employed in this historical context, it is understandable that it has largely been described as "localized, sporadic, unstructured, and individualistic."[37]

When we broaden our view to encompass adaptation, negotiation, and contest, however, a very different picture of workers' agency and its historical significance comes into focus. The overseer-state's historical trajectory emerges not just as the history of an institution in constant tension with those it sought to govern but also as a history *shaped by* workers' ubiquitous encounters with mechanisms of management and rule.[38] Through such encounters, laborers played a crucial role in influencing colonial policy, the attitudes of those in positions of authority, and the public discourse of both those who supported indenture and those who opposed it. Therefore, though indentured workers' responses to the overseer-state may have lacked a coherent ideology or transcolonial organization, they were hardly devoid of significance in the wider histories of labor, governance, and imperialism.[39] The same holds true for the engagement of slaves and apprentices with the apparatus of amelioration and apprenticeship, which shaped the character of the colonial state – in practice, policy, and public discourse – in the years prior to the widespread introduction of indenture.

Unraveling the meaning and significance of encounters with the overseer-state from the point of view of slaves, apprentices, and indentured laborers presents several challenges, methodological, conceptual, and archival. To begin with, the categories typically employed in the historical record often obscure the immense cultural diversity and variation of experience that characterized the population of slaves and indentured laborers across the British Empire. These categories, which appear across a broad variety of milieu – from

36 On the methodological issues associated with accessing indentured laborers' direct resistance to colonial authority, see Mahase, "Plenty a Dem Run Away," 467–8.

37 Ibid., 471.

38 Burton, *The Trouble with Empire.*

39 In contrast, for more than two decades now, those who have examined the final years of slavery in the British Empire have been keen to emphasize the long-term significance of enslaved Africans' responses to the opportunities for grievance and redress offered by the processes of amelioration and emancipation. See John Edwin Mason, "Slaves and Their Protectors: Reforming Resistance in a Slave Society, the Cape Colony, 1826–1834," *Journal of Southern African Studies* 17, no. 1 (March 1991), 104; Diana Paton, *No Bond but the Law: Punishment, Race, and Gender in Jamaican State Formation, 1780–1870* (Durham, NC: Duke University Press, 2004).

memoirs and autobiographical accounts to official reports to newspapers to courtroom testimony – were themselves cultural constructions and therefore subject to constant contestation and reinterpretation in the nineteenth century.[40] To some extent, the accounts demonstrate how vast variations in geographical origin, culture, dialect, social status, and a host of other elements were bridged by historical actors to co-opt, albeit under extreme coercion, a new, shared identity as "negroes," "slaves," "Indians," "Chinese," and "coolies."[41] These identities could be deployed or performed as a mechanism for solidarity, rather than merely being forced upon individuals as a means of oppression, with the result of "new scripts written upon old scripts, new meanings, and a new language."[42]

Another methodological issue arises from the secondhand and overtly biased nature of the vast majority of records wherein these subaltern groups "speak" (e.g. complaints and grievances).[43] Official documentation produced by the overseer-state presents a particular interpretive challenge. They originate with the agents, institutions, and protocols that, while implemented ostensibly with the purpose of paternalist protection, operated primarily to suppress and punish workers for a wide variety of alleged transgressions. The negative views of the enslaved and of indentured workers that prevailed among figures of official authority were deeply encoded into the production of such records, in ways both obvious and more subtle. They remain, nonetheless, the largest and most detailed accounts available of the experiences of enslaved Africans and indentured Indian and Chinese workers from this period. Incomplete, biased, and problematic though they may be, their reinterpretation offers a crucial pathway to avoid the permanent silencing of these voices.[44] Read "against the grain," they can provide crucial insights into the views of those who saw themselves as active subjects, even when they were often treated as passive objects.[45]

Given these considerations, while the volume's focus on governance and responses to it returns the state to the center of our historical understanding of what the British Empire was, it should be clear that it does so very much at

40 Paton, *No Bond but the Law*, 17.

41 Emilia Viotti Da Costa, *Crowns of Glory, Tears of Blood: The Demerara Slave Rebellion of 1823* (Oxford: Oxford University Press, 1997), 75.

42 Ibid.

43 The classic work on this topic is Gayatri Spivak's "Can the Subaltern Speak," in Cary Nelson and Lawrence Grossberg, eds., *Marxism and the Interpretation of Culture* (London: Macmillan, 1988), 24–8. The issue has been engaged across a broad swath of scholarship in history, postcolonial studies, and elsewhere.

44 Lightfoot, *Troubling Freedom*, 13.

45 Kale, *Fragments of Empire*, 4. As Stoler points out, we must understand what that "grain" is – reading the archive "for its regularities, for its logic of recall, for its densities and distributions, for its consistencies of misinformation, omission, and mistake" – before we can read "against" it. Stoler, "Colonial Archives," 100.

odds with early historians' assertions that the two were essentially synonymous.[46] What has long been presented, by its practitioners, and studied, by scholars, as a particularly *British* form of imperial rule, when examined through the lens of labor organization, emerges as a distinctly hybridized entity. The overseer-state borrowed from both Continental modes of rule and labor organization and, in Southeast Asia, from Chinese and Indian ones. Indeed, the key to its power and longevity was its flexibility and capacity to absorb and integrate established practices and structures. More specifically, British approaches to colonial labor regulation *asserted* staunch adherence to ideological precepts such as liberalism, rule of law, free markets, and moral governance. In practice, they were built on the cultural and structural foundation of previous labor systems, borrowing heavily from their attendant offices, procedures, and institutions. These latter were often conservative, coercive, and distinctly illiberal. The result was not a fundamental rewriting of the methods of labor organization that had existed previously to British rule in any given region but, rather, a palimpsest of governance inscribed over these prior systems, be they French, Dutch, Spanish, or Chinese. What emerged in Britain's tropical plantation and mining colonies of the nineteenth century was thus as much an *overwritten*-state as it was an overseer-state.

The prevalence of this hybridization complicates our current understanding of the British imperial state, and of the modern state more generally. Given the importance of both earlier forms of Continental imperial labor organization in the Caribbean and Chinese labor organization in Southeast Asia, the structures and methods of the overseer-state can hardly be labeled either wholly "modern" or as emerging directly from European models of the nation-state.[47] Although grounded in modern technologies of rule and organization, such as long-distance telegraph communication and steamship travel, the overseer-state borrowed extensively from a more traditional governing approach through coercive paternalism and from economic, social, and cultural modes introduced and disseminated by the Chinese throughout Southeast Asia in the eighteenth and nineteenth centuries. The most modern element of the overseer-state was the interdependence of epistemic oversight with regulatory oversight. Its legal authority to regulate labor and laborers, its cultural capacity to define labor as a discrete element of activity over which

[46] John Robert Seeley asserted that the crucial distinction between ancient empires and modern ones was that the former involved a dispersal of the population and the attenuation of their connection with the home country, while the latter, of which the British Empire was the epitome, was anchored instead in an extension of the state. John Robert Seeley, *The Expansion of England* ([1883]; repr. Cambridge: Cambridge University Press, 2010), 8.

[47] The classic work problematizing Eurocentric visions of modernity is Dipesh Chakrabarty's *Provincializing Europe: Postcolonial Thoughts and Historical Difference* (Princeton, NJ: Princeton University Press, 2000).

the state could claim authority, and its public project to delineate what constituted moral governance and just colonial rule were all mutually reinforcing. The overseer-state's epistemic project was made that much more necessary by its dependance, in the Caribbean, on older, more coercive, and centralized modes of Continental imperial rule and, in southeast Asia, on distinctly non-Western models of labor organization.[48]

Viewing the history of the nineteenth-century British Empire in light of the overseer-state therefore thoroughly embeds it in the history of European imperialism and of the interrelationship between Europe, the Caribbean, Africa, and Asia, rather than in the primarily British models of imperial power and expansion such as "informal" versus "formal" empire and "gentlemanly capitalism."[49] The overseer-state nonetheless has significance for these latter analytical frameworks as well. It contributes to our understanding of what the empire was in practice, why and how imperial hegemony expanded, the relationship between politics and economics in this process, and the influence of different parts of the empire on one another.

This volume also sheds new light on the legacies of slavery in post-emancipation societies and in the British Empire more broadly. Previous scholarship has emphasized how aspects of slavery persisted structurally in the societies, economies, laws, and cultures of post-slavery societies.[50] My goal, in contrast, is to demonstrate how the duration, strength, and character of these legacies were significantly shaped by the period of reform and amelioration in slavery's final decades, so much so that they were felt even in regions where African chattel slavery had not been practiced to any notable extent. The key development in this period was the integration of private labor organization with public oversight. The results of this process, which accelerated in the wake of emancipation, was not merely that labor organization became the purview of the colonial state. The colonial state, by assuming the authority once held by slave-owners, managers, and even overseers, became *primarily*

[48] On Britain's domestic project to create liberal subjects, see Joyce, *The Rule of Freedom*.

[49] John Gallagher and Ronald Robinson, "The Imperialism of Free Trade," *Economic History Review*, 6, no. 1 (1953), 1–15; P. J. Cain and A. G. Hopkins, "Gentlemanly Capitalism and British Expansion Overseas I: The Old Colonial System, 1688–1850," *Economic History Review*, 2nd ser. 39, no. 4 (1986), 501–25; P. J. Cain and A. G. Hopkins, "Gentlemanly Capitalism and British Expansion Overseas II: New Imperialism, 1850–1945," *Economic History Review* 40, no. 1 (February 1987), 1–26.

[50] See Holt, *The Problem of Freedom*; Lightfoot, *Troubling Freedom*; Richard B. Allen, "Slaves, Convicts, Abolitionism and the Global Origins of the Post-Emancipation Indentured Labor System," *Slavery & Abolition* 35, no. 2 (2014), 329–31. The domestic legacies of slavery are an animating concern of the prolific "Legacies of British Slave-Ownership" project, as demonstrated in the recent volume by Catherine Hall, Nicholas Draper, Keith McClellan, Katie Donington, and Rachel Lang, *Legacies of British Slave-Ownership: Colonial Slavery and the Formation of Victorian Britain* (Cambridge: Cambridge University Press, 2014).

a mechanism for labor organization. Over time, labor organization and colonial governance became so entangled that state authorities could not relinquish their power over the labor system without fundamentally weakening their overall authority. This helps explain why colonial administrators, although sometimes reluctant to assert their authority over both employers and workers in the initial decades of the overseer-state, were often disinclined to surrender it even the face of the scandals, public critiques, and official inquiries that increased in number and severity across the nineteenth century. Despite the obvious failings of the overseer-state, officials from colonial governors to local magistrates repeatedly rose to its defense on economic, moral, legal, and social grounds. In this regard, just as criticism and resistance to the overseer-state formed a key aspect of a wider attack on colonialism in the later nineteenth century, support for the overseer-state represented a crucial facet of the public and official justifications for the empire's continued operation and expansion.

In sum, while the ostensible goal of this volume is to help us better understand the history of race, labor, and governance in the British Caribbean, southern Africa, Mauritius, and Southeast Asia, it also contributes to much broader historical questions. Chief among these are: What is the nature of the colonial state, both conceptual and structural? How and why did it develop and expand over the nineteenth century? How can we define colonial authority, and how is it related to state processes? By extension, how did the British Empire operate (or fail to operate) as a coherent entity? In what ways was it coordinated in practice and concept, and where were its points of tension and fracture? What were the various ways in which colonial authority was negotiated, contested, and resisted, and what were the wider historical consequences of these acts? What role did ideology, and liberalism in particular, play in colonial governance? How did core principles of liberalism and a host of other crucial concepts such as freedom, justice, and order shape everyday encounters between individual workers and state agents of institutions? How, in turn, were public or official discussions and articulations of these principles and concepts shaped by these encounters? And lastly, what was the broader relationship between imperialism and labor, and how did it change over the course of the nineteenth century?

To effectively engage these questions, the book embraces a chronology that is broader and structured differently from the norm. Most studies of enslavement and emancipation in the British Empire end, for understandable reasons, in the 1830s and 1840s, while the majority of works on indenture begin at that point. This volume, in contrast, commences with the advent of "ameliorated" slavery in the early nineteenth century and concludes the substantive part of its analysis in the early twentieth, when indenture was finally abolished. This wide time span allows for a critical examination of both continuity and change in the systems of colonial labor organization and responses to them. Likewise, geographically, most studies restrict their examination to either the Atlantic or the Pacific Ocean World, and topically to one among enslavement, Indian indenture, or Chinese indenture and contract labor. Here, with the overseer-state as the analytical frame, both regions and all three institutions are examined. As with the wide chronological span, this broad geographical and topical remit allows me to tease out both similarities and contrasts in how racialized systems of state-regulated labor organization operated in different locales and with different groups.

Finally, the prior historical frameworks of either regional and social focus or of the labor diaspora have not established how labor management and its attendant state processes operated as a coherent system across the vast distances of Britain's tropical archipelago of colonies. In the innumerable ways that labor governance linked disparate parts of the empire, from the life-course of individuals to shared practices of governance to the ubiquitous public discourse on "the coolie," it was a quintessentially imperial phenomenon.[51] The study of the state's changing role in labor oversight therefore offers unique insights into what the British Empire was and into the interrelationship of historical processes at the local, regional, imperial, and global levels. Within these contexts, the engagement of workers themselves with the overseer-state was essential in determining how the local dynamics interacted with global changes, and how different regions of the empire were connected to the metropole and to each other. Approaching labor governance as a global system also allows for the more nuanced analysis of a host of other historical actors who, in previous studies, have served largely as one-dimensional foils against which the long struggle for rights and recognition by the enslaved and the indentured was arrayed. Accordingly, this study places the overseer-state not only in the broader canvas of the relationship between Britain, the Caribbean, southern Africa, Mauritius, India, and China, and between metropolitan authorities and their colonial counterparts, but also in the context of the global development of capitalist enterprise and its profound effect on the full spectrum of colonial societies. The overseer-state did not survive long into the twentieth century, but its legacies were profound. It helped establish the cultural and social diversity that characterize regions from the Pacific Islands to the Caribbean. It also set patterns of race, migration, governance, and labor that would persist long after the last indenture expired and the final ounce of "bitter strength" had been expended in the canebrakes of Trinidad, the gold mines of the Transvaal, and the rubber plantations of Malaysia.

[51] According to Kale, "focusing on Indian indentured immigration as an *imperial* labor reallocation strategy . . . casts into relief the webs of association – financial, governmental, individual, and affective – that connected the lives and liberties of imperial subjects all over the world" (Kale, *Fragments of Empire*, 6).

The volume's chapter structure reflects this long chronology and broad geographic remit, while remaining anchored in a focus on labor governance and responses to it. Chapter 1 explores the crucial period of late-stage slavery and the reform of the plantation labor system in the early nineteenth century. During this period, new state processes and their ideological adjuncts transformed the plantation workforce from private property that was controlled by owners into subjects of rule who were answerable to the state. These new mechanisms of labor regulation came to play a crucial role, structurally and conceptually, in anchoring colonial rule not just in the post-emancipation Caribbean but as far afield as Mauritius and South Africa. This process of reform was justified ideologically as a moral imperative, politically as a means of maintaining order and sustaining revenue, and culturally as a paternalistic uplift of the abused and exploited enslaved who were transitioning from property to Crown subjects.[52] Examining the transition from slavery to free labor through the lens of the overseer-state, the chapter clarifies the ascent of labor regulation to a key preoccupation of colonial rule, reveals plantation colonies as sites of experimentation in interventionist governance, and illuminates the evolving relationship between colony and metropole (and different colonies to one another). The analytical framework of the overseer-state also demonstrates how the changing character of colonial labor management entangled British and Continental European modes of imperialism, complicating our historical understanding of the role played by liberal ideology in British imperial governance and political discourse. The overseer-state, concretely and conceptually, bridged the histories of the British Empire and the French, Spanish, and Dutch empires, revealing how the development of labor control mechanisms in Britain's plantation colonies remained a European enterprise rather than merely a British one.

The overseer-state, from its earliest years, was reciprocally constructed by the rulers and the ruled, albeit from vastly asymmetrical positions of authority. Over time, slave-owners adapted to the changes in labor governance by trying to employ the new agents and processes to enhance their authority over their slaves. But enslaved men and women, too, saw opportunities to assert themselves in the new system. Chapter 2 examines how the employment of local official and judicial venues became a common practice as enslaved African-Caribbeans sought to engage the new rights and resources provided to them. They faced an uphill battle, since the discourse of racial inferiority was programmed into the system. Nonetheless, their actions forced all of those

[52] As Kale points out in her examination of indenture's Caribbean introduction, this process occurred simultaneously at the concrete level and at the conceptual level. The process of organizing labor economically and legally occurred in tandem with the "forging" of the definition of labor, and both were entangled in racial, social, gender, and political contexts. Kale, *Fragments of Empire*, 10.

involved to wrestle with the role of the state in regulating slavery, the balance between public order and individual rights, the use of coercion and violence within the new regulatory framework of ameliorated slavery, and the competing concepts of morality and justice. These interactions shaped the character of the overseer-state in a multitude of ways, from altering the approaches of local officials to different aspects of plantation life to serving as leverage for antislavery activists in Parliament, and even to prompting internal conflicts over how justice was defined and to what extent, if at all, enslaved Africans were entitled to it.

Chapter 3 argues that during the crucial transition from slavery to apprenticeship and thence to indenture and free labor in the 1830s, the state's oversight of colonial labor systems became one of the most prominent and powerful aspects of colonial governance. The first part of the chapter assesses the central role of the post-emancipation state in colonial labor management in Jamaica, Britain's most populous, politically prominent, and wealthy colony in the Americas. There, the ruling plantocracy, in collaboration with the administrative and judicial authorities with whom it was intertwined, successfully avoided undue metropolitan interference.[53] As had been the case in the Crown colonies, the Jamaican colonial government established control not only over the African-Caribbean workforce, first as slaves and later as apprentices, but also over plantation-owners and managers. Even without the metropolitan direction that had shaped labor policy more strongly in places such as Trinidad and British Guiana, Jamaican authorities adopted a regime of regulation and oversight that was very similar to that implemented in the Caribbean Crown colonies, becoming a kind of overseer-state writ small. The second section of the chapter explores the first attempts to introduce Indian indentured labor in British Guiana and Mauritius, examining the motivations for the adaptation of this centuries-old labor system to a nineteenth-century context. In the Indian Ocean World, the state apparatus of ameliorated slavery was merged with the preexisting models of coerced labor that had been employed in southern India and Ceylon, and with established practices of penal transportation.[54] This initial attempt to expand the indenture system from its modest origins, mired in mismanagement and public scandal, was a failure. This failure, in turn, prompted the expansion of state oversight, a pattern that had already become a central characteristic of the

53 The contrast between governance in chartered (aka "legislative") colonies and the newer, more centralized model of the Crown colony system is neatly summarized in Anthony De V. Phillips, "Emancipation Betrayed? Social Control Legislation in the British Caribbean (with Special Reference to Barbados), 1834–1876," *Chicago-Kent Law Review* 70 (1995), 1355–6.

54 For the permeability of indenture and convict labor, see Clare Anderson, "Convicts and Coolies: Rethinking Indentured Labour in the Nineteenth Century," *Slavery & Abolition* 30, no. 1 (2009), 93–109.

overseer-state during amelioration and would continue to be so across indenture's subsequent century of operation.

Chapter 4 assesses how indenture grew from its modest beginnings in British Guiana and Mauritius into a global labor system spanning the breadth of Britain's plantation colonies. With the parliamentary critics of slavery and indenture in abeyance and labor organization established as a keystone of colonial and imperial governance in the colonies where it was employed, the overseer-state was free to expand across the empire. It still faced structural, legal, and moral challenges. The most significant obstacle, for the supporters of indenture, was reconciling a system that was exploitative and inherently unfree with the discourses of liberalism, "free labor," moral colonization, and just rule. This, in many respects, was the imperial project in microcosm, and the responses of policy, practice, and public discourse adopted to defend indenture developed in tandem with the broader redefinition of the British Empire as a whole.[55] The Indian Rebellion of 1857 was a crucial moment in this process. The subsequent imposition of direct Crown rule over India greatly enhanced the state's control over the exportation of laborers, and the violence of the event provided public justification for the increasing intervention of the state to maintain stern discipline among the global diaspora of Indian workers.

Chapter 5, focusing primarily on Mauritius and British Guiana, examines the development of the overseer-state and responses to it in the middle decades of the nineteenth century, exploring the rising tensions that became increasingly apparent at the fulcrum of colonial labor governance in the latter half of the nineteenth century. At the center of this examination is the ongoing dialogue between indentured workers, magistrates, public commentators, and colonial administrators over the laws governing labor and the principles underlying them. I argue that, despite their position as the anchor of colonial rule in the plantation colonies and their commitment to their vision of just rule and public order, magistrates were not invariably the catalysts of the state's direct intercession in labor relations. That initiative frequently came from plantation workers themselves. Building on the protocols established during amelioration and apprenticeship, laborers brought grievances and petitions to magistrates nearly from the moment of indenture's introduction. As a counterpoint to the magistrates' perspective, this chapter examines, through the accounts of indentured laborers' engagement with state agents and institutions, how workers articulated their own visions of rights, justice, morality, law, and the changing role of the colonial state in labor relations. Even though their views lacked a coherent ideology, their actions had inherent political

[55] On the moral reform movement in India and its Atlantic World linkages, see Zoe Laidlaw, "'Justice to India – Prosperity to England – Freedom to the Slave!' Humanitarian and Moral Reform Campaigns on India, Aborigines and American Slavery," *Journal of the Royal Asiatic Society* 22, no. 2 (April 2012), 299–324.

significance in that they influenced both the practices of governance and the public discourse concerning them. Through their contestations with the overseer-state, indentured workers shaped the dynamics of colonial rule, too. By the 1860s and 1870s, the increasing dissonance between Indians' perceptions of justice and their legal entitlements and magistrates' hardening line toward labor discipline and public order had prompted more direct resistance on the part of laborers. State representatives, in response, would defend their actions with portrayals of Indian indentured workers as a population that was largely docile and benefitted from the colonial labor system, but which was veined through with moral failings and subject to the cynical influence of disruptive individuals. The fissures between the overseer-state and its charges, already apparent even in its early years, were growing into a yawning chasm as a system that billed itself as being supportive of free labor, liberal principles, and moral colonial rule increasingly abandoned its paternalist guise to advocate and practice coercion, the restriction of labor mobility, and, when deemed necessary, the violent suppression of workers' collective action.

Chapter 6 focuses on the British Straits Settlements and the Malay States, which were the sites of the overseer-state's last great expansion. This was arguably its most rapid and radical iteration yet. The elements of labor governance introduced there, although analogous to those implemented in other regions, had no historical antecedents in slavery, and the labor management infrastructure provided by the preexisting plantation system was modest. At the edge of the imperial frontier, where Chinese organizations and their attendant customs had long held sway, British laws and institutions struggled to gain a foothold. The febrile circumstances of British governance there were lent further urgency by the growing importance of the region to Britain's economic, political, and strategic hegemony in Southeast Asia. From its precarious state in the early 1870s, in the course of a few decades, Britain's toehold on the Malay Peninsula would solidify in the Straits Settlements and extend to encompass the Malay States. At the heart of this project would be the subsuming under government authority of the Chinese laboring population and the Chinese organizations that controlled their immigration and conditions of work. The rapid extension of state control over labor would transform one of the empire's most strategically vital cities and some of its most inaccessible and unruly territory from, or so British officials would claim, locales of lawless immorality to models of civilized behavior, orderly governance, and stable prosperity. The apparatus of the overseer-state would be grafted onto the structural elements of Chinese labor governance even as British rule was defined against it. As the overseer-state struggled to establish its political supremacy against highly resilient cultural and economic systems established previously by the Chinese Secret Societies and *kongsi*, its success or failure hinged increasingly on its ontological power to define moral governance and just rule. In this sense, British colonial authority in the Straits Settlements was more than merely anchored in regulation of the Chinese workforce; they were synonymous. Put another way, on the imperial frontier in Southeast Asia, labor control *was* sovereignty.[56]

What caused indenture, which had spread so rapidly across the empire in the wake of emancipation, becoming the backbone of the colonial labor system and the keystone of colonial governance, to be so rapidly abolished in the second decade of the twentieth century? Previous scholarship on this "second abolition" has asserted that a revived and reinvigorated humanitarian movement coincided with a series of public scandals over indenture and the increasingly vehement objections of the Indian and Chinese governments. Chapter 7 demonstrates how the model of the overseer-state prompts a very different perspective on indenture's end. I argue that the expansion of the indenture system created the blueprint for its own undoing. It did so in three primary ways. Firstly, it tied labor relations, labor immigration, and the moral and physical well-being of the indentured workforce indelibly to state agents and institutions of governance. Secondly, it entangled the operation of this labor governance in disparate regions of the empire, ensuring that issues arising in one region reverberated politically and economically throughout the system. And thirdly, its own processes of recordkeeping, adjudication, inquiry, and oversight provided a channel along which the suffering and discontent of those under its yoke could be communicated both to the public and to the highest levels of government.[57]

Employing the overseer-state as a context for the end of indenture also brings into sharper relief the agency of those under the system itself in its decline and eventual abrogation. When we refocus our lens on the role of the state and state processes, we find that whereas employers and managers had most commonly been the source of laborers' grievance in the first decades of the system, by the waning decades of the nineteenth century workers often directed their sharpest ire at the laws, agents, and institutions of the overseer state that underpinned it. Their testimony, demonstrations, and strikes provided the grist that the opponents of indenture could employ in public discourse, emphasizing the inequities of the system and its many contradictions to Britain's self-proclaimed principles of liberalism and moral colonialism. At the same time, workers throughout the empire were themselves

[56] My thanks to Catherine Hall for this particular observation, which was made at the "Short Histories of the British Empire, 1816–1856" workshop, hosted by the Institute of Advanced Studies, University College London, September 16, 2016.

[57] For the ways in which the expansion of British administration in India itself similarly created avenues by which India could resist British authority or turn the connections forged by colonial government into networks of nationalist activism, see Anil Seal, "Introduction," in John Gallagher, Gordon Johnson, and Anil Seal, eds., *Locality, Province, and Nation: Essays on Indian Politics, 1870 to 1940* (Cambridge: Cambridge University Press, 1973).

rejecting the overseer-state and the indenture system, with their rigid schema of multi-year contracts and heavily criminalized labor statutes. Instead, wherever possible, they chose more flexible arrangements, taking advantage of the growing demand for their labor to maximize their mobility and recompense. Their efforts were aided by the continued development of local intermediaries who sought to circumvent or replace state-organized avenues of recruitment and long-term contracts with arrangements more adapted to their specific environments and more amenable to potential workers.

Historians have long recognized that the post-emancipation decades were ones haunted by the legacies of slavery.[58] The book's conclusion asserts that the overseer-state, in terms of both labor governance and responses to it, was one of the most important of these legacies. The effects of the indenture system were particularly profound and widespread, most visibly in the social, political, and cultural dynamics of multiracial (but highly unequal) societies in Mauritius, the British Caribbean, and Malaya, and in the establishment of long-range, long-term labor mobility as the norm in a globalized system of labor transportation and organization. Through the overseer-state, the abiding impact of slavery and its aftermath were felt acutely even in places such as Malaysia, where plantation slavery had never been a prevalent practice. In the regions where the British imperial state was most powerful, the dynamics of governance and the history of slavery remained entangled well beyond the centenary of the slave trade's abolition.

When I asked, at a workshop in Berlin a few years ago, "What image of the British Empire emerges when we examine it through the lens of labor organization?" one response was "a distorted one."[59] All lenses bring some elements into focus while obscuring others, and the work before you is no exception. I have chosen to concentrate my analysis on the Crown colonies of the southern hemisphere, and specifically on those acquired in the later eighteenth and the nineteenth centuries, because it was there that African, Indian, and Chinese workers formed the vast majority of workers. The trajectory of labor governance in the white-settler colonies of Canada and Australia followed a very different path. In these locales, the state also took an increasingly central role in managing labor and labor relations, but it did so under strong influence from a working-class cohort that both successfully unified around an exclusionary white identity and effectively translated that collective identity into organized political action.[60] Consequently, although these regions witnessed significant labor migration from India and Asia, white workers remained the

58 See, for example, the various pieces in *The International Journal of African Historical Studies* 48, no. 2 (2015), Special Issue: Exploring Post-Slavery in Contemporary Africa.

59 Specifically, at the Colonial Agricultural Modernities Workshop, Wissenchaftskolleg zu Berlin in March 2018, which I had the pleasure of co-convening with Kris Manjapra.

60 Hyslop, "The Imperial Working Class Makes Itself 'White'"; Lake and Reynolds, *Drawing the Global Colour Line*; Money and van Zyl-Hermann, "Revisiting White Labourism."

majority and state power was deployed to maintain increasingly stern restrictions both on the mobility and rights of Asian and Indian workers and on immigration itself. State labor oversight of white workers in the white-settler colonies, though powerfully expressed through master and servant laws and the criminalization of labor offenses, tended to wane rather than wax as the nineteenth century wore on.[61] So, too, did the imperial penal labor system, at least with regard to white workers, as transportation declined with the concurrent growth the domestic penitentiary system.[62] Coerced labor extraction for non-white cohorts via the colonial penal system, on the other hand, remained a prominent expression of racialized state labor organization throughout the nineteenth century, operating in a matrix of laws and policies, moral discourse, social and cultural relations, and institutional frameworks that were entangled with the other elements of the overseer-state. Penal labor, however, has been a subject of focused study elsewhere.[63] For these reasons, neither subject comes under the purview of this volume, though a reexamination of them in light of the overseer-state may prove fruitful in future.

Women workers are also not a major focus of this study, though the agency of enslaved women does form a core consideration in Chapter 2. Gender was a crucial aspect of the indenture system, and the alleged paucity of women among successive cohorts of workers who arrived at plantation colonies around the empire was a source of perennial concern to administrators, who worried about the sustainability of the system and the potential for moral corrosion among an overwhelmingly male population of laborers.[64] But women's liminal legal identity, the general unwillingness of state officials to recognize the value of their work and include them in the official accounts of the colonial labor force, and their status as a minority contingent among an

[61] Michael Quinland, "Australia, 1788–1902: A Workingman's Paradise?" in Douglas Hay and Paul Craven, eds., *Masters, Servants, and Magistrates in Britain and the Empire, 1562–1955* (Chapel Hill: University of North Carolina Press, 2004), 240.

[62] James Willis, "Transportation versus Imprisonment in Eighteenth- and Nineteenth-Century Britain: Penal Power, Liberty, and the State," *Law & Society Review* 39, no. 1 (2005), 171–210.

[63] Most prominently in the work of Clare Anderson, "Convicts and Coolies"; Clare Anderson, "Transnational Histories of Penal Transportation: Punishment, Labour and Governance in the British Imperial World, 1788–1939," *Australian Historical Studies* 47, no. 3 (2016), 381–97; Clare Anderson, "The Andaman Islands Penal Colony: Race, Class, Criminality, and the British Empire," *International Review of Social History* 63, special issue 26 (August 2018), 25–43; Clare Anderson, *Convicts: A Global History* (Cambridge: Cambridge University Press, 2022).

[64] Marina Carter, *Lakshmi's Legacy: The Testimonies of Indian Women in 19th Century Mauritius* (Stanley, Rose Hill, Mauritius: Editions de l'Ocean Indien, distributed by African Books Collective, Oxford, 1994); Brij V. Lal, "Kunti's Cry: Indentured Women on Fiji Plantations," *Indian Economic and Social History Review* 22, no. 1 (1985), 55–71; Amba Pande, ed., *Indentured and Post-Indentured Experiences of Women in the Indian Diaspora* (Berlin: Springer, 2020).

already marginalized population all pose methodological issues that make it problematic to incorporate their history sufficiently in the current analytical frame. Although women's voices, agency, and circumstances – whether African, Indian, or Chinese – were rarely acknowledged by the apparatus of the overseer-state, the potentially disruptive influence of women workers to various schema of imperial labor management and the unfavorable moral affects of the gender imbalance of the indentured workforce were sources of perennial concern among colonial officials. This simultaneous absence and presence speaks to how powerfully gender shaped the operation of the colonial state apparatus, in matters of labor as elsewhere.[65] Consequently, the gendered aspects of colonial labor governance are dealt with at length in a separate article.[66]

As a final note, viewing the origins, development, and decline of the overseer-state as a cultural exchange shaped by a variety of historical actors – enslaved men and women, plantation-owners, indentured Indian and Chinese workers, anti-colonial activists, local magistrates, overseers, Chinese *towkays* and Indian *maistries*, to name but a few – in no way discounts its exploitative

[65] The scholarship on gender, imperialism, slavery, and labor is rich and voluminous. Of particular relevance here are Barbara Bush-Slimani, "Hard Labour: Women, Childbirth and Resistance in British Slave Caribbean Societies," *History Workshop Journal* 36 (Autumn 1983), 83–99; Ashrafi Faruqee, "Conceiving the Coolie Woman: Indentured Labour, Indian Women and Colonial Discourse," *South Asia Research* 16, no. 1 (Spring 1996), 61–76; Catherine Lewis and J. Hilary Beckles, *Centering Women: Gender Discourses in Caribbean Slave Society* (Princeton, NJ: M. Wiener, 1999); Maureen Elgersman Lee, *Unyielding Spirits: Black Women and Slavery in Early Canada and Jamaica* (New York: Garland, 1999); Henrice Altink, "Slavery by Another Name: Apprenticed Women in Jamaican Workhouses in the Period 1834–8," *Social History* 26, no. 1 (2001), 40–59; Verene A. Shepherd, *Maharani's Misery: Narratives of Passage from India to the Caribbean* (Barbados: University of the West Indies Press, 2002); Jennifer Morgan, *Laboring Women: Reproduction and Gender in New World Slavery* (Philadelphia: University of Pennsylvania Press, 2011); Gaiutra Bahadur, *Coolie Woman: The Odyssey of Indenture* (Chicago, IL: University of Chicago Press, 2013); Camillia Cowling, *Conceiving Freedom: Women of Color, Gender, and the Abolition of Slavery in Havana and Rio de Janeiro* (Chapel Hill: University of North Carolina Press, 2013); Mary E. Frederickson and Delores M. Walters, *Gendered Resistance: Women, Slavery, and the Legacy of Margaret Garner* (Urbana: University of Illinois Press, 2017); Sasha Turner, *Contested Bodies: Pregnancy, Childrearing, and Slavery in Jamaica* (Philadelphia: University of Pennsylvania Press, 2017).

[66] Sascha Auerbach, "'If You Flog Me, It Shall Cost You': Violence and Female Subjecthood in Britain's Colonial Labour Systems, 1820–1870," in Mark Condos and Reeju Ray, eds., *The Malevolent Engine of Empire: Colonial Violence Across Temporal, Spatial, and Trans-imperial Boundaries* (London: Routledge, forthcoming winter 2025). This builds on the outstanding work conducted already by Sasha Turner, Mary Turner, and several other key scholars. See, for example, Turner, *Contested Bodies*; Mary Turner, "The 11 O'Clock Flog: Women, Work, and Labour Law in the British Caribbean," *Slavery & Abolition* 20, no. 1 (1999), 38–58.

character. Rather, it is my hope that an approach that examines the reciprocal interactions between officials and workers, no matter how asymmetrical the power relations were, enriches our historical understanding of labor, race, and the state, their interaction, and their roles in shaping the social, economic, political, and cultural dynamics of colonial societies. In the encounters prompted by the overseer-state, we can find key precursors of international labor rights as well as of the global labor market that was its necessary corollary, animating elements of anti-colonial movements, and crucial contributions to the discourse and practice of free labor.[67] In the widest frame, my examination of these topics through the paradigm of the overseer-state contributes to the ongoing historical debates on the legacies of slavery, imperialism, and colonialism; how the modern world was shaped by the mass movement of peoples; and the evolving relationship between the Atlantic and Indian Ocean Worlds in the nineteenth and early twentieth centuries. Given the ubiquity of the state and encounters with it in Britain's global plantation–mining complex, putting the overseer-state at the center of analysis also helps to unify the currently disparate histories of Indian and Chinese labor migration and to clarify the deep and complex relationship between slavery, indenture, and imperialism. In light of the fierce public debates currently taking place in the UK, the US, and Continental Europe about labor and migration, and over the state's legal and moral authority to regulate them, the contemporary relevance of this history is painfully clear.

[67] Jonathan Connolly, "Indentured Labour Migration and the Meaning of Emancipation: Free Trade, Race, and Labour in British Public Debate, 1838–1860," *Past & Present* 238, no. 1 (February 2018), 85–119.

1

"Not Fit for the Enjoyment of Freedom"

Amelioration and the Origins of the Overseer-State, 1812–1834

In December 1825, the sugar plantation Portushope on the east coast of Demerara received a visit from Charles Herbert, one of the most powerful figures in the colony (see Map 1.1). Two years previously, Herbert had been appointed by the Crown to the office of Fiscal. This position was a legacy of the *Code noir* system that had governed the treatment of slaves when the region, on the north coast of South America, was under French control.[1] At an annual salary of £8,000, Herbert was, along with Lieutenant Governor General Benjamin D'Urban, the best paid government official in Demerara. To earn this extraordinary sum, in his capacity as the "Guardian and Protector of Slaves," Herbert faced a daunting task.[2] Working with his small staff of peripatetic Assistant Protectors, many of whom were drawn from the ranks of former army officers, he would ensure that the colony's first comprehensive slave code implemented under British rule was being properly followed, and would shepherd in the newly adopted policy of "amelioration." Approved by Parliament only after a fierce debate, amelioration was an interim solution meant to mollify the powerful antislavery lobby in Britain without alienating the Caribbean plantocracy or disrupting the economically vital sugar trade. Its constellation of laws, principles, and practices was intended to curb the worst abuses of plantation slavery and bring it more in line with the metropolitan vision of the British Empire as a moral, civilizing force.

Herbert had come to Portushope to speak to both the plantation managers and the plantation slaves about how these "new laws," as they were commonly referred to, would shape their lives in the years to come. He described his visit subsequently in a report to Governor D'Urban:

> I beg to report to your Excellency that I yesterday visited the estate *Portushope* on the east coast, and directed the managers from the neighbouring estates, and two or three of the head people [i.e. leaders of the enslaved workforce] from each property to be present. I then

[1] For a broader overview of the final decades of slavery in Guyana, see Alvin Thompson, *Unprofitable Servants: Crown Slaves in Berbice, Guyana, 1803–1831* (Mona: University of the West Indies Press, 2002); J. H. Lean, "The Secret Lives of Slaves: Berbice, 1819–1827," unpublished PhD thesis, University of Canterbury, 2002.

[2] Parliamentary Papers from 1826 covering the reports of the Fiscals are appropriately titled "Proceedings of the Fiscals … in Their Capacity as Guardians and Protectors of Slaves."

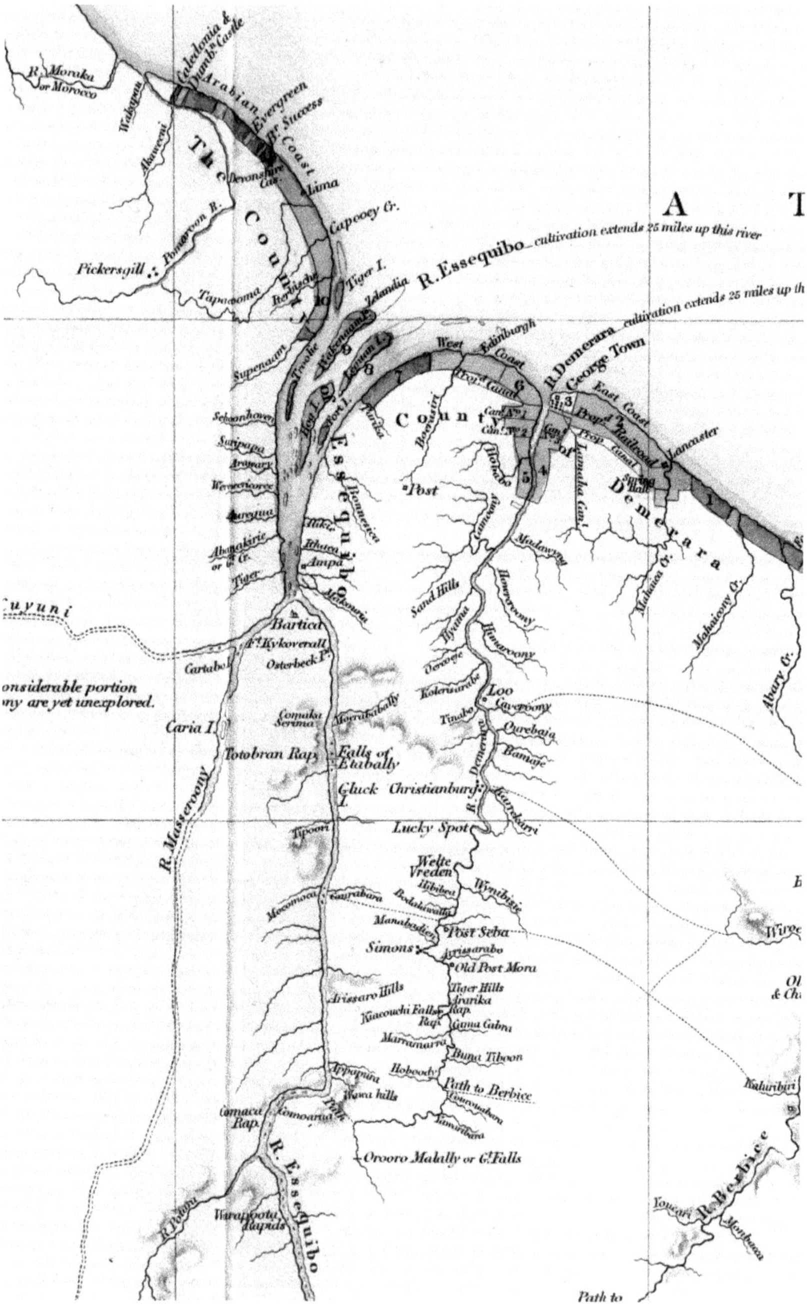

Map 1.1 Essequibo, Demerara, and Berbice, 1838.
Source: *The London Atlas of Universal Geography, Exhibiting the Physical & Political Divisions of the Various Countries of the World, Constructed from Original Materials* (London: John Arrowsmith, 1842).
Note: This map was compiled in 1838 by Crown Surveyor J. Hadfield, from prior surveys by others, and dedicated to the then-governor of the colony, Sir Henry Light.

L A N T I C
O C E A N
R. Berbice _ cultivation extends 35 miles up this river
Union
Belair
N. Amsterdam
Bestendighed
Bleyendall
Jahoeca
R. Canje
Corentyn
Coast
Mary's Hope
R. Corentyn
R. Nikirie or Nickerie
Eliza & Mary
Skeldon
Brandwagt
Haitiban
Liddel
Wikhy
Old Post
DUTCH COLONY
OF
SURINAM
Baboon I.s
Saranapoo
Oreala
Laytield
R. Wasiappo

Map 1.1 (cont.)

> explained to them that I was informed that they entertained mistaken ideas concerning the ordinance recently published, and called by the slaves, "the new laws." I explained to them (in plain language) the regulations concerning their labour, and the consequence of misconduct; that they must not imagine themselves exempt from either the one or the other; that it was expected they would perform their work cheerfully, and not from the fear of punishment, and that measures being adopted to render their situation comfortable, a suitable behaviour was expected from them. I told them that I would always take care of them in case of ill treatment; but I should discountenance any improper conduct; they all seemed sensible of my observations, and were pleased, and I have every reason to think it will have a good effect. I was induced to this measure as several people from that district had latterly shewn a disinclination to attend to their work, or submit to the authority of their managers, it [*sic*] may have the effect of correcting any mistaken ideas which negroes are apt to entertain of a "new law" and if any little discontent is checked by such means, it is far preferable to harsh measures.[3]

Within Herbert's statement, we can discern many of the core principles and practices that would constitute the overseer-state in the decades to come. The central message of his announcement was that the colonial government, in the guise of the Fiscal or an analogous official, would assume ultimate authority, and ultimate responsibility, for the character of life and work on the plantation. The new officials would mediate between management and labor, and it would be to them that workers would address any grievances and from them that redress, if deemed appropriate, would come. Such intervention came at a price. The state was now keeping a keen eye on slaves' behavior, and demanded their respect and their adherence to good order. Discontent or malingering would *not* be tolerated. Existing methods of plantation discipline – which comprised in the main the strict surveillance and regimentation of labor guided by codified regulations and enforced with corporal punishment, all of which operated within a context of customary practice – would not be dismantled but would rather come under the authority of the new state agents installed to oversee both the plantation workforce and their managers.[4]

Herbert embodied the new direction of this centralized, hierarchical state apparatus. His visits to the plantations and public addresses to their staff and enslaved workforce served as a visible demonstration of how the days of self-government in Britain's plantation colonies were waning. The abolition of the

3 Charles Herbert (Fiscal) to Gen. B. D'Urban (Lt. Gov. Demerara), December 21, 1825, HC Papers, *Further Papers Relating to the Proceedings of the Fiscals of Demerara and Berbice; in Their Capacity of Guardians and Protectors of Slaves and Their Decisions in All Cases of Complaints of Masters and Slaves*, 1826 (hereafter, *Complaints of Masters and Slaves*, 1826), 19.

4 Thomas Holt, *The Problem of Freedom: Race, Labour, and Politics in Jamaica and Britain* (Baltimore, MD: Johns Hopkins University Press, 1992), 38.

slave trade, an unprecedented intervention by Parliament into the social, economic, and political structure of Britain's global plantation complex, had shifted the balance of power throughout the empire. The seizure of new territory during the Napoleonic Wars, territory that was administered directly by the Crown rather than indirectly through colonial legislatures, had accelerated the shifting balance of power from the traditional planter oligarchy to Crown-appointed governors and new agents such as Fiscals.[5] In this rapidly changing terrain of colonial governance, how quickly the process of reform proceeded, and how decisively the newly appointed agents of imperial oversight would intercede in plantation life, would depend on the response of planters and slaves alike to "the new laws."

For the proprietors of sugar estates, incidents such as the Demerara Rebellion of 1823 demonstrated the dangers of meddling with the established practices of plantation slavery.[6] But for the powerful antislavery lobby in Britain, the violence in Demerara was instead an apt illustration of the rot at the heart of the Caribbean plantation system. The new crop of administrators in London, and their appointees in the colonies, had to tread a fine balance between mollifying the planters, who remained paramount in the economic and social order of the colonies, and alienating antislavery Members of Parliament (MPs), whose political power and influence on public opinion made them a force to be reckoned with. The stakes involved in this radical restructuring of the colonial state were very much evident to Herbert and his superior, Governor D'Urban. Both men explicitly identified the failure of the state to improve plantation conditions as the central catalyst of the 1823 revolt, and warned their superiors in Whitehall that history would repeat itself if officials did not respond effectively to the complaints of enslaved African-Caribbeans.[7]

Herbert's address at Portushope therefore offers an entry point for framing the origins of the overseer-state within the broader historical trajectories of labor and governance in the empire. Given the longevity of the offices created (or, rather, adapted) to manage the transition from slavery to free labor, we can see that the practices of amelioration, emancipation, apprenticeship, and indenture were not discrete, but contiguous and entangled.

5 Madhavi Kale, *Fragments of Empire: Capital, Slavery, & Indian Indentured Labor in the British Caribbean* (Philadelphia: University of Pennsylvania Press, 1998), 40–1.

6 The owners of sugar plantations, whether in residence or absentee, are typically referred to in the archival record as "proprietors," "estate owners," or "masters," the last even decades after the abolition of slavery.

7 *Complaints of Masters and Slaves*, 1826, 14. D'Urban, who had been appointed as the governor of Demerara in 1824, even went so far as to arrange for complaints to be directly solicited from slaves in pamphlets and newspapers and, to ensure that they were not overlooked, instructed them to register their grievances with local magistrates along with the assistant to the Fiscal. Caroline Quarrier Spence, "Ameliorating Empire: Slavery and Protection in the British Colonies, 1783–1865," unpublished PhD dissertation, Harvard University, 2014, 203.

Exploring the crucial transition period from slavery to indenture, this chapter makes three arguments. The first is that while indenture's position in the plantation economy may have echoed the practices of slavery, which had been primarily a private enterprise, the origins of its legal framework lay in the state apparatus introduced to manage the transition from slavery to free labor. Likewise, its ideological underpinnings drew on the justifications for this new apparatus. The central aspect of these new state processes and their ideological adjuncts was the transformation of the plantation workforce from private property that was controlled by owners into subjects of rule who were answerable to the state. The second argument is that these new mechanisms of labor regulation came to play a crucial role, structurally and conceptually, in anchoring colonial rule not just in the post-emancipation Caribbean but as far afield as Mauritius and South Africa. This radical process of reform was justified ideologically as a moral imperative, politically as a means of maintaining order and sustaining revenue, and culturally as a paternalistic enterprise to uplift the abused and exploited slaves who were transitioning from property to Crown subjects.[8]

A third, corollary argument made here is that during the amelioration period, plantation colonies became sites of experimentation in governance. More specifically, the expansion of state power through the introduction of the Crown colony system and the decisive intervention of the state into the dynamics of plantation labor organization, first with amelioration and subsequently with emancipation, were two interdependent processes.[9] The rapid upswing in the authority of a centralized colonial state (at the cost of colonial self-governance) was accomplished through its growing predominance in monitoring, organizing, and disciplining not just laborers but all of those involved in the plantation labor system, including planters, managers, and overseers. As a consequence, labor system regulation emerged not just as an aspect of British imperial sovereignty in the tropics but as its keystone.[10] Across the nineteenth century, this coordinated network of laws, administrators, institutions and practices

[8] As Madhavi Kale points out in her examination of indenture's Caribbean introduction, this process occurred simultaneously at the concrete level and at the conceptual level. The process of organizing labor economically and legally occurred in tandem with the "forging" of the definition of labor, and both were entangled in racial, social, gender, and political contexts. Kale, *Fragments of Empire*, 10.

[9] Their interrelation has long been recognized, though what this tells us about the nature of colonial governance and its dependence on labor control has remained unexplored. L. M. Penson, "The Making of a Crown Colony: British Guiana, 1803–33," *Transactions of the Royal Historical Society* 9 (1926), 109–10.

[10] My thanks to Catherine Hall for this insight, which was offered at the "Short Histories of the British Empire, 1816–1856" workshop, hosted by the Institute of Advanced Studies, University College London, September 16, 2016. As Lauren Benton argues, "territorial control was, in many places, an incidental aim of imperial expansion." Lauren Benton, *A Search for Sovereignty: Law and Geography in European Empires* (Cambridge: Cambridge University Press, 2010), 2.

would come to constitute the overseer-state.[11] It would enhance the effectiveness of colonial governance over local populations, increase the accountability of local state agents to directives from the metropole, widen the adaptability of state institutions to the responses of those under their suzerainty and, most importantly, allow the state to regulate and coordinate the empire's most valuable resource, its vast plantation labor force. New modes of recording, inspection, regulation, and enforcement introduced to colonial labor management in the 1820s would presage the adoption of similar policies and mechanisms in Britain by years or even decades.[12] Examining the transition from slavery to free labor and indenture through the lens of the overseer-state therefore clarifies the central role of labor management in colonial rule, reveals plantation colonies as a site of experimentation in enhanced governance, and illuminates the evolving relationship between colony and metropole (and of different colonies to one another).

The framework of the overseer-state also demonstrates how the changing character of colonial labor management entangled British and Continental European modes of imperialism and complicates our historical understanding of the role played by liberal ideology in colonial rule.[13] The overseer-state, concretely and conceptually, bridged the histories of the British Empire and the French, Spanish, and Dutch empires, demonstrating how the development of labor control mechanisms in tropical colonies was a European enterprise rather than merely a British one. The model for reform in Britain's plantation colonies was not liberalism, since the putative objects of reform, both enslaved Africans and their masters, fit poorly within the parameters of liberal subjecthood as they were understood at the time.[14] Instead, the coercive, interventionist, centralized state structures that were the legacies of Spanish, French, or (to a lesser extent) Dutch rule served as the structural basis for British legal reform in the possessions seized from these powers during the Napoleonic Wars.[15] The provenance of these laws explicitly evoked their Continental precedents. The first comprehensive slave code in the British Empire, the 1824 Amelioration Order in Council (Trinidad), was commonly referred to by contemporaries as the *Code noir*, the same term that was applied to its

[11] This follows on the argument made by Caroline Spence that "emancipation . . . would be a turning point in a process of centralization of metropolitan authority that would culminate in the 1860s." Spence, "Ameliorating Empire," 198.

[12] Patrick Joyce, *The Rule of Freedom: Liberalism and the Modern City* (New York: Verso, 2003), 14–15.

[13] See Duncan Bell, *Reordering the World: Essays on Liberalism and Empire* (Princeton, NJ: Princeton University Press, 2016), esp. ch. 4, 106–7.

[14] Natasha Lightfoot, *Troubling Freedom: Antigua and the Aftermath of British Emancipation* (Durham, NC: Duke University Press, 2015), 7.

[15] Christina Twomey, "Protecting Slaves and Aborigines: The Legacies of European Colonialism in the British Empire," *Pacific Historical Review* 87, no. 1 (2018), 11.

French antecedent.[16] The initial hope among metropolitan administrators was that such laws, while interventionist in nature, could be applied in the spirit of liberal governance, which relied to a great degree on moral self-reliance encouraged by didactic regulation.[17] These hopes would fade rapidly when confronted by a conservative plantocracy that saw the maintenance of racialized authority and plantation discipline as the bedrock of social stability and economic viability. The reluctance of enslaved men and women to unquestioningly accept the authority of the new structure of state-sponsored discipline and their frustration at the slow pace of emancipation, frustration that occasionally boiled over into violent resistance, also hastened the turn toward governing through coercion rather than by consent.[18] Amelioration and emancipation would be achieved only through the expansion of colonial governance in a manner that borrowed extensively from the Continental colonial systems and slave-plantation practices that formed its historical foundations. Like these antecedents, the new overseer-state would be paternalist in language, hierarchical in structure, interventionist in conduct, and punitive in action.

The Early Stages of Amelioration

Thirty years before Britain's abolition of the transatlantic trade in enslaved Africans and fifty years before the first attempts at "ameliorating" the condition of slaves across the British Empire, Adam Smith identified the chief legal obstacle to the state's direct intervention in the institution of slavery. As long as slaves were classified as private property, he argued, the agents of a constitutional state would be severely constrained in their ability to act. To "intermeddle ... in the management of the private property of the master," Smith asserted, would violate the laws guarding private ownership, and any official who did so would likely face the wrath of the colonial legislative body to which he was answerable.[19] The circumstances were very different in a colony ruled by an "arbitrary" government, where judicial officials could execute their duties without such accountability. Here, Smith pointed to the example of the French colonies, where the unrestrained power of the magistrates and their "common humanity" allowed them to more effectively protect slaves from abuse by their masters. This fear of

[16] Claudius Fergus, "The *Siete Partidas*: A Framework for Philanthropy and Coercion during the Amelioration Experiment in Trinidad," *Caribbean Studies* 36, no. 1 (Jan.–June 2008), 78.

[17] Martin Wiener, *Reconstructing the Criminal: Culture, Law, and Policy in England, 1830–1914* (Cambridge: Cambridge University Press, 1990), 11.

[18] The majority of their erstwhile advocates in Parliament still thought enslaved Africans to be incapable of either comprehending legal processes or employing them responsibly. Lightfoot, *Troubling Freedom*, 7.

[19] Adam Smith, *An Inquiry into the Nature and Causes of the Wealth of Nations, Book IV: Systems of Political Economy* (London: W. Strahan and T. Cadell, 1776), 179.

punishment, in turn, prompted French slave-owners to treat their slaves better, to the social and economic benefit of all involved. Such "gentle usage," Smith insisted, "makes the slave more faithful and more intelligent, and therefore doubly more useful."[20]

Smith's praise of French slaveholders belied the brutality that pervaded French plantation colonies, as it did in all European possessions where slavery was practiced.[21] His assessment of the contrast between the British system of slavery and that applied by the French, the Spanish, and the Dutch, however, was accurate on several points. Enslaved men and women did, indeed, enjoy legal protections under the latter that they did not possess in British colonies. And in colonies under the control of Continental European powers, an attitude of paternalism was key to both public discourse and legal practice with regard to enslavement. Unlike in British colonies, enslaved Africans and their owners were subject to a codified set of regulations governing how slaves could be treated, the conditions under which they labored, the rights of slaves, their avenues for grievance against their masters, the protocols for adjudicating these complaints and the enforcement of penalties against the latter when judgments went against them.[22] These laws were enforced by a cadre of powerful officials who received their instructions directly from their respective imperial centers.

When British policymakers, prompted in part by outbreaks of rebellion in the Caribbean slave colonies, took up the issue of improving the conditions of slaves there, they would look to the more centralized colonial governments of the French, the Spanish, and the Dutch to provide models for reform.[23] While the new system was hardly "arbitrary," in that its enforcers were still guided by law, they were not directly accountable to the planters whom they governed. Instead, it was the planters who became answerable to these new agents, who were, in turn, accountable to Crown-appointed governors. The result was a system that, while arguably no less coercive toward slaves than its predecessor was, did shift the ultimate authority for plantation management from the slave-owners to the state; the latter would hold the power of punishment over slaves and masters alike.[24] The lash was not discarded but rather passed from the hands of the planters and managers to the hands of a new agent tasked with overseeing *all* of those in the plantation system.

[20] Smith, *Wealth of Nations*, 179.

[21] Fergus, "*Siete Partidas*," 80.

[22] Matthew Wyman-McCarthy, "Perceptions of French and Spanish Slave Law in Late Eighteenth-Century Britain," *Journal of British Studies* 57, no. 1 (2018), 29–30.

[23] Ibid., 30–1.

[24] On the wider imperial juridical dynamics in which this was embedded, see Lauren Benton and Lisa Ford, "Magistrates in Empire: Convicts, Slaves, and the Remaking of the Plural Legal Order in the British Empire," in Lauren Benton and Richard J. Ross, eds., *Legal Pluralism and Empires, 1500–1850* (New York: New York University Press, 2013), 173–98.

The overseer-state that emerged in this process would be an amalgam of the older principles of royal and aristocratic paternalism, newer ideas of humanitarianism, the preexisting traditions of Continental slave regulation and the local judicial structure. Its power would be greatest in the Crown colony system that was implemented in the territories acquired during the Napoleonic Wars (e.g. Trinidad, British Guiana and St. Lucia), but its influence would extend well beyond them. The new system of laws, agents and principles established during the process of amelioration would also signal the beginning of the incremental but steady expansion of the imperial state's authority in older colonies where legislatures largely beholden to the plantocracy had long enjoyed considerable autonomy, particularly in matters of labor and plantation management.

This process began slowly, then accelerated rapidly in the mid-1820s. A crucial early step in expanding the imperial state's oversight of colonial labor systems involved one of the most effective new methods of modern governance, the census.[25] Following an Order in Council in March 1812, a new Crown-appointed agent was introduced to Trinidad, the "Registrar of Slaves." This official's duty was to collate two registers annually, one of all plantation slaves and one of all personal slaves. To compose these tallies, the Registrar was to collect, from each planter on the island, a report of all births, deaths, sales, and manumissions each year. In order to ensure the cooperation of the planters in this endeavor, it was stipulated by the Order that proper documentation was necessary to prove a master's claim over a slave. This introduced a novel and profoundly significant legal principle: for the first time in the history of the British Empire, the *default* status of all African-Caribbeans was that of freedom, whereas enslavement had to be proven through legally certified records.[26] As the Chief Justice of Trinidad stated bluntly when questioned a decade later by Royal Commissioners on the topic, "every man is presumed by law to be free, until he be proved to be a slave."[27]

With the appointment of the Trinidad Registrar and the implementation of the comprehensive "slave census," the imperial state, for the first time, began monitoring the slave population as individuals and intervening directly in the practice of slavery itself.[28] The goal was not to create practical avenues by which slaves could achieve freedom, and it would take some time before

[25] The first comprehensive census of England, Wales and Scotland was conducted in 1801.

[26] *Report of the Commissioners of Legal Inquiry on the Colony of Trinidad 1826*, 28 (hereafter *Trinidad Legal Inquiry 1826*). For the longer history of how the legal principles of slavery had changed as a result of the Somerset Case, see James Van Cleve, "*Somerset's Case* and Its Antecedents in Imperial Perspective," *Law and History Review* 24, no. 3 (Fall, 2006), 603–4.

[27] *Trinidad Legal Inquiry 1826*, 28.

[28] Initial registers recorded the name of the slave and their owners, and information was also collected on the former's occupation, age, family relations, and physical characteristics such as height and distinguishing marks. B. W. Higman, *Slave Populations of the British Caribbean, 1807–1834* (Kingston: University of the West Indies Press, 1984), 11–19.

enslaved African-Caribbeans would begin seeking, in any great number, manumission through documentary means. Instead, the purpose of the Order and other similar measures that were to follow throughout the British Caribbean was to manage the behavior of slave-*owners* and to hasten the end of the trade in enslaved Africans.[29] Spanish officials had maintained slave registers as a means by which slave-owners could be encouraged to keep mortality rates down, preserving a vital means of revenue for the Crown. The system also aided the accurate levy of taxes, given that such slaves were, legally, taxable property.[30] The Trinidad regulation, in contrast, was intended to discourage the importation of new slaves to Trinidad from another colony or their exportation elsewhere, both of which were forbidden without special license. Its implementation would prove problematic, and the number of slaves recorded in Trinidad would fluctuate significantly over the course of the next few years, planters accounting for this with claims that the initial registers were inaccurate.[31] Despite the mixed results, the appointment of a Registrar of Slaves and the keeping of the registers themselves were the first major steps in establishing a centralized state apparatus, its agents directly answerable to policy-makers in London, that would oversee the slave labor system in Trinidad. At the urging of antislavery interests in Parliament and against the protests of both planters in the colonies and their organized advocates in Britain, keeping detailed and updated registers of slaves in any colony where they were present would become a legal mandate throughout the British Empire by 1819.[32]

The direct intervention of the colonial state into the management of the plantation workforce in Trinidad had preceded the recognition of enslaved Africans as legal individuals by more than a decade. The reformed slave law code of 1800, known as "Picton's Code" after the governor who implemented it, imposed a wide array of strict and specific regulations on care for the physical well-being of the enslaved population. This was done with the justification that such practices would "promote the natural increase" of the population and, in doing so, diminish and eventually eliminate the need to maintain the labor force through importation.[33] These new regulations encompassed

29 James Stephen, *Reasons for Establishing a Registry of Slaves in the British Colonies* (London: Ellerton and Henderson, 1885), 12.

30 The model here was the 1789 *cédula real.* The Spanish system of governance is described in A. Meredith John, *The Plantation Slaves of Trinidad: A Mathematical and Demographic Inquiry* (Cambridge: Cambridge University Press, 1988), 8–17.

31 Stephen, *Registry of Slaves*, 28.

32 The keeping of a slave register began in Demerara and Essequibo in 1817; Berbice followed in 1818. www.ucl.ac.uk/lbs/project/estates-sources-notes/ (accessed April 13, 2021). These registers now form the most comprehensive and detailed record available of the institution of slavery in its final years.

33 Ordinance from Thomas Picton, Governor of Trinidad, June 30, 1800, reprinted in Appendix D, *Report of the Commissioners of Legal Inquiry on the Colony of Trinidad, 1826* (hereafter Picton's Code 1800), 158.

almost every aspect of the life of enslaved Africans on the plantations. Specific obligations for care and maintenance included the provision of "good and comfortable homes," supplying set amounts of meat (3 lb) and fish (4 lb) twice a week, the allotment of land for garden cultivation, supplying clothing twice a year, and setting aside time off of work for daily meals.[34] In addition, plantation owners were required to establish a hospital, its size proportionate to the number of slaves on the plantation; to clothe, feed, and lodge slaves that could no longer work due to age, accident, or sickness; and to allow them Sundays off for holiday. Stern limitations were placed on the severity and the manner of corporal punishment. Plantation owners or their proxies were permitted to administer a maximum of thirty-nine lashes, while managers or overseers were restricted to no more than twelve for any one offense. More severe punishments could be inflicted only by the governor's appointed district administrator, the Commandant.[35] The penalties for violation of this last edict were significant, set at fifty Trinidadian dollars (approximately £20). Even more harsh was the punishment for striking a slave with an edged weapon or a bludgeon. Conviction for that crime brought with it immediate confiscation of the injured slave and their sale "to some person of known humanity."[36]

As much as the historiography of emancipation has said about the character of freedom and rights following the abolition of the slave trade in 1806, Picton's Code points to a very different mechanism of government intervention by which enslaved Africans were reconfigured, legally and conceptually, from objects of property into subjects of rule. The first stage of British reform was to delineate strict parameters for how the bodies of the enslaved were to be maintained by their owners. Such measures echoed the earlier recognition by the Spanish state that the lives of the enslaved were of value, if only as an important commodity and source of revenue, and therefore needed to be preserved. Picton's Code also explicitly categorized the enslaved Africans of Trinidad as a distinct population that was defined through, and could therefore be regulated by, the state.[37] With the census, this cohort (and, subsequently, all slaves across the British Empire) were embedded in state oversight more specifically by installing a mechanism to count and record them as individuals. Both reforms were couched in humanitarian language, and given the public outcry over the wide-ranging abuses revealed by antislavery activists, this was easily reconcilable with their other consequence, which was to subsume under direct state authority the most important economic resource of tropical

34 Picton's Code 1800, 159.

35 Ibid.

36 Ibid.

37 On the creation of populations through the use of demographic data as a characteristic of the modern state, see Thomas Lemke, "The Government of Living Beings: Michel Foucault," in Thomas Lemke (with a preface by Monica J. Casper and Lisa Moore), *Biopolitics: An Advanced Introduction* (New York: New York University Press, 2011), 37.

colonies, their workforce. By taking on these new roles, the colonial state was transforming from an entity concerned largely with collecting revenue, maintaining order, and protecting property to one that was increasingly involved in monitoring populations, defining the conditions of life and work on the plantation, and preserving the bodies and health of the enslaved labor force.[38] Over time, the older focus of the state and its newer emphasis would prove to be highly complementary.

Picton's Code allowed the state to intervene directly into the behavior of slave-owners, but it was problematic to enforce for two reasons. The first was that Trinidad's magistracy was socially and culturally integrated with the planter oligarchy that were the putative targets of regulation and the second was the absence of any mechanism by which plantation slaves could appeal violations.[39] The subsequent establishment of the Registrar, an officer that was directly answerable to the Crown-appointed governor, lessened these obstacles, empowering the state in relation to a plantocracy that had formerly held near-total sway over plantation labor discipline. With the implementation of the 1819 Order in Council, the status of enslaved Africans, at least in law if not always in practice, changed. Although the immediate responsibility for their condition remained, as it always had, on their owners, this duty altered from one guided by customary practice to one regulated more comprehensively by law and monitored more strictly by state agents. The latter were directly supervised by metropolitan authorities and the colonial administrators they appointed. Even as slaves themselves were transitioning from property to Crown subjects, slave-owners, and the plantation managers and overseers they employed, were being legally redefined from property-holders largely unfettered by law to wardens increasingly answerable to it.

The newly empowered agents of the colonial state, such as the Registrar, in turn became the supervisors of those wardens. They were imbued with a host of powers – the fining of plantation-owners and the seizure of their property, for example – heretofore wielded only by governors, magistrates, or colonial legislatures. These early decades of reform brought the owners and managers of plantations under stricter legal regulation and closer scrutiny, albeit indirectly,

[38] Michel Foucault termed this form of authority "biopower," and identified it as a seminal stage in the growth of the modern configurations of power. It was the joining of disciplinary or "sovereign-juridical" power with this authority to control "biological processes: propagation, births and mortality, the level of health, life expectancy and longevity" that characterized the evolution of power in the nineteenth century. Michel Foucault, *The Will to Knowledge: The History of Sexuality Volume 1* ([1976]; trans. R Hurley, London: Penguin, 1998), 139–40.

[39] Closely advised by one of the colony's most prominent plantation-owners, Governor Thomas Picton himself was, at best, an ambivalent figure in the efforts to reform slavery. James Epstein, "Politics of Colonial Sensation: The Trial of Thomas Picton and the Cause of Louisa Calderon," *American Historical Review* 112, no. 3 (June 2007), 717.

from the imperial center. The reports produced by the Registrar subsequently became ammunition for antislavery elements in Parliament and, in the hands of a burgeoning metropolitan press eager for scandal and the readership it garnered, fodder for sensationalist accounts that emphasized the cruelty of slavery and the moral failings of slave-owners. The new laws also redefined enslaved Africans as individuals to be counted, classified, warded, and ruled via state processes, though their full recognition as Crown subjects with all attendant rights and protections would not arrive until nearly two decades later.[40]

In this early configuration, the overseer-state borrowed from the paternalistic traditions of eighteenth-century aristocratic rule, where noble landowners had assumed the customary duty for the care of those who worked their land.[41] Colonial plantation-owners, for their part, asserted that this concern was already central to their outlook, and that the state's intervention was therefore unnecessary.[42] The 1819 Order also anticipated the humanitarian reform of work conditions, housing, food, sanitation, and childrearing that would not be implemented in Britain itself until the mid-nineteenth century. The pioneering of such measures in the empire was made possible by the rising assertiveness of Crown rule in the face of planter resistance, by the influence of the antislavery lobby in Parliament, and by the common appeal of such measures to both Tory paternalism and liberal humanitarianism. Another key cultural and political impetus behind these reforms was the desire of imperial administrators to fulfill the mission of "moral imperialism." This had followed in the wake of the outlawing of the slave trade and the establishment of Britain's new self-declared national identity as the antithesis of Napoleonic injustice and despotism.[43]

Like much of the legislation that would be introduced after it, the Trinidad register of slaves was explicitly modeled on laws implemented by the prior occupiers, in this case, the Spanish *cédula real*, first adopted in 1789.[44] The "Spanish Laws" (also known as the *Code noir*), as they came to be called by contemporaries, would also serve as the structural precedents for the next major phase of reform, amelioration. The latter began in earnest with Lord Canning's resolution in the House of Commons, moved on May 15, 1823, "to adopt effectual and decisive measures for ameliorating the condition of the

40 For slavery as "one of the first instances of biopolitical experimentation," see Achille Mbembe, "Necropolitics," trans. by Libby Meintjes, *Public Culture* 15, no. 1 (2003), 21.

41 Ibid., 27–8.

42 *House of Commons Papers in Explanation of the Measures adopted by His Majesty's Government for the Melioration of the Condition of the Slave Population in the West Indies, and on the Continent of South America*, 1823–4 (hereafter, *Papers on Melioration*, 1823–4), 22.

43 On the latter, see Linda Colley, *Britons: Forging the Nation, 1707–1837* (New Haven, CT: Yale University Press, 1992).

44 For a more comprehensive catalog of the different Spanish laws in force at the time of Trinidad's capture in February 1797, see *Report of His Majesty's Commissioners of Legal Enquiry on the Colony of Trinidad*, 1827, 6.

slave population in his majesty's colonies."[45] Amelioration was a compromise between the goal of antislavery parliamentarians, led by Thomas Fowell Buxton, to eradicate slavery altogether, and the more conservative mindset of the West India Committee. The members of the latter, representing Caribbean planter interests in metropolitan circles, were determined to preserve as much of the institution as was possible.[46] This compromise was achieved by establishing the state, in the form of new Crown-appointed agents such as the Registrar, as the intermediary between the enslaved plantation workforce and plantation-owners, managers, and overseers. The state's accession as overseer for the plantation system was made morally defensible through the language of paternalism and protection. The reforms implemented, while providing the enslaved population with new legal rights and some avenues for redress against abuse, acceded to planter interests by retaining the coercive practices of slave labor management. Amelioration attempted to mollify antislavery interests in Parliament, on the other hand, by placing limitations on the authority of planters and managers. They now had to follow strict protocols in their punishment of plantation slaves or face fines and even, in rare cases, imprisonment.

The result of this attempt at compromise was widespread tension and dissatisfaction across the span of Britain's plantation colonies. Owners and managers from the Caribbean to South Africa and Mauritius persistently sought ways to undermine or avoid the new legal limitations on their authority. The enslaved population, meanwhile, chafed at the slow pace of reform and demanded their own versions of justice regardless of whether or not they fit the parameters of the new laws. As its agents struggled to deal with the recalcitrance of plantation managers on the one hand and the remonstrations of enslaved Africans on the other, the overseer-state would expand its power across the 1820s and early 1830s. In principle, the new laws would embody the paternalism that colonial administrators from Jamaica to London insisted was at the heart of British imperial enterprise.[47] In practice, the same violent suppression that had characterized pre-amelioration slavery would persist, with the authority to regulate and implement it passing from the hands of slave-owners to those of new Crown-appointed agents, albeit in a less severe incarnation.

Typical of the new system was the limiting of the maximum lashes to be inflicted on an enslaved African by their master, with strict guidelines on the offenses that justified such punishment, the necessity of witnesses, the means by which the lashes were delivered, and the careful recording of punishments.[48]

[45] House of Commons Debates, 15 May 1823, vol. 9, cc 285.

[46] Robert Luster, *The Amelioration of the Slaves in the British Empire, 1790–1833* (New York: Peter Lang, 1995), ch. 1.

[47] *Papers on Melioration*, 1823–4, 21.

[48] Amelioration Order in Council, 24 in *Appendix to Report of Commissioners of Enquiry on the Colony of Trinidad*, CO 318/29, 226. The limitations on physical punishment took their

Enslaved Africans were also granted conditional rights such as that to purchase their own freedom (i.e. manumission), to marry of their own free will, to open accounts with a savings bank (largely for the purpose of facilitating eventual manumission), to give evidence in courts of law, and to own and bequeath property.[49] The new regulations elicited howls of protest from slave-owners, especially in the legislative colonies such as Jamaica. There, elected representatives complained bitterly that the new laws, passed without their approval, were tantamount to the "encroachment of despotic power" on their liberties as Crown subjects and their rights as owners of private property.[50]

The protests of planters notwithstanding, the "Spanish Laws" in Trinidad, which were codified and expanded with an Order in Council in 1824, would serve as a model for amelioration throughout the empire. At their core was the reestablishment of a figure that had been the lynchpin of state labor regulation under Spanish rule, the Protector and Guardian of Slaves. This figure replaced the older office of *Procurador Syndic* of the Port of Spain. He assumed all the powers of the previous office and added to them the authority of a magistrate whose remit extended the length and breadth of the colony.[51] The Protector's duties were wide-ranging, from ensuring that the enslaved population was provided with proper food and housing to serving as the advocate for any slave who was brought to court on criminal charges. Among the most significant and time-consuming of his responsibilities was traveling to plantations in order to hear the complaints that any enslaved person was now entitled to make against a master, manager, or overseer for violation of the new laws. As amelioration was adopted throughout the Caribbean colonies, this latter task devolved onto a cadre of Assistant Protectors who would act with the authority of the Protector, provide regular reports of the conditions they encountered among the enslaved population, and receive their petitions for redress against alleged abuses.[52]

Although Trinidad would be the first to receive a comprehensive overhaul of its laws regarding slavery, Demerara, one of the three colonies that would eventually make up British Guiana, would also serve as an initial site for the experiment of amelioration. There, a compromise had been adopted by the Prime Minister, George Canning, and the Secretary for the Colonies, Henry

inspiration both from metropolitan ideas about penal reform and from experiments by "enlightened" planters such as Joshua Steele, who, in the second half of the eighteenth century, was proposing new ways of managing enslaved labor. Randy Browne, *Surviving Slavery in the British Caribbean* (Philadelphia: University of Pennsylvania Press, 2017), 47.

49 Fergus, "*Siete Partidas*," 86.

50 Jamaica House of Assembly to the Duke of Manchester, Gov. of Jamaica, December 11, 1823, *Papers on Melioration*, 1823–4, 27.

51 Draft of an Order in Council for Improving the Condition of Slaves in Trinidad (hereafter "1824 Trinidad Order"), *Papers on Melioration*, 1823–4, 141.

52 1824 Trinidad Order; *Papers on Melioration*, 1823–4, 143.

Bathurst, between the demands of Buxton and other reformers and the staunch resistance of the West India Committee. As a newly acquired Crown colony with a substantial enslaved population, it was an ideal site, or so it was thought by the colonial executive and metropolitan administrators, for the new experiment in state oversight and governance. The high stakes of amelioration and the consequences of rising tensions between the enslaved population, plantation-owners, and the burgeoning state apparatus operating as a mediator, however, would become apparent when a wave of disorder swept across the region. At the core of the debate that followed would be whether amelioration was the potential cause of widespread dissatisfaction among the enslaved population or a potential cure for it. The combination of an effective antislavery lobby and the support of metropolitan administrators, lent greater urgency by the actions of the enslaved themselves, would prove decisive in overcoming planters' stubbornness to release the reins of control and the ardent efforts of the West India lobby. The supporters of amelioration as a moral necessity and the most effective response to the increasing tensions in plantation colonies would prevail, prompting an expansion of state oversight over the plantation system and culminating in the centralization and consolidation of governance over the entire three-colony region (i.e. Demerara, Essequibo, and Berbice).

Initial attempts to revise the institution of slavery there met with little success. The responsibility for hearing slave complaints and ensuring that the laws regarding them were respected fell on the Fiscal, an official created when the colony had been under Dutch rule.[53] As in Trinidad, the original inspiration for this had come from the Spanish.[54] Under British authority, the Fiscal, retained at an annual salary of £3,000, proved largely ineffective at implementing any significant reform. As the Chief Magistrate in the colony, his duties were broad, and analogous to those of the Attorney-General of England.[55] Despite the urging of Governor (Lieutenant General) John Murray, the Fiscal tended to side with proprietors and dismiss slaves' complaints out of hand, or even to punish the latter when they came to state their grievances.[56] In this, the Fiscal, commensurate with his role under the Dutch system, prioritized the colony's traditional social order, in which the authority of owners to discipline their slaves was considered paramount, over paternalism or humanitarian concerns. These circumstances, where the officer tasked with enforcing the just treatment of enslaved Africans and addressing the abuses of slave-owners was little motivated to do either, were exacerbated by

[53] Emilia Viotti da Costa, *Crowns of Glory, Tears of Blood: The Demerara Slave Rebellion of 1823* (Oxford: Oxford University Press, 1997), 45.
[54] Da Costa, *Crowns of Glory*, 45.
[55] Henry Bolingbroke, *A Voyage to the Demerary* (London: Richard Phillips, 1809), 40.
[56] Da Costa, *Crowns of Glory*, 64. The Murrays were a family replete with high military office and positions of colonial influence.

the social and economic structure of Demerara. Even more so than in other regions of the British Caribbean, the colony was characterized by a minuscule white minority ruling over a vast population of enslaved Africans.[57] Since the instability of Demerara's economy and the concurrent frequency of defaults on plantation mortgages had resulted in widespread absentee landlordship, neither proprietors nor their representatives demonstrated any discernible interest in engaging proposals for reform.[58] Plantations were often directed by attorneys and managers without even the window-dressing of paternalism that the wealthy planter class in older, more established colonies might assert. Instead, these custodians had a strong motivation to return a profit and little impetus to support legislation that weakened their authority over their workforce.

In a pattern that would become common across the Caribbean in subsequent years, tensions between enslaved Africans and plantation authorities in Demerara, exacerbated by the foment over reform, escalated into open conflict. The end result would see the state further expand its oversight of the colonial labor system. The catalyst for the rebellion here emerged from the ongoing debate between abolitionists and the supporters of the plantocracy, represented by the West India Committee, over the conditions of slavery and what role the colonial state would play in their alteration. The Secretary for the Colonies, Henry Bathurst, had been confronted with a broad suite of changes proposed by Thomas Buxton, a close associate of William Wilberforce, in Parliament.[59] Many of Buxton's proposals would subsequently be enshrined in the 1824 Trinidad Order, but not before events in Demerara demonstrated the fragility of social order in the region. In contrast to Buxton and other antislavery advocates who, having run out of patience at the slow pace of progress toward emancipation, called for dramatic alterations to be implemented as soon as possible, Canning and other metropolitan officials took a more circumspect approach. Responding to Buxton's slate of proposed changes, the Prime Minister expressed eagerness to prepare the currently enslaved population to enjoy "civil rights and privileges," but was also mindful of "the safety of the colonies" and "the sacredness of private property."[60]

Here, the humanitarian impulse was at odds with pressure from the West India lobby. This tension, combined with the typical concern of colonial administrators over maintaining public order, prompted Bathurst to demur from many of Buxton's more radical recommendations. In May of 1823, in a letter to Governor Murray of Demerara, Bathurst stipulated the initial implementation

[57] Essequibo and Demerara had a population of approximately 80,000 in the early 1820s, of which 75,000 were enslaved Africans and only 2,500 were white Europeans. Half of the latter group lived in Georgetown, the capital of Demerara. Da Costa, *Crowns of Glory*, 217.

[58] Da Costa, *Crowns of Glory*, 46.

[59] May 15, 1823, *Hansard's Parliamentary Debates*, vol. IX, 1823 (London: Hansard, 1824), 273–4.

[60] *Hansard's Parliamentary Debates*, vol. IX, 1823 (London: Hansard, 1824), 277.

of only two of Buxton's proposed reforms, prohibiting the flogging of female slaves and the employment of the whip in the fields, either to encourage work or to serve as a symbol of the overseer's authority.[61] A few weeks later, a subsequent dispatch from Bathurst included a wider suite of changes, most important among them being the encouragement of religious instruction, a prohibition against separating families, and reforms to manumission.[62] Demerara's representative governing body, the Court of Policy, met in August to discuss these matters, which were much to the consternation of many planters. The latter resented the interference of metropolitan administrators over their management of a large and, to their mind, fractious slave population.[63] Although they agreed to implement the proposed reforms – as a body that was deliberative but not legislative, they could hardly refuse the instructions of the Colonial Secretary and the governor – they did not make their intentions public.[64]

This decision to confine the formal recognition of the first stages of amelioration within a close circle of governing officials and planters would prove fateful. Word of "the new laws" quickly spread among the communal information networks of enslaved plantation workers. Sentiment grew among them that, at the very least, their masters were denying them the rights to which they were now entitled, and perhaps even denying them their lawful freedom altogether. Fueled by patchwork knowledge gained from a variety of sources (including overheard conversations among the planters), by long-held hopes of freedom, and by the common tendency of rumors to amplify and distort over time and distance, some among the enslaved population became convinced that the monarch himself had instituted emancipation but that planters were refusing to comply. In August 1823, weeks of simmering tension boiled over into full-scale rebellion. Led by a small group that had coordinated their plans, several thousand enslaved Africans from scores of plantations across the colony rose up against their masters.[65] They burned plantation property, assaulted managers and overseers or put them in the punishment stocks, and seized guns and powder, but they largely refrained from serious violence.[66] Instead, in numerous confrontations with government officials, military officers, and other figures of authority, enslaved Africans demanded that they be granted the rights to which they believed the new laws had entitled them, the most prominent of them all being their right to freedom. "God had made them

61 DaCosta, *Crowns of Glory*, 178.

62 Ibid.

63 Ibid. See also Anon. ("A Landowner"), *Demerara After Fifteen Years of Freedom* (London: T. Bosworth, 1853), 56–7.

64 Minutes of the Proceedings of the Court of Policy of Demerara, August 7, 1823, *Papers on Melioration*, 1823–4, 115.

65 It is estimated that between 9,000 and 12,000 enslaved Africans from 60 plantations participated in the revolt. For a detailed account, see da Costa, *Crowns of Glory*, 178–206.

66 There were only two or three white fatalities overall. Da Costa, *Crowns of Glory*, 198.

of the same flesh and blood as the whites," one group told Governor Murray. "They were tired of being slaves to them . . . their good King had sent order that they should be free, and they would not work any more."[67] The uprising, though widespread, was poorly coordinated, and was quickly suppressed by the local military and militia forces. In contrast to the rebelling slaves, the military and the militia did not hesitate to employ deadly force. Over the course of a week in the waning days of August, about 200 enslaved Africans were killed in skirmishes. Another twenty alleged ringleaders on various plantations were given the briefest of summary trials before being executed, sometimes over the protests of their owners, in public rituals witnessed by their terrified comrades.[68]

The Demerara revolt brought the volatile situation in the colony and in neighboring Essequibo, where a population of some 2,500 white Europeans was dwarfed by 80,000 enslaved Africans, into sharp focus.[69] At the core of the heated discussions that ensued, from the plantations to Parliament, was what role the state would take, moving forward, in reforming slavery and managing the relationship between plantation-owners and their labor force. Planters across Britain's Caribbean possessions blamed the disorder in Demerara on amelioration and continued to resist unwelcome metropolitan interference in how they managed their private property (i.e. their enslaved Africans).[70] Parliamentary reformers, in contrast, saw events in the colony as a sure sign that slavery was an untenable institution, and that its eradication should be engineered not only in Crown colonies such as Trinidad and Demerara but in the older, self-governing ones as well (e.g. Jamaica).[71] Bathurst and the metropolitan colonial administration tasked with managing the process of amelioration remained reluctant to immediately enact the sweeping changes demanded earlier by Buxton and other antislavery advocates. They were nonetheless in agreement that a light-handed approach relying on the cooperation of plantation-owners would not work. The planters' continued recalcitrance in the immediate aftermath of the Demerara Rebellion was communicated in Governor Murray's insistence to Bathurst that, given the "unfortunate circumstances in which the colony is placed," amelioration could not proceed as planned.[72]

[67] Extract of a dispatch addressed to Earl Bathurst by Major-General Murray, dated Demerara, August 24, 1823, *Papers on Melioration*, 1823–4, 117.

[68] Da Costa, *Crowns of Glory*, 224. Murray explained in a public proclamation that it was the actions of the rebelling slaves themselves that had necessitated their "suffering all the horrors attendant on the existence of martial law." Proclamation by Gov. Murray, August 20, 1823, *Papers on Melioration*, 1823–4, 119.

[69] Da Costa, *Crowns of Glory*, 217.

[70] *Papers on Melioration*, 1823–4, 34.

[71] Holt, *Problem of Freedom*, 18–19.

[72] Despatch of Murray to Bathurst, August 31, 1823, *Papers on Melioration*, 1823–4, 120.

The Evolution of Amelioration in the Wake of the 1823 Rebellion: Protectors and Guardians

Amidst heated public discussions in Parliament and the British press over the Demerara revolt and its bloody suppression, and in the face of both the plantocracy's defiant refusal to cooperate with amelioration and the roiling discontent of the region's enslaved Africans, the state's intervention into plantation labor management accelerated. The first step was the embedding of a new cohort of powerful administrators as permanent mediators between plantation-owners and their enslaved workforce. George Murray was replaced as governor by Lieutenant General Sir Benjamin D'Urban, the former governor of Antigua. D'Urban significantly expanded both the accountability of the Fiscal and the mechanisms of oversight by the governor and metropolitan authorities, further centralizing the process of amelioration and delineating a clear hierarchy for its implementation and supervision. Henceforth, the Fiscal would be required to keep detailed records of all complaints made by slaves, which would be regularly transmitted, via the governor, to London. This oversight extended to the plantation-owners (referred to as "proprietors"), their representatives if the former were not in residence ("attorneys"), and their managers and overseers. By the end of 1824, in both Demerara and Essequibo, those in authority on the plantations were required to grant any slave who wished to complain a pass off of the plantation, and it was customary for the slaves to be informed of their right to file a grievance.[73]

From D'Urban's perspective, while the new system of recording allowed him to keep a closer eye on the activities of the Fiscal, the results were still not satisfactory. The new officer, Charles Herbert, seemed to be more concerned with maintaining plantation discipline than he was with addressing the complaints of enslaved Africans. Herbert insisted that, in order to preserve public order and prevent a repeat of the events of 1823, it was necessary to ensure that the system of pass and grievance did not enable "insubordination and misconduct on the part of the slave ... under the name of complaint."[74] D'Urban, in contrast, asserted that the state had to take a more forceful hand to ensure that slaves could freely lodge complaints against their managers and overseers without fear of retribution. To do otherwise would bring about "an end to all justice ... an end to hope," and would "end in universal desperation" of the

[73] George Bagot (Fiscal) to Gov. D'Urban, June 7, 1824, *Complaints of Masters and Slaves*, 1826, 15. By the end of 1824, in Demerara and Essequibo, it was "customary ... for proprietors and attornies [*sic*] of estates to give orders to the managers, and to inform the negroes that they have given such orders, at all times to furnish any negro who wishes to complain with a pass ... consequences of refusal on the part of a manager would be a severe reprimand or perhaps the loss of his situation."

[74] Charles Herbert (Fiscal) to Gov. D'Urban, December 22, 1825, *Complaints of Masters and Slaves*, 1826, 5.

kind that had prompted the 1823 revolt.[75] Maintaining the belief among enslaved Africans that they could find some measure of justice through the Fiscal and his assistants, D'Urban contended, was not only necessary under the requirements of the law, it was vital to restoring peace and order across the region.[76]

The next crucial expansion of amelioration in the Caribbean, which would be shepherded through by D'Urban, emerged from the fierce debate that the events of 1823 prompted in Parliament and from the concerns of imperial administrators over the precarious social stability of Britain's new Crown colonies in coastal South America. Both the debate and the concerns were exacerbated by the unwillingness of the plantocracy to accept stricter oversight of their affairs from the metropole. In neighboring Berbice, as with Demerara, British officials, on taking control of the colony, had retained much of its prior Dutch bureaucratic structure, including the office of Fiscal.[77] Several factors combined to thrust the treatment of enslaved Africans there into the public limelight and to prompt a sharp intervention into the regulation of conditions on its 140 plantations. The first was the growing worry among administrators, in the wake of the Demerara Rebellion, that failure to address the grievances of slaves, alongside continued toleration of cruel or excessive treatment, might trigger further uprisings. This was a particularly strong concern in Berbice, given its geographical proximity to the events of 1823. The second factor was the recalcitrance of planters in Berbice to emulate their colleagues in Trinidad by adopting Bathurst's recommendations for amelioration. The third was, ironically, the careful recordkeeping of the Berbice Fiscal, M. S. Bennett, who had occupied the office since 1809.[78] When Parliament, in the aftermath of the 1823 revolt and the reforms of 1824, had expanded its oversight of conditions in the plantation colonies, Bennett, on request, was able to provide detailed accounts of slave complaints and their resolution dating back to 1819.[79] The content of these reports became grist for the campaign of the antislavery lobby. They employed these records in a scathing and wide-ranging public

[75] Gov. D'Urban to acting First Fiscal George Bagot, June 5, 1823, *Complaints of Masters and Slaves*, 1826, 14.

[76] The governor even went so far as to insist that slaves who had not joined the revolt should be rewarded with particular attention to their complaints. D'Urban to Herbert, July 4, 1824, *Complaints of Masters and Slaves*, 1826, 16.

[77] The Fiscal had been part of the Dutch administration of Berbice since 1772 (Trevor Burnard, "A Voice for Slaves: The Office of the Fiscal in Berbice and the Beginning of Protection in the British Empire, 1819–1834," *Pacific Historical Review* 87, no. 1 [2018], 33). Berbice had been acquired by the British in 1803, though their rule was not officially confirmed until 1814. M. S. Bennett served as Fiscal from 1809 to 1826.

[78] Bennett to D'Urban, January 21, 1826, *Further Papers Relating to Slaves in the West Indies* (Demerara and Berbice), 1826, 3.

[79] This was in contrast to Demerara, where such records were not maintained prior to D'Urban's appointment as governor in 1824.

condemnation of planters' behavior in Berbice, the failure of the Fiscal to fulfill his duties, and the institution of slavery more generally.[80]

The charge was led in Parliament by William Smith (MP, Norwich), one of William Wilberforce's early supporters and a co-founder of the London Anti-Slavery Society (LAS), who delivered a fiery speech to the assembled MPs on April 20, 1826.[81] In it, he condemned both slave-owners for their brutality and the government for its inaction, while emphasizing the commendable paternalism of the Spanish laws and contrasting it with the lamentable negligence of the Dutch. It was deeply disturbing, Smith observed, that Roman Catholics (i.e. the Spanish), who had been declared immoral and incapable of wielding civic power responsibly in England, should have demonstrated themselves to be morally superior in their treatment of enslaved Africans in the Caribbean.[82] For all his condemnation, however, Smith stopped short of advocating full and immediate emancipation, asserting that, in their current state, enslaved Africans were "not fit for the enjoyment of freedom."[83] The blame for this lay not with slaves themselves but with slave-owners. The latter, through their cruelty and neglect, had abdicated their moral responsibility and so brutalized their slaves that it would be "dangerous to entrust them with liberty."[84] The neglect of slaves' physical state had been as severe as the disregard for their moral and spiritual needs, Smith lamented, with the result that "the cultivation of sugar was more injurious to human life than any other of the West-India productions."[85] By way of evidence, he quoted the statistics on mortality rates in various Caribbean colonies, which were directly proportional to the amount of sugar being produced in each.[86]

The failure of amelioration to address these dire circumstances, Smith maintained, was attributable to the lack of oversight from the metropole. This inattention had allowed men with close association to slave-owners, and even those who were slave-owners themselves, to occupy positions of authority in legal cases involving slaves.[87] To make matters worse, such men were, by dint of their lack of legal education, "unfit to administer justice" even among their fellow Europeans, let alone suitable to be "in-trusted [*sic*] with the protection of the blacks."[88] According to Smith, slavery had left slave-owners and slaves alike

80 Excerpts from the records were distributed via the publications of the London Society for the Abolition of Slavery, to which several references were made in the subsequent House of Commons debate on the topic. *House of Commons Debates*, April 20, 1826, v. 15, 521, 525, 527.
81 Founded in 1823, the official name was the Society for the Mitigation and Gradual Abolition of Slavery throughout the British Dominions. It was commonly known as the "London Anti-Slavery Society" or merely the "Anti-Slavery Society."
82 *House of Commons Debates*, April 20, 1826, v. 15, 509.
83 Ibid.
84 Ibid.
85 Ibid., 511.
86 Ibid., 512.
87 Ibid., 513.
88 Ibid., 508.

ignorant of good governance and incapable of moral action. The only solution was the intercession of Crown-appointed officers whose primary connection was to the metropole rather than to their fellow colonists. Berbice's plantation system required the oversight of a more powerful state apparatus–following paternalist principles, its new agents would assume responsibility for the moral uplift of slaves and their masters, as well as safeguarding the physical well-being of the colony's vital workforce.

Earlier that year, in response to the public outcry prompted by the LAS's publications of excerpts from his reports, Bennett, the Berbice Fiscal, had written to Governor D'Urban in defense of his conduct and to express alarm at the "garbled" and "inflammatory" character of the accounts. Bennett's statement did little to mollify the concerns of the antislavery lobby about where his sympathies lay. The Fiscal had defended the colony's planters and insisted that the enslaved Africans in Berbice received the best treatment of any in the British colonies. Slaves were in the habit of exaggerating, he had asserted; not only were the majority of the complaints unfounded but their initiation lay with the most demoralized among the population. "Nine times in ten," Bennett had written, "they proceed from the most indolent and worthless negroes on the estates, and are generally contradicted by the better-behaved negroes."[89] The Fiscal's protests notwithstanding, 1826 saw the imposition of the first consolidated slave code in Berbice, conducted along the lines of the Trinidad model first piloted (unsuccessfully) in Demerara.[90] As part of this reform, as had been the case in Trinidad earlier, a powerful new agent was introduced in both colonies to oversee the process of amelioration and to address the failings evident in the practices of the Fiscals. In Demerara and Berbice, a "Protector and Guardian of Slaves" would assume many of the duties formerly conducted by the Fiscals, such as soliciting complaints and advocating for enslaved Africans in the courts of law.

The introduction of the Protectors and the segregation of their powers from those of the Fiscals represented a more radical intercession in Demerara and Berbice than it had in Trinidad. The former territories, though their Dutch colonizers had modeled the office of the Fiscal on Spanish practice, possessed a far weaker tradition of paternalistic intervention into plantation affairs, had

89 Bennett to D'Urban, January 21, 1826, *Further Papers Relating to Slaves in the West Indies* (Demerara and Berbice), 1826, 3.

90 "An Ordinance for Promoting the Religious Instruction and Bettering the State and Condition of the Slave Population in His Majesty's Colony of Berbice," *Papers in Explanation of Measures for Melioration of Condition of Slave Population in W. Indies and S. America, Part II,* House of Commons Papers, 1826–7 (b), 202–19. Note: There are two parts of this, and this particular reference is drawn from the ninety-eight-page document that begins "Berbice" and that I am designating (b). There is another document, consisting of 200 pages, which I am designating (a).

not accorded slaves the same degree of legal rights as they had possessed under Spanish colonial rule, and operated in a more complex legal structure that was entangled with the legacies of their Romano-Dutch antecedents.[91] Because of this, the circumstances in Demerara and Berbice were accommodating to the conduct of the Fiscals, whose duties had been broad and somewhat amorphous in their remits as the Crown's legal advocates. When the Fiscals were given the additional role and title of "Protector and Guardian of Slaves" in 1824, the responsibility for ensuring obedience to the new laws on amelioration was to be conducted in addition to their established commitments. The Dutch legacy, the dependence of colonial governance on the cooperation of the plantocracy, and the already fraught state of race relations in the colonies, from the perspective of administrators and the planter interests represented in the Courts of Policy, made a light-touch approach to the Fiscal's new duties appealing.

The new Protector's role, in contrast, was explicitly paternalistic and focused solely on interceding between planters, managers, and the enslaved workforce. Under the oversight of colonial governors and their superiors in the Colonial Office, the Protectors were responsible for ensuring that the growing catalog of regulations was adhered to, that slaves' newfound rights were respected, and that their grievances were heard, investigated, and, when deemed appropriate, escalated to formal prosecution in the colonial court system.[92] Whereas the Fiscals were members of the colonies' elite and maintained close social ties with the plantocracy, the Protector, in theory, was supposed to be aloof from local allegiances, familiar with the regulations of the new slave code, and committed to their fair enforcement. In practice, however, the Protector remained under the direction of the Fiscal, who supervised his efforts and to whom all serious complaints had to be referred.[93] The result was a system whereby Fiscals and Protectors were motivated – by pressure from their superiors in the Colonial Office and by the increasing public scrutiny – to solicit complaints, but in which

[91] Both concerns were the subject of commentary in the House of Commons during the debate over amelioration there in 1826. *House of Commons Debates*, April 20, 1826, v. 15, 508–9.

[92] Burnard, "A Voice for Slaves," 34. Somewhat confusingly, the Fiscals of Demerara and Berbice, as of 1824, received the title of "Protector and Guardian of Slaves," hence references to "Protectors" in documents prior to 1826.

[93] Burnard, "A Voice for Slaves," 35. Further complicating the dynamics of slave complaints prior to 1814 was the Fiscals' vested financial interest in the process, since all slave owners against whom a case was brought were fined the considerable costs of the proceedings, regardless of the outcome. Costs for a typical case ranged between 50 and 100 *f.* (guilders), with the typical penalty on conviction *f.* 300. By comparison, the cost of a healthy, adult slave in 1826 was approximately *f.* 300–500. *Papers on the Protection of Slaves in Demerara and Berbice*, 1826, 110. The practice of awarding Fiscals a share of the fines was discontinued in 1814 and the Fiscal's salary was increased by £2,000 (to £8,000 total) to compensate for the loss in earnings. James Rodway, *History of British Guiana, from the Year 1668 to the Present Time, Vol. 2: 1782–1833* (Georgetown: J. Thompson, 1894), 104.

adjudication – supervised by Fiscals who were entangled with plantocracy interests and reluctant to directly challenge planters' authority over their workforce – heavily favored the interests of the owners, attorneys, and managers.

The Trinidad model and its attendant office of Protector and Guardian of Slaves, having been introduced in 1824 and expanded in 1826, was subsequently extended across the breadth of Britain's southern hemisphere Crown colonies. An 1831 Order in Council implemented the measures stipulated in the 1824 Order as far away as Mauritius, where a Protector had been introduced in 1829 as part of a comprehensive new slave code, and in the Cape of Good Hope (South Africa).[94] This geographical expansion was accompanied by the consolidation of state authority in the Caribbean and by the expansion in state personnel and resources across the colonies with significant populations of enslaved men and women. The year 1831 witnessed the amalgamation of the former colonies of Berbice, Essequibo, and Demerara into a single Crown colony, British Guiana, under the stewardship of Governor Benjamin D'Urban, the primary architect of amelioration in the region.[95] There and throughout the empire, in order to adequately cover the wide territory and the large number of plantations encompassed by even the smaller colonies, Protectors' efforts were bolstered by a small cohort of Assistant Protectors. They were often drawn, as were colonial governors, from the ranks of army officers who had fought in the Napoleonic Wars.[96] Such men, of whom there was a surplus at the conclusion of the conflict, were well-suited to the physical rigors of the job, which required them to travel extensively in their districts, visiting plantations and soliciting complaints from the enslaved workforce. Protectors supervised their efforts, sitting astride a new regulatory apparatus that, on paper, was overseen by the Fiscal or its analog, but in practice was accountable to the Crown-appointed governors and their metropolitan superior, the Colonial Secretary. What had begun as a regional experiment in centralized governance had become a coordinated system of inspection and investigation operated across the Crown colonies of the southern hemisphere. While this apparatus was internally fractured and unevenly enforced, it was nonetheless peripatetic and continuous in operation. Its implementation had coincided with a major restructuring of state power in British Guiana, and with the broader expansion of the new experiment in direct colonial governance through the Crown colony system.

94 *Order in Council for Consolidating the Several Laws for Improving the Conditions of Slaves in His Majesty's Colonies of Trinidad, Berbice, Demerara St. Lucia, the Cape of Good Hope, and Mauritius*, 1831, 2–4.

95 Penson, "The Making of a Crown Colony," 130–1.

96 These men had often served as regional administrators, known as "Commandants" or "Commandants of Quarters," in the transition period from wartime to peacetime governance.

Apprenticeship and the Merger of State Authority with Plantation Discipline

Even as planters' autonomy was being hedged around by new laws, new state agents, new institutions, and new practices, the overall interests of the overseer-state and those of the plantocracy with regard to the plantation workforce remained closely aligned. Both plantation proprietors and the new cadre of colonial officials shared a commitment to the continued productivity of the plantation economy and to the maintenance of order in the colonies. The path to reconciling planters' interest in maintaining authority over their enslaved workforce and the new colonial officers' desires to maintain public order and the principle (or at least appearance) of just governance lay in the preservation of a paternalist system (albeit with the state in the role as protector) coupled with a public discourse focused on improving the lives of the enslaved.[97] Planters and colonial officials alike also shared an interest in mollifying the antislavery lobby in London, whose calls for a rapid and fundamental transformation of the plantation system were widely considered by those in the plantation colonies themselves to be a threat to both public order and economic viability.[98]

The alignment of interests between plantation-owners and the overseer-state would become increasingly apparent as the process of emancipation reached its final stage, apprenticeship. This period witnessed the implementation of a constellation of laws designed to sustain the subordination of the newly emancipated plantation workforce under a paternalistic regulatory framework, and the introduction of a new set of officials and processes to enforce this subordination. The system was strongest in the Crown colonies, where direct rule had given governors and the Colonial Office more authority to apply reforms as they saw fit. Unlike in older legislative colonies such as Jamaica, where most laws were composed and enacted via elected colonial assemblies, planters in the Crown colonies could exercise their power only indirectly through consultative bodies. The typical process was that Crown-appointed governors, in consultation with advisory councils wherein planter interest was well represented, submitted legislative proposals, which were known as "ordinances," to the Colonial Office for approval.[99] The Colonial

[97] As members of the Legislative Council of Tobago remonstrated to the governor on the eve of emancipation, in any consideration of amelioration and "the slave question," the measures taken had to be "compatible with the security of the Master and beneficial to the slaves themselves," *Minutes of the Legislative Council of Tobago*, March 27, 1833, 81(161) [National Archives of Trinidad]. See also Lightfoot, *Troubling Freedom*, 11.

[98] As Diana Paton has written describing the process of amelioration in Jamaica, "protection worked within the limits of the needs of continued plantation production." Diana Paton, *No Bond but the Law: Punishment, Race, and Gender in Jamaican State Formation, 1780–1870* (Durham, NC: Duke University Press, 2004), 55.

[99] William A. Green, *British Slave Emancipation: The Sugar Colonies and the Great Experiment, 1830–1865* (Oxford: Clarendon, 1976), 76–8.

Secretary could also exercise legislative initiative from the metropole by issuing an Order in Council.[100] But the expansion of state power over the labor system had its analogs in the older plantation colonies as well. In both contexts, facing the rising tide of reform, planters reluctantly resigned themselves to emancipation and began developing ways of co-opting the new mechanisms of state labor governance rather than openly resisting their implementation.

Apprenticeship bridged the divide, legally and economically, between slavery and indenture. It served as the mechanism by which the practices, concepts, and institutions laid down during amelioration would pass to the indenture system in the wake of emancipation. Apprenticeship shackled former slaves with unbreakable labor contracts, binding them to their former owners through a matrix of regulations inherited from slavery and the early stages of amelioration. Since apprenticeship operated on the basis of a contract between employers and workers, rather than on the basis of ownership, as had been the case in slavery, it acquired its legitimation and structures of implementation directly from the state. Under this system, the involvement of the state in plantation workforce discipline extended well beyond what it had been under slavery or in the earlier stages of amelioration. During this transition from slavery to indentured and "free" African-Caribbean labor on the plantations, local officials would assume permanent, formal roles as inspectors, regulators, mediators, and enforcers of the new laws that defined plantation-owners as employers and plantation workers as their employees. What had started as an ad hoc system designed to shepherd the plantation colonies through a tumultuous period of change would become cemented as a permanent apparatus of state labor oversight.

In this "extreme version of state formation . . . [the] coercive role was played by the state rather than by either the market or the slaveowner."[101] While this change signaled the growing power of the overseer-state, the new configuration also stabilized the power of the plantocracy, which had frayed somewhat under the tensions of amelioration. The state would retain the official paramountcy over plantation labor relations that it had achieved in the 1820s, reducing the autonomy of planters and placing their treatment of their workforce under closer scrutiny. But plantation owners would adapt to the new circumstances, largely abandoning their open resistance and instead seeking to integrate themselves into the new systems of oversight. In doing so, planters and their managerial infrastructure would harness the powers of colonial labor governance to serve their own interests. This harmonized configuration of state oversight with labor management to ensure plantation order and productivity would outlast slavery by many decades, forming

[100] Ibid.
[101] Paton, *No Bond but the Law*, 54.

a central pillar of indenture and other colonial labor structures well into the early twentieth century.

In legislative colonies such as Jamaica, the diminution of planters' autonomy over their workforce was achieved through the appointment of special stipendiary magistrates.[102] These powerful judicial figures were typically trained in the London Inns of Court, and arrived well-versed in the law, though as outsiders to the social structure of the colony. They served as a vector for metropolitan moral and legislative priorities while also providing an avenue by which slaves and, subsequently, apprentices, freedmen, and indentured laborers could contest their treatment by the planter elite.[103] Although this paralleled the introduction of stipendiaries as key stabilizers of social order in the growing industrial cities of Britain, there were significant differences. In the reforms introduced under Robert Peel, which ushered in Britain's first professionalized and centralized police force, the adjudication of law and its enforcement were disaggregated. Every effort was made to distinguish between the new police, who were to be members of the community, unarmed, and endowed with no powers beyond those accorded to private citizens, and the military forces (hence the distinctive blue uniforms of the former).[104] In contrast, in the plantation colonies, the line between the new institutions of labor management and military authority was highly permeable. Governors, Protectors, and Assistant Protectors were drawn from the ranks of military officers; constables were armed with military rifles and were led by magistrates; and there was close coordination between military leadership and judicial authorities in responses to even minor disorder on the plantations.

Partly, this was an issue of practicality and financial restraint.[105] Especially in the Crown colonies, which were seized through military force during the Napoleonic Wars, appointing an aristocratic general as a governor offered continuity and made sense politically. But the practice was common in legislative colonies as well. In Jamaica, the Colonial Office tended to appoint inactive army and navy officers as magistrates because it was assumed that, thanks to their military service, they were accustomed to enforcing discipline.[106] The same held true of the common practice of appointing former district "Commandants" as the new Assistant Protectors of Slaves.[107] These men were familiar with the territory and its inhabitants, socially adjacent to planter

102 Ibid., 65–7.

103 Ibid., 71.

104 Clive Emsley, "Policing the Empire, Policing the Metropole: Some Thoughts on Models and Types," *Crime, Histoire & Sociétés/Crime, History & Societies* 18, no. 2 (2014), 7.

105 N. Gash, "After Waterloo: British Society and the Legacy of the Napoleonic Wars," *Transactions of the Royal Historical Society* 28 (1978), 149.

106 Holt, *Problem of Freedom*, 58.

107 See note 92.

society but not (in theory) beholden to it, and habituated to dealing with the enslaved population and maintaining public order. The end of the war had left Britain with a surfeit of qualified military officers and a dearth of employment for them, which added to the utility of integrating them into the new apparatus of civilian governance.[108] This close association of military personnel and labor governance also reflected the widespread belief that the reform of the plantation colonies, regardless of its paternalistic and humanitarian gloss, would be a coercive exercise conducted against an intrinsically discontented and potentially rebellious population.[109]

Both the merger of state authority and plantation interests and the subsuming of the latter's authority to that of the former in the coercive paternalism of the overseer-state were readily apparent in Berbice, Essequibo, and Demerara, which were administratively consolidated into British Guiana as of 1831.[110] The apprenticeship system, there as elsewhere in the British Empire, was implemented in 1834 as part of the Abolition Act 1833. Through legal fiat, slaves over the age of six became indentured laborers, bound to their plantations, and therefore to their former owners, by labor laws and employment contracts rather than by deeds of ownership. The goal of this transitional arrangement was to prevent any interruption of plantation productivity and to allow time for former slaves and slave-owners alike to adjust to the new economic, social, legal, and cultural circumstances that followed emancipation.[111] The process of transferring punitive power over the plantation workforce from former slave-owners to the state, in the form of magistrates, was hotly contested. As was the case across the plantation colonies, in British Guiana, new institutions and agents were at the core of this struggle over the "reconstruction of colonial law and government" in which the state assumed the duties of regulating social relations, maintaining plantation order, and punishing violators among a population where all of these responsibilities had formerly lain with owners and masters.[112]

[108] Gash, "After Waterloo," 147.

[109] This tendency ran in contrast to the metropolitan administration of colonial affairs, which saw a widening separation of the War and Colonial Offices. This process began in 1806, accelerated in 1825 with the establishment of a permanent undersecretary, and was largely complete by the time of Bathurst's retirement in 1827, at which point the Colonial Office had twenty-five permanent officials in post.

[110] All paternalism has an element of coercion. I mean here that it was *legally* coercive (or even punitive) and explicitly disciplinary.

[111] Mary Turner, "The British Caribbean, 1823–1838: The Transition from Free to Legal Status," in Douglas Hay and Paul Craven, eds., *Masters, Servants, and Magistrates in Britain and the Empire* (Chapel Hill: University of North Carolina Press, 2004), 314.

[112] William Green, "Apprenticeship in British Guiana, 1834–1838," *Caribbean Studies* 9, no. 2 (July 1969), 47.

Prior to 1833, slave-owners had wielded the power of summary jurisdiction over enslaved Africans on their estates in all but cases of the most serious crimes.[113] This equation changed with the arrival of a new governor, Sir James Carmichael Smyth, formerly a major general in the Royal Engineers. Smyth, in his previous post as governor of the Bahamas (1829–33), had long campaigned for the rights and protections of enslaved Africans, and had strongly opposed the corporal punishment of enslaved women in particular.[114] He was also a staunch advocate of centralized administration. He had not hesitated to resort to authoritarian means in order to achieve his goals of reforming slavery and castigating abusive slave-owners in his pursuit of what he saw as equitable treatment and moral governance. In Barbados, such measures had earned him the praise of his superiors in the Colonial Office and the ire of planters and their representatives in the colonial legislature. Once appointed to his new post in British Guiana, Smyth moved quickly to consolidate the state's oversight of plantation labor relations there. On his orders, twelve new Crown-appointed stipendiary magistrates, most with no prior experience of practicing law in the Caribbean, were installed. Their duty was to oversee the implementation of the Emancipation Act, making frequent visits to the estates, hearing the complaints of masters and apprentices, and adjudicating any issues that arose between the two.[115] Those magistrates who failed, in Smyth's estimation, to ensure the mild treatment of apprentices were promptly removed. Over time, the governor extended his control over this judicial cohort and, through them, the conduct of labor relations on the plantations. The use of the lash was a particular anathema to Smyth. In 1837, he ordered the stipendiaries to make detailed reports of cases where the apprentices had been sentenced to corporal punishment, and forbade its infliction prior to his personal review.[116] Smyth also insisted that the magistrates must be personally present for the application of lashes, even though extensive travel was required and the time between the sentence and its execution was often attenuated. Without expressly forbidding the practice, Smyth had made the corporal punishment of apprentices so procedurally onerous for the magistrates that, within a year of introducing his new guidelines, the infliction of lashes on conviction had declined dramatically.[117]

113 Green, "Apprenticeship," 48.
114 Smyth had gone so far as to suspend several Barbados magistrates that had ruled in favor of a slave-owner accused of cruelty against his female slaves, and had campaigned ardently, if unsuccessfully, for outlawing the corporal punishment of female slaves in the colony.
115 Green, "Apprenticeship," 51.
116 Ibid., 54.
117 Ibid.

Planter interests, expressed through the representative bodies of the Court of Policy and the Combined Court and wielding power over the colony's finances, balked at Smyth's heavy-handed approach, prompting a constitutional crisis. This became so serious that the Colonial Office intervened directly, urging both sides to reconcile their differences. Looming over these arguments about the limits on planters' authority, the rights of apprentices, and the magistrates' remit to govern plantation labor relations was the chronic labor shortage that had dogged the region for more than a decade. At the urging of Lord Aberdeen, the Colonial Secretary, a compromise was negotiated. The government lessened the tax burden on planters and granted them greater control over the colony's finances in return for their acquiescence to a more robust system of laws delineating the legal relationship between apprentices and employers. The Guyanese compromise, which was implemented at the tail end of emancipation, mirrored the Trinidad model, implemented during the earlier stages of amelioration. In both instances, "where labor shortages were most threatening, the crown dictated the terms upon which the essential relations between employers and laborers would be regulated."[118]

In other colonies, particularly in the legislative ones where the Crown wielded less direct authority and where planter interests were more thoroughly integrated into the local judiciary, the merger of state and plantation interests was accomplished with less acrimony, though not without controversy. In Jamaica, the stipendiary magistrates were sharply opposed by the planter elite, who resented the erosion of their autonomy, metropolitan interference in plantation life, and the potential for workers, first slaves and later apprentices, to challenge planters' authority in court. The new officials were criticized and undermined by the planters on a number of grounds, chief among them their position as outsiders ignorant of the colony's culture and social structure and their inferior class status vis-à-vis the plantocracy. In the few instances where men of color were appointed to the post, planters also employed race as an avenue of attack on their unsuitability to oversee and adjudicate the plantation system.[119] As a consequence of this dogged opposition, Jamaican magistrates never achieved the judicial independence that they enjoyed, with the support and stern oversight of Smyth, in British Guiana. In the former, as in other legislative colonies, the magistrates' powers were slowly but surely subsumed under the supervision of the established judiciary.[120] And unlike in British Guiana, in Jamaica, the lash remained a tool commonly employed to punish those who violated the new

118 Ibid., 63.

119 Paton, *No Bond but the Law*, 65. One example was Richard Hill, who was of mixed ethnic background, being the son of a prominent merchant and a woman of mixed African-Caribbean and Indian background. Frank Cundall, "Richard Hill," *Journal of Negro History* 5, no. 1 (January 1920), 37. See also Richard Hill, *Lights and Shadows of Jamaica History* (London: Ford and Gall, 1859).

120 Green, "Apprenticeship," 65.

array of laws governing plantation labor. Such compromise and integration was a predictable outcome when the smooth functioning of the plantation system remained a paramount concern for all of those in positions of authority.

The line between the overseer-state and the established mechanisms of governance, whether in Crown colonies or in legislative ones, was permeable. And whatever public dialogue was produced by Smyth or like-minded administrators about the rights and protections of slaves or apprentices, there can be no doubt that the majority of state exercise across the period of slavery, amelioration, apprenticeship, and, subsequently, indenture with regard to plantation workers remained punitive. Even as the state implemented reforms that codified a slave's right to complain of abuse, excessive punishment, or denial of basic needs, it also took up the responsibility for disciplining workers through a vast array of regulations that governed everything from work hours to abusive language. As late as 1829, one in every six enslaved Africans in Demerara and Berbice would be convicted and punished for some offense or another in any given six-month period.[121] By far the most common offenses fell under the vague categories of "neglect of duty" and "not doing a day's work."[122] The delineation of these and a host of other common offenses, many with equally nebulous definitions (e.g. "laziness and idleness" or "disobedience") lay almost entirely in the hands of the plantation managers. These laws would, over time, be modified to accommodate the status of plantation laborers as free workers rather than slaves. But the primary function of the colonial legal system would remain to punish recalcitrant or disobedient workers and to ensure that they fulfilled their labor obligations, albeit those stipulated by law rather than solely by the customary practices of plantation life. The effective result was the criminalization of any attempt by slaves, and, later, apprentices, to negotiate the terms of their labor and employment.[123]

Even as the state replaced plantation owners as the paramount authority on labor relations and statutes replaced customary practice in determining the boundaries of that authority, owners and managers adapted the racialized language of plantation discipline to the new systems of law and government oversight. The overseer-state, once direct resistance to it had failed, was harnessed by the overseers themselves to reinforce and legitimize their approach to labor discipline. In this, they enjoyed a distinct advantage over their workforce. This advantage stemmed from established racial hierarchies, the management's familiarity with legal processes, and their experience of dealing with state agents and government bureaucracy in a variety of capacities. At the level of personnel,

121 Of the 62,352 slaves in the colony, from January 1 to June 30, 1828, 10,054 were convicted of various offenses. *Report from the Protectors of Slaves in Demerara, Berbice, Trinidad, St. Lucia, and the Cape of Good Hope 1829* (hereafter *Report from the Protectors 1829*), 9.

122 Respectively, 2,121 and 2,144, from January 1 to June 30, 1828, *Report from the Protectors 1829*, 9.

123 Burnard, "A Voice for Slaves," 37–8.

the line dividing the plantocracy from the structures of governance was also often quite thin. Although the highest echelons of the overseer-state were typically filled by men without a direct linkage to the plantocracy, and both Protectors and their Assistants were forbidden, by law, to own slaves themselves, the picture at the next level down in colonial governance looked very different. For example, when Governor Smyth attempted to reform the treatment of slaves in British Guiana by removing the prosecution of petty offenses from the authority of planters and putting it instead into the hands of justices of the peace, his efforts were stymied by the recalcitrance of his judicial recruits, the majority of whom were themselves either planters or planters' attorneys.[124] The latter, unsurprisingly given their role as representatives of absentee planters, typically viewed slaves' complaints with a marked lack of sympathy. The close accord of state processes and planter interests was apparent in the more serious judicial processes as well as in the multitude of quotidian ones. In instances of suspicious death among the workforce (i.e. those not obviously due to sickness, age, or suicide), the coroner assigned to oversee the official inquiry was most commonly a manager from a neighboring plantation.[125]

The larger role in maintaining plantation discipline assumed by the state during the apprenticeship period not only reinforced the overall strength of the affair by enshrining customary practices in law and establishing institutions for the formal adjudication of labor relations, it also provided a host of new instruments for enforcement. These ranged from the establishment of an armed, uniformed constabulary and the construction of public prisons to replace the private estate lock-ups to the revival of the "pass laws" that had been one of the central pillars of the slave codes.[126] In at least one crucial respect, the formal rights of apprentices were a significant step *backwards* from the informal rights of slaves. The latter had, during the period of amelioration, adopted the practice of collective bargaining through the Protectors. But under the 1833 Act, such actions were criminalized. If three or more apprentices collectively disputed work conditions or, worse yet, defied their employers' orders openly, they could be charged with unlawful conspiracy and face up to six months' imprisonment with hard labor and thirty-nine lashes on conviction.[127] A protest by three or more workers that became disorderly and defied an official's directive to disband could result in an even more severe punishment of twelve months in prison with hard labour (ss. 5, 7).[128]

124 Green, "Apprenticeship," 49.

125 This practice persisted well into the later decades of the nineteenth century, despite the protests of some reformers about the resulting conflict of interests. Mr. Des Voeux's Letter, December 25, 1869, *Report of the Commissioners Appointed to Enquire into the Treatment of Immigrants in British Guiana*, PP 1871 (c. 393), 10.

126 Turner, "The British Caribbean," 317.

127 Ibid.

128 Ibid.

For their part, colonial administrators had always made explicit their priorities of maintaining public order and work discipline, and recognized that the shoring up of planter authority was the pillar of both.[129] This was couched in the language of coercive paternalism, which asserted that a population so unused to freedom and so prone to "indolence" required the steady and experienced hands of planters and managers to guide it.[130] Once they had faced the inevitable passing of the whip from private hands into those of the state, plantation owners and managers adapted to the new processes of enforcing discipline in a way that became readily apparent. This accommodation had begun during the process of amelioration, when some managers had encouraged slaves to complain to the Fiscals, knowing full well that the latter would, in almost all instances, affirm the managers' power and chastise the grieving parties. It was not unusual for managers to explicitly evoke the Fiscal's authority and claim his approval of their actions, in full awareness that the power of the new agents had become common knowledge among the plantation workforce.[131] This merger of state and private authority on the plantations was especially close in British Guiana, where the simultaneous expansion of the sugar industry, contraction of the slave trade, and outlawing of the movement of slaves between colonies in the 1820s had created an acute demand for labor.[132] In such circumstances, restricting the movement of such workers as could be obtained, preventing newly freed Africans from leaving the plantations, retaining the authority of planters and managers, and cementing mechanisms to enforce labor discipline and steady production on the plantations seemed, in the eyes of most officials (Smyth being an exception), urgently necessary for the colony's economic survival.

Though more visible and extreme in British Guiana, the cementing of this disciplinary regime during the apprenticeship period was evident across the plantation colonies. From the newer Crown colonies to the older legislative ones, plantation managers found ready allies in the new judicial officials appointed to mediate plantation labor relations and enforce discipline. In contrast to the Protectors of Slaves, who were willing to advocate for their charges when they deemed their grievances to have merit, the magistrates appointed to enforce the new regulations on plantation labor did so with great alacrity, and were often more likely to punish apprentices *for* complaining than

[129] Green, "Apprenticeship," 57; Lightfoot, *Troubling Freedom*, 11.

[130] Such language was written into the Abolition Act 1833, which mandated that "regulations should be framed and established for the maintenance of order and good discipline ... and for the prevention and punishment of indolence, or the neglect or improper performance of work." *Bill of the Abolition of Slavery throughout the British Colonies* 1833, s. 15, 7–8.

[131] One enslaved man testified that the manager "told him that he had full power from the Fiscal to do what he thought fit." *1826 Proceedings Fiscals*, Berbice (70).

[132] Green, "Apprenticeship," 60.

they were to find in their favor against managers.[133] In the wake of emancipation, across Britain's tropical possessions, the Crown dictated the legal parameters of plantation labor and enforced them, but those parameters were set according to the priorities of plantation owners and the perceived need to maintain social order.

With apprenticeship and emancipation, the task of protecting the rights of free African-Caribbean plantation workers would fall into the hands of stipendiary magistrates who were, by and large, sympathetic toward the needs of planters. But there was another legacy of amelioration that would persist into the post-emancipation era, complicating the dynamics of plantation management and workforce discipline. With the end of slavery and the transition to indenture in the late 1830s, the former Protectors of Slaves would assume a new role and title, that of Protectors of Immigrants. As had been the case with their predecessors, these men would operate in a parallel administrative hierarchy, answerable to colonial governors and, through them, to the Colonial Office. Like Protectors of Slaves had, Protectors of Immigrants would serve as advocates for indentured laborers, hearing their grievances and representing them in magistrates' courtrooms. In this capacity, the Protectors would sustain the principles of amelioration and serve as the eyes and ears of an empire-wide regulatory apparatus designed to sustain the image, if not necessarily the substance, of moral colonialism and respect for the rights of even the most modest subjects of the Crown.[134]

Conclusion

Historians have rightly recognized that, from the perspective of reformers' stated goal to materially improve the lives of enslaved Africans on the plantations, amelioration was a failure.[135] The regulations that were imposed largely sustained the disciplinary regime that had existed under slavery, so much so that the continued abuse of the plantation workforce, the recalcitrance of plantation owners to relinquish their authority, and the repeated outbreaks of disorder made full emancipation a moral and political necessity both from the perspective of antislavery campaigners committed to pulling out the institution of slavery root and stem and from that of metropolitan administrators determined to maintain public order. Despite this continuity of plantation discipline from the pre-amelioration period, amelioration heralded significant

[133] In Jamaica, for example, the eighteenth-century slave court had seen an acquittal rate of 25 percent, rising to 35 percent in the 1820s. By comparison, two key judges in the apprenticeship period acquitted well under 10 percent of apprentices in cases brought by their employers. Paton, *No Bond but the Law*, 77.

[134] *House of Commons Debates*, April 20, 1826, v. 15, 510–11.

[135] J. R. Ward, *British West Indian Slavery: The Process of Amelioration* (Oxford: Clarendon Press, 1988); Luster, *The Amelioration of the Slaves.*

changes in the character of the colonial state, the relationship between colony and metropole, and the role of metropolitan authorities and their appointed representatives in the management of plantation life. Abolition, amelioration, emancipation, and apprenticeship all required the assertion of metropolitan control over the governance of colonial labor systems to a heretofore unprecedented degree. This was particularly true of amelioration, which engineered a fundamental change in the balance of power between the state and the individual in the plantation economy, a change that encompassed enslaved Africans and plantation owners alike.

This process dovetailed well with the desire of an increasingly professionalized and hierarchical cohort of imperial administrators to maintain law and order, minimize the expensive deployment of troops to quell rebellion, and ensure the smooth flow of revenue and trade across Britain's sprawling colonial edifice. In the 1820s, these administrators had taken their marching orders from a series of metropolitan ministries that had tried to balance domestic demands for reform with the need for planters' cooperation, reluctant or otherwise. Such an approach proved impossible to sustain in the face of resistance and disruption by both planters and enslaved Africans. The former desired to maintain their autonomy, while the latter, encouraged by limited information and possessed of hope, that most dangerous of all emotions, anticipated freedom on a more accelerated timetable. The result was a largely uncooperative plantocracy that, when pushed, could effectively disempower an activist colonial governor (e.g. Smyth) and a plantation workforce that was willing, *in extremis*, to go into open rebellion when they believed that their owners were denying them the freedom that they had been promised.

Resistance on both sides of the equation prompted an expansion and strengthening of state control over the entire labor system. By the mid-1830s, the elements of the overseer-state and its attendant principles had been firmly established in British colonial policy and metropolitan discourse. Amelioration, emancipation, and apprenticeship had erected the structure of laws, practices, institutions, and concepts that would henceforth govern *all* contract labor in the colonies.[136] Plantation labor relations, the rights of workers, and the authority of employers were now fully codified rather than determined by a melange of local ordinances and customary practices. Punishments for violations were administered, in all but the most minor infractions, by judicial officials rather than by plantation managers and overseers. And a system of officials, accountable to the central colonial administration, had been established as the permanent intercessors between the plantocracy and the workforce. The overseer-state had become a lynchpin of

[136] Turner, "The British Caribbean," 322.

colonial governance, with its agents and processes exerting a powerful influence in plantation colonies across the breadth of Britain's empire.

This new edifice of labor governance, epitomized by the Abolition Act 1833, encompassed Protectors, punitive laws on labor, legal parameters on the authority of employers, a grievance process, a court system, and a cohort of new magistrates. The resultant overseer-state, although ostensibly as aspect of liberal policy, was nonetheless centralized, bureaucratic, and hierarchical.[137] It was built explicitly on Continental systems of labor management, most especially that of the Spanish empire in the Americas. Paternalistic and humanitarian in discourse, it was coercive and punitive in practice. The stern penalties for a vast range of actions, from collective bargaining to "improper" or "frivolous" complaints, by slaves or apprentices meant that a system founded on the liberal principle of protecting the rights of workers often denied the same rights in daily operation. Much of the debate that continued among MPs, colonial administrators, antislavery activists, and planters and their representatives revolved not around whether such intervention was necessary but, rather, around where its limits should lie. Arguments about plantation owners' failure to honor this obligation of paternalism, a failure that made state involvement necessary, served as an effective counter to those who tried to assert that respect for private property must take precedence over the rights and well-being of enslaved Africans.[138] As one MP pointed out during a particularly vehement House of Commons debate in 1826, private property was only sacrosanct to the point that owners acknowledged the moral obligations that accompanied it. Should owners transgress the limits of ethical ownership, the state was morally and legally bound to intervene. If cruelly beating one's horse in public was illegal and immoral, the MP insisted, how much more so was the abuse of one's slave?[139]

Despite this growth of the colonial state apparatus, it is understandable why, at first glance, the Colonial Office may have appeared uninterested in colonial labor and reluctant to regulate it or conduct anything but weak oversight vis-à-vis the plantation system.[140] This was certainly the case in the initial stages of amelioration, but it was much less so by the apprenticeship period. By the

137 On association between liberalism and imperial systems of rule, see Uday Singh Mehta, *Liberalism and Empire: A Study in Nineteenth-Century British Liberal Thought* (Chicago, IL: University of Chicago Press, 1999); Jennifer Pitts, *A Turn to Empire: The Rise of Imperial Liberalism in Britain and France* (Princeton, NJ: Princeton University Press, 2006).

138 As Diana Paton points out, this vision of paternalism was based on an idealized aristocratic model that was increasingly outdated in England, where urbanization had removed large numbers of the working-class from the traditional social hierarchies and their attendance structures of social control. Paton, *No Bond but the Law*, 66.

139 *House of Commons Debates*, April 20, 1826, v. 15, 513.

140 M. K. Banton, "The Colonial Office, 1820–1955: Constantly the Subject of Small Struggles," in Douglas Hay and Paul Craven, eds., *Masters, Servants, and Magistrates in Britain and the Empire* (Chapel Hill: University of North Carolina Press, 2004), 253.

latter's conclusion, it would be more accurate to assert that certain principles (e.g. protection and rights), processes (e.g. grievance, regulation of work hours and conditions), and concepts (e.g. free labor), while remaining in flux, were being prominently articulated in the ongoing dialogue between the metropole, colonial legislatures, lobbying groups, appointed officials, and plantation workers themselves. These elements were shaped by local conditions and varied significantly between colonies. There can be no doubt that the overseer-state was far stronger in the Crown colonies than it was in the older, legislative ones. But the basic ideas and structures formed a system that was, if hardly unvarying, nonetheless coherent and pervasive. Officials, laws, and practices first introduced in the Caribbean, by the end of the 1820s, had expanded throughout the empire and been adopted in Crown colonies as distant as the Cape Colony and Mauritius.[141]

Without this growing apparatus of colonial labor governance, neither amelioration nor emancipation would have been possible. With indenture, the state would become even more deeply involved in labor management, serving not only as the overseer but as the underwriter of a global system of recruitment, inspection, transportation, regulation, and, when deemed necessary, punishment. Amelioration, emancipation, and apprenticeship thus operated as a laboratory for experiments in state centralization and the oversight of liberal subjects, especially with regard to labor relations and the moral and physical well-being of the workforce. By the end of amelioration, it was widely accepted across the range of local and metropolitan colonial administrators that the state, in order to maintain social order, economic viability, and the principles of "civilized" colonial rule, needed to oversee the entirety of the labor structure for the sake of those who had the least amount of power in the system, be they slaves, apprentices, or freed African-Caribbeans.

In sum, we can see the laws on slavery, abolition, amelioration, emancipation, and apprenticeship as aspects of an interrelated, empire-wide system not only connecting geographically disparate colonies but also tying newer forms of governance to older paternalist ideas, and hybridizing those ideas with novel discourses of humanitarianism. These reforms constituted a conceptual and structural bridge between centralized, hierarchical modes of Continental colonial rule and the British approach to governance that, in the Napoleonic period, had labeled the former "tyranny" and praised its own approach as epitomizing "liberty."[142] In the years before and after 1834, the boundaries in

141 Tyler Yank, "Slave Protection and Resistance in Colonial Mauritius, 1829–1830," in Jeff Fynn-Paul and Damian Alan Pargas, eds., *Slaving Zones: Cultural Identities, Ideologies, and Institutions in the Evolution of Global Slavery* (Leiden: Brill, 2018), 224–5.

142 This contradiction was not lost on colonial legislatures. Their planter-dominated representatives, facing the raft of imposed regulations, spoke explicitly of "tyranny." *Complaints by Masters and Slaves*, 1823–4, 21, 27, 34.

code and practice (and in concept) that separated slaves from British subjects narrowed. This was not least because, with amelioration, the regulation of slaves was removed from the hands of their owners and placed in the same institution, and in the hands of the same authorities, that regulated free labor (i.e. the colonial magistracy). Such reforms met the desires of both abolitionists on one hand and Tory paternalists on the other. Both cohorts were busy laying the moral and philosophical foundations of what would become, by mid-century, the empire's "civilizing mission" and cementing Britain's self-promoted image as a moral colonizer that deserved its paramount position as the largest empire in the modern world. These designations would distinguish Britain's colonial enterprise, in its public discourse, from the extremes of religious zeal, commercial avarice, racial exploitation, or naked aggrandizement that allegedly characterized the imperial aspirations of its Continental rivals. Such competitors possessed the might to achieve colonial conquest, according to the defenders of *Pax Britania*, but only Britain, by dint of its commitment to liberty and rule of law, possessed the *right* to govern others on far distant shores. This image of liberal governance and commitment to free labor belied the coercive character of the overseer-state, but was consonant with the public discourse of just rule and moral colonization that accompanied the abolition of slavery throughout the empire. Even among the staunchest advocates of emancipation, there was widespread understanding that for the former slave colonies to be governed, the formerly enslaved workforce and their successors would have to be *ruled.*

This new state apparatus, powerful though it was, was rife with internal fractures and conceptual contradictions, and was itself closely observed by metropolitan officials eager to avoid scandal and by an attentive metropolitan press and readership that was equally keen to uncover it.[143] Slaves, and later, apprentices, would prove adept at harnessing the new protocols and forums to solicit the aid of new state agents, to assert their own ideas of justice, to publicly undermine the moral standing of planters, and to protest violations of the rights to which they felt they were entitled. Soon enough, a new cohort of free workers would find themselves, much as slaves and apprentices had, contesting their entitlements and negotiating their status across the legal and conceptual terrain of the newly established overseer-state. How and why slaves and apprentices sought to employ this system, which heavily favored the interests of slave-owners and employers and was far more likely to punish workers than it was to accommodate them, and what precedents their agency set for the indenture system that followed, are the topics of Chapter 2.

[143] Epstein, "Politics of Colonial Sensation," 714–16.

2

"To Go and Look for Law"

Early Responses to the Overseer-State, 1823–1836

Lodewyk, an enslaved African in the British Cape Colony of southern Africa, faced grim prospects when he was taken before a judge in 1827. His owner, Conrad Laubscher, and another young slave, Mentor, both testified that Lodewyck had struck Laubscher. For a slave who was convicted of striking a white man, even amidst the many reforms introduced by amelioration, the sentence remained death by hanging. Despite the potentially dire consequences, Lodewyk had voluntarily sought the intervention of judicial authorities after the confrontation with his master. The injury to Laubscher had been accidental, he testified, the result of an unfortunate series of events that had unfolded as the three men, journeying across the veldt with a wagon, had just woken up from their evening's rest. Laubscher had lost his temper as Lodewyk had tried to help him get dressed, and had begun to beat and kick him violently in a manner that Lodewyk knew to be forbidden by law. Still enraged, his master had gone to the wagon to get his gun, and Lodweyk, fearing that he would be shot, had grasped him around the waist to stop him. When the horses moved and the wagon shifted, Laubscher had fallen and cut his head on the vehicle's ironwork. Seeing his master's injury and fearing for his life, Lodewyk had run off, not fleeing justice but *seeking* it. Lodewyk knew that Laubscher had broken the law, and he knew where to go in order to plead his case.[1]

Lodewyk was arrested and subsequently tried in the district court of Cape Town. His case was conducted across three days, separated by a month's interim.[2] Lodewyk, Laubscher, Mentor, and various witnesses all offered testimony. Some of this supported Lodewyk's story, while other accounts were more ambiguous.[3] The Fiscal, the powerful, Crown-appointed official

[1] "He did not intend to desert," Lodewyk testified in court. "But . . . he knew where he would go, meaning that he would go to Cape Town to complain of his master's ill-usage." Appendix A, Return of Prosecutions For and Against Slaves from December 26 to June 24, 1827, *Protectors of Slaves Reports. Copy of Any Reports . . . from the Protectors of Slaves in the Colonies of Demerara, Berbice, Trinidad, St. Lucia and the Cape of Good Hope*, 1829 (hereafter *Reports from the Protectors*, 1829), 117.

[2] March 19, April 19, and April 24, 1827.

[3] Laubscher himself painted a very different picture of the event. He testified that Lodewyk had been impertinent (a common accusation), had struck him an unprovoked blow, had wrestled with him for the whip, and had declared defiantly that "it was of little consequence

who was responsible for prosecuting all serious charges against slaves in the colony, represented Laubscher. The Guardian and Protector of Slaves for the Cape of Good Hope, another influential Crown appointment who was tasked with representing the interests of enslaved men and women, organized Lodewyk's defense for the first half of the trial. The case was a weighty one, given the potential for capital punishment. Accordingly, at the request of the Guardian, a trained advocate, Mr. de Wet, was brought in as lead counsel for Lodewyk's defense on the second day of the trial. The dynamics of Lodewyk's case reflected the ongoing process of "amelioration," which, by the 1820s, had imbued the colonial state with direct and paramount authority over all issues involving slaves across the empire.[4] Crown-appointed officials were now responsible for ensuring both that order was maintained among the enslaved population and that their rights with regard to illegal punishment and abuse were respected.[5] The Fiscal, occupying an older, more established administrative post, was aligned more closely with the first task. The Protector, a more recently created office and one subsumed to the Fiscal in the official hierarchy, was responsible for the second. Thus the case did not pit Lodewyk against Laubscher so much as it arrayed the apparatus of the colonial state against itself in an adversarial trial over which of these two aims, order and the authority of the slave-owner or the rights and protection of the enslaved, would prevail.

At the trial's conclusion, Mr. de Wet astutely challenged the prosecution's case. The testimony of its primary witness, Mentor, must be discounted because Laubscher had promised the young man his freedom in return for his assistance. And since the criminal law required the reliable testimony of *two* witnesses in any capital conviction, this consideration alone was enough to prevent full conviction (i.e. merely on the basis of Laubscher's testimony). Beyond the failure of the case to meet the technical requirements of the law, there was the larger context of history to consider. As de Wet explained, the law requiring that any slave who struck their master must be executed "had been for a long time in disuse . . . the circumstances of the colony were much changed . . . this case was not of such atrocity as to call for so severe a punishment."[6] Law, history, and justice all demanded that Lodewyk be

whether he died to-day or tomorrow." Laubscher had only gotten his gun, he insisted, when he had witnessed Lodewyk "feeling in his pockets for a knife." *Reports from the Protectors*, 1829, 118.

4 For an overview of the legal structure of amelioration in the Cape Colony, see the seminal work of John Edwin Mason, *Social Death and Resurrection: Slavery and Emancipation in South Africa* (Charlottesville: University of Virginia Press, 2003), 46–58.

5 On the wider history of the colony during the emancipation period, see Pamela Scully, *Liberating the Family: Gender and British Slave Emancipation in the Rural Western Cape, South Africa, 1823–1853* (Portsmouth, ME: Heinemann, 1997); Wayne Dooling, *Slavery, Emancipation and Colonial Rule in South Africa* (Athens: Ohio University Press, 2007).

6 *Reports from the Protectors*, 1829, 119.

spared the gallows. This held true even if he *had* struck Laubscher in the manner alleged, which had not been proven beyond reasonable doubt. The presiding magistrate disagreed, and sentenced Lodewyk to death by hanging.

Lodewyk's trial was one of many thousands that was conducted across the British Empire over the course of amelioration and apprenticeship. His case illustrates the complexity of the state apparatus that was created to manage an enslaved workforce transitioning from the status of private property to subjects of the Crown.[7] Owners and managers had initially resisted this change, prompting metropolitan authorities to increase the state oversight of labor organization. This was achieved through the appointment of new agents, the passage of new policies, and the creation of new institutions. Over time, slave-owners adapted to these changes by trying to employ the new agents and processes as a means of enhancing their authority.

But those suffering under the yoke of slavery, too, saw opportunities in the new system. Going to "look for law" became a common practice as enslaved African-Caribbeans sought to engage the new rights and resources available.[8] They faced an uphill battle, since the discourse of racial inferiority was programmed into the system. Nonetheless, their actions forced all of those involved to wrestle with the role of the state in regulating slavery, the balance between public order and individual rights, the use of violence to coerce and punish, and competing concepts of morality and justice. These were minor cases, but they multiplied over time, shaping the nature of the overseer-state. The contests during these early years of reform would have a long legacy in the decades that followed.[9] The willingness of enslaved men and women to employ these new agents and processes greatly enhanced their significance as anchors of colonial rule, embedding figures like the Protectors and Guardians of Slaves as permanent mediators between slave-owners and the enslaved, enshrining these officials' authority over the labor system that lay at the heart of Britain's plantation colonies, and increasing the legal and administrative coherence across disparate regions.

[7] The transition has recently been examined in a comparative Atlantic World context in Alejandro de la Fuente and Ariela J. Gross, *Becoming Free, Becoming Black: Race, Freedom, and Law in Cuba, Virginia, and Louisiana* (Cambridge: Cambridge University Press, 2020).

[8] William Perry, manager of plantation Annandale (Demerara) to A. Mack Rae, attorney for plantation Annandale, May 23, 1829, 56. *Protectors of Slaves Reports: Copy of Any Reports … From the Protectors of Slaves in the Colonies of Demerara, Berbice, Trinidad, St. Lucia, the Cape of Good Hope and Mauritius*, 1831 (262) (hereafter *Protectors of Slaves Reports* 1831), 56.

[9] This lends further support to the argument made by Caroline Spence that "emancipation … would be a turning point in a process of centralization of metropolitan authority that would culminate in the 1860s." Caroline Quarrier Spence, "Ameliorating Empire: Slavery and Protection in the British Colonies, 1783–1865," unpublished PhD dissertation, Harvard University, 2014, 198.

The integration of state oversight with colonial labor discipline also changed the political and cultural implications of encounters between slaves, managers, and owners, and the expanding apparatus of colonial governance. Slavery had been defined by its opponents as a system that was undesirable not just because it was immoral but also because it provoked resistance and threatened public order at a time when policing was diffuse and the use of force to maintain stability was both financially draining and politically hazardous. To reformers, this resistance was morally understandable if not necessarily to be indulged, while to advocates of traditional planter authority, *any* recalcitrance on the part of enslaved men and women was to be met with a swift and definitive response. Mass demonstrations and violent resistance were intolerable to both reformers and traditionalists alike, though whether reform measures or slavery itself was to blame for such incidents remained a matter of debate. The public dispute over whether the Demerara Rebellion of 1823 had been caused by amelioration moving too quickly or by it not proceeding quickly enough was one example of this discourse in action. With the advent of amelioration and apprenticeship, resistance to the expanding suite of regulations or defiance of its enforcers took on a new meaning. Cooperation with the effort of reform and employment of legal protocols along the terms defined by colonial authorities were mandatory and commendable, respectively.[10] Demanding justice on their own terms, exaggeration, deception, frivolous grievances, or open defiance, on the other hand, were labeled, at best, immoral and, at worst, threats to public order.[11] Such acts, according to those in authority, merited an appropriately forceful response by a civilian government that was fused with its antecedents in military governance and the violent tools of slave discipline.[12]

Amidst these debates over the moral dimensions of slavery and resistance to it, the legal and political foundations post-emancipation rule in the plantation colonies were laid by the policies of amelioration, new institutions and agents of governance, and the increasing assertion of colonial executives and metropolitan authority over labor relations. It is these foundations, rather than the agency of the enslaved per se (which has been well documented elsewhere),

10 On the ways in which racial power dynamics are embedded in judicial documents, and the methodological issues this poses, see Ranajit Guha, "Chandra's Death," in Ranajit Guha, ed., *A Subaltern Studies Reader, 1986–1995* (Minneapolis, MN: University of Minneapolis Press, 1997), 34–8.

11 This was a natural extension of elite assumptions regarding the innate cultural deficiencies of African-Caribbean people. Natasha Lightfoot, *Troubling Freedom: Antigua and the Aftermath of British Emancipation* (Durham, NC: Duke University Press, 2015), 7; Thomas C. Holt, *The Problem of Freedom: Race, Labor, and Politics in Jamaica and Britain, 1832–1938* (Baltimore, MD: Johns Hopkins University Press, 1992), xxiii.

12 By the terms of the Emancipation Act 1833, plantation discipline, though adjudicated by stipendiary magistrates, would be administered by a new plantation police force composed of freed African Caribbeans and organized along military lines.

that constitute the focus of this chapter.[13] But the social and cultural practices that emerged from these foundations were profoundly shaped by the responses of enslaved Africans, and these deserve careful attention.[14] Such responses evolved over time and in relation to new policies and new protocols of governance. This interaction helped determine the character of the overseer-state in a multitude of ways, from altering the approaches of agents to different aspects of plantation life to serving as leverage for antislavery activists in Parliament and even to prompting internal conflicts, as Lodewyk's case did, over how justice was defined and whether or not the life of an enslaved African had any worth at all. The overseer-state, from its earliest years, was thus reciprocally constructed by the rulers and the ruled, albeit from vastly asymmetrical positions of authority. It would carry over older laws, concepts, and practices that had been established during late-stage slavery and combine them with novel elements introduced during amelioration.[15] This infrastructure of racialized labor governance, and the patterns of response that it generated, would persist across Britain's plantation colonies long after emancipation.[16]

[13] David Barry Gaspar, "Working the System: Antigua Slaves and Their Struggle to Live," *Slavery & Abolition* 13, no. 3 (1992), 131–5; Randy Browne, *Surviving Slavery in the British Caribbean* (Philadelphia: University of Pennsylvania Press, 2017), 44–71; Mary Turner, "The 11 O'Clock Flog: Women, Work, and Labour Law in the British Caribbean," *Slavery & Abolition* 20, no. 1 (1999), 38–58; John Lean and Trevor Burnard, "Hearing Slave Voices: The Fiscal's Reports of Berbice and Demerara-Essequebo," *Journal of the British Records Association* 27, no. 107 (2002), 120–33; Trevor Burnard, *Hearing Slaves Speak* (Georgetown: Caribbean Press, 2010); Trevor Burnard, "A Voice for Slaves: The Office of the Fiscal in Berbice and the Beginning of Protection in the British Empire, 1819–1834," *Pacific Historical Review* 87, no. 1 (2018), 30–54.

[14] For a discussion of how a focus on "resistance" has led scholars to overlook the complexities of power relations within subaltern communities, see Sherry Ortner, "Resistance and the Problem of Ethnographic Refusal," *Comparative Studies in Society and History* 37, no. 1 (January 1995), 175–6. On violence and resistance to it in British Guiana, see Browne, *Surviving Slavery*, 44–71; Diana Paton, *No Bond but the Law: Punishment, Race, and Gender in Jamaican State Formation, 1780–1870* (Durham, NC: Duke University Press, 2004), 159.

[15] On the wider relationship between law and race in the nineteenth-century Caribbean, see David V. Trotman, *Crime in Trinidad: Conflict and Control in a Plantation Society, 1838–1900* (Knoxville: University of Tennessee Press, 1986); Mindie Lazarus-Black, *Legitimate Acts and Illegal Encounters: Law and Society in Antigua and Barbuda* (Washington, DC: Smithsonian Institution Press, 1994); Paton, *No Bond but the Law*; James Epstein, "Politics of Colonial Sensation: The Trial of Thomas Picton and the Cause of Louisa Calderon," *American Historical Review* 112, no. 3 (2007), 712–41.

[16] For a recent discussion of the relationship between race, legal institutions, and the discourse of law in the Caribbean, see Juanita de Barros, "The Death of Molly Shultz: Race, Magic, and the Law in the Post-Slavery Caribbean," *Journal of Social History* 55, no. 2 (2021), 345–73. See also Alejandro de la Fuente, "Slave Law and Claims-Making in Cuba: The Tannenbaum Debate Revisited," *Law and History Review* 22, no. 2 (2004), 339–69.

The Complaint System during Early-Stage Amelioration

The most frequent and significant engagement of enslaved Africans with the overseer-state began with the merger of customary practice with official oversight and formal investigation, the latter incorporating magistrates and protectors, as an ancillary mechanism to direct discipline on the plantations. This coincided with the widening responsibilities of Fiscals and their analogs in the second decade of the nineteenth century and accelerated with the appointment of Protectors and Guardians of Slaves across Britain's Crown colonies in the mid-1820s.[17] The increased frequency of official inquiries was hardly the first encounter of enslaved Africans with legal proceedings, but it was only in this period that such contact became an integral part of plantation labor relations. Slave courts in British colonies dated back to the eighteenth century. Until the amelioration period, however, the granting of summary justice power to slave-owners for the punishment of most routine offenses meant that these venues were used on a very limited basis, and then almost always as direct extensions of the extant disciplinary regime of violence and terror.[18]

Although amelioration would significantly widen the opportunities for the enslaved to voluntarily engage the law, it is important to note from the outset that the overwhelming majority of encounters between slaves and the state in this period remained coercive and punitive. In any given colony, every year, as many as one-fifth of the entire enslaved population could face floggings, confinement to the stocks, or imprisonment for a vast array of causes. The bulk of the punishments inflicted were related to workplace discipline. In the first six months of 1828 in Berbice alone, for example, local magistrates authorized enslaved men and women to be punished on 4,829 separate occasions.[19] The most common offenses, by far, were those concerning the conduct of plantation work and the responses of the enslaved to the authority of managers and overseers.[20] Foremost among these were "neglecting duty and insufficient work" (1,232), "bad work" (819), "idleness, laziness and indolence" (444),

[17] Browne, *Surviving Slavery*, 44–71; Turner, "The 11 O'Clock Flog," 38–58; Lean and Burnard, "Hearing Slave Voices," 120–33; Burnard, "A Voice for Slaves," 30–54; Christina Twomey, "Protecting Slaves and Aborigines: The Legacies of European Colonialism in the British Empire," *Pacific Historical Review* 87, no. 1 (2018), 10–29.

[18] Diana Paton, "Punishment, Crime, and the Bodies of Slaves in Eighteenth-Century Jamaica," *Journal of Social History* 34, no. 4 (Summer 2001), 924.

[19] *Reports from the Protectors*, 1829, 40.

[20] For the ways in which the speech of enslaved men and women developed as a mode of challenging the authority of slave-owners in the antebellum American South, see William E. Wiethoff, "The Nature and Limits of Slave Insolence in the American South," *Quarterly Journal of Speech* 87, no. 2 (2001), 197–207; William E. Wiethoff, *The Insolent Slave* (Columbia: University of South Carolina Press, 2002).

"not coming to work on time" (376), "disobedience" (341), "insolence" (318), and "absenting from work" (258).[21]

Ultimately, the discretion to punish a slave on one grounds or another lay entirely in the hands of proprietors, managers, and overseers. Their decision in each case was based on customary practice, the individual in question, and how seriously plantation authorities took the issue. First or infrequent offenders could be punished for one of the lesser offenses such as "refusing to work," "not coming to work on time," "bad work," or "idleness, laziness and indolence," which were typically punished by short periods of confinement to stocks and rarely resulted in floggings.[22] The latter could only be inflicted on male slaves; corporal punishment, by the terms of the amelioration ordinances, was forbidden altogether for female slaves. Repeat offenders or those deemed troublesome by managers or overseers were more likely to face serious punishments for "neglecting duty and insufficient work" or "disobedience," the penalty for which was commonly the lash.[23] These punishments were administered on site, recorded, and later reviewed and approved by officials.

The infliction of these punishments remained the responsibility of plantation staff, though they were required to keep a careful accounting for subsequent examination by magistrates and Protectors. Slaves had little recourse in such matters unless they had grounds to claim that their treatment had violated amelioration regulations. In such instances, they could bring formal grievances against managers, overseers, or others in positions of authority. By the later half of the 1820s, the regulations governing amelioration required slave-owners and plantation managers to make their slaves aware that they had rights, the right to grieve among them. In the Caribbean Crown colonies, the Protectors and Guardians of Slaves and their Assistants regularly traveled to plantations in order to solicit slaves' complaints, and enslaved men and women were entitled to passes off of the plantation so that they could submit a grievance to the appropriate official. By 1830, slaves' "going to laws," while remaining far less common than their being summarily punished, had become a regular experience throughout Britain's slave-colony archipelago. This activity, which increased in frequency across the amelioration and apprenticeship periods, would become integral to indenture in subsequent decades. It represented yet another common element by which the overseer-state bound the disparate locales of Britain's plantation-mining colonies together with a coherent – albeit internally contested – system of shared laws, concepts, practices, and experiences.

21 *Reports from the Protectors*, 1829, 40.

22 Respectively, 26 out of 88, 35 out of 202, 96 out of 406, and 51 out of 255. *Reports from the Protectors*, 1829, 40.

23 Respectively, 302 out of 364 and 115 out of 256. *Reports from the Protectors*, 1829, 40.

Slaves quickly absorbed and adapted to the new legal landscape created by amelioration, recognizing that officials such as Fiscals and Protectors were now superior in authority to slave-owners and the managers and overseers of plantations.[24] In small but significant numbers, they sought redress for perceived abuses, contested the denial of rights and resources to which they believed they were entitled, and endeavored to harness the courts' authority to reinterpret customary practices as legal prerogatives. Through such actions, enslaved men and women helped establish local officials as arbiters and mediators between owners and plantation managers and their workforce. In a broader sense, both the slave-owners' employment of the law to discipline slaves and the slaves' employment of the grievance system to contest owners' or managers' abuses achieved the same result, albeit from different directions and much to the advantage of the owners and managers. These practices cemented the authority of the overseer-state in colonial labor systems.

The officials in charge of implementing amelioration insisted that the process of grievance was an integral aspect of ameliorating the worst aspects of slavery. Such changes, however, are exceedingly difficult to measure. Many of the abuses of power that were endemic as owners, managers, and overseers adjusted to the new regime of legal oversight would not have come to the attention of Fiscals and Protectors were it not for the initiative of enslaved men and women in submitting grievances. Formal legal prosecutions, on the other hand, which had to be first reviewed and approved, and later conducted, by an agent of the overseer-state on the basis of a complaint, were exceedingly rare. But these cases, though few in number, were historically significant. They reveal the complex and contested operation of the overseer-state with regard to individual rights and also illuminate how those with the least power, enslaved Africans, viewed the new regulations and the changing role of the state in slave-labor management. Their attempts to gain redress had political import as well, since they could filter up the chain of oversight and accountability, creating public scandals or triggering further reform.[25] The records of slave grievances contributed to the case assembled by antislavery activists for emancipation, highlighting the ubiquity of abuse and the continued

[24] Wayne Dooling, "Slavery and Amelioration in the Graaff-Reinet District, 1823–1830," *South African Historical Journal* 27, no. 1 (1992), 82; Browne, *Surviving Slavery*, 44–71; J. H. Lean, "The Secret Lives of Slaves: Berbice, 1819–1827," unpublished PhD thesis, University of Canterbury, 2002, 25–6.

[25] On the complexities of assessing the political significance of resistance among enslaved men and women, see Vincent Brown, "Social Death and Political Life in the Study of Slavery," *American Historical Review* 114, no. 5 (2009), 1234–5. On the wider use of legal arenas by enslaved men and women for political purposes, see Marcela Echeverri, "'Enraged to the Limit of Despair': Infanticide and Slave Judicial Strategies in Barbacoas," *Slavery and Abolition* 30, no. 3 (2009), 403–26; Karen B. Graubart, "*Pesa Más La Libertad*: Slavery, Legal Claims, and the History of Afro-Latin American Ideas," *William and Mary Quarterly* 78, no. 3 (2021), 427–58.

recalcitrance of owners and managers to amend their behavior as both law and morality demanded. Although the agency of the enslaved might have not directly prompted changes in policy or practice, it helped foster the cultural and political atmosphere in which such change became a moral imperative for all of those committed to the rule of law, just governance, and public order among antislavery activists, reformist metropolitan administrators, sympathetic Members of Parliament (MPs), and a small but vocal segment of the enfranchised British populace.

The potential of slave grievances to alter the public debates and trigger reform was aptly demonstrated in 1823. The filing of complaints had followed very quickly on the heels of policy changes such as the appointment of Fiscals, which made it possible, for the first time, for enslaved men and women to formally seek the aid of the law and to hold their owners accountable for violations of the amelioration regulations. The office of the Fiscal in the Dutch colonies, and its analog in formerly Spanish colonies, the *Procurador Syndic*, dated to the eighteenth century. Although their redesignation as Protectors of Slaves, or the appointment of a separate Protector, dated to 1824 in Trinidad and 1826 in Demerara, Essequibo, and Berbice, Fiscals and *Procuradors*, under the Dutch, Spanish, and British colonial administrations, had been overseeing the grievances of slaves for several decades previously.[26] However, prior to 1819 there had been no systematic tabulation or other recording of the complaints made by enslaved Africans under British jurisdiction.[27] But it is clear that by the time the formal, annual accounting of them began, the practice of filing grievances had become common, if hardly widespread.[28] Under pressure from the colonial governors and their superiors in London, Fiscals or their analogs in each colony were now tasked with investigating these complaints and reporting the outcome of their inquiries into the matter. The numbers of enslaved Africans who, via this avenue, became entangled in state processes as complainants or witnesses in any given colony each year were considerable. Each individual case often involved multiple complainants, and required officials to interview witnesses, most typically other slaves on the plantation, the manager, and the owner.

26 Turner, "The 11 O'Clock Flog," 38; Lean, "The Secret Lives of Slaves," 37–8.

27 This was done by the Fiscal, H. M. Bennett, at the request of the new President of the Courts of Civil and Criminal Justice, Henry Beard. As a qualified attorney, Beard well understood the value of careful documentation. Turner, "The 11 O'Clock Flog," 39.

28 Benjamin D'Urban, who was appointed Governor of Demerara in 1824, took this process one step further, by arranging for complaints to be directly solicited from slaves in pamphlets and newspapers, and by directing slaves to register their complaints with local magistrates along with the assistant to the Fiscal. He also made the recording of complaints and the forwarding of such reports to the governor an official policy. Spence, "Ameliorating Empire," 203.

By the mid-1820s, Berbice was annually witnessing several hundred instances of legal action being taken by slaves against their masters.[29] The case of Felix, a slave from plantation Scotland, was just one of several initiated in August 1822. Felix alleged that the manager of the estate regularly took the wives of the slaves for "connexion" (i.e. intercourse).[30] Felix's wife had been particularly abused for this purpose. To make matters worse, she had become pregnant as a result, and since the child had been born, "the manager is always punishing him [i.e. Felix] and his wife without cause." Ten slaves from Scotland had already complained to the owner of the plantation, Dr. Broer, who had promised to remove the offending manager, but no action had been taken. The Acting Fiscal of the colony, W. M. Scott, reported that he had proceeded to Scotland, accompanied by Dr. Broer, and questioned the manager and the other slaves about the matter. The consequences were worse for Felix than they were for the manager. The accused had blamed Felix for the whole incident, claiming that he had gone to the Fiscal only because he was trying to forestall facing punishment for incomplete work. As a result, Felix received the penalty that the manager claimed was due for his transgression, while the manager himself received a reprimand, accompanied by a recommendation from the Fiscal that he be discharged from service.

Felix's complaint, although resolved quickly at the time, would have a long afterlife in public discourse. Nearly four years later, when the abolitionist MP William Smith (Norwich) took up the cause of amelioration in a parliamentary debate, the plight of Felix and the other enslaved Africans at Scotland occupied center stage.[31] The miscarriage of justice in this case, where the manager was briefly dismissed but then rehired subsequently, was offered by Smith as a blatant demonstration of the failures endemic to the entire legal system in the colony and its neighboring territories. Most egregious among these, Smith maintained, was the close alliance between judicial officials and slave-owners. "He had proofs in abundance," he declared, that "nine out of ten persons appointed to guard against abuses were themselves the most interested in their continuance."[32] The local magistrates, often drawn from the merchant class, were a particular problem since "they were in every instance the friends,

[29] In 1824–5, there were 768 such cases. Burnard, "A Voice for Slaves," 52. For a broader overview of the final decades of slavery in Guyana, see Alvin Thompson, *Unprofitable Servants: Crown Slaves in Berbice, Guyana, 1803–1831* (Mona: University of the West Indies Press, 2002); Lean, "The Secret Lives of Slaves."

[30] "Examination of a Complaint Preferred by the negro *Felix*, belonging to plantation Scotland, against the Manager of said Estate," August 23, 1822, *Proceedings of the Fiscals of Demerara and Berbice in Their Capacity of Guardians and Protectors of Slaves*, 1826 (hereafter *Proceedings of the Fiscals*, 1826), 131.

[31] Smith was a close associate of William Wilburforce and one of the founding members of the London Society for the Abolition of Slavery in Our Colonies (f. 1823).

[32] William Smith, *House of Commons Debates*, April 20, 1826, v. 15, 508–9.

companions, and even relations of those who might be supposed the aggressors." "It could not be expected," the MP lamented, "that the slaves would derive much benefit from their interference."[33] The only remedy was to enact regulations by which all judicial officers in the slave-holding colonies would be appointed from the metropole, and those chosen must subsequently be prohibited from owning or employing slaves in either a domestic or a laboring capacity.[34]

Smith faced fierce resistance to his proposal, and the motion was, initially, voted down. Later that year, however, when a comprehensive new slave code, based on the Trinidad model, was adopted in Berbice, Smith's proposed reforms would constitute its central pillars. Firstly, the new code called for the appointment of a Protector and Guardian of Slaves as a discrete officer, disaggregated from the Fiscal who currently served in that capacity.[35] Secondly, those appointed to the new office could not own or employ any slaves. And lastly, the new Protectors could not have any vested interest, direct or indirect, related to slavery. This barred them not only from plantation or slave ownership but from holding any financial interest in the former (e.g. a mortgage on a plantation) and from serving as a plantation employee (e.g. as a manager or attorney). This absolute prohibition extended to the Protector's wife as well, and any violation of it was to result in immediate termination of office and forfeiture of salary.

Felix's complaint and the public scandal it generated had provided the justification necessary for Smith and his allies to assert greater metropolitan oversight over amelioration in British Guiana, and to enact reforms that changed the apparatus of governance with regard to slaves, their rights, and their grievances. A decade later, the power of public opinion and the crucial role played by the petitions of plantation workers in shaping it would be acknowledged by Henry Light, the governor of British Guiana in a dispatch to the Home Secretary, Constantine Phipps (the Marquess of Normanby), that was prominently reprinted in *The Times*. Commenting on the latest reports of abuses in the colony, Light assured Phipps that any British subject in the colonies who complained would receive redress. Such redress, however, was entirely dependent on the initiative of the aggrieved party. "The executive," Light explained, "can only remedy that which is brought to its notice."[36]

33 Ibid., 508.

34 Ibid., 513.

35 "An Ordinance for Promoting the Religious Instruction and Bettering the State and Condition of the Slave Population in His Majesty's Colony of Berbice," *Papers in Explanation of Measures for Melioration of Condition of Slave Population in W. Indies and S. America, Part II*, House of Commons Papers, 1826–7 (b), 202.

36 Copy of a dispatch from Governor Light to the Marquess of Normanby, April 13, 1839, reprinted in *The Times* (of London), December 7, 1839, 2.

Smith's decision to justify his demands for reform in the context of Felix's complaint ultimately says more about the priorities of reformers than it does about the views and goals of enslaved Africans. There were far more severe abuses, even in the same record that Smith had employed to such significant effect, that received no such public attention. Most notable among them was the testimony that Rosa (aka "Roosje"), an enslaved woman on plantation L'Espérance ("hope"), delivered on June 10, 1819. The manager, Mr. Grade, had instructed the driver, a freedman named Zondag, to flog Rosa for doing bad work. When Zondag reported that she was in an advanced state of pregnancy, the manager replied "never mind, flog her till the blood comes!"[37] Zondag duly administered the punishment, with the whip "doubled" (i.e. folded on itself to make a kind of cudgel).[38] Two days later, Rosa miscarried. Another enslaved woman, Marianna, who had served as midwife, reported that the dead infant had emerged with traumatic evidence of Rosa's punishment, including a broken arm, an eye put out, and a fractured skull.[39]

Neither Felix nor Rosa was likely to have held much hope that their respective testimony would have brought them significant redress, at least not directly. It was only on rare occasions that slave complaints were carried forward to prosecution by Fiscals or Protectors. A far more likely result was that they would be summarily dismissed and the petitioners chastised for their temerity.[40] The enslaved population was widely portrayed as being deceptive, prone to exaggeration, ignorant, and cunningly manipulative. Much of the new system of monitoring and processing complaints was designed to weed out frivolous claims and punish those who made them. In the early years of amelioration, Fiscals, with their close ties to the plantocracy, often seemed more dedicated to preserving the reputations of plantation owners against the alleged calumny of their slaves than they were to shielding the latter from abuse. Maintaining plantation discipline and

[37] "Complaint Jonas versus Grade, manager," June 10, 1819, *Fiscals of Demerara and Berbice*, 1826, 57.

[38] The practice of doing so, or of administering a flogging with the thick handle of the whip, which was outlawed under later ordinances, was a perennial cause of grievance among the enslaved since such punishment was more painful than a typical flogging and more likely to produce serious injury. See also the discussion of this case in Browne, *Surviving Slavery*, 66–7.

[39] On issues of gender, reproductivity, and the contest for control over enslaved women's bodies, see Sasha Turner, *Contested Bodies: Pregnancy, Childrearing, and Slavery in Jamaica* (Philadelphia: University of Pennsylvania Press, 2017).

[40] As several slaves of plantation Resolution testified in 1821, their manager was so disdainful of the grievance process that he not only punished those who complained but told them as he did it, "I put the licks on, if the Fiscal can take them off." "Complaint of Jack, Boast, Jem, Tancra, Trim, Harry and Peter, property of M. Jeffray," December 24, 1824, *Fiscals of Demerara and Berbice*, 1826, 93.

keeping the workforce in good order remained the paramount goal. One of the most common responses of Fiscals to those who brought grievances was to sharply question why they had not, in the first instance, reported abuses to the owner and sought redress that way before escalating the issue to outside parties.[41] It was not uncommon for these officers to accuse complainants of using the grievance process to avoid work or abrogate punishment, nor did they hesitate to recommend public, exemplary chastisement for such petitioners as a deterrent to others. The Berbice Fiscal, M. S. Bennett, summed up the view of many of his colleagues around the Caribbean and throughout the empire when he reported to the Lieutenant Governor of the colony in July 1823 that "although the complaints of slaves shall always command my ready and serious attention ... the duty is no less imperious on me to punish slaves, whose only motives in quitting their estates to prefer complaints proceed from idle and wanton dispositions, whose statements prove to be groundless and vexatious."[42]

The Evolution of Legal Engagement by Enslaved Africans in the 1820s

Despite the low chances of success, the considerable likelihood of punishment from the Fiscal or retribution from owners or managers, and the overwhelming focus of judicial authorities on prosecuting charges *against* slaves, by the late 1820s slave complaints had become a common occurrence across Britain's Crown colonies.[43] From Trinidad and Demerara to the Cape of Good Hope and Mauritius, enslaved men and women regularly petitioned the newly installed Protectors and Guardians of Slaves, seeking redress for a wide array of grievances. The most common causes of complaint can be broadly divided into three categories: grievances about work and work discipline, grievances about physical well-being, and grievances about their status vis-à-vis ownership and freedom. Specific complaints in the first two instances most commonly concerned excessive or unfair punishment for alleged failures of task performance, reassignment from a more preferable work-task to a more demanding one, inadequate recognition and care for illness, mistreatment of mothers and children, or failure to provide proper allowances of food or

41 "Complaint of Grace, Eliza, Flora, Eve, Daphna, Silvia and Hannah, belonging to plantation Prospect, property of the late Benjamin Jeffrey, deceased," September 4, 1823, *Fiscals of Demerara and Berbice*, 1826, 108.

42 *Fiscals of Demerara and Berbice*, 1826, 105. See also Report from G. J. Rogers, Registrar and Guardian of Slaves, Cape of Good Hope, to Lieutenant Governor Richard Bourke, January 6, 1827, *Reports from the Protectors*, 1829, 71.

43 Mary Turner, "The British Caribbean, 1823–38: The Transition from Slave to Free Legal Status," in Douglas Hay and Paul Craven, eds., *Masters, Servants, and Magistrates in Britain and the Empire, 1562–1955* (Chapel Hill: University of North Carolina Press, 2004), 303–4.

clothing.[44] Grievances in the last category tended to concern being moved from one locale to another against their will, unlawful sale or transfer, violation of a previous agreement to grant them freedom (e.g. as promised by a now-deceased owner), or illegal detainment or designation as a slave when the complainant was legally free.

Complaints in the first two categories (i.e. work and well-being) stemmed largely from customary rights and practices that had existed under pre-amelioration slavery.[45] As of the 1820s, many of these had been translated into legal entitlements, and colonial officials were under clear instructions to inform enslaved men and women of their rights and the mechanism by which they could make complaints. To facilitate this, Fiscals, Protectors, and their Assistants were peripatetic, traveling around their assigned regions, visiting plantations, and announcing their availability to hear grievances. Being aware that these rights existed and *proving* to authorities that they had been violated, however, were two very different matters. Well up to emancipation, it was a constant, often losing struggle for enslaved men and women to secure enforcement. There can be no doubt that the legal system remained oriented toward the rights of owners, employers, and managers, and firmly directed toward prosecuting the wards rather than the wardens. The third category of complaints, those involving the legal status vis-à-vis ownership or even enslavement itself, was a more novel proposition, though one not entirely without precedent in the wider context of European slavery in the Americas.[46] These complaints did not emerge from the longer tradition of customary practice. In the British Empire, prior to amelioration, cases in which slaves, of their own volition, had initiated legal proceedings to establish their freedom were all but unheard of.[47] Instead, such claims, few at first but increasing in number across the 1820s and 1830s, emerged from the slow accumulation of knowledge (albeit incomplete and often secondhand) among the enslaved about the changing nature of law and the new role of the state in overseeing slavery. In some colonies, by the later 1820s, these petitions against illegal enslavement or claims for rightful manumission constituted the *majority* of complaints lodged in any given period.[48]

[44] Emilia Viotti da Costa, *Crowns of Glory, Tears of Blood: The Demerara Slave Rebellion of 1823* (Oxford: Oxford University Press, 1997), 69–72.

[45] Da Costa, *Crowns of Glory*, 73; Browne, *Surviving Slavery*, 59.

[46] See, for example, Brian P. Owensby, "How Juan and Leonor Won Their Freedom: Litigation and Liberty in Seventeenth-Century Mexico," *Hispanic American Historical Review* 85, no. 1 (February 2005), 39–79.

[47] When these few instances had occurred, they had been at the behest of antislavery activists, as in the famed case of James Somerset. James Van Cleve, "*Somerset's Case* and Its Antecedents in Imperial Perspective," *Law and History Review* 24, no. 3 (Fall 2006), 601–2.

[48] Between August 1826 and June 1827, for example, there were seventy-three such complaints filed by enslaved men and women in the Cape of Good Hope. Appendix B, Return

These grievances were filtered through the lens of a system designed primarily to root out frivolous complaints and maintain labor discipline, and they were recorded by officials who approached the testimony of the enslaved with powerful prejudices.[49] Nonetheless, they remain the most voluminous and detailed accounts available of how slaves publicly presented themselves, their circumstances, and their views on a wide range of topics, among them rights, law, morality, and justice.[50] What is clear, even through this incomplete and highly problematic record, is that the increasingly frequent encounters between enslaved Africans and the agents and institutions of the overseer-state were catalysts for change. Enslaved men and women rapidly adapted their self-presentations to the evolving landscape of law and governance, even as the agents and institutions of the state, along with slave-owners and plantation managers, adapted to them as well. Each cohort involved, from magistrates to enslaved Africans to plantation attorneys, also shaped their responses to the dynamics of encounters with one another through the medium of the new state processes, reinterpreting customary practices as legal matters or presenting personal conflicts and perceived injustices as issues meriting the intervention of the state. Complaints and grievances to Fiscals and Protectors demonstrated that enslaved men and women were acutely aware of the new processes and agents. They also showed that this cohort was willing to voluntarily bring these authorities into their contests with owners, managers, and other authorities. Like the overseer-state itself, the patterns of response were a common element throughout the breadth of Britain's slave colonies.

Across the wide variation in complaints, testimony, and decisions, enslaved men and women were increasingly behaving like subjects bound by law rather than as legally ambiguous persons whose treatment was bound only by custom. They argued, with a high degree of precision, that owners, attorneys, managers, and drivers were obliged to follow the dictates of an ever-changing regulatory landscape. Enslaved men and women demonstrated a keen comprehension of both the new laws and the shifting terrain of official authority.

Slave complaints were also often remarkably detailed and extensive. Although they generally centered on one particular grievance, their testimony

of Complaints and Applications for Freedom That Have Been Made to the Guardian of Slaves in Cape Town, *Reports from the Protectors*, 1829, 122–31.

49 On the archival dynamics at play here, see Marisa J. Fuentes, *Dispossessed Lives: Enslaved Women, Violence, and the Archive* (Philadelphia: University of Pennsylvania Press, 2016); Sophie White, *Voices of the Enslaved: Love, Labor and Longing in French Louisiana* (Chapel Hill: University of North Carolina Press, 2019).

50 This public presentation was, no doubt, very different from their private identity, and must always be viewed as being performative to one degree or another. For the contrast between "public" and "private" transcripts, and the constraints on dissent in the former, see James C. Scott, *Domination and the Arts of Resistance: Hidden Transcripts* (New Haven, CT: Yale University Press, 1990), xi.

commonly mixed claims about unfair work demands, unwarranted or excessive punishment, deprivation or inadequate provision of resources, and denial of access to justice. When three slaves (unnamed) approached the Fiscal of Demerara in July 1824 to protest against their treatment by Blake, the manager of plantation Better Hope, they brought with them a long list of issues. These included being assigned work "beyond their power to perform," punishment when said work was not completed, being compelled to work during meal and rest hours, inadequate care for the sick, forcing the sick to work, and flogging the sick or putting them in the stocks.[51] The nine enslaved men – La Rose, Klaas, Comaad, Kees, Lubin, Tom, Sam, William, and Adam – belonging to Mrs. Ibon Sanders who came to complain to the Fiscal of Berbice in February 1819 similarly pressed their case across the full gamut of issues covered by the clauses of amelioration. These ranged from insufficient provisions and denial of clothing to overwork, excessive flogging, punishment with forbidden instruments (e.g. a heavy rope-end), abrogation of Sundays off work, illegal confinement with shackles (rather than the permissible stocks), and further punishment when they complained about their needs and improper treatment.[52] Their complaint prompted a detailed investigation, with the primary witness being Christian Mackreel, the overseer and superintendent of the wood-cutting gang to which the complainants belonged. Mackreel's refutations were every bit as detailed as the claims of the complainants had been. Across two days of testimony under oath, Mackreel gave exacting descriptions of how work was organized, the provisions supplied, and the methods of punishment. Mr. Sanders, the overseer explained, had been prone to punishing his slaves in excess, but Mrs. Sanders, his widow, was a scrupulous respecter of the law. Such punishments as had been administered conformed to the regulations, including those against Kees for "being impertinent" (thirty-nine lashes) and Tom for three days' absence from work (ten lashes).[53] The enslaved men and women did, however, achieve a concrete result. Mrs. Sanders was fined a total of *f.*1,500, plus court expenses of *f.*312 (the equivalent of £130 then or approximately £13,000 now) for violations of the amelioration ordinances with regards to the feeding and clothing of slaves and the abrogation of work on Sundays.[54]

[51] "Investigation of a Complaint preferred by Nine Negroes, the property of Mrs. J. Saunders," February 1, 1819, *Further Papers Relating to Slaves in the West Indies (Berbice and Demerara): Copies of the Record of the Proceedings of the Fiscals of Demerara and Berbice, in their capacity of Guardians and Protectors of Slaves*, 1826 (401), 5 (hereafter "Complaint against J. Saunders").

[52] "Complaint against J. Saunders, 5–6.

[53] Ibid., 6–7.

[54] Ibid., 8. The fine was levied in the Dutch currency of guilders (*f.*), with the exchange rate at the time being approximately fourteen guilders to the pound.

Another frequent element that began to appear in slaves' grievances in the early to mid-1820s was the claim that they were being punished for making complaints in the first place. Such was the case in the grievances against Blake and Sanders described just now. Although governors and other colonial administrators would express concern that the rights of slaves to complain must be respected at all costs, as their denial could prompt them to turn to more direct measures of resistance, Fiscals appeared to have little sympathy for these actions.[55] These officers, in the early years of amelioration, were far more concerned with ensuring that the authority and reputation of plantation-owners was maintained, and with preventing slaves from using the grievance process as a means of defiance. This principle would be expressed aggressively with exemplary, public punishments for slaves whose complaints were judged, by Fiscals or their equivalents, to have been groundless. Grievances they believed to be founded in slaves' desire to avoid either work or accountability for their previous violations of plantation discipline were treated with particular harshness.[56]

By such means, Fiscals collaborated with slave-owners to preserve the image of slavery as a paternalistic institution. They could not conduct their duties as required without reporting the substance of slave complaints, nor could they prevent such reports from circulating to MPs and thence to a concerned British public whose moral sensibilities were being inflamed by the rhetoric of the antislavery lobby. But by attributing grievances either to the dishonesty of slaves or, on rarer occasions, to the misbehavior of aberrant owners, managers, overseers, drivers, or other middlemen in the slave-labor system, Fiscals deflected blame from the institution of slavery as a whole. They also gave the impression that the reforms demanded by humanitarians and interventionist metropolitan officials were being implemented to the greatest degree that was practical, but that this program had its limits; the fraught state of labor relations and the inherently fractious character of the enslaved workforce, these officials insisted, demanded the conscientious respect of traditional authority by *all* parties.

Reform and the Failures of Amelioration in the Late 1820s

By the late 1820s, despite the best efforts of Fiscals and other officials involved in amelioration, the public reconciliation of slavery with the image of just rule and moral colonization was becoming increasingly problematic. Stories of abuse, the violence inflicted on slaves, and the failure of reform had continually

55 Da Costa, *Crowns of Glory*, 65.

56 Herbert to D'Urban, December 22, 1825, *Further Papers Relating to the Proceedings of the Fiscals in Demerara and Berbice in Their Capacity as Guardians and Protectors of Slaves*, 1826, 7–10.

fanned the flames of political opposition and public outrage. Amelioration had been operating for more than a decade, and yet had seemingly failed to bring about an end to the abuses of the slave-plantation system. The apparent failure of reform catalyzed changes in procedures for addressing slave complaints, in the tenor of complaints themselves, and in their results. In the early years of amelioration, the responsibility for handling complaints and overseeing all cases pertaining to slaves had typically fallen on the Fiscal or their equivalent (e.g. the Procurator-General). By the final years prior to emancipation, following the Trinidad model, all Crown colonies across the empire where slavery was practiced would be required to appoint a separate official, the Guardian and Protector of Slaves, to perform these duties. Although the Fiscal, in many instances, continued to supervise any resultant prosecutions, the Protectors and their Assistants became the primary points of official contact for enslaved men and women and the state and the primary mediators between slaves and owners, managers, and overseers.

Despite this important reform, metropolitan officials became increasingly dissatisfied with the progress of amelioration. This discontent was particularly acute in the case of Demerara, which had been a focus of concern since the initial failure of the first effort at amelioration and the outbreak of rebellion there in 1823. The extensive employment of judicial processes to punish slaves and the paucity of slave complaints was a especially problematic for metropolitan officials. George Murray, the Secretary of State for War and the Colonies, expressed his dissatisfaction with these circumstances to D'Urban, the governor of Demerara, in 1829. Murray criticized the behavior of the judiciary with regard to slaves, the inadequate and incomplete mechanisms for recording legal matters, and the general conduct of the Protector of Slaves, Aretas William Young. Murray conveyed particular alarm at the large percentage of the slave population that had suffered under legally sanctioned punishment in the first six months of 1829. This period saw 10,207 slaves out of a population of 61,626 receiving chastisement for one offense or another.[57] When considered in conjunction with the low number of complaints filed by enslaved men and women, he asserted, the conclusion was either that slaves were decidedly criminal or that they had no confidence in the likelihood of redress through official channels. "In either case," Murray concluded, "the result is much to be lamented."[58] He also voiced dismay at the vague nature of some of the most common charges leveled at slaves, particularly the extraordinary number that had been convicted of "neglect of duty" (2,055) and "not doing a day's work" (2,169).[59]

[57] "Despatch from Sir George Murray to Sir B. D'Urban," September 2, 1829, *Protectors of Slaves Reports* 1831, 20.
[58] Ibid.
[59] Ibid.

To address these issues, Murray insisted that the Protector make determined inquiries into why these charges were being brought in such great numbers and what their specific nature was. He also demanded that he be supplied with more detailed reports, and was especially keen for more specific information about who, among the plantation authorities, had been fined for the improper punishment of slaves. Young responded directly to Murray's criticisms, explaining that "the exercise of limited punishment is left to the discretion of the person in charge of the slave," and that it was to the benefit of the slaves, in cases of more serious crimes, that this remained the case.[60] Referring such matters to the colony's judiciary, rather than allowing punishment in situ, would have two negative results. The punishment on conviction would have been more severe and it would have fostered distrust of the Protector among the enslaved, who would see Young as complicit in their chastisement. "I am directed to defend slaves," he declared, "not to prosecute them."[61]

The concerns of Murray and of other metropolitan administrators and humanitarian reformers over the failure of amelioration were well borne out in the complaints that continued, in small but significant numbers, to be submitted by enslaved men and women throughout the late 1820s. Across the empire, they sought out Protectors and their Assistants in order to make complaints on a raft of issues, demonstrating how little had changed about the concrete experience of slavery despite a decade of reform. Continuing a pattern that had been apparent since the beginning of amelioration, many of these grievances aimed to see the unspoken contract of customary rights recognized as being now a matter of law.[62] In such complaints, enslaved men and women often demanded that owners fulfill their paternalistic duties by addressing their unfair treatment at the hands of managers or drivers.[63]

Several important differences, however, were apparent between the complaints in these later years and those that had typically been seen in the early 1820s, and in the consequences of slaves' engagement with state authorities. One major change was that in the later years of amelioration, the number of slaves asserting that their rightful freedom had been denied, either through

[60] Report from A. W. Young to Benjamin D'Urban, October 26, 1829, *Protectors of Slaves Reports* 1831, 22.

[61] Ibid.

[62] Da Costa, *Crowns of Glory*, 73.

[63] "Complaint of Grace, Eliza, Flora, Eve, Daphna, Silvia, and Hannah, belonging to plantation Prospect," September 4, 1823, 107 (complaint about unfair work demands and premature beating by driver); "Complaint of the negroes Romeo, Sandy, Sam, Brazil, Hannah and Rose, belonging to plantation Profit on the West Coast," October 21, 1823, 114 ("We have no attorney, or at least we hear of none"), *Fiscals of Demerara and Berbice*, 1826.

oversight or by intent, rose considerably. Such cases demonstrated how knowledge of the new laws, agents, and institutions of the overseer-state had become, across the empire, indispensable to enslaved men and women seeking their freedom. This was the case in October 1829 with Thomas, a twenty-three-year-old Demeraran slave who had belonged to S. Gravesande, now deceased. The complainant, a creole, explained that he was the son of Gravesande's brother, and that his putative master had never treated him as a slave, never requiring work from him or providing allowances of food or clothing.[64] Instead, he had been raised with his father and trained to be a carpenter. Thomas believed that he had never been registered as a slave, "and that he was always led to believe that he would be free."[65] The current predicament, he explained, arose over a quarrel between his father and S. Gravesande, the result of which was that the latter had left the administration of his estate and the execution of his will in the hands of the Orphan Chamber. The Chamber, a legacy of Dutch rule, was an official board charged to decide the fate of children who had lost one or both parents, a status for which Thomas, by dint of his deceased mother, qualified.[66] The authority of the Board, given that Thomas's father was still living and had even written a letter attesting to the truth of Thomas's claim, was somewhat questionable. Gravesande's appointment of them as his executors nonetheless granted them a say in Thomas' fate, and the Board seemed determined to press the matter.

Here, the implementation of careful recordkeeping and the appointment of the Registrar of Slaves, both key aspects of centralized administration under the "Spanish Laws" that had been carried over into British rule, proved to be vital.[67] By the principle established in the 1812 Order in Council, the most comprehensive measure of early ameliorative legislation, the default status of all African-Caribbean subjects of the Crown was that of freedom unless documentation registering them as slaves expressly proved otherwise.[68] The Protector's inquiry to the Registrar of Slaves revealed that, as Thomas had claimed, he had never been registered as a slave. With Thomas's legal status confirmed by the records and certified by one of the colony's most formidable officials, the Protector was confident in adopting measures to affect his manumission "without delay." Although the apparatus of the overseer-state operated primarily to preserve the authority of slave-owners and maintain the submission of the enslaved, as this instance demonstrated, it was also the

64 "Complaint of Thomas, a coloured slave, aged about twenty-three years, creole of this colony, belonging to the estate of S. Gravesande, deceased," Report from the Protector of Slaves, Demerara, October 12, 1829, *Protectors of Slaves Reports* 1831, 102.

65 Ibid.

66 R. W. Lee, "Romano-Dutch Law in British Guiana," *Journal of the Society of Comparative Legislation* 14, no. 1 (1914), 15.

67 Registrars had been an integral part of the Trinidad model of amelioration.

68 See the discussion in Chapter 1.

mechanism that made manumission possible, albeit only for those who could successfully navigate its ever-evolving protocols.

The advent of Protectors in the 1820s signaled another significant change in the resources available to the enslaved and in the potential outcomes of the complaints process. Although still largely supportive of owners' authority and reliant on established practices to sustain discipline, Protectors were more likely than Fiscals had been to intervene and recommend changes to slave-management practices. Fines for slave-owners, managers, or attorneys remained rare, but not unknown, and a few cases in each colony every year saw large penalties in circumstances that the Protectors deemed particularly egregious. These officials, although typically working under the general supervision of the Fiscals, were directly answerable to colonial governors and, via them, to metropolitan authorities. The latter, which included men like Murray, were exerting increasing pressure on Protectors to demonstrate that amelioration was addressing the worst abuses of slavery and rooting out the most flagrant offenders. Sustaining at least the appearance of moral governance and paternalistic care for an enslaved cohort who occupied the liminal space between private property and Crown subjects depended on such measures.

One example of severe consequences following on recognizable mismanagement occurred in December 1829, when F. G. Bayley of plantation La Belle Alliance in Demerara was fined the extraordinary sum of *f.* 1,400 (£100). The complainant in this case was William, a fourteen-year-old enslaved boy, who had delivered a detailed and damning portrayal of the various acts committed by drivers and overseers under the supervision of the manager. Their behavior, which was in glaring contravention of the amelioration regulations, included the use of a heavy iron punishment collar rather than a lighter tin one (*f.* 200), allowing the driver to carry a cat-o'-nine-tails while supervising work (*f.* 600), and inflicting more than one punishment for the same offense (*f.* 600).[69] Not content with merely punishing exemplary offenders, Protectors could be proactive, moving well beyond the boundaries of official regulations to insist on specific alterations in how slaves were treated. Earlier that year, the Protector of Slaves for Demerara had intervened in the disciplinary practices of the manager at plantation La Penitence. The case in question involved separating young infants from their mothers when the latter were confined in plantation "lock-ups" as punishment for labor-related offenses (e.g. "neglecting to work"). The manager insisted that this was out of paternalistic concern for the children, as "a precaution against vindictive feelings [i.e. against him], which might be exercised upon the infants."[70] The Protector, Aretas William Young, disagreed, insisting that

[69] *Protectors of Slaves Reports* 1831, 154. *f.* 14 = £1.
[70] Ibid., 108.

the "violent feeling" and "passion" the manager had referred to among mothers facing punishment stemmed from the prospect of separation from their offspring. It was therefore highly unlikely that it would be directed against the children themselves. The manager's argument was unsupported by evidence, Young insisted further, since there was not a single instance of an infant suffering injury of death as a result of a mother's anger at confinement or spite against the manager. Condemning such separations as "altogether unnatural," the Protector ordered the practice to be discontinued, and warned of further legal measures on disobedience of his command.

Slave Complaints and the Authority of the Overseer-State

These cases and many others like them received a detailed accounting in annual reports delivered to colonial governors and subsequently communicated to metropolitan officials. Through them, slave complaints were becoming an arena in which the state itself, the progress of amelioration, and the work of Fiscals and Protectors were being judged and evaluated by their superiors, Parliamentarians, antislavery activists, and, via the latter's publication of excerpts, the British public. In this context, given the widespread skepticism toward the honesty of enslaved men and women, frivolous complaints and exaggerations were described by Protectors and the officials who directed them as an unavoidable aspect of daily experience. Public scrutiny and a sense of professional accountability, as much as the legal responsibility to enforce the new regulations, was why a careful investigating and subsequent accounting of each complaint was considered necessary, even in an environment allegedly rife with exaggeration and duplicity. Once a slave's grievance had been confirmed to be unfounded, as was most often the case, it could be dismissed without prompting any outcry that justice had not been done. Owners, managers, overseers, and drivers, in contrast, were held to a higher standard of legal and moral responsibility, since their transgressions, if proven, undermined the image of racial superiority and the paternalistic façade that justified both ameliorated slavery and colonial rule more broadly.

In these fraught dynamics, subject to both official and public scrutiny, Protectors' primary commitment was to the mechanics of governance rather than to the humanitarian ideals that, at least in theory, lay behind the ongoing reform of slavery. This explains how they could, on the one hand, condemn owners and managers for excessive violation of amelioration regulations while, on the other hand, continuing to evince strong negative opinions about the enslaved men and women whose rights and well-being it was their putative duty to preserve. These officers, many of whom came from a military background (much like their superiors, the colonial governors), were, first and foremost, members of a hierarchical, centralized bureaucracy to whose higher administrators they were accountable and within which they had a defined set of responsibilities.[71] They were organizational functionaries, conservative in their support of public order, coercive paternalism, rule of law, and the schema of racial hierarchy that pervaded, with regional variations, across Britain's slave colonies. There is no evidence that Protectors evinced humanitarian leanings, supported emancipation, or held any particular sympathy for the plight of Africans, enslaved or otherwise. Their official titles notwithstanding, their guiding principle was not the "protection" of slaves – they were, after all, complicit in maintaining a regime that enforced plantation discipline through violence and terror. Instead, to fulfill their professional duties effectively, they had to cement the state as the highest authority across Britain's archipelago of slave colonies, ensuring that everyone in the system, be they enslaved men and women, drivers, managers, owners, or proprietors, accepted its suzerainty. For them, public order and moral governance did not merely require respect for the new laws and officers, they were synonymous. Protectors' primary mission was to preserve and enhance the overseer-state itself. Ensuring that the rights of slaves were respected was a means to an end, rather than an end unto itself.

One demonstration of this commitment to the paramountcy of the state in labor relations was that, by the late 1820s, egregious violations of the law or disrespect toward its enforcers had become a doubly serious offense in the view of the Protectors and their superiors. Such behavior implied disregard not only of moral governance but also of the apparatus that had been erected to implement it. It was more understandable, in their eyes, for slaves to manipulate legal protocols, given their inherent immorality and limited capacity for comprehension. But open defiance on the part of slave-owners or plantation managers and overseers was considered wholly unacceptable. When William Perry, the manager of plantation Annandale in Demerara, contravened the explicit instructions of the Assistant Protector for the region, Captain E. Bishop, the response was swift and unambiguous. In May of 1829, Pollux, an enslaved man on Annandale, had demanded "a pass to go and look for law."[72] He was duly granted one and made his complaint to Bishop regarding what he viewed to be unfair punishment. In return, Pollux received a note for Perry indicating that the Protector would come when he could, and that the manager was "not to molest complainant" in the interim. When Bishop arrived ten days later to find that Pollux, against his express orders, had been confined to the plantation hospital, the Assistant Protector responded with a blistering attack on Perry. "Now you have *committed yourself* [emphasis theirs]," he exclaimed to the manager. "You have punished the man before he was tried. *I will give you law. I will show you law. I will first write to Mr. McRae* [the

[71] William Aretas Young, the Protector for Demerara, and Captain E. Bishop, his chief Assistant Protector, were both former British Army officers, as were many of their colleagues in the Caribbean, the Cape Colony, and Mauritius.

[72] William Perry to A. McRae, June 10, 1829, *Protectors of Slaves Reports* 1831, 56.

estate's attorney] *to know* if he authorizes you to act in this manner, and I will then prosecute you. You *gentlemen* seem to treat the Protector of Slaves with a great deal of *levity*."[73]

Perry and McRae only compounded their initial error by subsequently attacking Bishop's character and professional commitment to public order and proper authority on the plantation. In a letter to Aretas William Young, Bishop's superior officer, they accused the latter of extorting a monetary reward from them to compensate Pollux, an act that McRae asserted was a "dangerous tendency to the colony in general" and "likely to be subversive of all subordination."[74] Bishop himself responded with an equally damning assessment of Perry and McRae, insisting that he had only been attempting to mollify Pollux with the goal of preventing further acrimony or litigation. To suggest otherwise was "a mischievous attempt of perverting the intentions of the Assistant Protector, who in the main complaint actually *favoured* the master."[75] Bishop called on Young to demonstrate his support in this matter, as it was crucial to the conduct of his duties.[76] Young assented, declaring Pollux's confinement "illegal and unjust," though in private he cautioned Bishop to avoid any future attempts at informal resolution of plantation conflicts.[77] "A cool and dispassionate manner," the Protector concluded, would deflect any suspicion that Bishop was prioritizing an affront to his authority over redressing a slave's grievance.

As serious as the consequences were for managers and proprietors who set themselves in open defiance against Protectors or other aspects of the overseer-state, the consequences were far greater for those within the apparatus itself who failed to perform their duties to the satisfaction of the metropolitan authorities. Such instances aptly demonstrated the growing power and cohesion of centralized authority and oversight that tied together the infrastructure of Colonial Office administrators, Crown-appointed colonial governors, Fiscals and Protectors of Slaves, appointed magistrates, and the coterie of assistants that worked under them. As much as the overseer-state was scrutinizing the workings of slavery and mediating between proprietors, attorneys, managers, drivers, and the enslaved workforce, its own agents were facing ever-stricter auditing for the apparent failure of amelioration to address abuses. Slave complaints could highlight this disjuncture in dramatic ways, indirectly exerting a powerful influence on how Protectors conducted their duties and triggering a chain reaction of accountability for those who fell short of professional expectations. Such was the potential cost for those shepherding

73 Ibid., 55.

74 A. McRae to Aretas William Young, May 30, 1829, *Protectors of Slaves Reports* 1831, 56.

75 E. Bishop to Aretas William Young, June 10, 1829, *Protectors of Slaves Reports* 1831, 55.

76 Absent such backing, Bishop insisted, "protection to the slaves in remote country districts becomes a mere farce," *Protectors of Slaves Reports* 1831, 1831, 55.

77 Aretas William Young to E. Bishop, June 15, 1829, *Protectors of Slaves Reports* 1831, 57.

a reform program that was so prominently in the public eye, and that served as one of the most visible barometers by which the success or failure of moral and paternalistic colonial rule more broadly was being judged in the metropole.

In 1830, Aretas William Young, ex-army officer, former acting governor of Trinidad, and Protector and Guardian of Slaves for Demerara, became the most prominent casualty thus far to be sacrificed on the public altar of moral and professional accountability. In a blistering response to his reports of slave complaints from 1829, George Murray, the Secretary of State for War and the Colonies, accused Young of gross misconduct. Murray was particularly disappointed at Young's failure, in the vast majority of instances, to seek witnesses beyond the complainant, "from whom the truth is least likely to be elicited," and the target of their complaint."[78] This lackadaisical practice of investigation was compounded by the Protector's neglect of his other chief duty, which was to ensure that all due consideration and support was given to the *process* of slave complaints. "There is no appearance of assistance or of advice, or indeed of opportunity, having been afforded to the Slaves to substantiate their allegations," Murray wrote.[79] In consequence of Young's general negligence, "it was in very few instances that the claims of justice and the provisions of law seem to have been satisfied." So blatant was the Protector's abdication of his responsibilities, Murray concluded, that the ordinances governing slavery in the colony were, at least in the aspects dependent on Young's competence, "almost devoid of practical effect."[80] The Protector, at Murray's insistence, was relieved of his duties and recalled to London, where he would be subject to formal review. Young's employment in imperial administration was not terminated subsequently, but he never again held responsibility over enslaved men and women, ending his career in the smallest, remotest, and least populated of Britain's remaining North American colonies, Prince Edward Island.

Pollux's case and the castigation of Young demonstrate how slave complaints, indirectly and in the aggregate, could influence the dynamics of the overseer-state. A decade into amelioration, Protectors were willing to punish extravagant violations that were brought to their attention via slaves' complaints, and metropolitan authorities could sternly censure Protectors who failed to respond to such complaints in a manner consonant with moral governance, rule of law, and paternalistic obligation. Nonetheless, the bias of all those in the system, from Murray to the colonial governors to the Protectors and Assistant Protectors, against enslaved men and women remained exceedingly strong, especially in regard to their engagement with the protocols of grievance and redress. For Murray, enslaved men and women remained "those

78 Sir George Murray to William D'Urban, November 30, 1830, *Protectors of Slaves Reports* 1831, 115.
79 Ibid., 121.
80 Ibid., 122.

from whom the truth is least likely to be elicited."[81] Protectors across the empire, likewise, continued to express contempt for their charges. Fiscals and Protectors frequently translated these negative views of the enslaved into direct action, writing scathingly of complaints that they thought were manipulative or frivolous and punishing those slaves who put them forwards. Such matters were treated with particular harshness in the early years of amelioration. Well into the mid-1820s, it was not uncommon for these officials, after establishing through interviews with the targets of complaint (most frequently the overseer, driver, or manager), their superiors (typically the manager, attorney, or proprietor), other slaves on the plantation in question (whose testimony was treated with general skepticism), or the authorities on neighboring plantations, to order a flogging for the complainant.

Slaves that complained en masse or mobilized their cohort to support their grievance were treated with even greater severity. Such was the case when Caesar, Duncan, Hero, Baccus, Watt, Hector, Jeffery, Welcome, and Smith, of plantation New Forest in Berbice, attempted to seek redress for overwork, unfair punishment, and denial of food in June 1822. Caesar offered the main complaint, and was supported by his compatriots who, in turn, called upon "the whole gang of the plantation to prove the way they are treated by their manager; and they state the whole gang were ready to come to town to his Honor the Fiscal to make their complaint and seek redress."[82] The Fiscal swiftly responded to this threat against public order, traveling the next day to New Forest and examining the manager, the overseer, and a number of other slaves. Their testimony was not recorded, but the Fiscal's conclusion was that Caesar and his coworkers had engineered this mass protest, and the accompanying potential for public unrest, merely to avoid punishment themselves for failing to do their assigned tasks and for defying the orders of the manager. The complainants were subsequently flogged "in the presence of the whole gang; who were all reprimanded for their disorderly behaviour."[83] In extreme cases, where the complainant was determined, by the counter-testimony of witnesses and plantation authorities, to be an especially troublesome individual, the negative consequences of an investigation of their complaint could be even more dramatic. When Tobias, of plantation Friends in Berbice, escaped the stocks to file a complaint that he had been unfairly

81 It is also worth noting that the specific case that had done the most to convince Murray of Young's dereliction of duty was that of a female, creole slave-owner, Mary Lowe. Sir George Murray to William D'Urban, November 30, 1830, *Protectors of Slaves Reports* 1831, 118–19.

82 "Examination of a complaint preferred by the negroes Caesar, Duncan, Hero, Baccus, Watt, Hector, Jeffery, Welcome, and Smith, belonging to plantation New Forest," June 11, 1822, *Proceedings of the Fiscals*, 1826, 121.

83 Ibid., 121. See also 105, where Mr. Ross was declared by Bennett to be "a proprietor of respectability and a good owner of slaves."

punished, denied water in the stocks, and forced to drink his own urine, the testimony of two other enslaved men from a neighboring plantation proved to be his undoing. They claimed that Tobias had snuck onto their grounds and killed a goose, and had later been punished for practicing obeah. The attorney, the manager, and the overseer of Friends all asserted that he was "a very bad character, and disliked by all the other negroes on the estate."[84] With their collective assent, Tobias was sold at public auction.

The Formal and Informal Uses of Law Among Enslaved Men and Women

Given such clear prejudices toward the slaves' complaints, the state's nearly unwavering support of owners' authority (absent an egregious violation of the law), and the potential for punishment either or from the managers, or from both, for grievances deemed to be unfounded, spiteful, or disruptive to public order, why did enslaved men and women continue to engage the state at all? These were not spontaneous acts, devoid of intent. Complaints required a significant amount of planning, which often involved organizing corroborating witnesses, mobilizing coworkers with similar grievances, and even securing physical evidence (e.g. manacles or other tools of punishment). Their substance demonstrated considerable familiarity on the part of enslaved men and women with the general outlines of the law and the mechanisms of enforcement.[85] Such familiarity is hardly surprising, given that informing slaves of their rights, updating them on relevant changes to the law, and explaining the process by which they could file complaints was one of the core duties of Fiscals, Protectors, and their Assistants.[86] The detailed and often very specific testimony, whether that of the complainant or of witnesses, demonstrated the relative effectiveness of this campaign to keep slaves informed of their rights. Regardless of accusations that slaves

[84] "Examination of a complaint preferred by the negro Tobias, belonging to plantation Friends," September 4, 1822, *Proceedings of the Fiscals*, 1826, 132.

[85] It was very common for slave complaints to refer to specific regulations or to the protocols of grievance. For example, when Romeo, of plantation Profit, made a complaint on behalf of himself and five other slaves, he explained that the justification for seeking out the Fiscal was the absence of higher authority on the plantation to whom they could complain about the abuses of the manager. "We have no attorney," he explained, "or at least we hear of none, and we have not seen one for five months." "Complaint of the negroes Romeo, Sandy, Sam, Brazil, Hannah and Rose, belonging to plantation Profit on the West Coast," October 21, 1823, *Proceedings of the Fiscals*, 1826, 114.

[86] Colonial magistrates, too, played a role in informing the enslaved about the law and legal procedures relevant to them. Lauren Benton and Lisa Ford, "Legal Panics, Fast and Slow: Slavery and the Constitution of Empire," in Dan Edelstein, Stefanos Geoulanos, and Natasha Wheatley, eds., *Power and Time: Temporalities in Conflict and the Making of History* (Chicago, IL: University of Chicago Press, 2020), 299–300.

exaggerated or outright fabricated accounts of abuses on the plantation, their claims that certain acts were in contravention of the law were typically quite precise.

Slaves themselves, through long years of experience, would have known that their complaints were highly unlikely to prompt an official prosecution, let alone a conviction.[87] If formal redress was so exceedingly rare, the answer as to why complaints remained a common practice must lie in the informal results. What had developed over the period of amelioration was a culture of grievance, and though the consequences of any given complaint were unpredictable, the act of filing one and giving testimony could still serve a variety of purposes from the perspective of the complainant. One of the most common reasons to make a complaint was to seek confirmation that what had formerly been a customary practice was now a matter of legal regulation in which the representatives of the state had the final say. The most common of these arose when there was a disagreement about whether or not a task had been completed, which often involved a difference of opinion between a slave's and an owner's or manager's perception of what was a reasonable or fair expectation within a certain time frame. Such matters had, prior to amelioration, been governed by custom. Enslaved men and women had lacked access to any formal avenue for redress if punishment was inflicted contrary to these customary expectations.[88]

The installation first of Fiscals, and later of Protectors, gave enslaved men and women an opportunity to seek official mediation in these disputes. The same held true for the distribution of resources, the granting of time off from work, and various other small allowances that had been integral to plantation life for many years (e.g. the use of small plots of land for personal or communal gardening). Some of these customary rights were codified in various ordinances, most notably with the comprehensive overhaul of the slave laws along the Trinidad model in 1824. The expansion and evolution of these laws brought more of the mutual obligations between slaves and owners, proprietors, and managers from the realm of custom to the realm of regulation and

[87] J. H. Lean has estimated that of the 2,000 complaints made to the Fiscal and Protector in Berbice, only 30 percent resulted in punishment of the defendant. Lean, "The Secret Lives of Slaves," 69. Especially in the earlier years of amelioration, managers were quick to recognize this and use it as a means to discourage complaints. As Swift, an enslaved man in Berbice, testified to the Fiscal in 1823, "manager says 'if you go to complain to Melville or Kewley [i.e. the estate attorneys], they will only send you back, and you will get flogged. The manager says, 'you are fools for going,' and this makes us afraid; for if the attornies [*sic*] go, we are afraid to talk, because after going away we get severely punished." "Complaint of the negroes Wallace, Swift and Pompey," November 10, 1823, *Proceedings of the Fiscals*, 1826, 115.

[88] An informal system had existed in which, during disputes, neighboring managers or local officials were called in to mediate in order to avoid a work stoppage. But this, too, was governed by custom rather than by law prior to the 1820s. Turner, "The British Caribbean," 304.

state oversight. The hours of the work day, the right to days off of labor and for domestic tasks, the manner and degree of allowable punishments for certain offenses, and the provisioning of food and clothing all fell within this category. Other customary rights could simply be reaffirmed through the declaration of officials after due investigation of a complaint. These latter ranged from fundamental concerns such as the time fairly allotted to any given work-task, to the seemingly trivial, such as slaves' access to non-essential resources.

Bringing complaints could have immediate and concrete consequences. Although the most common outcome was that the complainant was reprimanded and, not infrequently, assigned lashings in response to the counter-testimony of plantation authorities, a complaint that was supported by multiple witnesses and against which the defendant could not produce an adequate explanation could have a number of positive results.[89] These could vary from the granting of additional resources (e.g. food, clothing, housing, firewood) to the firing of an unpopular manager, overseer, or driver.[90] In the earlier years of amelioration, it was a typical practice that any time a slave brought a complaint before a Fiscal against an owner or manager, the latter was fined, regardless of the outcome.[91] Initially, this was intended to underwrite the cost of the Fiscal's salary. In 1820s Berbice, the typical cost of processing a complaint was *f.* 50–100 (about £4–8 at the time).[92] If the case against the owner or manager was proven, fines could range anywhere from *f.* 300 to *f.* 600 for any single offense. Given that complaints often involved multiple alleged offenses, these costs could add up to a considerable amount. The more serious the complaint, the higher the fine. By the end of the 1820s, the potential cost for an egregious violation of the amelioration regulations could be high indeed. In the Cape Colony, in 1827, one slave-owner, Johannes Christian, was fined the extraordinary sum of £30 (approximately £2,000 in current value) in consequence of a complaint filed by a female slave named Eva. Eva had offered a dramatic account of how she had been trussed up helplessly before being savagely beaten with an illegal instrument of punishment, all merely for her unsatisfactory bread-making.[93]

89 These outcomes, it should be noted, were not mutually exclusive with chastisement or lashings for the complainant.

90 Fiscals and Protectors did not have the authority to force an attorney or proprietor to dismiss another employee of the estate, but they could strongly recommend it, with the unspoken intimation that further complaints *would* result in fines.

91 Burnard, "A Voice for Slaves," 35.

92 *f.* 14 = £1.

93 "The Secretary of State of the Cape District *versus* Johannes Christian for severely flogging his female slave Eva," Appendix A, Return of Prosecutions for and against Slaves, January 29, 1827, *Reports from the Protectors*, 1829, 115. In Eva's case, the instrument was a particularly cruel one, a "sambok," described as "a species of whip made from the hide of the hippopotamus or rhinoceros." The sambok (more typically "sjambok"),

Her testimony was lent weight by the evidence of a medical examination, which provided details of significant injuries consistent with her account.

It might, at first glance, seem counterintuitive that enslaved men and women, who demonstrated a clear understanding of the new regulations and their limits, would risk lashings or even punitive sale by bringing complaints over what appeared to be small issues.[94] In some cases, however, these informal entitlements had been custom for many years and could, in the long run, prove vital to their survival. When Maurant, Joseph, Secondo, Frank Mackay, Fanny, Susan, Daly, Cuba, Coffy, Qualo, Elias, Quamy, and Fanny of plantation Plegt Ankar complained to the Fiscal of Berbice in July 1822, their grievances focused on how the manager, Jon Quarles, had appropriated the chickens and ducks they raised to supplement their meager rations.[95] The Fiscal, after attending Plegt Ankar and making all appropriate inquiries, admonished Quarles that, were more complaints forthcoming in future, he would face criminal prosecution. In the presence of the assembled workforce of the plantation, he was also instructed to give a pass off of the plantation to any who wished to file a grievance and to pay full value for any birds he had seized. Such a public admonishment effectively secured a crucial, customary entitlement as a legal one, in precedent if not in code, while also reminding the manager that the final say in any contests with the plantation workforce lay not with the plantation authorities but rather with the Fiscal.

The grievance system allowed slaves to test the boundaries of their rights and to contest what they considered to be unfair or illegal treatment, be it denial of resources, overwork, excessive punishment, violation of customary practice, or any number of other transgressions. Prior to the amelioration period, slaves could seek the intervention of managers against drivers, or of proprietors or their attorneys against managers, but the decision to do so lay entirely at the discretion of the superior parties in that equation.[96] With the expansion of the complaint system via the older Fiscals and the newly appointed Protectors, such complaints, even if unsuccessful, added pressure on those same parties to address the issue in a manner that mollified the aggrieved. Cursory dismissal of such grievances could prompt slaves to escalate

a heavy, tapered truncheon originally designed for herdsmen to drive cattle with, would remain a common instrument of punishment for much of South Africa's history.

94 Not that any sale was ever truly voluntary, it should be noted.

95 Coffy's testimony was key to their complaint since he was a domestic slave, and explained that he was the one personally responsible for seizing any birds he found in their dwellings, with specific instructions from Quarles to tell them, should they press their claim, "that the fowl had no business in his yard." "Examination of a complaint preferred by the negroes Maurant, Joseph, Secondo, Frank Mackay, Fanny, Susan, Daly, Cuba, Coffy, Qualo, Elias, Quamy, and Fanny, a girl, the property of John Quarles, plantation Plegt Ankar," July 5, 1822, *Proceedings of the Fiscals*, 1826, 125.

96 In both Berbice and Demerara, there are indications that slaves protested to the Fiscal prior to the 1820s. Browne, *Surviving Slavery*, 56.

the disagreement by seeking out these new agents, with consequences ranging from restoration of resources or affirmation of rights to, albeit on rare occasions, chastisement or dismissal of plantation employees and even financial penalties for offenders (this last only after a formal prosecution supervised by higher officials such as the Fiscals). Slaves' keen awareness of this new avenue of negotiation was apparent as early as 1819, when the accounts of them employing the *threat* of formal complaint as a tactic began to appear.[97] In circumstances either where slaves didn't have direct access to proprietors or their attorneys (a not uncommon occurrence), or when their initial attempts to bring a complaint to them about a manager had been rebuffed, the filing of a formal grievance could force their response on the issue.[98] Such complaints called attention to the failure of owners in fulfilling their paternalistic obligations and challenged agents of the overseer-state to address these failures by enforcing the law.

Since it was a Fiscal's or Protector's duty to perform due diligence on every complaint made, the process itself compelled slave owners, managers, and others in positions of authority over slaves to give testimony justifying their actions. In these investigations, enslaved men and women proved adept at providing detailed and damning descriptions of abuse and deprivation.[99] Even if managers, attorneys, and proprietors effectively rebutted them and the case was found in the latter's favor (as was typical), the entire affair became a matter of public record. Reports of excessively cruel punishment, willful denial of

[97] It was reported that Minkie, a female slave in Berbice, responded to her owner's statement that she deserved a flogging with "if you flog me, it shall cost you plenty of money." Minkie's threat was not an empty one as in the formal proceedings that her complaint initiated, the Fiscal found in her favor and fined her owner. "Investigation of a complaint preferred by the Negress Minkie, the property of Thomas C. Jones," February 12, 1819, *Records of the Proceedings of the Fiscals of Demerara and Berbice, in Their Capacity of Guardians and Protectors of the Slaves*, 1826, 9. (Note that this is the twenty-page document.)

[98] Enslaved men and women were often at pains to explain that they had brought their complaint to higher authorities only after repeated, unsuccessful attempts to secure the intervention of attorneys or proprietors. "Complaint of Grace, Eliza, Flora, Eve, Daphna, Silvia and Hannah, belonging to plantation Prospect," September 4, 1823, *Proceedings of the Fiscals*, 1826, 108–9; "Complaint of the negroes Romeo, Sandy, Sam, Brazil, Hannah and Rose, belonging to plantation Profit," October 21, 1823, *Proceedings of the Fiscals*, 1826, 114; "Complaint of the negroes Wallace, Swift, and Pompey," November 10, 1823, *Proceedings of the Fiscals*, 1826, 115.

[99] Browne, *Surviving Slavery*, 59. The construction of legal narratives has attracted extensive attention from a wide spectrum of scholars. The seminal historical work remains Natalie Zemon Davis, *Fiction in the Archives: Pardon Tales and Their Tellers in Sixteenth-Century France* (Stanford, CA: Stanford University Press, 1987), especially 2–5. See also Sally Engle Merry, *Getting Justice, Getting Even: Legal Consciousness Among Working-Class Americans* (Chicago, IL: University of Chicago Press, 1990), 10–11. See also Toni M. Massaro, "Empathy, Legal Storytelling, and the Rule of Law: New Words, Old Wounds?" *Michigan Law Review* 87, no. 8 (August 1989), 2099–2127.

resources, overwork, sexual assault, and a host of other immoral acts were laid at the feet of such men. Although slaves' accusations were most commonly judged to be untrue at the conclusion of an investigation, the exhaustive catalog of alleged abuses challenged the image that planters and their advocates in Parliament were trying to maintain of slavery as a paternalistic exercise in which owners generally treated their slaves humanely. When communicated to the public by antislavery activists who were endeavoring to rouse the national conscience, these accounts also undermined the officials tasked with reform and threw doubt on the amelioration program as a whole. As the Fiscal for Berbice, M. S. Bennett, lamented to the governor, Benjamin D'Urban, in 1826, the "garbled statements" of slave complaints disseminated in Britain and the "inflammatory manner" in which they were communicated to an attentive public not only "excited indignation" against him personally but also prompted "the most unfounded prejudice against individuals of respectability [i.e. planters, attorneys, and managers] in this colony."[100] The slave complaints for Berbice became such a cause célèbre in Parliament at one point that the members of the Council of Government for the colony themselves called upon the Fiscal to compile a fuller and more detailed account of them, including the defense of those accused, for communication to the Secretary of State for the Colonies.[101] This was in hopes of countering the "unqualified attacks" that planters feared "will be levelled against the West India character" in Parliament. While the "refutations" Bennett provided might have reassured his superiors that he was duly investigating complaints and that the targets of such calumny were innocent, they were of little consequence to the public campaign mounted by antislavery activists.[102] Those who distributed pamphlets or made condemnatory speeches employing the material of slave complaints were hardly obliged to mention countervailing testimony from owners or managers.

Adding strength to this litany of abuses was the similarity of complaints across a broad swath of Britain's imperial possessions, including not just multiple colonies within the Caribbean but also the Cape Colony and Mauritius. Partly this similarity emerged because the abuses of slavery shared many common elements between regions (e.g. corporal punishment,

[100] M. S. Bennett to B. D'Urban, January 21, 1826, *Further Papers Relating to Slaves in the West Indies, Demerara and Berbice: Copies of the Records of the Proceedings of the Fiscals of Demerara and Berbice in Their Capacity as Protectors and Guardians of Slaves* 1826 (401) (hereafter *Further Papers, Slaves in the West Indies, Fiscals of Demerara and Berbice* 1826) 3.

[101] Proceedings of the Council of Government, Berbice, January 11, 1826, Further Papers, Slaves in the West Indies, Fiscals of Demerara and Berbice 1826, 1826, 20. (Note that this is the twenty-page document.)

[102] M. S. Bennett to B. D'Urban, January 21, 1826, *Further Papers, Slaves in the West Indies, Fiscals of Demerara and Berbice* 1826, 3.

discipline through terror, forced confinement, denial of resources). But the processes of the overseer-state itself also helped to foster an image of slavery as a persistently abusive institution even in regions with very different modes and practices of enslavement. Over time, the coordination of ameliorative regulations across the empire shaped the form and substance of grievances in similar ways between colonies. Slaves, informed of similar rights, and provided access to analogous officials, complained of similar issues and in a similar manner. The investigative and reporting protocols for grievances, which took a common form across the empire, also enhanced this apparent coherency and ubiquity. As more and more colonies adopted the Trinidad model and appointed their own Fiscals and Protectors who, in turn, initiated detailed investigations of slaves' complaints, these portrayals of abuse multiplied and coalesced around common themes despite the vast differences of geography, culture, social structure, and customary practice.[103]

Whether or not enslaved men and women were aware of the potential consequences of their testimony is very difficult to determine.[104] Slaves were, by and large, not literate, and the colonies, unlike mid-Victorian Britain, did not generate a raft of cheap, local newspapers that featured extensive coverage of trials in the local courts.[105] Nonetheless, the informal networks of communication by which information was shared between plantations was extensive.[106] The details of slave testimonies; the comprehensive character of their complaints; and the frequency of their assertions that managers and proprietors had abdicated their responsibilities or acted in ways that directly contravened either customary practice or law, or both, all suggest that enslaved men and women were cognizant of the moral standards of their audience (the Fiscals and Protectors) and of the value that plantation authorities placed on public reputation. Much like the laments of working-class men and women before local magistrates in Victorian London, the grievances put forth by slaves were both legalistic and publicly performative, translating issues of morality and custom into matters necessitating official attention and intervention, even if the formal verdict rarely went in their favor.

103 When Rosina and Eva, two enslaved women in the Cape Colony, brought complaints of excessive punishment to the Fiscal in 1827, they organized corroborating witnesses, used physical evidence (the marks they bore), and asserted that the instrument employed had been improper, much as slaves in Demerara, Berbice, Jamaica, and elsewhere throughout the empire had been doing for more than a decade previously. Appendix A, Return of Prosecutions For and Against Slaves, January 27 and February 1, 1827, *Reports from the Protectors*, 1829, 115.

104 Randy Browne asserts that enslaved men and women were "clearly aware of the radical potential of amelioration," but it is very difficult to ascertain, based on the evidence available, to what degree this was the case. Browne, *Surviving Slavery*, 67.

105 Sascha Auerbach, *Armed with Sword and Scales: Law, Culture, and Local Courtrooms in London, 1860–1913* (Cambridge: Cambridge University Press, 2022), ch. 1.

106 Da Costa, *Crowns of Glory*, 179.

The cumulative effect of slave complaints, the metropolitan concerns with the failures of amelioration that they helped make visible, and the continued discontent of the enslaved population that had resulted were demonstrated by the response of Parliamentarians and administrators as colonies across the empire reformed the local laws on slavery in the later 1820s. The deficiencies of the Trinidad model, in both design and implementation, were the central focus of a Commission of Inquiry sent to Mauritius in 1828 in order to examine conditions there and to address the proposed revisions to the Mauritian slavery laws.[107] Mauritius was among those possessions that, like Berbice and Demerara, had been seized during the Napoleonic Wars and, like them, operated within the legacy of a centralized, Continental legal system of slave regulation. The commissioners were forceful in their insistence that the Trinidad model could not serve as an appropriate guide, criticizing it on a number of grounds. The first of these was that the proposed fusion of the post of Protector and Guardian of Slaves with the existing office of Procureur Général was untenable for several reasons. Most important among these, the commissioners asserted, was the tendency of this officer to punish slaves for their complaints and to consistently advocate against them in criminal cases where he served as the public prosecutor.[108] Only the appointment of a separate official as a Protector and Guardian "whose duty and attention would be exclusively directed to the interest of slaves" could ensure that slaves enjoyed "confidence in support of their just rights from an officer."[109] This conscientious conduct of their official duties would, in turn, increase the likelihood that enslaved men and women would remain orderly and continue to respect the authority of proprietors. The commissioners also strongly objected to the tendency, in Caribbean colonies, to treat complaints made en masse by slaves as a "rebellion" and to punish the complainers accordingly.[110] Another cause of great concern was an issue that had come up repeatedly in communications between Fiscals, Protectors, and metropolitan administrators and that had made its way into parliamentary debates – the frequent punishment of slaves for allegedly frivolous complaints. The commissioners were adamant in their insistence that "no punishment can be justly incurred for a complaint which is simply ill-founded, or which may fail from want of proof."[111] Such punishment could be inflicted, at the judge's discretion, only

[107] The chief commissioner was William McBean Colebrooke, a career Army officer who would later serve as Lieutenant-Governor of the Bahamas, overseeing its transition from slavery to emancipation and apprenticeship in the mid-1830s.

[108] "Observations of the Commissioners of Inquiry upon the proposed Ordinance in Council, for improving the Condition of the Slave Population in Mauritius," May 19, 1828, 17.

[109] Ibid.

[110] Ibid., 21.

[111] Ibid., 24.

in instances of "false accusation wilfully made," which would be rare in any case, given that the majority of complaints, the commissioners insisted, were "well founded."

The overhaul of the Mauritian laws vis-à-vis slavery, as with similar measures in the Caribbean, largely transferred the overall authority for enforcing labor discipline from owners to state agents without significantly reducing the strength of the disciplinary apparatus itself. To justify these changes, the commissioners consistently framed the new laws not in the light of the presumed immorality of enslaved men and women but in the context of the presumed immorality of owners and managers. Any moral failings on the part of the former, they asserted, "is the effect of their condition, for which the masters themselves are responsible."[112] This central tenet of the Trinidad model, and amelioration overall, was just as strong in Mauritius as it had been in the Caribbean. Although sustaining plantation discipline among enslaved men and women remained the priority, the new laws and regulations brought slave-owners and managers under the authority of the overseer-state even as they brought slaves under the same aegis. In Mauritius and the Cape Colony, as in Demerara, Berbice, and across the archipelago of Britain's tropical possessions, slave complaints would form a keystone of this process.[113] They called the attention of Protectors to abuses, provided the necessary evidence of legal violations, and contributed, over time, via official reports and accounting to the growing narrative of slavery as an immoral practice that was incompatible with the self-declared ideals of moral colonization and just rule that were increasing central to public and official discourse on empire in the post-abolition period.

Conclusion

The apparatus of law, officials, and processes that constituted amelioration was never intended to empower enslaved men and women. Its purpose was to maintain social order among a vast and discontented workforce, to mollify the demands of antislavery campaigners by addressing the worst abuses of the institution, and to sustain both aims by installing a regime of oversight and mediation whose officers were accountable to metropolitan authorities and their appointed governors in the colonies. Those who implemented amelioration held fast to the belief that slavery could be reformed in a manner that made it commensurate with racialized paternalism, just governance, and moral

112 Ibid., 23.

113 In the Cape Colony, the dissatisfaction of the Colonial Secretary, William Huskisson, with the progress of amelioration prompted him to demand more vehement action and a more detailed accounting of what measures the district Guardians of Slaves had taken to address the abuses enumerated in slave complaints. Letter from Huskisson to Lowry Cole, Governor of Cape Colony, April 22, 1828 in *Reports from the Protectors*, 1829 (158).

colonialism. Design and implementation, however, are two very different things. Amelioration provided slaves with direct access to, and explicit knowledge of, a system of grievance that they could use in a variety of ways. While enslaved men and women recognized that their legal status was changing in ways that brought them closer to their erstwhile masters, the latter often still perceived their power as largely untrammeled, a perception that filtered down to managers and overseers. These authorities, with the implicit sanction of proprietors, continued to behave with impunity toward their enslaved workers, even to the point of taunting them and daring them to file complaints. Such behavior was galling to colonial officials and antislavery activists when they encountered it in the detailed reports generated by the Protectors. They understood that the authority of the owners and other plantation authorities needed to be maintained, but their arrogance and abuse had to be checked, since the former encouraged order but the latter was the most common catalyst of open resistance. One could punish slaves, chastise them, and still seek the state's support. But one could not behave arbitrarily and humiliate them without consequence.

By engaging the complaints process, slaves were presenting themselves as subjects with rights, rather than property that could be wantonly abused.[114] This self-presentation fitted more easily into the discourse of moral rule and the proclaimed goals of amelioration than the behavior of the owners, managers, and drivers that were the targets of complaints and grievances did. This concordance enhanced the degree to which slaves' engagement with the new apparatus of rule and labor management influenced the changing role of the state in slave colonies. This was not because their complaints were likely to result in fines or other penalties against their abusers, but rather because slaves' assertion of their rights was more in accord with the vision espoused by the architects of amelioration than the static self-perception of plantation-owners, managers, and overseers was, given that the latter cohorts typically wished only to yoke the authority of the state to their own established disciplinary practices.[115]

Even if enslaved men and women could not foresee how their complaints might influence law or governance in the broader frame, their accounts constituted a highly visible and comprehensive challenge to the façade of paternalism maintained by slave-owners. They also contested, implicitly if not explicitly, the notion that the agents to whom they made their complaints

[114] Da Costa, *Crowns of Glory*, 72–4. On the wider dynamics of this in the Americas, see Michelle A. McKinley, *Fractional Freedoms: Slavery, Intimacy, and Legal Mobilization in Colonial Lima, 1600–1700* (Cambridge: Cambridge University Press, 2016).

[115] When a group of enslaved men in Demerara told Lieutenant Governor John Murray, during the 1823 revolt, that "God had made them of the same flesh and blood as the whites," they were, unknowingly, echoing the clarion call of abolition etched so famously on Josiah Wedgewood's ubiquitous medallions, "Am I not a man and a brother?" Major-General Murray to Earl Bathurst, August 23, 1823. *Melioration of the Condition of the Slave Population in the West Indies, and on the Continent of South America*, 1823–4, 137–8.

were properly fulfilling their publicly declared role as "protectors and guardians." In this light, the repeated assertions of Fiscals, Protectors, and Assistant Protectors that slaves were inherently deceptive, that their testimony was either exaggeration or fabrication, and that they were intentionally manipulating the complaint process out of cunning or spite emerges as a defensive reaction to the narrative of persistent humiliation, deprivation, torment, and brutal violence propagated by these accounts. In order to sustain the image of moral and just governance through amelioration, and to defend their own conduct of their duties, the vast majority of slaves' grievances *had* to be countered by competing testimony, treated as suspect from the outset, or dismissed outright as the creations of immoral actors with no respect for truth and no comprehension of law. This strategy was effective only up to the point that metropolitan officials, antislavery parliamentarians, and humanitarian reformers secured access to the testimony itself. After that, such accounts could be, and were, deployed as powerful evidence that slavery remained an unjust and violent institution that the state was not merely tolerating but *abetting* through its new roles as regulator, mediator, and adjudicator.

As with the challenges to Protectors' authority mounted by managers and proprietors and with the often blistering assessments made by Colonial Office administrators, slave complaints put the overseer-state itself on public trial. These grievances called local officials to account for the widespread and continuing failure of amelioration to reform the institution of slavery. They also forced those in authority to reckon with the ideas of morality, justice, and fairness and to recognize that, with the growing public and official recognition of the cruelties inherent in slavery, the status of enslaved men and women with regard to law and the state had been irrevocably altered. This was dramatically demonstrated when Lodewyck, the Cape Colony slave discussed at the beginning of the chapter, faced capital punishment for allegedly striking his master, Laubscher. The presiding magistrate had taken a conservative path, following the letter of established law rather than the changing landscape of practice and perception on the issue of slaves and their rights, and had sentenced Lodewyck to hang. But the case was subsequently reviewed on appeal by the Lieutenant-Governor, General Sir Richard Bourke. In his next posting as Governor-General of New South Wales, he would lead the charge to reform the brutal treatment of convicts there.[116] Bourke, the man who would ultimately be held accountable by Parliament, his superiors in the Colonial Office, and antislavery activists in Britain for how enslaved men and women were treated in the courtrooms of Cape Town, reversed the sentence.[117] As the advocate defending Lodewyck had

[116] Sandra Blair, "The Felonry and the Free? Divisions in Colonial Society in the Penal Era," *Labour History* 45 (November 1983), 1–2.

[117] *Reports from the Protectors*, 1829, 120.

declared in a public courtroom, "the circumstances of the colony were much changed."[118]

The introduction of formal grievance procedures and the expansion of access to law, although providing enslaved men and women with a means to demand rights and challenge abuse, also served an ideologically stabilizing function by providing a safety valve for dissatisfaction. It occupied a middle ground between passive resistance and active rebellion, offering individuals the visceral satisfaction of seeking justice and redress, even if those efforts often ended in disappointment.[119] Encounters with the state via complaints, petitions, and court cases helped accustom enslaved men and women to their new roles as subjects of rule rather objects of ownership, a changeover that owners and managers often stubbornly refused to acknowledge. As with the expanded power of the state in regulating slave labor and the creation of new agents and institutions to monitor the institutions across the empire, these dynamics constituted another significant legacy of the amelioration period. In the decades after 1834, the ubiquitous petitioning and sporadic demonstrations of indentured laborers would have similar consequences vis-à-vis the overseer-state and its critics. They would provide ammunition for anti-indenture campaigns, emphasizing the incompatibility between the practice of indenture and the principle of moral colonial rule; channel dissent; and incorporate workers into the schema of merged state authority and private interest that governed colonial labor systems. The constant friction between indentured workers and the regulatory apparatus would, ultimately, provide the justification to sustain the disciplinary machinery originally developed to manage plantation labor and maintain public order in the final years of slavery. When substantial cohorts of indentured laborers began to arrive in plantation colonies across the empire during the latter half of the 1830s, the overseer-state would be ready for them.

[118] Ibid., 119.

[119] John Edwin Mason, "Slaves and Their Protectors: Reforming Resistance in a Slave Society, the Cape Colony, 1826–1834," *Journal of Southern African Studies* 17, no. 1 (March 1991), 104.

3

"A Most Imperfect Act of Abolition"

Apprenticeship and Early Indenture in the Atlantic and Indian Ocean Worlds, 1834–1842

Amelioration, emancipation, apprenticeship, and the (re)introduction of indenture all required the state at the local and imperial levels to assume unprecedented new roles in the regulation of labor. The coordinated set of practices, laws, institutions, and principles that resulted constituted, in function if not in name, a coherent state apparatus. This overseer-state was dedicated to the supply, organization, and control of coerced and semi-coerced labor across Britain's tropical colonies. How coherent was it and what were its constituent parts? Douglas Hay and Paul Craven have offered some useful guidance to addressing the legal dimension of this question, arguing that abolition, emancipation, and indenture were among the key areas in which the British metropolitan government, in contrast to its general practice of leaving labor regulation up to colonial authorities, "took a pronounced and continuing interest."[1] The statutes governing indenture were part of a constellation of labor laws that together constituted a "global web of closely related language, doctrine and social practice."[2] They were a key facet of the many "legal ligaments" that, since the eighteenth century, had made the empire "a thinkable whole" for both contemporaries then and historians since.[3] Supporting and implementing this framework of laws and policies, Alan Lester has argued, was an "imperial governmental assemblage."[4] This consisted of interlinked metropolitan governmental departments (the Colonial Office foremost among them) that interfaced with an empire-wide network of colonial administrations that, in turn, collaborated and communicated with one another.[5] During the crucial transition from slavery to apprenticeship

[1] Douglas Hay and Paul Craven, "Introduction," in Douglas Hay and Paul Craven, eds., *Masters, Servants, and Magistrates in Britain and the Empire, 1562–1955* (Chapel Hill: University of North Carolina Press, 2004), 13.

[2] Ibid., 2.

[3] Ibid., 2.

[4] Kate Boehme, Peter Mitchell, and Alan Lester, "Reforming Everywhere and All at Once: Transitioning to Free Labor Across the British Empire, 1837–1838," *Comparative Studies in Society and History* 60, no. 3 (July 2018), 689.

[5] M. K. Banton, "The Colonial Office 1820–1955: Constantly the Subject of Small Struggles," in Douglas Hay and Paul Craven, eds., *Masters, Servants, and Magistrates in Britain and the Empire, 1562–1955* (Chapel Hill: University of North Carolina Press, 2004), 253.

and thence to indenture and "free labor" in the 1830s, the state's oversight of colonial labor systems became one of the most prominent and powerful aspects of this assemblage, forging shared links of practice and principle that more closely tied the metropole to the former slave colonies and those colonies to one another.[6] Together, this set of policies, the practices that were disseminated between different colonies, the principles that guided them and shaped public discourse on colonial labor, and the various colonial officials and institutions tasked with enforcing the new regulations all constituted the overseer-state.

With this pan-colonial "governmental assemblage" in mind, this chapter first examines how the overseer-state evolved during the final years of slavery and the period of post-emancipation apprenticeship. The latter, which saw ex-slaves transition to a status analogous to indentured laborers, was particularly important in setting precedents for the wider adoption of Indian and Chinese indenture across the British Empire in subsequent years. The central role of the post-emancipation state in colonial labor management was especially evident in Jamaica. There, the ruling plantocracy, in collaboration with the administrative and judicial authorities with whom it was intertwined, successfully avoided undue metropolitan interference.[7] As had been the case in the Crown colonies, the Jamaican colonial government, dominated by its legislative assembly, established control not only over the African-Caribbean workforce, first as slaves and later as apprentices, but also over owners and managers. Even without the metropolitan direction that had shaped labor policy in places such as Trinidad and British Guiana, Jamaican authorities adopted a regime of regulation and oversight similar to that implemented in the Crown colonies, becoming a kind of overseer-state writ small. This convergent evolution between legislative and Crown colonies further demonstrates the degree to which racialized labor governance, in the waning years of slavery, developed into a coordinated and cohesive state system that anchored colonial authority across Britain's tropical possessions.

The final section of this chapter explores the first attempt to implement Indian indentured labor in British Guiana and Mauritius, examining the motivations for the adaptation and reintroduction of this centuries-old labor system. In the Indian Ocean World, the state apparatus of ameliorated slavery was merged with the preexisting models of coerced labor that had been employed in southern India and Ceylon, and with established practices of

[6] Walton Look Lai, *Indenture Labor, Caribbean Sugar: Chinese and Indian Migrants to the British West Indies, 1838–1918* (Baltimore, MD: Johns Hopkins University Press, 1993), 51.

[7] The contrast between governance in "chartered" (aka "legislative") colonies and the newer, more centralized model of the crown colony system is neatly summarized in Anthony De V. Phillips, "Emancipation Betrayed? Social Control Legislation in the British Caribbean (with Special Reference to Barbados), 1834–1876," *Chicago-Kent Law Review* 70 (1995), 1355–6.

penal transportation. The introduction of Indian indenture in Mauritius and subsequently in British Guiana resulted from a collaboration between planters eager for a subordinated labor force to replace apprentices, a Colonial Office that was keen to maintain both revenue and social order in the plantation colonies, and opportunistic private investors seeking to profit by connecting a newly available labor source with a newly created labor demand. This initial attempt to expand the indenture system from its modest origins, mired in mismanagement and public scandal, was a failure. This failure, however, was short-lived, and quickly prompted a rapid expansion of state oversight. The ineffectiveness of the public critique of indenture to do anything beyond briefly delaying the expansion of a state-regulated labor system reveals how deeply embedded indenture became, in a very short time, within the schema of imperial and colonial governance. In this period, from Jamaica to Mauritius, labor regulation continued to operate as a laboratory for experiments in enhanced colonial governance, linking the Atlantic and the Indian Ocean Worlds and establishing models that would later spread across the breadth of Britain's tropical colonies. These experiments firmly embedded labor management in the discourse and practice of imperial rule. For those involved in policy and practice, an expanded apparatus of state labor oversight was increasingly seen not as a temporary, ad hoc measure but as a moral, social, and economic necessity. By the early 1840s, the overseer-state, initially meant as an interim stage in the transition from slavery to free labor, had become a central and permanent element of colonial administration.

The Apprenticeship Period

How did the British state, constituted at the metropolitan and colonial levels, in the process of abolishing slavery, become the overseer of a vast, exploitative labor system that indelibly linked the Atlantic and the Indian Ocean worlds?[8] It did so region by region, and on the grounds that only an enhanced state apparatus could preserve public order, ensure the steady operation of plantation economies, and deliver on imperial administrators' vision of continued moral colonial rule in the aftermath of emancipation. The most long-lasting legacies of slavery, in this regard, were the legal structures left in the wake of amelioration and emancipation's operation as a moral foil against which successive regimes of "free labor" could be positively evaluated, regardless of their flaws. In light of slavery's brutalities, which had been made public knowledge by an abolition campaign that spanned a half-century, any new labor system, even one characterized by racial subordination, punitive labor

[8] For Britain as an "anti-slave state," see J. R. Oldfield, "After Emancipation: Slavery, Freedom and the Victorian Empire," in David Brown and Miles Taylor, eds., *The Victorian Empire and Britain's Maritime World, 1837–1901* (London: Palgrave Macmillan, 2013), 43–63.

regulation, corporal punishment, overwork, deceptive recruitment, and violence, could be presented by its advocates as an improvement over what had preceded it. At the ideological level, the two systems that succeeded slavery, apprenticeship and indenture, could be justified as progress toward liberalism colonial governance because, on paper, those within them were free workers bound by contract, rather than property. As such, in public discourse, these systems jibed with both humanitarianism and the growing public commitment of British politicians and imperial administrators to liberalism.[9]

For tropical commodities to flow across the empire following the principles of "free trade," however, the labor force of colonial agriculture had to be maintained. Absent slavery, and under the assumption that neither free African-Caribbeans nor imported Indian subjects would labor sufficiently without coercion, the burden of organizing and controlling this vast workforce would fall on the state.[10] A structure of recruitment, regulation, and, when necessary, coercion was necessary for economic reasons and still consonant with moral colonialism because the overarching principle was not the inhumanity of slavery but the commendable rule of law over free, albeit inherently underproductive, individuals. As Jonathan Connolly has written, "free trade required an unfree labour market."[11] Although it was grounded in liberal ideology, the overseer-state, in structure and practice, would thus continue to echo the more conservative imperial labor models of Spain and France that had been incorporated into British colonial rule during amelioration.

Introduced in the wake of emancipation by colonial authorities working under metropolitan oversight, the system of "apprenticeship" constituted the next stage in the evolution of the overseer-state. Legally, apprenticeship redefined freed slaves, involuntarily, as indentured laborers. By such means, they were tied to their former masters via an unbreakable contract of six years' duration, in the case of "praedial" or "field" slaves; or of four years, in the case of "non-praedial" (e.g. "household") slaves. Under the terms of this contract, workers were compelled to labor for forty-five hours a week in return for

[9] According to Jonathan Connolly, "[f]ar from disclaiming interventionism, theorists and administrators embraced regulated migration as a means of structuring the imperial economy. State-sponsored labour migration was a form of 'free trade imperialism,' to use Bernard Semmel's term, in which the ends of liberal political economy (redistribution of productive labour) would be achieved through large-scale state intervention (a highly regulated system of indentured labour migration)." (Jonathan Connolly, "Indentured Labour Migration and the Meaning of Emancipation: Free Trade, Race, and Labour in British Public Debate, 1838–1960," *Past and Present* 238 [February 2018], 94).

[10] De V. Phillips, "Emancipation Betrayed?" 1351.

[11] Jonathan Connolly, "Indenture as Compensation: State Financing for Indentured Labor Migration in the Era of Emancipation," *Slavery & Abolition* 40, no. 3 (2019), 461. See also William A. Green, "Emancipation to Indenture: A Question of Imperial Morality," *Journal of British Studies* 22, no. 2 (1983), 119; Phillips, "Emancipation Betrayed?" 1349.

provisions, housing, and basic medical care.[12] Apprenticeship fulfilled the demands of humanitarians, who insisted that the plantation workforce be employed as "free" workers, while also addressing the need for continued plantation production, a priority of both plantation-owners and colonial administrators. Like amelioration before it, the new system required the state to assume a central role in labor organization by operating as the coercive force tying former slaves to the plantations.[13]

Despite the prominent insistence of its proponents that this system constituted "free labor," its operation was anything but free from the viewpoint of workers themselves. The state's intervention was thought necessary, from the metropolitan perspective, because it provided time for the legal and financial structures of the Caribbean to adapt to the post-emancipation labor landscape.[14] Colonial executives and other opponents expressed doubts, through channels official and public, that the traditional planter class would be willing to abandon old habits of intimidation. In such circumstances, new laws such as those governing apprenticeship could provide yet another means of continued coercion. Despite this opposition, the coercive aspects of apprenticeship were made politically palatable in part because planters were able to successfully lobby for their view that freed African-Caribbeans, absent any countervailing force, would revert to their natural state of sloth.[15] This negative assessment, which ignored the centuries-long dependance of the plantation economy on the extraordinary labor output of its enslaved workforce, would persist well into the post-emancipation period.[16] Its prevalence was apparent even in the public speeches of abolitionists. As subscribers to a Protestant ideology that elevated useful work to a paramount virtue, they shared the abhorrence of the Victorian middle class toward idleness, whether it be that of paupers in Britain or of freed slaves in the Caribbean.[17] The strand of liberal thought espoused by some prominent Colonial Office administrators,

[12] O. Nigel Bolland, "Systems of Domination after Slavery: The Control of Land and Labor in the British West Indies after 1838," *Comparative Studies in Society and History* 23, no. 4 (October 1981), 594.

[13] Diana Paton, *No Bond but the Law: Punishment, Race, and Gender in Jamaican State Formation, 1780–1870* (Durham, NC: Duke University Press, 2004), 54.

[14] For example, at the time of emancipation, a monetary shortage in the Caribbean posed a serious obstacle to the widespread adoption of a wage-labor system. William A. Green, *British Slave Emancipation: The Sugar Colonies and the Great Experiment, 1830–1865* (Oxford: Clarendon Press, 1976), 130.

[15] Green, "Emancipation to Indenture," 100–1.

[16] It was aptly summarized by Anthony Trollope, who wrote, in his widely read travelogue of the Caribbean colonies, that "the negro's idea of emancipation was and is emancipation not from slavery, but from work." Anthony Trollope, *The West Indies and the Spanish Main* (London: Chapman & Hall, 1860), 89.

[17] David Eltis, "Abolitionist Perceptions of Society after Slavery," in James Walvin, ed., *Slavery and British Society* (London: Palgrave Macmillan, 1982), 192–213.

namely that freed African-Caribbeans would make rational economic choices and opt for skilled work or leasehold farming over plantation labor, did little to mollify these concerns.[18] From the metropole to the Caribbean colonies, whether one feared idleness or anticipated that newly emancipated workers would pursue alternative work, the most direct solution seemed self-evident. In order to ensure the continued productivity of plantations and the accompanying social stability, all while still implementing emancipation, former slaves would have to be bound to their former owners as employees. This proposed configuration, as a contractual relationship between Crown subjects rather than a matter of ownership, required an enhanced state apparatus to regulate and oversee it.

Caribbean apprenticeship, occupying the legal, economic, and moral middle-ground between slavery and free labor, borrowed elements of both amelioration and indenture. From the former, it replicated the traditional exchange of the majority of a given worker's labor for food, housing, and basic medical care. Following the patterns of indenture, it tied workers to the plantation through contracts that were breakable only by their employer. Apprenticeship also preserved the most potent coercive elements of amelioration. These were the use of punitive law to enforce labor discipline and the transfer of authority for that discipline from planters and managers to state officials in the form of special magistrates. The latter would assume the roles of "judge, teacher, and task-master," serving as the lynchpin of a legal system that regarded former slaves as "children needing to be re-educated as laborers and resocialised as citizens."[19]

This "extreme version of state formation" would continue the process that had begun with amelioration.[20] The overseer-state, operating through the magistrates and their superiors, the colonial governors and metropolitan officials, would guide the transition of former slaves from property to Crown subjects. While ostensibly guarding the fledgling subjects' newfound rights in principle, in practice, this apparatus of governance would prioritize the needs of their employers, the image of just colonial rule, and the preservation of public order. It would also perpetuate the integration of military governance and discipline with civilian labor control. Military officers would continue to fill the ranks of those administrators tasked with overseeing apprenticeship, from governors to special magistrates, and military patterns of punishment (i.e. public floggings, their number specific to the offense, administered with official

[18] De V. Phillips, "Emancipation Betrayed?" 1351. The anticipation that freed African-Caribbeans would show little enthusiasm for reassuming their former roles on the plantations did, indeed, turn out to be accurate (W. Manuel Riviere, "Labour Shortage in the British West Indies after Emancipation," *Journal of Caribbean History* 4 [May 1972], 3).

[19] Thomas Holt, *The Problem of Freedom: Race, Labour, and Politics in Jamaica and Britain* (Baltimore, MD: Johns Hopkins University Press, 1992), 56–7.

[20] This phrase is from Paton, *No Bond but the Law*, 54.

sanction) would continue to be employed. The integration of military and civilian governance in this arrangement was explicit. The necessity to preserve public order by controlling apprentices via a strengthened state would be publicly compared by colonial officials to the necessity of controlling soldiers through similar means and with similar purpose.[21]

The apprenticeship system would lay the final legal foundation-stone for the edifice of indenture by incorporating the venerable tradition of master and servant law into the practices of colonial labor management. Master and servant laws had constituted the legal framework for free labor since the sixteenth century in both Britain and its colonial possessions.[22] Prior to the amelioration period, however, the magistrates who adjudicated this framework had played a very limited role in slavery and slave labor management. The authority to dispense summary punishment of slaves, who were legally designated as private property and therefore were not subject to master and servant laws, had rested instead with their owners and their employees. Amelioration had changed that equation by interposing magistrates' authority between slave owners and the infliction of punishment for any formal transgressions of the laws governing slaves' work and comportment. In the wake of emancipation, the introduction of apprenticeship and the concurrent adoption of master and servant law as its primary legal scaffolding completed the legal transformation of enslaved workers into indentured laborers. The new workforce would be free Crown subjects in principle, but entirely subordinated in practice, albeit by contract and labor statutes rather than merely by the will and property rights of their masters.

Although the specifics of master and servant law, which dated to Elizabethan times, varied across period and location, there were three defining characteristics. The first was to establish employment as a matter of private contract or formal agreement between employer and employee, defined by an exchange of either wages or their equivalent for work.[23] The employer had the right to direct the employee and the employee was obliged to acquiesce, within the boundaries of the contract. The second characteristic established summary enforcement (i.e. trial without jury) of contracts by either magistrates or their analogs, with only cursory supervision by higher justices.[24] The last central characteristic of master and servant law was to establish an asymmetry of punishment for breaches of contract between employer and employee. An employer, in such circumstances, was vulnerable only to payment of damages.

[21] Testimony of John Jeremie, Esq., Chief Justice of St. Lucia, April 19, 1836, *Report from the Select Committee on Negro Apprenticeship in the Colonies*, 1836, 2.

[22] A full treatment of master and servant law can be found in Douglas Hay and Paul Craven's authoritative anthology: Douglas Hay and Paul Craven, eds., *Masters, Servants, and Magistrates in Britain and the Empire, 1562–1955* (Chapel Hill: University of North Carolina Press, 2004).

[23] Hay and Craven, "Introduction," 1.

[24] Ibid.

An employee, by contrast, should they be summarily convicted of contract violation, could face fines, corporal punishment, or imprisonment as well as forfeiture of wages for work already performed.[25] In essence, this established workers' violations as a criminal offense, with commensurately harsher punishments, while employers' violations remained a civil affair, though summary justice under British law did not make such hard and fast distinctions.[26] Across Britain and its empire, master and servant laws thus "constructed employment relationships as contractual relationships between formally [i.e. legally] unequal parties," despite their ostensible legal equality as free Crown subjects.[27]

Absent any persistent labor organization or financial capacity to employ legal advocates, there could be no systematic resistance to the strengthening of master and servant law as the successor to the power that planters had once wielded over their private property. The newly emancipated population of African-Caribbeans were thoroughly subordinated within this new web of regulations. Along with the stern laws against unlawful assembly, such measures all but abrogated any individual bargaining power or possibility for peaceful demonstration and collective resistance. African-Caribbeans thus emerged from slavery with no clear path to improving their position economically, legally, or politically unless they left the plantations – just the avenue that apprenticeship was designed to obstruct. This structurally disadvantageous position was made worse by a prevalent discourse among policymakers that the only palatable solution to the decline of private authority over the colonial workforce was the expansion of state authority over it.

Continuing the trend that had been characteristic of amelioration, with emancipation and apprenticeship, policing labor and laborers through a variety of legal measures both direct and indirect rapidly rose to become one of the chief responsibilities of colonial governance. These activities included a robust array of coercive and punitive measures such as preventing labor mobility through the stern policing of vagrancy, regulating the exchange of plantation labor for rent (on pain of eviction), punishing absenteeism with imprisonment and hard labor, and treating any collective action as an unlawful disruption of the peace (or even as sedition). New laws and novel applications

25 Ibid., 2; Ravi Ahuja, "Review – Making the Empire a Thinkable Whole: Master and Servant Law in Transterritorial Perspective" (review of Douglas Hay and Paul Craven, eds., *Masters, Servants and Magistrates in Britain and the Empire, 1562–1955* [Chapel Hill: University of North Carolina Press, 2004]), *International Review of Social History* 52, no. 2 (August 2007), 288.

26 Ahuja, "Review – Making the Empire," 288. That contract violations and other labor offenses were designated, in the Acts passed to govern them, as triable by summary justice with a set range of penalties brought them into the category of non-indictable offenses.

27 Ibid. This distinguished apprentices, and later indentured workers, from women, who were entitled to protection under the law but could not, at the time, enter into contracts of employment (or, indeed, most legal contracts, since they did not enjoy the status of fully independent legal entities).

of old ones ensured the subordination of the laboring population spatially beyond the boundaries of the plantations and chronologically beyond the period of slavery. Such circumstances set apprentices on a direct collision course with the overseer-state even as some administrators, most notably Lord Glenelg, the Colonial Secretary, had been seeking to change the public face of government. These officials had sought, via apprenticeship, to inculcate habits of orderly and lawful behavior among former slaves and to establish themselves in the role of paternalist intermediaries between labor and management. Instead, the ground-level agents of the expanded and enhanced overseer-state, magistrates foremost among them, would become the focus of criticism and defiance by both former slaves and the metropolitan reformers that claimed to be their advocates.

Jamaica: The Overseer-State Writ Small

The increasingly strained relations between the state and the emancipated African-Caribbean population were common between different colonies despite variations in the structure of governance and the degree of metropolitan oversight. During amelioration, much of the initiative for the expansion of the state apparatus had come from the metropole, and its implementation was most visible in the Crown colonies, where direct rule granted metropolitan officials the strongest say in regulating labor. During apprenticeship, in contrast, the expanded mechanism of labor governance evolved simultaneously along two parallel paths. Metropolitan proposals played a key role, especially in Crown colonies, while in other instances, new regulations resulted from the local initiative of proprietors eager to keep former slaves tied to plantation work. Even in colonies where metropolitan authority was relatively attenuated, however, the laws, principles, and practices that characterized the overseer-state elsewhere became an integrated aspect of rule. The older legislative colonies still required metropolitan assistance and guidance, despite their penchant for jealously guarding their semi-autonomy.[28] Any new colonial statutes required the approval of the home government and colonial structures of labor governance needed both financial and logistical support to populate their expanding suite of officials. By the time of emancipation and

[28] Though this was, in the long term, a losing battle in the wake of emancipation. For the general trajectory of Jamaica's legislature and the failure of effective self-government in the period between emancipation and the introduction of Crown rule in the wake of the 1865 Morant Bay Rebellion, see Ronald V. Sires, "Constitutional Change in Jamaica, 1834–60," *Journal of Comparative Legislation and International Law* 22, no. 4 (1940), 178–90; C. V. Gocking, "Early Constitutional History of Jamaica: (With Special Reference to the Period 1838–1866)," *Caribbean Quarterly* 6, no. 2/3 (1960), 114–33; Christer Petley, "Slaveholders and Revolution: The Jamaican Planter Class, British Imperial Politics, and the Ending of the Slave Trade, 1775–1807," *Slavery & Abolition* 39, no. 1 (2017), 53–79.

apprenticeship, state oversight of both the colonial workforce and their employers had become the de facto norm, regardless of whether it emerged from metropolitan proposals or local impetus.

This dynamic was aptly demonstrated in Jamaica, where the new apparatus of labor regulation installed during amelioration and emancipation operated as a kind of overseer-state writ small. Jamaica's relative legislative autonomy allowed planters to strengthen the legal apparatus of labor discipline while simultaneously resisting the encroachment of metropolitan imperial authority. The Jamaican Assembly, dominated by planter interests, refused to appoint a Protector of Slaves.[29] The authority of the state to regulate the plantation workforce instead remained in the hands of local judicial officials and was most visibly expressed through the expansion of the penal system, which was composed of some sixteen institutions by 1820. Such prisons served as collection points for runaway slaves, replacing the ad hoc system of privately hired slave-catchers with a more systematic, state-run edifice for discouraging absconders and ensuring their return, when caught, to their original owners.[30] These institutions also served as a mechanism to temporarily quarantine disruptive or potentially rebellious slaves, working in tandem with the continued employment of flogging and the stocks to enforce plantation discipline.[31] Under the regime of the "creole state," coercion, deployed through this penal system and an expanded cohort of magistrates armed with an extensive regulatory arsenal, would maintain discipline among the plantation workforce.[32] As was the case with Fiscals and Protectors elsewhere, many of the new Jamaican magistrates would be drawn from the ranks of former military officers and would be appointed by the Colonial Office. Metropolitan administrators viewed this cohort as most appropriate to the task since they were accustomed to dispensing the kind of stern discipline (e.g. corporal punishment) that was required to keep a fractious African-Jamaican population in line.[33] At the ground level, such discipline would be maintained by constables recruited from among plantation drivers and freedmen.[34] At the same time that this state disciplinary apparatus was being erected to reinforce planters'

[29] Anon., *Slave Law of Jamaica: With Proceedings and Documents Relative Thereto* (London: James Ridgeway, 1829), 169.

[30] Ibid., 90.

[31] Between 1821 and 1825, 66 percent of prison terms for the enslaved were accompanied by flogging, most commonly at the beginning and the end of the sentence. B. W. Higman, *Slave Population and Economy in Jamaica, 1807–1834* (Cambridge: Cambridge University Press, 1976), 70.

[32] Paton, *No Bond but the Law*, 28–9.

[33] Holt, *The Problem of Freedom*, 58.

[34] Ibid., 57.

authority over their enslaved workforce, the avenues by which the enslaved themselves could potentially harness the state's new powers to prevent abuse were being constrained. Enslaved men and women in Jamaica could, as elsewhere, submit complaints of ill-treatment. But in the absence of a Protector, such complaints were instead processed by a Council of Protection comprised of the same magistrates who were responsible for enforcing the regulations on labor discipline. So potent had become the state's power over the enslaved in Jamaica, and so readily did Jamaican authorities resort to the lash and the prison, that the noted abolitionist Fowell Buxton, in a fiery 1831 parliamentary address, condemned the Jamaican system as the "most execrable" in existence, and the one that most epitomized the "moral devastation of slavery."[35]

Strengthening the state's authority over the African-Jamaican population had been a long-term project. Watershed moments had come in the late eighteenth century, when the military forces there had been expanded, and in the second decade of the nineteenth century, when the laws on slavery had been consolidated and revised.[36] These measures were commensurate with Jamaica's place as the keystone of Britain's Caribbean possessions. It was the empire's most populous and valuable colony in the Western hemisphere and the locus of its economic and military power in the region. This prominence was apparent in both metropolitan politics and culture – Jamaica was well-represented by the West India lobby in Parliament and "synonymous with the West Indies" in the public eye.[37] The maintenance of social and economic stability there was, accordingly, a paramount consideration for the local elite and metropolitan authorities alike.

But the reinforcement of coercive resources over the largest enslaved population in the British Caribbean, which dwarfed the white European residents by a factor of nearly twenty to one (approximately 311,000 vs. 15,000 in 1800), represented only one-half of a wider expansion of state power in the colony.[38] Much like the Colonial Office authorities had in their dealings with the slave-worked Crown colonies across Britain's tropical possessions, the Jamaican elite recognized that maintaining discipline among the immense enslaved workforce, although crucial, was alone insufficient to assure public order.[39] During the amelioration period, the plantocracy had also begun to expand the state's

35 *House of Commons Debates*, "Slavery in the Colonies," May 24, 1832, v. 13, cc 47.

36 Paton, *No Bond but the Law*, 28.

37 Green, *British Slave Emancipation*, 128.

38 As of 1834, the population of Jamaica was classified officially as follows: 15,000 "white"; 45,000 "free coloured and free black"; and 311,070 slaves. Green, *British Slave Emancipation*, 13.

39 This was especially the case given the large number and immense scale of Jamaican plantations. By 1820 there were 5,349 slave-worked properties in Jamaica, of which nearly a quarter (1,189) contained more than 100 enslaved Africans.

authority to govern *slaveholders*, a process that would continue through the emancipation and apprenticeship period. Owners who abused their slaves could be fined and even lose their property, should their violations prove serious enough. The main targets of such legislation were those owners considered by the largely white plantocracy to be the least fit for the paternalistic role expected of them. As a consequence, slaveholders who were poor, female, or African-Caribbean frequently fell afoul of the new regulations.[40] As with other aspects of the Jamaican overseer-state, the tendency to single out female slaveholders of color for particularly close monitoring and harsh punishment mirrored the practices in those colonies under more direct supervision from the metropole. Such cases often attracted the attention of authorities out of all proportion to their small representation in the overall cohort of slave-owners.[41]

Efforts to prevent, via state oversight, cruelty among slaveholders dealt with one potential catalyst for dissatisfaction and disorder as well as deflecting public criticism from antislavery activists in the metropole. The Jamaican overseer-state also installed legal mechanisms to deal more directly with the potential negligence of slave-owners in maintaining appropriate discipline. The consolidated slave code of December 1816 included laws forbidding unlawful assembly and the unauthorized carrying of weapons by slaves, and made the abetting of one slave's escape by another a crime.[42] By disciplining both slaves and slave-owners, and by incorporating the free African-Jamaican population into the disciplinary apparatus, the Jamaican elite hoped to secure the colony from the disorder and occasional rebellions that periodically swept across other Caribbean slave colonies.[43] Bussa's Rebellion in Barbados, which began in April 1816, stood as a particularly visible example of the danger posed by an enslaved population whose simmering discontent had been fanned to flames by the rumors of emancipation.

The comprehensive overhaul of Jamaica's slave laws in December of the same year was intended to forestall future uprisings by codifying the customary rights of slaves and safeguarding against the abuses or neglect of incompetent masters. At the same time, the reforms were also designed to cement the authority of slave-owners via a strengthened state apparatus. The revision

40 Paton, *No Bond but the Law*, 29.

41 One of the most attenuated investigations of slave-code violations heard in 1829 Demerara involved a freed African-Caribbean woman, Mary Lowe. Legal proceedings were subsequently instituted in order to strip her of all ownership. Return of Complaints made to the Protector from May 1 to October 31, 1829, *Reports from the Protectors of Slaves in the Colonies of Demerara, Berbice, Trinidad, St. Lucia, the Cape of Good Hope and Mauritius*, 1831, 72–6.

42 Articles LX and LIX of the 1816 Act for the Subsistence, Clothing and the Better Regulation and Government of Slaves (57 Geo. III. cap. 25), reprinted in Anon., *Slave Law of Jamaica*, 94–5.

43 Paton, *No Bond but the Law*, 28.

and consolidation of the Jamaican slave code during the early amelioration period foreshadowed many of the regulations that would later be implemented throughout the Caribbean. These included mandatory supply of provisions, limits on corporal punishment, set holidays and mealtimes, explicitly naming the killing of a slave as a capital crime, stern punishments for the mutilation of slaves, facilitating slaves' ability to file grievances with a justice of the peace, compulsory support for infirm or elderly slaves, manumission protocols, the outlawing of iron collars, and a host of other measures that would later become standard under the Trinidad model of ameliorated slavery in the mid-1820s.[44]

As was the case in the similarities between the Jamaica slave code and the Trinidad model, new regulations and practices subsuming labor discipline under state control, with magistrates as the intermediaries, circulated freely between different colonies in the 1820s and 1830s. Antigua was another pioneer in this regard. In December 1834, the legislature there passed an act that made labor contracts valid merely by oral agreement with two witnesses present. The same measure implemented severe punishments, including imprisonment with hard labor, for absenteeism.[45] Employers, in contrast, were subject only to a maximum fine of £5 for any contract violation. Although the first Antiguan act was subsequently disallowed by the British government, a second act, which was nearly as disadvantageous to workers as the first one had been, was passed and approved the next year.[46] Another post-emancipation Antiguan innovation was to merge the roles of employer and landlord, tying free workers to poorly paid plantation labor through control of their tenancy and the threat of eviction. Emancipated slaves, who had viewed housing and the free use of provision grounds for small-scale gardening as entitlements, and who had seen those entitlements confirmed as rights under amelioration, had expected to enjoy the same privileges when they became free. Instead, former slaves in Antigua found themselves paying rent and having their wages garnished to cover it, or being threatened with eviction if they refused to work on their former masters' estates.[47] By the early 1840s, similar systems had been adopted in Jamaica, British Guiana, Barbados, and across the Caribbean.[48]

44 Articles I–XXX, 1816 Act for the Subsistence, Clothing and the Better Regulation and Government of Slaves (57 Geo. III. cap. 25), reprinted in Anon., *Slave Law of Jamaica*, 1–11.

45 Bolland, "Systems of Domination after Slavery," 594–5.

46 Under the new act, verbal or even merely implied contracts were sustainable for a year's length, with the occupation of dwellings as prima facie evidence that such a contract existed between a tenant and their landlord/employer. Ibid., 565.

47 Ibid., 595.

48 Douglas Hall, "Flight from the Estates Reconsidered: The British West Indies, 1838–42," *Journal of Caribbean History* 10 (January 1978), 16–23.

As amelioration transitioned into emancipation and apprenticeship, the expansion of state control over labor thus proceeded from two directions, top-down via metropolitan initiative, oversight, and the host of new agents introduced (e.g. Fiscals and Protectors), and from the bottom-up via the initiative of colonial legislatures. In the latter instance, new regulations and practices or adaptations of older ones instituted in one colony spread rapidly not just to neighboring regions but wherever slavery had been practiced in the empire. In the wake of emancipation, pass laws, which had precluded slaves from leaving their plantations without specific permission and documentation, were revived and merged with the centuries-old legal tradition of vagrancy laws.[49] The new statutes were employed for a variety of purposes, from binding workers to specific employers – whereby a laborer who was prevented by vagrancy laws from leaving their current plantation even temporarily would be a priori unable to find new employment – to punishing obeah or other traditional spiritual practices.[50] The new uses of the vagrancy laws introduced in Jamaica were propagated throughout the Caribbean and integrated into the control of labor mobility as far away as Mauritius and the Cape Colony.[51] Although the post-emancipation overseer-state was not always as explicitly hierarchical as it had been under amelioration, the rapid dissemination of labor control regulation, along with continued metropolitan oversight and the key roles played by new administrative agents, demonstrated how it remained both coherent and coordinated throughout the empire.

Much as had been the case during amelioration, metropolitan authority during the apprenticeship period played varying roles depending upon the status of the colony vis-à-vis governance. In Crown colonies such as British Guiana, the Colonial Office directly supervised the conditions of apprenticeship, intervening, through governors and Protectors, to hedge abuses of authority by proprietors and managers.[52] In the older, legislative colonies such as Jamaica, local authority prevailed, albeit administered by Crown-appointed magistrates, and the resulting treatment of apprentices was harsh enough to draw both official concern and public opprobrium.[53] Master and servant laws and vagrancy laws were particular points of contention, with the

[49] Vagrancy laws had been strengthened in Britain to control the burgeoning population of paupers. Nicholas Rogers, "Policing the Poor in Eighteenth-Century London: The Vagrancy Laws and Their Administration," *Histoire sociale/Social History* 34, no. 47 (May 1991), 127–47.

[50] Act for the Punishment of Idle and Disorderly Persons, Rogues and Vagabonds, and Incorrigible Rogues, 3 Vict. c. 18 (Jamaica, 1839).

[51] Richard B. Allen, *Slaves, Freedmen, and Indentured Laborers in Colonial Mauritius* (Cambridge: Cambridge University Press, 1999), 63.

[52] William A. Green, "Apprenticeship in British Guiana, 1834–1838," *Caribbean History* 9, no. 2 (July 1969), 62.

[53] Green, "Apprenticeship in British Guiana," 62.

Colonial Office and antislavery activists in Parliament mounting a determined campaign to ensure that they were applied leniently and that neither the letter nor the spirit of abolition was violated in the process.[54] This campaign to improve the conditions of emancipation and apprenticeship had a particularly limited effect in Jamaica. There, Lord Sligo, the governor, labeled the measures adopted by the planter-dominated legislature "a most imperfect Act of Abolition," a designation that was later employed with pointed effect by critics in Parliament.[55]

Resistance and Responses to Apprenticeship

New methods of labor control, grounded in new laws and in the expanded power of the state, catalyzed new forms of response and resistance. From the very beginning, the terms of apprenticeship had been a bitter disappointment to a population that had anticipated full emancipation. In Essequibo, British Guiana, public announcements of the new law and its terms in early August 1834 had been met by enslaved men and women with outrage and disbelief, even when delivered by relatively trusted figures such as parish priests. John Halloway Duke, rector of the Trinity Parish in the heart of the cultivated coastal region, had carefully enumerated the conditions of their upcoming apprenticeship to his congregation. He had informed them that most would be obliged to work seven and a half hours a day on their plantations and would be bound by contract to that work for six more years.[56] The response from assembled parishioners was unequivocal. "They said they could not be bound," one spokesmen declared; "the King had freed them, and they could not be bound."[57] The manager of plantation Belle Alliance was confronted with the same response after spending two hours trying to explain the new regulations to an assembled crowd of emancipated men and women. Some in attendance expressed suspicion that this was merely another local ordinance, since it was inconceivable to them that such measures could be "the law of the King."[58]

Discontent at the prospect of continued servitude to their former masters spread rapidly with each new announcement, and more vociferous demonstrations followed soon after. Eventually, a crowd of several hundred enslaved

54 Green, "Emancipation to Indenture," 100.

55 Fowell Buxton, "Apprenticeship in the Colonies," House of Commons Debate, March 22, 1836, vol. 32, cc 453.

56 Although the exact location of Trinity Parish has been lost in the records, in all likelihood it corresponded with the location of the Holy Trinity Church, which was near plantation Anna Regina.

57 Appendix A, Trial of Damon and Others, *Papers on the Abolition of Slavery Throughout the British Colonies, Part II: Jamaica, Barbados, British Guiana, and Mauritius, 1833–1835*, 1835 [hereafter *Abolition of Slavery* 1835], 195.

58 Appendix A, Trial of Damon and Others, *Abolition of Slavery* 1835, 201.

men and women from Trinity Parish left their plantations en masse and assembled in the local churchyard. They protested the new law, raised homemade flags bearing the cross of St. George, and declared to those who challenged them that they would indeed be free. When told by the local justice of the peace that they must disperse, one of the crowd, Frederick, responded, in a refrain that echoed the pronouncements common in the Demerara Rebellion of the previous decade, that "it was not the true law; they were all freemen, and would not be bound."[59] This demonstration, although no violence ensued beyond a brief scuffle with local constables, came at great cost to those who were later identified as its instigators and ringleaders. Of the thirteen men subsequently arrested, tried, and convicted for unlawful assembly, riotous conduct, and disturbing the peace, one (Damon) would be hanged; three (Frederick, Fothergill, and Bob) would be transported for hard labor in the penal colony of New South Wales; and ten more (Adonis, Chance, Sandy, Billy, Peter, Sandy, Homer, Caesar, Laurence, and Sam) would receive between 50 and 200 lashes and a month's imprisonment.[60]

The most substantial account of responses to the apprenticeship system comes from James Williams, a Jamaican apprentice from Penshurst, St. Ann's Parish, in the north-central part of the island. Williams portrayed the conditions of apprenticeship in great detail, describing the conditions of work, his treatment by his employer (whom he referred to, following convention, as "master" or "massa"), and the system of punitive labor discipline. From the very outset, he asserted that the circumstances of apprenticeship, by almost any measure, were worse than those of slavery had been. Williams enumerated a broad range of laments, from the attitude of masters to the denial of provisions to the harsh administration of punishment. He opened his account with a portrayal of Jamaican employers as cynically determined to wring the most labor possible out of their former slaves, in open defiance of the emancipation that had been forced on their colony by metropolitan authorities. Unable to strike directly at those in London, whom they blamed for their predicament, aggrieved employers instead vented their frustration on their new employees. "The master take spite," Williams wrote; "I have heard my master say – 'Those English devils say we [i.e. Williams and his comrades] be free, but if we is to be free, he will pretty well weaken we, before the six and the four years [i.e. of apprenticeship] done; we shall be no use to ourselves afterwards.'"[61]

Williams's account was a scathing indictment of both the apprenticeship system and the plantation-owners who wielded it against the newly freed African-Caribbean workers. One figure emerged from the account even

59 Ibid., 188.
60 Ibid., 197, 204.
61 James Williams, *A Narrative of Events since the First of August, 1834* (1837; repr. Durham, NC: Duke University Press, 2001), 5.

more villainously portrayed than the former masters did – the magistrates tasked with enforcing the new laws on labor. Williams demonstrated a keen understanding of the terms of apprenticeship and the boundaries of legal treatment, and repeatedly sought the intervention of local judicial authorities to protect himself from the abuses of employers. He was also determined to see that the customary entitlements he had been granted during amelioration were still respected during apprenticeship. These included the right to work his own land, protection from excessive flogging, halting the flogging of apprentices too ill to work, and providing medical care for the sick. Long years of experience had left Williams with a detailed awareness of what his rights were and when they were being violated, and he did not hesitate to deploy that knowledge against his new employer.[62] It also allowed him to level accusations of specific violations, chief among them the particular cruelties visited on those who were imprisoned in the workhouses, illegal floggings, and the infliction of severe corporal punishment on women, the outlawing of which had been a core tenet of amelioration.[63]

Such knowledge was made nearly useless, however, by the failings of the judicial system tasked with safeguarding them. The magistrates, in Williams's account, repeatedly acted with arrogant disdain, and demonstrated blatant bias toward employers, even to the point of guiding them on what types of charges would most effectively bring their apprentices to heel.[64] So arbitrary was the treatment of apprentices and other former slaves at the hands of local magistrates that Williams, at one point in his account, having been repeatedly stymied in his attempts to seek protection under the law, confronted the magistrate directly on his misbehavior. "I say," the apprentice declared: "if I have been twenty times before you [i.e. the magistrate, Mr. Rawlinson], you ought to do justice 'twixt I and massa. He said, He do justice. I told him, You don't do justice."[65] One of the most heinous figures in Williams's account was Mr. Hilton, the court clerk, who amused himself by tormenting men and women imprisoned in the workhouse (almost exclusively for alleged labor violations) so mercilessly that even his own wife, in vain, entreated him to desist.[66]

Williams's account was just one of many reports of abuse emerging from the post-emancipation Caribbean. Abolitionists in the metropole were quick to seize on them in order to castigate the government and spur more its more forceful intervention on labor conditions. In March 1836, Fowell Buxton, who had succeeded William Wilberforce as the leader of the abolition movement in Parliament, delivered a withering condemnation of apprenticeship, singling

62 Ibid., 13.
63 Ibid., 14–16, 19.
64 Ibid., 6, 7.
65 Ibid., 19.
66 Ibid., 17.

out the legal system and the behavior of magistrates for particular calumny. They were to be faulted on two interrelated grounds: first for their callous treatment of African-Caribbeans and second for their failure to appropriately discipline the white population. Together, these amounted to an abandonment of their central duty, that of offering justice in a region where its provision was both a moral obligation and the only effective prophylactic to mass insurrection. "Nothing was more distinctly proven," Buxton told the House of Commons, "than that there was one law for the West-Indies for . . . the negroes, and another for the white population."[67] As had been the case with the failings of amelioration, the plight of African-Caribbean women was a particular point of concern. Mirroring metropolitan discourse, however, where women's frequent use of local courtrooms was either ignored or disparaged, the key role African-Caribbean women had played in bringing the abuses of managers and overseers to light through engagement with the grievance process was never publicly acknowledged.[68] They merited paternalistic compassion as passive victims of abuse, not support as active and canny employers of their newfound rights.

Fowell's broadside was part of a series of damning public attacks on how the Colonial Office, by facilitating apprenticeship without sufficient oversight, had failed to deliver on the grand promises of emancipation. These sharp criticisms had begun almost from the moment that the new system had been installed and, with the Essequibo apprentice strike of 1834 as a further impetus, they had catalyzed a parliamentary inquiry in 1835. The findings of that investigation prompted Lord Glenelg, then the Colonial Secretary, to firmly instruct the governors of the Caribbean colonies that the system by which justice was administered in regard to apprentices needed immediate revision. The "diversities of practice" that were apparent across different colonies had to be addressed with dispatch, and the number of special magistrates with jurisdiction over apprentices had to be increased to address the demand for their services.[69] Even more importantly, those in post who had "any interest in apprenticed labour" needed to be removed from office and no one with such interests should be appointed in future.[70] These measures, Glenelg declared, were necessary to fulfill "the spirit of the intentions by which Parliament was governed in passing the Act for the Abolition of Slavery."[71] Only by such means could Glenelg's goal of achieving legal equity for African-Caribbean

[67] Buxton, "Apprenticeship in the Colonies," cc 458.
[68] Sascha Auerbach, *Armed with Sword and Scales: Law, Culture, and Local Courtrooms in London, 1860–1913* (Cambridge: Cambridge University Press, 2021), 218–80.
[69] Glenelg to the Governors of the West India Colonies, June 15, 1835, *Abolition of Slavery* 1835, 8.
[70] Ibid.
[71] Ibid.

freedmen and, in time, establishing a free society in which they played a stabilizing role be achieved.[72]

More systematic assessments by historians in recent decades have revealed a mixed picture of reforms in the immediate post-emancipation period. There were general improvements in working conditions, which ranged from a steep decline in corporal punishment to a significant accumulation of wages.[73] In some territories, Trinidad and Guiana in particular, employers, desperate to keep workers on the plantations, went to great lengths to make the prospect attractive, such as building new residences or offering high wages. These gains, however, need to be balanced against the various means employed by planters to leverage their authority over apprentices. Chief among these were offsetting wages with rent and the employment of forcible evictions either as a threat to secure labor or as a punishment for withholding it.[74]

Accounts composed at the time of the alleged benefits of apprenticeship fell largely on deaf ears. The sensational stories of mistreatment, on the other hand, were met by a receptive public audience that had been primed to judge planters harshly by the long campaign for amelioration and emancipation. The abuse of the apprenticeship system by estate proprietors, recounted publicly by their critics in Parliament, put the Colonial Office and the government of which it was a very visible aspect in an acutely vulnerable position. Prior to the period of amelioration, the cruelties enumerated by abolitionists could be laid almost exclusively at the feet of plantation-owners. The increasing amount of government oversight implemented in the 1820s, however, had been accompanied by an higher level of accountability for the systems' failures or persistent abuses. This, in turn, led to calls by antislavery activists for more state intervention (and therefore even greater government accountability). Both planters and the majority of metropolitan administrators shared the opinion that an enslaved population that had for so long been subject to coercion by private means needed to remain under the firm oversight of an equally powerful, if more just and equitable, state apparatus. This reflected not only widespread doubt about the moral and social capacities of African-Caribbeans but a general anxiety, among the Victorian middle and upper classes, about the character of the lower orders and their potential for public mayhem in the absence of stern governance.[75] The system of special magistrates had been installed to oversee the transition, preserve social order, prevent abuses by employers, protect the rights of apprenticed workers, and, through didactic

[72] Holt, *The Problem of Freedom*, 181.
[73] Green, *British Slave Emancipation*, 135.
[74] Riviere, "Labour Shortage," 5–9.
[75] Testimony of John Jeremie, Esq., Chief Justice of St. Lucia, April 19, 1836, *Apprenticeship in the Colonies*, 1836, 2.

justice, help inculcate former slaves with values and practices commensurate with their new status as free subjects.[76]

The results, however, according to Buxton and the public accounts criticizing apprenticeship, were the exact opposite of what had been intended. And the failures of apprenticeship system, much like the failures of amelioration before it, were largely placed at the feet of the overseer-state, of which the magistrates were the most visible representatives. For many African-Caribbeans, the freedom they had granted, once diluted by apprenticeship, now revealed itself to be just a new iteration of servitude. Not only did they remain bound to their former employers by unbreakable contracts but they remained subject to a brutal regime of corporal punishment for labor offenses. To add insult to injury, they had been stripped of the customary rights that had been codified under amelioration.[77] Appeals to the magistrates allegedly installed to guard their rights had been in vain, and in some colonies reports emerged that the treatment of those found guilty of labor offenses was even *more* brutal than it had been under ameliorated slavery. The stories coming from Jamaica, given its prominence in the public eye, were particularly damning, even though the Colonial Office's ability to mitigate the behavior of planters there was attenuated by a weak executive, a powerful and established plantocracy, and a largely autonomous legislature.[78] Although official inquiries indicated a general decline in corporal punishment, largely due to the procedural necessity of a magistrates' intercession, there was widespread feeling among the freed population in the Caribbean and among the antislavery lobby in the metropole that the brutalities of slavery persisted still.[79] And this was hardly just a matter of perception. With the backbone of apprenticeship as a foundation, government administrations across the Caribbean, in both Crown and legislative colonies, had implemented a raft of local regulations allowing them to maximize the economic leverage of employers over their workers and to minimize their costs. Customary rights guaranteed by law under amelioration, such as the right to occupy dwellings and to raise garden crops or animals on unplanted land, were either turned into privileges requiring payment or forbidden altogether.[80] Over time, the response of freed African-Caribbeans was exactly what both planters and the government had hoped to avoid. Often, when the availability of land and their economic

[76] Holt, *The Problem of Freedom*, 56–7.

[77] Hall, "Flight from the Estates Reconsidered," 17.

[78] De V. Phillips, "Emancipation Betrayed?"1355.

[79] Green, *British Slave Emancipation*, 135.

[80] In the Essequebo apprentice strike of 1834, one of the key catalysts of apprentices' dissatisfaction had been the widespread slaughter, by plantation-owners, of the hogs kept on private grounds. The keeping of animals by slaves had long been a customary right, but it was not guaranteed under the new laws governing apprenticeship and free labor. Appendix A, Trial of Damon and Others, *Abolition of Slavery* 1835, 194.

resources made it possible, they left the plantations to become small freeholders.[81] In circumstances where this was not feasible, or if a desire to remain in their established communities persisted, former slaves insisted on working along terms that they found more agreeable, but which did not at all suit the planters' needs.[82]

In contrast to the amelioration period, however, when the frustration of enslaved men and women was typically expressed against plantation authorities, it was increasingly representatives of the state that were held directly responsible for the failings of apprenticeship. A key cause of the flight from the plantation labor by African-Caribbeans, according to a broad spectrum of critics, including apprentices themselves, was the neglect of magistrates to address the ubiquitous abuses and denial of rights that had accompanied apprenticeship. Instead of inculcating a respect for law and the magistrates who enforced it, apprentices had grown mistrustful and even defiant of a magistracy that, in the accounts of Williams and other critics, seemed to be every bit as cruel and arbitrary as their former masters had been.[83] These failings, as Buxton had vehemently insisted in Parliament, were the responsibility of the government, not the planters. Regardless of the "diversities in practice" that Glenelg had bemoaned, apprenticeship, much like amelioration before it, was perceived by its detractors to be a system organized and overseen from the metropole, and its failings were the failings of the state itself to honor the promises of emancipation. The complex relationship and delicate balance of power between the Colonial Office, governors, and colonial legislatures were no more important to Buxton and antislavery activists than they were to the apprentices who expressed their discontent through the grievance system or collective demonstrations.[84] Both groups demanded an end to the alleged abuses of apprenticeship from the higher authorities who had introduced the system in the first place.

81 Woodville K. Marshall, "Notes on Peasant Development in the West Indies Since 1838," *Social and Economic Studies* 17, no. 3 (1968), 252–63.

82 Examples of these terms include being paid by the job or task rather than by the day. Hall, "Flight from the Estates Reconsidered," 18.

83 According to Paton, [i]t is particularly ironic that this form of gradual emancipation brought apprentices into such direct conflict with the state. After all, the architects of emancipation wanted Jamaican (and other) slaves to be educated into trusting the state – respecting the rule of law – as well as wanting to perform wage labor. Indeed, the two goals were inseparable . . . [but] at the height of the colonial state's efforts to portray itself as the protector of the interests of the masses, Jamaican workers' daily experiences of state representatives demonstrated that this protection worked within the limits of the needs of continued plantation production. (Paton, *No Bond but the Law*, 54–5) See also Green, *British Slave Emancipation*, 139–40, 144.

84 Green, *British Slave Emancipation*, 161.

The catalyst for change was a well-orchestrated assault that took place simultaneously in the colonies themselves, in metropolitan politics, and in the court of public opinion that linked the politically active members of both locales. Fowell Buxton's anti-apprenticeship campaign, initially stymied by a parliamentary committee that produced a relatively optimistic assessment of the system, resumed its charge in late 1836. In the vanguard were the leaders of the most radical wing of the antislavery lobby, Joseph Sturge, secretary of the Birmingham Anti-Slavery Society, and John Scoble. The latter would shortly establish the British and Foreign Anti-Slavery Society (BFASS) as a vehicle for coordinating political opposition to the apprenticeship system.[85] The fight against apprenticeship advanced along three fronts: detailed published reports drawing from the delegations' Caribbean visit (see below) and official documentation; a petitioning campaign directed at Melbourne's Whig government and supplemented with delegations to the Colonial Office; and mass meetings against apprenticeship (with Birmingham as the epicenter of the movement). As a final offensive, to add specific substance to their critique, the opponents of apprenticeship would brave the lion in its den. In October 1836, Scoble and Sturge organized a highly publicized tour around the Caribbean colonies in order to gather evidence.[86] This last measure, in particular, aroused the ire of colonial governors, who asserted that such political grandstanding was certain to sow discontent among both the colonial legislatures and the apprentices themselves.[87]

The speed and vehemence of the multi-pronged campaign against apprenticeship proved to be a source of embarrassment for the government and put the colonial governors on the defensive. These parties, whom Buxton and his allies had held most responsible for the abuses they recounted, were confronted by an awkward situation. They could not ignore the intensifying calls for the abrogation of apprenticeship; nor could they arbitrarily rescind their pledges to estate-owners that the system would be sustained until its official termination date (for formerly praedial slaves) in 1840. Adding urgency to the matter was widespread anxiety among both planters and governors that the whistle stop Caribbean tour of Scoble and Sturge would foment discontent and possibly violent disorder among apprentices.[88] In March 1838, Glenelg bowed to political pressure and engineered a compromise bill that would address the chief complaints of the antislavery lobby – such as guaranteeing the continuation of customary allowances that had become common during

[85] Izhak Gross, "Parliament and the Abolition of Negro Apprenticeship," *English Historical Review* 96, no. 3080 (July 1981) 562–3.

[86] They were accompanied by two colleagues, William Lloyd and Thomas Harvey. The specific colonies of focus were Antigua, Montserrat, Dominica, St. Lucia, Barbados, and Jamaica, though Sturge also traveled to British Guiana.

[87] Green, *British Slave Emancipation*, 154.

[88] Ibid., 156.

amelioration and the total abolition of flogging – while still preserving the institution of apprenticeship.[89]

When word of the impending reform reached the colonies shortly after, it provoked an immediate reaction. Planters objected on two primary grounds: first, that the bill undermined the general principle of colonial legislative autonomy; and second, more specifically, that the proposals would increase the power of metropolitan-appointed governors and stipendiary magistrates over colonial assemblies and the more traditional judiciary drawn from the plantocracy and their allies.[90] Fears of losing their remaining powers of self-rule and growing unease at agitation among the apprentices ultimately prevailed over anxieties about a premature end to apprenticeship. Plantation-dominated governing bodies across the Caribbean, beginning with the Barbados Assembly in May, agreed to abolish the system.[91]

The struggle over apprenticeship illustrated the increasing centrality of labor regulation in colonial and imperial governance. It also demonstrated how the autonomy of Caribbean colonies in these matters was eroding as the Colonial Office, its representatives, and the wider dynamics of metropolitan political conflicts superseded the suzerainty of the traditional plantocracy. In its aftermath, the political turmoil over how labor relations would be configured in the post-emancipation Caribbean, and who would have the authority to configure them, would escalate to the point of a constitutional crisis. This conflict pitted the Colonial Office against colonial legislatures in a political battle royale to determine who would have the ultimate authority to shape labor governance once apprenticeship ended. This contest centered on a general principle, which was the limits of the Colonial Office's authority to dictate legislation, and on a more specific legal issue, which was the laws on vagrancy and contract. The latter two were crucial to labor relations since they operated as the principal means by which planters hoped to shackle free African-Caribbeans to the plantations.[92] Glenelg's attempts to mitigate the effects of these laws on emancipated workers and, in doing so, to enhance metropolitan control over *all* colonial legislation ran into fierce resistance from colonial legislatures, led by the Jamaican assembly.[93] In the ensuing political melee, the colonies were able to claw back some degree of autonomy, and the Prime Minister, Lord Melbourne, was briefly forced to resign.[94]

After reaching an apex with Melbourne's temporary resignation, the conflict between the Colonial Office and the colonial legislatures rapidly deescalated. Beneath all this political tension was an underlying common principle that

89 Ibid.
90 Ibid., 157.
91 Ibid.
92 Green, "Apprenticeship in British Guiana," 63.
93 Holt, *The Problem of Freedom*, 108–11.
94 Green, *British Slave Emancipation*, 170–1.

bound London to Kingston and to the plantations themselves. As the dust cleared from Glenelg's failed effort at imperial labor governance, what remained was the conviction that white racial hegemony endured as the cornerstone of political, social, and cultural stability in the Caribbean, and that the plantations required subordinated labor to preserve their economic viability.[95] The continued resistance of colonial legislatures to the centralization and coordination of labor relations by the overseer-state remained a rearguard action. First with amelioration, then with emancipation, subsequently with apprenticeship, and lastly with the abolition of apprenticeship, metropolitan authorities had made a series of decisive interventions into the colonial labor system. Driven forward by the recalcitrance of planters in the legislative colonies to relinquish control, the persistent remonstration of the workforce at their conditions, fears of public disorder, and the need to stave off political attacks against the morality of its colonial oversight, the overseer-state had repeatedly expanded its remit. The resolution of disagreements over post-emancipation labor governance in a grudging agreement between the Colonial Office and colonial legislatures that apprenticeship must be abolished prematurely set the stage for its next iteration. With the antislavery lobby mollified and the power of those metropolitan administrators who were willing to confront planter-controlled legislatures over the rights of emancipated African-Caribbeans on the wane, colonial and metropolitan interests were once again coming into alignment.[96] The oversight of labor in the colonies had been established as a permanent responsibility of the Colonial Office and its representatives in the empire. Regardless of the détente of the post-apprenticeship period, the state's authority over labor was on the ascendance. Henceforth, it would be spearheaded from above by governors and Protectors drawn from a military background and from below by planters who sought to harness the new regulatory framework as a tool for subordinating the newly emancipated workforce.[97]

[95] Green, "Emancipation to Indenture," 100–1.

[96] In 1839, Glenelg would be replaced as Colonial Secretary by Lord Mulgrave, the Marquess of Normanby and former Governor of Jamaica, who was more adept at dealing with the plantocracy and navigating the fraught political terrain that had become characteristic of the office. Such was the confidence of the government in Mulgrave that he had been appointed to restore order in the wake of the 1831–2 Jamaica rebellion. Wibur D. Jones, "Lord Mulgrave's Administration in Jamaica, 1832–1833," *Journal of Negro History* 48 (1963), 46.

[97] Four of the five principal Caribbean executives governing during the apprenticeship period were military officers. They were General Sir Lionel Smith (Barbados 1833–6, Jamaica 1836–9 and later Mauritius 1840–2), Major-General Sir Evan John Murray-MacGregor (Barbados 1836–41), Major General Sir James Carmichael-Smyth (British Guiana 1833–8), and Vice-Admiral Howe Peter Browne (Jamaica 1834–6).

"The Asian Model" and the First Experiments in Indian Indenture

The debacle of the apprenticeship system had driven a wedge between metropolitan authorities and colonial governors on one hand and the established plantocracy in Jamaica and the other legislative colonies on the other. In the process, largely thanks to the anti-apprenticeship campaign mounted by Scoble, the issue of colonial labor had remained firmly in the public eye and a central concern among administrators and legislators in London. Apprenticeship had also further alienated a freed African-Caribbean workforce from both the proprietors who wished to employ them and from the government that was trying to portray itself as their protector. This tense situation was exacerbated by the concerns over the labor supply in Britain's tropical colonies, which plantation-owners claimed was jeopardized by the end of apprenticeship. The post-apprenticeship "labor crisis" was portrayed by estate proprietors and their advocates as an objective lack of available plantation workers. To what extent it was simply the result of African-Caribbean freedmens' unwillingness to accept the conditions set by planters and of the restrictions placed by different colonies on the movement of workers both within them and between remains a matter of much debate among historians.[98]

In some regions, it is clear that the expansion of sugar cultivation combined with some decrease in the supply of available laborers allowed planters and local administrators to present the case convincingly as one of dire need.[99] Two such locales were British Guiana and Mauritius. In both colonies, plantation proprietors and local officials, in cooperation with metropolitan authorities, instituted measures to deal with an expansion of land under sugar cultivation along with, or so they claimed, a decrease in workers available (or just willing) to cultivate it.[100] The replacement workforce needed to be suited to large-scale agriculture, unthreatening to the political hegemony of white Europeans, and amenable to the disciplinary regime of sugar cultivation. The complexities of processing cane, along with its unremitting schedule, made it an activity that, according to planters, required workers to be under strict control and constant supervision. To ensure productivity and social stability, and to guard against further public controversy, this labor force would be carefully managed through an extensive framework of labor regulations and state oversight, the foundations for which had already been laid during late-stage amelioration and apprenticeship. In the wake of the tumultuous and politically bruising apprenticeship period, the powerful stakeholders in both government and private enterprise shared a common goal. This was to obtain a workforce that was industrious, affordable, relatively docile and, most of all, that posed little or no threat to the social or

[98] Madhavi Kale, *Fragments of Empire: Capital, Slavery, and Indian Indentured Labor in the British Caribbean* (Philadelphia, PA: University of Philadelphia Press, 1998), 48–51.
[99] Connolly, "Indentured Labour Migration," 99.
[100] Riviere, "Labour Shortage," 2.

economic status quo. The latter had already been disrupted by both wide-scale demonstrations and persistent, low-level grievances on the part of apprentices.

Having been embroiled in two controversies over the issue of labor in the Caribbean, first with the failings of amelioration and subsequently with the scandal of apprenticeship, metropolitan authorities would proceed with caution. This time, policymakers would take a more circumspect route to present their oversight of colonial labor systems as just and commensurate with the idea of "free labor." The architects of the overseer-state's next evolution would not forget the most important lesson that late-stage slavery, amelioration, and apprenticeship had offered, a lesson that would soon be reinforced by the expansion of summary justice among the working class in Britain itself. This was that, given the opportunity, workers *would* grieve, persistently and vehemently, even when there was no justice to be had. But it was only when their complaints were mobilized as ammunition for political opponents of the system, or when workers became so outraged that they resorted to collective resistance, that such grievances became a serious problem in terms of public opinion, public order, or both.

With such lessons in mind, Colonial Office administrators recognized that the organization of a new labor force could not be left merely to estate proprietors and their advocates in colonial governments. The public scandal over the abuses of apprenticeship had made such a path politically untenable. From the planters' perspective, some level of metropolitan support was necessary in any case. The considerable costs involved, and the sentiment among them that any dearth of labor was attributable to policy dictated from London, seemed to mandate both official sanction and financial underwriting from the imperial center as a starting point for any new system of labor. The actions of former slaves in the apprenticeship system, moreover, made it clear that, absent state coercion, planters lacked the leverage to force freed African-Caribbeans to work in the manner they preferred or at the wages that would make sugar sufficiently profitable. Such anxieties over profit were exacerbated by the loosening of tariffs and monopolies and by the implementation of other measures to promote free trade in the early 1840s.[101] Even as the metropolitan state, animated by a growing commitment to economic liberalism, was easing the regulation of imperial trade, those overseeing imperial affairs were growing *more* willing to regulate labor conditions, and to do so in a manner favorable to colonial employers.[102]

The new experiment in colonial labor organization and governance would be implemented by a collaboration in which the London-based network of

[101] Riviere, "Labour Shortage," 3; Holt, *The Problem of Freedom*, 122–3; Green, *British Slave Emancipation*, 170; Sunanda Sen, "Indentured Labour from India in the Age of Empire," *Social Scientist* 44, no. 1/2 (January–February 2016), 40.

[102] Boehme et al., "Reforming Everywhere and All at Once," 694–5.

governmental departments interfaced with a global network of colonial governments that, in turn, were in communication and coordination with one another. For this "imperial governmental assemblage," managing the transition from apprenticeship to other types of coerced or free labor was the chief preoccupation in 1837–8.[103] As had been the case since the end of the nineteenth century, discussions at all levels of government, both metropolitan and colonial, about the future of the empire were entangled with questions about labor organization.[104] To address this issue, the distributed but coordinated apparatus of the overseer-state would engage three major imperatives through policy, investment, and administration at the imperial and colonial levels. The first would be a global redistribution of labor; the second would be to identify the moral dimensions of different kinds of labor; and the third would be to reconcile the preservation of public order with the need to maintain colonial revenue and a desire to sustain a public image of moral rule.[105] Added to these imperatives among metropolitan administrators would be an enthusiasm for collaborating not with the traditional plantocracy that had proved so obstructionist to reform previously but with the newer crop of cosmopolitan, entrepreneurial investors based in London. This latter cohort had interests dispersed across the empire and was eager to take advantage of the opportunities presented by the decline of tariffs and monopolies. In this collaboration, the discourses of "free trade" and "free labor" would appear prominently. But over time, as criticisms of the system mounted, the practices of labor recruitment, transportation, and organization would increasingly be characterized instead by restriction, regulation, and stern control through local and imperial governance.

In the years running up to emancipation, the Colonial Office, in close consultation with other metropolitan officials and colonial governors, had considered various schemes to redistribute labor around the empire.[106] These deliberations were undergirded by evidence from a series of investigative commissions assigned to consider the interrelated issues of an expanding colonial sphere and an inadequate labor supply. Chief among those consulted was the governor of Ceylon, Wilmot Horton, who was a staunch advocate of free trade and a keen supporter of migrant Indian labor.[107] Ceylon had witnessed the first large-scale effort to import Indian labor via state support; since the turn of the century, the Ceylonese government had employed

103 Ibid., 689.

104 Trevor Burnard and Kit Candlin, "Sir John Gladstone and the Debate over the Amelioration of Slavery in the British West Indies in the 1820s," *Journal of British Studies* 57 (October 2018), 760.

105 Boehme et al., "Reforming Everywhere and All at Once," 694.

106 James Stephen, the Permanent Undersecretary of the Colonial Office, and Thomas Elliott, the first Agent General for Emigration, were particularly instrumental in these efforts. Boehme et al., "Reforming Everywhere and All at Once," 697–9.

107 Ibid., 699.

workers brought from southern India for public works projects.[108] In the 1820s, the practice of exporting Indian labor overseas had expanded to include the French colony of Réunion, which shared an isolated patch of the western Indian Ocean with the British colony of Mauritius, approximately 600 miles east of Madagascar. By 1830, more than 3,000 Indian workers from Karikal and Pondicherry had arrived in Réunion.[109] In his previous post as the Undersecretary of State for War and the Colonies (1821–8), Horton had been in a good position to evaluate the colonial labor issue and consider how the vast labor supply of southern India might be utilized to address it. As Glenelg and other metropolitan officials considered various responses to the colonial "labor crisis," Horton's was one of the voices calling most enthusiastically for the government to expand the experiment in Indian indenture across the vast distances of the empire.[110] The Ceylonese labor traffic constituted one major antecedent of the state-organized transportation and employment of Indian workers overseas. The practices of the criminal justice system in the empire were another. These had seen colonial administrators utilizing Indian convict laborers to help build the infrastructure of new territorial acquisitions across Southeast Asia.[111] Before the first indentured laborers arrived on the shores of Mauritius, thousands of Indian prisoners had been transported to penal colonies in Bencoolen, the Straits Settlements, and Burma.[112] Mauritius, soon to be one of the two colonies where Indian indenture was first trialed on a large scale, received more than 1,500 such prisoners between 1815 and 1837.

Even as territorial expansion supported by the imperial state apparatus had helped create the demand for colonial labor, the *surplus* of available workers was itself at least partly the result of Britain's aggressive, state-supported economic expansion into the markets of South Asia. This effort had been buoyed by both private and public investment and by the expansion of mechanized textile production in Britain. The flooding of India with cheap manufactured goods from British industry had severely disrupted the Indian village economy, leaving many thousands of former farmers, agricultural workers, and small craftsmen without employment.[113] By the beginning of

[108] Roland Wenzelhuemer, "Indian Labour Immigration and British Labour Policy in Nineteenth-Century Ceylon," *Modern Asian Studies* 41, no. 3 (May 2007), 581.

[109] Hugh Tinker, *A New System of Slavery: The Export of Indian Labour Overseas, 1830–1920* (London: Oxford University Press, 1974), 61.

[110] Boehme et al., "Reforming Everywhere and All at Once," 699.

[111] Clare Anderson, "Convicts and Coolies: Rethinking Indentured Labour in the Nineteenth Century," *Slavery and Abolition* 30, no. 1 (March 2009), 95.

[112] Richard B. Allen, "Slaves, Convicts, Abolitionism and the Global Origins of the Post-Emancipation Indentured Labor System," *Slavery & Abolition* 35, no. 2 (2014), 335.

[113] The disintegration of the Indian village handcraft industries as a result of the influx of cheap manufactured articles from Britain, in conjunction with a series of crop failures, famines, and other environmental catastrophes (at times also exacerbated by British

the nineteenth century, this cohort might have comprised as much as 15 percent of the total population of the southern Indian states.[114] In Bihar and Utter Pradesh, from whence the majority of indentured laborers would originate, this situation was exacerbated by the East India Company's extensive land-tenure reform of the late eighteenth century. The shift from communal village cultivation to cash-crop agriculture and the expansion of the *Zamindari* landlord system, both of which allowed the East India Company to increase tax revenue while keeping administrative costs low, had inflicted a state of permanent debt on to the Indian peasantry.[115] Migration, both within India and, with the introduction of indenture, beyond it, provided an opportunity to escape this dire economic status.[116]

One of the major participants in the opening up of Indian markets to "free trade," which helped to create the burgeoning pool of potential laborers, was also a key figure in the expansion of Indian indentured labor from a limited, local project into one that spanned the breadth of the British Empire. John Gladstone (b. 1820), a Scottish-born Liverpool merchant speculator, former slaveholder, and father of the future Liberal Prime Minister, embodied the opportunistic enthusiasm for liberalized long-distance trade that had prospered on the disruptions of the Napoleonic period and the decline of the East India Company's monopolistic hold on the subcontinent.[117] So pivotal was the elder Gladstone in the introduction of indenture to British Guiana that, to this day, the system is still referred to there as "The Gladstone Experiment."[118] At the forefront of Liverpool merchants' efforts to make inroads in South Asia and expand their presence in Caribbean markets, his assiduous efforts to acquire land had rapidly elevated him, by the early 1820s, into the ranks of the largest landowners in Demerara.[119] Gladstone's initial effort to secure indentured laborers for his sugar estates there, organized in 1836, built on the heels of the first British sugar colony to employ Indian indenture on a large

efforts to capitalize the agricultural system), had created a vast pool of landless agricultural laborers in South Indian districts. Wenzelhuemer, "Indian Labour Migration," 582.

114 D. Wesempura, *Indian Immigrant Plantation Workers*, 15, cited in Wenzelhuemer, "Indian Labour Migration," 582.

115 Gayan Prakash, *Bonded Histories: Genealogies of Labor Servitude in Colonial India* (Cambridge: Cambridge University Press, 1990), 101–37.

116 Anand A. Yang, *The Limited Raj: Agrarian Relations in Colonial India, Saran District, 1793–1920* (Berkeley: University of California Press, 1989), 181–97.

117 Purba Hossain, "'A Matter of Doubt and Uncertainty': John Gladstone and Post-Slavery Labour in the British Empire," *Journal of Imperial and Commonwealth History* 50, no. 1 (2022), 52–80.

118 Tota C. Mangar, article in *Sabroek News*, May 8, 2003, cited in M. G. Manton, "The Rise of the British Managing Societies in North Eastern India 1836–1918," unpublished MPhil thesis, School of Oriental and African Studies, 2017, 35.

119 S. G. Checkland, "John Gladstone as Trader and Planter," *Economic History Review* 7, no. 2 (1954), 216.

scale, Mauritius. Following successful efforts by Indian-based British firms to export labor to Réunion, the new system was trialed in nearby Mauritius, a formerly French sugar colony that had been seized by the British during the Napoleonic Wars. After a brief, aborted effort in 1829 to bring indentured Indians there at the behest of the then governor, Sir Charles Colville, the project was recommenced in 1834. That year, in August, a contingent of thirty-nine workers arrived on the island and were assigned to sugar plantations. This renewed effort was an immense success, in the eyes of planters, and by 1838 the number of Indian indentured laborers in Mauritius had swelled to 19,700.[120] An added benefit, from the planters' perspective, was that the new Indian workforce undermined the economic position of African-Mauritian apprentices, whose numbers dwindled as the ranks of their indentured replacements rose.[121]

When James Stephen, the counsel for the Colonial Office, raised concerns that the importation of indentured Indian workers might have a negative effect on the social and economic trajectory of the newly emancipated African-Mauritians, he was overruled by the Colonial Secretary, Glenelg, and by the governor of Mauritius, William Nicolay. The latter was keen to prevent was keen to prevent African-Mauritians from gaining any economic leverage in Britain's newest colony, and defended his position with an appeal to the principles of competition in a free labor market. This stance ignored the clear evidence that the volatile labor landscape in Mauritius was almost entirely the consequence of state intervention in the sugar trade. The metropolitan government had facilitated a labor demand by granting Mauritian sugar exports tariff equality with sugar from West India, a policy that had prompted a cultivation boom on the island, where the land under sugar production had doubled and the cost of slaves had quadrupled by 1830.[122] Far from being driven by the dynamics of free trade and a free labor market, as its proponents insisted, indenture, itself a state-engineered policy, addressed an issue that previous policies had themselves created.[123]

As the traffic in Indian labor expanded, the Indian government, mindful of the public and official scrutiny of colonial labor issues that characterized the period, began to take an interest in its regulation. The year 1830 witnessed the first attempt at monitoring the traffic in the name of ensuring that its practice was commensurate with the principles of free labor and moral colonial rule.

120 R. Kuczynski, *Demographic Survey of the British Colonial Empire* (Oxford: Oxford University Press, 1949), cited in Marina Carter, "The Transition from Apprenticeship to Indentured Labour in Mauritius," in Michael Twaddle, ed., *The Wages of Slavery: From Chattel Slavery to Wage Labor in Africa, the Caribbean and England* (London: Routledge, 1993), 123.

121 Boehme et al., "Reforming Everywhere and All at Once," 703.

122 Ibid.

123 Tayyab Mahmud, "Cheaper Than a Slave: Indentured Labor, Colonialism and Capitalism," *Whittier Law Review* 34 (2012), 4–5.

Potential emigrants were required to appear before a magistrate and declare that they were engaging in their contracts voluntarily. These contracts were for five-years' duration with a set monthly wage (Rs. 8) and the provision of rations.[124] With the exportation of indentured workers to Mauritius accelerating rapidly across the decade, in 1837 the Government of India instituted a broad suite of regulations to bring the burgeoning trade in overseas labor export more firmly under state oversight. It began to monitor the conditions of exported laborers at their destinations, to allow recruitment only by officially licensed agents, to inspect potential recruits for health at the port of embarkation and to provide a medical officer on transport ships, to dictate the conditions of transport, and to subsidize the costs of the new labor organization and transportation apparatus.[125] This expansion of the indenture system was made possible by the confluence of several previous innovations in governance. Chief among these were the extension of direct Crown rule over colonial possessions (including Mauritius itself), the willingness of Indian government officials to take on the task of monitoring and regulating the system, and the amenability of imperial officials such as the governor of Ceylon (Wilmot), in the era of amelioration and emancipation, to become directly involved in the minutiae of colonial labor organization.[126]

The legacies of ameliorated slavery and apprenticeship were also clear in the moral discourse employed to justify indenture and the transportation of Indian workers across vast distances. When John Gladstone placed his proposal for importing Indian laborers to his Guyanese estates before Glenelg, the Colonial Secretary, he outlined the terms of indenture in a paternalistic tone. The new workforce, he explained, would be employed and provided for along terms that mirrored their predecessors' circumstances on the plantations. Food, provisions, and clothing would be supplied, as would regular medical service, all at the expense of their employers.[127] Recognizing the need to care for the soul as well as for the body, Gladstone also emphasized that employers would offer schooling for the children of workers and religious instruction for their parents. Gladstone's efforts to radically expand the export of Indian indenture by transporting workers across two oceans were aided by his close personal connections in government. The interest that he and Wilmot shared in the potential of Indian labor developed in tandem, and the two were in regular communication throughout the 1820s and 1830s.[128] Gladstone was also a strong supporter of increased state authority over the plantation

124 Tinker, *A New System of Slavery*, 61.
125 Ibid., 64.
126 Kale, *Fragments of Empire*, 41.
127 Letter from John Gladstone to Messrs. Gillanders, Arbuthnot, and Co., January 4, 1836, 2. Copy of a Letter from John Gladstone to Lord Glenelg, with enclosures, 1838 (hereafter Gladstone to Glenelg, 1838).
128 Checkland, "John Gladstone," 224.

workforce, particularly in the wake of the 1823 Demerara Rebellion, which had centered on his own estates and in which one of his own slaves, Jack, had been identified as a primary instigator.[129] The relationship between Gladstone and Wilmot was a prominent example of the new kind of alliance between cosmopolitan, imperial capital on one hand and metropolitan colonial administrators' enthusiasm for free trade and free labor, in word if not in deed, on the other. In an environment where relations between the more traditional plantocracy and officials in London had been soured by the long political conflict over slavery, the collaboration of the imperial state with cosmopolitan capital would open the door for this latest experiment in colonial labor and its governance.

In the expansion of the indenture system, key among the companies epitomizing this alliance was the Scottish firm of Arbuthnot, Gillanders, and Co. This firm, through their base in Calcutta, had already arranged the exportation of a sizable contingent of Indian indentured laborers to Mauritius. They were therefore well situated to organize a similar effort to recruit and transport laborers for Gladstone's estates in British Guiana.[130] Once introduced to British Guiana, the indenture system quickly took hold. Year-round production, fertile soil, and a significant amount of undeveloped land gave it the potential to be the most productive sugar colony in the British Caribbean, with labor being the one resource not available in plentiful supply.[131] In the wake of emancipation and the end of apprenticeship, the number of African-Guyanese working in the plantations dropped precipitously, and would continue to do so throughout the 1840s. Many former slaves and apprentices became smallhold farmers or migrated to the capital, Georgetown, to take on work in the trades.[132] There is much historical debate on whether this was due to the rise of the village economy and a desire to escape the memories of slavery and the abuse of the plantations or rather due to the arbitrary treatment of workers by plantation-owners after slavery (i.e. the iniquities of apprenticeship, refusal to pay competitive wages, measures to cut labor costs).[133] The latter seems more likely. The inability of planters to keep former slaves was a failure of emancipation and apprenticeship to improve conditions of plantation work satisfactorily; otherwise, it would be

129 Ibid., 225–6.

130 Letter from Messrs. Gillanders, Arbuthnot, and Co. to John Gladstone, June 6, 1836 in Gladstone to Glenelg, 1838. By this time, Gladstone possessed no fewer than seven estates there (*Success*, *Wales*, *Waller's Delight*, *Covenden*, *Hampton Court*, *Vreedenhoop*, and *Vreedstein*) in addition to his extensive holdings in Jamaica. Checkland, "John Gladstone," 223.

131 Green, "Apprenticeship in British Guiana," 46.

132 The most common of these trades involved working as carters, porters, mechanics, warehousemen, and domestic servants. By 1844, the number of free African-Guyanese working on the plantations had dropped to 30 percent of what it had been a decade previously, while the population of Georgetown, the capital, doubled from 1838 to 1844. Riviere, "Labour Shortage," 11.

133 See Hall, "Flight from the Estates Reconsidered," 9–11.

difficult to explain the continuing reluctance of African-Guyanese to work on estates even half a decade after emancipation.[134]

Regardless of the reasons for the flight from the plantations, John Gladstone and other supporters of the scheme were eager to bring in indentured Indians. Doing so would allow them both to expand their sugar production and to abrogate their dependency on what Governor Henry Light of British Guiana would later describe as "the caprice of the negro."[135] It was not the absence of labor overall, but rather the refusal of the freed African-Guyanese workforce to work under the terms that, in the eyes of the planters, would allow them to expand their production and maintain their estates at a profit that made the importation of Indian workers so desirable. Gladstone emphasized this alleged "labor crisis" in British Guiana when he appealed to Glenelg for approval of his labor importation scheme, insisting that "unless such [i.e. indenture] or other means are adopted to promote the emigration of free labourers to be employed in their future cultivation, their productive advantages are likely to be greatly diminished if not wholly lost to the Mother Country."[136] Despite the reservations of some in the Colonial Office, Gladstone's scheme was approved. With it, indenture had taken a major step in its transformation from a limited, regional practice into a globe-spanning institution.

The First Anti-Indenture Campaign

Although John Gladstone's plan to bring indentured Indians to Guiana in modest numbers was approved, authorities in London were initially reluctant to expand the system further. In part, this hesitancy stemmed from the mounting political opposition to the importation of indentured Indians among metropolitan antislavery activists. At the head of this burgeoning anti-indenture campaign were the perennial opponents of ameliorated slavery and, subsequently, apprenticeship, Thomas Buxton and John Scoble. Scoble had founded the BFASS in 1839 in response to the growing concern among former abolitionists over the abuses of the apprenticeship system. Hot on the heels of his successful lobbying against that system, he now set his sights on indenture. The initial salvos appeared in the *British Emancipator*, the journal that had been the primary clearing house for abolitionist writing since it commenced publication in 1837. The first prominent anti-indenture article, organized by Buxton himself, was published in January 1838, and

134 Ibid., 11.

135 Henry Light to Earl Grey, May 3, 1848. Quoted by R. E. G. Farley, "Aspects of the Economic History of British Guiana, 1781 to 1852," unpublished PhD thesis, London University, 1958.

136 Gladstone to Glenelg, February 28, 1838, in Gladstone to Glenelg, 1838.

decried the government's sanctioning of five-year indentures for Indian workers arriving in British Guiana, labeling it "a modified slave-trade."[137] After visiting British Guiana once again to gather evidence, Scoble published another article that painted the system in the worst possible light. Calculated to evoke outrage among readers, the piece emphasized the terrible conditions of indenture in the colony, which had prompted frequent escape attempts and a high mortality rate among the workers.[138] Scoble's full broadside against the system was published subsequently in 1840. Although John Gladstone appeared as the primary villain, much of the harshest criticism was reserved for the various officials, both metropolitan and colonial, that had aided and abetted his scheme. Glenelg and the coterie of special justices in British Guiana received especially severe condemnation. Far from protecting the rights and safeguarding the well-being of the immigrants, as was their task, Scoble declared, the latter had turned a blind eye to the exploitation, abuse, and even shocking levels of mortality among their erstwhile charges.[139]

In contrast to how metropolitan authorities had handled criticisms of amelioration, they could not simply pawn the blame for the abuses of indenture off on the immorality of plantation-owners. The scheme had been developed in a collaboration between Glenelg's colonial oversight and planters in Mauritius and British Guiana. The special magistrates whose appointment was directed by the Colonial Office were at the heart of the system. The criticism of indenture, which was underwritten by the government, approved by metropolitan officials, and supported by positive reports from magistrates, put the overseer-state itself at the center of the problem. Therefore it was on its officials that the responsibility for addressing abuses fell. Scoble was also able to use the self-same tools of the overseer-state, the reports of magistrates and the dense communication between the Colonial Office and the colonial governors on colonial labor organization, as evidence of the state's failure to protect both the interests of its Indian subjects and those of emancipated Africans in both colonies. Among the most damning statements that Scoble employed was one from F. R. Prinsep, the secretary to the government of India. Prinsep had written in an official report that "the methods adopted for procuring labourers to engage for service in the colonies and places beyond the sea are productive of serous frauds and have led to much oppression ... the system is a source of serious injury and abuse, rather than of benefit to the labourers."[140] Equally negative appraisals came from other officials, including William Nicolay, the governor of Mauritius,

137 *The British Emancipator* II (January 3, 1838), 21.
138 Kale, *Fragments of Empire*, 24.
139 John Scoble, *Hill Coolies: A Brief Exposure of the Deplorable Condition of the Hill Coolies in British Guiana and Mauritius and of the Nefarious Means by Which They Were Induced to Resort to These Colonies* (London: Harvey and Darnton, 1840), 11–13.
140 Ibid., 25.

and a special justice (Charles Anderson) from India, both of whom asserted that kidnapping and fraud were common practices employed by labor recruiters.[141] "The whole system has been characterized by the grossest fraud and cruelty," Scoble vehemently declared, "and has been sustained by the most infamous tyranny and oppression."[142]

Much like amelioration and indenture themselves did, opposition to these systems was helping to forge greater coordination between different colonies, and between them and the metropole, over the issue of labor regulation and the state's obligations to mediate between plantation employers and their workforce. Scoble's publications were bolstered by the agitation of Anglo-Indian reformers who were led by a collection of religious figures and local officials.[143] Many of the most vocal activists resided in Calcutta, a primary recruiting point of the laborers destined for Mauritius and British Guiana. The British government's response to this dual-pronged attack was to appoint a parliamentary commission of inquiry, whose chairman and most prominent member was Theodore Dickens, a Calcutta-born solicitor.[144] Although the formal report of the Dickens Committee, as it came to be known, was not submitted to Parliament until October 1840, the extensive evidence collected, which was drawn from a wide range of witnesses including indentured laborers themselves, was printed in March 1839.[145] The practices of coerced recruitment, perilous health conditions on transport ships, poor treatment on the estates, and a host of other problems revealed were enough to prompt the Governor-General of India's council to suspend all overseas emigration of laborers.[146]

This suspension was temporary, however, and followed not by abrogation of the trade but instead by a series of modifications to it. These reforms sought to implement for indentured laborers what amelioration had done for enslaved Africans. At their core was the extension of state authority over the new labor system through increased regulation and oversight. A Protector of Immigrants, analogous to the Protector of Slaves, was introduced to Mauritius in 1842, shortly after Indian immigration resumed in 1841.[147] The first of these Protectors was Charles Anderson, whose criticism of indenture as a magistrate

141 Ibid.

142 Ibid., 24.

143 Tinker, *A New System of Slavery*, 65; Connolly, "Indentured Labour Migration," 91.

144 *Hill Coolies and Indian Labourers. Report of the Committee to Enquire into Alleged Abuses in Exporting from Bengal to Other Countries*, PP 1841, XVI, Nos. 287 and 483. See also *Hill Coolies. Copies of Papers Respecting the Exportation of Hill Coolies, Received from the Government of India*, PP 1841, No. 427.

145 Tinker, *A New System of Slavery*, 66.

146 Act XIV, May 28, 1839.

147 Act XV "for regulating the emigration of the native inhabitants of the territories under the Government of the East India Company to the Island of Mauritius."

in India had been quoted in Parliament and subsequently employed to great effect by Scoble. Anderson did not confine his efforts to Mauritius itself, but instead undertook oversight of the entire system from origin to destination. After visiting India, he submitted a detailed report of his findings and recommendations, the latter of which entailed the expansion of formal state oversight through the appointment of new agents and through granting enhanced powers to those already in place. Anderson's proposed policies would more closely coordinate the apparatus of labor governance between the point of supply, India, and the territories of destination, which were primarily Mauritius and British Guiana. Chief among these proposals for broader state involvement was his recommendation that government agents be appointed in India to monitor the process of recruitment and transportation. These agents would act for the government of Mauritius, but be answerable to the governments of the presidencies from which the workers would emigrate (Calcutta, Madras, and Bombay).[148] Anderson's proposed reforms were put into effect, and, subsequently, similar arrangements would be made in British Guiana. In what would become a persistent pattern, at each step, the expansion of the indenture system was accompanied by an expansion of the state apparatus to monitor and regulate it, entangling the growth of this global labor system with the growing authority and coordination of colonial and imperial labor governance.

The attack on indenture mounted by Scoble, Buxton, and the cohort of India-based activists had ended in the reform, rather than the abolition, of indenture for several reasons. The first is that antislavery activists, although willing to campaign against the more visibly coercive and exploitative elements of the indenture system, were nonetheless invested in the idea that free labor was superior to slave labor. The contrast between the two had been key to the antislavery campaign from its early days, so unless indenture could be effectively defined *as* slavery, it was very difficult to oppose it using the same moral discourse employed in the opposition *to* slavery. As a counter to criticism, those who supported the system could argue that the work, wages, medical services, and housing offered by the allegedly voluntary engagement of indenture contracts was far preferable to the poverty, hunger, and hopelessness that characterized life for the legions of unemployed in southern India.[149] The institutional backbone of the overseer-state, established during amelioration and apprenticeship, had also provided the means necessary to address the most serious issues raised by the early critics of indenture. In response to accusations of coercion and kidnapping, a more rigorous system of state regulation and monitoring was implemented.[150] At the ground level, the role and the authority of magistrates and Protectors to oversee the system were expanded, while at

[148] Tinker, *A New System of Slavery*, 75.
[149] Kale, *Fragments of Empire*, 36.
[150] Connolly, "Indentured Labour Migration," 93.

the administrative level, Colonial Office officials and colonial governors who were well-acquainted with the issues of labor management demonstrated a clear willingness to intervene in order to address alleged abuses by recruiters and employers.

Another reason that indenture would persist and expand despite the campaign against it was that the system appeared, in the eyes of both state officials and estate proprietors, to address some of the major economic and political issues confronting the plantation colonies in the wake of emancipation and the termination of apprenticeship. It was clear that former slaves were not remaining on the plantations willingly, and the one attempt at a more coercive system, apprenticeship, had been a notable failure. In response, indenture seemed to provide a capable, affordable, and subordinated workforce amenable to the strict regime of plantation sugar production. This particularly suited the interests of cosmopolitan, metropole-based imperial wealth of the kind represented by Gladstone and his allies in government.[151] Men like Gladstone and his collaborators, Arbuthnot and Gillanders, could benefit both from acquiring the labor force to increase sugar production and from investment in the indenture scheme itself, which offered another way to profit from Britain's expanding control over India and its consequent opening up as a market.

Another reason that indenture survived the determined attack by Scoble and his allies was because it aligned on a number of levels with the ideological and cultural strains that were becoming dominant in British political discourse and in the attitudes of metropolitan officials toward the empire. The most direct of these alignments was between indenture and the commonly made argument, among economic theorists and imperial administrators, that state-sponsored schemes of labor migration were an advisable and effective means of intervention in the imperial economy.[152] The apparent contradiction between this and the growing enthusiasm for "free trade" was reconciled through the insistence, by Gladstone, Wilmot, and other advocates, that indentured labor was "free" in the sense that workers entered into their contracts voluntarily. Supporters of indenture, when confronted with reams of evidence that recruitment was coercive and deceptive, had a solution ready to hand. They simply stressed the importance of reforming the system to ensure that magistrates or other officials could monitor the recruitment process more closely.

151 At the time of emancipation, more than 40 percent of the compensation given to slave-owners for amounts of £500 and above in British Guiana (the average award for an enslaved person there being just over £50) went to absentee landlords. Nicholas Draper, "Rise of a New Planter Class? Some Countercurrents from British Guiana and Trinidad, 1807–33," *Atlantic Studies: Literary, Cultural and Historical Perspectives* 9, no. 1 (2012), 69–71.

152 Connolly, "Indentured Labour Migration," 94, 104; Connolly, "Indenture as Compensation," 449.

The expansion of state oversight allowed metropolitan authorities to reconcile what many believed was, and were urged by estate proprietors to see as, an economic necessity with the humanitarian considerations trumpeted by the antislavery lobby and a concerned public. This was part of the broader turn toward moral colonial rule, the concept of Britain's paternalistic "civilizing mission," and its erstwhile status as a defender of liberty and rule of law. These principles, which were championed with increasing prominence in everything from official communication to parliamentary speeches and public political commentaries, emerged in part from the emancipation campaign and in part from the long contest against Napoleonic "tyranny." Gladstone and Wilmot had preached to this choir effectively with their insistence that indenture would benefit the Indian workers involved, economically and culturally. Such engagement with the project of paternalistic uplift helped bridge the political rift between estate proprietors, colonial governors, and metropolitan officials that had developed during the bruising political melee over emancipation and apprenticeship. And it did so in a way that enhanced the powers of metropolitan officials and the economic fortunes of the cosmopolitan imperial capital becoming predominant in the new Crown colonies more so than it did the traditional, more conservative planter interests in the older legislative ones. From the standpoint of metropolitan officials and colonial governors, on a more practical level, indenture had proven useful in undercutting the economic and political leverage of the freed African-Caribbean and African-Mauritian population.

Contrasting views on race also played a part in the persistence of indenture and its relative resilience against criticism. Among antislavery activists and the British public, there was far less natural sympathy for Indian subjects than there had been for enslaved Africans. The former had not suffered for centuries under the yoke of slavery, nor had they experienced the level of cruelty and inhuman punishment reported to have been the daily lot under that system. And the amount of moral uplift necessary, and therefore visible in its absence, was less extreme. The new cohort of laborers were not Africans, who were thought by many to be incapable of properly wielding or even comprehending their newfound economic freedom, let alone of political participation.[153] They were Indians, who had already been successfully incorporated into the military and other elements of Britain's imperial apparatus via the East India Company.[154] In contrast to the image of Africans, enslaved or free, as being fractious, violent, untrustworthy, lazy, immoral, and dishonest, Indians were described by the supporters of

[153] Holt, *The Problem of Freedom*, 56.

[154] As had African-Caribbeans, though in more limited numbers. See David Lambert, *Soldiers of Uncertain Rank: The West India Regiments in British Imperial Culture* (Cambridge: Cambridge University Press, 2024).

indenture as being naturally docile, industrious, and welcoming of authority and good governance. They were, in short, ideal subjects for a paternalistic overseer-state that would guarantee the protection of their rights as Crown subjects, regulate the terms and conditions of their recruitment and employment, and guide their integration into plantation life in a manner commensurate with moral colonization and just rule.

Conclusion

By the 1840s, the role of the state in the colonial labor system had changed dramatically. This development was the culmination of several decades of persistent expansion and adaptation that had begun with the outlawing of the slave trade; continued through amelioration, emancipation, and apprenticeship; and persisted with the introduction of indenture. Supervision through a host of powerful agents and administrators who had set labor organization as a central duty of governance, the dictation of labor policy, and intervention between employers and workers on a level unimaginable in the metropole had become a central and permanent aspect of imperial policy and colonial governance. This operated through a coherent, coordinated apparatus with magistrates serving as the lynchpins. Policy was sometimes dictated from the imperial center, but often developed through the interaction between Colonial Office administrators, colonial governors, cosmopolitan capital interests, and the various planter-dominated consultative and representative bodies in the colonies themselves. Each had different goals and all were forced to respond to the concerted efforts of antislavery activists and the negative public opinion they could marshal. The various parties favoring different colonial labor schemes diverged on a wide variety of issues, chief among them the role of freed African-Caribbeans in the post-emancipation polity and the degree of autonomy that plantation colonies should enjoy in deciding how to manage their affairs. Regardless of their differences, they shared a common interest in maintaining Britain's paternalistic image as a moral colonizer while sustaining the political, social, and economic viability of her tropical colonies.

Over time, the path to resolving the differences of those who supported the new experiments in colonial labor organization and mollifying its critics converged in the expansion of state control, managed either top-down from the metropole or bottom-up from local initiatives. Across the period of apprenticeship and the early experiments in indenture, the state established itself as a permanent mediator between free laborers and employers, much as it had been between slave owners and slaves during amelioration. It was tasked with setting hiring and work conditions and preventing abuse, but also with enforcing labor contracts and disciplining workers. Regardless of humanitarian opposition and the desire, by at least some metropolitan officials, for a configuration that gave freed African-Caribbeans a more equitable place in the schema of colonial society, the measures introduced sustained white racial hegemony and granted employers a decisive advantage in labor relations. Concerns over public order and the necessity of stern plantation discipline prompted the state to collaborate with planters by suppressing demonstrations and collective bargaining and by criminalizing labor offenses. The insistence of some metropolitan officials that such stern policing of workers was incompatible with just governance, and their fears that contract and vagrancy laws, in particular, could become tools of oppression, were not heeded.[155]

As methods of labor regulation and organization were shared between different colonies, the expanding apparatus of the overseer-state forged crucial and novel links not just between India, Mauritius, and British Guiana, but between all these regions and the metropole, and across the vast distances of Britain's colonial possessions. Labor organization was fast becoming one of the quintessential aspects connecting disparate locales, practices, and concepts in the British Empire. It also operated at the forefront of crucial debates about policy and guiding principles, among them free labor, free trade, the limits of Crown authority, paternalism, and individual rights. In the process of harmonizing the practice and principles of colonial labor organization, the overseer-state was pioneering methods of governance and shaping the nature of the modern British imperial state. In certain regions, British Guiana and Mauritius in particular, it had become the most ubiquitous and publicly visible aspect of governance. It had also become the task by which, in the regions formerly defined by slavery and now increasingly worked by indentured laborers, the success of the British imperial system in its self-declared goals of moral colonization and just governance was being assessed. The careers of even the most powerful officials could be made or broken by how well they handled these matters.

Indenture, the first attempt at a state-sponsored, state-regulated colonial labor system, was built on the prior practices of convict labor transportation, amelioration, and apprenticeship. The initial trial was on a limited scale, but it survived its first test, emerging as a system that served the needs of many stakeholders for an affordable, subordinated replacement for slaves and apprentices, and with a coherent justification that combined the principles of free labor, racialized paternalism, and the civilizing mission. Across the mid-Victorian period, indenture would rapidly expand throughout the empire. Having proven that connecting the labor supply of India to the labor demand of Mauritius and British Guiana was desirable for reasons both economic and political, the next iteration would help create the world's first global labor market. It would be directed by the same collaboration of state and private

[155] Green, *British Slave Emancipation*, 165 n. 5.

capital that had made the initial experiment possible. Exactly how the overseer-state expanded, the new roles taken on by state agents in colonial labor organization, and the broader implications of the indenture system for the relationship between the state, industry, and capital in the second half of the nineteenth century are the topics of Chapter 4.

4

"A System Entirely Favorable to the Poorer Class of Natives"

Health, Moral Reform, and Coercion in the Indenture System, 1840–1864

In 1840, Charles Anderson, a judicial official assigned to Mauritius, delivered a detailed proposal to the government in Whitehall. He did this on behalf of a group of cosmopolitan investors and landholders with interests in Mauritius, foremost among whom was Charles Arbuthnot of Arbuthnot, Gillanders, & Co.[1] Arbuthnot and his colleagues were eager to see a reversal of the policy, adopted the Government of India in May of 1839, forbidding the overseas emigration of Indian manual laborers.[2] This ban, prompted by reports of abuse that had been brought to light by antislavery activists, had halted the steady flow of workers that had been arriving since 1836 in Mauritius, Demerara, Réunion, and Ceylon.[3] Anderson's patrons proposed a collaboration between the governments of India and Mauritius in order to restore the movement of "free emigrants" to the latter. Although the term "indenture" was never employed, the proposal enumerated a long series of conditions that would bind the newly arrived workers to their employers and ensure that the laborers would not become "an onus upon society" by abandoning their estates precipitously.[4] This system would be underwritten by the Mauritian government with an initial investment of £20,000.[5] Recruitment, transportation, assignment, employment, wages, provisioning, and health would all be closely monitored by agents in both India and Mauritius. These agents would be assigned by a self-styled "Emigration Committee" composed of Anderson's patrons, working in consultation with the appropriate state authorities. The entire endeavor would be closely overseen by the Indian government via a new

1 The other parties signing the proposal were Edward Chapman, Henry Barlow, C. C. Brownrigg, John P. Rowlandson, and Robert Bullen.
2 Act XIV of the Governor-General's council, May 29, 1839.
3 Hugh Tinker, *A New System of Slavery: The Export of Indian Labour Overseas, 1830–1920* (London: Oxford University Press, 1974), 69.
4 Charles Anderson, *Outlines of a Plan Submitted to Her Majesty's Government for the Purpose of Establishing an Authorized Committee to Regulate and Carry on the Introduction of Indian Laborers at Mauritius* (London: Nichols, 1840), 3.
5 Ibid., 9.

officer specially appointed for this purpose.[6] This proposed emigration arrangement, the Committee asserted, would be of considerable benefit to the new workers themselves, providing, as work on the sugar estates of the island already had for their predecessors, great improvements in their "social condition . . . health, appearance, and habits of industry."[7]

Writing from the Steven's Hotel, in the heart of London's fashionable Mayfair district, Anderson was happy to reassure any official or potential critic who might find defects in the proposal. The matter was one of utmost urgency, he insisted, since the continuance of the ban on Indian emigration would soon "reduce that fertile colony to an unprofitable waste."[8] His claims of expertise on the conditions of life, labor, morality, and governance in Mauritius would, to any representative of the metropolitan government, have appeared well founded. Anderson had, after all, been appointed by that self-same administration as a special magistrate in Mauritius. There, like his counterparts across Britain's plantation archipelago, he had been tasked with overseeing and reporting on the colony's transition from slavery to emancipation by way of the apprenticeship system. The arguments put forward by Anderson, Arbuthnot, and others with a vested interest in securing labor for the plantation colonies found favor with Lord Stanley, the Colonial Secretary. Emigration resumed from India to Mauritius in 1842, with Anderson appointed as the new Protector of Immigrants. This office and its wide-ranging duties and powers had evolved from its prior iteration, the Protector and Guardian of Slaves.

Under the resumed system of immigration, the first shipment of new laborers arrived at the capital city of Port Louis, Mauritius, in January 1843. By the end of the year, 30,218 Indian men and 4,307 Indian women had passed through the port, comprising the most recent additions to an Indian migrant cohort that, across the succeeding six decades, would total nearly half a million.[9] During the same period, approximately 1.5 million Indian laborers would emigrate to the Atlantic and Indian Ocean colonies of various European powers (primarily the British-controlled territories), while another 5 million Indian workers would be transported to other colonies around the Bay of Bengal (primarily to Ceylon, British Malaya, and Burma).[10] They would be joined by a much smaller contingent of Chinese indentured laborers, numbering some 16,000 in the British colonies, destined primarily for the Caribbean.[11] Greatest of all would be the migration of Chinese workers to Southeast Asia across the later decades of the

6 Ibid., 5.
7 Ibid., 11.
8 Ibid., 16.
9 Tinker, *A New System of Slavery*, 76. The total number of Indians to arrive in Mauritius from 1838 to 1924 was 455,000. David Northrup, *Indentured Labor in the Age of Imperialism, 1834–1922* (Cambridge: Cambridge University Press, 1995), 53.
10 Ibid.
11 Ibid., 25. Spain made much greater use of Chinese labor, as did the United States.

nineteenth century – more than 5.7 million to the Malaysian Peninsula alone.[12] In this process, institutions of governance, metropolitan and colonial, would regulate and manage a system of coerced labor that, while inflicting a far lower mortality rate than slavery had in a previous era, would exceed the nineteenth-century transatlantic trade in enslaved Africans in numbers, in the scope of circumstances, and in the distance traveled.[13]

With the antislavery lobby significantly weakened in the Caribbean context and labor organization established as a key aspect of colonial and imperial governance, the overseer-state could now expand into a global apparatus.[14] In some colonies where it was introduced, indentured labor would rise to become the dominant form of plantation work. In these locales, the merger of state power and planter authority would constitute the central nexus of colonial rule. Even in those territories where indentured labor was a smaller segment of the workforce, however, it would still operate as the anchor for colonial systems of labor control. Its apparatus of regulations, institutions, practices, and agents would provide the property-holders and their allies in the government with the leverage necessary to shape the circumstances for the entire agricultural labor force. The significance of indenture was further enhanced by its entanglement with the acceleration of private and public investment in colonial enterprises. The development of the global indenture system, the expansion of the imperial state, the economic growth of imperial commodities, and the collaboration between the imperial and colonial state and the cosmopolitan capital all went hand in hand.

The reconciliation of indenture, which would remain a perennial source of scandal and public controversy, with Britain's self-proclaimed commitment to liberalism, free labor, moral colonization, and just rule was achieved in four ways. First, by the establishment of "the coolie," in public dialogue and official policy, as a figure on whom the allegedly paternalistic mission of colonial governance could be inscribed. A corollary to this was the construction of allegedly villainous middlemen, immoral recruiters chief among them, as the primary foil for efforts to promote free labor in the tropical colonies. Popular stereotypes of Africans, African-Caribbeans, and African-Mauritians

[12] Ibid., 61.

[13] The transatlantic trade in enslaved Africans encompassed between 12 million and 13 million individuals, but took place over a 400-year period. For a general overview of the trade, see www.gilderlehrman.org/history-resources/teacher-resources/historical-context-facts-about-slave-trade-and-slavery.

[14] British antislavery would eventually revive in new forms later in the century, and there is a lively historical debate over the degree to which it was sustained in the political discourse of the Atlantic World during the 1840s and 1850s. See Hannah-Rose Murray, *Advocates of Freedom: African-American Transatlantic Abolitionism in the British Isles* (Cambridge: Cambridge University Press, 2020); Kate Rivington, "The London Emancipation Society and Transatlantic Abolitionism in the Civil War Era, 1859–1865," *Slavery & Abolition* 43, no. 4 (2022), 798–818.

as inherently incapable of contributing to the social, economic, and moral progress of colonized regions also played an important role in these dynamics. The second path to reconciling indenture with just rule was the public redefinition of planters and plantation discipline. Plantation proprietors, redeemed as collaborators with the state in this program, would cease to be key targets for efforts at reforming labor practices (as they had been during amelioration) and would instead become partners in the grand project of imperial free labor. Meanwhile, building on the groundwork that been laid with the pro-slavery lobby during the period of amelioration, plantation labor discipline would be portrayed not as an engine of cruelty and exploitation, as it had been painted by antislavery activists, but as a mechanism for inculcating industrious habits and moral advancement. Regimes of inspection, which operated as systems of surveillance and punishment, would be presented through the language of "protection," thus morally legitimizing and reinforcing the powerful legal and judicial mechanisms of labor control that had been radically expanded during amelioration. The last path to reconciling indenture with morality in policy, public dialogue, and practice was the reconfiguration of the most visible figures of the colonial labor control apparatus – primarily magistrates, Protectors, and other local officials – not as enforcers of stern labor discipline but rather as the paternalistic guardians of workers against those who would exploit them, be they unscrupulous recruiters or abusive plantation-owners.

Critics and would-be reformers from London to Calcutta would dog the overseer-state's expansion, but the Government of India would prove to be an even more intractable opponent.[15] Entangled in their own efforts to govern and reform the rapidly expanding colony where, in the wake of the Napoleonic Wars, they found themselves hegemon, Indian government officials would become increasingly concerned over what was rapidly becoming one of their most valuable resources and the most problematic cohort of their subjects, a vast pool of indebted, agricultural laborers. In dealing with the tripartite issue of labor supply, public criticism, and the complexities of Indian rule, the overseer-state would adopt new methods of governance and new financial instruments, strengthen its systems of surveillance and control in the colonial context, develop novel discourses of race and morality, and repurpose old institutions into powerful new roles. In the process, the overseer-state would emerge not just as a global, interconnected system of labor organization but as

[15] By the terms of the Government of India Act 1833, the Governor-General of Bengal was designated as the Governor-General of India. In conjunction with the newly designated "India Council," the "Governor-General in Council" was empowered with exclusive legislative authority over all of British India. In practice, the East India Company's executive body, the Board of Directors, continued to exert considerable authority over both policy and day-to-day governance. For a succinct overview of these changes, see M. B. Hooker, "The East India Company and the Crown, 1773–1858," *Malaya Law Review* 11, no. 1 (1969), 1–37.

a mechanism for the generation and dissemination of official information and public portrayals. Its epistemic processes, regardless of the coercion and abuse inherent to indenture itself, aligned the system with the discourses of free labor, moral colonization, liberalism, and just governance.

Skeletons in the Woods and Cane-Pieces: Debt, Contract, and the Crisis of Indian Vagrancy in the 1840s

The 1840s witnessed the development, through a collaboration between the Colonial Office, colonial governments, cosmopolitan investors, and local planters, of an empire-wide apparatus of labor recruitment, transportation, and plantation discipline. At its core were three elements that required the state to mediate between workers and their employers: debt, contract, and the policing of vagrancy. The first was a particularly potent means of controlling an agricultural labor force and rural social relations more generally, as both early indenture in the colonization of Britain's Atlantic North American colonies and its employment in Britain itself had demonstrated.[16] Debt's key role in the development of the global indenture system stemmed from the rapid growth of an indebted peasantry in late-eighteenth-century India. There, the reform of land tenure implemented by the East India Company had restructured landlord–tenant dynamics.[17] Whereas such dynamics had formerly been bound by custom in long-term relationships and had been organized around village communities, the introduction of Permanent Settlement established a land-owning class, the *zamīndāris*, whose primary impetus was to maximize their annual income.[18] This, in turn, forced the Indian peasantry to focus on cash crops rather than subsistence farming in order to meet the demands of their increasingly estranged and profit-minded landlords.[19] The resulting debt accumulation drove the peasantry into reliance on an

[16] On the former, see David W. Galenson, "British Servants and the Colonial Indenture System in the Eighteenth Century," *Journal of Southern History* 44, no. 1 (1978), 41–66; David W. Galenson, "White Servitude and the Growth of Black Slavery in Colonial America," *Journal of Economic History* 41, no. 1 (1981), 39–47; David W. Galenson, "The Rise and Fall of Indentured Servitude in the Americas: An Economic Analysis," *Journal of Economic History* 44, no. 1 (1984), 1–26. On the latter, see Chris Briggs, "The Availability of Credit in the English Countryside, 1400–1480," *Agricultural History Review* 56, no. 1 (2008), 1–24.

[17] Thomas Metcalf, "The British and the Moneylender in Nineteenth-Century India," *Journal of Modern History* 34, no. 4 (1962), 390–7; Bipasha Raha, "Moneylenders and Peasants: Credit Relations in Rural Bengal, 1793–1885," *Proceedings of the Indian History Congress* 68 (2007), 640–7.

[18] Gyan Prakash, *Bonded Histories: Genealogies of Labor Servitude in Colonial India* (Cambridge: Cambridge University Press, 1990), 101.

[19] Ibid., 128.

intermediary group, moneylenders (*sahukār*).[20] The growing cohort of indebted peasants also filled the ranks of those willing, often out of desperation, to entertain the promises offered by labor recruiters that relief awaited them doing work of which they knew not, in lands they knew not of, and of whose distance from home they had only the faintest comprehension.

Debt, regulated by the state, would also be the primary tool by which the initial intakes of Indian laborers to Mauritius and British Guiana were tied to plantation labor. This was not debt in the conventional sense of money lent and subsequently owed with interest. Rather, this was an obligation of agricultural workers who emigrated with some level of state and private underwriting to remain in continuous employment or face accumulating fines owed to the *state*. The path by which this form of state-regulated debt-coercion was implemented in the indenture system was somewhat roundabout, but it rapidly became a crucial and ubiquitous aspect of it. The scandal of early indenture and the abuses highlighted by antislavery activists and revealed in the Dickens Committee report had made the multi-year indentures desired by planters politically untenable. William Ewart Gladstone, the Colonial Secretary (and future prime minister) in the mid-1840s, had held firm in his support of one-year contracts.[21] The issue subsequently fell under the authority of Sir George Grey, who was appointed as the Colonial Secretary under Lord John Russell's government in 1846. Grey, a Whig of the Liberal stripe, wrestled with the competing demands of planters for a dependable workforce and the need to avoid further scandal over the issue of Indian immigration to the plantation colonies. His approach to the organization of Indian labor was strongly shaped by his perspective on race and its relationship to industry and idleness, articulated in his two-volume work *The Colonial Policy of Lord John Russell's Administration*. In it, Grey argued that the great failing of abolition was that it had not included provisions to compel African-Caribbeans to "submit to steady and continuous labour."[22] Far from the liberal principles holding that individuals would work for their own self-interest, Grey took a more conservative, Hobbesian stance, bemoaning the absence of forceful state intervention to compel labor and protect the social equilibrium.[23] Absent either coercion or necessity, he wrote, men would work only the minimum amount necessary to live "a comfortable existence." A greater failing still was that neither emancipation nor apprenticeship went far enough in morally uplifting the formerly enslaved population by

20 Ibid., 138.

21 Tinker, *A New System of Slavery*, 83.

22 George Grey, *The Colonial Policy of Lord John Russell's Administration, Vol. 1* (London: Richard Bentley, 1853), 54.

23 On Hobbes' defense of coercion as a morally acceptable means of enforcing obedience to contracts, see Luciano Venezia, *Hobbes on Legal Authority and Political Obligation* (London: Palgrave Macmillan, 2015), 126–7.

inculcating "motives to industry" or by providing education and religious instruction.[24] This error was compounded, Grey insisted, by the state's failure to enforce public order through the creation of an effective colonial police force.[25]

The key question here, from the perspective of a prominent colonial administrator very much in both the public and the official gaze, was how such "continuous labour" and moral uplift could be achieved via coercion while maintaining a nominal commitment to the principle of free labor. Grey's argument was that the state, via the imposition of sterner paternalistic regulation, must be the prime mover in ensuring that the colonial labor system operated smoothly and that the workers within it were prompted to "industry." This stance became policy when, following his suggestion, Ordinance 22 of 1847 was approved by the Mauritian governor (Sir William Maynard Gomm) and legislative council. The ordinance compelled Indians in the colony either to enter into work contracts or to pay a monthly tax of four shillings. Those who failed to comply faced imprisonment along with fines that accumulated at the rate of *6d.* a week.[26] So harsh was this legislation that it prompted protests both from Thomy Hugon, who had replaced Charles Anderson as Protector of Immigrants in 1847, and from the directors of the East India Company.[27] Such opposition notwithstanding, the policy adopted throughout the Crown colonies, following the pattern established in the preceding decade, the policy adopted in one territory via a collaboration between Colonial Office officials and planter interests rapidly became common throughout the Crown colonies.[28] Debt was thus transformed into a tool of state-sanctioned coercion, justified by the moral necessity of inculcating habits of "industry" among a population allegedly prone to idleness and disorder. This system also had the advantage of being a familiar one to the laborers themselves, given the proliferation of debt bondage across India in the wake of Permanent Settlement.

These measures did not quiet the demands of planters for long-term contracts that would guarantee a stable, subordinated labor force and justify the considerable investment required to recruit, transport, and maintain it. Absent the landlord and moneylender structure and the social bonds that had tied peasants to their localities in India, the debts imposed for failure to sign

24 Grey, *The Colonial Policy*, 56.

25 Ibid.

26 Tinker, *A New System of Slavery*, 84. This was roughly a quarter to a third of a field laborer's daily wages. G. E. Cumper, "Labour Demand and Supply in the Jamaican Sugar Industry, 1830–1950," *Social and Economic Studies* 2, no. 4 (1954), 48.

27 Tinker, *A New System of Slavery*, 82, 84.

28 Trinidad, at the suggestion of the Colonial Office, had also adopted a policy of compulsory engagement and fines for refusal in 1846. Walton Look Lai, *Indenture Labor, Caribbean Sugar: Chinese and Indian Migrants to the British West Indies, 1838–1918* (Baltimore, MD: Johns Hopkins University Press, 1993), 55–6.

contracts proved nearly impossible to collect.[29] The detention of offenders was impractical and counterproductive, moreover, since imprisoned workers could not provide labor. Unable, for the time being, to gain sanction for a return to long-term contracts, colonial governments instead turned to more indirect means to tie Indian workers to their employers, constrain their mobility, and ensure their "industry." Vagrancy laws, having been employed in Britain since the fourteenth century, were implemented with increasing vigor in the plantation colonies.[30] As with the laws on absenteeism and vagabondage that had been integrated into the Abolition Act, these measures authorized the arrest and imprisonment of any individuals found wandering without employment.[31] Revived as indenture expanded in the 1840s, they constrained workers' mobility in two interrelated capacities. Firstly, vagrancy laws prevented workers from leaving one plantation for another in order to seek better pay, keeping wages artificially low by precluding competition between plantation-owners. And secondly, they tied laborers to their places of employment even beyond the expiration of their short-term contracts. Denied permission to move from one plantation to another while they were employed, the securing of new employment on a different plantation was, in practice, nearly impossible.

These coercive measures were justified by what colonial governors, Henry Light of British Guiana and Lord Harris of Trinidad in particular, portrayed to the Colonial Office as a humanitarian crisis among Indian immigrants. The context for this was the economic depression that had overtaken the Caribbean sugar industry in the wake of the Sugar Duties Act 1846. Passed at the same time as the Corn Laws were repealed, the 1846 Act equalized duties between sugar imported from British colonies and that imported from foreign ones. Planters across the Caribbean faced the dual pressures of declining profits and increasing regulatory obligations to house, feed, and care for their imported laborers, the latter in addition to the initial outlay of a mandatory head tax on new arrivals.[32] Indian immigrants, already dissatisfied with the poor conditions of work on the plantations, chafed at the stagnating or reduced wages offered by their employers. Some chose to leave the plantations rather than continue such onerous work for what they

[29] Ibid., 56.

[30] The first English vagrancy statute was passed in 1349. W. Chambliss, "A Sociological Analysis of the Law of Vagrancy," *Social Problems* 12 (1960), 68.

[31] Mary Turner, "The British Caribbean, 1823–1838: The Transition from Slaver to Free Legal Status," in Douglas Hay and Paul Craven, eds., *Masters, Servants, and Magistrates in Britain and the Empire, 1562–1955* (Chapel Hill: University of North Carolina Press, 2004), 316–17.

[32] William A. Green, *British Slave Emancipation: The Sugar Colonies and the Great Experiment, 1830–1865* (Oxford: Clarendon Press, 1976), 278.

saw as inadequate pay.[33] In a vicious cycle, as Indian laborers expressed their dissatisfaction either by refusing to sign extensions on their short-term contracts or by absconding after having signed them, planters were increasingly disinclined to invest in imported labor if it was accompanied by a significant flight risk.[34]

The situation was particularly acute in British Guiana, which had seen the importation of thousands of Indian laborers to work on the lands newly brought under sugar cultivation in the previous decades. This expansion had come a time when the sugar market was rising and when sales were protected by the import duties on foreign sugar. Facing a planter elite that claimed such dire circumstances that they could not afford to pay their taxes, and finding himself overseeing a colony that appeared to be on the verge of economic collapse, Governor Light recast the conflict between planters and their labor force over wages and work conditions as a humanitarian crisis. This assessment was made possible by another key element of the overseer-state, medical inspections. These inspections had become an increasingly crucial source of information and a means by which the social, economic, and cultural portrayals of plantation colonies were shaped for colonial governors and metropolitan officials alike. The facility to conduct them was a legacy of the cholera pandemics of the 1830s, when colonial governments, at the insistence of metropolitan officials, had begun (albeit with some reluctance) to implement sanitary measures similar to those adopted in the metropole.[35] These patchwork efforts would not become systematic and consolidated until mid-century. In the interim, the responsibility for collecting data, collating it, and reporting to the governor was assigned either to local magistrates or to ad hoc health inspectors. In the case of British Guiana, the duty to assess the sickness and mortality rates among immigrant workers fell to George R. Bonyun, a British doctor who had arrived only recently in the colony. These workers were broken down in official discourse into three groups: "Africans," "Madeirans" (i.e. Portuguese), and "Indians."

Bonyun classified the incidence of sickness and death by geographic circumstances, distinguishing between both coastal districts and those on islands and river-banks, and between Demerara/Essequibo and Berbice. The doctor was

33 This was an assessment made relative to conditions in the years before the downturn in the sugar market, and not in absolute terms. Wages for indentured plantation work in Trinidad in 1872, which averaged 25 cents (1½ shillings) a day, were still approximately three times what could be earned in Eastern India for the typical labor in either an agricultural or an industrial setting. Murdoch to Hulbert, June 19, 1872, CO 318/67.

34 Evidence of Benjamin Hawes, Under Secretary of State for the Colonies, April 5, 1848, *Reports from Committees – Sugar and Coffee Planting*, PP XXIII, Pt. III, November 18, 1847–September 5, 1848, 107 (hereafter *Reports from Committees – Sugar and Coffee*).

35 Juanita de Barros, "Sanitation and Civilization in Georgetown, British Guiana," *Caribbean Quarterly* 49, no. 4 (December 2003), 70.

careful to point out the specific causes of poor health, alluding to the epidemic of yellow fever that had caused high mortality among some cohorts, emphasizing that some groups arrived at the colony in better health than others did, and indicating that certain locales (e.g. river banks) were inherently more unhealthful than others (e.g. sea coasts). Regardless of this specificity about geography and his recognition that an immigrant's state on arrival was a key predictor of health outcomes, Bonyun's descriptions of sickness and mortality among plantation laborers heavily conflated the effects of disease and climate with moral issues and vagrancy (also known as "vagabondage"). He categorized and ranked each of the main immigrant laboring cohorts in the colony with a combination of allegedly intrinsic racial characteristics, cultural predilections, and physical attributes. Madeirans, although not suffering from any particular moral defects, were, in his estimation, "the most sickly," and Bonyun estimated an annual mortality rate of 7 percent, with an overall decrease of approximately 40 percent of the population in the previous six years.[36] In comparison, the doctor reported that African immigrants did not seem to suffer the debilitating effects of either disease or climate, and therefore, of all the groups examined, were the most suitable and promising prospects for future immigration.[37]

Bonyun further divided the Indian immigrant workers into two categories based on their port of embarkation, "Madras Coolies" and "Calcutta Coolies," and evaluated them on a comparative scale. The latter, coming from the center of British authority in India, he described as second only to Africans in their suitability as planation laborers, and far superior to their south Indian confreres. Compared to the arrivals from Madras, the Calcutta contingent were "generally of a higher caste of Coolies, are more cleanly in their persons, stricter in their religious observances with regards to food, fonder of dress, and more industrious."[38] "Calcutta coolies" were even superior in comportment, evincing a "bright, clean and gay aspect," whereas the immigrants from Madras "have a dirty, lurid, ragged appearance."[39] But the greatest failings of the Madras workers, according to Bonyun, lay in their character and behavior. "They are very much given to vagabondage," the doctor explained, "and are extremely filthy in their persons and habits, eating every species of garbage, even to the extent of picking up the putrid bodies of animals from the nastiest trenches, cooking and eating them mixed with curry."[40] As a result of these moral and physical defects, Bonyun reported,

[36] British Guiana, Appendix No. 2, Report of George R. Bunyon, Demerara, January 6, 1848, *Reports from Committees - Sugar and Coffee*, 245.
[37] Ibid., 246.
[38] Ibid., 245.
[39] Ibid.
[40] Ibid.

the Madras contingent suffered from a mortality rate four times that of the Calcutta arrivals.[41]

Grey, the Colonial Secretary, responded to this report in the same vein, addressing the concrete issues of public health in tandem with the more nebulous ones of moral reform. The state's intervention was urgently needed, he wrote in a missive to Governor Light, in the form of more public hospitals, more effective vagrancy laws, and, potentially, the establishment of workhouses to which "all vagrants and beggars might be compelled to resort."[42] None of those involved in the discussion, Light, Grey, or Bonyun, despite the last's willingness to talk at length about issues of caste, religion, and personal hygiene, made any mention of the work conditions on the plantations themselves or the deleterious health effects of long-distance maritime voyages. Nor did they venture possible reasons why – beyond "vagabondage," a lack of industriousness, and general moral failings – immigrant workers from Madras were apparently quitting the plantations in such numbers. In short, the possibility that the economic and social conditions of the Indian plantation labor system *itself* were to blame for the high mortality rate was never considered; nor was the abandonment of a scheme now so crucial to the labor supply. Instead, much as had been the case with the amelioration of slavery, which had occupied an analogous position twenty years previously amidst a similar reported crisis that threatened the plantation economy, the only viable solution was robust state intervention. This, Grey and Light asserted, would come in the form of government regulation, sterner policing of "idleness," and state investment in the measures necessary to address the most pressing threats to health and the most acute moral failings among the workforce.

Facing a similar situation in Trinidad, Governor George Harris expressed an even greater eagerness to expand the state oversight of Indian immigrants.[43] Harris painted an extraordinary picture of the humanitarian crisis there, the dire failings of government to rectify the situation, and the absolute necessity, on both moral and economic grounds, of immediate public intervention via coercive paternalism. Indian workers, he informed the Colonial Secretary, were "naturally dissolute," "depraved in their habits," and prone to "vagabondage and licentiousness."[44] He insisted that only "zealous and unceasing care"

[41] The influence of "scientific racism" on Bonyun's perspective was especially prevalent in his analysis of the children of mixed-race unions. British Guiana, Appendix No. 2, Report of George R. Bunyon, Demerara, January 6, 1848, *Reports from Committees – Sugar and Coffee*, 246.

[42] Grey to Light, March 29, 1848, *Reports from Committees – Sugar and Coffee*, 249.

[43] George Harris, a Liberal, was the son of the former Commander-in Chief of the Madras Army.

[44] Harris to Gladstone, July 30, 1846, in *Reports from Committees – Sugar and Coffee*, 263. William Gladstone, the future Prime Minister, preceded Grey in the office, serving from 1845 to 1847.

and "close supervision" by the government would safeguard their well-being, ensure their productivity, and prevent them from having a deleterious effect on the moral and social fabric of the colony. Consequently, Harris initiated the most sweeping reform of the regulations on labor to be seen since emancipation. These included measures that covered almost every aspect of the work and life of Indian immigrants, and were backed by a stern apparatus of surveillance and policing. The proposed policies were developed in close consultation with a special official, appointed by the governor, to directly oversee the integration of the Indian labor force into plantation life. Major James Fagan, a retired military officer from Bengal, would serve as the first (and last) "Coolie magistrate" in Trinidad.[45] Together, Harris and Fagan developed a set of special laws that standardized wages, delineated the specific allocations of food and clothing that plantation owners were required to supply to workers, specified the hours and type of labor permitted, set a detailed standard of worker housing, and organized regular medical inspections. The reproductive state of the population would also be carefully recorded, with twice-yearly reports submitted to the governor on the number of women in each "coolie gang" and the number, gender, and age of any children.

Although these measures were couched in paternalistic terms, the bulk of effort devolving onto the "Coolie magistrate" and the colonial state apparatus concerned the strict policing of the laborers' mobility and strengthening the power of estate-owners over their workforce. Such regulations were necessary, Harris asserted, because, "no one requires stricter surveillance of conduct at work than the Indian labourer, whose propensity to lie down and smoke while at work, and to seize every available opening for evading it, is proverbial."[46] Indian laborers could henceforth not leave their estates without a pass; police constables were authorized to interrogate any worker they encountered and, should they not possess proper documentation, to return them to their estates at the owner's expense.[47] Another method Harris introduced to prevent the "wilfully lazy and drawling performance of work" was to extend labor contracts beyond their listed date of expiration in order to make up for time lost due to poor effort.[48] Such dereliction would be recorded via a register kept by the plantation manager. These documentary records served to further bind workers under the authority of estate owners. The guidelines issued by the governor expressly discouraged the hire of those who lacked an official certificate of discharge from their previous employers. This certificate was provided only when the worker had fulfilled their contract to the satisfaction of their employer, including making up for any "lost" days.

[45] *Immigration of Labourers into the West India Colonies*, PP 1846, XXVIII (691-11), 144.
[46] "Trinidad Cooly Regulations," in *Reports from Committees – Sugar and Coffee*, 265.
[47] Ibid., 263.
[48] Harris to Gladstone, July 30, 1846, in *Reports from Committees – Sugar and Coffee*, 265.

The cumulative effect of these regulations was to ensure that laborers could not leave the plantations that had first hired them until the owner and the manager permitted them to do so, regardless of what their contracts said. Estate owners and managers were also encouraged to promote the "religious and social improvement" of their workers.[49] Taken together, Harris claimed, these regulations constituted a "liberal but uniform system of pay and treatment in respect to the coolie labourers."[50] The necessity of this, and of the standardization of wages in particular, was not couched in terms of the economic benefit to the estate owners, which was considerable. Rather, Harris upheld it as a means of preserving public order by preventing the "dissatisfaction" among workers that "invariably result[s] from the cessation of what men, from being long in receipt of [them], regard as rights."[51] Indian labor, in his opinion, could succeed in Trinidad only if the trajectory of amelioration, which had seen customary rights codified as legal ones, was reversed; if any notions of different entitlements between the workers on various plantations were quashed; and if the entire workforce were subject to "just and constant surveillance by the Cooly [*sic*] magistrate."[52]

Grey, who had succeeded William Gladstone as Colonial Secretary, was unequivocal in his response, and demanded that Harris' regulations, already in the process of implementation, be rescinded without delay. He sharply questioned the "wisdom and justice" of such measures, and objected even more strongly to the gross overreach of autonomy they represented, given that "the enactment of laws is manifestly not within the province of the executive government of Trinidad."[53] Although Harris acceded to the demands of his superior, it was only under vehement protest and with an even more stringent reprisal of why expanded state oversight was the *sine qua non* for successfully introducing Indian labor to Trinidad. Employing paternalistic language and horrifying descriptions of the consequences of absconding and vagabondage, he insisted that stern government oversight was a moral, humanitarian, and economic necessity. His proposed regulations, Harris asserted, were the only way to check the advance of "ignorance and vice," halt the spread of disease and destitution, and make the colony prosperous. This expansion of the state's authority over its Indian labor force was irrefutably necessary to ensure that, in time, the island's population would improve mentally and morally, becoming fit to help "civilize the fine and extensive continent in its vicinity."[54]

49 "Trinidad Cooly Regulations," in *Reports from Committees – Sugar and Coffee*, 265.
50 Ibid., 267.
51 Ibid.
52 Harris to Grey, February 21, 1848, in *Reports from Committees – Sugar and Coffee*, 274.
53 Grey to Harris, September 15, 1846, *Reports from Committees – Sugar and Coffee*, 267.
54 Haris to Grey, February 21, 1848, *Reports from Committees – Sugar and Coffee*, 277.

Although not presented in such hyperbolic terms as those employed by Harris, the threat to the health, morality, public order, and economic progress posed by Indian labor immigration was a common issue articulated by local officials across Britain's plantation colonies in the 1840s. Even in those locales, such as Jamaica, that received very small numbers of Indian immigrants, stipendiary magistrates tasked with overseeing them found cause to complain of their alleged gambling, their drinking of rum, and their unwillingness to adopt local customs of dress (or, indeed, any clothing at all).[55] These concerns were countered by those who supported Indian immigration with arguments that Indian workers fared far better in British plantation colonies than they did in their regions of origin. Such claims were strongest in those colonies where the practice of importing Indian labor had been most thoroughly established, where other alternative sources of plantation labor (e.g. emancipated Africans) were limited, where the sugar economy continued to be profitable, and where the cost of labor importation was lowest. Mauritius was the foremost among the regions where planters extolled the virtues of indenture for the workers themselves. Such positive portrayals were exemplified in the Rawson Committee report. As Parliament's most extensive inquiry into the conditions of Indian immigration to Mauritius and the Caribbean to follow its resumption in the mid-1840s, it provided a prominent avenue for the promulgation of these views. In testimony after testimony, plantation owners in Mauritius emphasized that by every possible measure – from health, food, lodging, and medical care to the redress of ill-treatment or injustice – Indian laborers benefited from immigration.

Across the plantation colonies, as Indian immigration and its consequences generated a raft of official reports, magistrates and medical officers served as the eyes, ears, and assessors of the physical, moral, and cultural state not just of Indian workers but of the entire transcolonial laboring cohort. Indian immigrants were not judged in isolation but relative to the habits and character of other plebian cohorts, most commonly emancipated Africans and, in the Caribbean, Madeirans (Portuguese). Liberated Africans' unwillingness to work as plantation laborers, or at least not in the continuous manner desired by estate-owners, and their preference for buying small plots of land for market-gardening or other modest farming pursuits, were common causes of concern. As with the assessments of Indian workers, the level of anxiety over the habits of emancipated Africans expressed by magistrates and, through their reports, colonial governors was relative both to the desirability of their labor and to the judgments leveled against Indian workers. In Trinidad and British Guiana, where the "crisis" of Indian vagabondage was trumpeted loudly and

[55] Report of W. F. Bell (Stipendiary Magistrate) to Governor Bruce, May 1845, "State of the Labouring Population in the West Indies and Mauritius," *Papers Relating to the Labouring Population of the British Colonies – West Indies and Mauritius* (hereafter *Rawson Committee Report*), PP 1846 (691), 8.

where disease had taken a significant toll on both them and Madeiran immigrants, Africans, particularly those imported as free laborers, were praised for their physical robustness and adaptability to local conditions.[56] The tendency of African-Caribbean freedmen to prefer freehold, subsistence farming was regrettable, but not damning of the population as a whole, local officials insisted. In Mauritius, by comparison, where planters' demand and praise for Indian immigrants were both widely expressed, Africans were roundly condemned by local magistrates for their lack of industry, moral failings, and low potential for social and cultural uplift.

Taken together, the raft of official reports and inquiries generated by the resumption of Indian immigration constituted a significant reconfiguration of the racial hierarchies, as defined in policy and both official and public discourse, in the plantation colonies. This reconfiguration was conducted via the interlocking elements of the overseer-state: magistrates, medical inspectors, colonial governors, and their superiors in the Colonial Office. All of those contributing to the effort were concerned about the economic and moral trajectory of colonial society. This concern revolved around the key characteristics by which a liberal vision of moral colonialism and "progress" – economic, social, and cultural – was constructed. Chief among these characteristics were labor discipline, sobriety, religious observance, financial responsibility, and orderly conduct. Regardless of the short-term issues associated with their reintroduction, with some exceptions (e.g. Jamaica), there was general agreement that Indian immigration would be the keystone of future advancement.[57] Even in those regions (such as Trinidad) where the importation of liberated Africans was considered economical and, to some, preferable, the limited supply available and their allegedly inherent racial unsuitability for moral, social, and economic "progress" made them unviable as a long-term solution to the post-emancipation labor shortage.[58] The presumed necessity of large-scale Indian immigration made the physical and moral state of that population a crucial priority. This priority could be addressed, or so officials from the lowest to the highest insisted, only through stern government oversight. Africans, these same officials claimed, could never be inculcated with the "habits of industry, frugality and obedience so highly necessary to their eventually becoming useful members of the community."[59]

[56] Bunyon to Harris, January 6, 1848, *Reports from Committees – Sugar and Coffee*, 246.

[57] In Jamaica, planters argued that the importation of "uncivilized" African and Indian workers not only was unnecessary given the availability of emancipated Africans in the colony but would be detrimental to the social and economic progress achieved thus far by the latter. Thomas C. Holt, *The Problem of Freedom: Race, Labor, and Politics in Jamaica and Britain, 1832-1938* (Baltimore, MD: Johns Hopkins University Press, 1992), 201.

[58] Russell to Metcalf, September 27, 1839, excerpted in Anon. ("A Landowner"), *Demerara After Fifteen Years of Freedom* (London: T. Bosworth, 1853), 41.

[59] J. Regnard, Stipendiary Magistrate (Mauritius), to George F. Dick, Colonial Secretary (Mauritius), December 19, 1845, *Rawson Committee Report*, 352.

The expanded apparatus of the overseer-state played a crucial role in this process of constructing the official and public discourse on race, labor, and immigration. Indians' long-term suitability as a plantation workforce hinged on the efficacy of laws and regulations in molding them into useful, productive, obedient, moral subjects of rule, succeeding with them where it had failed with emancipated Africans. The legacies of amelioration and apprenticeship loomed large in this project. Thanks to the growth of state oversight that had accompanied this regulatory edifice, the necessary mechanisms of labor control were already in place, and were being reinforced with new personnel (e.g. medical inspectors) and new powers (e.g. the invigorated vagrancy laws). Its agents were also the primary assessors of its success (or failure) in its stated aims. Measures to police mobility, to standardize wages and working conditions, and to install documentary protocols of recording and surveillance could all be justified, as they had been with apprenticeship, via paternalistic concern for the physical and moral well-being of Indian immigrants.[60]

With only the vestiges of the once-powerful antislavery movement remaining to challenge this program, and with a Colonial Office that had access only to information generated by the self same apparatus of colonial labor governance, state agents and planters in situ were free to dominate the portrayals of life and work in the sugar colonies. In the reports offered by magistrates, medical inspectors, and colonial governors, economic assessment and moral assessments went hand in hand. Because emancipated Africans in British Guiana, Mauritius, and Trinidad showed a disinclination for subordinating themselves to plantation discipline, they were portrayed as lazy and as lacking the potential to become useful members of the community. Their preference for economic and social independence from the plantation structure, over time, would be employed by their critics as a justification for their marginalization in the political and cultural schema of post-emancipation societies.[61] In this configuration, plantations and their owners, once vilified by the antislavery lobby as economically and morally retrograde, were reconfigured as engines of economic and cultural progress. Those who would work these plantations and, in doing so, submit to their attendant disciplinary regime of state oversight, moral education, hygienic provision, and social subordination would contribute to the grander vision of social and economic advancement. Emancipated Africans, by their refusal, would remain mired in inherent indolence, ignorance, and penury.

This intertwining, via the processes of the overseer-state, of the economic and moral status of different racial groups was illustrated, in microcosm, by the alleged "crisis" of vagabondage among Indian laborers in the Caribbean sugar colonies. In the late 1840s, this crisis and its attendant humanitarian calamity

[60] Tinker, *A New System of Slavery*, 107.
[61] Holt, *The Problem of Freedom*, 182.

served as the immediate catalyst for the general expansion of regulatory powers over Indian immigrants, and for the restriction of their labor mobility most specifically. The dynamics of this crisis, however, shared many elements with the "moral panics" that would promulgate in mid-Victorian Britain.[62] The latter would generate sensational narratives to justify the rapid expansion of surveillance and policing over specific populations deemed to be a threat to the health and morality of the community.[63] Having implemented the new measures, state authorities could then claim victory over the dangers to the public weal, leaving in place an enhanced apparatus of control and monitoring of the targeted groups. In British Guiana, where Light described vagabondage in dramatic terms, the careful recording of immigration numbers, the discrepancy over time between workers being introduced to the estates and those who remained there, and the systematic accounting of sickness and mortality made by the newly appointed medical inspector, Dr. Bonyun, all indicated that some aspects of the crisis were being conveyed with relative accuracy. Imported workers from certain cohorts *were* leaving the estates, and the incidence of sickness and mortality *was* considerable. What is more open to question is the confinement of these issues primarily to Indian immigrants, the interrelation of mobility and health, and the reasons behind their incidence. Looking at the statistics, it becomes apparent that sickness and mortality among imported workers on the one hand and abandonment of the estates on the other, while conflated in the accounts presented by Light and Harris to the Colonial Office, were two quite separate affairs with very different causes at their root.

The detailed statistics gathered by Dr. Bonyun in British Guiana demonstrated that workers brought from Madras were falling ill and dying at a much greater rate than those from Calcutta, and also that they were quitting the estates in far greater numbers – 33.5 percent for the former (i.e. the Madras workers) from 1844 to 1847 versus 7.2 percent for the latter (i.e. the Calcutta

62 A "moral panic," as defined by Stanley Cohen, occurred when "a condition, episode, person or group of persons emerges to become defined as a threat to societal values and interests; its nature is presented in a stylized and stereotypical fashion by the mass media; the moral barricades are manned by editors, bishops, politicians and other right-thinking people; socially accredited experts pronounce their diagnoses and solutions; ways of coping are evolved or (more often) resorted to; the condition then disappears, submerges or deteriorates and becomes more visible." Stanley Cohen, *Folk Devils and Moral Panics* (1972; repr. Abingdon: Routledge, 2002), 1. Moral panic theory in the Victorian British context has been revised and refined in Judith R. Walkowitz, *City of Dreadful Delight: Narratives of Sexual Danger in Late-Victorian London* (Chicago, IL: University of Chicago Press, 1992), 5–6.

63 In the Victorian British context, Stuart Hall, in addressing the "garrotting" panic, has emphasized the increased state control that such events enable and legitimize. See Stuart Hall, Chas Critcher, Tony Jefferson, John Clarke, and Brian Roberts, *Policing the Crisis: Mugging, the State, and Law and Order* (1978; repr. London: Macmillan, 1984), 25–52.

workers).[64] The assessment of absconding and mortality together is telling in itself as it showed that the medical inspector's priority in his reporting reflected the priorities of the governor. Their shared goal was determining the overall loss in labor more than it was in addressing the humanitarian issue of survival for immigrants. More telling still were three other key observations from Bonyun. The first was that Madeirans had mortality rates that matched or exceeded those of the "Madras coolies," the second was that both groups fared poorly in the same geographic locales (river banks), and the third was that both cohorts suffered from intermittent fevers.[65] Although they shared similar profiles of health, sickness, and mortality, however, there was no reported incidence of "vagabondage" among the Madeiran workers, nor were they described has having the same poor habits of diet and hygiene attributed to the Madras cohort. In sum, despite the assertions by Bonyun, Light, and Harris, there was little evidence to demonstrate that the poor health outcomes of Madras immigrants were directly attributable to their departure from the plantations in violation of their contracts (i.e. to "vagabondage").

This does leave open the question of why workers were abandoning their employers, given that the latter were required to provide them with wages, housing, and medical care. Here, Harris' description of the dire financial state of the sugar industry and his proposed response to the vagabondage crisis were revealing. Sugar revenues in Trinidad were plummeting in response to the repeal of tariff controls on foreign imports to Britain, resulting in a more than 10 percent decline in tax revenue from 1846 to 1847 alone.[66] The economic pressures on plantation-owners were compounded by the high cost of imported Indian labor, for which they were required to pay a head tax, and for whom they had to maintain a certain minimal level of provisioning, housing, and basic healthcare.[67] These circumstances, which prevailed across the Caribbean, had driven Trinidadian estate-owners into arrears in wage payments. The failure to pay wages had, in turn, prompted Indian workers to leave the estates in significant numbers.[68] This situation was exacerbated by the poor working conditions and the lack of adequate health provision. Plantation hospitals, according to local agents, had much worse health outcomes than publicly funded district hospitals did. But when asked by Governor Light to support a modest tax rise in order to fund an increase in the number of hospitals and improvements to the general infrastructure of the colony, planters protested loudly, pleading poverty.[69]

64 Bunyon to Harris, January 6, 2848, *Reports from Committees – Sugar and Coffee*, 245–6.
65 Ibid.
66 From £62,703 to £55,107, a difference of £7,596. Harris to Grey, February 21, 1848, *Reports from Committees – Sugar and Coffee*, 271.
67 Ibid., 276.
68 Ibid., 274; Green, *British Slave Emancipation*, 200.
69 Extract from the Minutes of the Court of Policy of British Guiana, January 6, 1848, *Reports from Committees – Sugar and Coffee*, 252–3.

What Harris and Light labeled vagabondage and immorality on the part of Indian workers appears, in this context, to have been little more than a desperate response to unpaid wages and inadequate medical care in a time of rampant illness. The true crisis was one of finance, made acute by the cessation of tariff protection and the chronic overextension of credit that had left planters in a state of unsupportable debt.[70] In such circumstances, and with a waning antislavery lobby unable to hold them to account, planters could justify to colonial executives their unwillingness to support improvements to the colony's medical infrastructure. This edifice, already inadequate to deal with the rapid population growth and other issues fueled by poorly organized labor immigration, failed even more dramatically in the face of increasing disease rates.

The proposed solutions by colonial governors followed a familiar pattern – they demanded an expansion of state control over the entire labor system. Harris's proposed regulations, which were sweeping in character, in addition to providing further means of tying workers to plantations, were also intended to address the neglect by employers that was a key factor driving Indian workers to break their contracts and abscond. Under such rules, planters would have been subject to a stern regime of government inspection requiring them to see to the needs of their workforce and to pay them at a standardized rate. As with the regulations passed during amelioration, the state, through such measures, would extend its supervision not just over plantation workers but over plantation management as well, with the similar goal of ensuring revenue, maintaining public order, and avoiding official scrutiny and public scandal. The conflation of moral and humanitarian arguments with economic assertions that the sugar colonies would become uncompetitive without more state oversight and investment from the metropole was clear from Harris's summation of conditions in Trinidad. Thanks to underregulated and underfunded immigration, the population of the colony, he wrote, was daily advancing both in numbers and "in ignorance and vice."[71] Jails overcrowded with the newcomers would soon become breeding grounds for disease; the public hospital was so unhygienic that patients were turning gangrenous; and "the lunatics and the idiots wander at large about the streets." Only the "fostering care of Great Britain," Harris concluded, could ensure that the population of Trinidad would return to prosperity and become a fit beacon to "civilize" its surrounding environs.[72]

[70] The overextension of credit in the early 1840s was a particularly sore point for Governor Light. Evidence of Sir Henry Light, March 13, 1849, *Report from the Select Committee on Ceylon and British Guiana*, PP 1849 (297), 1.

[71] Harris to Grey, February 21, 1848, *Reports from Committees – Sugar and Coffee*, 277.

[72] Ibid.

Both the expansion of the public health system mooted by Light and Harris's proposal for a radical overhaul of the state's intervention into labor matters came to naught. The first failed because Guyanese planters, reeling from declining profits in the wake of the Sugar Act, balked at the additional taxes required to fund it. The second failed because Grey could not countenance such an enlargement of Trinidad's coercive state apparatus, especially at the demand of local authorities whose own power, and with it autonomy over labor matters, would have grown commensurately.[73] Given the relentless attacks on Jamaica's coercive, post-emancipation labor regulations mounted by Buxton and others and the still-recent scandals that had accompanied the initial experiments in indenture, granting more control to colonial authorities *sans* oversight was politically unpalatable to the Colonial Office.

More successful was the effort by Crown-appointed colonial executives to implement a stronger regime for the inspection, oversight, and policing of workers. The response to the vagabondage crisis across the plantation colonies was to increase the power of vagrancy laws, a measure justified as a moral imperative to address the uncivilized habits of Indians and their tendency toward idleness. With their labor contracts redefined as the sole element permitting them residence, and their role constrained to that of either agricultural worker or vagabond, Indian laborers effectively became a separate legal class, subject to a raft of local ordinances that other workers were not.[74] These regulations became ubiquitous across British plantation colonies, ensuring that the restriction of Indians' internal mobility, their subordination to employers' demands and judgments of labor value, and their hedging in through official monitoring were a common lot regardless of their locale. Such a pattern held true in both Crown colonies and legislative ones – Mauritius adopted similarly strict measures with regard to worker mobility and documentation, as did Jamaica.[75]

[73] Guyanese planters, through the Court of Policy, ardently petitioned Parliament to *reduce* the cost of the government, even as they protested the Colonial Office's failure to allow sterner regulations to be employed against vagabondage "to prevent squatting and idleness." *Report from the Select Committee on Ceylon and British Guiana*, PP 1849 (297), xxiii.

[74] Richard C. Allen, *Slaves, Freedmen and Indentured Laborers in Colonial Mauritius* (Cambridge: Cambridge University Press, 1999), 63.

[75] In Mauritius, Ordinance No. 21 of 1843 prevented imported agricultural laborers (who were overwhelmingly Indian) from working outside the sector without government approval. Ordinance No. 22 of 1847 required Indian immigrants whose contracts had expired to carry documentation attesting to their status. Subsequent ordinances that were passed between 1848 and 1852 expanded these restrictions through a host of measures. Among these included authorizing the arrest, without warrant, of any Indian immigrant lacking either a current employment contract or evidence of their status as a contract-expired worker and the empowering of employers to withhold certificates of discharge (i.e. contact expiration) if they were unsatisfied with the work of the laborer in question. Allen, Slaves, Freedmen and Indentured Labourers, 63. A further act passed in 1864 defined desertion, already punishable under master and servant law, as vagrancy, putting

Though neither Light nor Harris initially received the support they demanded from the Colonial Office, the twin issues of cost and mobility that had accompanied the resumption of Indian labor immigration had been firmly established in official discourse. Woven into the dire descriptions of wandering, destitute coolies; hospitals overflowing with the sick and the starving; and the bodies of dead workers accumulating in the cane-breaks were equally ominous predictions from governors about the economic failure and the inevitable moral and cultural decline of the Caribbean colonies, should government support not be forthcoming.[76] As Harris had written, only a cheap and sustained labor supply, bound by various means to their employers, closely controlled through regulation, and under strict surveillance by an expanded state apparatus could ensure that these territories would remain orderly, humane, and profitable.[77] Such measures, he insisted, jibed with the moral aim of colonial governance, which was to recast the Indian immigrant worker from "a mere animal whose labour is valuable" into "a useful colonist, an industrious and worthy citizen."[78]

By 1851, the combination of gloomy economic reports, the apparent public health crisis, and the persistent lobbying by colonial governors and planter interests had prompted a reversal of Colonial Office policy with regard to Indian immigration to the Caribbean. Grey, the Colonial Secretary, acceded to three-year contracts of indenture as a temporary measure, and the full period allowed for residence by Indian immigrants was doubled from five to ten years.[79] Accompanying these three-year contracts was an obligation for each immigrant to serve an additional two years under indenture unless they bought themselves out for a hefty sum.[80] The offer of free return passage to India was rescinded. The shackling of Indian immigrants with weighty bonds of contract obligation was accompanied by increased state oversight and regulation. This encompassed every aspect of the system, from recruitment

those workers who left the estates without proper permission and documentation in even greater legal jeopardy. Douglas Hay and Paul Craven, "Introduction," in Douglas Hay and Paul Craven, eds., *Masters, Servants, and Magistrates in Britain and the Empire, 1562–1955* (Chapel Hill: University of North Carolina Press, 2004), 42. On the Jamaican vagrancy laws, see Holt, *The Problem of Freedom, 184–5.*

76 Harris, writing to Grey in February 1848, asserted that, in the last 7 months, 250 Indian laborers died in hospital "and a great many in other places" with "the skeletons of Coolies being found in the woods and cane-pieces." Harris to Grey, February 21, 1848, *Reports from Committees – Sugar and Coffee*, 274.

77 Ibid., 271.

78 Ibid., 276.

79 Green, *British Slave Emancipation*, 280; Donald Wood, *Trinidad in Transition: The Years after Slavery* (Oxford: Oxford University Press, 1986), 136; Alan H. Adamson, *Sugar without Slaves: The Political Economy of British Guiana* (New Haven, CT: Yale University Press, 1972), 52–6.

80 Amounting to £2 10*s*. per year. Green, *British Slave Emancipation*, 280.

in India to transportation overseas to the plantation work itself. Colonial governments established emigration depots in Calcutta, overseen by emigration agents, in accordance with the government of India's Emigration Acts.[81] These depots were complete with cooking sheds, sanitary facilities, and provisions for medical care. A Protector and a medical officer were required to inspect each depot once a week to ensure that all relevant regulations were being met and that prospective emigrants were in good physical condition. These officers would also confirm that recruits had engaged their contracts voluntarily and comprehended where they were going and what would be expected of them once they arrived.[82] Meanwhile, at their colonies of destination, many of Harris' proposed regulations for Indian labor were eventually adopted in both Trinidad and British Guiana.[83] In 1854, following the Mauritian example, three-year contracts became the permanent standard in Caribbean colonies as well, as did the commutation fee (now raised to £5) for those workers wishing to avoid the mandatory two-year extension.[84] In 1862, the standard length of contract was raised again to five years.

Supporting this coordination of labor governance between India, Mauritius, and the Caribbean colonies was the state's more substantial commitment to underwriting the finances of indenture and increased coordination between the Colonial Office, individual colonial governments, and the Government of India. The investment in Indian immigration and the expansion of state oversight represented a further evolution of the metropolitan attitudes and official policies driving the growth of the overseer-state. What had begun, with amelioration and emancipation, as a combination of humanitarian commitment to mollify antislavery activists and a liberal interest in free labor was now developing into balder economic pragmatism and a grudging recognition that paternalistic oversight of the colonial labor force was necessary both for moral reasons and to preserve public order.[85] This evolution would cement indenture as the backbone of the labor force in British Guiana, Trinidad, and Mauritius. It would also embed the state as the central actor in the larger schema of colonial labor systems across the Caribbean and Indian Ocean colonies while simultaneously elevating labor regulation to the keystone of colonial rule throughout Britain's tropical

[81] The primary legislation here was Act XV of 1842, which regulated emigration to Mauritius from Calcutta. Act XXI of 1843 lifted the bans on emigration to other colonies, and subsequent acts in 1857 and 1859 imposed regulations for the conditions of passenger ships leaving from Indian ports.

[82] The latter was established through an interview conducted, in the prospective migrant's own language, by the Protector of Emigrants. "Questions Put by the Protector to Emigrants Proceeding to the West Indies," Appendix No. 53, *12th General Report of the Colonial Land and Emigration Commission*, PP 1852, XVIII (1499), 188.

[83] Green, *British Slave Emancipation*, 280.

[84] Tinker, *A New System of Slavery*, 85.

[85] Look Lai, *Indentured Labor, Caribbean Sugar*, 51.

archipelago. The 1850s and 1860s witnessed the harmonization of attitudes, policies, and practices with regard to labor, migration, health, and the maintenance of public order in these regions. This synchronization was necessary because of the accelerating migration of Crown subjects between different colonies, and because of the increasingly vital role that this cohort played in colonial economies. For a transcolonial labor immigration system to operate in an orderly fashion, workers could not have one legal status in their colony of origin and a radically different one at their destination. Accordingly, metropolitan and colonial officials, plantation-owners, and cosmopolitan capital investors would collaborate to create a coordinated *imperial* labor system that combined elements of ameliorated slavery, apprenticeship, indenture, and convict labor.

By 1870, British Guiana alone had expended more than £1.8 million on the importation of Indian laborers.[86] This cost was covered by a combination of taxes on commonly imported goods (borne largely by the general populace), direct investment from planters, and government loans supported by both colonial and metropolitan authorities.[87] The financial instruments that governed the colony's taxation system enabled the state to economically bolster plantation operation. They also connected the plantation system to mechanisms of metropolitan investment, both private and public, which were reorganized to underwrite labor importation.[88] Much of this newly reorganized structure for financing transcolonial labor importation drew on Mauritius for its model, where a seemingly inexhaustible demand for Indian workers had seen the annual numbers of arriving immigrants jump from 5,395 in 1848 to 29,946 a decade later.[89] The results were dramatic. Building on an improving sugar market, the influx of labor allowed new lands to be brought under cultivation, doubling the value of the exported product in Mauritius from 1852 to 1857 and nearly trebling it in Trinidad from 1855 to 1857.[90] These profits, in turn, allowed planters and colonial governments to funnel more money into the support of further immigration, making them less dependent on underwriting from the metropole.[91] At the same time, other British colonies,

[86] Jonathan Connolly, "Indenture as Compensation: State Financing for Indentured Labor Migration in the Era of Emancipation," *Slavery & Abolition* 40, no. 3 (2019), 457.

[87] Ibid., 456.

[88] Ibid., 451–2.

[89] Tinker, *A New System of Slavery*, 95. Much of this growth took place in the 1850s – the number of Indian laborers having remained relatively steady from 1845 to 1852 (46,000 to 44, 632). *Mauritius – Report of the Committee Appointed to Inquire into the State of the Indian Immigrants*, PP 1845 (641), 15.

[90] Jonathan Connolly, "Indentured Labour Migration and the Meaning of Emancipation: Free Trade, Race, and Labour in British Public Debate, 1838–1860," *Past & Present* 238, no. 1 (February 2018), 110–11.

[91] Mauritius' dramatic rise in surplus revenue had allowed it to defray the immense cost of the indenture system in the early 1840s. *Mauritius – Report of the Committee Appointed to Inquire into the State of the Indian Immigrants*, PP 1845 (641), 14.

witnessing the positive economic results of Indian labor, began their own modest immigration programs. They were joined by French colonies, which, having outlawed slavery in 1848, initiated their new Indian immigration schemes with British oversight and sanction. By the 1860s, Indian laborers were arriving by the thousands annually in St. Lucia, Réunion, Dutch Guiana, and Natal, even as numbers continued to rise rapidly in established destinations such as Mauritius, British Guiana, and Trinidad.[92] In the latter two colonies, they were joined by thousands of Chinese indentured workers who were organized by British firms operating out of the treaty ports of Amoy (Xiamen), Canton, and Hong Kong.[93]

From the perspective of planters across the plantation archipelago, indentured Indians offered another structural benefit beyond the continuous labor needed for growing and processing sugarcane – the artificial reduction of wages for plantation work.[94] These workers were deliberately assigned to the lower-paid, low-skill tasks that constituted the bulk of plantation labor. They also provided a ready supply that abrogated the demand for emancipated Africans on the estates. Thus, in colonies where indentured Indians became the backbone of the sugar industry (e.g. British Guiana and Trinidad), indenture served as the economic leverage by which planters and their allies in the colonial government could determine the economic parameters of the *entire* agricultural workforce, both free and indentured.[95] Even in colonies that employed relatively modest numbers of indentured Indians, such as Jamaica, the system depressed agricultural wages, pushing the African-Caribbean workforce further into economic and social marginalization.[96]

By the 1850s, the combination of contract extension, punitive labor laws, and vagrancy laws had ensured that Indian laborers, once arriving at their destination, were fully entangled in a coercive system that was undergirded by state agents, institutions, and policies, but could be wielded in practice by estate-owners and managers. This provided the subordinated, continuous labor force that plantation-owners had been insisting, since emancipation, was necessary for the economic viability of their estates. The process of recruitment and transportation, however, remained a crucial concern. Control over it was a point of contention between estate-owners and officials, who wished for greater freedom and autonomy to increase their labor supply, on the one hand and, on the other, the Government of India, which was acutely

92 Tinker, *A New System of Slavery*, 96–7.
93 Northrup, *Indentured Labor*, 55.
94 This depression in wages as a result of increasing labor supply was one of the triggers of the strike by African-Caribbean workers in British Guiana during the winter of 1847–8. Evidence of Sir Henry Light, March 13, 1849, *Report from the Select Committee on Ceylon and British Guiana*, PP 1849 (297), 1.
95 Green, *British Slave Emancipation*, 581, 592.
96 Holt, *The Problem of Freedom*, 127.

sensitive to accusations that it was failing in its paternalistic obligations to safeguard the well-being of Crown subjects. This anxiety was exacerbated by a series of public scandals that occurred in the 1850s, leaving the Indian Government on the defensive.[97] Tensions were particularly high in the wake of the 1857 Indian Rebellion, which saw both a significant rise in the number of Indians willing to emigrate and increasing demands from planters (Mauritian ones in particular) for more laborers.

With planters now viewed by the Colonial Office and its appointed executives as potential political allies and crucial co-investors in the project of free labor, the plantation system redeemed as the mainstay of economic and social progress in the colonies, and Indian immigrants portrayed as suitable replacements for freed African-Caribbeans, a new villain was needed if further state intervention (and its attendant costs) was to be effectively justified. Such a moral foil was readily available in the middlemen who had been designated as a dire threat to the moral and orderly operation of indenture early on in the system's life span. These villainous intermediaries identified by colonial officials in the new labor system fell into two primary groups. Foremost among them were Indian recruiters known as "crimps" and *kanganis*. Crimps operated in situ, recruiting from Indian villages in the interior and delivering them to points of debarkation on the coast. *Kanganis* were returned workers who organized subsequent migrants from among their kin, villages, and localities and served as leaders of these new recruits when they arrived at the estates. The latter had sprung up initially in the context of labor migration from southern India to Ceylon, later becoming a common element as the system spread to Mauritius and the Caribbean.[98] Another group of middlemen was the *sirdars*, who were also involved in the recruitment process, but operated primarily as headman on the estates themselves, in a capacity analogous to that of the *kanganis*. These middlemen collected fees both from employers and from the workers whose recruitment, transportation, and labor they helped organize.

The issues with recruitment, and with exploitation of vulnerable, ill-informed Indian villagers by unscrupulous middlemen, first came to prominent light with the Dickens Committee report of 1841. The report had been so damning that it had prompted the temporary suspension of labor emigration by the Government of India. Emigration was resumed only after a raft of additional regulations and protections had been imposed, including the appointment of emigration agents at the point of departure and Protectors of Immigrants in the colonies of destination. In this regard, much of the initial

[97] The most damning of these took place in 1856, when inadequate facilities, disease, exposure, and general neglect resulted in a nearly 50 percent mortality rate (273 out of 697) for two shiploads of Indian workers brought to work on two islands off the northern coast of Mauritius. Tinker, *A New System of Slavery*, 90–1.

[98] Tinker, *A New System of Slavery*, 93.

expansion of the apparatus of inspection and regulation both in India and in Mauritius and the Caribbean had been triggered by concerns over the alleged criminality and immorality of what the committee described as "native crimps, styled *duffadars* and *akotties*."[99] The Dickens Committee report was rife with testimony describing the deceit, coercion, and extortion practiced by Indian recruiters who would go to any lengths to secure potential workers and who were merciless in their extraction of money from them. These accounts followed a common thread across a broad spectrum of witnesses, from magistrates and police officials to ships' captains and workers themselves. In government communications across the 1840s and 1850s, *sirdars*, too, were portrayed as venal, callous exploiters of their fellow Indians, even though, when called to give official testimony, they often asserted that they were themselves victims of abuse from owners and managers.[100]

In the face of widespread negative accounts and condemnation, in both official testimony and press reports, the Dickens Committee report called for the entire transportation process to be "superintended by government officers and medical men."[101] This, the report's authors asserted, was the only certain way to avoid the "waste of human life and misery that … will approach to those inflicted on the negro in the middle passage by the slave trade." The lack of clear boundaries of authority between colonial executives in the colonies of destination and the Indian government, along with differences of approach to governance overall, made the coordination of an integrated, harmonized system regulating a worker's transition from one colony to another impossible to achieve.[102] Even as the laws on labor and movement within plantation colonies were coalescing around a common structure of contract law, vagrancy law, policing, and the standardization of wages, health, housing, and provisioning (monitored through official inspections), the regulatory system as applied to recruitment and transport remained patchwork.[103]

The establishment of direct Crown rule over India in the wake of the 1857 rebellion changed this equation. At the core of this next expansion of the overseer-state was a figure who would drive forward both the legal reform of British imperialism and the ideological underpinnings of imperial rule, Henry Maine. Maine is best known as the prophet of "indirect rule."

99 PP 1841, *Hill Coolies and Indian Labourers. Report of the Committee to Enquire into Alleged Abuses in Exporting from Bengal to Other Countries*, Session 1 (45) (hereafter *Dickens Report 1*), 5.

100 Testimony of Sheik Manick, October 1, 1838, 46–8; Testimony of Boodoo Khan, October 1, 1838, 49–50, *Dickens Report 1*; Green, *British Slave Emancipation*, 279.

101 *Dickens Report 1*, 9.

102 Bruce Knox, "The Queen's Letter of 1865 and British Policy towards Emancipation and Indentured Labour in the West Indies, 1830–65," *Historical Journal* 29, no. 2 (June 1986), 366.

103 Tinker, *A New System of Slavery*, 104.

This encompassed the abandonment of a liberal agenda, an embracing of the fundamental cultural irreconcilability between European and non-European societies, and an understanding that self-rule through "traditional" institutions in regions of colonization would avoid the inherently destabilizing effects of contact between modern (i.e. European) and "primitive" (i.e. non-European) societies.[104]

This framework for understanding the inherent tensions of European colonization would, at first glance, make Maine an odd candidate for engineering the harmonization of regulations on Indian emigration. His advocacy of reform there stemmed rather from his training and predilection in jurisprudence, and from his firm belief that the transition from custom to contract lay at the heart of progress from primitive societies to modern ones.[105] Maine's object was to remove the discrepancies that existed between the various emigration schemes that governed the movement of Indian subjects from India both to elsewhere in the British Empire and to those territories controlled by other European powers (e.g. French colonies).[106] Under his guidance as the Law Member of the Governor-General's Council in India, the Indian government passed Act XIII of 1864. This codified and standardized the entire system of Indian emigration, with a particular focus on the process of labor recruitment, inspection, and organization for transportation.[107] All recruits were henceforth to be interviewed by a magistrate in their home districts; all recruiters had to be officially licensed and bound by a stern set of regulations undergirded with the threat of fines or imprisonment; and a strict set of rules was established for the operation of emigration depots in the Indian port cities.

The 1864 Act expanded the direct oversight of state agents as well, enhancing and defining the powers of the Protectors of Emigrants and replacing commissions with salary provisions for emigration agents, thereby abrogating the motivation for overrecruitment or coercion on the latter's part.[108] The permissible treatment of emigrants while aboard ship was similarly enumerated in great detail. Lastly, to address pervasive concerns of sexual immorality among Indian immigrants in their colonies of destination, the gender proportions were carefully delineated to mandate no fewer than 25 women to every contingent of 100 men. The culmination of this raft of regulations was the standardization of practice not only across the British Empire but between India, the empire, and other European colonial possessions as well. At the same

104 Karuna Mantena, *Alibis of Empire: Henry Maine and the Ends of Liberal Imperialism* (Princeton, NJ: Princeton University Press, 2010), 6.

105 Henry Maine, *Ancient Law: Its Connection with the Early History of Society, and Its Relation to Modern Ideas* (London: John Murray, 1861), 46.

106 Tinker, *A New System of Slavery*, 104.

107 Basdeo Mangru, "Indian Government Policy towards Labor Recruitment for the Sugar Colonies, 1838–1883," *Journal of Third World Studies* 9, no. 1 (Spring 1992), 123–4.

108 Emigration Act 1844.

time, more ad hoc practices of local recruitment were now firmly embedded in formal protocols, duly regulated by mechanisms of licensing, inspection, and judicial oversight. Act XIII thus ably achieved Maine's dual goals of legal harmonization and of cementing a definitive shift from customary practice to contract law, at least in that aspect of colonial governance that applied to the recruitment and transportation of labor.[109]

In the passage of Act XIII, revised attitudes toward Indians and their governance in the wake of the 1857 rebellion dovetailed with earlier arguments about the need for state oversight as a prophylactic to the villainy of middlemen in the immigration system. Advocates continued to describe Indian immigrant cohorts on the whole as being obedient and docile, fit material to serve as the plantation workforce. But descriptions of their character and habits increasingly emphasized their fundamental differences from their European counterparts in both character and habit, presenting them no longer as suitable partners for achieving social and economic progress in the plantation colonies.[110] A second assumption popularized in the wake of 1857 was the Indian capacity for sedition, the potential for which stemmed from bad characters seeded among the general population.[111] Both circumstances justified enhanced state power over Indian subjects, whether in India itself or among the expanding cohort of immigrant laborers across the empire. Efforts to "civilize" the Indian population in the plantation colonies, as in India itself, would be scaled back, while mechanisms for extracting labor through punitive laws, under the guise of contracts and allegedly "free labor," would be reinforced. At the same time, concerns over the potential threats to public order posed by Indians would be countered with an increasingly potent structure of policing and state oversight of the entire labor process from recruitment to the plantation itself.[112] Both efforts would be justified by a combination of paternalistic concern for vulnerable Crown subjects, the need to purge villainous middlemen, and the looming danger of seditious elements in an otherwise orderly and docile cohort.

In these reforms of the overseer-state, the Caribbean labor system once again operated as a laboratory of governance, setting the precedent for

[109] This also coincided with the passage of the first federal immigration law in the US, the 1864 Act to Encourage Immigration, which was similarly focused on the issue of contracts.

[110] Mantena, *Alibis of Empire*, 4–5.

[111] Thomas R. Metcalf, "The Impact of the Mutiny on British Attitudes to India," *Proceedings of the Indian History Congress* 23 (1960), 24–31; Kim A. Wagner, "'Treading Upon Fires': The 'Mutiny' Motif and Colonial Anxieties in British India," *Past & Present* 218 (February 2013), 159–97.

[112] Ian Kerr, "Labour Control and Labour Legislation in Colonial India: A Tale of Two Mid-Nineteenth Century Acts," *South Asia: Journal of South Asian Studies* 27, no. 1 (2004), 21–2.

developments that subsequently spread across the empire and beyond. The Indian government's Act III of 1863 and Act IV of 1865 extended the indenture system – with its multi-year contracts, recruit depots, Protectors of Labour, and standardization of pay, provisioning, and housing – to the tea industry of Assam.[113] In India itself, Act VIII of 1859 and Act IX of 1860 had already stipulated the appointment of special magistrates to oversee labor relations in the colony's largest public works project, the construction of the Bhore Ghat railway incline.[114] Like the special magistrates appointed to supervise labor relations in the post-emancipation Caribbean and Mauritius, these officials were granted summary power over both workers and their employers, but their authority over the former far exceeded that over the latter. By the terms of the Acts, magistrates could order employers to pay workers any monies owed or, in lieu of this, to seize the goods of the employer by warrant and to sell them to cover the arrears.[115] Although the extension of state supervision was ostensibly intended to ensure public order and continued progress of the massive undertaking in the wake of a violent wage dispute, the strongest aspect of the new laws criminalized contract violation on the part of laborers. Magistrates were empowered to summarily either fine or compel to labor, without possibility of appeal, any worker in breach.[116] Continued refusal could prompt imprisonment for up to two months with hard labor. The state's power over the Indian labor force more generally was further expanded through the Police Act 1861 (Act V of 1861), which authorized the Inspector General of Police to dispatch additional forces to "any railway, canal, or other public work or any manufactory or commercial concern," in order to maintain order.[117] As was already the case in the post-emancipation Caribbean, in India, increasingly punitive laws for the enforcement of labor contracts were backed up with a more expansive, centralized, and aggressive system of labor surveillance and policing. The deployment of police power to quell worker unrest would become a common occurrence in subsequent decades, setting the precedent for a similar trend in Britain itself across the final quarter of the nineteenth century.[118]

113 For a detailed account of the system's implementation in Assam, see Rana P. Behal, *One Hundred Years of Servitude: Political Economy of Tea Plantations in Colonial Assam* (Delhi: Tulika Books, 2014). See also Tinker, *A New System of Slavery*, 101–2.

114 Kerr, "Labour Control," 14–15. These Acts were based, as had been those governing apprenticeship in the Caribbean, on the much older master and servant laws.

115 Ibid., 15.

116 William Theobold, *The Legislative Acts of the Governor General of India in Council, from 1834 to the End of 1867, Vol. III, 1859–1861* (Calcutta: Thacker, Spink and Co., 1868), 342–4. At its peak in January 1861, the endeavor employed a workforce of 42,000 (Kerr, "Labour Control," 10).

117 Kerr, "Labour Control," 21–2.

118 V. A. C. Gatrell, "Crime, Authority, and the Policeman State," in F. M. L. Thompson, ed., *The Cambridge Social History of Britain 1750–1950, Vol. 3: Social Agencies and*

The expansion of the state's oversight and coercive power over labor could be found in Britain's African colonies as well. One colony alone, Natal, saw the importation of some 160,000 indentured Indians in the second half of the nineteenth century.[119] Facing increasing public criticism, state authorities responded there, as they had elsewhere, by installing a Protector of Indian Immigrants empowered to hear workers' complaints and to investigate grievances. But pass laws, the distance to the Protector's office in Durban, and other barriers both regulatory and practical ensured that laborers' primary experience of the state was through the heavy hand of penalties levied on alleged contract violations and other civil offenses.[120] Sugar and tea planters' abuse of their Indian workers, despite numerous damning reports and repeated scandals, went largely unchecked.[121]

These trends of enhanced government labor oversight in regions of significant Indian immigration stood in stark contrast to what happened in colonies where the collective political power of white laborers was mobilized, the most notable being Australia and Canada. In the latter, as in Britain itself, enfranchisement and union organization among white workers facilitated effective pushback against attempts to strengthen the legal leverage of employers over labor. The lines of racialized labor division became evident in culture in tandem with the growing contrast between the state's rising involvement in regulating non-European labor on the one hand and the *integration* of the white labor force into political dynamics on the other.[122] One clear consequence of this was the *decriminalizing* of labor offenses in Britain and the white-settler colonies, a trend that contrasted with the increasingly punitive labor laws in the Caribbean, Mauritius, India, and other regions where African, Indian, or Chinese labor predominated.[123] In a self-reinforcing cycle, white workers, who had justified

Institutions (Cambridge: Cambridge University Press, 1990), 262, 265–7. One particularly telling trend was the rising conviction rate for common law rioting, which increased from 59 percent at mid-century to 89 percent by the 1890s (ibid., 267).

119 Rick Halpern, "Solving the 'Labour Problem': Race, Work and the State in the Sugar Industries of Louisiana and Natal, 1870–1910," *Journal of Southern African Studies* 30, no. 1 (March 2004), 24–7.

120 Ibid., 27.

121 Patrick Harries, "Plantations, Passes and Proletarians: Labour and the Colonial State in Nineteenth-Century Natal," *Journal of Southern African Studies* 13, no. 3 (April 1987), 376–7; Tinker, *A New System of Slavery*, 247–8.

122 On Canada, see Paul Craven, "Canada, 1670–1935: Symbolic and Instrumental Enforcement in Loyalist North America," in Douglas Hay and Paul Craven, eds., *Masters, Servants, and Magistrates in Britain and the Empire, 1562–1955* (Chapel Hill: University of North Carolina Press, 2004), 214–18. On Australia, see Michael Quinlan, "Australia, 1788–1902: A Workingman's Paradise?" in Douglas Hay and Paul Craven, eds., *Masters, Servants, and Magistrates in Britain and the Empire, 1562–1955* (Chapel Hill: University of North Carolina Press, 2004), 226–31, 245–7.

123 In the UK, the legal power of employers over their workers remained strong, but it suffered significant setbacks in the third quarter of the nineteenth century with the

their need for political power with reference to their innate racial superiority over non-white workers, particularly in terms of their commitment to liberalism, rule of law, and democratic governance, would then employ their newfound power to demand further legal restrictions on the rights and mobility of non-white workers.[124] Alleged racial disparities propagated in the cultural sphere thus became concrete dynamics in law and politics, which, in turn, lent further evidence to discourses of racial difference. First marginalized by cultural and social practices and subsequently persecuted by labor law, free African, Indian, and Chinese workers found that their purported incompatibility with the schema of post-emancipation colonial liberal governance became a self-sustaining process and a self-fulfilling prophecy.

The expansion and codification of a coercive contract-labor system targeted at the expanding system of global migration was hardly confined to the British Empire. Even as Act XIII of 1864 set the terms for Indian immigration to other European colonies, the US, fast on the heels of its own Emancipation Proclamation, was also establishing a framework for legally subordinating workers from abroad with its first federal immigration law. "An Act to Encourage Immigration," following the impetus set by President Abraham Lincoln, authorized workers in foreign countries to pledge their first twelve months of wages to repay transportation expenses, and made such contracts enforceable in the United States even if they were signed on foreign soil.[125] Slowly but surely, a global system of contract-bound, migrant labor, drawn primarily from India and China, was developing, with Britain at the vanguard and enjoying a near-monopoly over the supply. It was made possible by the extension of European hegemony over South and Southeast Asia, the concurrent social and economic crises that colonialism catalyzed (e.g. widespread indebtedness among the Indian peasantry), and the falling costs of trans-oceanic transport.[126] This system, built on a much older tradition of local and regional labor migration, was underwritten by a combination of public and private investment, and enforced through the expanding authority of governments eager to fill the labor demand left in the wake of emancipation.

These structural changes, which made a global system economical from a European perspective, worked in tandem with the deployment of ideological precepts that justified the system on moral grounds. Henry Maine's assertions

passage of the Master & Servant Act 1867 and the British Employer and Workmen Act 1875 (Douglas Hay, "England 1562–1875: The Law and Its Uses," in Douglas Hay and Paul Craven, eds., *Masters, Servants, and Magistrates in Britain and the Empire, 1562–1955* [Chapel Hill: University of North Carolina Press, 2004], 116).

124 The most potent demonstration of this was in the various pass laws and exclusion acts revived for African, Indian, and Chinese workers in Canada, South Africa, and Australia.

125 Edith Abbott, "Federal Immigration Policies, 1864–1924," *University Journal of Business* 2, no. 2 (March 1924), 133.

126 Northrup, *Indentured Labor*, 52, 65.

of both the fundamental difference of Indians from Europeans and the need to protect their traditional society from the destabilizing influence of European modernity would go on to become the central pillar of British colonial governance in Asia and Africa during the second half of the nineteenth century.[127] The contract, and the labor contract in particular, so central to Maine's vision of civilization, would form a crucial bridge between the otherwise incompatible cultural and social systems of Europe and India. Championed as a mechanism both fair and comprehensible, with appropriate state supervision, to proprietor and peasant alike, it would allow the British and other European colonial powers to tap into the vast labor supply of India and transfer it to colonies across the globe while still adhering to the empire's declared mission of moral uplift.

As had been the case with the initial introduction of indenture in the late 1830s, the expansion of the state's power of regulation and oversight, the imposition of multi-year contracts, and the harmonization of rules regarding recruitment and transportation still needed to be defended against those who condemned indenture as a new form of slavery. They also needed to be reconciled with overarching ideas about liberalism, paternalism, moral colonization, and just rule by the officials who composed and implemented them. To achieve this end, administrators in the colonies and the metropole, along with advocates of indenture among the intermingled cohort of colonial estate-owners and cosmopolitan financial interests invested in the plantation and labor transportation infrastructure, echoed the conceptual reconfigurations of the state's role in labor organization that had accompanied emancipation in the Caribbean. They justified the expansion of the overseer-state and its growing authority over an expanding global labor migration with references to freedom, individual choice, and the opportunity offered for Indians to escape poor conditions in India itself.[128] This process of reconciliation had begun with the Dickens Committee, where those with a stake in the plantation economy and its ancillary industries were well-represented among both the committee members and the witnesses interviewed.[129] Despite the generally critical tone of the report and its emphasis on the abuses rampant in recruitment, the committee's conclusion had emphasized that "it is the right of all men to trade in free labour, and especially of him whose only property is his capacity to labour, to sell that commodity to the best profit."[130] To restrict Indian indenture, supporters of the system argued, was to deny Indians both

127 Mantena, *Alibis of Empire*, 7.

128 Holt, *The Problem of Freedom*, xii–xiii.

129 Although the single largest contingent was composed of leaders of the Calcutta reform movement (Reverend James Charles, Russomoy Dutt, and Theodore Dickens, the chairman), the members also included W. Dowson, a Calcutta merchant who was a participant in the "coolie trade." Tinker, *A New System of Slavery*, 66.

130 *Dickens Committee Report*, 9.

the freedom to which all Crown subjects were entitled and the opportunity for economic benefit that was at the heart of "free trade" and "free labor."[131]

Only an enhanced state apparatus, such arguments went, empowered both at the metropolitan level and in the colonial context with the extension of Crown rule over India, could guarantee the freedom and rights of Indian subjects. One advocate of the system even went so far as to catalogue, in great detail, the sufferings of Indians under East India Company rule, enumerating the long list of famines that coincided with it and quoting a prominent official's assessment that the East India Company's governance had been "one of the most extortionate and oppressive that ever existed in India."[132] At the same time, once laborers were bound to their plantations by contract, coercion was asserted by planters, colonial governors, and metropolitan officials to be a fundamental necessity. It was, they argued, the only way to overcome the alleged racial predilections that prompted Indians toward absconding and vagabondage, proclivities that did themselves and the economy on which they were dependent great harm.[133] In a pattern that would become characteristic of Britain's imperial expansion in the second half of the nineteenth century, the language of liberalism and humanitarianism was thus deployed in inverse proportion to its presence in the policies and practices of indenture.

Conclusion

The quarter-century that followed indenture's introduction saw its expansion across the empire's plantation colonies, transforming it from a limited, regional labor system into an expansive, global one. The growth of the overseer-state that accompanied this expansion, justified by the need to protect the rights and freedoms of Indians as Crown subjects, allowed metropolitan officials, working in conjunction with colonial executives and plantation owners, to dictate the terms of work and life for the imported labor force. The subordination of Indian workers, in turn, facilitated the overseer-state's indirect control over the entire colonial labor system of the plantation colonies, from determining the wages for free laborers to setting the standards of provisioning, housing, work hours, and medical care on the plantations and chivvying employers into conformity with new regulations. Even as

[131] Kale, *Fragments of Empire*, 35; Colonial Land and Emigration Committee (CLEC), March 1858, para. 24 cited in Knox, "The Queen's Letter," 361.

[132] Appendix VII, "Objections of the East India Company to the Unconditional and Permanent Emigration of Labourers from East India to Guiana," Anon. ("A Landowner"), *Demerara*, 54–6.

[133] "Those who will labour without the compulsion of force or the pressure of want in any country are few – and fewest of all among Asiatics and Africans in Tropical climates." CLEC to Merivale, December 15, 1858, CO 218/220 fos. 361–78, cited in Knox, "The Queen's Letter," 359.

African-Caribbeans' abandonment of the plantations and the financial crisis of the sugar industry made Indian immigration with government underwriting an economic necessity, or so its proponents argued, the alleged cultural and physical failings of Indian immigrants themselves made the imposition of stern governance a moral imperative. The identification of exploitative middlemen permeating the recruitment system and the scandals provoked by poor conditions of transportation prompted rising calls to extend government regulation into these aspects of the labor system as well.

In the wake of 1857, arguments that Indians were incompatible with "progress" and anxieties about their potential for public disorder prompted further enhancement of colonial labor discipline. At the same time, the Crown's assumption of rule over India facilitated greater government oversight and the regulatory harmonization of the labor exportation system. This oversight expanded in tandem with the system itself as it encompassed newer destinations within the empire as well as colonies under the rule of other European powers. Labor regulation, throughout these decades, continued to develop as the anchor of British colonial rule in its tropical plantation colonies. This was true in a structural dimension, as indenture provided the economic leverage necessary for colonial executives, judicial officials, and estate-owners and managers to control the entire plantation labor structure and ensure the viability of an increasingly volatile sugar economy. It also anchored the ideological dimension of colonial rule as it reconfigured Indian workers on plantations into key targets of governance. Governor Harris's 1846 program for a vast overhaul of the labor regulatory structure in Trinidad, prompted by arguments that the government must collaborate with estate-owners to fill the demand left by the termination of African-Caribbean apprenticeship, would prove prophetic. Initially rejected by metropolitan officials, his proposed reforms would, in a few short years, become common practice from British Guiana and Trinidad to Mauritius and Assam.

The growing entanglement of cosmopolitan private and public finance, the collaboration across different colonial administrations, and the increasing coordination between metropolitan authorities and colonial executives allowed the British imperial state to assume ever greater control of a global labor market in indentured Indians. It also helped cement indenture as a quintessentially modern system embedded in new technologies of bureaucratic governance (e.g. inspection, accounting, and standardized documentation in particular), transportation, finance, and capitalized agriculture. Indenture and its attendant regulatory systems bound Indian workers directly through a coordinated apparatus of laws, institutions, agents, and practices. They also indirectly controlled free African-Caribbean, Portuguese, and other plantation workers through the economic and political leverage that the subordinated labor force of indenture provided. The structural changes in debt-bondage, inspectorial regimes, documentary protocols, and the policing of mobility within plantation colonies themselves were complemented by the increasing government oversight of labor recruitment and transportation across the empire. Changes in the character and enforcement of labor contracts also reverberated throughout the vast span of Britain's imperial edifice.[134] These changes accelerated after 1857, as Henry Maine's arguments about the centrality of contracts and the necessity of legal standardization between different regions provided the blueprint for a harmonized labor exportation system across the British Empire and even to other European colonies. His assertion of the essential differences between Indians, Africans, Asians, and Europeans and the consequent need to shield the former from the disruptive influences of modernity – beyond the mutually beneficial bridge of the labor contract – offered a powerful moral justification for enhancing the state's authority and expanding its infrastructure to oversee this system.

The growth and reform of the indenture system and its attendant state processes reconfigured the Indian immigrant worker as a distinct figure – legally, economically, socially, and culturally – in this new imperial labor system. The "indentured coolie" combined aspects of the free laborer, the settler, the slave, the convict, and the vagrant. They were technically free, but hemmed in by an increasingly powerful and multilayered apparatus of law, inspection, documentation, and policing. Economically, they most closely resembled plantation slaves in their roles; legally, they were subject to many of the punitive regulations that were applied to convict workers; and socially, at least until 1857, they were portrayed as free laborers and potentially as settlers who would contribute to the progress of colonized regions. Their cultural identity, according to those with the authority to define their place in colonial society – most commonly colonial executives, metropolitan officials, magistrates, memoirists, or journalists – was malleable. When advocates of indenture sought state support of the system, they portrayed indentured Indian workers as industrious and docile. But when colonial executives demanded greater government underwriting and an expansion of the coercive legal apparatus, they described the same cohort as idle, sickly, prone to absconding, and potentially fractious.

The expansion of indenture and its attendant state systems, and the underwriting of the institution by colonial governments in collusion with metropolitan authorities, cosmopolitan capital interests, and the plantocracy had consequences that extended well beyond the status and experiences of Indian workers in the empire. Emancipation and the subsequent expansion of the indenture system altered the social, legal, economic, political, and racial hierarchies of plantation colonies, most especially at the top and bottom levels. The traditional plantocracy in places such as British Guiana, Trinidad, and Mauritius remained powerful, but they were forced to trade a significant

134 Hay and Craven, "Introduction," 32–3.

amount of their autonomy in order to enlist the political and financial support of colonial governors and their metropolitan supervisors in the project of recruiting and managing their workforce.[135] Their direct authority over their workers was also superseded, legally, by that of Protectors and magistrates. Freed African-Caribbeans, at the same time, saw the potential to leverage their labor power into economic benefit and some level of political recognition undermined by the large-scale importation of a cheaper, fully subordinated Indian workforce.

This continuous interlinkage and exchange of schemes of regulation, concepts of paternalism and morality, institutions of inspection and policing connected India to the Caribbean and Mauritius, as well as the colonial vision of governance and reform to the metropolitan one. The 1840s and 1850s saw the acceleration of these connections with the colonial state's enhanced role in regulating plantation work, the harmonization of indenture contracts, the government's heightened oversight of recruitment and transportation, and the increasing merger of state support and private capital in the creation of a global market in indentured labor. Accompanying the rising power and prominence of the overseer-state, however, was increasing visibility and accountability for its alleged failings. Even as labor control became an anchor of colonial governance from British Guiana to Assam, the indentured labor system would face stiffening resistance from the workers on the plantations and growing criticism from a wide spectrum of opponents. At the height of its power, the overseer-state would soon become a lightning-rod for challenges to Britain's self-styled image as a moral colonizer, its self-declared goal of just rule, and its self-proclaimed dedication to safeguarding the rights and well-being of its most vulnerable subjects.

[135] Another general trend undercutting the power of the traditional plantocracy was the rising numbers and influence of absentee estate-owners drawn from the ranks of cosmopolitan investors. Nicholas Draper, "The Rise of a New Planter Class? Some Countercurrents from British Guiana and Trinidad, 1807–33," *Atlantic Studies* 9, no. 1 (2012), 71–2.

5

"Man, in His Natural State . . . Must Either Be Led by Conviction, or by Force"

Magistrates, Workers' Agency, and State Violence, 1840–1873

In 1871, on the road to plantation Devonshire Castle in British Guiana, five Indian men were shot dead. Their names, according to the coroner's report written subsequently, were Maxidally, Kaulica, Baldeo, Beccaroo, and Auckloo. We can be assured that in this, at least, the records were neutral and factually accurate. The other conclusions of the Coroner's Court about the circumstances of their deaths were profoundly shaped by the integration of the judicial system, magistrates' authority, discourses of race and public order, and the apparatus of colonial labor discipline. Local courts, in British Guiana as elsewhere in Britain's former slave colonies, served as the uneasy mediator between planters' interests on the one hand and those of the plantation workforce on the other. The coroner's inquest in this instance stood as a stark example of the entanglement between colonial governance and plantation management. The deaths of these five men would be attributed, in the official record, to their unlawful and riotous conduct, their refusal to disperse after the requisite time following the reading of the "riot act" (45 minutes, give or take), and their assault on the attending constables with their agricultural instruments ("hakia sticks"). In contrast to the alleged perfidy of the deceased, their killers would be lionized. "[If] not for the brave actions of the constables," the inquest's key witness testified, "the entire colony would have descended into violence and rapine."[1] At the heart of the complaint that had taken the five men and several hundred of their fellow workers from Devonshire Castle to the magistrate's courtroom and back to the plantation road where five of them would perish was the same figure that would subsequently deliver this testimony. This was the stipendiary magistrate who had commanded the armed constables that fired the fatal shots, Henry Loughran. Both parties had brought to his courtroom, an epicenter of tension in the colonial labor system, differing visions of justice, the rights of workers, the authority of plantation managers, and the role of state agents in labor management. These

[1] Testimony of Henry Loughran, October 11, 1872, *The Coolie Riots in Essequebo: A Report of the Proceedings and Evidence at the Inquest on the Bodies of Five Rioters, Killed by the Fire of the Police (Carefully Corrected and Collated with the Official Records)* (Georgetown: The Colonist Office, 1872) (hereafter *Inquest on the Bodies*), 140.

visions would find expression in the daily interactions between magistrates, managers, and workers that became a ubiquitous aspect of life in Britain's plantation colonies across the second half of the nineteenth century. With five men dead on a plantation road, the public would make its own judgments, as, no doubt, would the wider community of Indian indentured laborers in the colony.

With the fatal clash in British Guiana as its illustrative capstone, this chapter, focusing primarily on Mauritius and British Guiana, examines the development of the overseer-state and responses to it in the middle decades of the nineteenth century. In this period, labor governance expanded to become the single most extensive, and among the most expensive, aspect of colonial rule in the plantation colonies. The fulcrum of these dynamics, in Mauritius, British Guiana, and across Britain's archipelago of former slave colonies, was the Stipendiary Magistracy. This cohort served not only as the intermediary between workers and plantation owners and managers but also as the intercessors between the latter and the colonial executive. The were, furthermore, the means by which official information about the plantation system was generated for transmission and dissemination between colony and metropole. In this capacity, magistrates wielded the authority not just to interpret and enforce labor law but to define the moral dimensions of labor relations and labor governance. Given that such labor was at the core of the social, economic, political, and cultural dynamics of these territories, and that the Indian workers whom magistrates supervised became the single largest population cohort in British Guiana and Mauritius, and one of the largest in several other plantation colonies, this meant that the interactions between workers and magistrates, in many respects, defined what colonial rule *was* in these regions.

Although similar in their structures of state authority and labor regulation, Mauritius and British Guiana provide an illuminating comparison, demonstrating how local conditions and responses could alter the dynamics of labor governance in some respects and fail to do so in others. As explored in Chapter 4, in British Guiana, a relative abundance of imported Indian labor; the successful portrayal of vagrancy and vagabondage as acute social, public health, and economic crises; the absence of alternatives to plantation work for Indian immigrants; and the close collaboration between magistrates and planters all left workers little room to contest the authority of the overseer-state. In Mauritius, by comparison, planters' frenzied competition with one another and with small landowners over a limited pool of workers; the availability of alternative avenues of employment; and dense, extensive networks of community support initially provided Indian indentured laborers with a much greater degree of latitude in their responses. In both locales, however, magistrates' authority expanded over time, allowing them more direct authority over workers and a more central role in plantation labor discipline. Their role vis-à-vis laborers, whether in alleged scarcity or abundance, remained the same – to constrain mobility, preserve public order, inculcate moral habits, and, in doing so, to fulfill the mission of ostensibly just governance while ensuring the economic viability of the plantation system.

Over time, magistrates across the colonies where indenture was employed came to both occupy and embody the highest level of authority to which workers had access, superseding the middlemen of the system as well as the managers and proprietors of the estates. As such, magistrates also increasingly became a focus of workers' efforts to negotiate and contest the plantation discipline system. In this process, workers' adherence to magistrates' authority also became a crucial litmus test for colonial officials' evaluations of Indian laborers as moral, rational beings and fit subjects of liberal rule. The Indian Rebellion formed a crucial context for these interactions since it reframed the meaning and significance of Indian responses to state authority. With humanitarian influence on the wane and concerns over the potentially disruptive impact of a growing Indian indentured population on the rise, the colonial judiciary, while still attempting to rein in the excesses of planters, became more committed than ever to the coercive disciplining of the Indian labor force. This was particularly true in British Guiana, where the fear of rebellion excused, in the public and official eye, even the most brutal repression.

Drawing primarily on the voluminous official records of the interaction between magistrates, workers, estate proprietors and managers, and other colonial officers, this chapter explores the rising tensions that became increasingly apparent at the fulcrum of colonial labor governance in the latter half of the nineteenth century. This inflection point was the ongoing dialogue between indentured workers, magistrates, public commentators, and colonial administrators over the laws governing labor and the principles underlying them. I argue that, despite their position as the anchor of colonial rule in the plantation colonies and their commitment to their vision of just rule and public order, magistrates were not invariably the catalysts of the state's direct intercession in labor relations. That initiative frequently came instead from plantation workers themselves. Building on the protocols established during amelioration and apprenticeship, laborers began bringing grievances and petitions to magistrates nearly from the moment of indenture's introduction. The records of these efforts were written from the perspective of the magistrates, but they attest to the agency of workers. Fragmentary and problematic though they may be, they offer crucial insights into the viewpoints of the many hundreds of thousands who toiled under indenture's heavy yoke. As a counterpoint to the magistrates' perspective, this chapter examines, through the accounts of indentured laborers' engagement with state agents and institutions, how workers articulated their own visions of rights, justice, morality, law, and the changing role of the colonial state in labor relations. Even though their views lacked a coherent ideology and their conceptualizations of the political did not jibe with those of planters or magistrates, their actions had inherent political significance. They influenced both the practices of governance and the public discourse concerning it.[2] Through their contestations with the overseer-state, indentured workers, too, shaped the dynamics of colonial rule.

With the broader evolution of magistrates' and workers' interactions established, the final section of the chapter returns to that fatal day in British Guiana in order to address three crucial questions. Firstly, how did a labor demonstration evolve into a violent clash and how was it subsequently reinterpreted in the official record as the early stages of bloody, colony-wide rebellion, barely averted by the allegedly heroic actions of the magistrate Loughran and his constables? Secondly, how was violence committed against indentured workers by representatives of the state reconciled with the discourses of liberalism, moral colonization, and orderly rule? And thirdly, how did this incident, its intertwining with state processes, and its subsequent discussion in public discourse demonstrate the ascendance of magistrates and their authority as the keystone of governance across Britain's plantation colonies for the rulers and the ruled alike? By the 1860s and 1870s, I argue, the increasing dissonance between Indians' perceptions of justice and their legal entitlements and magistrates' hardening line toward labor discipline and public order prompted more direct resistance on the part of laborers. State representatives, in response, would defend their actions with portrayals of Indian indentured workers as a population that was largely docile and benefited from the colonial labor system, but that was veined through with moral failings and subject to the cynical influence of disruptive individuals. The fissures between the overseer-state and its charges, already apparent even in its early years, would widen into a chasm in this period. A system that billed itself as supportive of free labor, a free labor market, liberal principles, and moral colonial rule increasingly abandoned its paternalist guise to advocate and practice coercion, the restriction of labor mobility, and, when deemed necessary, the violent suppression of workers' collective action.[3]

[2] This follows on the urging of Dipesh Chakrabarty to seek a more heterogenous perspective on the modern state and its attendant institutions. Chakrabarty has advocated moving beyond the assumption of European iterations as the invariable model, in order to instead "provicialize or decenter . . . concepts such as citizenship, the state, civil society, public sphere, human rights, equality before the law, the individual," and to recognize that "the field of the political is not singular." Dipesh Chakrabarty, *Provincializing Europe: Postcolonial Thought and Historical Difference* (Princeton, NJ: Princeton University Press, 2000) 3–4, 149.

[3] For an overview of the broader turn toward a more coercive legal system across the empire (especially Ireland, India, Nigeria, and South Africa) in the second half of the nineteenth century, see Christopher M. Roberts, "From the State of Emergency to the Rule of Law: The Evolution of Repressive Legality in the Nineteenth-Century British Empire," *Chicago Journal of International Law* 20, no. 1 (January 2019), 1–61.

Magistrates as the Lynchpin of the Overseer-State

Well before the Devonshire Castle killings thrust Henry Loughran into the limelight, magistrates had become acutely aware of the key roles they occupied in the burgeoning apparatus of the overseer-state and the degree to which these roles exposed them to public and official scrutiny. Three decades previously, in 1843, one of Loughran's predecessors, the stipendiary magistrate and former Assistant Protector of Slaves in Mauritius, Percy Fitzpatrick, was prompted by repeated incidents of negative press coverage to defend himself to his superior, the Colonial Secretary of the colony.[4] The latter, along with the governor, was the highest government official on the island, representing the authority of, and answering directly to, the Colonial Secretary in London. Fitzpatrick was responding to the public attacks made on him and his colleagues and by the Mauritian press, which had sharply criticized the magistrates' increasingly assertive oversight of labor relations in the colony. At the heart of his defense was the assertion that magistrates' supervision was indispensable to the moral and economic survival of the plantation system. As Fitpatrick explained, "as long as Mauritius requires labourers, stipendiary magistrates or officers with similar or even greater powers must be there, not only to protect the working classes from the innumerable wrongs of which they would be the victims, but also to protect the employers of these men from the results of their own vices."[5] From his position of wide supervision, which encompassed both workers and planters, Fitzpatrick vigorously asserted the crucial role of the magistracy in the colony's governance. He also vehemently rejected accusations of bias and attempts to smear the judiciary by linking their efforts with the legacy of slavery. The faults of indenture, he insisted, "lay not with the magistrates, but in the institution itself."[6]

Magistrates' roles as the lynchpins of the plantation system in Mauritius developed as part and parcel of two key transitions in the colony's history. The first was its passage from a French to a British schema of law and governance and the second was the evolution of its primary labor composition from Francophone slavery to British ameliorated slavery and subsequently to a mixture of free African and indentured Indian labor. Mauritius, the last

[4] Fitzpatrick was originally from Dublin, Ireland, and, like many higher officers in the administration of territories acquired during the Napoleonic Wars, came from a military background. His career in the civil service had been preceded by his work as Assistant Surgeon for the 51st Regiment. He remained on half-pay (typical for officers not on active service) until 1832, when he was appointed as Assistant Protector of Slaves, subsequently being posted as a Special Justice to oversee amelioration in 1836, and finally ascending to the position of stipendiary magistrate in 1839. Blue Book for Mauritius 1842, 353.

[5] Stipendiary Magistrate Fitzpatrick to Colonial Secretary (of Mauritius) Dick, March 15, 1843, Stipendiary Magistrates Records, Magistrates Correspondence 1841–5 (National Archives of Mauritius).

[6] Ibid.

inhabitable area of the world to be discovered and populated by humans, was first colonized by the Dutch in the mid-seventeenth century, passed into French hands in 1715, and was subsequently seized by Britain during the Napoleonic Wars.[7] Its fertile volcanic soil, good natural harbor, and strategic position astride the sea lanes connecting southern and eastern Africa to the Indian subcontinent and Southeast Asia all made it valuable territory. In the eighteenth century, fueled by the growing demand for sugar and worked by slave-labor, Mauritius became one of France's most profitable colonies, and served as a strategically vital port and resupply point in a vast and otherwise nearly landless stretch of the Indian Ocean. It would serve the same role in the British Empire as well. In the 1840s, the judicial system of this remote locale included over a dozen magistrates and their attendant clerks. By the 1860s, this system had grown to constitute the backbone of governance, encompassing ten district magistrates, ten stipendiary magistrates, a police magistrate, and a magistrate assigned to manage the immigration depot in the capital, Port Louis.[8] Working under them was a veritable army of clerks and Indian interpreters, as well as constables seconded to attend their courts. This robust administrative scaffolding was responsible for supervising a population of over 313,000.[9] By the 1880s, the Mauritian magistracy was adjudicating some 20,000 cases annually, or an average of 57 cases per 1,000 residents.[10] The Mauritian magistrates' court system was proportionally far larger, and significantly more active, than its metropolitan counterpart, equalling in size the Police Court Magistracy of London, whose legal authority extended over nearly four million residents.[11]

District magistrates were responsible for the prosecution of criminal charges, largely those brought to them by local police, and for the adjudication of various civil and commercial disputes. Due to the legacy of the island's French legal tradition, most notable in the continued operation of some aspects of the Napoleonic Code, it was difficult for British magistrates to serve in this latter capacity during the initial period of British rule. As a consequence, in the first decades after Britain took control of the colony, the District Magistracy was staffed largely by Mauritians possessed of some

[7] Perry J. Moree, *A Concise History of Dutch Mauritius, 1598–1710: A Fruitful and Healthy Land* (London: Routledge, 1998).

[8] C. M. de Joux, *The Mauritius Almanac and Civil Service Register for 1865* (London: Harrison and Sons, 1865), 26–36.

[9] The Mauritius Civil Service Almanac 1862, 193.

[10] Matthew Lange, "Embedding the Colonial State: A Comparative-Historical Analysis of State Building and Broad-Based Development in Mauritius," *Social Science History* 27, no. 3 (Fall 2003), 405.

[11] The population of London, according to the 1871 census, was 3,840,595. London's outer regions were under the jurisdiction of unpaid justices of the peace, but the metropolitan administrative boundary was co-terminus with its police districts and, prima facie, the authority of the Metropolitan Police magistrates.

French legal training. This branch of the judiciary operated with significant autonomy from the rest of the colony's British-run administration.[12] The Stipendiary Magistracy, in contrast, whose responsibility was overseeing the plantation system and its labor force, was from its inception deeply integrated within the wider matrix of British colonial rule. Its members were thoroughly embedded in a cosmopolitan cohort of officials that spanned the empire. A typical Mauritian stipendiary magistrate in this early stage of British rule was of metropolitan, Mauritian, or British Caribbean origin and had served as a clerk in either the magistracy or another aspect of colonial governance (e.g. the Colonial Secretary's office) before being appointed to their post.[13] By mid-century, much of this initial contrast had lessened, with remnants of French law being progressively overwritten by successive reforms, both arms of the magistracy coming firmly under the oversight of the colonial executive, and individual justices drawn from either French or British backgrounds and moving freely between the district and stipendiary cohorts.[14]

Modeled on the Protectors of Slaves, the institutional origins of colonial stipendiary magistrates lay in the processes of amelioration, abolition, and emancipation.[15] They had been appointed initially in the second decade of the nineteenth century to oversee the new regulations governing plantations, their enslaved labor force, and the conduct of owners and managers. As such, stipendiaries formed the administrative mechanism by which plantation colonies had managed the initial reform of slavery, the transition from slavery to apprenticeship subsequently, and finally the implementation of a free labor system that included both emancipated Africans and indentured Indians. By the 1840s, the Stipendiary Magistracy had become a permanent and indispensable facet of colonial administration across the plantation

12 Lange, "Embedding the Colonial State," 405.

13 For example, Charles Alexander Findlay Stuart Farquharson had served as an Assistant District Clerk (Riviere du Rampart), the Inspector of Distilleries (Mauritius), a Corresponding Clerk in the Colonial Office (Mauritius), and a district magistrate (Seychelles) before assuming the post of stipendiary magistrate for the district of Flacq in 1864. *The Mauritius Almanac and Civil Service Register for 1865* (London: Harrison and Sons, 1865), 34.

14 Such movement was generally from stipendiary to district, since the latter, with wider jurisdiction and higher pay, was considered the superior position in the colony's judicial hierarchy.

15 In Mauritius, the special magistrates were installed following Order in Council of 1834 to enforce new laws on apprenticeship. There were sixteen in 1837, covering the nine districts into which Mauritius had been administratively subdivided in order to facilitate enforcement and clarify the limits of individuals' jurisdiction. Subsequent to the end of apprenticeship, these special magistrates were retitled as "stipendiary magistrates," a process that was similarly followed across the former slave colonies. Moses D. E. Nwulia, "The 'Apprenticeship' System in Mauritius: Its Character and Its Impact on Race Relations in the Immediate Post-Emancipation Period, 1839–1879." *African Studies Review* 21, no. 1 (1978), 91.

archipelago. In Mauritius, as in other colonies, by mid-century, their responsibilities had expanded to supervising the immigration system, ensuring adherence to the wide array of regulations on laborers' work and health (e.g. housing, medical care, and provisioning), hearing the grievances put forth by both Indian indentured laborers and their employers, providing regular reports to the governor on the state of immigrants in the colony, and conducting regular inspections of the sugar plantations. The Indian workers who occupied the majority of stipendiaries' attention comprised the single largest cohort of the colony's population by the 1850s.[16] By the end of the century, they would constitute its majority.[17]

The expansion of the overseer-state in Mauritius played out along similar lines, and with similar justifications, as it did in British Guiana and throughout the Caribbean, but with important variations. Mauritius was among the very first of the colonies to receive indentured laborers in significant numbers, and the first to experience a public scandal concerning them. It was also in much closer proximity to India, and therefore more directly connected with the economy, society, governance, and culture of that region. Lastly, compared to many other plantation colonies, there had been fewer slaves residing in Mauritius and a smaller proportion of that population were agricultural laborers.[18] Therefore, amelioration and apprenticeship did not catalyze the same dramatic expansion of the state apparatus required to regulate plantation labor relations that it did elsewhere. Instead, it was the 1840s and its accompanying waves of Indian indentured immigration that saw the period of fastest growth in the government oversight and regulation of the plantation labor system. The catalysts for this growth were nearly identical to those in British Guiana – an alleged crises of vagabondage and the supposedly pernicious influence of Indian middlemen known as *sirdars* (trans. "headmen" or "chiefs"). The arguments for expansion of indenture and its attendant regulatory structure were also similar – economic justification combined with alleged concern for the well-being of workers, and their physical well-being in particular. And the results were the same – the imposition of much sterner regulations on mobility and employment, and the

[16] In 1846, they comprised a third of the colony's population. Richard B. Allen, *Slaves, Freedmen, and Indentured Laborers in Colonial Mauritius* (Cambridge: Cambridge University Press, 1999), 58.

[17] In 1861, agricultural laborers on the sugar estates, the vast majority of whom were Indian indentured immigrants, numbered 84,727. *Mauritius Civil Service Almanac 1862* (Port Louis: E. Dupuy & P. Dubois, 1862).

[18] For example, whereas the enslaved population of the three colonies that would eventually compose British Guiana was over 100,000, the vast majority of whom were classified as "field laborers," on the eve of emancipation, slightly more than 20,000 enslaved men and women in Mauritius were plantation field laborers. "Abstract of District Returns of Slaves in Mauritius at the Time of the Emancipation in the Year 1835," HA 73 Committee of Council Appointed to Inquire into the Subject of Immigrant Labor in Mauritius, 1844 (hereafter, Immigrant Labor in Mauritius 1844) (National Archives of Mauritius).

intercession of magistrates more deeply into labor relations. In Mauritius, however, Indian workers enjoyed a key advantage. The small size of the emancipated African-Mauritian agricultural labor force, when combined with a rapid growth in the island's sugar economy, created a situation of acute labor demand. This, and the presence of African-Mauritian smallholders who could offer alternative employment, provided Indians in Mauritius with considerable leverage, at least initially, in shaping their conditions of employment.

The efforts of the Indian workforce to assert their agency were made more effective by the awkward position that the newly empowered stipendiary magistracy occupied. Committed, by nature of their training and professional outlook, to rule of law and public order, they struggled to reconcile the expectations of their superiors to fulfill this commitment with the competing demands of their duties. Tasked with overseeing a rapidly changing legal, economic, and social landscape, they faced pressure from employers to discipline allegedly wayward workers and to support the growing sugar economy, on one hand, and pressure from workers to respect their rights and address their grievances, on the other. In contrast to their colleagues in British Guiana, Mauritian magistrates were initially much less willing to be co-opted into planters' desired schema of state-backed plantation discipline. Their belief that a harsh system of discipline would only discourage labor immigration, their desire to disassociate themselves from the moral taint of slavery, their resentment at planters' attempts to impinge on their judicial independence, and their paternalist ideals all shaped their initial approach to mediating labor relations. In the immediate post-emancipation period, magistrates operated less as unproblematic facilitators of planter authority and more as a contested choke-point in the system of plantation discipline.

The strained relationship between magistrates and indentured Indians, and the formers' willingness to abet an increasingly stern apparatus of labor governance, would only develop over time. This tension increased in tandem with the rapidly growing population of indentured laborers, the latter's persistent efforts to leverage the demand for their labor into more favorable conditions of work and pay, and the planters' dogged campaign to define workers' responses as immoral, threatening to public order, and incompatible with rule of law. Magistrates' responses were guided both by their perennial professional skepticism was guided both by the perennial professional scepticism toward the testimony of the lower orders and by pervasive racial stereotypes that depicted Indians, especially in their encounters with legal authorities, as fractious and untrustworthy.[19] Armed with an overweening

[19] This was similarly hardwired into the legal dimension of nineteenth-century labor law in British India. Michael Anderson, "India 1858–1930: The Illusion of Free Labor," in Douglas Hay and Paul Craven, eds., *Masters, Servants, and Magistrates in Britain and the Empire, 1562–1955* (Chapel Hill: University of North Carolina Press, 2004), 430.

confidence in their judgment and autonomy and beleaguered by the ubiquitous complaints of workers, the cavilling of planters, and the probing inquiries of their superiors in the metropole, magistrates, over time, assumed more and more direct power over, and commensurately more public accountability for, labor discipline in the colony. Indentured workers, in turn, adapted their own approaches to compensate for magistrates' increasing authority and hardening attitudes.

In the first decades after emancipation, stipendiary magistrates' approach to enforcing labor regulations reflected the attitudes of their superiors in the Colonial Office and the colonial executive, both of whom were acutely aware – much like Percy Fitzpatrick was – of public scrutiny and the politically sensitive character of labor governance in the former slave colonies. As a consequence, the initial efforts by Mauritian planters to introduce a harsh system of coercive regulation were largely unsuccessful. For Mauritius, a small, isolated colony thousands of miles from both the African and the Indian coasts, emancipation presented a serious logistical challenge. Given its rapidly expanding sugar industry and its significant remove from Britain's Atlantic and Indian Ocean territories, there would be no easy remedy to a labor shortage if emancipated Africans decided to leave the plantations en masse. To compensate for this, when Mauritius implemented the apprenticeship system tying former slavers to a mandatory period of "free" labor on their old plantations, it was accompanied by a proposal to introduce the harshest arsenal of labor laws yet seen in the empire.[20] This constellation of measures included defining *any* period of unemployment by former slaves as "vagrancy," criminalizing unemployment, and instituting a system of forced servitude.[21] Any adult "vagrant," as unemployed former plantation workers were defined, under the age of sixty was required to find gainful employment immediately, and on failure to do so could be forced to labor on public works. Violators of these regulations faced punishments of up to three months' imprisonment on first offense and a year's on the second, with continued failure to secure employment making them liable to a sentence of forced labor on either plantations or manufactories for up to three years. When word of these proposals reached London, however, the government disallowed the measures, asserting that, as free laborers, apprentices could not be hedged in so severely.[22]

The alleged labor shortage in the face of expanding sugar cultivation, combined with the metropolitan government's refusal to subordinate the African-Mauritian population under a harsh labor regime, prompted planters to turn to Indian indentured labor as a potential solution. As described in Chapter 4, this effort expanded rapidly in the decade following emancipation.

20 Ordinance 17 of 1835.
21 Nwulia, "The 'Apprenticeship' System in Mauritius," 92.
22 Ibid., 93.

The rate of labor importation nonetheless failed to satisfy the demands of Mauritian planters. In the mid-1840s, they once again appealed to the Colonial Office to support increased labor importation. They also sought to strengthen the legal apparatus that abrogated open competition between planters, shackled free workers to the plantations, reduced their mobility, and prevented them from using the demand for labor to their advantage. To achieve this empowerment of the overseer-state, planters deployed arguments similar to those they had used to justify the failed attempt to impose coercive legal restrictions on African-Mauritian apprentices in the mid-1830s. Indian workers, or so planters maintained, were inherently idle and could be transformed into productive subjects only through an enhanced apparatus of state-overseen labor discipline.

To these older arguments offered by Mauritian planters were added a number of key elements that paralleled the discourse deployed by their counterparts in the Caribbean. The convergence of planters' justifications in the two regions demonstrated how the expansion of the overseer-state and the institution of indenture in particular were composed not just of a shared apparatus of legal control but also of a common discourse legitimizing it. Among the most important of these common arguments was the elevation of the contract as an inherently moral mechanism that served the interests of worker and planter alike and the conflation of economic, moral, and public health arguments against vagrancy and vagabondage. Other shared elements of planter discourse included the determination to restrict worker mobility while supporting the principle of "free labor" and the identification of *sirdars* as a corrupting element in an otherwise amenable Indian cohort. These arguments were further overlaid – as had been the case during the periods of late-stage slavery, amelioration, and apprenticeship – with planters' assertions of paternalistic concern for their workforce and the insistence that the labor "crisis" demanded immediate and forceful intervention by the state to prevent economic collapse. At the epicenter of this intervention and the resulting tensions across the Mauritian plantation system would be the newly empowered Stipendiary Magistracy.

Both the colonial executive and the magistracy demonstrated an acute awareness of the key role played by Indian immigration and its regulation in the economic and social development of Mauritius. This sensitivity to just how much was at stake prompted the first systematic inquiry into the operation of the indenture system there. The initial cohorts of Indian immigration had been supported by the Mauritian government, which worked with planters to underwrite the costs of immigration and to organize a regular deduction from their pay to cover the cost of return passage. But the poor legal oversight of the system, fraud and wage-robbery by unscrupulous recruiters, the selection of recruits unsuited to agricultural labor, and a host of other issues soon catalyzed a public scandal. Alarm at widespread reports about abuse and corruption prompted the Indian government to ban immigration to Mauritius from 1838 to 1841. Prior to this suspension, the initial cohorts of Indian workers, referred to as "Old Immigrants," had signed multi-year contracts of up to five years in length.[23] To mollify the concerns of Indian government officials, the "New Immigrants" arriving when the ban was lifted in 1842 were typically brought over on contracts of only one year, albeit with the possibility of multiple renewals ("reengagements") at their consent. The reengagement terms of Old Immigrants were similarly of short duration, though the ability of both cohorts to return to India was hindered by the stipulation that their entitlement to passage back at government expense required them to remain steadily employed for five years.[24]

By 1844, only three years after the Indian government had reopened labor immigration to the island, Indian indentured workers had already become the backbone of the plantation labor force. With many of the original contracts of the Old Immigrants having expired and with New Immigrants and reengaged Old Immigrants on short contracts constituting an ever-higher percentage of the workforce, sugar estate proprietors had begun to advocate for a reexamination of the current policies. A government inquiry conducted that year offered them a platform to make their case for the reform of labor governance to both the colonial executive, who would be responsible for instituting new regulations, and the stipendiary magistrates, who would be tasked with enforcing them. As a sign of their growing importance in shaping and implementing colonial labor policy, the stipendiaries themselves were given the responsibility of collecting evidence. The bulk of this would consist of testimony from planters and estate managers who had a powerfully vested interest in the continuation and expansion of the indenture system.

The 1844 inquiry would guide the adoption and enforcement of new policies in the subsequent years. At the core of planters' testimony were four primary arguments for the sterner regulation of Indian immigrants. The first and most pervasive was that the economic viability of the sugar industry depended upon the long-term retention of experienced agricultural laborers. Almost unanimously, planters insisted that new workers were all but useless for the first six

23 This initial cohort, first requested by the Government of Mauritius from the Indian Government, received Rs. 5/- per month in pay, as well as rations, clothing, living quarters, and basic medical care. Pravina Bhim Sain, "A Study of the Problems Faced by Indian Indentured Labour in Mauritius Due to Violation of Contract, 1834–1878," *Proceedings of the Indian History Congress* 41 (1980), 813.

24 They could return at their own expense, and with no requirement to reimburse the government for the cost of their passage from India, a situation sometimes lamented by government officials who felt compelled to reduce the costs of the system whenever possible. In the face of planters' persistent lobbying, the entitlement to free return passage was abrogated in 1851, along with the automatic deduction from wages that covered it. Sain, "Indian Indentured Labour," 818.

months of employment, remained suitable only for light work in the months immediately following that period, and became productive enough to justify the expense of their cost (importation and maintenance) only after a full year.[25] The second was the paternalist assertion that long-term engagement on the same plantation was of financial and moral benefit to Indians as well as being of economic and practical benefit to planters. Contracts of several years' length, such as had been characteristic of the Old Immigrants, brought a number of salutary consequences for workers. Chief among these were the greater likelihood of accumulating savings, the acquisition of good work habits, cleaner residences, the opportunity to raise animals for profit, and the accumulated goodwill of planters motivated to retain steady workers. In contrast, as one Flacq proprietor asserted, those on short engagements "neglect their houses, keep no stock, acquire habits of indifference and indolence, and are fit for nothing at the end of the year."[26]

The third argument repeated ad nauseum by planters and managers was that the common tendency of Indian workers to miss days of labor (absenteeism), to leave the estate either for days at a time or permanently (desertion), and to wander around the island with no fixed employment (vagrancy or vagabondage) were all the result of their innate moral failings. Over and over again, planters referred to "idleness" and a nearly universal "love of change" as indelible aspects of the Indian character. This assessment was echoed with equal conviction by Charles Anderson, the Protector of Immigrants and a key witness in the inquiry, who insisted that even high wages could not overcome these racial propensities. "Indians are naturally lazy," he told the committee of inquiry, "opposed by disposition and habit to constant labor. To the idle, money is no return for the sacrifice of their ease."[27] According to Anderson and others, the Indians' tendency toward vagabondage also posed an acute risk to their health. Severed from the rudimentary medical provision that estates were required, by law, to supply, wandering Indians apprehended by the local constables were often "in a dying state," and had to be nursed back to well-being at public expense in the civic hospital.[28]

The final argument commonly deployed by the planters and managers interviewed was that the peripatetic tendencies of Indians were grossly

[25] Evidence of M. Margault Decourcay, Bon Air (Pamplemousses), October 22, Immigrant Labor in Mauritius 1844, 1; Evidence of Mr. Baudot, Poudre D'or (Riviere du Rampart), October 22, Immigrant Labor in Mauritius 1844, 5; Evidence of M. Blancard, Beauchamp (Flacq), October 22, Immigrant Labor in Mauritius 1844, 9; Evidence of Mr. Rudelle, La Barraque (Grand Port District), October 29, Immigrant Labor in Mauritius 1844, 18.

[26] Evidence Mr. Blancard, Beauchamp (Flacq), October 22, 1844. Immigrant Labor in Mauritius 1844.

[27] Evidence of Charles Anderson, Protector of Immigrants, December 1844, Immigrant Labor in Mauritius 1844, 66.

[28] Ibid., 66.

exacerbated by the nefarious practices of *sirdars*. The greed of these experienced Indian headmen knew no bounds, they insisted, and they were relentless in the exploitation of those under their influence. Knowing that they would receive a bonus for delivering new bands of men to estates thirsty for labor, these work-bosses "induce laborers by false promises and delusive prospects to leave [their current employer], and then sell them to some other planter, regardless of the men's interest."[29] "The employment of Sirdars," one Pamplemousses planter asserted, "is at the root of the evil," while his colleague from Plaine Wilhelm decried them as "a great curse to the Island."[30] One of the most damning accounts of *sirdars*' alleged perfidy came from the sole Indian proprietor interviewed, who told the committee that "they are like leeches. They bleed the laborers and rob the Masters of their men."[31] The practices of unscrupulous *sirdars* were aided and abetted by unprincipled planters. Such men were willing to take on new workers even when they lacked the necessary paperwork proving the lawful termination of their previous contracts. This widespread practice of labor poaching was known as "*embauchage*" (which translates as "hiring").[32]

According to planters and managers, as a result of these issues and the widespread use of short-term labor contracts, the continued viability of the Mauritian sugar industry was in serious jeopardy.[33] Any supposition that Indian laborers were using the demand for their services as leverage to secure higher wages, that is to say, that they were engaging the free labor market that had been so touted as central to indenture's moral superiority over slavery, was roundly dismissed. Even as witnesses insisted that Indians' "love of change" was an intrinsic racial characteristic, they also asserted that stability of labor on the plantations was an achievable goal. The crux of the problem, according to managers and planters, was the inducement to desert provided by *sirdars* and *embauchage*. Should such temptation be removed, they argued, Indian workers were perfectly capable of finding contentment, health, moral improvement, and even substantial financial reward on plantations where they remained long

29 Evidence of Mr. West, The Vale (Pamplemousses), October 22, 1844, Immigrant Labor in Mauritius 1844.

30 Ibid. Evidence of Mr. Riviere, Palma (Plaine Wilhelm), November 12, 1844, Immigrant Labor in Mauritius 1844, 47.

31 Evidence of Mr. Tiroumondy, Bon Espoir (Riviere du Rampart), November 5, 1844, Immigrant Labor in Mauritius 1844, 41.

32 Evidence of Mr. Jamin, Savannah and Eastwick Park (Savanne), Chauvot (Riviere du Rampart), and Victoria (Flacq), November 5, 1844, Immigrant Labor in Mauritius 1844, 30.

33 Planters often lost large swathes of their labor force just when they needed them the most, and were forced to leave their estates to go hunting for new bands of workers rather than ensuring that their crop of sugarcane was properly harvested and processed. Evidence of Mr. Rudelle, La Barraque (Grand Port), October 29, 1844. Immigrant Labor in Mauritius 1844.

term and developed a mutually beneficial relationship with their employers. Restriction of worker mobility was thus presented by planters as far more than an economic necessity for the survival of the Mauritian sugar industry. In their testimony, it became a profound moral obligation, the benefits of which to workers far exceeded whatever might be lost through the abrogation of a free market for their labor. Under the insidious influence of *sirdars* and the unscrupulous practice of *embauchage*, such a market could never truly be free in any case, merely exploitative to either a lesser or a greater degree.

In response to this moral imperative, estate proprietors called for an extension of labor contracts ("Contracts of Service") from one year to five years.[34] Anticipating, by decades, Henry Maine's focus on the contract as the mediator between Europeans and non-Europeans, planters enshrined the contract as the primary mechanism by which employers would exert a civilizing influence over their workforce and through which the inherent cultural differences between Indians and Europeans could be bridged.[35] Such contracts were inherently fair and moral, they maintained, and the pervasive disregard for them by Indian workers only further demonstrated both their immorality and their ignorance. Planters argued that the essence of free labor lay not in the ability of laborers to move between employers and seek better wages but rather in their ability to voluntarily sign Contracts of Service. By extension, the height of immorality was workers' rampant violation of these agreements or, worse yet, their willingness to work *sans* any signed contract at all.[36]

Given these circumstances, planters insisted that the state had a moral obligation to enforce the contract system. Stipendiary magistrates, they asserted, would continue to play a crucial role as mediators between employers and their workforce, ensuring that the workers' rights were respected, protecting them from abuse, and arbitrating any disagreements over wages, contracts, or work conditions.[37] Magistrates' chief priority, however, must be to ensure that *all* workers signed proper Contracts of Service, that no employers took them on without this and other elements of official documentation (e.g. tickets of discharge from their former employers), and that violators of either requirement were disciplined appropriately. Since all indentured workers were already required to certify any new engagements before the stipendiaries, this represented a natural extension of the latter's current responsibilities. Such expressions of paternalism by planters belied a much more coercive structure at the heart of labor governance in

[34] Evidence of Mr. Baudot, Paudre D'or (Riviere du Rampart), October 22, 1844, Immigrant Labor in Mauritius 1844, 7.

[35] See discussion in Chapter 4.

[36] Evidence of Mr. West, The Vale (Pamplemousses), October 22, 1844, Immigrant Labor in Mauritius 1844, 15.

[37] Evidence of Mr. Rudelle, La Barraque (Grand Port), October 29, 1844, Immigrant Labor in Mauritius 1844, 22.

Mauritius. As in British Guiana and other former slave colonies, the authority of magistrates in Mauritius over the plantation workforce was undergirded by the stern regulations on desertion, vagabondage, and "idleness" that persisted as the legacy of ameliorated slavery and the apprenticeship system. These ordinances criminalized labor offenses and severely constrained workers' mobility through a strict regimen of documentation and surveillance.[38]

Magistrates, for their part, confident in their ability to intervene in a manner that benefited both workers and planters, were eager to expand their role in labor governance. In their own testimony, they called for a far more dramatic extension of their authority over the plantation system than that suggested by proprietors, albeit in a paternalistic rather than a coercive guise. Given the pervasiveness of what those on the 1844 Commission referred to as "the Grand Maroonage" (i.e. mass desertion) that was afflicting Mauritius, greater judicial oversight was required not merely over the workers but over employers and, most especially, over *sirdars* and other middlemen in the system.[39] Only by such measures could the moral progress of the colony as a whole be sustained and its economic viability assured. Of equal importance was the inculcation, through the stern enforcement of contractual obligations, of the moral habits that allowed liberal society and its attendant freedoms for the individual to coexist with the social and economic well-being of the community. As the magistrate Severin Seignette explained, "man, in his natural state . . . must either be led by conviction, or by force."[40] Where the former was lacking, the latter, in the form of magistrates' authority, would need to be deployed. Reviving the pass laws that had criminalized the mobility of slaves, Seignette proposed that any time a worker left their assigned estate for any reason, and for whatever length of time, he be required to carry a ticket from his employer justifying his absence. Said document could be demanded by any state officer. "By these means," the magistrate expressed confidently, "vagrancy will diminish or

38 The Order in Council of September 17, 1834 was a key piece of legislation in this regard. Nwulia, "The 'Apprenticeship' System in Mauritius," 90–1.

39 On colonists' perennial fear of maroonage, see Clare Anderson, "The Politics of Punishment in Colonial Mauritius, 1766–1887," *Cultural and Social History* 5, no. 4 (2015), 412. For discussions of vagrancy, see Anderson, "Politics of Punishment," 418–19; Satyendra Peerthum, "History of the Vagrant Depot of Grand River North West (1864–1886)," in Vijaya Teelock, ed., *The Vagrant Depot of Grand River, Its Surroundings and Vagrancy in British Mauritius* (Port Louis: Aapravasi Ghat Trust Fund, 2004), 88–93.

40 Evidence of Severin Seignette, Stipendiary Magistrate, November 30, 1844, Appendix, Immigrant Labor in Mauritius 1844, 150. Severin was originally from La Rochelle, France. Like Percy Fitzpatrick, his colleague, he had served as a special magistrate during amelioration before being appointed as a Stipendiary in 1839. Blue Book for Mauritius 1842, 353.

entirely cease."[41] Such measures, far from being contrary to the principle of free labor, were "sanctioned by the most liberal Nations of the Earth."[42]

Seignette further proposed that magistrates be granted the authority to cancel contracts outright, "thus rendering justice to the parties," be they workers or employers. Much like the planters had, the magistrate singled out *sirdars* for particular opprobrium. They fed off of the innate greed of workers, who were "weak-minded people," and in doing so were the "ruin" of planters both financially and morally, beggaring them with their exorbitant fees and corrupting them by demanding bribes for the provision of workers.[43] Reprehensible, too, were the cohort of "interpreters" and "speculators" that had accompanied the recent tranches of immigrants. Only an empowered magistracy could compensate for these insidious influences, Seignette insisted, and restore the earlier, idyllic state of affairs in which workers had "acted with a natural and free will, expressing honestly their demands."

Seignette's colleague, H. M. Self, went one step further, advocating more expansive powers for magistrates over employers and workers alike. To ensure "justice to the labourers," he insisted, if contracts were to be extended to multi-year affairs, magistrates should be empowered to fix wages in accordance with the typical rates of pay from year to year.[44] To halt *embauchage*, and the vagrancy and desertion it fostered, magistrates should also be authorized to impose fines as high as £20 on any employer, "of no matter what class or condition, who should be found harbouring or employing a Deserter or Absentee."[45] In this measure, Self tangentially acknowledged a key concern that the planters had stated explicitly: the significant competition for labor posed by former "Old Immigrants" and African-Mauritian small land-owners whom Indian workers sought out as alternatives to employment on the plantations.[46] Given that the practice of taking on laborers without engagements was more common among these lesser landholders, such a regulation would have fallen most heavily on them rather than on the large-scale plantation owners. The latter, who actively poached entire bands of laborers, could absorb such penalties if necessary, while the small cultivators whose economic survival was precarious to begin with could not. For the magistrates, workers' mobility and the competition for their labor among employers were justified neither by the principles of liberalism nor by those of a free labor market.

41 Evidence of Severin Seignette, 151.

42 Ibid., 152.

43 Ibid., 146–7.

44 Evidence of H. M. Self, Stipendiary Magistrate, November 25, 1844, Appendix, Immigrant Labor in Mauritius 1844, n.p.

45 Ibid.

46 Evidence of Mr. Jamin, Savannah and Eastwick Park (Savanne), Chauvot (Riviere du Rampart), and Victoria (Flacq), November 5, 1844, Immigrant Labor in Mauritius 1844, 32.

Instead, they represented a combination of immorality, irrationality, and illegality that was incompatible with public order, social stability, and economic progress. For magistrates, stern, paternalistic judicial oversight of the entire labor system was the *sine qua non* of just and moral colonial rule in Mauritius.

Charles Anderson, the current Protector of Immigrants, a former justice of the peace and stipendiary magistrate, and arguably the most prominent state representative interviewed by the committee, echoed many of the negative views of Indian laborers offered by planters and magistrates.[47] He shared their belief that a reinvigorated state apparatus, one whose control over labor extended from the point of origin to the plantations themselves, was urgently needed. Laborers hired by the new government-licensed agents now operating in India would provide recruits with an honest appraisal of terms and conditions of work, ensuring that those who emigrated would be suitable for plantation labor and predisposed to find long-term satisfaction with their lot.[48] The system of documentation and magistrates' oversight must also remain rigorous, both to protect the workforce from unscrupulous *sirdars* and planters and to make certain that laborers remained with the proprietors who had underwritten the costs of their immigration. For all his faith in government oversight, Anderson was dubious that sterner policing alone would lessen desertion. "An Indian once a maroon [i.e. deserter]," he told the committee members, "always remains so."[49]

By the mid-1840s, stipendiary magistrates' authority, in line with their demands and the continuing complaints from planters about the prevalence of desertion and vagabondage, had been extended to encompass a wide scope of labor governance. Powers that they had formerly wielded by custom had been expanded and codified through a succession of ordinances. Their original duties to adjudicate all complaints brought by either workers or proprietors remained the centerpiece of magistrates' daily duties, along with certifying the engagements of new labor contracts and ensuring that the latter were entered into only after the earlier engagements had been completed. As had been the case since the Order in Council of 1839 (Article 8), magistrates had the authority to cancel Contracts of Service if they judged that the terms had been violated by either the worker or their employer. By mid-century, however, magistrates were taking a much more direct role in the management of plantation discipline. They were empowered to remove *sirdars* from their roles, to compel workers to return to their estates, and to deploy a raft of other coercive measures in

47 Blue Book for Mauritius, 1842 (National Archives of Mauritius).
48 Ibid., 67.
49 Ibid., 66.

order to make sure that workers honored their contracts.[50] These measures included consigning workers to the stocks or docking them up to a month's pay.[51]

In succeeding decades, stipendiary magistrates in Mauritius and across the former slave colonies took on a number of new roles. Through a succession of ordinances, colonial legislatures in plantation colonies, looking to Mauritius and British Guiana for precedents, extended magistrates' authority not only over the plantation system and labor relations involving *all* workers, be they indentured or free, but into a broad range of activities involving their growing Indian and Chinese populations. By mid-century, stipendiaries in Mauritius had become the de facto and de jure overseers of the entire Indian population, responsible for governing their work conditions, their legal status as residents, their mobility between employers, and even their health and well-being. Procedurally, this authority was expressed through their ubiquitous adjudication of complaints by workers and managers, their certification of Contracts of Service, and their prosecution of workers for the substantial raft of labor-related offenses, alleged contract violations, and the ever-present vagrancy charges.

Magistrates' growing authority was backed not just through new regulations but also through the expansion of resources available to them and of institutions under their purview. By 1865, each of the ten stipendiary magistrates in Mauritius earned £300 annually and was granted an additional £150 in "horse and house allowance."[52] Beneath them worked a senior clerk (paid £150–£250 annually), one or two junior clerks (£100–£150), an interpreter (£60–£100), and a messenger (£24–£36). Additionally, there were typically two police constables assigned to each court, serving as bailiffs and delivering or executing warrants as needed. In 1864, a Vagrant's Depot was established in Grand River, with a stipendiary assigned to supervise it, making weekly inspections and ordering punishments for violators when deemed necessary.[53] This institution replaced the more ad hoc treatment of deserters via the Government Depot for indentured labor immigrants that had been set up in 1843 under the oversight of the Protector of Immigrants. Across the plantation colonies, the Protectors remained a crucial aspect of labor governance, were paid substantially more (in Mauritius, £1,000 plus £100 in expenses, annually), and occupied a higher position on the governmental table of precedency than magistrates did.[54] Despite such recognition, the trend over time was for

[50] Stipendiary Magistrate Jules Reynard to Colonial Secretary (Mauritius) George F. Dick, May 29, 1843, Stipendiary Magistrates Records, Magistrates Correspondence 1841–5.

[51] Remarks, Establishment of the Stipendiary Magistrates of the District of Grand Port, Mauritius Blue Book 1850, n.p.

[52] Almanac 1865, 34.

[53] Anderson, "Politics of Punishment," 419.

[54] Almanac 1865, 34.

Protectors' duties vis-à-vis labor to become more focused and constrained even as those of the stipendiaries became more expansive. The close association between stipendiaries and Protectors remained evident in the professional background of the latter, who, by long-standing tradition, were typically drawn from the ranks of the senior stipendiaries.[55] By the 1860s, however, Protectors had largely ceded the role of monitoring workers and mediating conflicts to their judicial confreres.[56]

In Mauritius, as in other plantation colonies, with Indian workers rapidly growing to become a plurality, and in some cases a majority, of the population, criminal justice also operated increasingly as an extension of plantation discipline. This system was overseen by the stipendiaries' superiors in the judicial hierarchy, the district magistrates. The vast majority of the criminal charges that the latter adjudicated were brought against the colony's Indian population. District magistrates were well-accustomed to dealing with this cohort as they almost invariably served as stipendiaries for several years before being promoted to their new posts. The two judicial cohorts were largely responsible for monitoring the same population, the primary difference being in the types of activities they dealt with and the strength of the disciplinary tools at hand. Granted the responsibility for adjudicating more serious offenses and armed with the authority to inflict higher fines and longer terms of imprisonment, district magistrates administered the boundaries of conduct, while stipendiaries played a more ubiquitous role in daily affairs. The latter were involved, on a regular basis, in the everyday operation of plantations and oversaw the behavior, discipline, movement, and documenting of *all* workers and of most aspects of the plantation labor system, from contracts and finances to health and provisioning. District magistrates became involved only at the extremes of workers' behavior, such as acts of violence or theft, disruptions of public order (e.g. drunkenness), or threats to public safety (e.g. unsafe driving of carts or other vehicles, cruelty to animals, the setting of illegal fires). As criminal offenses, these violations were deemed serious enough to involve constables and merit the possibility of significant fines or lengthy imprisonment on conviction. The latter was a punishment that, unless the worker was deemed truly irredeemable or incontrovertibly guilty, a planter or manager was unlikely to pursue, given the loss of labor it entailed. Though

55 Charles Anderson, mentioned earlier, was originally a stipendiary magistrate. Similarly, Henry Nicholas Duverger Beyts, who assumed the role in 1861, had spent two years as a magistrate's clerk before serving a further five years as a magistrate in a succession of districts around the colony. Almanac 1865, 44.

56 The parallel evolution of stipendiaries and Protectors stretched back to the period of amelioration, as the powers of the special magistrates originally appointed to oversee it had been modeled on those of the Protectors of Slaves. Mary Turner, "The British Caribbean, 1823–1838: The Transition from Slave to Free Legal Status," in Douglas Hay and Paul Craven, eds., *Masters, Servants, and Magistrates in Britain and the Empire, 1562–1955* (Cambridge: Cambridge University Press, 2004), 315.

even in cases of imprisonment, the state found ways to make such workers productive, as hard labor was de rigueur in most convictions.[57]

The careful statistics collected annually by each branch of the magistracy attested to this contrast between the daily involvement of the stipendiary magistrates and the more constrained but severe interventions of the district magistrates. In the 1860s, it was not uncommon for a single district in Mauritius to have thousands of workers every year file complaints against their employers with stipendiary magistrates, and for those employers to, in turn, submit many hundreds of complaints against them (see Table 5.1). By comparison, the typical district magistrate, even in the busiest and most populous district (Port Louis), prosecuted fewer than 2,000 Indians each year, the vast majority for driving offenses, while in the other districts, a few hundred prosecutions annually was more the norm.[58]

Table 5.1 *Complaints to the stipendiary magistrate, Mauritius, 1866*[59]

District	# of complaints servant vs. master	# of individuals complaining (if known)	# of complaints master vs. servant	Court fees paid by servants	Court fees paid by masters
Flacq	909	4 004	743	£800 16*s.*	£74 6*s.*
Grand Port	1 838		702	£367 12*s.*	£70 4*s.*
Plaines Wilhems	524		317		
Pamplemousses	2 583		589	£516 12*s.*	£58 18*s.*
Savanne	2 173		1 073	£434 12*s.*	£107 6*s.*

[57] Report by F. M. Randall and Stipendiary Magistrate Pearce to the Colonial Secretary (Mauritius), George F. Dick, March 20, 1841, Stipendiary Magistrates Records, Stipendiary Magistrates Correspondence, Port Louis, 1841–5.

[58] In 1874, the criminal court at Port Louis, the capital, convicted 1,697 Indian men and 36 Indian women, the most common offense being the contravention of driving regulations (1,093), followed distantly by unlawful possession of stolen property (249), larceny (145), and blows and wounds (121). The criminal court at Grand Port, another populous district, demonstrated a similar pattern, with 846 (793 men, 53 women) out of a total 1,016 prosecutions being against Indians, the most common offenses being road contraventions (177), larceny (149), drunkenness and disturbance (89), assault (73), and keeping a fire in a hut (62). In Moka that same year, the criminal court convicted 580 Indians (542 men and 38 women) out of a total 688 convictions. In Plaines Wilhems, the numbers were 143 (141/2) out of 166, respectively, and in Black River, a mere 73 (6/13) out of 86 total convictions. Records of the Magistrates (Mauritius), RA 2230 (National Archives of Mauritius).

[59] Stipendiary Magistrates Records, Stipendiary Magistrates Correspondence, 1867–8 (National Archives of Mauritius). The standard fee for complaints by servants against masters was 4s., while the standard fee for masters against servants was 2s.

Magistrates' commitment to plantation discipline, rigorous application of the law, maintenance of public order, and vision of just governance were not confined to Indian workers, even if they were the focus of most daily efforts. They were confident in their role as the arbiters of moral rule over the colony as a whole, and more than willing to extend their authority over proprietors and the entire cohort of those involved in sustaining the sugar industry. The frequent solicitation of stipendiaries' advice by colonial governors and the expanding suite of regulations governing plantation management became a self-reinforcing cycle. As new policies were mooted, the colonial executive sought the opinion of magistrates, who invariably advocated the increase of their own authority and the expansion of their oversight. When, in Mauritius, Ordinance 21 of 1854 authorized planters to deduct two days' wages for every day a worker was absent (the infamous "double-cut"), the governor turned to the stipendiaries for their views on its merits and liabilities. The magistrate Alexander Magard responded with an expansive analysis not just of the causes of absenteeism and possible solutions but of the larger social and moral issues that shaped Indian workers' behavior in the colony. The increased deduction of wages, Magard insisted, would only worsen the problem of absenteeism.[60] Magard's colleague in Flacq, J. Jeffroy, was even more vehement in his objection to the "double-cut" penalization for absence. Such "harsh measures are not even advocated by the most intelligent Planters," he insisted, "both from humane motives" and because they were dubious that such means would reduce desertion.[61]

Woven throughout these discussions were increasingly explicit expressions by magistrates that indenture and the plantation system, *sans* their stern oversight, tended toward corruption and immorality. This slow rot, they suggested, stemmed from the failings of everyone involved in the system, apart from the magistrates themselves. The innate moral weaknesses of Indian workers were certainly lamentable. Indian workers, wrote one magistrate in 1855, were possessed of a "natural idle disposition" combined with an "aversion for regular and assiduous labor."[62] The only solution to desertion and absenteeism, he insisted, was "more repressive means to check said offenses." But no small part of the moral, legal, and social issues that accompanied the expansion of indenture stemmed from the greed of unscrupulous proprietors and the influence of insidious middlemen, among whom relentless competition for a limited and febrile pool of laborers encouraged unethical practices and cavalier treatment of the law. *Sirdars* remained a perennial source of complaint for magistrates, who

60 Alexander Magard, Stipendiary Magistrate, to the Governor of Mauritius, August 13, 1855, Stipendiary Magistrates Correspondence 1855.

61 J. Geffory, Acting Stipendiary Magistrate (Flacq) to J. Dowland, Colonial Secretary (Mauritius), August 14, 1855, Stipendiary Magistrates Correspondence 1855.

62 Freemantle, Stipendiary Magistrate to Acting Colonial Secretary (Mauritius), August 15, 1855. Stipendiary Magistrates Correspondence 1855.

bemoaned their pernicious influence on workers and their relentless efforts to lure them off one estate and onto another.

By mid-century, such rogues had been joined by a new villain, the "Job Planter" or "Contractor." These shadowy figures, according to the magistrate Edward Martindale, owned no property themselves, and sought their fortune through the organized poaching of laborers from estates. They operated through a colony-wide network of sub-recruiters, "sowing disorder on Estates where all seemed tranquil before, unsettling the minds of the labourers, and exciting some by false promises to desert."[63] Job Planters easily defrauded the key concrete mechanism of magistrates' authority over the workforce, official documentation, by providing laborers with tickets of engagement and certificates of discharge from contracts gleaned from other workers. Barring the implementation of stricture measures against them, Martindale argued, such men, already "a scourge to the Colony," would prove to be "destroyers of all law and order among the Indians."[64] In subsequent years, such requests for the extension of regulatory authority over estate proprietors in general and Job Planters and Contractors in particular would remain a common theme in magistrates' communications with their superiors.[65]

As vehement as their condemnation of Job Planters was, the most common cause of magistrates' concern and the group over which they most consistently sought greater authority was Indian workers themselves. Indians' increasing engagement with the courts over time, largely through the complaints process, and their greater familiarity with the laws and regulations governing their labor were causes of particular concern. In the Stipendiary Courts, wrote the magistrate James Wildman, "summonses are often maliciously taken out by persons who fail to appear on the [adjudication] day or who have no just cause for complaint."[66] The ubiquitous practice of workers bringing complaints against their employers was even more alarming to those tasked with addressing them. Such complaints were often delivered en masse by dozens, scores, or even hundreds of workers at a time. These gangs of workers (or "lumps," as one magistrate called them) would collectively halt work and march to the courthouse to deliver a coordinated set of grievances at the magistrate's doorstep. Such broad-ranging complaints, conveyed by so many individuals and involving so many witnesses, were viewed by magistrates as being nearly impossible to adjudicate fairly. They were emblematic of the problems posed to plantation productivity, public order, and rational governance by Indians' inherently

63 Edward Martindale, Stipendiary Magistrate, to the Colonial Secretary (Mauritius), August 23, 1855, Stipendiary Magistrates Correspondence 1855.

64 Ibid.

65 Stipendiary Magistrate Reneuf (Pamplemousses) to the Colonial Secretary at Port Louis, July 9, 1867, Stipendiary Magistrates Correspondence 1867–8.

66 James Wildman, Senior Stipendiary Magistrate to the Colonial Secretary (Mauritius), February 15, 1867, Stipendiary Magistrates Correspondence 1867–8.

disruptive character and behavior. Workers' tendency of "rushing 'en bande' to complain," according to the magistrate Charles Farquharson, was "an evil which creates considerable disorder and indiscipline on the Estates, and not infrequently clouds the true state of things with an impenetrable veil."[67] The only solution, he maintained, was to charge *every* individual involved the 4-shilling court fee required, a policy that would certainly have produced a windfall for the courts, the busiest of which were already collecting hundreds of pounds annually in fees (see Table 5.1).[68] Even the Indian interpreters attached to the courts insisted that the central feature of these complaints was exaggeration and outright duplicity.[69]

The shift in tenor of magistrates' views on the Indian population followed a clear trajectory. In their earliest vilification of unprincipled planters and grasping *sirdars*, and in their later critique of contemptible Job Planters and mendacious, disruptive workers' complaints, magistrates often couched their calls for more authority and oversight in paternalistic terms. The enhancement of their role in labor relations, they insisted, was necessary to protect Indian laborers both from unfair practices and from their own moral failings. In this, they were hewing their predecessors' vociferous assertions that "Indians should be regarded as free men on a perfect equality of legal rights with all others of Her Majesty's subjects."[70] Over time, however, as the Indian workforce grew in number, became ever more crucial to the island's economy, and occupied more and more of magistrates' time with complaints, contract violations, absenteeism, desertion, vagrancy, and criminal offenses, the focus of magistrates official and public commentary changed in tone. This was apparent in the 1840s with their descriptions of Indians alleged "idleness" and "love of change" as the primary obstacles to stable plantation production. By the mid-1850s, adding to these moral failings, magistrates commonly pointed to Indians' disregard for law, disrespect for contracts, and cynical manipulation of the mediation process (e.g. through frivolous or unfounded complaints against their employers) as crucial issues. And for all magistrates' continued assertions of paternalistic concern for worker's rights and well-being, their official and public pronouncements underscored an increasingly powerful belief that indenture and the orderly conduct of those under its contracts were the indispensable core of the Mauritian plantation economy.

As had been the case in British Guiana and elsewhere, as slavery became, over time, a more distant reference point, Mauritian magistrates' negative

[67] Charles Farquharson, Stipendiary Magistrate (Flacq) to the Colonial Secretary (Mauritius), May 10, 1867, Stipendiary Magistrates Correspondence 1867–8.

[68] Ibid.

[69] Testimony of Ramdoss, interpreter at the Stipendiary Magistrate's Court (Flacq), January 17, 1868, Stipendiary Magistrates Correspondence 1867–8.

[70] Percy Fitzpatrick, Stipendiary Magistrate, to George F. Dick, Colonial Secretary (Mauritius), June 22, 1841, Stipendiary Magistrates Correspondence 1841–5.

views of Indians and their conviction that only stern and consistent discipline could ensure moral progress, social stability, and economic viability became more and more prominent. Their occasional challenges to managers, proprietors, Job Planters, and other figures wielding power in the plantation hierarchy were in no way an attack on the plantation system itself and the subordination of the Indian labor force that sustained it. Rather, they represented an effort by these officials to *sustain* the system by curbing, with the fair and judicious exercise of their own authority, what they saw as the sometimes illegal, frequently unethical, and often arbitrary conduct prompted by a competitive labor market. Magistrates' oversight, in their own view, was the only sure pathway to just and moral governance that benefited all of the colony's residents, not least by safeguarding the policies and practices that made immigration and indentured labor a viable option for Indian workers and a tolerable one for the Government of India.

Workers' Responses in Mauritius

Taken from another perspective, that of the workers involved, magistrates' records offer a very different view of the evolving relationship between the overseer-state and those it governed. Although the increasing coerciveness of the system is clearly evident, so, too, is the agency of Indian laborers and their astute adaptation to the shifting hierarchies of authority that shaped plantation life in Mauritius. Workers, through frequent engagement with magistrates, keenly tracked and effectively responded to the changing structure of authority in the plantation system. Strikes and direct resistance were ineffective and ran the risk of harsh prosecution. As such, they were rarely deployed in the initial decades of indenture. Instead, workers' responses typically consisted of appeals to the magistrates, mass grievances, and the strategic deployment of mobility as leverage. These measures were employed in a complex relationship with their own authority figures (*sirdars*), plantation managers, and the colony's African-Mauritian community. Indentured workers' responses, in many ways, demonstrated continuity with the practices of ameliorated slaves and, later, apprentices, for whom the magistrates, in their earlier incarnation as Protectors of Slaves and special magistrates, had also been a key counterbalance to the authority of planters. In these negotiations, indentured laborers were not merely pragmatic but also asserted their own notions of justice, rights, and morality, contesting both the practices of plantation discipline and the principles of free labor and just governance that served as its ostensible underpinnings. Workers' agency thus helped shaped both the concrete conduct of the overseer-state and its ideological justifications.

Read from the viewpoint of the workers, the 1844 Mauritian inquiry into the indenture system referenced earlier in the chapter offers one clear demonstration of just how quickly workers adapted to the changing labor landscape of the colony. What managers and magistrates derided as a racialized "love of change" can be seen instead as a rational response to opportunity. With long-term contracts in abeyance and proprietors eagerly competing for their labor, laborers employed their newfound mobility to seek better conditions and better pay from other employers. And unlike slaves and apprentices before them, indentured workers in Mauritius had an attractive alternative to plantation work. By 1838, freed African-Mauritians, who comprised one-fifth of the colony's population, had become formidable landowners in their own right, controlling between 16 percent and 20 percent of the island's agricultural wealth.[71] They were joined by a contingent of "Old Immigrants" who, following the conclusion of their multi-year contracts, had used their savings to purchase their own modest parcels of land.[72] Working for this cohort of small-scale agricultural employers appealed to Indian workers since they did not require contracts of any sort and they were willing to pay competitive wages.[73] Some Indians who left the plantations also found work with African-Mauritians in a variety of other capacities, most commonly as assistants or personal servants, while others went to the towns or to Port Louis, the capital, to ply a trade or work as hawkers.[74]

Planters' condemnation of African-Mauritian and Indian small proprietors for harboring "vagabonds" and their demands that sterner legal measures be imposed to punish employers who made hires *sans* official Contracts of Service were couched with a combination of paternalism and alarmism; they expressed concern for workers while voicing dire predictions about the potential collapse of the plantation system. But these objections, while dissimilar in tone, were both based on the underlying argument that Indian workers were incapable of making moral or rational decisions about their labor and that harsh measures were required to lessen the appeal of alternative avenues of employment. Despite the common advocacy of indenture under the principles of "free labor," the competition for such labor was thus presented as one of the main causes of illegal and unscrupulous behavior among workers and planters alike. Magistrates, for their part, were well aware that most alleged "vagrants" and "deserters" had simply taken on work elsewhere under informal agreements.[75] Nonetheless, they supported a stern regulatory response to these practices.

[71] On patterns of land ownership in post-emancipation Mauritius, see Allen, *Slaves, Freedmen and Indentured Laborers*, 79–135.

[72] Evidence of Mr. Riviere, 9695–9696, Immigrant Labor in Mauritius 1844.

[73] The 1844 Inquiry revealed strong evidence of planters' collusion to keep wages standardized at around 5 rupees a month and, in doing so, to reduce any motivation for workers to leave one plantation for another in hopes of higher wages.

[74] Evidence of Mr. Jamin, Savannah and Eastwick Park (Savanne), Chauvot (Riviere du Rampart), Victoria (Flacq), Immigrant Labor in Mauritius 1844, 32.

[75] Testimony of H. M. Self, Stipendiary Magistrate, November 25, 1844, Appendix, Immigrant Labor in Mauritius 1844.

They did so in the name of public order, moral reform (i.e. inculcating habits of industry and combating "idleness"), and the planters' economic needs. Magistrates also evinced a firm conviction that for their own good and that of their community, Indian workers must respect both the law and the judicial authority through which it was implemented. Disagreements over work conditions had to be mediated by the magistrates – any other course of action taken by laborers was deemed both illegal and immoral.

Beyond leaving the estates to work for small proprietors or seek other forms of more flexible employment *sans* contracts, Indian workers adopted a number of different strategies to leverage power in an environment characterized both by increasing labor demand and by increasing judicial oversight. The most common and widespread was their tendency to negotiate the terms of their service collectively in bands numbering from a few dozen to over a hundred. Such bands typically operated under the leadership of a *sirdar* who represented the workers both to employers and to the magistrates who oversaw and ratified their contracts. Potential employers were faced with the option of hiring either the entire group or no one at all. Facing limited alternatives, most obliged.[76] Such bands, having signed on at the same time, would also announce their intention to depart as a group when their contracts neared an end. This put additional pressure on proprietors, for whom such mass departures were extremely disruptive, to reengage them at higher pay or under better conditions.

Workers also responded directly to attempts at monitoring their movement through documentary methods, the most common being the requirement to have a signed and ratified ticket of discharge from the previous employer before they could engage with a new one. Intentionally misplacing tickets, using the tickets of other workers, or altering the tickets were all common strategies, though the first of these became increasingly risky as laws mandating some form of documentation, on pain of arrest and imprisonment, were introduced by mid-century. One widespread practice was to erase the name of the employer from their current employment certificate in order to demonstrate their availability for engagement elsewhere. Such a tactic also abrogated any possibility of confirmation through inquiry with their former master, since the altered certificate offered no clue as to who that might have been.[77] Laborers also sometimes made a verbal commitment to a proprietor, but subsequently refused to ratify the agreement before a magistrate unless certain terms were met.[78]

76 Evidence of Mr. Riviere, 9696, Immigrant Labor in Mauritius 1844.

77 Evidence of Mr. West, The Vale, Pamplemousses, October 22, 1844, Immigrant Labor in Mauritius 1844, 15.

78 Evidence of Mr. Riviere, Palma Plaine Wilhelm), November 12, 1844, Immigrant Labor in Mauritius 1844, 50.

Another strategy deployed by workers was to contest the measure of time stipulated in their contracts. As the termination of multi-year engagements approached, different bands would assert that, according to their own standard of dating (e.g. lunar months), their period of employment had expired and they were free to leave the estate. Planters and managers, on the other hand, hewed to a fixed idea of time based on the common European standard of numerical months independent of the lunar cycle. When workers pressed the issue, plantation authorities could threaten to bring a case to the magistrate's court, where a judgment favoring the managers (the typical outcome) could cost the workers penalties to their wages or an involuntary extension of their contracts to recover the lost labor.[79]

When considering the various responses workers employed to counter an increasingly rigid and coercive labor regime, *sirdars*, the perennial villains of magistrates' accounts, appear in a new light. In the adaptation of workers' agency to the rising authority of magistrates and the increasing suite of regulations, and in magistrates' response to workers' tactics of mobility and negotiation, the *sirdars* played a crucial role. It was these "headmen" who often bargained, on behalf of a band, with employers to determine the conditions for engagement. And it was *sirdars* who managed the official certification of that engagement before the magistrate, although each individual worker was required to attest personally as well. Vilified by employers and magistrates alike as the primary instigators of *embauchage*, ruthless exploiters of workers for their own gain, and saboteurs of both social order and the rule of law in the colony, *sirdars* remained the key point of interface between laborers and higher authorities, whether in the courtrooms or on the plantations.

The increasing power of *sirdars* was made possible by the continual operation of indenture over its first decade in Mauritius, and by the abrogation of long-term contracts in the early 1840s, when immigration resumed after the temporary ban imposed by the government of India. The persistent growth of indenture allowed those who entered the system early on (i.e. the "Old Immigrants") to accumulate both financial resources and experience of the labor immigration and governance system.[80] The switch from long-term to short-term contracts in a period of growing labor demand created a more fluid labor environment where movement between employers from year to year became the norm rather than the exception. In this environment, *sirdars* operated as the organizers of mobile bands, taking best advantage of their knowledge of the labor pool in India and of the labor conditions in Mauritius.

[79] Evidence of Mr. Rudelle, La Barraque (Grand Port), October 29, 1844, Immigrant Labor in Mauritius 1844, 19.

[80] The "Old Immigrants" are reported to have accumulated hundreds, and in some rare cases thousands, of rupees in savings across the course of their multi-year contracts.

The typical routine was for them to offer potential employers the engagement of a band on condition of a bonus paid directly to them, proportionate to the number of laborers under their purview.

The increasing vilification of *sirdars* in magistrates' commentary and in the public dialogue of proprietors and managers was accompanied by the overseer-state's concrete efforts to supersede their role in the Mauritian labor landscape. By the mid-1840s, magistrates had been empowered to remove *sirdars* from their positions, should they contravene the increasingly stern and expansive suite of labor regulations. This was not an effective solution to undermining their authority, however, since it was a general practice for bands to appoint a new *sirdar* in the absence of one. Instead, magistrates worked to replace the influence of *sirdars* with their own. They did so by encouraging workers to appeal to them directly, by actively intervening in labor disputes, by holding managers to public account for obvious or egregious contract violations, and by publicly declaring their opposition to employers' arbitrary behavior or abuse of power. Magistrates' vociferous opposition to the "double-cut" was one prominent example of this. Their determined pursuit of employers who defaulted on payment to workers, to the point of the seizure and sale of their property to recover wages in arrears, was another.[81]

As with their intercession into the behavior of workers on the issues of "maroonage," "idleness," "vagrancy," and "love of change," magistrates justified their moves to regulate *sirdars* and reduce their influence over workers in moral terms. Couching their increased legal authority in the language of paternalism made their disciplining of these either self-appointed or communally elected headmen appear to be neither a response to the latter's growing economic leverage in an allegedly "free labor market" nor an attempt to hem in a strategic response to planters' insatiable demand for labor. Instead, state intervention was portrayed as a moral and economic imperative. Cutting *sirdars* out of the equation of labor management would, according to magistrates, both protect laborers from their "secrete motives of Interest," on the one hand, and save "the poor Planter ... from complete ruin," on the other.[82] *Sirdars* also provided magistrates and planters alike with a convenient scapegoat for the failings of indenture, and reconciled the strengthening of state intervention with the principle of free labor. With *sirdars*' pernicious influence replaced by magistrates' salutary oversight, these arguments ran, indenture would provide planters and the colony as a whole with the necessary workforce at competitive wage rates. Of equal importance, this substitution would render Indians "more perfect labourers" in the process, ensuring their smooth

[81] Report from Renouf, Stipendiary Magistrate (Pamplemousses) to the Colonial Secretary (Mauritius), July 9, 1867, Stipendiary Magistrates Correspondence 1867–8.

[82] Evidence of Severin Seignette, Stipendiary Magistrate (Port Louis), November 30, 1844, Appendix, Immigrant Labor in Mauritius 1844.

incorporation into a morally just, socially stable, and economically profitable schema of colonial productivity.[83]

Although magistrates' saw their rising authority as a natural outgrowth of their paternalism and dedication to moral governance, indentured workers' agency was crucial in this process. By mid-century, they had adapted their strategies to recognize that stipendiary magistrates were now the ultimate authority in the plantation labor system; the increasing prominence of stipendiaries' courtrooms as locales of labor mediation was as much due to workers' willingness to employ them as it was to magistrates' efforts to make them so. And while employers' complaints against their workers were a common occurrence, it was workers' complaints against their employers, which exceeded the former by multiples in terms of numbers and by orders of magnitude in terms of the individuals involved, that made the courts' labor mediation a daily affair (see Table 5.1). Looking at the scale of the state's involvement in plantation labor relations, the number of complaints filed by workers against employers at the Pamplemousses Stipendiary Magistrate's Court in 1867 (2,583) is impressive enough. This number, however, belies an even more extraordinary level of entanglement between the plantation workforce and the stipendiaries. Whereas slaves or apprentices had typically complained either as individuals or in relatively small groups of a half-dozen or so, indentured workers often complained in the same format in which they negotiated their contracts – en masse as a "band." Any given complaint could involve dozens or even scores of individual workers who would leave the plantation together, march to the local courtroom, and crowd the courtyard of the stipendiaries' venue, barraging the clerk with their appeals. It was not uncommon for groups of fifty, sixty, or more to coordinate such mass complaints.[84]

Much as enslaved men and women and apprentices had before them, Indian indentured laborers voluntarily engaged the magistrates' courtrooms for a broad variety of reasons. Most commonly, they brought complaints against their employers. The most typical causes of official complaints were unpaid wages. Other common catalysts for grievance included excessive work and failure to provide adequate provisions. Such complaints were often accompanied by a litany of other concerns as workers took the opportunity to publicly air their dissatisfaction with the general conditions of employment on any given

[83] "The advantage [of long contracts of indenture] was a more regular and constant application to labour, and thus they obtained such a practice in their Employment, which of itself, must have rendered them more perfect 'labourers.'" Ibid.

[84] Some magistrates saw the assembly of so many aggrieved workers alone as a serious threat to public order. In 1844, one Mahebourge Stipendiary even ordered a petitioner who had publicly exhorted sixty-three of his coworkers to press their cases put into the stocks as a punishment for his "insolent conduct in the presence of the many people assembled." Harrison, Stipendiary Magistrate, to the Colonial Secretary (Mauritius), December 2, 1844, Stipendiary Magistrates Correspondence 1841–5.

estate. As was the case during amelioration and apprenticeship, it was very difficult for petitioners to convince magistrates that the substance of their grievance was valid, and it was a common outcome for the workers themselves to be punished for bringing unfounded or "frivolous" cases. But the process of complaint itself could often bring some level of informal resolution. This helps explain why workers filed grievances in such great numbers despite the high likelihood that the official verdicts would be against them.

It was common for *sirdars* to play a variety of pivotal roles in these complaints. *Sirdars* could be the instigators of grievances, either leading a group of laborers in their petition or convincing them to approach the magistrate themselves. Workers, for their part, could support their *sirdar*, or in the latter case could blame them for forcing them to bring a false complaint against their employer. These complaints could become a forum in which workers sought the magistrates' intervention in conflicts with either their employers or their *sirdar*, or, in some cases, with both. Magistrates were particularly severe on *sirdars* whom they surmised from workers' testimony were encouraging their subordinates either to file complaints in an effort to leverage their employer or, worse yet, to abscond. The typical punishment for a complaint judged to be groundless by the magistrate was the loss of a week's wages and a short period of imprisonment with hard labor. In contrast, the magistrate Peter Regnard, on more than one occasion, penalized workers in allegedly "malicious" complaints much more severely. In such cases, his standard sentence was the deduction of a month's wages for the complainants, and for the *sirdar*, two weeks' imprisonment and the permanent loss of their position and its accompanying wages.[85]

Besides the wide range of issues and the use of formal procedures to obtain informal redress, the engagement of indentured workers with local courtrooms shared another crucial feature with the precedents established by slaves and apprentices in previous decades. The cases that Indian workers brought against their employers, although typically revolving around specific claims of misuse or contract violation, were frequently couched in moral terms and employed the language of justice and rights. Such was the case in the exhaustive efforts of Tiagrassen, Ibrahim Said, and Miguel, three Indian indentured laborers in the service of Mr. Dubois D'Unilae of the Plaine Wilhelm district. All three asserted that while they had been absent from D'Unilae's estate on three months' punishment duty (breaking stones in the Port Louis prison, known as the "bagne"), their employer had sold their personal livestock of pigs and fowls. After multiple attempts to seek redress via the usual channels, the three men, representing a much larger group of fifty-five Indian laborers, had taken the

[85] Peter Regnard, Stipendiary Magistrate, to George F. Dick, Colonial Secretary (Mauritius), May 25, 1845; Peter Regnard, Stipendiary Magistrate, to George F. Dick, Colonial Secretary (Mauritius), May 29, 1845, Stipendiary Magistrates Correspondence 1841–5.

extraordinary measure of sending a written petition to the Colonial Secretary of Mauritius. The latter had appointed stipendiaries Francis Randall and William Pearce to investigate the issue. Testifying before them in 1841, Miguel explained that every time a grievance on the subject was brought before the local magistrate, his employer would mobilize other workers on the estate to bring a counter-complaint, accusing him and his comrades of insulting D'Unilae's wife.[86] The three men painted a dire picture in which their employer not only robbed them of their property but attempted to frame them for vandalism, refused to pay their wages, and repeatedly bribed other workers to undermine their efforts at gaining redress. Both Tiagrassen and Said complained bitterly of being denied "justice" no matter to whom they turned, the latter to such a point of despair that he would soon drown himself.[87] The magistrates, after extensive interviews with all three men, rejected their claims as absent of proof.

The complaint of the three workers ultimately failed, but the complex and convoluted interplay of moral narratives, the employment of witness evidence, and the use of legal protocols and language in this case and others like it are revealing. They demonstrate how intertwined the plantation system had become with stipendiary courtrooms, and how familiar workers had become with the judicial authorities who were responsible for governing their labor. This entanglement was the result both of magistrates' top-down efforts to expand their authority over the plantation system and the lives of indentured Indians more generally, and of the latter's voluntary engagement with the growing apparatus of state labor regulation. At the heart of this apparatus lay the magistrates and their courtrooms. Serving as forums for workers to contest the authority of their employers, demand pay and better conditions, or negotiate the terms of contracts, the increasing court usage advanced the magistrates' goals as well. Stipendiaries used workers' complaints as an opportunity to expand and solidify their authority. Every case offered a chance for magistrates to remind both workers and their superiors that *they* were the ultimate arbiters of the plantation labor system and that any attack on their independence would be to the detriment of the colony's legal, social, and moral fabric.[88] Prosper D'Epinay, the Procureur and Advocate General of Mauritius, and therefore its highest authority on all matters of legal practice and doctrine, expressed his support for this stance with a vigorous defense of magistrates'

[86] Report by Francis Minoch Randall and William Pearce, Stipendiary Magistrates, to George F. Dick, Colonial Secretary (Mauritius), March 20, 1841, Stipendiary Magistrates Correspondence 1841–5.

[87] Ibid.

[88] The "independence of justice," argued Magistrate Percy Fitzpatrick, was "a quality … precious to the public" and to reduce it would undermine their faith in the system, forcing them to "plead before a shadow." Percy Fitzpatrick, Stipendiary Magistrate, to George F. Dick, Colonial Secretary (Mauritius), June 22, 1841, Stipendiary Magistrates Correspondence 1841–5.

autonomy in 1851. Above all, he wrote, magistrates must respect one another's decisions. Any internal conflict, should the Indian workforce get wind of it, would undermine their judicial authority, weakening the keystone of public order in the colony.[89]

By the 1860s, the entanglement of courts and plantations had become so ubiquitous that stipendiary magistrates were requesting the imposition of additional fees in order to lessen the deluge of workers' court summonses. The original purpose of free summonses, the magistrate James Wildman wrote to the Colonial Secretary, had been "to enable the poor and ignorant classes to obtain justice easily."[90] But for African-Mauritians, the circumstances had changed so much in the course of the generation since emancipation that such "protection" was no longer necessary, while Indian workers now appeared so abundantly as suitors in the District Courts that their close familiarity with both "law and language" must be taken as a given. Originally intended as a shield, for both cohorts, summons had become a sword, "maliciously taken out by persons who fail to appear on the cause day or who have no just cause for complaint."[91] Wildman's comments were emblematic of the souring tone and increasing tension between magistrates and workers. This downward trajectory in how colonial officials approached Indian laborers was embodied in the evolving attitude of D'Epinay. The Procrereur and Advocate General was himself a former slave-owner whose older brother had been one of the most notorious supporters of slavery and vociferous advocates against amelioration and emancipation in Mauritius.[92] Although circumspect in his opinions on immigration during its initial decade, by the 1850s, D'Epinay made no secret of his negative views of Indians as participants in legal forums, or of his belief that most of their complaints could be dismissed out of hand because they did not make "credible witnesses."[93]

89 Letter by Prosper D'Epinay, Procureur and Advocate General, November 28, 1850, Stipendiary Magistrates Correspondence 1850.

90 James Wildman, Stipendiary Magistrate, to the Colonial Secretary (Mauritius), February 15, 1867, Stipendiary Magistrates Correspondence 1867–8.

91 Ibid.

92 Amid some controversy, D'Epinay had been appointed to the post provisionally in 1836 by the governor of the colony, Sir William Nicolay. "State of the Mauritius," House of Commons Debates, February 15, 1836, Hansard's vol. 31, 416. His brother, Adrien D'Epinay, had once described the Protector of slaves as being "the enemy of slavery, the enemy of our institutions, the enemy of our colony" and was responsible for whipping his fellow Mauritians into a frenzy of resistance against amelioration and, indeed, any interference by British authorities into the treatment of slaves in Mauritius. Vijaya Teelock, *Bitter Sugar: Sugar and Slavery in 19th Century Mauritius* (Moka: Mahatma Gandhi Institute, 1998), 11.

93 Letter signed Prosper D'Epinay (Attorney General) dated January 7, 1851, Stipendiary Magistrates Correspondence 1867.

In contrast to their worsening views of Indians over time, magistrates' assertions that they were the guardians of the colony's moral, social and economic welfare only increased in tandem with their growing authority over this cohort. They also continued to express a strong interest in preserving indentured labor as an institution, insisting that it benefited both Indian workers and the colony as a whole. But much like their direct superior, D'Epinay, stipendiaries' vocal statements about Indian immigrants' morality and the shifting of their portrayal of them from an economic boon to a social blight were increasingly apparent in the 1850s. By the 1860s, the generation of stipendiaries that had begun their careers as special magistrates in the 1830s, shepherding through amelioration, emancipation, and apprenticeship, had retired. The growing concern of their successors that Indian workers posed a threat to public order, morality, and even public health was increasingly apparent in both policy and practice. Magistrates were employing the coercive measures they had acquired in previous years with greater frequency. At their urging, a system of depots had been established throughout the island to house the many hundreds of Indians arrested each month for vagrancy and related charges. Even this expansion proved insufficient to deal with a problem that, according to stipendiaries, reached crisis levels in the 1860s.[94] Gone was the hope expressed in earlier decades that magistrates could, through didactic adjudication, inculcate liberal self-discipline and moral habits to Indians. Where this instruction had failed, fines, the stocks, depots, and prisons would have to suffice. Interwoven with this general shift in magistrates' discourse from paternalistic reform with elements of coercion to unabashed enthusiasm for coercive regulation was a more specific mistrust of Indians' increasing, and increasingly immoral, engagement with legal venues. Clearly evident in official discourse, in policy, the increasing mistrust evinced by magistrates and other officials toward Indians was expressed in specific regulations implemented to prevent deception, fraud, forgery, and the other illegal practices deemed by authorities to be widespread among indentured laborers by the 1860s.[95]

Both the ascendency of the magistrates as the fulcrum of the overseer-state and the rising tensions between them and the growing population of Indian workers were common features of Britain's plantation colonies across the empire. Similar conditions bred similar responses and the commensurate

[94] Alfonse De Boucherville, Senior Stipendiary Magistrate (Port Louis) to the Colonial Secretary, October 15, 1867, Stipendiary Magistrates Correspondence 1867–8.

[95] The Labour Law of 1867, for example, mandated that all tickets of discharge from employment, a document that also served as an informal proof of identity and evidence of right of residency, had to include the bearer's photograph. This was intended to prevent workers or sirdars from employing the tickets belonging to other individuals in order to illegally secure new engagements, a practice magistrates and other officials alleged to be widespread. Allen, *Slaves, Freemen, and Indentured Laborers*, 65.

contestations. The powerful cohesion of labor discipline, criminal justice, inspectorial regimes, regulatory structures, and institutional backbone (e.g. Vagrants Depots) that constituted the overseer-state in Mauritius was characteristic of other former colonies as well. British Guiana had witnessed the same expansion of magistrates' authority and the turn to coercion even earlier, where planters and magistrates had employed an alleged crisis of vagabondage and public health to enhance the disciplinary regime applied to the ballooning Indian labor force. In Assam, which imported thousands of Indian indentured workers to man its vast tea plantations, a comparable structure of laws, officials, and institutions was introduced in the 1860s. There, a contract system fused the state and the plantation management in ways similar to that seen in Mauritius and British Guiana, with regulations stipulating long-term contracts, government inspections of plantations, and criminalizing labor offenses such as absconding or refusal to work.[96] The implementation of this system there was justified, as it was elsewhere, with a discourse that portrayed Indian workers as "slothful" and prone to absconding.[97] Planters' demands for the implementation of heavy penalties for work-related offenses made explicit references to similar measures adopted previously in other colonies where Indian indenture had been introduced.[98] Government oversight, as in Mauritius and British Guiana, was deemed necessary not because the system itself was cruel and exploitative but in order to preserve public health and to compensate for "human nature" leading some in positions of authority – but only a minority, officials insisted – to abuse their power.[99]

The overseer-state in Trinidad, which received the largest number of indentured Indian laborers after British Guiana and Mauritius (over 147,000 by 1917), followed a pattern akin to that in British Guiana. The special magistrates installed to oversee amelioration were reestablished as stipendiary magistrates in 1841, and long-term contracts, once opposed by the Colonial Office, became the norm in the 1850s. Trinidad took regulation one step further, trying to implement a "pass law" similar to that employed during slavery, but the measure was disallowed by the Colonial Office.[100] By the final decades of the nineteenth century, in any given year, between one-third and one-fifth of the laborers in British Guiana and Trinidad would face prosecution at the hands of magistrates.[101] Whereas the Indian government had once contested with

96 Rana P. Behal, "Coolie Drivers or Benevolent Paternalists? British Tea Planters in Assam and the Indenture Labour System," *Modern Asian Studies* 44, no. 1 (2010), 32–3.
97 Ibid., 36.
98 Prabhu P. Mohapatra, "Assam and the West Indies, 1860–1920," in Douglas Hay and Paul Craven, eds., *Masters, Servants, and Magistrates in Britain and the Empire, 1562–1955* (Chapel Hill: University of North Carolina Press, 2004), 463.
99 Behal, "Coolie Drivers," 44.
100 Mohapatra, "Assam and the West Indies," 460.
101 Ibid., 468.

former slave colonies over laws that opened their subjects to abuse, by the 1860s Indian regulations were instead following the legislative patterns set in indentured colonies.[102]

The expansion of the overseer-state, with magistrates at its core, was hardly confined only to those regions where indentured labor became common. To maintain the burgeoning plantation-mining complex, the latter half of the nineteenth century witnessed a vast migration of workers, both free and indentured, drawn from the length and breadth of the British Empire, and transported across an equally wide span of territory. From Fiji to Jamaica, from the Cape Colony to British Malaya, this vast cohort traveled and worked under the eye of the state. Indenture and the system of regulations, officials, and institutions through which it was conducted, originally introduced to govern labor on sugar plantations, expanded in tandem with the spread of the plantation system into other regions and commodities such as tea and rubber. The advent of direct Crown rule in India and Jamaica after their rebellions in 1857 and 1865 accelerated this process.[103] A system of parallel ordinances in different colonies progressively empowered magistrates to oversee the contracts of indentured workers, inspect their places of work, hear their grievances, punish their alleged transgressions, and deliver periodic reports on the workings of the labor system to colonial officials both in situ and in the metropole. In some regions, the ordinances governing magistrates' authority were built on the foundations of ameliorated slavery; in others, they emerged from master and servant law; and in some, they depended on a fusion of the two legal traditions. The implementation of regulations based on British labor law to govern Indian workers in the second half of the nineteenth century, however, typically stripped such legislation of the clauses that, in their domestic iterations, were intended to safeguard laborers from cruelty and ill-treatment.[104] As the institutional memory and legal principles of amelioration receded into the past, the guise of paternalistic protection that colonial labor governance once wore was flensed off to reveal the harsher, more explicitly coercive matrix that had always lain at its core.

[102] On prominent example of this was Act VI of the Bengal Council 1865 (mod. 1882). Behel, "Coolie Drivers," 32.

[103] In Jamaica, for example, which had relatively few indentured laborers, magistrates performed similar functions to those they had in Mauritius and British Guiana with regard to the freed African-Jamaican workforce. They were peripatetic, moving from plantation to plantation in order to inspect them and hear workers' grievances; they were responsible for adjudicating the growing array of labor offenses; they inspected jails and workhouses to which offenders were sent; and they drew up periodic reports on work conditions in the colony. As with Mauritius (and London), Jamaica was divided into several judicial districts, each under the charge of a stipendiary magistrate appointed (and removed, if necessary) only by the Colonial Secretary. These magistrates were assisted by unpaid justices of the peace, who were appointed by the governor.

[104] Anderson, "India 1858–1930," 423–33.

Magistrates, Direct Resistance, and State Violence

By the 1860s, wherever Indian or Chinese labor was imported in significant numbers, magistrates and the regulatory edifice they oversaw had become the mechanism by which workers' contractual obligations were enforced, their mobility constrained, their alleged labor transgressions punished, and whatever leverage they might have exerted abrogated. Magistrates insulated planters and the colonial plantation system more generally from the, to their minds, potentially adverse effects of a "free labor market" – labor competition, rising wages, and workers' collective bargaining tactics foremost among them. During a period of expanding production and increasing demand for colonial planation products, but also one of declining sugar prices, such intervention was justified, to colonial executives and their masters in the Colonial Office, as necessary to protect the economic survival of the plantation economy. With magistrates occupying such a pivotal role not just in labor management but in the wider experience of Indian laborers across the archipelago of Britain's plantation colonies, it is small wonder that they also became a focus of workers' resentment and frustration. Indentured laborers employed the complaint system to demand what they saw as their rights even as they sought new ways to subvert the coercive measures deployed against them. In these grievances, it became increasingly common for workers to contest not just their employers' treatment but also their treatment by magistrates and other state authorities. Workers' complaints about officials were often combined with broad assertions that colonial legal systems themselves invariably favored plantation authorities and denied workers any semblance of justice.

This entanglement of colonial law and plantation management allows us to challenge the tendency of social historians to view contestation by indentured workers as apolitical and the tendency of historians of colonial politics and governance to ignore workers' perspectives altogether.[105] Indian workers' engagement with the overseer-state, their articulation of their own vision of rights and justice, and the subsequent incorporation of these contests into the public discourse of both proponents and critics of indenture (and its fusion with colonial law and governance) gave these protests considerable political significance even if they lacked a cohesive and explicit political ideology. Reading workers' contestation in this way also counters one of the key racialized narratives of colonial authority, which was that only Europeans were capable of "legitimate" (in the official mind) employment of legal institutions

[105] As Hugh Tinker writes, "the history of Indian indenture is filled with incidents of protest, leading to violence, the [*sic*]most significant feature of these incidents is their shortsightedness ... when the story of one protest has been told, the story of all is told." Hugh Tinker, *A New System of Slavery: The Export of Indian Labour Overseas, 1830–1920* (London: Oxford University Press, 1974), 226.

and the language of rights, whereas African-Caribbean and Indian usage of them was invariably immoral, ineffective, and antithetical to public order.

Although these tensions were, in part, the result of a growing Indian population in the plantation colonies, the rising dependence of the plantation economy on that population's legal and economic subordination, and the increasing intervention of the state in colonial labor systems, the intensification of direct confrontations between workers and magistrates was also attributable to a crucial change in the cultural and political context of indenture. Behind the shift in magistrates' attitudes, the turn toward coercion, and the abandonment of claims by colonial authorities that Indians could be incorporated into the "civilizing mission" of moral colonial rule lay the decline of ameliorated slavery and emancipation as the touchstones for the state's oversight of colonial labor systems. These antecedents were overwritten by the 1857 Indian Rebellion, which reshaped both magistrates' interpretations of Indian response to governance and the wider cultural context through which they and other officials viewed the morality of coercion. The events of 1857 provided a powerful justification for the deployment of force to maintain plantation discipline and labor governance.[106] At the most extreme manifestations of such reasoning, magistrates could now defend using coercive measures against laborers' mass demonstrations or direct resistance by asserting that they were fighting sedition and preventing rebellion.[107]

The Indian Rebellion provided colonial authorities dealing with indentured laborers what the history of slave rebellions had in the context of slavery – a ubiquitous, violent, and intractable menace meriting a swift and terrible response with all the tools at the state's disposal. The justifications for state violence were lent further reinforcement by the 1865 Morant Bay Rebellion. This event reignited the spectre of slave rebellions that had long been integral to British colonial governance in the Caribbean while ensuring that the importation of Indian labor, despite the violence of 1857, remained an alternative to African-Caribbean labor from the perspective of planters and colonial officials alike. The long history of slave rebellions, an entrenched anti-black racial discourse, and the growing assertiveness of free black labor in the Caribbean prompted most British observers to assert that Indians remained more amenable than Afro-Caribbeans were to smooth incorporation within imperial labor schema. Widespread apprehension that replacing the plantation

[106] This presaged the more general turn toward violence that Martin Thomas has argued characterized colonial policing of strikes and other types of economic protest between the wars. Martin Thomas, *Violence and Colonial Order: Police, Workers and Protest in the European Colonial Empires, 1918–1940* (Cambridge: Cambridge University Press, 2012), 2.

[107] For the justification of violence on the imperial frontier, see Elizabeth Kolsky, "The Colonial Rule of Law and the Legal Regime of Exception: Frontier 'Fanaticism' and State Violence in British India," *American Historical Review* 120, no. 4 (October 2015), 1219.

economy with a "peasant democracy" of African-Caribbean smallholders would be a political and economic catastrophe had, after all, been a primary motivation for importing Indian workers to begin with.[108] These circumstances presented magistrates, governors, and other colonial authorities with a powerful rhetorical tool for reconciling coercion with the discourses of liberalism moral colonization, and orderly rule. In the state's new role as supervisors of a coercive, but technically free, contractual labor system, the most extreme form of coercion, direct violence committed against indentured workers, required such reconciliation in a manner that the violent suppression of enslaved Africans had not.[109] Since local courts provided ample avenues for formal grievances by workers, magistrates could readily portray resistance pursued *beyond* these forums as a threat to the entire edifice of colonial law and governance.[110]

Magistrates' ability to frame workers' direct resistance to authority as dangerous and subversive was dramatically demonstrated in 1872, when five indentured Indian workers – Maxidally, Kaulica, Baldeo, Beccaroo, and Auckloo – of Devonshire Castle plantation in British Guiana were shot dead while protesting against work conditions and their treatment at the hands of the colonial judiciary.[111] These men had been part of a larger group of workers

[108] William A. Green, "Emancipation to Indentured: A Question of Imperial Morality," *Journal of British Studies* 22, no. 2 (Spring 1983), 120.

[109] This was explicitly recognized in the report of a Parliamentary Commission convened in the year before the Devonshire Castle killings. "The obligations of the slave are enforced by violence," the commissioners explained in their report, "while the obligations of the indentured labourer, like those of the free labourer, are only to be enforced by law, and his rights he is invited and encouraged to defend." Report of the Commissioners Appointed to Enquire into the Treatment of Immigrants in British Guiana, PP 1871 (c. 393) (hereafter Treatment of Immigrants), v. 4, 102. On liberalism and colonial rule, see Eric Stokes, *The English Utilitarians and India* (Oxford: Oxford University Press, 1959); Karuna Mantena, *Alibis of Empire: Henry Maine and the Ends of Liberal Imperialism* (Princeton, NJ: Princeton University Press, 2010); Uday Singh Mehta, *Liberalism and Empire: A Study in Nineteenth Century Political Thought* (Chicago, IL: University of Chicago Press, 1999); Theodore Koditshek, *Liberalism, Imperialism and the Historical Imagination* (Cambridge: Cambridge University Press, 2011); Andrew Sartori, *Liberalism in Empire: An Alternative History* (Berkeley: University of California Press, 2014).

[110] As Walter Rodney explained in his pioneering study of the Guyanese working people, "the particular stereotype of the murderous and ungovernable Coolies was activated as a virtually self-fulfilling prophecy, given the heavy-handed, authoritarian responses of those in power. When workers sought to protest peaceably, they were backed into a position of frustration and violence." Walter Rodney, *A History of the Guyanese Working People, 1881–1905* (Baltimore, MD: Johns Hopkins University Press, 1981), 158.

[111] For a fuller account of the incident, see Sascha Auerbach, "Of Rights and Riots: Indenture and (Mis)Rule in the Late Nineteenth-Century British Caribbean," *English Historical Review* 137, no. 589 (December 2022), 1662–92.

that had first sought to bring a case in court against their manager, whom they alleged had abused them in contravention of the law. Having failed to gain a sympathetic hearing there, the protesting workers had subsequently blockaded the road to Devonshire Castle, demanding that the magistrate, Henry Loughran, reconvene the court there and grant them their rights. Loughran refused, ordering the workers to disperse and threatening them with arrest if they did not comply. When the workers held their ground, Loughran ordered his armed constables to advance and arrest the "ringleaders." In the resulting clash, which pitted a small squad of Loughran's men against a group of several hundred workers, although no specific order was given, the constables opened fire, killing five and wounding several more. In the official inquiry that followed, magistrates and colonial administrators defined the collective protest of the Devonshire Castle workers, even though such protests were largely absent anything beyond threats and public demonstration, as violent sedition and an antecedent to a bloody, colony-wide rebellion. Murderous violence against these workers committed *by* colonial authorities, on the other hand, was framed by both the local magistrate and his superiors as a just, moral, and proportionate response that had been necessary to preserve order and protect the lives (and virtue) of white residents.[112]

Much of the discursive reconfiguration of the labor contest on Devonshire Castle into an incipient rebellion was carried out via the colonial justice system that was itself both a vehicle for and a key focus of the workers' grievances.[113] In this process, the fusion of plantation discipline and colonial governance became starkly visible. Managers and plantation overseers not only enjoyed a privileged voice in legal venues but occupied many of its most influential roles.[114] The first stage of this rewriting of a protest into a rebellion was the Coroner's Court inquest following the killing of the five indentured workers. A Coroner's Court was a temporary judicial body convened to conduct an investigation into any deaths deemed out of the ordinary. The witness testimony offered there, which was published in *The Colonist*, the main press organ of British Guiana, would remain the constant point of reference for all subsequent discussions of what had happened at Devonshire Castle and in the surrounding district (Essequibo) in the days leading up to the killings. Far

[112] For the colonial state's normalization of its own violence in India, see Kolsky, "The Colonial Rule of Law," 1216. For "violence" as a historically constructed category, see Elizabeth Kolsky, *Colonial Justice in British India: White Violence and the Rule of Law* (Cambridge: Cambridge University Press, 2010), 2–4; Tracey Banivanua-Mar, *Violence and Colonial Dialogue: The Australian-Pacific Indentured Labour Trade* (Honolulu: University of Hawai'i Press, 2007), 2–3.

[113] Mr. Des Voeux's Letter, December 25, 1869, Report of the Commissioners Appointed to Enquire into the Treatment of Immigrants in British Guiana, PP 1871 (c. 393), 10.

[114] Diana Paton, *No Bond but the Law: Punishment, Race, and Gender in Jamaican State Formation, 1780–1870* (Durham, NC: Duke University Press, 2004), 71–7.

from being independent entities, Coroner's Courts were dominated by those with a vested interest in the plantation system. They were assembled by local justices of the peace, and at the time of the Devonshire Castle killings, one-third of all justices of the peace in British Guiana were resident managers on sugar estates.[115] The four-person jury for such proceedings was drawn from the other employees of the estate, often with the manager of the neighboring plantation serving as the coroner who oversaw and directed the inquest.

Due to both his rank and his key role in the incident, the figure wielding the greatest power in the proceedings was Henry Loughran, a local stipendiary magistrate. Loughran had been commanding the force of constables that had confronted the workers of Devonshire Castle. His version of events, more so than any other, shaped both the official and the public accounts that followed. As was made clear by a discussion over procedure at the beginning of the inquest, he was the true authority in the court, effectively managing the conduct of an inquiry into his own actions and those of his constables.[116] Other central figures who offered substantial testimony included Loughran's clerk, John Blake, and the manager of Devonshire Castle, Peter Abel. All three concurred that events were set in motion not by ongoing tensions between managers and the plantation workers but rather by the violent predilections of agitators among the latter.

The Devonshire Castle killings and the subsequent inquiry occurred at a time when indenture and colonial labor governance was once again beginning to come under intense public and official scrutiny. In the 1850s and 1860s, the indenture system had expanded rapidly across the empire from its initial introduction in Mauritius and British Guiana (Map 5.1). As the apparatus of laws, institutions, and officials tasked with overseeing it grew commensurately, those opposing the system either for political or for humanitarian reasons were able to use the accumulating reports of workers' grievances, labor disruption, and negative press coverage to question the morality and practicality of indenture. The perceived injustices of colonial labor governance and the discontent it might foment among Indian workers were taken up directly in the first sustained government critique of the system to appear subsequent to the events of 1857 and 1865. It was indentured workers themselves who had prompted this investigation by staging a wave of protests across British Guiana in late 1869 and early 1870. In the late 1860s, planters' attempts to drive down wages by importing a surplus of immigrant labor had brought

115 Treatment of Immigrants, 81–2. John Edward Jenkins, *The Coolie: His Rights and Wrongs* (New York: George Routledge & Sons, 1871), 213.

116 When the absence of the fourth juror had prompted the coroner's call for a delay, Loughran cited the specific statute and insisted that the proceedings move forward. The former deferred to the magistrate's judgment and the inquest commenced. *Inquest on the Bodies*, 4–5.

Map 5.1 British Guiana, c. 1880
Source: Courtesy of Mathilde Grimaldi.

tensions to a boiling point.[117] A serious confrontation between workers and police at plantation Leonora in August 1869, as would be the case in the Devonshire Castle incident, had been preceded by months of workers' grievances and discontent over the arbitrary cutting of wages, contract violations, overwork, and other mistreatments (see Map 5.2).[118] The Leonora

[117] Basdeo Mangru, "Indian Militancy on Sugar Estates: The 1869 Leonora Episode," *Guyana Journal* (October 2007), n.p. www.guyanajournal.com/indian_militancy_leonora.html (accessed October 25, 2017).

[118] These measures had been implemented by a new plantation manager who had formerly made a career of overseeing cotton-plantation slaves in the antebellum US South. Ibid.

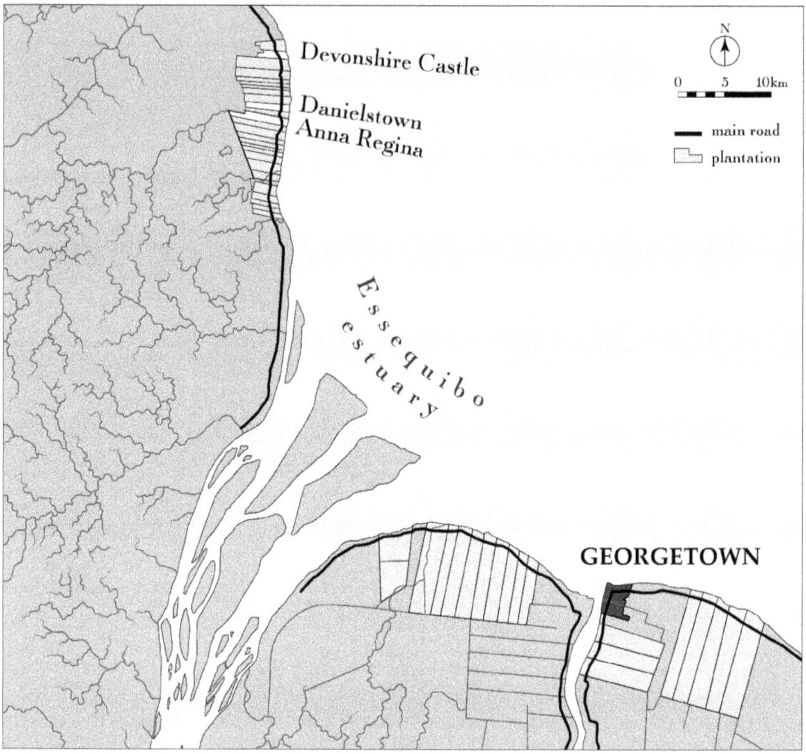

Map 5.2 The Essequibo plantations and Georgetown, c. 1880
Source: Courtesy of Mathilde Grimaldi.

clash between 300 workers and local constables had been followed by a series of labor disturbances at more than half a dozen other plantations across the colony in subsequent months.[119]

Demonstrating the internal tensions in colonial governance that were exacerbated by the debate over indentured labor, criticism of the system in this period emerged vociferously from within the Guyanese magistracy itself. Partly in response to this, a Parliamentary Commission was convened in 1871 to investigate the conditions among Indian immigrants to the colony.[120] As indenture in the colony came under increasing scrutiny, albeit only from a minority of judicial officials and local journalists, some critical observers blamed the planters and managers for destabilizing labor relations on the

[119] These included Farm, Chateau Margot, Success, Mon Ropos, La Jolousie, Gladstone Hall, Uitvlugt, and Non-Pareill.

[120] The letter was included, in full, as the first piece of documentation in the Commission's report. Treatment of Immigrants, 1–14.

estates. With wage cuts and arbitrary deductions, such arguments held, proprietors had prompted their workers to respond through grievances, wage demands, work stoppages, and full-scale walkouts.[121] These reproaches fell on deaf ears, and the main Guyanese newspaper, *The Colonist*, instead broadcast the most sinister picture possible of the indentured Indian workforce. Its commentary linked the cohort explicitly with the Indian Rebellion, asserting that participants in the most brutal episodes of 1857 had infiltrated the workforce of local estates. Guyanese plantations, the paper reported, were full of "Sepoys who bore parts in the memorable tragedies of Cawnpore and Delhi [i.e. the Indian Mutiny of 1857]," and the danger of their collusion in a full-scale uprising put all white residents in mortal peril.[122] The governor of British Guiana, Sir John Scott, in his communications with the Colonial Secretary, eschewed such hyperbole. But he expressed considerable alarm about the many agitators allegedly present on the plantations and the serious danger that "a combination among the whole of the coolies would be formed."[123] The Colonial Office, responding to these alarming reports, agreed, as a precaution, to headquarter the Second West India Regiment in British Guiana.[124]

Following the Leonora incident, in the public debate over whether indenture in British Guiana was immoral and abusive, prompting widespread discontent, or whether it was just and orderly, with the only dissatisfaction emerging from seditious malcontents, the former view had won out. This had been accomplished primarily through the success of colonial officials and the local press – both entangled with the planter class and invested in the colony's continued profitability through indenture – in redefining the temporal and geographical context of workers' demonstrations from the realm of labor relations to that of violent rebellion and in recasting unhappy workers as conspiring mutineers. In doing so, they had neatly reconciled the violent suppression of indentured laborers with the principles of liberalism and moral rule. While some in the British establishment, post-Peterloo, might balk at the killing of unarmed demonstrators, in the wake of 1857 few would question the necessity of using force to quell the opening stages of a bloody, colony-wide rebellion.

In the days preceding the violence at Devonshire Castle, the consequences of maintaining the status quo on the sugar estates while giving only a cursory nod toward laborers' complaints would become clear. The work of the 1871

121 *The Royal Gazette*, September 24, 1869, cited in Mangru, "Indian Militancy." A particular issue was the abuse of Ordinance 9 of 1868, which allowed plantation authorities to arbitrarily deduct wages for work that had not been completed to their satisfaction.

122 *The Colonist*, October 4, 1869, cited in Mangru, "Indian Militancy."

123 Scott to Granville, no. 47, April 22, 1870, cited in Mangru, "Indian Militancy."

124 The West India Regiment was composed primarily of Afro-Caribbean troops under the command of white British officers.

Commission had raised expectations among the indentured workforce, who had sought out those involved and besieged them with their grievances.[125] The failure of reform had only amplified their widespread discontent with both affairs on the estates and a judicial system that was so fully subsumed to planters' interests that it served only as a rod of punishment and never as a mechanism for justice.[126] Far from being a spontaneous outbreak of violence, the final conflict between workers and police was the culmination of several months of rising tension at Devonshire Castle, tension that emerged from the same concerns that had prompted workers' grievances prior to the 1871 Commission. As several witnesses testified during the course of the coroner's inquest that followed, the main complaints of the indentured Indian workers concerned the labor conditions (pay especially), on one hand, and their belief that they were being denied justice and the rights to which they were entitled, on the other. Such complaints were endemic to the indenture system, as they had been in the post-emancipation apprenticeship system and in mid-century Mauritius.[127] And even if the details of colonial governance were often beyond their knowledge, laborers were generally familiar with key local authorities. The rights to petition the local magistrate in contract grievances and to approach the local Immigration Agent with such complaints, in particular, were familiar to the indentured workforce.[128] Skepticism among workers that, given the close relationship between magistrates and plantation managers, such grievances would be taken seriously was equally common.[129] Though from the published account of the Devonshire Castle inquiry, the correspondence between local officials and higher administrators, and the manner in which the incident was subsequently reported to the public in both British

[125] George William Des Voeux, *My Colonial Service in British Guiana, St. Lucia, Trinidad, Fiji, Australia, Newfoundland, and Hong Kong, Vols. 1 & 2* (London: John Murray, 1903), 135.

[126] The powerful influence of the planter interest on magistrates' decisions, Des Voeux had explained to Earl Granville, would have been apparent to even the most casual and uninformed observer, since estate managers were commonly allowed to sit on the bench with the latter during the conduct of their trials. Des Voeux to Granville, December 15, 1869, *Report of the Commissioners Appointed to Enquire into the Treatment of Immigrants in British Guiana* (London: Her Majesty's Stationary Office, 1871) (C. 393), 5. Although the ratio of employers' prosecutions versus workers' prosecutions varied between colonies, it exponentially favored the former in both success rate and severity of penalties. Brij V. Lal, "Understanding the Indian Indenture Experience," *South Asia: Journal of South Asian Studies* 21, no. 1 (1998), 226.

[127] Paton, *No Bond but the Law*, 160–1.

[128] Tinker, *A New System of Slavery*, 193, 223.

[129] Edward Jenkins recounted the response of one worker to his suggestion that he take his complaints of beatings and withholding of food and wages before the local magistrate. "O massa, no good go mahitee [magistrate]. Mahitee know manahee [manager] – go manahee's house – eat um breakfast – come court – no good Coolie go court – mahitee friend manahee: always for manahee, no for Coolie." Jenkins, *The Coolie*, 103.

Guiana and Britain, one would hardly have known that workers had any understanding of the indenture system, or any intention to resolve their complaints peacefully. Across the empire, the dismissal of such complaints as frivolous, and the categorical rejection of alternative ideas of "justice," had been commonplace in colonial authorities' treatment of former slaves and immigrant workers for many decades prior.[130]

The structural obstacles that hampered indentured workers' conduct of complaints against their employers – the need for interpreters, illiteracy, and the high costs of legal representation foremost among them – worked in tandem with the widespread racial prejudices expressed by colonial officials to heavily stack the odds against any success via formal channels. The situation in British Guiana was particularly egregious. Members of the 1871 Commission decried a system in which estate overseers pursued their duty to see tasks completed on the plantation and to secure fines or imprisonment against workers charged with labor offenses with equal vigor.[131] So weighted against indentured laborers were the legal protocols that, according to the official immigration ordinances, they were not even allowed to give evidence on their own behalf in such cases.[132] Though magistrates commonly ignored this moratorium and allowed defendants to give evidence, as one observer commented, "no emigrant [was] so deficient in the instinct of justice" as to mistake such *performance* of legal equality for its substance.[133] The same observers who criticized a legal framework that treated indentured Indians as criminal defendants in prosecutions for labor offenses, however, were also quick to portray the same cohort as inherently incompatible with British legal procedures and principles.[134] Even when their lack of language facility and their ignorance of the relevant laws could be overcome, Indians' "notorious profligacy of deceit" remained an insurmountable obstacle to their legitimate engagement with local magistrates and their courts.[135]

130 Imperial authorities elsewhere had made some effort to accommodate "customary law," but efforts by relocated populations in slave and former slave societies to translocate forms of conflict resolution and their own sense of justice were invariably dismissed as indicators not of legal consciousness but of their inherent "barbarism." Paton, *No Bond but the Law*, 161.

131 Jenkins, *The Coolie*, 235.

132 Ibid., 236.

133 Ibid., 237.

134 Ravi Ahuja, "Review – Making the Empire a Thinkable Whole: Master and Servant Law in Transterritorial Perspective" (review of Douglas Hay and Paul Craven, eds., *Masters, Servants and Magistrates in Britain and the Empire, 1562–1955* [Chapel Hill: University of North Carolina Press, 2004]), *International Review of Social History* 52, no. 2 (2007), 288. That contract violations and other labor offenses were designated, in the Acts passed to govern them, as triable by summary justice with a set range of penalties brought them into the category of non-indictable offenses.

135 Jenkins, *The Coolie*, 235.

Consistently deriding indentured laborers' interaction with the state as being irrevocably tainted by their inherent immorality was one thing, but ignoring it altogether was impossible, both in daily governance and in the continual stream of reports that it produced. Indentured workers' ubiquitous encounters – both voluntarily through grievances and involuntarily through managers' and planters' initiatives – with the latticework of laws, rights, and formal procedures were what had sustained the colonial state, its legal institutions, and the agents of law, policing, and inspection as the primary mediator between workers and employers.[136] Whereas former slaves and their descendants often employed slavery as the cultural (or, in the 1830s and 1840s, experiential) touchstone for their understanding of "freedom" and their protests against being denied their vision of its benefits, indentured laborers more commonly expressed their ideas in relation to this subsequently installed state apparatus.[137] Indentured workers' encounters with the evolving practices of post-emancipation plantation labor organization began with their recruitment in India and continued throughout their sojourn in British Guiana. These experiences helped propagate a self-awareness of rights that, along with a recognition of their status as British subjects and parties in Contracts of Service, shaped their responses to both employers and state agents.[138] The reaction of the Devonshire Castle workers and their confreres on other plantations to perceived injustices were in line with this contractual identity. Indentured workers had a concrete and specific conception of what their rights were in these circumstances, and they were determined to exercise them, as their bringing a case to court and their demands to see their rights respected on the plantation road demonstrated. Many of their actions evinced a desire to

[136] Paton, *No Bond but the Law*, 54.

[137] For the former, see Gad Heuman, "'Is This What You Call Free?': Riots and Resistance in the Anglophone Caribbean," in Gad Heuman and David Vincent Trotman, eds., *Contesting Freedom: Control and Resistance in the Post-Emancipation Caribbean* (Oxford: Macmillan Caribbean, 2005), 107–13.

[138] This was the case in other regions where Indian labor – free, indentured, and contract – was employed. Rsemarijn Hoefte, "Different Modes of Resistance by British Indian and Javanese Contract Labourers in Suriname," in Gad Heuman and David Vincent Trotman, eds., *Contesting Freedom: Control and Resistance in the Post-Emancipation Caribbean* (Oxford: Macmillan Caribbean, 2005), 155. On the issue of contractual identity, see Thomas Holt, *The Problem of Freedom: Race, Labor, and Politics in Jamaica and Britain, 1832–1938* (Baltimore, MD: Johns Hopkins University Press, 1992), 5; Natasha Lightfoot, *Troubling Freedom: Antigua and the Aftermath of British Abolition* (Durham, NC: Duke University Press, 2015), 96–101; Alessandro Stanziani, *Labour on the Fringes of Empire: Voice, Exit and the Law* (New York: Palgrave Macmillan, 2018), 143. For resistance and violence more specifically, see Radica Mahase, "Plenty a Dem Run Away': Resistance by Indian Indentured Labourers in Trinidad, 1870–1920," *Labour History* 49, no. 4 (November 2008), 465–80; Maurits S. Hassankhan, Brij V. Lal, and Doug Munro, eds., *Resistance and Indian Indenture Experience: Comparative Perspectives* (New Delhi: Manohar, 2014).

engage state agents and institutions of rule, albeit on their own terms and in line with their own expectations of justice, rather than to defy them or deny their authority. Although labeled disruptive or seditious malcontents, demonstrating Indian workers were acting as liberal subjects, albeit according to their own understandings of rights rather than the understanding of magistrates or their employers.

In light of such engagement, it became crucial for colonial authorities, in their own accounts composed in the wake of fatal state violence against demonstrating workers, to obscure or delegitimize such efforts. A narrative of just and moral colonial rule was difficult to sustain if those killed were recognized as merely protesting against perceived contract violations or demanding a fair hearing from unbiased judges. To establish this narrative of just rule and proportionate response, contrary to the evidence readily available, the Devonshire Castle incident was rewritten as the first stage of a murderous, colony-wide rebellion, fomented by conspiring renegades with no cause for grievance, and barely averted by the valiant and timely intervention of the local judiciary and constabulary. Over time, this portrayal, constituted across a range of government correspondence and newspaper stories, became the official account of events. Like the 1871 Commission, the Devonshire Castle inquiry performed a powerful ideological function, and it did so through explicit references to the 1857 Indian Rebellion as the most compelling context for interpreting Indian workers' behavior.

This was particularly visible in the magistrate Loughran's concluding testimony at the coroner's inquest following the Devonshire Castle killings. He was effusive in his descriptions of his constables' conduct on that fatal day, declaring that "great praise is due to each and every one of those gentlemen for their manly and courageous conduct in assisting to suppress the riot."[139] Although Loughran was "deeply grieved" at the death of the five "misguided and unfortunate coolies," the magistrate was adamant that the residents of the entire district owed their continued existence, and the women their virtue, to the policemen's heroic acts. "I believed then as I do now that the firing of the rifles saved the lives of not only the few supporters of law and order that were present from immediate destruction," he told the jury. "I further believed that if the coolies had overcome the police the county of Essequebo would have become a scene of murder, rapine, and pillage."[140] The jurors were fully in accord, returning a verdict of "justifiable homicide" and adding that, in their opinion, "but for the discharge of the rifles . . . the riot would have extended over the whole district."[141] The coroner's inquest had exonerated Loughran

[139] Testimony of Henry Loughran, October 11, 1872, *Inquest on the Bodies*, 37.

[140] Ibid., October 12, 1872, 38.

[141] Statement of the Jury (Philip Smith (foreman), J. A. Bascom, P. J. Rohlehr), October 14, 1872, *Inquest on the Bodies*, 38–9.

and his constables, and through the proceedings' publication in the pages of *The Colonist*, the narrative of a barely averted rebellion would become entrenched in public discourse. Loughran and the plantation authorities, in their testimony, were keen to ascribe the behavior of the workers to the undue influence of agitators in their midst. These alleged ringleaders served the same functional purpose that *sirdars* had in Mauritius. They allowed authorities to justify the continuation of indenture and Indian immigration as conducive to public order and amenable to just rule. The faults lay not with the system but only with certain immoral individuals within it, and this problem could be rectified through the stern application of law.

Ultimately, it was the responsibility of Kimberley, the Colonial Secretary, to summarize the events at Devonshire Castle for the Prime Minister, his Cabinet, and other crucial decision-makers in the British government. This final, crucial communication would set the tone for how those with the greatest investment in the orderly governance of Britain's empire would interpret what had happened in Essequibo. The discussion of the event came at a critical juncture in the development of Britain's empire-wide indentured labor system, the state's roles and obligations therein, and the implications for Britain's commitment to just rule and the guardianship of its subjects' rights. It coincided with both the elevation of magistrates as the overseers of this global labor edifice and the expansion of the system into newly colonized regions.[142] With an empire-wide plantation-mining complex that was anchored in indenture and its ancillaries, and having already conducted a parliamentary inquiry that had vindicated the system in British Guiana, both the colonial administration there and the Colonial Office in London were more heavily invested than ever in the indenture system. Defending the legality and morality of it, dismissing resistance as the work of unscrupulous agitators, and justifying violent suppression of protests as necessary but unfortunate would, in the decades that followed, become all but second nature to the officials involved.[143] Kimberley hewed to the assertions that Loughran had made in the coroner's inquest. The potential for a colony-wide revolt under the leadership of seditious ringleaders had, indeed, loomed over the events at Devonshire Castle on that bloody day in September.[144] He passed this interpretation of a nascent rebellion on to the India Office, which had direct responsibility for regulating the global system of Indian indenture at its source.

From a district magistrate's testimony in a far-flung colonial courtroom to the center of Britain's imperial edifice, a labor demonstration had been rewritten into a tale of averted rebellion and justifiable killing, the fault for which lay

[142] Sunil Amrith, *Crossing the Bay of Bengal: The Furies of Nature and the Fortunes of Migrants* (Cambridge, MA: Harvard University Press, 2013), 101.

[143] Rodney, *Guyanese Working People*, 158–9.

[144] Kimberley to the Officer Administering the Government, August 4, 1873.

firmly with a few malcontents who had agitated an otherwise docile – albeit weak-minded and prone to immoral influence – indentured workforce. This explanation rested on judicial and administrative processes that severed the events at Devonshire Castle from the context of ongoing labor resistance and workers' ubiquitous grievances, linking them instead to the 1857 Indian Rebellion, Morant Bay, and the history of slave uprisings in the Caribbean. And at the pivot of both how the incident itself had unfolded and how it was subsequently reinterpreted in official and public discourse was a representative of the Stipendiary Magistracy whose authority formed the backbone of the overseer-state and the anchor of colonial rule more generally in the plantation colonies.

Conclusion

Loughran's central role in the Devonshire Castle killings and their subsequent official and public recounting was an apt demonstration of how magistrates across the empire shaped both the structural and the cultural dimensions of governance in the plantation colonies. In the 1820s and 1830s, first as special magistrates overseeing ameliorated slavery and apprenticeship and later as stipendiaries overseeing indenture, these officials were at the vanguard of colonial labor governance. They served as the mediators between managers and workers, as the primary interface between both cohorts and the state apparatus, as the enforcers of labor regulation, as the inspectors of the plantation system, and as the primary avenues by which information about workers and their conditions was transmitted to both the colonial executive and to the metropole. The character of their interventions varied over time and between locales. In the Caribbean, magistrates' authority became fused with plantation discipline very early on, and they were integral to creating the impression of a crisis that merited a swift and decisive state response. In Mauritius, by contrast, magistrates in the 1840s espoused the principles of free labor, emphasized the contrasts between indenture and slavery, stressed the "civilizing" influence of good governance on Indian workers, and enshrined themselves as the protectors of their rights against rapacious *sirdars* and immoral proprietors. Over time, magistrates there and across the empire steadily abandoned their advocacy of paternalistic oversight in favor of direct coercion. Following the precedent set in British Guiana, by the 1860s, Mauritian magistrates were leading the charge to tighten restrictions on labor mobility and to impose a more rigid schema of worker surveillance and documentation.

In the Caribbean, the trajectory of increasing coercion continued its upward trend, rising to a point in the 1870s where even the outright killing of Indian workers by constables under a magistrate's authority could be justified as consistent with moral rule and as necessary to maintain public order. In part, the evolving roles and attitudes of magistrates reflected their changing social, economic, and political contexts. The expansion of sugar cultivation in both the Caribbean and Mauritius, widespread concerns over the alleged unsuitability of African-Caribbeans for moral self-rule, and the Indian Rebellion of 1857 were all key aspects of these contexts. Together, they created an environment where the rapid growth of an Indian indentured workforce, the need for the state to oversee that workforce, and the empowerment of magistrates to direct that oversight all seemed merited to colonial governors, to their superiors in London, and to magistrates themselves. Reconciling the multiplying stories of abuse and the increasing employment of coercion with liberalism, moral rule, and just colonial governance was also achieved by magistrates in their role as the gatherers and conduits of information about immigration, plantation management, and the physical and moral state of the Indian immigrant population. The mistreatment of workers that was revealed through the same governmental systems designed to monitor the Indian workforce was laid by magistrates at the feet of rogue proprietors, corrupt labor recruiters, or a host of villainous middlemen, the *sirdars* being the most prominent and allegedly the most corrosive to moral and social order.

Such figures served as a foil for the magistrates and the overseer-state in which they were increasingly central. These contesting groups were cast as archetypes, with greedy planters and conniving middlement embodying the the failings of human nature or inherent racial flaws. Against them, magistrates presented themselves as paradigms of public order, justice, and moral probity. In this configuration, magistrates and their superiors, the local Colonial Secretaries and governors, portrayed the state as a paternalistic, inherently moral force, and the indenture system that it governed as intrinsically beneficial both to the individual and to the community. Thus, through both the concrete structure and the public conceptualization of the overseer-state, freedom and the "free labor" market in the plantation colonies, although championed in principle, were not implemented in practice. Instead, colonial labor, through the collaboration of magistrates and plantation managers, was increasingly organized around the rigid timetable of sugar production, the allegedly inherent fairness of labor contracts, and the purported benefits of the civilizing mission, all of which depended on state oversight.

But Indian workers themselves, much like slaves and apprentices before them, played a crucial part in shaping the role of magistrates and the broader character of the overseer-state. In Mauritius and in other plantation colonies, collective walkouts, contestation of contracts, seeking new employers and new terms of employment, filing complaints, forging documentation, and a host of other tactics were employed to preserve whatever leverage could be had in an increasingly harsh and restrictive labor system. For workers, these were necessary adaptations meant to preserve their mobility and maximize their negotiating position. Making complaints about contracts and daily ill-treatment on the plantations offered them a public platform to air their own views of fairness and just treatment. These assertions often fell on unsympathetic ears. Magistrates retained the authority not just to enforce the law but to define the *moral* implications of state oversight, workers' responses to it, and the labor system more generally. In the wake of 1857 and the context of alleged exploitation by *sirdars*, magistrates increasingly portrayed Indians as inherently immoral and disorderly, publicly eschewing any hope of their incorporation as liberal subjects who could be trusted to act properly without state coercion. Instead, by the 1860s, magistrates across the empire consistently depicted Indians as helpless victims, idle wastrels, or threats to public order and morality. Indians' engagement of legal venues on their own terms, or their developing of alternative uses for them as forums for labor negotiation, stood among the most unforgivable of all their sins. These efforts threatened what magistrates valued most – their ability to control the narrative in their own judicial domains and, in doing so, to stand as the arbiters of law and morality for workers and planters alike.

In British Guiana, Indian workers' persistent contestation of conditions on the plantations and their challenges to planters and the state that supported them prompted a parliamentary inquiry. At the core of discussions in the press and political circles were three interrelated issues: What were the comparative benefits and liabilities – economic, social, and moral – of indentured labor? Where did the balance lie between protecting the rights of Indian subjects and ensuring economic viability? And what level of force was the state justified in employing to preserve public order?[145] A year after the inquiry had reported on the many merits of indenture and the state's paternalistic supervision of Indian workers, the final question was answered dramatically in the fatal clash that left five men dead on the road to Devonshire Castle, while the perpetrators walked away lauded for their heroic acts. With the magistrate Loughran's portrayal serving as the authoritative account, the conclusion reached in British Guiana and London was predictable. The real problem lay with a small minority of seditious ringleaders and overzealous managers. Were these issues to be addressed with more interventionist regulation, as Downing Street had strongly advised in a dispatch to Governor Scott shortly before the Devonshire Castle killings, "the immigration of coolies may be made fruitful of good."[146]

Such faith in the efficacy of reform would have been cold comfort to those shot dead on the road to Devonshire Castle. The killings and the trajectory of inquest and court cases that followed were, nonetheless, small but perceptible blows to a system whose many tensions, over subsequent decades, would

[145] Catherine Hall, Keith McClelland, and Jane Rendall, *Defining the Victorian Nation: Class, Race, Gender and the Reform Act of 1867* (Cambridge: Cambridge University Press, 2000), 198–202.

[146] *Times* (of London), November 20, 1872, 4.

continue to prompt contest and discord. The rampant iniquities of indenture would drive a steady stream of public criticism and legal challenges from humanitarians, antislavery campaigners, judicial contrarians, and Indian activists that grew in volume across the decades preceding the First World War. These voices of opposition often explicitly referenced the gnawing, low-level resistance on the part of workers themselves, for whom the brutality and injustice of colonial labor organization were all too apparent. The official narrative of indenture's civilizing mission notwithstanding, workers' frequent contestations of the system could not be erased from the official record, nor could the cumulative political impact of their actions and the state's often violent reaction be ignored.[147] Efforts by officials in London and the empire to reconcile moral colonization, safeguarding subjects' rights and the civilizing mission, with the violations of all of these principles in state coercion and violence proved increasingly problematic as the decades wore on.[148] Seen in this light, the deaths of Maxidally, Kaulica, Baldeo, Beccaroo, and Auckloo on a plantation road in British Guiana were not a coda but a prelude. The Devonshire Castle massacre presaged the centrifugal forces of popular demonstration, violent suppression, moral condemnation, and administrative exhaustion that would prove instrumental in the end of indenture fifty years later. Before that end, however, labor governance would play a pivotal role in Britain's newest arena of rapid colonial expansion, Southeast Asia. There, the overseer-state would continue to evolve and adapt, serving not just as the anchor of colonial rule but as the core of sovereignty on the imperial frontier.

147 At plantation Rose Hall 1913, a clash between police and indentured workers resulted in fifteen deaths (fourteen workers and one policeman). The incident was serious enough to spur the Indian government to action and helped catalyze the abolition of indentured in 1917.

148 The reconciliation of liberal ideals with authoritarian practices in the imperial legal system is a central consideration in Martin J. Wiener, *An Empire on Trial: Race, Murder, and Justice under British Rule* (Cambridge: Cambridge University Press, 2009), 4–5; Mark Doyle, *Communal Violence in the British Empire: Disturbing the Pax* (London: Bloomsbury Academic Press, 2016), 9–10.

6

"They Must Know Their Master, and He Must Know Them"

Labor Governance and Sovereignty on the Imperial Frontier in Southeast Asia, 1867–1890

In the mid-nineteenth century, the British Straits Settlements seemed like a most unlikely candidate for a successful experiment in colonial labor governance. At the edge of the imperial frontier, where Chinese organizations and their attendant customs held sway, British laws and institutions struggled to gain a foothold. The colonial boomtown of Singapore was regularly disturbed by demonstrations that sometimes descended into rioting, while the Malay interior frequently witnessed clashes over control of its lucrative tin deposits. British officials blamed the former on the pernicious influence of Chinese Secret Societies, and the latter on the fierce rivalry between Chinese mining concerns known as *kongsi* or *congsi* (translation: "company").[1] In 1876, following the latest in a long series of violent disturbances among the peripatetic Chinese workforce in Singapore, a government inquiry was convened to examine the causes and possible solutions. According to the composers of the final report, the power of the Secret Societies and their attendant *kongsi* was exacerbated by the acute weakness of British governance over the region. "The vast majority of Chinamen who come to work in these Settlements," they lamented, "return to their country not knowing clearly whether there is a Government in them or not."[2]

The elements of British colonial labor governance introduced there, although analogous to those implemented in other regions, had no historical antecedents in ameliorated slavery.[3] Chattel slavery, likewise, could neither serve as a moral foil to justify the state's assumption of authority over labor nor provide the legal

[1] For an overview of the history of the *kongsi* in the region, see Carl A. Trocki, *Opium and Empire: Chinese Society in Colonial Singapore, 1800–1910* (Ithaca, NY: Cornell University Press, 1990).

[2] *Labour Commission Report 1876, Straits Settlements Legislative Council Proceedings* (SSLC), cited in R. N. Jackson, "Grasping the Nettle: First Successes in the Struggle to Govern the Chinese in Malaya," *Journal of the Malaysian Branch of the Royal Asiatic Society* 40, no. 1 (211) (July 1967), 133.

[3] Although the topic has not generated the same level of interest and investigation as it has in the Atlantic World, the historiography of enslavement and the slave trade in the Indian Ocean World has become an increasing focus of historical scholarship in recent decades.

and institutional scaffolding for labor management. There *was* a pervasive system of labor importation and organization that had been operating successfully since the 1820s, but it was controlled by local Chinese leaders and based on diasporan Chinese patterns of culture and governance. In addition to the absence of structural precedents or moral justifications based on plantation slavery, the expansion of the overseer-state in the Straits faced a number of additional challenges very different from those encountered previously in the Caribbean and Mauritius. The majority of the population that would be brought under its authority did not consist of Indian immigrants who would be locked into long-term indentures on sugar plantations. Instead, Chinese contract-laborers on relatively short-term periods of employment would be the focus as they worked in a wide array of capacities from tin-mining to pepper and gambier farming. This cohort, while accustomed to operating within a hierarchical and rule-bound system of their own, were unfamiliar with and highly skeptical of the principles and practices of European state oversight. Adding to this panoply of obstacles, the expansion of colonial state oversight of the labor system faced a social, cultural, and political terrain that was profoundly inhospitable to centralized governance of the kind Britain had imposed in the former slave colonies. On the eve of the overseer-state's introduction in Southeast Asia, there was no precedent of Continental European state structures on which to build; British authority over the region and its burgeoning Chinese population was tenuous at best; civil disorder was more the norm than the exception; and even the small European commercial elite was resentful and resistant to concerted state regulation.

Despite the challenging circumstances, there were compelling reasons for British administrators to solidify colonial rule there. Foremost among these was the growing importance of the region to Britain's economic, political, and strategic hegemony in Southeast Asia. Singapore was the primary port of the Straits Settlements (see Map 6.2) and one of the fastest-growing cities in the region.[4] Obtained by the East India Company in 1819, the once quiet island of 1,000 residents had grown, by 1860, to a thronging population of 80,000, the vast majority of whom were immigrants from the southeastern provinces of China.[5]

For an overview of work on the history of the Dutch slave trade in the region, see Markus Vink, "'The World's Oldest Trade': Dutch Slavery and the Slave Trade in the Indian Ocean in the Seventeenth Century," *Journal of World History* 14, no. 2 (2003): 131–77. See also G. J. Knapp, "Slavery and the Dutch in Southeast Asia," in G. Ostinidië, ed., *Fifty Years Later: Antislavery, Capitalism, and Modernity in the Dutch Orbit* (Pittsburgh, PA: University of Pittsburgh Press, 1996). For a broader assessment, see Richard B. Allen, "Satisfying the 'Want for Labouring People': European Slave Trading in the Indian Ocean, 1500–1850," *Journal of World History* 21, no. 1 (March 2010), 45–73.

4 The first British settlement on the Malay peninsula was established not in Singapore but in Penang by Captain Francis Light, working under the auspices of the East India Company, in the late eighteenth century.

5 Jackson, "Grasping the Nettle," 130.

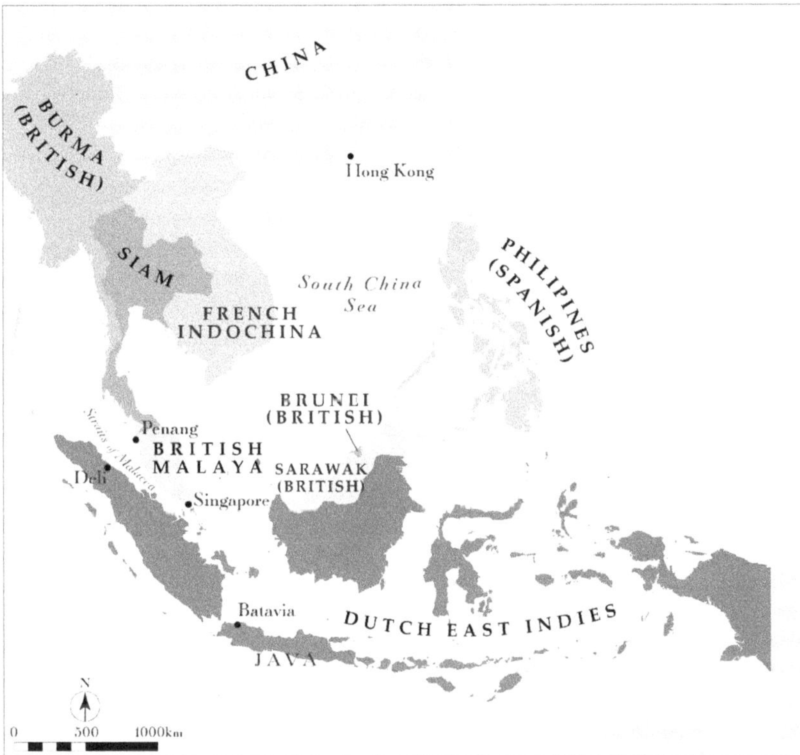

Map 6.1 Southeast Asia in 1895
Source: Courtesy of Mathilde Grimaldi.

This meteoric growth, which would continue throughout the later nineteenth and early twentieth centuries, was driven primarily by the large-scale immigration of Chinese workers from a weakened Qing Empire on the one hand and by the influx of wealth from British and cosmopolitan Chinese investors on the other. Singapore served as the entrepôt for sojourners from China, India, and other parts of Southeast Asia; as the exportation center for the vast mineral and agricultural wealth of the Malay Peninsula; and as the administrative and military seat of British authority in the region. Its economic value was matched by its strategic importance. With its excellent natural harbor and fortified position guarding the southern entry to the Malacca Strait, the "Lion City" founded by Stamford Raffles was crucial to Britain's suzerainty over the flourishing maritime trade between China and India.

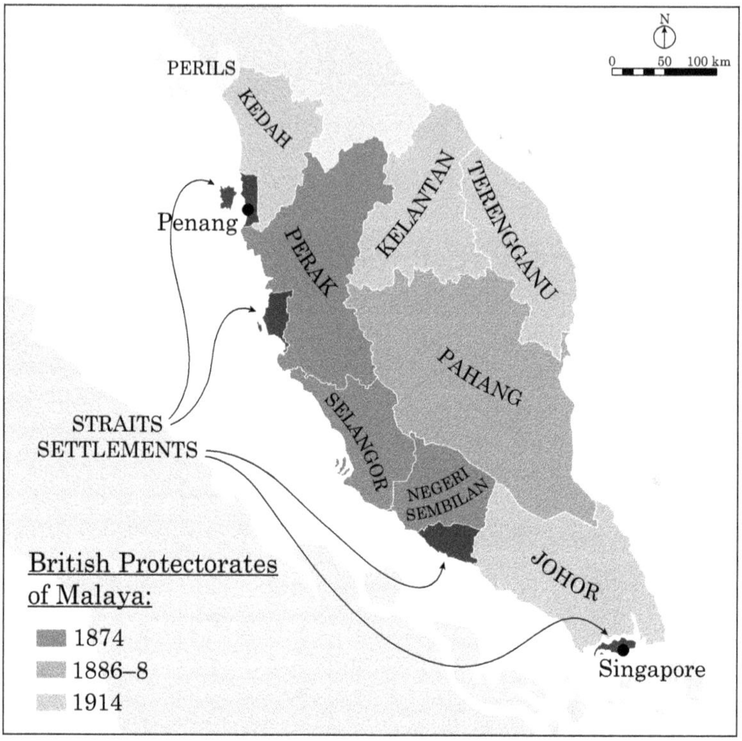

Map 6.2 The Straits Settlements and the British Protectorates of Malaya
Source: Courtesy of Mathilde Grimaldi.

Despite its seeming unsuitability as a site for experimentation in enhanced colonial governance, this region would witness the overseer-state's last great expansion and its most rapid and radical iteration.[6] From its precarious state in the early 1870s, in the course of a few decades, Britain's toehold on the Malay Peninsula would solidify in the Straits Settlements and extend to encompass large swathes of the interior as well. At the heart of this project would be the subsuming under government authority of the Chinese laboring population and the Chinese organizations that controlled their immigration and conditions of work. Whereas,

[6] The Straits Settlements comprised Singapore, Malacca, Dinding, and Penang. Perak, Selangor, Negiri Sembilan, and Pahang were established as the Federated Malay States in 1896, but came under indirect British rule in the 1870s with the appointment of British Residents to oversee their administration as "protected" states (Map 6.2). On the Resident system as employed in India, see Michael Fisher, *Indirect Rule in India: Residents and the Residency System 1764–1858* (Delhi: Oxford University Press, 1991).

in other regions, the expansion of state labor governance was morally justified in relation to chattel slavery, in the Straits, Chinese Secret Societies and their allegedly pernicious influence over the workforce would serve instead. These Societies would be first co-opted and then suppressed, allowing for the millions of Chinese workers that were the lifeblood of the region's prosperity to be incorporated into an extensive regimen of state oversight. Instead of opposition to chattel slavery, debt-slavery as practiced by the Societies would be a crucial focus of colonial paternalism.[7] The rapid extension of state control over labor would transform one of the empire's most strategically vital port cities in Asia and some of its most inaccessible and unruly territory from, or so British officials would claim, locales of lawless immorality to models of civilized behavior, orderly governance, and stable prosperity.

The apparatus of the overseer-state would be grafted onto the structural elements of Chinese labor governance even as British rule was defined against it. As discussed in Chapter 7, the expansion of colonial labor governance in the Straits Settlements would set the precedents, both morally and structurally, for its extension over the other Malay States through the Protectorate system.[8] Whereas in the plantation colonies of the Caribbean and Mauritius, state agents and institutions replaced British and European estate proprietors at the top of the colonial hierarchy, in Singapore and Malaya, they would replace the Secret Societies and their affiliated *kongsi*. The Societies were, according to colonial officials, an "*imperium in imperio*" (i.e. a government within a government), and the continuity of their authority was mutually exclusive with British suzerainty over the region.[9] The locale where these dynamics developed – on the edge of the imperial frontier where the precedents of European colonial rule were tenuous and the antecedents of British colonial labor organization were altogether absent – and the foil for their creation,

[7] Lynn Hollen Lees, *Planting Empire, Cultivating Subjects: British Malaya 1786–1941* (Cambridge: Cambridge University Press, 2017), 95.

[8] As Lynn Hollen Lees has emphasized, British colonial authority on the Malay peninsula was a complex and multilayered affair. In the Malay States, British officials, well into the early twentieth century, showed considerable willingness to respect local customs and authority in hopes of securing the willing cooperation of Malay rulers and elites. Ibid., 167–9; J. Norman Parmer, "The British Legacy," *Wilson Quarterly* 11, no. 5 (1987), 54–69. The moral equation of slavery would differ when applied to the Malay States as well, since British officials made the abolition of debt slavery a signifier of just colonial rule there. This, along with other encroachments on their authority, created much resentment among Malay chieftains, a sentiment expressed most dramatically in the assassination of J. W. W. Birch, the first British Resident of Perak, in November 1875.

[9] *Report of the Commissioners appointed under Act XXI of 1867 to enquire into "The Penang Riots,"* 4 (hereafter PRCR) (National Library of Singapore).

Chinese culture and governance, powerfully shaped the character of the overseer-state there.[10] As the overseer-state struggled to establish its political supremacy against highly resilient cultural and economic systems established previously by the Chinese Secret Societies and *kongsi*, its success or failure hinged increasingly on its ontological power to define moral governance and just rule. In this sense, British colonial authority in the Straits Settlements was more than merely anchored in regulation of the Chinese workforce; it was synonymous with it. On the imperial frontier in Southeast Asia, labor control *was* sovereignty.[11]

"Imperium in Imperio": The Introduction of the Overseer-State and Attempts at Accommodation with Secret Societies, 1867–1875

The development of the overseer-state in the Straits Settlements, and with it the expansion of British hegemony over the region and its labor supply, began in earnest in 1867. Prior to this period, the governance of the region operated as an extension of the governance of India. Indian government officials in Calcutta were largely content to work through the structures of Chinese labor organization that had grown in tandem with the region's rising Chinese immigrant population. This was particularly the case before 1857, when neither the British government in London nor the East India Company, both acutely sensitive to the potential financial and political costs involved, saw significant benefit to enhancing British authority further in the Malay Peninsula.[12] For the first few years of Singapore's development after 1819, it was run largely by officials seconded from the Indian civil service, who brought with them the methods of indirect rule employed extensively throughout the rural regions of India.[13] In practice, this meant leaving most everyday affairs

[10] The imperial frontier has long been a topic of concerted historical study, and has recently become an analytical lens unto itself as historians seek to understand the complex and permeable boundaries of political sovereignty and cultural and economic hegemony. See Richard Price, *Making Empire: Colonial Encounters and the Creation of Imperial Rule in Nineteenth-Century Africa* (Cambridge: Cambridge University Press, 2008); Benjamin D. Hopkins, *Ruling the Savage Periphery: Frontier Governance and the Making of the Modern State* (Cambridge, MA: Harvard University Press, 2020); Thomas Simpson, *The Frontier in British India: Space, Science, and Power in the Nineteenth Century* (Cambridge: Cambridge University Press, 2021).

[11] My thanks to Catherine Hall for this observation, which was made at the "Short Histories of the British Empire, 1816–1856" workshop hosted by the Institute of Advanced Studies, University College London, September 16, 2016.

[12] Leon Comber, "Chinese Secret Societies in Malaya: An Introduction," *Journal of the Malayan Branch of the Royal Asiatic Society* 29, no. 1 (May 1956), 151.

[13] Lees, *Planting Empire*, 3.

in the hands of local leaders. In the Straits, as was the case in India, colonial administrators typically had little formal experience with, or respect for, local customs. The British administration in Singapore would not have a high official with substantial knowledge of Chinese language and culture in post until the 1870s.[14]

In the intervening decades, the primary work of daily governance and labor organization, following patterns established in other Chinese communities throughout Southeast Asia, lay in the hands of the Secret Societies.[15] Structured along the lines of region (in China), dialect, and profession, the Societies organized labor importation and distribution.[16] Immigrants arrived in the ports of the Straits Settlements, where they found well-established Chinese communities. Through the oversight of Society leaders working in conjunction with labor importers and employers, new workers were distributed to European and Chinese-owned plantations in the Straits or to the Malay interior, where Chinese *kongsi* ran a thriving tin-mining industry with nominal deference to the Malay chiefs on whose land the tin deposits lay.[17] Britain's control of Singapore was crucial to this arrangement, particularly after the establishment of the Treaty Port system. This arrangement, which was forced on the Qing Dynasty in the wake of the Opium Wars, greatly reduced the Chinese

[14] Cheng Siok-Hwa, "Government Legislation for Chinese Secret Societies in the Straits Settlements in the Late 19th Century," *Asian Studies* 10, no. 2 (1972), 262.

[15] The establishment of the Secret Societies in the Straits Settlements dates to approximately the third decade of the nineteenth century, arriving first in Malacca from Thailand, then Penang, before finally being firmly established in Singapore around 1850. The exact origins of the Secret Societies in the Straits Settlements are difficult to determine. In part, this is due to the Societies' demands for strict secrecy among their members and the absence, prior to 1870, of any European official in the region who spoke Chinese and was familiar with Chinese culture. But the primary reason for this lacuna is that all of the records of the largest and most important of these organizations, referred to as the "Ghee Hin," were destroyed when they were suppressed by the British in 1890. Comber, "Chinese Secret Societies," 149–50.

[16] The modern scholarship on Chinese "Secret Societies" is voluminous. See, for example, Tai Hsuan-Chih and Ronald Suleski, "Origin of the Heaven and Earth Society," *Modern Asian Studies* 11, no. 3 (1977), 405–25; Cai Shaoqing, "An Overview of the Secret Societies in China during the Late Qing Period," *Cina* 21 (1988), 39–47; David Ownby, "The Heaven and Earth Society as Popular Religion," *Journal of Asian Studies* 54, no. 4 (1995), 1023–46. For a historical perspective on their contemporary forms, see An Chen, "Secret Societies and Organized Crime in Contemporary China," *Modern Asian Studies* 39, no. 1 (2005), 77–107.

[17] Rupert Emerson, *Malaysia: A Study in Direct and Indirect Rule* (Kuala Lumpur: University of Malaya Press, 1964), 26.

government's control of emigration and encouraged investment in labor transportation by both European and cosmopolitan Chinese interests.[18] As was the case in the Caribbean, Australia, western Canada, and wherever else cheap labor was in demand, British administrative structures and European (largely British) steamship companies facilitated the passage of workers from zones of recruitment to regions of employment.[19]

Although the steady transfer of Chinese laborers via the Treaty Ports to Singapore addressed the need for workers on the estates and tin mines, and the integrated recruitment and labor organization of the Secret Societies maintained the system at little administrative cost to the British, this arrangement came with its own problems from the perspective of colonial officials who were interested in both revenue and public order. Tin-mining was a profitable enterprise, and it was carried out far from the eyes of British officialdom.[20] The internecine rivalries between different regional and dialect groups, which had grown in intensity in China itself as the Qing Dynasty's rule was increasingly disrupted by European colonial incursions and internal fractures, accompanied the expansion of Chinese mining enterprises into the Malay interior.[21] The continued breakdown of order on the Chinese mainland, and the corrupt

[18] The Treaty Port system was enshrined in the Treaty of Nanking, which followed the conclusion of the First Opium War in 1842, and the Treaty of Bogue in 1843. In addition to ceding Hong Kong to the British in perpetuity, they were granted practical administrative control, legal independence ("extraterritoriality"), and most favored nation status in Shanghai, Canton (Ghuangzhou), Ningpo (Ningbo), Foochow (Fuzhou), and Amoy (Xiamen).

[19] Persia Crawford Campbell, *Chinese Coolie Emigration to Countries within the British Empire* (London: King & Sons, 1923), 1–3.

[20] For an overview of the economic aspects of Chinese mining in Southeast Asia, see Anthony Reid, "Chinese on the Mining Frontier in Southeast Asia," in Eric Tagliacozzo and Wen Chin Chang, eds., *Chinese Circulations: Capital, Commodities, and Networks in Southeast Asia* (Durham, NC: Duke University Press, 2011), 21–36.

[21] Chinese immigrants into the Straits Settlements came primarily from the maritime provinces of Kwangtung and Fukien. These two regions were at the epicenter of European incursions, the concurrent decline of Qing authority, and growing factional conflict among rival ethnic groups (William A. Pickering, "The Chinese in the Straits of Malacca," *Fraser's Magazine*, October 1876, 440). More specifically, the various cohorts could be broken down into five primary groups based on region and dialect:

> the Cantonese from the old prefectures of Kuang-chou-fu and Chao-ch'ing-fu in Kwangtung province; the Hokkiens from the old prefectures of Ch'lian-chou and Chang-chou, including Amoy, in Fukien province; the Teochius (or Hoklo) from the coastal regions and the delta areas of the Han River (including Swatow and Ch'ao-yang) in northeastern Kwangtung Province; the Hakkas (or Khehs) from all three provinces and also the southernmost parts of Kiangsi and Hunan; and the Hailams (or Hainanese) from the island of Hainan. (G. W. Skinner, *Chinese Society in Thailand: An Analytical History* [Ithaca, NY: Cornell University Press, 1957], 37–9)

and arbitrary practices of the Manchu Qing government, which many in southeast China viewed as foreign and invasive, had fed the rising importance of the Secret Societies. Amidst the challenges to Qing authority, these organizations served as vehicles to obtain employment, resolve conflicts, provide social support, and offer conflict resolution to large swathes of the population.[22]

On the Malay Peninsula, the Secret Societies, and the *kongsi* mining concerns that operated under their auspices, employed armed enforcers both to keep order among their own workers and to protect their interests from rivals, be they local Malays or rival *kongsi*.[23] The laborers in the *kongsi* were technically free, but were controlled through a system of debt-bondage known as the "credit-ticket" system, an arrangement structurally similar to indenture. To give their employers powerful leverage over their workers, new recruits were advanced the cost of passage and had to subsequently work off what was owed.[24] Although typically short in duration, one year being the most common length of contract, this arrangement was analogous to the indenture system that Britain had been employing across its empire since the abolition of slavery. The primary difference was that the credit-ticket system was controlled by private Chinese interests (i.e. the Secret Societies). Nominally, these were under the jurisdiction of the Government of India, as the paramount authority in the Straits. But geographic distance and attenuated lines of communication, a paucity of personnel on the ground, and almost complete ignorance of Chinese language, culture, and customs meant that British officials, in practice, exerted almost no direct authority over labor recruitment and organization, the tin-mining *kongsi*, and the Secret Societies that oversaw both.[25]

By mid-century, this arrangement of Chinese-controlled labor supply and organization, which had proceeded largely unregulated for several decades, was posing a growing conundrum for British officials in the Straits Settlements. The Chinese presence had, by this time, grown to constitute nearly half of the population of Singapore, a quarter of the population of Penang, and

22 The origins of the first Secret Society, known as the "Hung League" or "Heaven and Earth Society," are a source of much debate among historians since they are entangled with myth and arose during a very turbulent period of Chinese history. The most commonly related story is that the Hung League was founded in the early eighteenth century as a resistance movement against the K'ang Hsi, the second ruler of the Manchu dynasty, possibly as a response to his destruction of a Shao Lin monastery and the killing of the monks residing there. W. A. Pickering, "Chinese Secret Societies and Their Origin, Pt II," *Journal of the Straits Branch of the Royal Asiatic Society*, 3 (July 1879), 1–18; Comber, "Chinese Secret Societies," 148.

23 Emerson, *Malaysia*, 27.

24 For an overview of the credit-ticket system, see Pamela Crossley, "Dependency and Coercion in East Asian Labor, 1800–1949," in David Eltis, Stanley L. Engerman, Seymour Drescher, and David Richardson, eds., *The Cambridge World History of Slavery* (Cambridge: Cambridge University Press, 2017), 540–61.

25 Siok-Hwa, "Chinese Secret Societies," 264.

a significant cohort in Malacca as well.[26] With an Indian government that was remote, preoccupied with pressing affairs on its own soil, and largely uninterested and uninformed about affairs in the Straits, both the power of the Secret Societies and the accompanying social issues of a diverse and sometimes fractious Chinese population were becoming increasingly visible and disruptive. Violent clashes between rival groups, which had been intermittent since the 1820s, were growing in frequency and seriousness.[27] The entrenched structure of the Secret Societies and *kongsi* had long played an indispensable role in organizing the Chinese labor force and in maintaining the profits of Straits agriculture and the Malay tin-mining industry. But the internecine strife and apparent exploitation of Chinese workers ran counter to the British colonial administration's self-declared principles of moral governance and their desire for a particular vision of public order in a region that was increasingly vital to British strategic and economic interests in Southeast Asia.[28]

Calls rose from various quarters, most notably from the European and Chinese merchant community in Singapore and from the judiciary in the Straits Settlements, to curb the Secret Societies. The English-language press was especially vociferous in their condemnation of the Societies and their alleged promotion of illegal gambling among Singapore's swelling Chinese population.[29] Although the police force doubled between 1845 and 1865 (from 188 to 385), in part to deal with the issues blamed on the Societies, bribery and intimidation made them ineffective.[30] At the heart of the Straits government's inability to effectively address the growing influence of the Societies was the Indian government's inattention. Its officials were largely unconcerned about the social issues of its most distant territorial responsibility, unwilling to expend funds or commit personnel in that direction, and generally opposed to the cost and inconvenience of implementing restrictive legislation. Indicative of this was the tepid response to the outbreaks of violence, attributed to rivalries between Secret Societies, that occurred in 1854 and 1857. Despite the alarming reports of the Straits Settlements governor, Edmund Augustus

[26] Respectively, 27,988 out of 52,891 in 1850; 24,188 out of 107,914 in 1851; and 10,608 out of 62,514 in 1852. M. B. del Tufo, *Malaya (Federation) Superintendent of Census* (London: Crown Agents for the Colonies, 1949), appendix C, 584.

[27] Singapore had witnessed disturbances, attributed by British officials to the Secret Societies, in 1824, 1846, 1851, and 1854. Comber, "Chinese Secret Societies," 150.

[28] On the Colonial Office's efforts to balance colonial self-governance with the general tendency of employers to enact exploitative labor legislation in the wake of 1834, see M. K. Banton, "The Colonial Office, 1820–1955: Constantly the Subject of Small Struggles," in Douglas Hay and Paul Craven, eds., *Magistrates, Servants, and Magistrates in Britain and the Empire, 1562–1955* (Chapel Hill: University of North Carolina Press, 2004), 251–302.

[29] *Pinang Press*, May 29, reprinted under "Penang," in the *Singapore Free Press and Mercantile Advertiser*, June 18, 1852, 3.

[30] Ibid.

Blundell, about the threat posed to persons and property, the sole substantive measure adopted in response to the turmoil was an attempt to co-opt the headmen of the Secret Societies by designating them as special constables.[31] The Straits government's ability to monitor and restrict the Societies, and the Chinese population more generally, was further hampered by a police force that was composed almost entirely of Malays and Indians, among whom Chinese language was all but unknown, and a civil administration equally at sea with regard to Chinese culture and customs.[32]

The year 1867 signaled the beginning of the end of the Secret Societies' unchallenged authority over the Straits' Chinese population and the continued inattentive governance of this growing cohort. That year, after nearly a decade of petitioning by the British merchant community, the Government of India's laissez-faire administration was terminated and the Straits Settlements were reconstituted as an independent Crown colony.[33] Henceforth, its executive, who would be appointed and work under the direct supervision of the Colonial Office, would be empowered to convene a legislative council, staff various administrative posts, appoint committees, manage revenue and finance, and pass such ordinances as they saw fit. Colonel Harry St. George Ord, the first governor of the newly designated Crown colony, arrived in Singapore in 1867.[34] Like many of his predecessors in other Crown colonies, Ord came from a military background and, like them, one of his most challenging tasks in his new post would be finding a balance between the expectations of the Colonial Office, the demands of the local elites (represented in the legislative council), and what he perceived to be his responsibilities toward the population he governed. A key concern in the latter regard was the large Chinese laboring cohort that, until his arrival, had been managed largely by the Secret Societies and treated with impunity by the small European mercantile community. European merchants, their disdain notwithstanding, recognized the Chinese population's crucial twofold role as the colony's main workforce and its primary source of direct revenue via taxes on opium and alcohol.[35]

31 *Straits Settlements Annual Report 1861–2*, 3. For Blundell's response, see Rajesh Kai, "The 1857 Panic and the Fabrication of an Indian 'Menace' in Singapore," *Modern Asian Studies* 47, no. 2 (2013), 376.

32 Jackson, "Grasping the Nettle," 131.

33 C. B. Buckley, *An Anecdotal History of Old Times in Singapore, Vol. 2* (Singapore: Fraser & Neave: 1902), 755.

34 Previous governors had been appointed by the East India Company (1826–59) and the India Office (1859–67).

35 Diana S. Kim, *Empires of Vice: The Rise of Opium Prohibition Across Southeast Asia* (Princeton, NJ: Princeton University Press, 2020), 128. Duties were collected via "revenue farms," which entailed granting sole right to collect them to an individual or group in return for a fixed sum paid annually to the government. Revenue had also been generated in this manner for "gambling farms" prior to their abolition in 1826. Directly or

The new governor faced the daunting prospect of, after decades of relative non-interference, fulfilling his role as the colony's chief representative of the Crown and the embodiment of its colonial mission. Singapore's European merchant community was the first to contest his authority. Coordinated through the Straits Settlement Association (established in 1868), they began a steady campaign of protests to the Colonial Office, one that would continue unabated throughout Ord's tenure. The Colonial Office, in turn, would clash with the governor on many occasions over his six years in office.[36] But when Ord took up his post in 1867, these problems still lay in the future. A more immediate obstacle confronted his efforts to extend state authority. Coinciding with his arrival was the outbreak of a fresh wave of violence in Penang, which would prove to be a watershed moment in official attitudes and responses toward the Chinese population in the Straits.

What became known as the "Penang Riots of 1867" began in Georgetown, the capital, on August 3, and continued for ten days before the newly appointed Lieutenant-Governor of Penang, Archibald E. H. Anson, negotiated a settlement between the combatants.[37] In the immediate aftermath, a government commission appointed to investigate the riots attributed them to a rivalry between two Chinese Secret Societies, the Ghee Hin and the Toh Peh Kong (alternatively, Tua Pek Kong), and their allies, the White Flag and the Red Flag societies. The latter included both Malay members and south Indian contingents referred to as "Klings." The numbers involved were considerable, as each society could count thousands of members in the capital and the surrounding region.[38] Although eyewitness reports and press coverage in the aftermath described widespread violence and slaughter, an accurate accounting of the injuries, deaths, and property damage was never produced. At the time, the causes of the conflict were also poorly understood. More recent analysis has attributed them to a combination of long-running ethnic tensions exacerbated by contestation over control of the extraordinarily lucrative opium trade.[39] The most important consequence of the event was not the destruction wrought, the injuries inflicted,

indirectly, the heads of the Chinese Secret Societies managed the majority of the revenue farms in the Straits.

36 John Legge, "The Colonial Office and Governor Ord," *Journal of Southeast Asian Studies* 29, no. 1 (March 1998), 2.

37 Mahani Musa, "Malays and the Red and White Flag Societies in Penang, 1830s–1920s," *Journal of the Malaysian Branch of the Royal Asiatic Society* 72, no. 2 (1999), 164.

38 These may have been as high as 25,000 for the combined forces of the Ghee Hin and White Flag, 3,000 for the Toh Peh Kong, and 1,000 for the Red Flag, with the numerical disparity compensated for by the Red Flag's large stock of firearms. Musa, "Malays and the Red and White Flag Societies," 163.

39 For the former, see ibid., 151–61. At the time, in the Straits Settlements, opium accounted for 30–60 percent of locally collected revenue and 40–50 percent of total revenue annually, according to government reports. Carl A. Trocki, "Opium and the Beginnings

or the lives lost (if any). Rather, it was that the disturbances focused official attention on the Secret Societies just at the moment when the region had achieved independence from the Indian government and had come under direct Crown rule. In the figures of Ord and Anson, the Straits and Penang were now under the authority of newly empowered governors for whom the riots posed the first test of their administrative ability to realize their visions of public order and moral rule.

The efforts of these officials and their successors in the Straits took place in the context of a broader trend toward a more professionalized and robust apparatus of colonial authority across Britain's southern hemisphere colonies. In the years following 1857, the authority of the Colonial Office and the colonial governors under their supervision expanded at a rate not witnessed since the conclusion of the Napoleonic Wars. India was the largest and most notable territory brought under direct rule, with Jamaica following in the wake of the 1865 Morant Bay Rebellion.[40] Conversely, the change in the Straits' status in 1867 also took place on the eve of Britain's expansion of its African territories, which would often be accomplished through methods of indirect rule.[41] The balance between centralized-metropolitan authority (e.g. the Colonial Office), centralized-colonial authority (e.g. Crown-appointed governors), local officials (e.g. magistrates), and the power of local elites, whether European, African, or Asian, both formal (e.g. through nominated or legislative councils) and informal, would vary considerably from colony to colony.[42] Nonetheless, the apparatus of government, in the form of executives, their attendant administrations, magistrates, police forces, and various institutions of rule – such as courtrooms, customs depots, and prisons – saw significant growth.[43] This was a common thread across Britain and the British Empire, extending also to the white-settler colonies of Canada and Australia as they

of Chinese Capitalism in Southeast Asia," *Journal of Southeast Asian Studies* 33, no. 2 (June 2002), 298.

40 Other Crown colonies constituted in the 1870s and 1880s included Fiji (1874), the Transvaal (1877), and Basutoland (1884).

41 See, for example, J. C. Myers, *Indirect Rule in South Africa: Tradition, Modernity, and the Costuming of Political Power* (Rochester, NY: University of Rochester Press, 2009).

42 This was true even within Crown colonies, since some retained nominated councils and others retained legislative councils with varying degrees of power and influence.

43 For an overview of this process, see Lauren Benton, *Law and Colonial Cultures: Legal Regimes in World History 1400–1900* (Cambridge: Cambridge University Press, 2002), 167–209; John McLaren, "The Uses of the Rule of Law in British Colonial Societies in the Nineteenth Century," in S. Dorsett and I. Hunter, eds., *Law and Politics in British Colonial Thought* (New York: Palgrave Macmillan, 2010), 71–90. On the antecedents, see Helen Taft Manning, "Who Ran the British Empire, 1830–1850?" *Journal of British Studies* 5, no. 1 (1965), 88–121.

developed their economies, expanded formal control over indigenous lands, and moved toward federation and eventual autonomy.[44]

In the Straits, for Ord and his successors, the more specific question was how to achieve, by their own standards and with the tools of governing available to them, a morally acceptable compromise between the tendency of local elites, be they Secret Society headmen or European planters, to exploit their workforce and those workers' tendency to resist mistreatment in disruptive ways. Particularly in the wake of the Indian Rebellion of 1857, with its abject lesson in the consequences of colonial *mis*rule, colonial governors recognized that good government, revenue generation, and public order were mutually dependent, and saw their role as achieving the latter two through the former. In the aftermath of the 1867 riots, colonial administration in the Straits predictably became entangled with paternalistic oversight of the laboring population, much as had been the case in the Caribbean during the period of ameliorated slavery and in Mauritius during the growth of indenture.

The equally powerful intertwining of attitudes toward governance with ideas about race generated in the processes *of* governance was very much apparent in Anson's response to the events of 1867. The decisions made in the wake of the riots relied primarily on two sources of information. The first was the report of an official commission assembled and chaired by Anson to gather evidence about the causes and character of the disturbance. The second was *Thian Ti Hui: The Hung-League or Heaven and Earth League*, a work of scholarship on the history of the Chinese Secret Societies composed by the pioneering Dutch Sinologist Gustav Schlegel. Together, *Thian Ti Hui* and the Penang Riots Committee Report (PRCR) constituted the first concerted efforts to understand the operation and impact of the Chinese Secret Societies in Southeast Asia. They would remain for many years after as crucial touchstones for public discussions and official policies toward them, with *Thian Ti Hui*, in particular, being frequently referenced by British officials.[45] Both documents acknowledged that the Secret Societies had begun as institutions to preserve the spiritual and cultural practices of Chinese communities living abroad, but that they had developed into something far more pervasive, and potentially threatening to European colonial authority, in the years before the 1867 riots.

Schlegel, although he published his book in English, was Dutch, and worked as the official interpreter of Chinese to the government of Batavia (in the Dutch East Indies, aka the Netherlands-Indies). Having begun lessons in the Chinese language in Leiden at the age of nine, he had continued his study in China itself in 1861 before taking a job the following year as an interpreter in

[44] Bryan D. Palmer, "Nineteenth-Century Canada and Australia: The Paradoxes of Class Formation," *Labour/Le Travail* 84 (Fall 1996), 16–36.

[45] Jean Elizabeth DeBernardi, *Rites of Belonging: Memory, Modernity, and Identity in a Malaysian Chinese Community* (Pasadena, CA: Stanford University Press, 2004), 55, 66.

the Dutch colonial supreme court of Batavia (see Map 6.1). *Thian Ti Hui* was primarily a work of interpretive analysis, based on troves of documents seized by the Dutch police from the Secret Societies in Batavia. It was, at the time and for many decades after, considered to be the authoritative work on the Societies. It consisted primarily of detailed translations and analysis of their origins, their principles of organization, and the various oaths, statutes, and rituals that governed their members. Schlegel's work, though hardly objective, was largely dispassionate in its approach, and strove to interpret the Societies within their philosophical and historical context, as he understood it from his decades-long study of Chinese language and culture. The author acknowledged the coercive recruitment practices of the Societies, their willingness to resort to violence against their rivals, and their explicit commitment (in principle if not necessarily in practice) to severely punish members who were disloyal or who broke the sacred oaths of secrecy. But Schlegel refrained from overly moralistic assessments. He compared the Societies to what he saw as their closest European counterpart, the Freemasons. Their, to European eyes, stern methods were a logical reaction to the violence and corruption of Qing rule. The Societies, he insisted, whatever they might appear as to outside observers, were profoundly devoted to Chinese concepts of honor and virtue.

Schlegel's observations on the political implications of the Societies, and their potentially disruptive influence to European colonial authority, were confined to the introduction of *Thian Ti Hui*, and were highly ambivalent in their conclusions. The Chinese were "the most reasonable and cool of all Eastern races" and their "reverence for authority *when judiciously enforced* . . . is one of their chief characteristics."[46] Such tendency toward order, however, was manifest only when the laws in question were carefully explained and justified, and when they did not explicitly challenge Chinese customary practices. This commitment to resisting unjust rule was an essential aspect of Chinese history and of the Secret Societies in particular, and as a result, "they will submit less to tyranny than any other Eastern nation."[47] The problems facing Singapore, in particular, and the "unruliness of her Chinese population," were therefore the result of "defects in her [i.e. Singapore's] own Government."[48] The absence of Chinese-speaking officials had left the Chinese population in ignorance of government policy, and as a consequence, they still regarded themselves as Chinese subjects first and foremost. Therefore, the keys to effective colonial governance were knowledge and communication on the part of officialdom, and the most advisable approach was to take "due regard . . . to the prejudices of the nation" and to

46 Gustav Schlegel, *Thian Ti Hui – The Hung-League or Heaven and Earth League: A Secret Society with the Chinese in China and India* (Batavia: Lange & Co., 1866), xl.
47 Ibid., xlix.
48 Ibid.

"explain to [the Chinese population] the necessity or expediency of a new law or regulation."[49]

Thian Ti Hui, though academic in its tone and structure, had profound political implications for shaping how British administrators approached governing the Chinese population in the Straits. It provided a detailed and compelling intellectual justification for two key opinions expressed commonly in British official discourse. The first was that the Chinese saw themselves as a people apart and somewhat aloof from colonial governance, and the second was that they saw resistance as a moral response when laws were deemed arbitrary or hostile to their culture. These positions, along with Schlegel's elaboration of the intense coherence of the Societies through their secrecy, their complex structure of oaths and statutes, and their harsh punishment of transgressors, would emerge again and again in discussions over how Chinese populations in the Straits and throughout the British Empire were to be governed henceforth.

Schlegel's work also clearly delineated the essential cultural differences that allegedly divided the Chinese and Chinese culture in Southeast Asia irrevocably from Europeans and European culture.[50] The Chinese, according to Schlegel, were hierarchical, and potentially amenable to good governance, but only if they judged it to be fair by their own standards and in accord with their own cultural precepts. In sum, in the right circumstances, the Chinese could be persuaded to obey European laws, but never to adopt a European outlook. Schlegel's perspective also jibed with the arguments of Henry Maine and other British observers writing about India in the wake of 1857, and with the general retreat, in favor of more indirect modes of rule, from colonial efforts to integrate and acculturate non-Europeans.[51] The need for compromise in the face of such intractable cultural differences was made clear by Schlegel, in terms that could be read as either ominous or merely fatalistic. Eradicating the Secret Societies, he insisted, was "a sheer impossibility," and therefore it was up to "those in power to judge if [their] existence is dangerous for the tranquility of a colony or state or not."[52]

The committee assembled and chaired by Governor Anson of Penang in the wake of the 1867 riots reached a clear determination on this question. The Societies, they concluded after a lengthy investigation and voluminous witness testimony, were "unscrupulously evil," "barbarous," and "extremely dangerous

[49] Ibid., xl.

[50] Such essentializing of difference would also be a key aspect of how European scholarship portrayed the Middle East in the same period. See Edward Said, *Orientalism* (New York: Routledge and Kegan & Paul, 1978).

[51] Karuna Mantena, *Alibis of Empire: Henry Maine and the Ends of Liberal Imperialism* (Princeton, NJ: Princeton University Press, 2010), 6–7.

[52] Schlegel, *Thian Ti Hui*, xl.

to the peace and welfare of the community."[53] Their most dangerous aspect was that they operated as a government unto themselves for the Chinese population. This "*imperium in imperio*" fulfilled a multitude of roles normally occupied by the state. These included collective offense and defense for members, the provision of social welfare, care for those killed or wounded in service, the delineation of rules of conduct, and conflict resolution both internally among Society confreres and externally in disputes with members of other Societies.[54] Schlegel's account had focused on the history of the Societies and on their basis in Chinese culture and philosophy, only engaging their current political significance tangentially and steering away from excessive moral judgments. The PRCR, in contrast, was concerned *primarily* with the political and moral implications of the Societies for the governance of the Straits. The Societies, they emphasized, were inherently revolutionary in origin and character, intrinsically violent in practice, criminal in conduct, and utterly alien in custom. The largest of the organizations in the Straits, the Ghee Hin, estimated to have 25,000–26,000 members, was singled out for particular condemnation. New members, the committee asserted, were bound to their induction oaths by drinking one another's blood, and failure to answer calls to fight or to attend important ceremonies could be punished with floggings, amputations, or even beheadings.[55]

Although the PRCR could produce no direct evidence that the more extreme punishments had ever been inflicted in the Straits, the commissioners expressed confidence that this was only because the witnesses they interviewed, many of whom were Society members themselves, had concealed the worst features of their organizations.[56] Another highly notable and worrisome feature of the Societies was their ability to bridge racial divides in the colony. The primary protagonists in the riots, the Ghee Hin and the Toh Peh Kong, were largely Chinese in membership. Their allies, in contrast, the White Flag and the Red Flag, respectively, were constituted of Malay and "Kling" (i.e. southern Indian) members. In Georgetown, the capital of Penang, the allied groups occupied the same quarters of the town in relative harmony, their collaboration cemented by the induction of a key cohort of the Malay–Kling contingent into the Chinese Societies.[57] Given British officials' keen awareness of the threat that coordinated opposition could pose to their authority, particularly in a political environment as febrile as the Malay Peninsula was, such cooperation of ethnically diverse groups under Chinese leadership was a dire prospect indeed.

53 PRCR, 6, 16.
54 Ibid., 4.
55 Ibid., 5, 6.
56 Ibid., 6.
57 Ibid., 9, 10.

In the face of what they viewed to be a clear and present danger to the social, political, and moral fabric of the colony, the PRCR's strong recommendation was that the Societies be suppressed.[58] Such a firm response was consistent with the government's actions taken in the immediate aftermath of the Penang Riots. These had seen the leaders of the Societies forced to pay hefty fines to compensate those whose property had been damaged, and to the government directly to offset the expense of quelling the disturbances.[59] The already considerable authority of the colonial executive in the Crown colony system was further enhanced by the Straits Legislative Council's passing of Act XX of 1867, "an Act for the Better Preservation of the Peace."[60] This empowered the governor to issue a proclamation of emergency in cases of public disturbance (or anticipation of them). Under such circumstances, in contradiction to British constitutional principles, any Chinese alien or naturalized citizen could be summarily deported without a right of appeal. The government was quick to deploy these extraordinary powers, despite considerable opposition, most notably from the colony's own Chief Justice, Sir Peter Maxwell.[61] More than three dozen Chinese residents were transported, some for sentences exceeding two decades; two were deported; and four were sentenced to death, though these were later commuted to imprisonment for life.[62]

This harsh response against the Societies' leadership and those whom the government held most responsible, however, did little to lessen the overall influence of the organizations. Having assessed the situation more thoroughly, the Penang Riots Committee recognized that full suppression of the Societies might prove impossible. Given the size of the Societies, the relatively small policing and administrative structure of the fledgling colony, and the difficulties in distinguishing between members and non-members of a group alien in custom and language to European officials, this was an understandable conclusion. Accordingly, the PRCR recommended a raft of legal measures to

58 Ibid., 16.

59 Specifically, the fines were $SD5,000 to the family of a soldier killed, $SD60,000 in property compensation, and $SD10,000 to the government. These were extraordinary sums given that, at the time, the average Chinese laborer in the Straits earned between 50 and 70 cents a day.

60 Jack Jin Gary Lee, "Plural Society and the Colonial State: English Law and the Making of Crown Colony Government in the Straits Settlements," *Asian Journal of Law and Society* 2 (2015), 230. Act XX of 1867 (Act for Better Preservation of Public Peace) enabled the forcible disarming of the population within designated districts and the deportation, without trial, of any Chinese alien or naturalized British subject.

61 Maxwell referred to them as "extraordinary" and "unconstitutional." *Report of the Proceedings of the Straits Settlements Legislative Council*, August 28, 1869, 21. See also *Straits Times*, April 10, 1869.

62 Ord to Colonial Office April 27, 1868 (CO 273/18), July 24, 1868 (CO 273/19), January 6, 1869, cited in Negandiram Rajendra, "The Straits Settlements, 1867–1874," unpublished MA thesis, Australian National University, 1976, 230 n. 109.

constrain the Societies. The first and most important of these, which would be enshrined in Ordinance XIX of 1869, passed by the Straits Settlements Legislative Council (SSLC), was to bring the leadership and membership of these organizations under state oversight. The Act "to Provide for the Suppression of Dangerous Societies" incorporated several key steps toward this end. The most significant of these mandated the formal registration of all Societies of ten or more persons, a prohibition on the administration of oaths, and the requirement for official notification of any meetings.[63] The regulations on the disclosure of information were especially detailed, as registered Societies had to provide not only a full list of all members and officers, including their names, addresses, and occupations, but also a copy of all rules governing the Society, a list of all payments required and sources of income, copies of any obligations or promises, an explanation of all signs and passwords, and a description of all ceremonies.[64] Lastly, Ordinance XIX placed a significant financial burden on the Society leadership, empowering the governor to require from them, as sureties to keep the peace, bonds of up to 1,000 Singapore dollars.[65]

Ordinance XIX was the opening salvo of a decades-long effort by the Straits government to suppress the Secret Societies. It also had the functional effect of bringing a large proportion of the working population under indirect state oversight by definitively elevating the authority of the British colonial administration over that of the Society leadership. Ordinance XIX represented a pragmatic compromise between the impossibility, with the resources at hand, of directly governing the Chinese working population or eliminating the Societies entirely and the goal of Ord and Anson to reduce the threats they posed to public order. Whether the rank and file of the Chinese workforce would now be aware that they were under British suzerainty is difficult to determine. But, given the stern punishments meted out to their comrades, there can be little doubt that it would have been painfully obvious to the Society leadership.

In attempting to address the issue of the Societies, the colonial government, having finally achieved independence from Indian supervision and now in the hands of colonial executives committed to a more interventionist character of rule, faced two key problems. The first was that the Secret Societies were inextricably entangled with the economic functioning of the Straits, and with the generation of government revenue in particular. Pulling up these institutions root and branch was simply not practical given the resources at the disposal of the Straits government. The second, as commentators both then and subsequently acknowledged, was that the growing Chinese population was the key to the wealth and

[63] Siok-Hwa, "Chinese Secret Societies," 264 n. 7.
[64] Ibid.
[65] Ibid.

productivity of the region.[66] Not only did they supply the labor to toil on European-owned plantations and to mine the rich tin reserves of the Malay interior but they were also the primary consumers of opium. The proceeds from the latter, generated by the annual sale of "revenue farms," constituted more than 45 percent of the colony's total revenue by 1875.[67] This salient fact would hardly have been lost on the members of the 1867 Riots Commission, who represented a cross-section of Penang's cosmopolitan commercial elite, and were led by a governor for whom the finances of the region were of paramount concern.[68] For both practical and economic reasons, therefore, the Chinese could not simply be ejected from the colony. For Ord and Anson, as would be for their successors, the central conundrum was how to properly govern the expanding Chinese population and thus maintain the colony's growth and prosperity while simultaneously undermining the influence of the Secret Society leaders. Bringing them, and with them the Chinese labor force, under state control was made more difficult by the general attitude of the Colonial Office, whose officials were resistant to placing the Straits and the Malay States under the aegis of more concerted, and therefore more expensive, official administration.[69]

Schlegel's scholarly treatise and the PRCR provided policy guidelines to Governors Ord and Anson for the years immediately following the disturbances of 1867.[70] Both documents had focused on cultural and social explanations for the Secret Societies and their ongoing conflicts. Contrary to their arguments, however, the underlying causes of the Penang Riots and the even more serious disturbances that followed in subsequent years were confined

66 Pickering, "The Chinese in the Straits of Malacca," 442.

67 Although Malay miners had pioneered tin-mining in the region, their labor was constrained by small-scale production and its part-time integration with agricultural work (largely rice-growing). By the time the Straits were established as a Crown colony, the tin-mining was done primarily by the Chinese, who implemented a year-round labor regimen and employed more advanced and large-scale mining methods. John Gullick, "The Economy of Perak in the Mid-1870s," *Journal of the Malaysian Branch of the Royal Asiatic Society* 83, no. 2 (December 2010), 32. For opium revenue, see Cheng U. Wen, "Opium in the Straits Settlements, 1867–1910," *Journal of Southeast Asian History* 2, no. 1 (March 1961), 52.

68 The remaining eight commission members besides Anson included two of the proprietors of one of Penang's largest agricultural estates (Prye Estates), whose products were consumed in large part by the Chinese workforce; Foo-Tye Sin, originally a tin-miner himself and now a co-owner of one of the colony's most successful ship's chandler's (Tye Sin Tat & Co.); and Nina Merican Koordin, a prominent Tamil merchant and estate-owner whose family had emigrated from Tamil Nadu in the 1820s with Captain Francis Light, the colony's first superintendent. PRCR, 19.

69 Khoo Kay Kim, "The Origin of British Administration in Malaya," *Journal of the Malaysian Branch of the Royal Asiatic Society*, 39, no. 1 (1966), 62–4.

70 DeBernardi, *Rites of Belonging*, 55, 66.

neither to intractable ethnic hostilities nor to a general mistrust of overarching political authority and a consequent focus solely on internal cultural rules and Society loyalty. Equally important had been economic competition over control of the tin mines in the hinterlands, and of the lucrative opium, alcohol, and gambling concessions buoyed by the expanding Chinese population.[71] In the Malay States, this contestation would be mapped onto regional rivalries between Malay chieftains, whose wealth was also entangled in control of these essential resources and whose power depended on the Chinese mining companies (*kongsi*) and their Secret Society allies for both labor and protection.[72] In many respects, the Chinese Secret Societies and their associated *kongsi*, in the nearly completely deregulated environment of the Straits Settlements and the Malay States, embodied the same laissez-faire, free-market system that many prominent figures in the British government and commercial interests were themselves ardently advocating.[73]

This collaboration between Secret Societies, *kongsi*, and Malay chieftains had been operating quite successfully, and profitably, for several decades by the time of the 1867 riots.[74] How then to explain why these disturbances rose in frequency subsequently, and why they triggered a forceful reaction in policy toward the Secret Societies? The answer lies in the growth of the regional economy itself, in the changing structure of colonial governance and the attitude of its leadership, and in the need of the latter, in the face of rising disorder, to justify more forceful state intervention. As the potential revenue of the interrelated structure of mining, agriculture (e.g. the rice-farming that provided workers with their primary foodstuff), opium, alcohol, and other supporting commercial endeavors rose with the increasing Chinese population, competition over control of these concerns rose in tandem.[75] Attempts to maintain public order, meanwhile, substantially raised the cost of government, making the revenue gained from the "farming" of opium and the collection of tin-mining duties all the more necessary for maintaining the colony's finances. The timing of these events was crucial. The 1867 riots coincided with the establishment of independent governance of the Straits and its placement in the hands of colonial executives (e.g. Ord and Anson) who both felt that *ruling*

[71] The origins of Chinese tin-mining in the Malay States date to the 1820s. R. N. Jackson, *Immigrant Labour and the Development of Malaya, 1786–1920* (Singapore: Government Press, 1961), 32. Singapore itself operated as a free port, hence the need to sell the rights to collect duties on opium, alcohol, and gambling through annually renewed "revenue farms."

[72] Gullick, "The Economy of Perak," 36–7. Jackson, *Immigrant Labour*, 36–7. It is important to note here that the British maintained control of land tenures and much of the legal system, which ensured that British commercial interests were protected (Lees, *Planting Empire*, 40–1).

[73] Trocki, "Opium and the Beginnings of Chinese Capitalism," 301–4.

[74] Ibid., 301.

[75] The total revenue collected by the government rose rapidly from $SD1,538,854 in 1875 to $SD2,361,300 in 1880 and $SD3,508,074 in 1885. Wen, "Opium in the Straits Settlements," 52.

the Chinese population was a moral imperative and that only an enhanced colonial state could provide an acceptable framework for ordering the social and political dynamics of the colony.

As the growing Chinese population and the rising economic and strategic importance of the region prompted official inquiries and more scholarly investigations (e.g. Schlegel's) of Chinese society in the Straits, a dire image of its social and political fragility emerged. Much like in Mauritius, South Africa, and other Caribbean colonies, which were subject to similar official scrutiny in the wake of emancipation, the Straits were portrayed as lacking the stabilizing influence of a European middle class capable of liberal self-governance. In its absence, influential officials such as Ord would assert, a more robust state apparatus was required to step in and provide stability, maintain public order, create a safe environment for investment and development, and mediate relations between a small property-owning elite and a much larger, non-European workforce.[76] Without a strong state to preserve order, this reasoning held, Chinese and Malays alike would turn one of the central principles of British rule – and its widest contrast with Continental colonial system – into its greatest weakness. This principle, which was crucial to the public justifications of indenture as well, was the alleged recognition of legal equality among all Crown subjects and a concurrent commitment to nonracialized forms of governance. A more robust approach to colonial governance in Malaysia, which would transgress these principles with regulations that were racialized both *de jure* and de facto, was justifiable only within the schema of allegedly moral governance when the potential of non-Europeans to provide a stabilizing element was dismissed.[77] That dismissal, in turn, was grounded in broader discourses about race, and in the specific portrayal of the non-Europeans that did wield power – be they Society headmen, local Malay rulers, or *sirdars* – as ineffective, immoral, disruptive,

[76] The advocacy of more despotic, rather than representative, forms of governance in the colonial context had a long intellectual tradition in liberal political discourse, and had been a position held by John Stuart Mill, among others. See Uday S. Mehta, "Liberal Strategies of Exclusion," in Frederick Cooper and Ann Laura Stoler, eds., *Tensions of Empire: Colonial Cultures in a Bourgeois World* (Berkeley: University of California Press, 1997), 56–86.

[77] The only exceptions were Chinese merchants that openly declared their interest in seeing the Societies suppressed and fully supported the imposition of British modes of governance and structures of investment and commerce. This would become a pattern both throughout the empire and in Britain itself. Only Chinese men that completely rejected Chinese culture and embraced Western traditions in politics, culture, and economic activity could be seen as moral and beneficial to the local community. And even then they were often targets of suspicion and hostility. Sascha Auerbach, "Margaret Tart, Lao She, and the Opium-Master's Wife: Race and Class Among Chinese Commercial Immigrants in London and Australia, 1866–1929," *Comparative Studies in Society and History* 55, no. 1 (2013), 43–51.

and even seditious. When the latter were granted liberal freedoms but lacked the moral restraint required to wield such freedoms responsibly, disorder and violence were the inevitable result. As the author of an influential official report on the Societies asserted in 1869, "ambitious, turbulent and clever men [acquire] power and make it widely felt . . . they may form leagues for almost any purpose without Government knowing or caring, and engage in hostilities on a scale with which it is wholly powerless to cope."[78]

In this regard, it was not just the periodic, and increasingly frequent, outbreaks of disorder that were a problem; even the order that Societies were able to provide was defined through the informational processes of colonial governance as the *wrong type* of order. It was based on Chinese cultural and political norms, allegedly antithetical to European notions, and dependent on the influence of men who were, to quote the PRCR, irredeemably "evil" and "barbarous."[79] The central concern, as Schlegel's scholarship and numerous official reports maintained, was not that the Chinese population was inherently disorderly but rather that they were dominated by immoral leadership, shaped by undesirable cultural influences, and currently un*governed*. Stronger state oversight in the Straits was therefore deemed necessary to constrain the power of disruptive individuals within a population that was otherwise orderly and amenable to colonial rule, as had been the case with ameliorated slaves, apprentices, and indentured Indians. Thus was increasing the power of the state apparatus to monitor and prosecute the Chinese workforce in the Straits with legislation that applied solely to them reconciled with the insistence that British colonial rule was characterized there, as elsewhere, by its commitment to free markets, racial equality, and just rule according to liberal principles.

Schlegel's somewhat ambivalent conclusions about the dangers of the Secret Societies, reconstituted in more urgent terms by the PRCR and the *Report Upon Chinese Secret Societies* composed by SSLC in 1869, provided the immediate justification for sterner action against the Secret Society leaders who were accumulating wealth and influence.[80] In the wake of the 1867 riots, the Straits government, with Ord at its head, pursued three interrelated goals: undermine the power of Secret Society headmen, subsume the labor system under government authority, and co-opt the Chinese labor force into its vision of just governance. These would need to be accomplished with tepid support from the Colonial Office and against resistance from the local commercial elite. The latter group, while eager to preserve public order, was resentful of increased

[78] F. S. Brown, *Report upon the Secret Societies*, SSLC, August 28, 1869, lxx.

[79] Order was, in any case, largely a discursive element given the degree to which everyday rule, as experienced by those under colonial authority in Southeast Asia, could be "duplicitous, theatrical, despotic, highly personalized, and masculine." Jonathan Saha, *Law, Disorder, and the Colonial State: Corruption in Burma c. 1900* (Basingstoke: Palgrave Macmillan, 2013), 2.

[80] *Report upon the Secret Societies*, lxxiii.

government regulation and openly hostile to increased government expense. As had been the case elsewhere, the overseer-state would generate a moral panic, claim a moral imperative for reform, and deploy a paternalistic discourse to justify sterner and more expansive regulatory oversight and, ultimately, more coercive forms of governance. Even as its officials publicly espoused a free labor system and contrasted the legal equality of Chinese workers in the colony with the racialized hierarchy of other European colonizers, they would implement ever-greater restrictions on their status and mobility.[81] The threat of international competition for labor from neighboring colonial powers would increase the urgency of this project while simultaneously serving as an additional reason for expanding British authority in the name of regional security.

In the midst of ongoing debates over the practical and moral implications of governing the growing Chinese population of the Straits, further rioting broke out in Penang and Singapore in 1871 and 1872. The police forces at hand proved inadequate to the task, requiring the deputization of Secret Society leaders and European residents as well as, in some instances, the intervention of military forces to restore order. These incidents prompted the government to expand the emergency powers it had assumed in 1869, to extend their application in perpetuity, and to enlarge and reorganize the colonial police force.[82] By late 1872, though calls both from within the government and from the Straits European and Chinese mercantile communities for complete suppression of the Societies continued, *détente* had prevailed.

Although a modest extension of state authority and the co-optation of the Society leadership had achieved a temporary lessening of tensions between British officials and the burgeoning Chinese population, the peace remained an uneasy one. One factor threatening to disturb this equilibrium was labor demand in the Straits and the Malay States, which continued to rise as agriculture and mining operations expanded, with Penang and Singapore the primary entrepôts for new cohorts. This kept both labor immigration and the Secret Societies, who continued to serve as the main organizing force for newly arrived Chinese workers (known as *sinkehs*) and Indian workers, as a key issue

[81] Chinese workers were never granted the rights of British subjects. This made them vulnerable to extreme measures such as summary deportation (colloquially referred to as "banishment"), which was employed regularly in the final decades of the nineteenth century and the early decades of the twentieth. See, for example, the petition by Ng Ah Wok against the banishment of her husband, Cheow Ah Keong, Records of the High Commissioner for the Federated Malay States and Brunei, 1087/97, March 13, 1997 (National Archives of Malaysia); Lees, *Planting Empire*, 164.

[82] These measures included amending the Preservation of Peace Ordinance 1870 (247), the Dangerous Societies Ordinance of 1869, and the Police Force Ordinance 1871 (234). *The Acts and Ordinances of the Legislative Council of the Straits Settlements, 1 April 1867 to 7 March 1898.*

in policy discussions.[83] The typical arrangement for importation remained much as it had been since mid-century, with prospective immigrants either paying passage money from southern China in advance or traveling on credit, or a mixture of the two.[84] In the last case, they were obliged either to transfer their debt to a local sponsor (e.g. a Secret Society) or, more commonly, to work it off with their employer. These employers comprised primarily mine operators and agricultural estate-owners, who would also provide clothing and other necessities, only paying wages once the passage cost had been covered (which could take between six months and a year).[85] This "credit-ticket" system was analogous to indenture, but operated through private means, and was handled via Chinese organizers known as *kheh-taus* (sometimes "Kay Tows") or "coolie-brokers."[86]

By the time that the 1867 riots and subsequent disturbances brought a newly empowered colonial government's attention to the issue of Chinese immigration, the system had evolved to deal with the increasing numbers of new arrivals. A network of *kheh-taus* served as intermediaries between employers, whether European or Chinese, and prospective workers, organizing transportation in return for fees paid by the employer, by their agent in the port, or by the prospective immigrant (in advance or on credit). With the rise of labor demand and associated profits in the "coolie trade" after mid-century, the Secret Societies became more directly involved.[87] The early 1870s saw repeated appeals from prominent Chinese commercial elites for the government to regulate this "coolie traffic" on humanitarian grounds.[88] They expressed

83 The Hokkien *sinkeh* translates as "newcomer" or "new friend."

84 The rate of passage money, when paid in advance, could vary from as low as $SD7 or $SD8 (about 30 shillings) for immigrants from Amoy and Hong Kong to as high as $SD12 for immigrants from Swatow. *Report of Committee Appointed to Consider and Take Evidence upon the Condition of Chinese Labourers in the Colony*, 1876, Papers Laid Before the Legislative Council by Command of His Excellency the Governor, November 3, 1876, SSLCP, Appendix 22 (hereafter *1876 Committee Report*) (also filed as CO 275/16), ccxlii.

85 Planters maintained agents in the port towns to acquire new laborers from the *Kheh-taus*. *1876 Committee Report*, ccxliv; Jackson, *Immigrant Labour*, 44.

86 From the Hokkien "kheh" (guest) and "tau" (head). Ching Wan Yen, *Ethnic Chinese Business in Asia: History, Culture and Business Enterprise* (London: World Scientific Publishing, 2013), 20 n. 27.

87 Ibid., 22–3. In 1876, a typical band of ten to twenty men would be charged $SD7–$SD8 (in advance) or $SD12–$SD14 (in credit) each to transport, and could be supplied to an employer for $SD17–$SD20 per worker. The difference between the former and the latter constituted the profit of the *Kheh-tau* in the transaction. *1876 Committee Report*, ccxliii, ccxliv.

88 The first direct petition to the governor on the subject was in May 1871. It called for the implementation of a "general scheme of protection" that would include the appointment of a government officer to superintend the arrival of new immigrants and hear their complaints about any mistreatment. *Part I: Chinese Immigration, Report of the*

concern that incoming cohorts of *sinkehs* were being obtained through coercion, deception, and outright abduction, and that these contingents included a significant criminal element of *samsengs* (translation: "gangsters") who were prone to absconding.[89] The reforms discussed mirrored those adopted in other regions where the overseer-state had previously extended its authority over the workforce: immigrant depots, the registration of immigrants, written and certified Contracts of Service, and the creation of an official labor inspectorate.[90] Staunch opposition from the European members of the Straits Legislative Council, who threatened mass resignations in protest, and concern in the Colonial Office over such a radical expansion of state oversight prompted delays to any serious reform.[91] The departure of Ord, whose tenure was characterized by repeated clashes with the European commercial elite of the Straits, and the installation of his successor, Sir Andrew Clarke, who took up his post with a more conciliatory frame of mind, spelled the end of the first, aborted attempt to implement the overseer-state in the colony.[92]

By the mid-1870s, however, three events would have catalyzed a rapid change of course in policy, laying the foundation for the dramatic extension of British authority over the Malay Peninsula. Central to this shift would be the reorientation of governance from co-opting Society leaders and monitoring the workforce to suppressing the former and directly regulating the latter. In the process, the state's oversight of the Chinese labor force would become the fulcrum through which British authority was solidified in the Straits Settlements and extended beyond them into the tin-rich hinterlands of the Malay States. The first catalyst to this change was the departure of Governor Ord and his replacement by Sir Andrew Clarke. The new governor, as with so many of his colleagues, came from a military background. The eldest son of the governor of Western Australia, he arrived with more than two decades of experience as a military surveyor and engineer, and possessed an extensive record of government service in Tasmania, Victoria, the Gold Coast, and in

Commission Appointed to Enquire into and Report on the Question of the State of Labour in the Straits Settlements and the Protected Native States, 1890 (hereafter *1890 Labour Commission*), 4. The most significant of these was submitted in 1873. Its five signatories included Tan Seng Poh and Cheang Hong Lim, who controlled one of the largest opium revenue farms on the entire peninsula; his brother-in-law, one of the dominant gambier and pepper plantation-owners in the region; and Whampoa, a successful shipping merchant and the only Chinese member of the SSLC. *Petition from Chinese Merchants Relative to the Treatment of Chinese Immigrants*, June 22, 1873, CO 275/16.

89 The official commission appointed to investigate the 1872 Singapore riots attributed them, in part, to the presence of "a large body of rowdies, or *Samsengs* – a perpetual menace to the peace of the community." Part I: Chinese Immigration, *1890 Labour Commission*, 4. See also *Straits Times Overland Journal*, March 28, 1872, 4.

90 *Annual Report for the Straits Settlement 1871*, 114–15.

91 Part I: Chinese Immigration *1890 Labour Commission*, 5.

92 CO to Clarke, January 3, 1873, CO 273/71.

England as Director of Works at the Admiralty.[93] Despite his initial efforts to placate the legislative council and European commercial interests by delaying the implementation of Ordinance X of 1873, Clarke shared Ord's enthusiasm for an enhanced state apparatus that would bring a British vision of moral order and just governance to the Malay Peninsula. Clarke also arrived with greater support from the Colonial Office than his predecessor had enjoyed, and therefore possessed more latitude to alter policy.[94] The second catalyst was the increasing concern of British officials with an ongoing conflict in the Malaysian interior between rival alliances composed of Malay chieftains, Chinese *kongsi*, and Secret Societies. This series of regional conflicts, which became known as the "Larut Wars," threatened the designs of British investors with strong ties to the government in London.[95] The plans being mooted at the time included a trans-peninsular telegraph line that would connect Burma to the Straits Settlements, forming a crucial node in a wider network linking Britain, Australia, and Southeast Asia; a railway project; and further development of the region's lucrative tin deposits.[96]

Neither the ongoing conflict in the hinterlands nor the interests of politically connected British investors, nor Clarke's willingness to pursue more interventionist policies alone was sufficient to explain the dramatic expansion of British authority over the region, and over its Chinese population in particular. Although plans for investment carried their own political weight, the concrete presence of British financial capital in the Straits Settlements themselves was modest, and outside of them (i.e. in the Malay States), was minimal prior to 1896, despite growing pressure from Penang investors for expansion into Perak and other regions.[97] The strategic importance of Singapore had, likewise, yet to become a key concern.[98] These changes do make sense, on the other hand, in light of the changing cultural and political context within which

93 Betty Malone, "Clarke, Sir Andrew (1824–1902)," *Australian Dictionary of Biography, Vol. 3* (Manchester: Manchester University Press, 1969), 409–11.

94 Ord's tenure was characterized by continual friction with the Colonial Office, particularly over his tendency toward administrative overreach. Kim, "The Origin of British Administration," 64.

95 On the interrelation of imperial governance and City finance, see P. J. Cain and A. G. Hopkins, "Gentlemanly Capitalism and British Expansion Overseas II: New Imperialism, 1850–1945," *Economic History Review* 40, no. 1 (February 1987), 1–26.

96 Kim, "The Origin of British Administration," 78.

97 Ibid., 57. Penang investors had been eager to expand into Perak, with British security, for some time, with both agricultural and merchant interests at the forefront. See Lees, *Planting Empire*, 32–7.

98 Plans were being drawn up in the 1870s to fortify the harbor and install coastal defenses, and the potential vulnerability of the city to rival colonial powers was recognized, but British authorities were confident that they had sufficient maritime strength in the region, and the Straits Settlements were a minor consideration compared to India or the Treaty Ports.

British governance of the region was operating. By the time of Clarke's arrival, the issues of public order, Chinese immigration, and the allegedly nefarious influence of Secret Societies both in the Straits Settlements and in the Malay States were thoroughly entangled in official discussions and public discourse. This was clear across a wide variety of manifestations, including communications between the governors and the Colonial Office, press accounts, the conclusions of government commissions and inquiries conducted in previous years, and the burgeoning scholarly works on the region and its various communities. Schlegel's study and the 1867 Riots Commission were the two most prominent examples of the last two elements. Both painted an image of the Straits as being buoyed by Chinese capital, dominated by Chinese culture, and populated by those who were answerable to Chinese authority, but who only paid lip service to British law and colonial rule.

In this context, and amidst rising colonial revenue and sharpening competition for labor, the compelling reason to establish the overseer-state emerged from the growing sense within the colonial government itself that the Malay Peninsula was the frontline of an escalating conflict between Chinese culture and British culture. This conflict was occurring across Southeast Asia, but was particularly urgent in the Straits Settlements due to the rapidly expanding Chinese population and the commensurate growth in the power and influence of the Secret Societies.[99] State processes themselves would define labor control in the Straits Settlements as the terrain on which British colonial authorities would demonstrate the superiority of their culture and therefore their right to govern the region. The state would also retain, at least initially, the authority to define the success or failure of that project. The first stage of this project to expand British colonial authority had already been successfully accomplished with the establishment of Crown governance in 1867, the co-opting of Society leadership to mitigate internecine conflict in Penang and Singapore, and the generation of damning narratives about the impossibility of reconciling Secret Societies with British visions of moral rule and just governance. When Clarke succeeded Ord as governor in 1873, the most pressing issue was the ongoing disturbances in the Malay States, which had brought tin-mining operations to a standstill.[100] Given the pervasive involvement of Straits-based Secret Societies and their *kongsi*, this conflict was potentially threatening to the tenuous equilibrium that had been achieved with Ord's reforms.[101]

99 "The Straits Settlements were important to Britain for only one major reason – commerce." Kim, "The Origin of British Administration," 56.

100 R. N. Jackson, *Pickering, Protector of Chinese* (Kuala Lumpur: Oxford University Press, 1965), 20.

101 Ibid.; Legge, "The Colonial Office and Governor Ord," 6.

Clarke, who arrived in post with the belief that he had the authority to intervene more aggressively than his predecessor had in the affairs of both the Straits and the neighboring Malay States, deployed a powerful new resource. After decades of the East India Company rule and five years of Crown colony status, the Straits government had finally appointed an administrator with extensive knowledge of Chinese language, customs, history, and culture. This official, who would play an instrumental role in shaping this history of the colony and the character of its government, was William Pickering. Pickering (b. 1840), the Nottinghamshire son of a trade-association official who was fluent in Mandarin and several local dialects, had spent much of his life thus far working on ships and in the ports of south China and Southeast Asia. He was hired by Ord in 1871 to serve as the first official Chinese Interpreter to the Government of the Straits Settlements.[102]

Pickering, possessing extensive experience as a mediator between government agents, European merchants, and various Chinese communities across Southeast Asia, quickly became indispensable to Ord and his successors. Sent to Penang to intervene in the ongoing Larut Wars, he made direct contact with the rival leaders of the Secret Societies and persuaded them to allow British arbitration.[103] Much attention has been given, historically, to the Treaty of Pangkor (1874) that resulted from this intervention. It signaled the formal commencement of Britain's indirect rule over the Malay States through the installation of British "Residents" (i.e. advisors) who would counsel the Malay leaders.[104] Far more significant, however, was the Pacification Commission that followed in 1875, again with Pickering as its prime mover. This Commission provided the true resolution to conflict in the region by dividing control of the tin mines between the two different Societies that had been at the core of affairs there.[105] This control was accompanied, perforce, by a division of the lucrative opium and gambling concerns. These allowed the *kongsi* to recover the capital they had invested in labor directly from the imported Chinese laborers themselves.[106] With Pickering at its vanguard, the "forward movement" of Britain's extension of colonial authority over the Malay States would continue for the rest of the century. But the anchor of British rule in the region remained the Straits Settlements and the key challenge remained the governance of its Chinese workforce. Here, too, Pickering would play a key role, both building on and strengthening the mutually reinforcing dynamic of scholarly inquiry and policy that had emerged from Schlegel's work and the 1867 PRCR.

[102] Jackson, *Pickering*, 3–5.
[103] Comber, "Secret Societies," 153.
[104] Lees, *Planting Empire*, 18–19.
[105] These were the Ghee Hin, who had also been at the center of the 1867 Penang Riots, and the Hai San. Comber, "Secret Societies," 2.
[106] Jackson, *Pickering*, 39.

"In an English Country They Must Conform to English Rules": Coercive Paternalism and the Expansion of the Overseer-State, 1876–1890

With stability returning to the region in the wake of the Larut Wars, the Straits government could now turn to the ongoing challenge of the Societies and the Chinese workforce over whom they held sway.[107] The first attempt to deal with this issue under Clarke's tenure was Ordinance VI of 1874.[108] This modest measure instituted regulations on the maritime transport of passengers, the maximum capacity of ships, and the conditions of travel, allowing for government inspection at the port of debarkation. The following year saw the assassination of J. W. W. Birch, the first Resident (i.e. colonial administrator) of the Malay state of Perak, by a Malay chieftain allied with the Sultan of Perak. The local Malay rulers resented Birch's efforts to extend British authority over the region, and particularly his plans to deny them their customary revenues in return for fixed annuities.[109] Birch was one of the highest-ranking imperial officials to ever suffer such a fate, and his killing brought even more official attention to the febrile situation in the Malay Peninsula.

In 1876, Andrew Clarke was succeeded by William Jervois as the new governor of the Straits Settlements. That same year, Singapore was once again rocked by violent demonstrations, this time of an expressly anti-government character.[110] In the wake of the 1876 riots, which lent the question of governing the Straits' Chinese population urgent weight, the colonial state would turn toward more coercive measures, justified by paternalist discourse. Jervois would abandon efforts to co-opt the Secret Society leadership. Instead, the Straits government would follow the patterns set previously in the Caribbean and Mauritius. Identifying insidious middlemen as the primary

[107] The Treaty of Pangkor, the Pacification Commission, and the establishment of the British Resident system were the keystones of this resolution. Ernest Chew, "Swettenham and British Residential Rule in West Malaya," *Journal of Southeast Asian Studies* 5, no. 2 (1974), 166–78.

[108] An Ordinance for the Regulation of Passenger Ships, October 5, 1874, *Acts and Ordinances of the Legislative Council of the Straits Settlements from 1 April 1867 to 1 June 1886, Vol. I* (hereafter *Acts and Ordinances*) (London: Eyre & Spottiswoode, 1886), 607–13.

[109] Barbara Watson Andaya and Leonard Andaya, *A History of Malaysia*, 2nd ed. (Honolulu: University of Hawai'i Press, 2001), 166; Gullick, "The Economy of Perak," 33. The proposed system was eventually put in place anyway in 1877 (Gullick, 33).

[110] The government had given the franchise for a new sub-post office to two Straits-born Hokkiens. Such offices were essential for the transmission of both correspondence and remittances between Chinese communities. A group of Teochew merchants feared that the new sub-postmasters would abuse their "monopoly" on this vital resource through extortion, and roused the local community to attack and destroy the office. A series of clashes with police and a local economic boycott by the Teochew merchants followed, ending with the conviction of several merchants and the deportation of a local Teochow leader. Jackson, *Pickering*, 56–9.

threat to the physical and moral health of workers, the burgeoning overseer-state, with Pickering at its vanguard, would install a new regulatory apparatus to decisively supersede the authority of Society leaders over the Chinese workforce.[111]

As had been the case in 1867, two documents generated and disseminated by state processes would provide the guidelines for a new, more interventionist approach to the Secret Societies and labor governance. The first of these documents was the report of the committee appointed by Jervois in June 1876 to ascertain the state of Chinese immigration. Explicitly paternalist in its approach, its remit was to examine the condition of Chinese workers in the Straits in order to determine "whether any legislation is necessary with a view to their protection."[112] With Jervois under considerable pressure from the Colonial Office to address widespread reports of abuse, it was clear from the outset that a significant expansion of the government's authority over the Chinese population was a foregone conclusion, and that the primary purpose of the committee was to provide more specific guidance and moral justification for it.[113] The committee highlighted several abuses in the "credit-ticket" system, the most important of which concerned the immoral actions of the *kheh-tau* "coolie-brokers" and other nefarious characters that preyed on Chinese immigrants. Kidnapping was rife, they insisted, as evidence from the Chinese interpreters and the police in the primary ports of entry demonstrated. Other forms of milder coercion were equally prevalent, chief among them that the *kheh-taus* could divert workers involuntarily to alternative destinations. This could be for a number of reasons, but the primary one was that demand for their labor at the promised port of debarkation might not be high enough to garner the profits that the *kheh-tau* sought. In the interim, the workers themselves could be confined against their will in primitive barracoons for days or even weeks.[114] The final "blot" on the current system of Chinese labor immigration, the committee contended, was the spread of prostitution, primarily via Chinese women held in "a state of slavery."[115] Such "vice and crime [were] the natural concomitants of such a system ... in every part of the world to which the Chinese emigrate."

The committee blamed this host of problems on both the lack of government oversight and on the disengagement of the workforce with state institutions and officials. Chinese immigrants, who constituted "the industrial backbone" of the colony, looked not to the Straits government as the primary

[111] The quote in this section's heading is from W. A. Pickering, quoted in Jackson, *Pickering*, 56.

[112] *1876 Committee Report*, ccxlii.

[113] CO Despatch No. 74, May 3, 1875; No. 114, June 26, 1875. The committee was composed of John Douglas, W. W. Williams, and S. Dunlop, the Inspector of Police.

[114] *1876 Committee Report*, ccxliii.

[115] Ibid., ccxliv.

authority but instead to the Secret Societies. In order to address these critical flaws and allow Chinese labor in the Straits to be, "as far as the Immigrant is concerned, the freest imaginable," the committee recommended that the entire labor and immigration system be brought directly under state purview. The specific reforms mirrored those implemented previously in the former slave colonies: the appointment of a government Protector to monitor the system and mediate between workers, recruiters, and employers; the establishment of official immigrant depots at the ports of entry; the introduction of binding, written Contracts of Service to be certified by the Protector; and the mandatory licensing of "coolie-brokers" and other recruiting agents, with penalties enforced for noncompliance.[116] Such measures would be supported and reinforced through the passage of a new Ordinance "protecting Chinese Immigrants and Emigrants," and the system would be made sustainable through a government-sponsored program for training personnel in the Chinese language. With the 1876 committee, as had been the case in the Caribbean and Mauritius, the cumulative expansion of the state apparatus supplied the evidence of abuses that, in turn, demanded the expansion of the same apparatus further in order to address them. This equation required a very selective appraisal of the labor system, one that emphasized some aspects while ignoring others, and that offered solutions that did not undermine the colony's two pillars of prosperity, cheap Chinese labor and opium.

The many evils of these Societies had been made abundantly clear by the findings of the 1867 PRCR, which was cited at great length as the definitive authority on their insidious workings.[117] This issue was compounded by the policies of the government itself, which left them in almost complete ignorance of this crucial segment of the Straits population. The mutual lack of engagement between the state and the Chinese workforce was, the committee insisted, of great detriment to Chinese workers themselves, and the key hindrance to their incorporation within the British schema of colonial rule. The Chinese workers were respectable, hardworking, and essential to the prosperity of the colony. Despite these positive qualities, and the "independence" that distinguished them so clearly from "the Indian coolie," absent the aegis of British governance, they remained incapable of responding to alleged mistreatment except through appeals to the Secret Societies.[118] The latter were, as evidence cited from the 1867 PRCR confirmed, inherently violent, exploitative, and utterly incompatible with European modes of law and just governance.

The committee's report catalyzed a raft of ordinances that largely echoed the measures of labor regulation introduced previously in the Caribbean and Mauritius. The most significant of these were Ordinance I of 1876 (Indian

[116] Ibid., ccxlviii.
[117] Ibid., ccxliv.
[118] Ibid., ccxliv.

Immigrants' Protection), which was paralleled by Act V of 1877 from the Indian Legislative Council; Ordinance II of 1877 (Chinese Immigration Ordinance); and Ordinance III of 1877 (Crimping).[119] The measures introduced a coordinated system of inspection, registration, licensing, and contracts for both Chinese and Indian laborers, supervised by a staff composed of a Protector and Assistant Protectors. Oversight of the Chinese population was transferred from the authority of the police, whose involvement had been largely confined to instances of crime and disorder, to an official whose responsibility was to oversee the entire labor system, from recruitment and contracts to workers' grievances and well-being. These officials would replace the Secret Societies as the primary authority to whom workers were answerable.

The position of Protector of Chinese in the Straits, much like its analogs in the Caribbean and Mauritius, combined a number of specific roles and more general powers. They managed the grievances of the Chinese population, which rose rapidly to number in the thousands annually; they monitored the licensing of recruiters and "coolie-brokers"; they approved contracts; they inspected the new government immigration depots; and they submitted regular reports to the governor on the state of the Chinese laboring population and the operation of the immigration system.[120] Like their counterparts in the Caribbean and Mauritius, Straits Protectors were also given the responsibility for prosecuting workers, recruiters, or employers for any violations of the new regulations. The penalties, on conviction, for recruiters who employed force, fraud, or deceit were the harshest among these, set at a maximum of a year's imprisonment or a fine of $SD500 (Singapore dollars).[121] Although these ordinances did not criminalize specific labor offenses (e.g. "bad work" or "insolence"), as had been the case elsewhere, workers convicted of contract violations nonetheless faced stern punishments of up three months' imprisonment or fines the equivalent of 100 US dollars.[122] The Straits Protector, responding to the concerns of the 1876 committee, was also given additional authority as a "registering officer" under the Contagious Diseases Ordinance (CDO). This status empowered the official to monitor the conduct of prostitution in the colony, and charged them with insuring that women were not directly coerced into the practice.[123]

119 The original Act (Ordinance I of 1876) had to be suspended, then revised, then reinstated finally in Ordinance XII of 1876. See *1890 Labour Commission*, 37 and notes.

120 Most of these measures were introduced via Ordinance III of 1877 (An Ordinance to Amend the Law Relating to Crimping, and to Make Better Provision for the Protection of Emigrants). *Acts and Ordinances*, 683–6.

121 Sec. 1, Ordinance III of 1877, *Acts and Ordinances*, 683.

122 Sec. 9, Ordinance III of 1877, *Acts and Ordinances*, 685.

123 Ng Siew Yoong, "The Chinese Protectorate in Singapore, 1877–1900," *Journal of Southeast Asian History* 2, no. 1 (1961), 89. The CDO, which required brothels and their employees to be registered and inspected regularly, had been introduced in 1870.

In Singapore, the first man chosen to occupy this new position of immense influence in the Straits government was the same person who had served as the administration's primary source of information about the Chinese population for nearly a decade already, W. A. Pickering.[124] His vision for the state's role in the lives of Chinese workers, and in the Malay Peninsula more broadly, was laid out in a series of published articles. Serving as both guidelines for policy and public justifications for the same, they focused on three key propositions. The first was that the Chinese, while inherently orderly, followed a culture that was antithetical to European modes of rule. The second was that, for the good of the entire population under its authority, Britain had a moral imperative to transform the region from one dominated by Chinese and Malay culture to one where English culture was paramount. The third was that it was by asserting both British institutions of government and the British ideology of governance over the inhabitants of the Straits and the Malay States, and over the Chinese laboring population in particular, that Britain's preeminence would be achieved. Establishing British legal and cultural authority over the Chinese workforce was thus presented as involving interdependent and mutually reinforcing processes – if laws were to be effective, they must make sense to those most likely to feel their force. As Pickering had declared in the wake of the 1876 Singapore Riots, "in an English country, they [i.e. the Chinese] must conform to English rules."[125]

The first of these articles was composed in 1876 while Pickering was on leave in London and was subsequently published in the popular literary journal *Fraser's*.[126] The piece, like Schlegel's book and the 1867 PRCR, would become a ubiquitous touchstone for policy discussions in subsequent years. In it, Pickering offered the moral case for suppressing the Societies and establishing British suzerainty over the Malay States. The author took the extension of "regular and just government" over both as a given, and of benefit to British commerce and the current inhabitants of the region.[127] Directly referencing Schlegel's work and the 1867 PRCR, Pickering asserted that the British had a "moral duty to protect the Malays from majorities of Chinese, and to protect the turbulent Chinese from massacring each other . . . the peace and safety of our colonies demand that the British Government take an active and chief part in their rule and protection."[128] While condemning the Secret Society leadership, whom he accused of deliberately encouraging rioting "as a profit-making exercise," and insisting that their suppression was a necessary precursor to

124 Dr. N. B. Denys was appointed Assistant Protector for Singapore and E. Karl became Assistant Protector for Penang.

125 W. A. Pickering quoted in Jackson, *Pickering*, 56.

126 *Fraser's Magazine for Town and Country.*

127 Pickering, "The Chinese in the Straits of Malacca," 435. The article was reprinted subsequently in the *Straits Times*.

128 Ibid., 438, 442.

establishing British law and culture in the region, he praised the general Chinese population. "When governed firmly and justly," Pickering argued, "no people on earth are more amenable to law."[129] The key to such firm and just governance was "knowledge of the people to be governed."[130] Pickering compared the difficulties of governing the Chinese to those faced by Britain when ruling the Irish. Both, he insisted, had long associated strong government authority with injustice.[131]

Pickering's subsequent articles, published in the journal of the newly established Straits Branch of the Royal Asiatic Society (SBRAS), endeavored to expand that knowledge by elucidating the workings of the Societies. As in his *Fraser's* piece, the focus was on the contrast between British and Chinese culture, and on how the Chinese population had to be prised away from the latter and co-opted into the former if the region was to know peace and prosperity. The first of the two articles, which appeared in the inaugural issues of the *Journal of the Straits Branch of the Royal Asiatic Society* (*JSBRAS*) in July 1878, was primarily a summary of Schlegel's work, though it was not without its political subtext. The second article, which followed a year later, was much more explicitly political in its tone and far more critical of the Straits Chinese population. They were, Pickering wrote, "the scum of the Empire," and could never truly be reconciled to British modes of governance. This was because the English, through centuries of sacrifice, had become devoted to the ideal of "freedom." In contrast, the Chinese were held in check only by "dread ... and ever present power, either in the shape of his Government, his clan, or the village elders."[132] In such circumstances, there were only two possible courses of action. The first was to recognize and maintain the Secret Societies. The preferred course, however, was "exceptional and more stringent legislation for an exceptional population."[133] But since the government had already eschewed the latter, its only recourse was the former (i.e. accommodation with the Societies).

Pickering's change of opinion was at odds not only with his earlier writing, which he acknowledged explicitly, but also with the report he had submitted just the previous year to the SSLC on the "kidnapping of *senkehs*" [*sic*]. This report was unequivocal in its condemnation of labor governance in the Straits. The frequency with which *kheh-taus*, in collusion with the Societies, practiced deception and outright coercion, and the lack of state oversight, Pickering wrote, "cannot be called creditable to any government ... supposed to be based on the principles of justice and freedom."[134] This report, and the general

129 Ibid., 441–2.
130 Ibid., 439.
131 W. A. Pickering, "Chinese Secret Societies and Their Origin," *Journal of the Straits Branch of the Royal Asiatic Society* 1 (July 1878), 66.
132 Pickering, "Chinese Secret Societies and Their Origin, Pt II," 10.
133 Pickering, "Chinese Secret Societies and Their Origin, Pt. II" 11.
134 "Report by Mr. Pickering on Kidnapping of *Senkehs*," SSLCP, February 23, 1877, iii.

context in which the two *JSBRAS* articles were published, is revealing about the underlying purpose of Pickering's writing and helps explain his apparent *volte face* on the Societies. The SBRAS had been created in 1877, with Pickering himself as one of its founding members. Supported by other officials in the colonial administration, the society's goal was "collecting and recording scientific information in the Malay Peninsula and Archipelago."[135] Ostensibly an academic institution, in operation, the SBRAS had "the utilitarian purpose of gathering more knowledge to facilitate British rule in Malaya."[136] Given Pickering's strong stance in both the *Fraser's* article and the kidnapping report, the *JSBRAS* pieces appear less as a surrender to unavoidable reconciliation with the Societies and more as a criticism of the state's inaction and a call to arms. This interpretation is lent considerable weight by his attribution, in the kidnapping report, of the government's lassitude to "our over-anxiety not to interfere with the liberty of the Chinaman, and to abstain from vexatious regulations, which might impede free immigration of labour into these colonies."[137] In this formulation, the demand for labor was being allowed to trump the state's paternalistic obligations. State oversight of the labor system in the Straits, building on the precedents set in the Caribbean and Mauritius, was being presented as a moral imperative. Even more so than had been the case there, however, the overseer-state as envisioned by Pickering would combine legal, economic, social, and cultural authority in order to remake the colony in his particular image of just rule, moral governance, and rational, liberal labor management.

As the newly installed Protector of Chinese, Pickering was in a strong position to implement the expansion of labor governance that he had long argued was so crucial to the solidification of British colonial authority in the Straits. Although he presided over a significant expansion of the state vis-à-vis labor (the Chinese Protectorate, described later), Pickering was ultimately stymied by the political influence of a commercial and property-holding elite that feared doing anything to hinder Chinese immigration, the lifeline of the colony's prosperity. By expanding the authority of the overseer-state, however, Pickering had, unwittingly or not, created a means by which the state could control the labor importation process for the benefit of employers. The new agents, institutions, and ordinances could not directly prevent the illegal diversion of workers bound for their estates and mines to alternative locales. But they did provide an avenue to prosecute any Chinese middlemen who

[135] Choy Chee Meh née Lum, "History of the Malaysian Branch of the Royal Asiatic Society," *Journal of the Malaysian Branch of the Royal Asiatic Society* 68, no. 2 (269) (1995), 87. Among the other founding members were W. E. Maxwell, who later became the Colonial Secretary; A. M. Skinner, the Colonial Treasurer; C. J. Irving, the Resident Councillor, Malacca; and two magistrates, N. B. Denys and D. F. A. Hervey.

[136] Meh née Lum, "History of the Malaysian Branch of the Royal Asiatic Society," 89.

[137] "Report by Mr. Pickering on Kidnapping of *Senkehs*," iii.

interfered with the smooth delivery of new workers to the Straits. Such regulations as would strengthen this state oversight, in the name of "protection," and would relieve the political pressure from the Colonial Office to address the "evils" of the current system, were acceptable to all involved, from the colonial executive to European estate-owners to the Chinese *kongsi* who controlled the opium and mining industries. The type of stringent regulations that Pickering favored, however, found little support. With the resolution of the Larut Wars and the lessening of public disturbances in both frequency and severity, suppression of the Secret Societies also lost its political urgency. They remained, as even Pickering was forced to acknowledge, a crucial aspect of the labor immigration system, being both the primary mechanism for maintaining order among the Chinese workforce and also key collaborators and underwriters of the *kheh-taus*. In the Straits, Pickering's advocacy for paternalistic regulation of the Chinese labor system as the epitome of moral and effective governance had been effectively countered with arguments for the freedom of laborers and the benefits of undiminished immigration.

Pickering's appointment in 1876 was rapidly followed in 1877 with the official inauguration of the "Chinese Protectorate" as a new agency of labor governance in the Straits Settlements. The initial Protectorate was composed of the Protector himself, based in Singapore, an Assistant Protector, based in Penang, and the small contingent of officers and clerks that worked underneath them.[138] As an agency dedicated solely to the governance of a racially designated cohort of immigrant laborers, and given the immense size of that cohort, the Straits Chinese Protectorate was unique in the history of the British Empire.[139] By the late 1880s, Protectorate officials would be responsible for supervising an annual intake of over 160,000 new arrivals.[140] This authority was exercised in principle, though hardly unvarying in practice, since the limited resources of personnel available made direct supervision of so massive a cohort impossible.

138 It was officially constituted the Chinese Branch of the Secretariat, under the direct supervision of the Colonial Secretary (Singapore). In 1881, in Singapore, in addition to the Protector, it included a Boarding Officer, an interpreter, and three Chinese clerks. In Penang, it had a similar structure, albeit with only one Chinese clerk and a Detective. *The Singapore and Straits Directory for the Year 1881* (Singapore: Mission Press, 1881), 43, 79.

139 The Protectors of Slaves's remit was determined by the legal status of their charges, who occupied the liminal space between property and person. The duties of the Protectors of Immigrants that succeeded them encompassed both Indian and Chinese immigrants, as well as all those who arrived under contracts of indenture (e.g. Fijians).

140 At the height of Chinese immigration to the Straits, in 1887–8, the Protectorate in Singapore examined some 167,900 new Chinese arrivals on board vessels at the various landing depots. Table A: Table of Chinese immigrants arrived and inspected at Singapore, 1877–1890, *1890 Labour Commission*. The total Chinese arrivals the following year numbered 181,716. Jackson, *Immigrant Labour*, 76.

Though exceptional in scale and specific remit, the Protectorate was hardly without precedent. It combined, in a single entity, many of the functions exercised previously by the various Protectors of Immigrants, Fiscals, special magistrates, and stipendiary magistrates over ameliorated slavery and indenture in the Caribbean, South Africa, and Mauritius.[141] And, as with its earlier analogs in these locales, the goal of the Protectorate in the Straits, while operating under the guise of paternalism, was to facilitate the smooth provision of labor to the colony. Much of the sprawling system of recruitment, transportation, and distribution remained unchanged beyond the installation of state officials as regulators, monitors, and, when necessary, mediators between workers, recruiters, and employers. Pickering very rapidly implemented a protocol of official supervision that began with the licensing of recruiters (at the point of origin) and immigrant depots (at the ports of destination) across the region, where the new ordinances authorized the most serious penalties against violators, and persisted, in one form or another, as long as the laborer remained in the colony.[142] By the late 1870s, every ship arriving at a Straits port carrying new workers was required to be inspected by an officer of the Protectorate prior to debarking its passengers. The official would explain the role of the state in the labor system, solicit any complaints, and either release them (if they had paid their passage) or arrange their transport to the immigration depot (if passage debt was owed). Every labor contract was witnessed and registered by a Protectorate official, who reminded the new arrival that they did not need to join a Secret Society since the government was ready to hear any grievances and provide protection.[143]

While such state protection was offered, the threat of state *prosecution* was similarly made clear, should Chinese workers prove disruptive. As Pickering explained, the chief goal of the new legislation was "to bring the newly arrived Chinese into immediate contact with the Government, and to make them feel there is the power both to protect them and keep them in order."[144] This power was also felt in the government's efforts to ensure that the flow of immigrants to the Straits was not diverted to its competitors. When higher advances and wages offered in the Dutch tobacco plantations of Deli (Sumatra) proved attractive to both Chinese labor recruiters and the foremen of Chinese labor gangs, Pickering instituted new measures to

[141] The Protectorate also had additional powers, such as the authorization to designate certain parts of Singapore harbor anchor points for ships carrying immigrants in order to ensure ease of inspection and prevent illegal offloading. The Protectorate, until 1894, was also responsible for registering all brothels and all prostitutes working in them, and for conducting regular inspections of the former. Yoong, "The Chinese Protectorate," 89.

[142] Jackson, *Pickering*, 68.

[143] Ibid.

[144] W. A. Pickering, quoted in Jackson, *Pickering*, 68.

obstruct the redirection of workers there. This was done with the justification that such diversion was involuntary and that the terms of service were more exploitative there than they were with Straits employers.[145] Lacking the personnel that would have been required to carefully monitor the entire labor system, much of the Protectorate's power was implemented at the level of recruitment and in the initial stages of arrival. Beyond that point, the state's intervention, much like with ameliorated slavery and indenture, depended on the initiative of the workers themselves. The new regulations allowed workers to bring a case, via the Protectorate, before a local magistrate.[146] Very quickly, Chinese laborers began to use the leverage that the Protectorate afforded them to bring complaints against recruiters and employers.[147]

In the decade following the creation of the Protectorate, the use of the "credit-ticket" system of debt-bondage among Singapore-bound immigrants went into steady decline, falling from 2,653 of 9,776 total arrivals in 1877 (27 percent) to 8,152 of 96,230 (8.5 percent) in 1890.[148] At the same time, labor demand continued to drive up the overall level of Chinese immigration, a trend further exacerbated by a rapid rise in the price of tin and a resultant mining boom.[149] The dramatic increase in immigration across the region coincided with a significant expansion of the overseer-state and a turn toward more coercive methods in a pattern similar to that witnessed previously in the Caribbean and Mauritius. As elsewhere, new regulations were implemented in order to protect the interests of employers, constrain workers' mobility, and punish laborers viewed as being insufficiently productive. In 1882, the SSLC passed Ordinance I (Labour Contracts). This measure instituted a form of state-regulated indenture among Chinese workers, allowing employers to bind them to three-year contracts and mandating severe punishments for absconding.[150] Similar to analogous ordinances passed in the Caribbean, Southern Africa, and Mauritius, labor offenses such as disobedience, negligence, and damage to an employer's property were criminalized.[151] Breach of contract on the part of the employer faced the harshest penalty of all, with the convicted facing either a fine of up to $SD100 or imprisonment of up to six months.[152]

145 Jackson, *Pickering*, 70.
146 *Straits Settlements Government Gazette* 1878, p. 8. *Annual Reports of the Chinese Protectorate for 1877.*
147 One of the most common was that the latter had employed a rattan or other form of corporal punishment.
148 Table A, *1890 Labour Commission.*
149 Jackson, *Immigrant Labour*, 41.
150 Ordinance I of 1882 (Labour Contracts), *Acts and Ordinances*, 1076.
151 Ibid., 1081.
152 Ibid., 1082.

In contrast to the harnessing of state authority to enforce contracts and work discipline, efforts to expand the remit of the Protectorate to encompass regular inspections of estates or other places of employment met with concerted resistance from the colonial executive and from employers themselves. Evidence for poor conditions in Penang was provided by a local magistrate, W. Egerton, who had witnessed, firsthand, the degree to which unhappy workers were willing to suffer repeated terms of imprisonment for absconding rather than return to employers who mistreated them. Egerton explained in an official report that persistent abuse by "tindals" (i.e. work-gang foremen) was to blame for the serial absconders he encountered in his court.[153] Pickering voiced similar concerns, and argued that the powers of the Protector of Chinese should be expanded to include inspection and control, thereby matching the authority of the Protector of Indian Immigrants. The latter had been appointed in 1876 to oversee the colony's modest but growing population of Indian indentured workers.[154] Although he supported the expansion of the Chinese Protectorate to deal with the rapidly ballooning number of immigrants, the colony's new governor, Frederick Weld, demurred on granting them additional powers. Their necessity was doubtful, he argued, and such onerous new duties might put unsustainable strain on an agency whose resources were already stretched thin.[155]

By the end of the 1880s, the powers of the overseer-state had significantly enhanced the authority of employers over their Chinese workforce and had undermined the influence of Chinese middlemen, placing them under a rigorous system of government licensing and inspection. Subsequent to their initial encounters with Protectorate officials on arrival, however, Chinese workers did not have ready access to an avenue for filing grievances against their employers for mistreatment. Ironically, this left "free" Chinese workers under multi-year contracts in a worse position vis-à-vis complaints against their employers than indentured Indian workers occupied. With the peripatetic Protectors of Indian Immigrants conducting regular inspections of estates, the latter had frequent opportunities to voice their grievances.[156] Pickering, his successors, and other officials within the Straits government would continue to campaign for expanded state authority to oversee Chinese workers and regulate their treatment by recruiters and employers. Despite

153 Minute by W. Egerton, September 6, 1886, enclosed in CO 273/143 No. 11, January 10, 1887.

154 Minute by W. A. Pickering, November 29, 1886, No. 11 enclosed in CO 273/143, 2.

155 Weld to Secretary of State, January 10, 1887, No. 11, CO 273/143, 3.

156 A Protector of Indian Immigrants (but not a fully staffed Protectorate) had been created in 1876 under the auspices of Act I of 1876, "An Ordinance for Regulating the Immigration of Native Labourers from British India." The complaints system aside, Indian workers faced an even harsher regime of enforcement with regard to labor offenses. See Chapter 7.

their efforts, the structure and practice of Chinese labor immigration would not see significant change until the abolition of the credit-ticket system in 1914. Successive governors were generally reluctant to incur the expense of an expanded apparatus to manage labor itself or to implement regulations that would potentially intimidate prospective immigrants or threaten the interests of employers. The Straits government's conservative approach to labor regulation in the 1880s and 1890s was exacerbated by growing tensions with the Chinese government.[157]

By 1890, in the face of increasing demand, decreasing supply, and the resistance of Chinese officials, the priorities of the Straits government had shifted definitively away from paternalist efforts at reforming the Chinese immigration system and toward sustaining it and mitigating its rising costs to employers. This change in focus was aptly demonstrated in 1890, when the Chinese Secret Societies were formally dissolved, but the *kheh-tau* system was allowed to continue without further hinderance.[158] Likewise, when a major government inquiry was launched into Chinese labor in 1890, its primary task, unlike previous committees on the topic, was not to address complaints or investigate abuses. Instead, its explicit purpose was to devise "a scheme for encouraging immigration and thereby supplying the demand for labour."[159] The sweeping recommendations of the committee for expanding the state apparatus of inspection, implementing more severe penalties against employers, empowering magistrates or the Protector to cancel contracts in cases of maltreatment, and confining recruitment in China to officially licensed agents who were accountable to European employers rather than to Chinese brokers were all rejected.[160] The Protector of Chinese himself, F. Powell, concluded that the proposed reforms were impractical, given the recalcitrance of the Chinese government to cooperate.[161] And the committee's own final words made clear their reluctance to interfere overmuch in the current system. The government should continue to check the worst abuses, but it could, by its own efforts, neither provide the needed workforce nor create favorable conditions for their immigration. The responsibility to foster such an amenable environment lay with employers. There was, the report concluded, "no royal road to plentiful and cheap labour."[162]

157 Introduction, *1890 Labor Commission*, 16.
158 Ordinance I of 1889.
159 Introduction, *1890 Labour Commission*, 3.
160 Ibid., 27–33.
161 Powell argued that even if "theoretically . . . immigration under the direct conduct of the Government would be satisfactory," it was, in a practical sense, not feasible in the current political climate. Ibid., 71.
162 Ibid., 68.

Conclusion

The 1890 committee demonstrated both the extent and the limits of the overseer-state on the Malay Peninsula. Government officials and institutions had replaced the Secret Societies as the ultimate authority in the labor system. Through their oversight of immigration, contracts, and labor discipline for hundreds of thousands of Chinese workers, this apparatus of labor governance had become the anchor of British colonial authority in the Straits and the Malay States. Its legal power to define the rights, status, and obligations of recruiters, employers, and workers was mutually reinforced by its cultural power to define the alleged differences between Chinese and British approaches to governance and labor management. Both veins of authority had been made possible by the transition of the Straits Settlements to a Crown colony. This had been accompanied by an increasing reliance on a modern mode of governance in which scientific knowledge, bureaucratic processes, and political power were fused.[163] These modes entailed the state itself as an engine generating expertise about those under its rule, and employing that knowledge as justification for particular policies and approaches. In the Straits Settlements, such knowledge generation was directly entangled with concrete expressions of political power, in terms of both personnel and institutions. But both this knowledge and, by extension, the colonial authority it undergirded remained incomplete and constrained. The Secret Societies would never be eliminated entirely, even if their influence in the Straits was drastically reduced, and the various clan associations among the Chinese population remained a potent cultural and social force.[164]

The overseer-state had operated in this mode since its origins in ameliorated slavery, but its ultimate expression was found in the Straits Settlements post-1867. The interaction between the works of Schlegel, the 1867 PRCR, Pickering's articles, the SBRAS, and the creation of the Straits Chinese Protectorate epitomized the entanglement of scientific knowledge and official knowledge that came to characterize colonial governance in the second half of the nineteenth century. At the core of this entanglement was a state that funded and disseminated the works of policy-relevant scholarship even as officials such as Pickering adopted roles as objective, rational investigators of the territories and populations they administered. From this mutually reinforcing process of knowledge generation and rule emerged a compelling argument about the Chinese Secret Societies, a series of policies to deal with them,

[163] Patrick Joyce neatly summarizes the ideas about this fusion that have emerged from sociology, history, cultural studies, and political science in recent years. Patrick Joyce, *The State of Freedom: A Social History of the British State since 1800* (Cambridge: Cambridge University Press, 2013), 27–38.

[164] Lees, *Planting Empire*, 272–5.

and the attendant apparatus of labor immigration control that would permanently replace the Societies' authority.

Ultimately, the issue with the Societies and the labor immigration system they managed was *not* that they were either disorganized or ineffective. Both Schlegel and Pickering insisted that the Chinese were an inherently orderly and governable people. The persistence of the *Kheh-tau* and the "credit-ticket" systems were likewise a testament to their resiliency and their necessity for maintaining the labor supply of the entire region. Instead, the argument that emerged from the interlinked scholarly and governmental processes was that the Societies were based on an essentialized Chinese culture that was inherently antagonistic to British rule, and that they fostered the authority of villainous middlemen who were irreconcilable with a British vision of just and moral governance. Once this corrupting influence was excised and the networks of immigration brought under the careful oversight of the state, the entire labor system could operate for the mutual benefit – moral, social, and economic – of all involved.

The demonization of Chinese Secret Societies in Straits culture and policy would leave a powerful and lasting legacy. For more than half a century afterwards, anxiety over "Triads," "Tongs," and other clandestine groups would circulate around the British imperial world, reappearing as far away as Canada and eventually arriving in the metropole itself.[165] The belief that all Chinese communities were somehow connected via sinister channels to constitute a global, anti-Western conspiracy would become one of the most persistent of all anti-Chinese tropes. It would manifest in everything from anti-immigration policy to popular fictional characters such as the Insidious Dr. Fu Manchu.[166] Linked to it would be the common argument, first articulated in the Straits as "*imperium in imperio*," that Chinese communities could never be assimilated into European culture and would remain forever resistant to European modes of governance. In Australia, Canada, South Africa, and Britain itself, such assertions would serve, as they had in the Straits, as justification for the increased state oversight and coercive governance of Chinese communities.

For all the potency that the overseer-state developed through these entangled processes of knowledge generation and governance, its expansion of authority over the labor system and its development as the anchor of colonial control across the Caribbean, Mauritius, and Southeast Asia also left it vulnerable. The situation in the 1890s was analogous, in many ways, to that faced by the overseer-state at its inception in the 1820s. The state had assumed the power to regulate labor systems across the empire, but with such authority also

165 Sascha Auerbach, *Race, Law, and "The Chinese Puzzle" in Imperial Britain* (New York: Palgrave Macmillan, 2009), 60.

166 Ibid., 73–80.

came accountability for its failings. Embedded within its ability to generate measures of its own success through official reports and inquiries was also the potential to reveal the scale of abuses that persisted. In the Straits, as in the Caribbean and Mauritius, the response of colonial officials to reports of exploitation and injustice was to shift the blame to nefarious, non-European middlemen. As the state became more and more deeply enmeshed with the processes of labor recruitment, transportation, and regulation, however, it became more and more difficult to avoid some measure of responsibility for their worst aspects. The larger the overseer-state became as an entity, the larger a target it presented for both critics and for those who sought to contest the fusion of state power and employers' authority over their workers. The distance between the authority *claimed* by the state and its limited ability to *enforce* such policies only exacerbated its exposure to criticism. This discrepancy left it open to blame, through either official or public channels, both for the issues of labor that remained unaddressed and for those that the state had tried and failed to ameliorate. In the early decades of its existence, the overseer-state could always defend even its most coercive aspects as representing progress from the previous system of chattel slavery. In the decades prior to the First World War, when forced to defend "the new slavery" that it had, according to its critics, helped foster, the overseer-state would not be so successful.

7

"They Have Made the Government Arbitrary Enough"

The Decline of the Overseer-State, 1870–1904

In 1870, John Edward Jenkins arrived in British Guiana to investigate "the coolie question" at the behest of two of Britain's preeminent humanitarian organizations, the Aborigines Protection Society (APS) and the British and Foreign Anti-Slavery Society (BFAS).[1] Jenkins was accompanying a parliamentary commission of inquiry assembled to assess Indian and Chinese indenture in the wake of a series of prominent complaints against it. At the core of the most serious of these criticisms, he explained, were unfavorable comparisons to African chattel slavery, the perfidy of labor recruiters, and, above all, the misuse of state power by government officials. Government officials, critics maintained, had thoroughly neglected their paternalistic obligations toward workers, and had instead aligned themselves with the interests of estate proprietors. As a consequence, indentured laborers were "wronged by law and against the law – daily injured and unable to obtain redress, because of combinations between unjust magistrates, hireling doctors, and manoeuvring planters – dying unchecked and unreckoned."[2] In *The Coolie: His Rights and His Wrongs* (1871), his widely read account of the commission's inquiry, Jenkins emphasized just how crucial the issue of indenture as practice and policy was, whether in British Guiana, the British Empire, or beyond.[3] In a colony whose economy was based on plantation commodities, indenture lay at the heart of "capital and energy and commercial progress." Across the plantation colonies of the empire, the system, entangled with "the fortunes of peoples whose future is one of the gravest problems of humanity," was pivotal in determining the social, cultural, and economic advancement of the

1 The original Anti-Slavery Society, whose official name was The Society for Affecting the Abolition of the Slave Trade, was disbanded in 1838, following the end of the apprenticeship period, and reconstituted subsequently as the BFAS. Andrea Major, *Slavery, Abolitionism and Empire in India, 1772–1843* (Liverpool: Liverpool University Press, 2012), 321–2.

2 John Edward Jenkins, *The Coolie: His Rights and His Wrongs* (New York: George Routledge and Sons, 1871), 3.

3 "In the United States of America and in Australasia," he wrote, "the movement already commenced for the importation of Eastern labour foreshadows a time when this will be among the greatest of social-political subjects." Jenkins, *The Coolie*, 5.

millions of Indian and Chinese workers who filled its ranks.[4] Since workers arrived "of their own free will," however, Jenkins insisted that comparisons to slavery were without merit.[5] Instead, "bound under a wonderfully complicated system, with legal balances and checks," indenture brought Chinese and Indian workers both "material prosperity" and "moral progress."[6] In sum, indenture, with careful state oversight, was not only the epitome of modern governance but the path to prosperity and the avenue of uplift by which liberalism, rule of law, and British virtue would be planted in the hearts and minds of colonized peoples, thenceforth to flourish.

Forty years after Jenkins's rosy assessment, a vastly different picture of indenture and the state's management of colonial labor was offered by Gopal Krishna Gokhale to India's governing body, the Imperial Legislative Council. Gokhale, one of the senior leaders of the Indian National Congress, shared Jenkins's commitment to liberalism, his moderate political stance, and his understanding of indenture through the lenses of law, morality, social progress, and governance. But his conclusions about the institution were the polar opposite of those reached in *The Coolie*. Indenture was the functional successor to slavery, Gokhale insisted, and so similar that "even the negro, only just then emancipated, scorned [it]."[7] The system was so persistently rife with abuse that it had "troubled ... the conscience of the Government" since the very beginning. Its many failings, legal and moral, had been made evident by the British government's own repeated inquiries. These had prompted the periodic suspension of indenture, often for years at a stretch, on multiple occasions and in every colony where it had been introduced. Mohandas K. Gandhi, whom Gokhale had mentored for a time, was even blunter in his assessment. Writing in March 1916, on the eve of indenture's final abolition by the Indian government, he described it as being "perilously close to slavery," and as a "hideousness" irreconcilable with the "interest of humanity."[8]

Why was indenture, which had spread so rapidly across the empire in the wake of emancipation, becoming the backbone of the colonial labor system and a keystone of colonial governance, abruptly abolished in the second decade of the twentieth century? Previous scholarship on this "second abolition movement" has reflected Gokhale's emphasis on the "conscience of the government." Such arguments hold that a reinvigorated humanitarian movement coincided with a series of public scandals over indenture, its decreasing economic viability, and the increasingly vehement objections of the Indian

[4] Ibid., 3.
[5] Ibid.
[6] Ibid., 298, 299.
[7] Gopal Krishna Gohkale, Resolution in the Imperial Legislative Council, March 4, 1912.
[8] "The system of indenture," Gandhi concluded, "is so demonstrably degrading to [Indians] as a nation that it must be stopped at any cost." Mohandas K. Gandhi, "Indentured Labour," in *Mahatma Gandhi: His Life, Writings and Speeches* (Madras: The Cambridge Press, 1917), 92.

and Chinese governments. By the decade prior to the First World War, indenture had also become a public embarrassment both for the imperial government in London and for a series of colonial administrations.[9] This political millstone was made heavier by growing grassroots opposition to what its detractors deemed "the new slavery." Public criticism of the indenture system had served as a rallying cry for the new alliance of Liberal and Labour interests and as a key animating force in the political mobilization of unionized white labor both across the empire and in Britain itself.[10] The second abolition, much like the first, emerges from this formulation as a political initiative accelerated by a domestic social movement and culminating in a major policy reversal.

This chapter, employing the overseer-state as an analytical framework, approaches the second abolition from a different perspective. I argue that the expansion of the indenture system created the blueprint for its own undoing. It did so firstly by tying labor relations, labor immigration, and the moral and physical well-being of the indentured workforce indelibly to state agents and institutions of governance. It did so secondly by entangling the operation of this labor governance in disparate regions of the empire, ensuring that issues arising in one region reverberated politically and economically throughout the system. And it did so thirdly through its own processes of recordkeeping, adjudication, inquiry, and official accountability, which provided a channel along which the suffering and discontent of those under its yoke could be communicated to both the public and the highest levels of government.

Politically dependent on its association with "free labor," indenture was, by its critics, increasingly defined as a "new slavery." While its supporters defended it as a vehicle for "freedom" and "civilization," its opponents successfully portrayed it as coercive and corrupting, not the epitome of liberal ideals but its antithesis, not the apex of good governance and just rule but its nadir. In a vicious cycle, every effort to investigate and reform the system produced more evidence of its abuses and failures. Without the convenient moral foils of either slave-owners or allegedly rebellious slaves to justify its practices, and with the shibboleth of perfidious middlemen now incorporated into its regulatory apparatus as licensed operators, those who governed the indenture system could not deflect accountability for its failures, be they moral or economic. The indenture system was thus caught in a trap of its own making.

9 Hugh Tinker, *A New System of Slavery: The Export of Indian Labour Overseas* (London: Oxford University Press, 1974), 310–41; David Northrup, *Indentured Labour in the Age of Imperialism, 1834–1922* (Cambridge: Cambridge University Press, 1994), 144–8; Karen A. Ray, "Lakshmobai and the 'Ladies': Women's Labour and the Abolition of Indentured Immigration from India," *Labour, Capital and Society/Travail, capital et société* 29, no. 1/2 (April/November 1996), 138–40.

10 Sascha Auerbach, *Race, Law, and "The Chinese Puzzle" in Imperial Britain* (New York: Palgrave Macmillan, 2009), 15–50.

Employing the overseer-state as a lens for reappraising the end of indenture also brings into sharper focus the agency of those under the system itself in its decline and eventual abrogation. Prior accounts of the anti-indenture movement have given, at best, a tertiary role to Chinese and Indian workers. Low-level resistance was common since indenture's inception, such scholarship has asserted, but it was not a significant catalyst of its abolition.[11] When we refocus our gaze on the role of the state and state processes, however, we find that whereas employers and managers had most commonly been the source of laborers' grievance in the first decades of the indenture system, by the waning decades of the nineteenth century workers were often directing their sharpest ire at the laws, agents, and institutions of the overseer-state. Their testimony, demonstrations, and strikes provided the grist that the opponents of indenture could employ in public discourse, throwing the inequities of the system and its many contradictions of Britain's self-proclaimed principles of liberalism and moral colonialism into sharp relief.[12] At the same time, workers throughout the empire were themselves resisting the overseer-state and rejecting the indenture system, with its rigid schema of multi-year contracts and heavily criminalized labor statutes. Instead, wherever possible, they chose more flexible arrangements, with less state oversight, taking advantage of the growing demand for their labor to maximize their mobility and recompense while avoiding entanglement with state agents and institutions. Their efforts were aided by the continued development of local intermediaries who sought to circumvent or replace state-organized avenues of recruitment and unyielding, long-term contracts with arrangements more adapted to their specific environments and more amenable to potential recruits.

"Despotism Tempered by Sugar": Early Critiques of Indenture from the Colonial Magistracy

The end of indentured labor, which had constituted a central pillar of plantation labor and colonial governance more broadly in Britain's tropical colonies since the 1840s, began in earnest in 1869. It started in one of the two colonies where the system had first been introduced on a wide scale, British Guiana.[13] At the core of the forty-decade journey to indenture's abolition during the First World War stood the same dynamic that had anchored the overseer-state since

[11] See, for example, the excellent accounts in Maurits S. Hassankan, Brij V. Lal, and Doug Munro, eds., *Resistance and Indian Indenture Experience: Comparative Perspectives* (New Delhi: Manohar, 2014).

[12] Prabhu P. Mohapatra, "Assam and the West Indies, 1860–1920: Immobilizing Plantation Labor," in Douglas Hay and Paul Craven, eds., *Masters, Servants, and Magistrates in Britain and the Empire, 1562–1955* (Chapel Hill: University of North Carolina Press, 2004), 474.

[13] The other being Mauritius.

amelioration: the relationship between local magistrates, estate proprietors, and workers. As long as the first two groups cooperated to maintain the subordination of the third, the system survived. This collaboration could be tense at times – as Gokhale would later emphasize, criticism of indenture, both internal and external, had repeatedly prompted its suspension – but the commitment of magistrates and property-owners to sustaining indenture had been the key to the system's proliferation and persistence across the empire since the 1830s. In 1869, that uneasy alliance began to fray. The "conscience of the Government" would receive a rude shock, one administered by its own officials, but catalyzed by the actions of workers themselves and their disagreement with a colonial magistrate.

In July 1869, a group of Indian indentured laborers from plantation Leonora on the west coast of Demerara brought before the local magistrate a wage complaint against their deputy-manager.[14] This was a common occurrence, both in British Guiana and throughout the indenture system. Equally common was the magistrate's decision to dismiss the complaint. In this instance, however, the situation rapidly escalated. The Leonora workers downed tools, assaulted the deputy-manager, and staged what was, depending upon one's perspective, a strike, a demonstration, a "disturbance," or a riot.[15] Foreshadowing the fatal confrontation that would take place at the neighbouring plantation, Devonshire Castle, two years later, the magistrate summoned a group of armed constables to confront the workers.[16] In this instance, however, the arrival of rifle-armed police was enough to defuse the situation.

Although the Leonora confrontation concluded without further violence, the subsequent political fallout was considerable. With the 1857 Indian Mutiny and the long history of Caribbean slave rebellions as a backdrop, the incident, widely reported in the Guyanese press, revived perennial anxieties about insurrection that were prevalent among the small European population of the colony.[17] At the request of the governor, the local police forces were supplemented with additional armed units, composed primarily of African-Caribbean constables, some of whom were veterans of the West India regiments.[18] This reform may explain why armed constables were so readily

[14] Jenkins, *The Coolie*, 100.

[15] George William Des Voeux, *Experiences of a Demerara Magistrate 1865–1870*, ed. Vincent Ruth (Georgetown: The Daily Chronicle Limited, 1948), 113.

[16] See Chapter 6.

[17] Anne-Marie Lee-Loy, "Introduction," in Joseph Beaumont, *The New Slavery: An Account of the Indian and Chinese Immigrants in British Guiana* (1871; reprint edition [online] The Caribbean Press, 2011), 4–5.

[18] Jenkins, *The Coolie*, 101. For background on the West India Regiments, see David Lambert, "'[A] Mere Cloak for Their Proud Contempt and Antipathy towards the African Race': Imagining Britain's West India Regiments in the Caribbean, 1795–1838," *Journal of Imperial and Commonwealth History* 46, no. 4 (2018), 627–50.

at hand two years later when serious disruption once again arose among the region's indentured Indian workforce. But it would not take that long for the consequences of the laborers' disruption on Leonora to be felt. The affair galvanized demands for reform of the indenture system among those closest to the ground in the apparatus of Guyanese colonial labor governance. Chief among these proponents were the local Immigration Agent-General, James Crosby; Joseph Beaumont, the Chief Justice of the colony; and the colonial administrator and former magistrate Sir George William Des Voeux.[19]

Des Voeux was the first out of the gate with a lengthy report submitted to Lord Granville, the Colonial Secretary, in December 1869. He employed the Leonora incident as an illustration of the fundamental flaws – both moral and legal – that pervaded the indenture system. Des Voeux – who would later serve as governor in Fiji, Newfoundland, and Hong Kong – insisted that the most glaring faults arose from the close association between government agents and planters, and the resulting failure of the former to discharge their paternalistic obligations to the indentured Indian and Chinese population. The most blatant example of the state's overall neglect was the conduct of plantation medical officers, whom Des Voeux portrayed as venal, incompetent, avaricious, and utterly disregarding of workers' well-being. Although ill-treatment at the hands of such figures was a source of great resentment among the indentured population, Des Voeux argued, magistrates' corrupt practices were a problem "of even greater importance to the immigrants than that of the doctors."[20] These judicial officials, as a group, were almost entirely cowed by the plantocracy, due to the latter's near-monopoly on economic and political power and to their superior social position. The pressure on magistrates to decide every case in favor of the planters or their managers was intense, as any opposition might cost them their position. Making matters worse was the direct encroachment of the plantocracy into the justice system through the frequent installation of estate managers as justices of the peace. In such "invidiously distinct positions," these men were even permitted to remain on the bench when trials involving their own estates were conducted.[21] The one figure who might intercede to preserve judicial independence, the Crown-appointed governor, remained idle even in the face of the most egregious abuses of power.

19 James Crosby, during the course of his long career, became an iconic figure among the indentured Indian workforce. So strong was his reputation for advocacy that more than half a century later the term "Crosby," or "Krazbi," was still being employed as the popular designation for all Immigration Agents in the colony. Peter Ruhoman, *Daily Chronicle* (British Guiana), March 24, 1934, excerpted in William Des Voeux, *Experiences of a Demerara Magistrate, 1863–1869* (Georgetown: The Daily Chronicle Ltd., 1948, a reprint of part one of William Des Voeux, *My Colonial Service* [1903]), Appendix II.

20 Des Voeux to Granville in *Demerara Magistrate*, 118.

21 Ibid., 123.

The cumulative result of the planters' undue influence across the length and breadth of the labor governance system in British Guiana, according to Des Voeux, was that indentured workers were "reduced to a position . . . not far removed from slavery."[22] These intolerable circumstances had generated a profound sense of injustice among the indentured labor force, to the great detriment of peace and public order in the colony. To address these and the other issues he had enumerated in his letter to Granville, Des Voeux proposed a dramatic expansion of magistrates' authority and independence. At the core of these reforms would be a cohort of new superior judges who would combine criminal and civil jurisdiction. With such powers, they would assume unassailable legal oversight in all cases involving employers and workers, whether indentured or free. These judges would be empowered to summarily punish estate proprietors, managers, and even their own colleagues for illegal stoppages of wages, unjustified arrests, or the false imprisonment of workers.[23]

Joseph Beaumont, the former Chief Magistrate of British Guiana, was even more scathing of planters' abuse of power and the state's failure to curb it, and proposed even more radical and far-reaching reforms in his popular and much-cited 1872 work, *The New Slavery*. Through their dual control of the Court of Policy, the colony's primary legislative organ, and the Combined Court, its financial instrument, a "mercantile oligarchy . . . founded on the traditions of slavery" ruled in a manner best described as "despotism tempered by sugar."[24] Beaumont roundly condemned the British, Indian, and Chinese governments for aiding and abetting the planters and their allies in the colonial government to engineer "coolie immigration" with the goal of subordinating and replacing the labor of African freedmen.[25] The magistrate described indenture in the harshest possible terms as "a monstrous, rotten system, rooted upon slavery, grown in its stale soil, emulating its worst abuses, and only the more dangerous because it presents itself under false colours, whereas slavery bore the brand of infamy upon its head."[26] Yet despite his condemnation, Beaumont, like Des Voeux, did not call for indenture's abolition, but rather for its dramatic reform along a number of lines. At the core of his proposed changes lay the same measures that Des Voeux had advocated: a strengthening of the judicial oversight of employers and a significant drawdown of criminalized

22 Ibid., 119.

23 Ibid., 129–30.

24 Joseph Beaumont, *The New Slavery: an Account of the Indian and Chinese Immigrants in British Guiana* (1871; repr. ed. [online] The Caribbean Press, 2011), 30. Beaumont was, in all likelihood, evoking Anthony Trollope's famous characterization of the government of Demerara as "a mild despotism, tempered by sugar." Anthony Trollope, *The West Indies and the Spanish Main* (1860; repr. New York: Caroll & Graf, 1999), 162.

25 Beaumont, *The New Slavery*, 32.

26 Ibid., 35.

labor offenses. Failure to address the many faults of the current system, he warned, would have dire consequences for public order in the colony.

Although the rights of indentured laborers were frequently mentioned in the writings of both Beaumont and Des Voeux, neither magistrate called for what had proved to be, in Britain, the only reliable means of protecting workers' rights, namely collective bargaining, the pooling of resources to engage professional advocates against legal reforms that advantaged employers, and, ultimately, workers' enfranchisement and their representation in the legislature.[27] In many respects, their efforts echoed the impetus to ameliorate Caribbean slavery in the 1820s. Then, as well, the overseer-state had been touted as a vehicle for the inculcation of morality and civilization on owners and workers alike. And then, as well, it was the agents and processes of colonial labor governance (e.g. the annual reports of Fiscals and Protectors and Guardians of Slaves) that most visibly demonstrated the need for its reform. The difference in the early 1870s, as Des Voeux and Beaumont both emphasized, was that, even to the workers, the state itself, be it corrupt magistrates or an uncaring governor, were just as often the object of antipathy as the managers and proprietors were. If poor labor governance fostered disorder and resentment, the arguments of the magistrates asserted, then good governance through the expansion and strengthening of the overseer-state would encourage the opposite by reforming the behavior and characters of the planters, the workers, or both.

Much as the advocates of amelioration had half a century earlier, Beaumont and Des Voeux called for an overhaul of colonial administration and adjudication vis-à-vis the indentured workforce, articulating a vision of just and dispassionate governance anchored in an independent and reinvigorated magistracy. And like the earlier arguments for ameliorated slavery, apprenticeship, and the introduction of indenture, the magistrates' critique and proposed reforms were a distinct amalgamation of the contrasting principles that animated much of British governance both colonial and domestic. On the one hand, they remained enmeshed in an overarching commitment to liberal economic and social tenets, chief among them the benefits of free labor and the financial advantages of immigration to workers, employers, and the colony as a whole. At the same time, however, their demands for the expansion and strengthening of the state's intervention in labor relations and social conditions – from enhanced judicial oversight of employers to guaranteeing "an adequate supply of women" among immigrant cohorts – in order to preserve public order and the well-being of workers were more characteristic of the humanitarianism and Progressivism that pervaded urban social and sanitary

[27] Douglas Hay, "England, 1562–1875," in Douglas Hay and Paul Craven, eds., *Masters, Servants, and Magistrates in Britain and the Empire, 1562–1955* (Chapel Hill: University of North Carolina Press, 2004), 105–6, 115–16.

reform in the metropole.[28] Like the latter, their advocacy conflated the issues of moral and physical degeneration, and in both milieu, magistrates operated as prominent advocates of reform and the fulcrums of its enforcement.[29]

At the heart of the magistrates' justifications for their centrality in mediating labor relations and safeguarding those at the lowest end of the social order, however, was a conservative vision of paternalistic judicial authority reminiscent of the eighteenth-century English gentry.[30] In this formulation, they alone possessed the experience and expertise to serve as the guardians of those incapable of protecting themselves, be they indentured workers in the Caribbean or working-class women in the slums of London.[31] Shorn of any attendant support for policies that would grant workers any additional rights, secure access to independent advocates, or enable collective bargaining, the magistrates' proposed reforms maintained the agents of the overseer-state (i.e. themselves) as the mediators between employers and workers and as the sole avenue for the latter to seek redress. The authors' clear discomfort at the prospect of indentured workers striking or demonstrating in large numbers was evident, and Des Voeux's petition was itself animated by what he saw as the dire implications of one such event. In their view, the only viable solution to magistrates' misconduct, even in a system where this had been a perennial weak point from its inception, was to accord these pivotal officers full independence from the local matrix of authority and to grant them even more power over an even wider range of economic and social practices.

The assault on his own professional colleagues and the governor that supervised them would cost Beaumont dearly. After a protracted struggle with Governor Francis Hincks and the planters' lobby over a host of issues ranging from the adjudication of wage disputes to the conviction and imprisonment of a local newspaper editor for allegedly libelous comments about James Crosby, the Immigration Agent-General, Beaumont was removed from his post.[32] He would never hold another significant public office. Des Voeux, who had taken a less strident tone and had stayed within the channels of official

[28] Beaumont, *The New Slavery*, 36; Jules P. Gehrke, "A Radical Endeavor: Joseph Chamberlain and the Emergence of Municipal Socialism in Birmingham," *American Journal of Economics and Sociology* 75, no. 1 (2016), 23–57.

[29] On the metropolitan context, see Sascha Auerbach, *Armed with Sword and Scales: Law, Culture, and Local Courtrooms in London, 1860–1913* (Cambridge: Cambridge University Press, 2021), 141–74.

[30] Douglas Hay, "Patronage, Paternalism, and Welfare: Masters, Workers, and Magistrates in Eighteenth-Century England," *International Labor and Working-Class History*, 53 (1998), 27–48.

[31] Auerbach, *Sword and Scales*, 218–80.

[32] Basdeo Mangru, "The Hincks-Beaumont Imbroglio: Partisan Politics in British Guiana in the 1860s," *Boletín de Estudios Latinoamericanos y del Caribe* 43 (Diciembre de 1987), 111.

accountability, was able to continue his peripatetic imperial careering.[33] Although they both lost their direct influence in the affairs of British Guiana, the harsh light they had shed on indenture in the Caribbean would leave a lasting legacy. Catalyzed by the Leonora demonstration and amidst growing concern over the threats to public order posed by the specter of a fractious and discontented indentured workforce, the magistrates' ardent critiques of colonial labor governance would prove to be the beginning of a new wave of public and official reappraisals of the system. As part of his proposed suite of reforms to enhance the power of the overseer-state in the face of magistrates' corruption and planters' immorality, Des Voeux explicitly called for a parliamentary commission to investigate the situation in British Guiana. In this regard, at least, his success likely well exceeded his expectations. With two of its own appointees so prominently condemning the misconduct of state processes in the colony, and with a host of complaints about indenture being raised throughout the empire, the Colonial Office could not long ignore the responsibility laid at its feet. Within a few years of the publication of Des Voeux's appeal to Granville, a new round of government inquiries had been initiated across the colonies where indenture was practiced. Meanwhile, Beaumont's scathing assessment of "the new slavery" rapidly became a popular catchphrase in public discourse (and remains so in contemporary scholarship).[34] Indenture, championed by its proponents as a laudable example of free labor, would soon become indelibly tainted by this prominent association with its anathema.

"Watchful Supervision on the Part of the Government": Official Enquiries in the 1870s and 1880s

The first major government inquiry into indenture in the 1870s was a direct result of the Leonora demonstration and Des Voeux's subsequent letter to Granville. Hot on the heels of a significant civil disturbance, the magistrate's systematic condemnation of labor governance in British Guiana was too trenchant, and too public, to be ignored. The British Guiana Commission "to Enquire into the Condition of Immigrants" was a three-man affair, composed of a High Court judge from Bombay, a barrister, and the Immigration Agent-General of Trinidad (i.e. James Crosby's counterpart). Their investigation, conducted over the course of several months, was comprised of a series of interviews with proprietors, managers, judges, and other colonial officials involved in the oversight of the labor system (including James Crosby).

[33] In a similar vein, see Laurence Brown, "Inter-colonial Migration and the Refashioning of Indenture Labour: Arthur Gordon in Trinidad, Mauritius and Fiji," in David Lambert and Alan Lester, eds., *Colonial Lives Across the British Empire: Imperial Careering in the Long Nineteenth Century* (Cambridge: Cambridge University Press, 2006), 204–27.

[34] For example, in the title of Hugh Tinker's landmark study of indenture, *A New System of Slavery*.

Despite the key role played by workers in catalyzing Des Voeux's response, and regardless of his focus on workers' dissatisfaction, no indentured laborers were called as witnesses.

Dealing with Des Voeux's claims was the first order of business to be addressed in the final report. Published in 1871, it began by reprinting Des Voeux's letter to Granville and then providing a step-by-step refutation of it and its author. Des Voeux, the authors insisted, was entirely unreliable as a witness. Questioned about his sweeping and damning accusations against the magistracy, medical officers, and immigration agents, he could provide no documentation to support his claims. Worse yet, during the commission's interview, "his memory had very constantly slipped and still did very constantly betray him."[35] An exhaustive examination of official records produced no evidence of the many abuses he had outlined. On the contrary, such documentation as was produced indicated that the laws governing labor and laborers *were* being applied as intended. Arguably the most severe of the magistrate's accusations, that illegal arrest and detention were common throughout the colony, was completely unsupportable.[36] The Commission similarly dismissed Des Voeux's claim that the adjudication of workers' cases had been hopelessly corrupted by the "invidiously distinct position" of estate managers as justices of the peace. His accusation that these men were allowed to remain on the bench during cases concerning their own estates was "highly coloured, if not exaggerated."[37] The report's authors also dismissed the charges of misconduct Des Voeux had made against immigration agents, his decrying of the careless investigation of workers' complaints, and his assertions about callous behavior by estate medical officers.[38] The cumulative result was to paint his wide-ranging critique as a personal diatribe from a rambling, untrustworthy, and somewhat vindictive malcontent. "We must express a decided opinion," the commissioners wrote, "that Mr. Des Voeux was ill-advised in bringing under any circumstances a series of charges, so vague, so sweeping, and so little admitting of satisfactory proof as those we have hitherto discussed."[39] With the Commission's verdict, the harshest criticism yet of the overseer-state, composed by one of its prominent members, had been comprehensively refuted using the voluminous evidence that its own validatory processes had generated.

The British Guiana Commission, while definitively rejecting Des Voeux's accusations, did find some faults with the colony's system of labor governance.

[35] PP 1871, *Report of the Commissioners Appointed to Enquire into the Treatment of Immigrants in British Guiana* (1871 *Report of the British Guiana Commission*), c. 393 (London, 1871), 18.

[36] Ibid., 21.

[37] Ibid., 24.

[38] Ibid., 26–7.

[39] Ibid., 29.

Chief among these was the regulation that covered the extension of a worker's indenture in instances where they had been imprisoned or had deserted.[40] The commissioners also asserted that, on the whole, magistrates' sentences against laborers were too severe, though the report denied that this was due to their deference to planters' interests.[41] The best way to address the issues that existed, even if Des Voeux's descriptions of them were gross exaggerations, was with further extension of state oversight. The commissioners recommended reforms to the system, emphasizing, in particular, the importance of reinstating the power and independence of the Immigration Office as a fully recognized department of the government.[42] The most important consequence of this would be to reestablish the authority of the Immigration Agent-General (aka "Protector"), whose power had been subsumed by Governor Hincks.[43] In similar vein, the commissioners advised that the state should adopt direct supervision over the medical practitioners responsible for the health of the indentured population. Overall, the Commission's report mirrored Des Voeux's central argument: indenture was a laudable institution that guaranteed the continued economic survival of the colony and could easily be made both appealing to workers and morally acceptable through the appropriate expansion of government oversight.[44]

In many ways, the most significant consequence of the commission was that it facilitated the production of yet another popular treatise on indenture, John Edward Jenkins's *The Coolie: His Rights and Wrongs*. Much like Des Voeux's letter and the findings of the Commission, this volume, while criticizing some aspects of the indenture system and recommending modest reforms, portrayed the institution as necessary for the colony's prosperity and largely beneficial to the Indian workers involved. Jenkins was also in line with other commentators in asserting that overmighty planters were the source of most problems, and that an expansion of the state's oversight offered the most effective solution.[45]

[40] The Commission's objection here was that the Register of Imprisonments and Desertions kept by each estate was allowed to serve as the sole source of evidence to determine the period of additional indenture. Such a document, the authors insisted, was "of second-rate value as evidence" since it was controlled entirely by the estate manager, uncorroborated by any other documentation, and maintained solely with the purpose of providing evidence in cases of desertion or imprisonment. *British Guiana, Report of the Commissioners, The Commission of Inquiry into the Treatment of Immigrants in British Guiana, v. IV* (hereafter *British Guiana Commission Report v. IV*) (Georgetown: The Colonist Office, 1871), 117. Note: This was a version of the 1871 Report reprinted by the offices of *The Colonist*, in most ways identical to the official government version but formatted slightly differently.

[41] *British Guiana Commission Report v. IV*, 23

[42] Ibid., 373.

[43] Tinker, *A New System of Slavery*, 241.

[44] *British Guiana Commission Report v. IV*, 373, 380.

[45] Jenkins, *The Coolie*, 158.

Another possible tack for reform would be to dilute the political power of estate-owners. The author-barrister opined that incorporating the colony's Portuguese population into the political system, and even extending this participation to a select constituency of creole black or "coloured" (i.e. of mixed racial background) residents who possessed both "property and education," would somewhat balance out the power of the plantocracy and lessen class tensions.[46] But he stopped well short of advocating any political representation or direct participation by Indian or Chinese immigrants. It was, as Des Voeux, Beaumont, and the commissioners had all agreed, the duty of the government both to encourage the prosperity of its colonies by securing the required Indian workforce and to operate "as a powerful and comparatively [im]partial outsider ... to see that justice shall be done to those who are the instruments of profit."[47] Thus did the collective scrutiny of the indenture system, from Beaumont's treatise to the Commission to Jenkins's widely read account, reach consensus that its failings were primarily the failings of state processes, and the responsibility for repairing and maintaining it lay with the state agents and institutions. Even in a wider ideological environment that favored less state regulation of trade and commerce, supervising colonial labor immigration and sustaining the labor system itself remained, now more than ever, matters of state oversight.

Although there was much agreement across the different accounts of indenture in British Guiana, there was also a crucial difference between them. The British Guiana Commission had largely ignored the rising dissatisfaction and agitation among the Indian workforce with the conduct of indenture and with the state's (mis)handling of their grievances. In contrast, this widespread discontent was clearly engaged in Des Voeux's opening argument, in Beaumont's treatise, and in Jenkins's *The Coolie*. All three authors asserted that workers were increasingly directing their ire and sense of injustice as much, if not more so, *at the state itself* as they were at the employers whom it abetted. For the first time in the history of indenture, this pervasive sense of dissatisfaction and injustice among workers had catalyzed not just one but three different influential and powerful figures, two of them important colonial officials, to make both official and public remonstrations over the failings of colonial labor governance. The British Guiana Commission, even if it had failed to directly address workers' growing opposition to the overseer-state itself, was also nonetheless a watershed moment in the burgeoning public recognition of how the state apparatus was failing to fulfill its promises to protect the rights and well-being of indentured laborers. A labor demonstration, triggered by workers' unhappiness with the results of wage arbitration by a local magistrate, had been a crucial antecedent to this, the longest and most thorough official government inquiry yet conducted into indenture.

[46] Ibid., 71–2.
[47] Ibid., 157.

Throughout this period of scrutiny, the events of 1857 still reverberated across official discourse and were indelibly associated with the potentially disruptive consequences of a dissatisfied Indian population.[48] In such circumstances, pervasive rumblings of discontent could not be, as they had in the past, simply dismissed as the inconsequential plaints of a population racially predisposed toward hyperbole and lament. As they had been with this tranche of critical assessments in British Guiana, Indian workers' dissatisfaction with labor governance were also important catalysts of the next two serious investigations into the indenture system, which took place in Mauritius and Natal.

In Mauritius, the increasingly heavy-handed approach of the colonial magistracy both increased popular discontent and generated evidence of alarming levels of prosecution. These, combined with advocacy by a prominent member of the planter class, goaded the colonial administration into action. As in British Guiana, the state's response consisted largely of reaffirming indenture as a flawed, but ultimately necessary and moral system whose workings could be salvaged with more vigorous centralized oversight. In the 1860s, a confluence of conditions in Mauritius had created an acute sense of crisis among both planters seeking indentured workers and the governor, Sir Henry Barkly, who was eager to maintain the colony's revenues.[49] The island was facing rising competition in the labor market, a precipitous decline in the numbers of immigrants, and the ongoing effects of a malaria epidemic that had claimed 40,000 lives from 1867 to 1868. The concern this prompted among planters and the governor was exacerbated by their unfavorable position vis-à-vis the extant Indian population of the colony. This was composed largely of experienced "Old Immigrants" (i.e. those whose initial contracts of indenture had already expired) who were keen to seek better terms of subsequent employment and explore economic opportunities beyond the plantations.[50] In response to this multiplicity of issues affecting the labor supply, with Barkly's collusion, Mauritian planters engineered the passage of increasingly repressive labor laws. The goal was to force the island's existing Indian population to remain trammeled within the plantation indenture system. These regulations simultaneously restricted the mobility of Indian indentured workers while empowering police and magistrates to monitor their movements and punish violators. The harshest of these was a regulation passed in 1869 that allowed Indian workers a span of only eight days after the termination of their indenture, or of any other contract, before subjecting them

[48] Sascha Auerbach, "Of Rights and Riots: Indenture and (Mis)Rule in the Late Nineteenth-Century British Caribbean," *English Historical Review* 137, no. 589 (December 2022), 1662–92.

[49] The numbers of Indian immigrants arriving annually had dropped from an apex of approximately 40,000 in 1858–9 to just over 10,000 in 1860–1. Marina Carter, *Servants, Sirdars, and Settlers: Indians in Mauritius, 1834–1874* (Delhi: Oxford University Press, 1995), 26.

[50] Brown, "Inter-colonial Migration," 213–16.

to a fine of £2 or seven days' imprisonment along with classification as a "vagrant."[51] The cumulative result of these harsh new regulations, all designed to ensure the availability of cheap, experienced laborers for the estates, was a dramatic increase in the arrest rate of Old Immigrants. In 1869, with police officers combing the island in organized hunts for "vagabonds," more than 20 percent (30,824) of the colony's Indian population was arrested for vagrancy.[52]

Seeking respite from the relentless police patrols in the inaccessible hill country inland from Port Louis, the Old Immigrants encountered an unexpected ally in the form of Adolphe de Plevitz, the Paris-born Polish manager of a plantation in the Nouvelle Découverte district. De Plevitz, who had secured his position as manager through a marriage to the estate proprietor, and had formerly worked in the colony's Forests Department, was an anomaly among his colleagues. He refused to employ indentured Indian workers and allowed his own laborers to give notice when they pleased.[53] Working together, the Old Immigrants and De Plevitz collated a petition, signed by 9,401 workers, that catalogued their grievances.[54] The focus of their discontent was labor governance in the colony, which "deprived them of that freedom which all other inhabitants of Mauritius enjoy."[55] The new regulations on official documentation (i.e. identification and passes for travel) were the most onerous of these, leaving them liable to imprisonment for hard labor for conducting any number of mundane activities.[56] The situation was made even more intolerable by the aggressiveness of police in enforcing the new laws. In their zeal to arrest alleged vagabonds, the petitioners asserted, dozens of Indian workers would be rounded up, arrested, and sentenced en masse to imprisonment with hard labor. The result was that the Old Immigrants were "thus at the mercy of the police," and even if arrested and sentenced without just cause, they had no redress.[57]

[51] Richard B. Allen, *Slaves, Freedmen, and Indentured Laborers in Colonial Mauritius* (Cambridge: Cambridge University Press, 1999), 63.

[52] Tinker, *A New System of Slavery*, 242.

[53] Ibid., 243.

[54] For the broader historical context of colonial petitioning, see Richard Huzzey and Henry Miller, "Colonial Petitions, Colonial Petitioners, and the Imperial Parliament, ca. 1780–1918," *Journal of British Studies* 61 (April 2022), 261–89.

[55] "Petition of the Old Immigrants of Mauritius, Presented on 6th June, 1871," reprinted in PP 1975 *Report of the Royal Commissioners Appointed to Enquire into the Treatment of Immigrants in Mauritius* (C. 1115) (hereafter *Mauritius Commission* 1875), 2.

[56] "Petition of the Old Immigrants," *Mauritius Commission* 1875, 2–3. One of the most onerous of these regulations was Ordinance No. 31 of 1867, which specified the need for a pass to be obtained from the police inspector of the district in which the applicant lived. These boundaries were moved not infrequently, and since most Indian workers were of limited, if any, literacy and had no access to official maps, determining their home district was often problematic in the extreme.

[57] "Petition of the Old Immigrants," *Mauritius Commission* 1875, 3.

To support the Old Immigrants' assertions of rampant injustice, the petition was appended with sixteen detailed, personal accounts of the abuse and indignity that different signatories had suffered at the hands of police and magistrates. These tales of woe inflicted by the apparatus of the colonial state ranged from the piteous to the absurd. Dilloo, a market gardener, related how police had entered his dwelling, without warrant, demanding the papers of all residents. Although his house had burned down recently, Dilloo had managed to save the all-important documentation attesting to the legality of himself and his wife. Their children, aged nine, twelve, and thirteen, had not been so lucky, their paperwork having been lost in the fire. All three were arrested as vagabonds and remained imprisoned for three days.[58] Ramluckhun, another gardener, was arrested and imprisoned on the very morning of his wedding. It was never clear to him the justification for this, since all of his papers were in order. He was released by the magistrate only after several days of remonstration.[59]

The accounts appended to the petition also starkly related the infamous "vagrant hunts" that police organized to secure mass arrests of those lacking the proper paperwork. Abeluck described how two dozen of his fellow market-gardeners had repeatedly applied to the police inspector in Pamplemousses district for passes to conduct their business. At the offices, they were "always being turned out with violence, without any reason being given."[60] The petitioners deduced that they had made a mistake, and instead applied for passes in the neighboring Moka district, which they promptly received. Sometime later, their homes were surrounded by more than a dozen police officers who, ignoring the papers they had obtained in Moka, arrested and imprisoned them for several days. Over the next week, the unlucky band was transported in custody, often without any food, sometimes on foot and sometimes by rail, to a series of magistrates and police stations in the districts of Pamplemousses, Port Louis, and Plaines Wilhelm. At the end of this odyssey, which Abeluck estimated had covered 220 miles, they appeared once again in the Moka police court. The magistrate there informed them that they did, indeed, reside in Pamplemousses. After several more appearances at that district's police court over the course of the next two weeks, and having been repeatedly turned away "with violence," the peripatetic group were finally awarded the necessary passes to travel for their trade.

While Abeluck and his fellow market-gardeners were receiving their involuntary tour of the Mauritian jails and police courts, another signatory was paying dearly for his participation in the campaign to protest against rampant

58 Account of Dilloo, Old Immigrant, No. 82,500, gardener, in "Petition of the Old Immigrants," *Mauritius Commission* 1875, 3.

59 Account of Ramluckhun, gardener at Nouvelle Découverte, in "Petition of the Old Immigrants," *Mauritius Commission* 1875, 3.

60 Account of Abeluck, Old Immigrant, No. 268,683, on the Colville Estate belonging to Mr. Desenne, in "Petition of the Old Immigrants," *Mauritius Commission* 1875, 6.

injustice in the colony. Apprehended while traveling the roads from Nouvelle Découverte to Pamplemousses, Hookum explained to the arresting officer that he had been returning home from signing the Old Immigrants' petition to the governor. Unmoved by this defense, the police sergeant bound him, marched him to the local police station, forced him to fetch water and clean the establishment, and then imprisoned him overnight without food.[61] The next day, the magistrate sentenced him to four days' incarceration with hard labor.

The petition composed by de Plevitz and the Old Immigrants of Mauritius is notable in several regards. First and foremost, it stood out as the single largest act of collective response made thus far by Indian workers to the apparatus of colonial labor governance – the signatories represented approximately 5 percent of the colony's entire Indian population at the time. A second distinctive feature of the petition was that it made no mention of estate proprietors, managers, or overseers. The sole cause of complaint was the treatment that the signatories had received at the hands of the colony's police and magistrates. Another notable element was the depth of knowledge evident both in the Old Immigrants' engagement with the state and in the nature of their grievances as articulated in the individual accounts. Although de Plevitz, himself an estate manager, undoubtedly brought some level of expertise to the composition of the petition, his own knowledge of labor governance would have been limited. He did not himself employ indentured laborers and, though he served as the unofficial advocate of the Old Immigrants, he had never personally faced arrest, questioning, adjudication for documentary violations, or imprisonment.

The storehouse of expertise provided by the Indian signatories, in contrast, would have been extensive. Encounters with various government officials and institutions – the magistrates, police, and police courts in particular – had been part and parcel of the everyday life of Indian immigrants for several decades. Ramluckhun, Abcluck, and their compatriots all demonstrated a keen understanding of the laws and their implications, even though both the specific regulations and their methods of enforcement were in a state of rapid flux. Their accounts evinced a particularly sharp comprehension of the hierarchies of colonial authority; the divisions of police and magisterial jurisdiction; the processes of documentation, police questioning, and magistrates' adjudication; and the potential avenues for appeal. A life lived in the ever-present shadow of the overseer-state had taught them hard lessons in its operation, and even if their leverage during specific contests was minimal, their experiences left them very well equipped to dissect its iniquities and catalog its injustices. For these men and their compatriots, the apparatus of the state itself was the problem in Mauritius. The only "humane" course of action, the petition concluded, was repeal of the laws that had caused so much anguish to so many. These laws, the

61 Account of Hookum, in the service of Messrs. Pellereau & Co., Pamplemousses, "Petition of the Old Immigrants," *Mauritius Commission* 1875, 4.

petitioners were keen to point out, directly contravened the British constitutional principle that *all* subjects of the Crown were entitled to the same rights and protections, regardless of whether or not they were "of European birth or descent."[62]

De Plevitz amended his own observations to the Old Immigrants' petition, and his contribution was equally damning of how labor was being governed in the colony. Hemmed in by laws that prevented their mobility, hindered their independence to seek new employment, and hounded them with potential arrest for "vagrancy" within a week of their contract's termination, "an Old Immigrant's life is rendered so miserable that the vast majority of them are driven in despair to re-engage on the master's own terms."[63] Such "tyranny and oppression" was justified, he wrote, by a hypocritical representation of Indians as infantile and incapable of rational decision-making, and therefore requiring "a paternal government having arbitrary authority and exercising it benevolently to promote the welfare of its children." "They have made the Government arbitrary enough," de Plevitz observed, "but how far it is paternal the facts of this petition show." The ultimate effect of the law and its enforcement, the blame for which de Plevitz laid squarely at the feet of the governor, Barkly, and the colony's magistracy, was not only to deprive the Indian immigrant of his rights but to reduce him "to the position of a Helot [i.e. a slave]."[64]

As had been the case in British Guiana with the public excoriations delivered by Des Voeux and Beaumont, the colonial state in Mauritius had been condemned for supporting a labor system that more closely resembled slavery than it did free labor. Such associations were rhetorical rather than practically verifiable in the concrete legal structures governing Indian and Chinese labor. Although the labor laws left indentured and contract workers profoundly exposed to exploitation and persecution, they neither designated laborers as property nor explicitly denied them the wide array of rights to which all Crown subjects were entitled. Chief among these were the rights to enter into contracts, to bring legal suits, to file grievances, and to be free from punishment without due process. That the direct and forceful comparison to slavery had now been made independently in two widely disparate locations, however, demonstrated how far indenture, once touted as the antidote to the moral stain of slavery, was being prominently and publicly condemned as its vile resurrection.

Similarly to the Leonora demonstration and its political fallout in British Guiana, the Old Immigrants' petition catalyzed what would become the most

62 "Petition of the Old Immigrants," *Mauritius Commission* 1875, 3. This assessment was reinforced with de Plevitz's observations, which were amended to the petition. "The Labour Laws," he wrote, "have wholly deprived the poor Indian immigrant ... of the rights of citizenship, have almost put him without the pale of humanity, and reduced him to the position of a Helot."

63 De Plevitz, "Observations," *Mauritius Commission* 1875, 10.

64 De Plevitz, "Observations," *Mauritius Commission* 1875, 9.

broad-ranging inquiry yet into Mauritian labor governance. The island occupied a particularly crucial space in the overseer-state, since it was the first place where large-scale Indian immigration and indenture had been practiced; it had, by far, the largest Indian laboring population of any British colony outside of India itself; its judicial system was arguably the most interventionist of any colony's in terms of prosecuting labor offenses; and in the earlier decades of the indenture system, it was often to Mauritius that other colonies' administrations had looked for precedents and guidance on how Indian immigration and labor were to be organized and governed.[65] The primary locus of the indenture system as a state-supervised endeavor had since shifted to the Caribbean, and to British Guiana in particular. But Mauritius still loomed large in official policy as an ongoing experiment in large-scale labor transportation and regulation playing out on India's doorstep.

Even in a locale so central to the continuing development of the overseer-state, and despite the size of the petition's constituency and the prominence of its delivery, the appeal of the Old Immigrants for justice might still have been quietly ignored were it not for its timing. The petition landed not on the desk of Henry Barkly but instead on that of his successor as governor, Sir Arthur Gordon. As he had in his prior appointment as the governor of Trinidad, Gordon sought to deal with the problem of labor supply by expanding the government's role, citing the more proactive policies employed in the Caribbean as a foil for Mauritius's current crisis.[66] To his mind, the near total absence of state supervision over contracts and health care among the Indian indentured population lay at the root cause of the problem and a wholesale reform of the indenture system in the colony was therefore urgently required. The failings of indenture stemmed from the failings of the state, which was too harsh in some regards (e.g. the labor laws and the vagrancy regulations) and too lax in others (e.g. monitoring work conditions on the plantations). The Old Immigrants' petition jibed well with Gordon's concerns, adding weight to his lobbying for reform, which culminated in another official investigation into indenture.

In the preface to its final report, the resulting Royal Commission on "the treatment of immigrants in Mauritius" explicitly referenced, as the catalysts for its investigation, the Old Immigrants' petition and the commentary pamphlet de Plevitz had published subsequently. It also borrowed extensively from the precedents set with the earlier British Guiana Commission into the same subject, even down to the personnel involved. The Commission was led by

[65] In 1860–4, of the 72,960 Indian contract laborers in the colony, 15,191 were prosecuted at a conviction rate of 77.6 percent. From 1865 to 1869, there were 69,165, of whom 12,903 were prosecuted, at a conviction rate of 73.9 percent. Allen, *Slaves, Freedmen, and Indentured Laborers*, 66.

[66] Arthur Gordon, *Mauritius: Records of Private and Public Life, 1871–1874, Vol. 1* (Edinburgh: R. & R. Clark, 1894), 58.

Sir William Frere, the judge of the Bombay High Court that had steered the British Guiana inquiry. He was joined by Darnell Davis, a Demeraran historian and writer who had served as the secretary and author of the report in British Guiana, and who would serve the same function on the Mauritius Commission.[67] The authors called for a host of reforms across almost every aspect of the indenture system, from the methods of pay and the monitoring of contracts to the provision of health care and the treatment of vagrancy. The report was particularly harsh toward the magistracy, which had demonstrated both "great recklessness" in convicting and imprisoning Indian workers and "great negligence" in their oversight of labor contracts.[68]

At the core of the Commission's vision for a reinvigorated overseer-state in Mauritius, one more in line with the operation of labor governance in the Caribbean, was the centralization of power in an independent Immigration Department. Its staff not only would assume from magistrates the role of certifying and supervising labor contracts but also would regularly install themselves at the local courts in order to more carefully mediate the relationship between the plantation workforce, estate managers, and the judicial system.[69] Magistrates' authority was to be further curtailed by requiring them to be itinerant, holding their courts at local police stations once a month and thus being within easy reach of all the estates under their authority, and through the reduction of their jurisdiction over wage cases from those not exceeding £50 in dispute to those not exceeding £30.[70] The Commission also recommended that the state's authority to punish both negligent proprietors and wayward workers be expanded further, with such power accruing, as had been the case with the proposed reforms of the magistrate's roles, to the Protectors of Immigrants.

Delays in the conduct of the Commission's inquiry, along with Gordon's departure, in pursuit of career advancement, to a new post in Fiji, would blunt the impact of the Commission's report.[71] But the condemnation of the current vagrancy laws as "harassment" had a sobering effect on the conduct of the overseer-state in Mauritius.[72] In the subsequent decade, even though the Indian population declined by only 10 percent, the number of prosecutions under the labor laws fell by two-thirds.[73] Beyond its concrete effect on labor governance in the colony, the report, along with the Guiana Commission and

67 Tinker, *A New System of Slavery*, 241, 249. The third member of the Commission was Victor A. Williamson, a lawyer familiar with the Caribbean context. Ibid.
68 *Mauritius Commission* 1875, 584.
69 Ibid., 590.
70 Those in excess were to be handled by superior judges, as before. Ibid.
71 Brown, "Inter-colonial Migration," 218.
72 Allen, *Slaves, Freedmen, and Indentured Laborers*, 68.
73 Though it should be noted that the conviction rate rose to 85 percent in the same period. Allen, *Slaves, Freedmen, and Indentured Laborers*, 66.

the indictments leveled by Des Voeux and Beaumont, constituted a growing chorus of criticism against indenture. In it, planters figured prominently, but the apparatus of colonial governance was itself held increasingly responsible for the system's endemic issues. These critiques of the oversteer-state emerged from its own mechanisms of information-gathering and dissemination. At their heart were the complaints of indentured workers themselves about how the state was failing to respect their rights and entitlements to justice as subjects of the Crown. The proposed solutions were also coalescing around similar points, which was not surprising considering the peregrination of reform-minded administrators such as Des Voeux, Gordon, and Frere. Indenture as a system could be sustainable, economically and morally, and could fulfill its promise of revenue and prosperity only if magistrates, the lynchpins of labor governance, were brought under stricter and more centralized control; if the oversight and disciplining mechanisms of the state vis-à-vis contracts and conditions on the plantations were enhanced; and if workers themselves were given more direct and frequent access to forums for grievance and redress.

As the developments in both British Guiana and Mauritius demonstrated, however, the cumulative effect of the increased oversight of the overseer-state *by* the overseer-state was to generate even more evidence of the system's many injustices and abuses. This process also refocused accountability for these issues onto the conduct of state officials and the operation of state institutions, amplified the voices of critics, and expanded their audience both public and official. Fast on the heels of Old Immigrants' petition in Mauritius, yet another government inquiry was triggered by the complaints of Indian workers. In 1871, representatives of the Government of India wrote to the Secretary of State for India in Whitehall. Their goal was to bring to the attention of the metropolitan government the complaints of ill-treatment made by a group of Indian workers returning to Calcutta from the South African colony of Natal on the transport ship *Red Riding Hood*. Their grievances, the authors wrote, were so precise and so damning of certain employers that the matter demanded official investigation.[74] In the inquiry that was subsequently conducted by the Natal colonial government, the witnesses were drawn primarily from the ranks of estate managers and overseers, who vigorously defended their treatment of workers. They relied on the detailed records of their account books to demonstrate that Indian laborers were paid properly, fed sufficiently, given adequate sick time and medical care, and assigned only reasonable tasks.

[74] Government of India to the Duke of Argyll, Secretary of State for India, August 17, 1871, Appendix B, *Report of the Coolie Commission, Appointed to Inquire into the Condition of the Indian Immigrants in the Colony of Natal* (hereafter *Natal Commission* 1872), reprinted in the Third Session, Sixth Council, L. C. No. 1 (Pietermaritzburg: Keith & Co., 1872), 47.

Some of those interviewed, however, offered a very different picture of life on the Natal estates. These witnesses emphasized the abuses inherent in the system and identified the faulty operation of the colony's labor governance apparatus as the primary cause of Indians' widely held grievances. The first of those whose testimony undercut the narrative of a moral and well-regulated Indian colonial labor system was H. C. Shepstone, who had served as the Coolie Immigration Agent from July 1864 to June 1870. Echoing the comments made in the Mauritius report, Shepstone pointed to the imbalance of power between the magistrates' courts and the agents as the chief reason for dissatisfaction among workers. Whereas Indian laborers regarded the latter as their protectors, and expected immediate redress when they petitioned such agents, in truth, "the Coolie Agent has no power whatever."[75] Instead, this official could only recommend that the workers go to the magistrate with their grievances, "which they are averse to do." The depth of this aversion, and its causes, were made clear by one of the few Indian witnesses interviewed during the inquiry. Rangasammy, a former *sirdar* who had gone on to become a hotel-keeper, had lived in Natal for nearly nine years. Magistrates, he explained, could sometimes collude with the most abusive proprietors, issuing floggings without sufficient cause. The situation was made worse by the language barrier, which forced the magistrates to depend on interpreters who routinely distorted workers' depositions. "If we say, 'My wife was ill-treated,' he [i.e. the interpreter] renders it, 'My wife was kicked,'" Rangasammy explained.[76] "In consequence of this interpretation, the Magistrate gets angry, and says we are liars." The hotel-keeper's criticism of the magistrates and the interpreters in government employ was echoed in the statements of the returning Indian workers that had triggered the inquiry and in those of the Indians still residing in the colony. They asserted that they were routinely denied the wages they had contracted for, beaten savagely with a variety of implements, and forced to work when sick. Although magistrates were repeatedly made aware of these issues, the petitioners explained, these officials did nothing to stop the abuse.[77]

In their response to the Natal government's inquiry, the Government of India downplayed the raft of positive reports from managers, focusing instead on the original complaints by the *Red Riding Hood* passengers and on the accounts of the few resident Indians interviewed during the investigation. The Natal government was held fully accountable for the abuse of Indian immigrants, with the withholding of wages and the absence of any redress for workers' grievances being particularly heinous examples. The laborers in question, the Indian government representatives asserted, had been engaged

[75] Testimony of H. C. Shepstone, July 6, 1872, *Natal Commission* 1872, 36.

[76] Testimony of Rangasammy, June 23, 1872, *Natal Commission* 1872, 27.

[77] Statement of Ramasamy, *Natal Commission* 1872, 31; Statement of Baboo, *Natal Commission* 1872, 52.

by agents working under the auspices of the Natal government and assigned to employers by similar means. Therefore, it remained entirely the colonial government's responsibility to see that they were treated fairly. Indian government officials further castigated their colleagues in Natal for the "very perfunctory manner" in which the inquiry itself had been conducted.[78] They were alarmed that many of the most serious charges had gone largely unaddressed, and were particularly aghast over the failure to properly investigate the claim that, on one estate, four laborers had hanged themselves in order "'to escape the annoyance of being compelled to work when sick, and of being beaten."[79] The Government of India forwarded the entire report, along with its own representative's comments, to Lord Kimberley, the Colonial Secretary, indicating that, in light of the "unsatisfactory circumstances" in Natal, a complete prohibition on emigration there from Bengal Presidency was being seriously considered.

Through the Natal investigation, the complaints of Indian workers had once again reached the ears of the highest officials in the British imperial government. These cast further aspersions on an indenture system already under assault from various quarters, and held yet another colonial administration to account for the failures of labor governance. The ink on the Government of India's scathing letter to Kimberley had barely dried when an even more damning account of the overseer-state's failings was produced by its increasingly robust and critical mechanisms of reporting and accountability. J. Geoghegan, Undersecretary to the Government of Bengal, returning from a period of leave to find the issue of labor immigration much under discussion, decided to investigate the matter personally. He undertook a comprehensive survey of its history, its current configuration in various colonies, and the evolution of government policy and of the state's role in labor recruitment and management. Geoghegan's broad-ranging and compelling report, titled "Note on Emigration from India," would henceforth become a perennial reference point for the Indian government's approach to the labor emigration issue.

Geoghegan cast the ongoing debate over Indian labor as a legal and moral battle between the Government of India and the planters of Mauritius. The former, he asserted, strove to protect its subjects and ensure their fair treatment, while the latter sought at every turn to undercut their wages, saddle them with the costs of their own emigration, and otherwise bind them into indenture and plantation work in contravention of the principles of free migration and free labor.[80] At the core of his report was a detailed charting of the

[78] Proceedings of [the Indian] Government, Public, No. 589, dated May 5, 1871, *Natal Commission* 1872, 64.
[79] Statement of Baboo, *Natal Commission* 1872, 52.
[80] J. Geoghegan, *Report on Coolie Emigration from India* (hereafter *Geoghegan Report*), House of Commons Papers, 1874, 14.

inexorable expansion of state oversight across the previous three decades. New regulations, new agents, new institutions, and new procedures had been implemented as Indian labor was introduced to new colonies, and as the Government of India and authorities in London repeatedly intervened out of paternalistic concern for emigrants. The circumstances prompting the state's direct involvement in colonial labor organization had ranged from the mundane, such as one Mauritian employer's effort to avoid regulation by classifying immigrant workers as passengers, to the tragic.[81] A prominent example of the latter was the reports that, on ships transporting Indian emigrants to the West Indies in the 1850s, the mortality rates had been in excess of 30 percent. This dire situation had prompted a comprehensive investigation into workers' state of health on recruitment; provision of rations, water, and medical supervision en route; and conditions of accommodation and supervision at the ports of arrival.[82] The result had been a suite of new regulations covering almost every aspect of labor transport, from the ventilation of ships and the proper placement of privies to the professional qualifications of shipboard medical officers to the quantity of turmeric (½ oz) and coriander seeds (2 drams) each emigrant was to be provided with daily.[83]

Geoghegan's detailed report demonstrated the important interrelationship between the accounting, regulatory, and accountability functions of the overseer-state, which epitomized the operation of a coordinated, modern, bureaucratic apparatus of labor governance on a scale never before witnessed in the British context. The parallel expansion of recordkeeping and reporting by which the results of new regulations (or evasion of them) could be measured had been crucial to the growth of the colonial state's authority over labor since the Fiscals and Protectors had first been required to submit detailed annual summaries of amelioration's progress across the colonial sphere. By such means, in the succeeding decades, an empire-spanning loop of regulatory feedback on labor policy and its implementation had been created, where the events and subsequent state response in one region formed the basis for new regulations and procedures throughout the entire apparatus of colonial labor control.[84] Geoghegan's report thus neatly outlined not just how the overseer-state had grown into a comprehensive, coordinated entity stretching from India to Natal to St. Lucia but also how that entity had, by dint of its own system of accountability, been implicated in the steady series of scandals and

81 The Mauritius Dock Company was the violator, in this instance. *Geoghegan Report*, 23.
82 Ibid., 24.
83 Ibid., 25–7.
84 For example, Act XIII of 1864, a comprehensive measure passed by the Government of India, consolidated many of the previous ordinances regarding Indian labor emigration, which had often been passed in response to the particular circumstances in new colonies of destination or to address specific issues that had arisen in geographically disparate regions. *Geoghegan Report*, 37–40.

calamities that had plagued indenture from its inception. Geoghegan himself made full use of the volumes of condemnatory evidence that had accumulated just in recent years, employing the work of Beaumont and Jenkins, and the report of the British Guiana Commission, to catalog the many failings of law and governance there. Geoghegan found that at their core, as Beaumont and the commissioners had emphasized, was a colonial magistracy that was largely subservient to the plantocracy, an Immigration Department lacking the knowledge and authority needed to properly safeguard Indian workers, and a colonial executive reluctant to address even the most egregious abuses.

The multiplying accounts of the overseer-state's failure to fulfill the paternalistic obligations that had long served as indenture's moral justification in both public and official discourse provided powerful ammunition to its critics. Opponents of the system were quick to seize on the records of the state's responses to tragedy, such as the need to implement stricter regulations on flammable cargo after 300 Indian emigrants died when the *Shah Jehan* caught fire at sea in 1859, as evidence of its perennial incapacity to protect those for whom it had assumed increasing oversight and responsibility.[85] Such was the case in July 1875 when "the coolie traffic," as it was commonly called, once again became a topic of debate in Parliament. The issue was raised by Henry E. J. Stanley, a historian and translator of numerous volumes about Portuguese explorers in the fifteenth and sixteenth centuries. Lord Stanley of Alderly, as he was titled, employed the recently published report by the Royal Commission on Mauritius to castigate Lord Carnarvon, the Colonial Secretary, for his egregious failure to address the multitude of gross abuses in what "was only the Slave Trade by another name."[86]

As culpable as the planters were in the abuses endemic to the labor system there, it was the gross negligence and corruption of magistrates, aided and abetted by the colonial governor and by a lack of proper oversight from the Colonial Office, that had fostered such a lamentable state of affairs. Carnarvon's defense of the system, that labor demand in the Caribbean and in other colonies should take precedence, and that "coolie importations, if it can be administered under due safeguards, should be favoured by the Government," were of little account. In Stanley's eyes, such an assertion sadly echoed, "the considerations which brought negro slaves to America for the relief of the Mexicans and Caribs, who were fast dying out under labour imposed upon them."[87] Carnarvon, facing withering and precise criticism that was backed by information that his own government was producing in ever-greater amounts, could only emphasize his earnest commitment to reform the system in light of the report by the Mauritius Commission.

[85] Ibid., 28–9.
[86] House of Lords Debates, July 19, 1875.
[87] Ibid.

With new protestations coming from a revived Anti-Slavery Society in Britain and from as far afield as a representative of the French Creole population of Martinique, such a tepid defense was unlikely to mollify the growing cohort of magistrates, administrators, and politicians expressing doubt that indenture could be reconciled with Britain's constitutional principles or with its self-declared role as a moral colonizer and guardian of the rights of its colonial subjects. The intervention of Lord Kimberley, Carnarvon's political colleague and predecessor as Colonial Secretary, in the debate with Stanley was similarly unconvincing. "There were, no doubt, two sides to this question, the bright side and the dark one," Kimberley insisted, "but it would be unfair, unjust, and impolitic – and, indeed, most disadvantageous to the planters and to the Coolies, if they should rush to the conclusion that because abuses had occurred that there was no hope of a better state of things."[88] With such statements, both Carnarvon and Kimberley simply confirmed, at the highest levels of Britain's imperial government, the argument made by Des Voeux, Beaumont, de Plevitz, and, most tellingly, by the demonstrators at Leonora plantation, the Old Immigrants of Mauritius, and the Indian workers returning to Calcutta aboard the *Red Riding Hood.* These arguments held that, whatever the promise or faults of indenture, it was a structure that the state itself had organized and for which the state was ultimately accountable. Exactly who within the apparatus of colonial governance was to blame for the persistent reports of abuse and exploitation was still a matter of debate as officials at different levels, from local magistrates to the Colonial Secretary, sought to deflect responsibility. Although planters were complicit, they could no longer serve as the primary culprits in sustaining a system that had once been touted as the antidote for slavery, but was now being openly described by critics as its reincarnation.

"Nefarious Traffic": State Overreach and the Decline of Indian Indenture in the Straits Settlements

In the 1880s and 1890s, the economic, political, and cultural climate within which the debate over indenture and the state management of emigration and colonial labor systems was occurring changed dramatically. The decline of the Caribbean sugar industry and increasing competition with other European colonies in Southeast Asia prompted colonial governments to tighten their control over Indian and Chinese labor. British authorities justified these measures by fostering an atmosphere of crisis over kidnapping and other coercive methods allegedly employed by the unscrupulous agents of their Continental competitors. In the midst of this moral panic, however, the revival of humanitarian opposition and antislavery activism in Britain and India made it increasingly difficult for British authorities to differentiate their own labor

[88] Ibid.

practices from those they were demonizing. At the same time, the enhancement and expansion of coercive regulations in an effort to immobilize labor and keep wages artificially depressed prompted a new wave of grievances and demonstrations from Indian and Chinese workers. These events made the dissatisfaction of the workforce clear to British officials, public commentators, and political opponents of indenture. They also starkly illuminated the contrast between the repressive measures of control being deployed against workers and the principles of free labor, liberalism, and moral colonization that British authorities employed to defend their methods of labor governance. Well before the prewar scandals and the concerted political opposition from the Indian and Chinese governments finally doomed indenture in the British Empire, the system's own expansion and increasingly coercive operation had prompted widespread resistance both from within and from without.

The mid-1880s saw the beginnings of a long decline in the Caribbean sugar industry, the most prominent of several causes being the expanded production of cheaper beet sugar elsewhere.[89] In a highly diversified imperial agricultural economy, this decline did not result in a concurrent decrease in the demand for labor. The need for a cheap, subservient workforce remained strong throughout the tropical colonies of both Britain and other European powers, particularly those of France, Spain, Portugal, and the Netherlands. In the Caribbean, moreover, falling sugar prices prompted planters, in collusion with colonial officials, to redouble their efforts at keeping labor costs low. Indenture, with its many regulatory mechanisms by which additional work could be extracted at no extra cost (e.g. the "double-cut") and by which higher labor demand could be prevented from driving up wages (e.g. involuntary contract extension via vagrancy laws), was well suited to the task. While the immigration of Indian and Chinese workers to the Caribbean remained consistent until the final years of the nineteenth century, the area that saw the most rapid colonial development, and with it the fastest rising demand for labor, was to be found in Indian Ocean colonies such as Mauritius, Réunion, and Ceylon, and in Southeast Asia.[90] In the last-mentioned region, the epicenter of growing labor demand, and therefore the focus of efforts at labor emigration and regulation, was in the Straits Settlements. As discussed in Chapter 6, on the Malay Peninsula, by

89 The cane sugar price declines from a peak of 21 shillings per hundredweight (cwt) in 1881 to 13 shillings in 1890 and 11 shillings in 1896. Whereas at the beginning of that period the UK was importing twice as much cane as beet sugar (732,000 tons vs. 398,000), by the end of it, beet sugar imports were nearly four times those of cane sugar (1,144,000 tons vs. 382,000) and the overall imports of the latter had dropped to three-fifths of its 1882 level. C. Y. Shephard, "The Sugar Industry of the British West Indies and British Guiana with Special Reference to Trinidad," *Economic Geography* 5, no. 2 (April 1929), 151. See also Sunanda Sen, "Indentured Labour from India in the Age of Empire," *Social Scientist* 44, no. 1/2 (January–February 2016), 67–9.

90 Mohapatra, "Assam and the West Indies," 457; Sen, "Indentured Labour," 69.

the second half of the nineteenth century, the growing Chinese workforce had become too essential to the economy and too thoroughly integrated with the existing structures of agriculture and resource-extraction for their exclusion to be practical. This was despite the widespread belief among administrators that Chinese laborers were unlikely subjects for cultural assimilation, difficult to effectively govern and, ultimately, an impediment to "progress and civilisation."[91] After 1867, when the Straits government achieved functional independence from the Government of India, its focus was on addressing what it viewed as the most disruptive elements of the Chinese population (i.e. the Secret Societies).

In these circumstances, the importation of Indian indentured workers offered a solution to two pressing problems. The first was the continued demand for labor, which was already strong in the burgeoning sugar and tobacco industries, and would wax acutely with a rubber boom that began in the 1890s. The second was the desire, openly articulated at the highest levels of the colonial government, for a stabilizing element to counterbalance the growing Chinese presence in the region.[92] To British officials, Chinese immigration was an unfortunate necessity, but one that would resolve itself in due time. Whereas Chinese workers were essential for tin-mining, that industry was not anticipated to last forever, nor did Chinese immigrants tend to settle in the region long term.[93] In contrast, the agricultural sector was "the real future of the country," and the same qualities that made Chinese workers suitable for mining, such as their tendency to sojourn rather than to settle, made them less suitable than Indian workers were, since the latter were more likely to bring their wives and their families and to remain permanently. The other great advantage of Indian over Chinese immigrants was that the former, as British subjects, were already accustomed to British rule. Just as asserting state control over the Chinese workforce had anchored colonial authority in the short term, increasing the size of the permanent Indian workforce, and with it the proportion of the population that was "well-behaved and docile," was touted by British officials as the key to its long-term stability.[94]

[91] Jerningham to the Earl of Clarendon, March 9, 1869, in *Correspondence Respecting the Emigration of Chinese Coolies from Macao* (London: Harrison and Sons, 1871), C. 403.

[92] As the Governor of the colony, Frederick Weld, wrote in 1887, "I am anxious for political reasons that the great preponderance of the Chinese over any race in these Settlements, and to a less marked degree some of the Native States under our administration, should be counterbalanced as much as possible by the influx of Indians and other nationalities." Frederick A. Weld, Governor of the Straits Settlements to H. T. Holland (created Lord Knutsford, 1888), Secretary of State for the Colonies, No. 397, September 24, 1887, CO 273/45.

[93] *Report of the Commissioners Appointed to Enquire into the State of Labour in the Straits Settlements and the Protected Native States* (Singapore: Government Printing Office, 1891) (hereafter *1890 Labour Commission*), 66.

[94] Ibid.

As had been the case in other colonies where Indian indenture had been introduced, the extension of direct state control over the workforce through an increasingly coercive array of regulations would be implemented under the guise of paternalism. Officials would justify these reforms as a response to an alleged crisis threatening the physical and moral well-being of the immigrant population. In British Guiana and Mauritius, this crisis had taken the form of a moral panic over vagrancy and public health, with nefarious *sirdars* cast as the primary villains. In the Straits, the issue would be kidnapping, and the villains would be unscrupulous recruiters. Acrimonious debate over indentured emigration would drive a decades-long contest between the Government of India and colonial authorities in the Straits Settlements over which party wielded the final say in labor governance on the Malay Peninsula. The result would be a system of labor laws every bit as repressive as those found in Mauritius or British Guiana. But despite such harsh measures, the actions of workers themselves and the wider context of the labor market in Southeast Asia would undermine the ability of the overseer-state to control the mobility and the conditions of labor in the region.

The initial furor over Indian emigration to the Straits Settlement, which served as the catalyst for more concerted state oversight, began shortly after the colony had achieved administrative independence from the Government of India in 1867. In 1870, W. J. Hathaway, a prominent administrator in the southern Indian district of Tanjore, published allegations in the local English-language newspaper that an organized system of kidnapping was in operation for the purposes of transporting Indians to Penang.[95] Much to the alarm of Indian officials and the public, Hathaway asserted that it was not just men who were being abducted for labor; children were being seized for the same purpose and girls were similarly being snatched in order to serve as prostitutes. The official cited, as evidence, an 1869 court case that saw seven people convicted for conducting this "nefarious traffic."[96] At the core of the alleged cabal was a villainous *maistry*, the term applied to recruiters of Indian labor for work in distant regions. To strengthen the government's hand at shutting down what Hathaway claimed was a well-organized system of kidnapping, he asserted that *all* labor emigration from India to the Straits Settlements was currently illegal, since the territory had been explicitly excluded when the pertinent legislation governing such matters was passed by the Government of India (Act XIII of 1864).[97] Although this had made sense at the time, since the Straits Settlement had yet to achieve independence from the Indian government, since 1867, the elision had left the colony in legal limbo with regard to labor emigration.

95 *1890 Labour Commission*, 36.
96 David Chanderbali, *Indian Indenture in British Malaya: Policy and Practice in the Straits Settlements* (Leeds: Peepal Tree, 2008), 87.
97 *Geoghegan Report*, 59.

The result was the temporary suspension of Indian emigration to the Straits and a protracted conflict between the Indian and the Straits governments over how Indian labor recruitment, transportation, and organization were to be regulated in the colony and who would bear the costs of enforcing those regulations. The issue was not resolved until 1872, when the first Crown-appointed governor of the Straits Settlements, Sir Harry St. George Ord, with the colony's planters howling at his door about the imminent collapse of the sugar industry due to an acute labor shortage, capitulated to the demands of the Indian government.[98] As stipulated by Act XIV of 1872, labor emigration from India to the Straits was legalized, with Ord agreeing to fund a system of official oversight similar to that already installed for other colonies where Indian indenture had been introduced. In line with the stipulations applied by Act XIII of 1864, the key figures in this system would be paid by the Straits government but subject to the approval of Indian officials. Based in the ports of embarkation (Negapatam being the primary one), a Protector of Emigrants, working with local magistrates, would ensure that each recruit had signed their contract voluntarily and in comprehension of what it entailed, while an Immigration Agent would oversee the recruitment system, arrange for the lodging of workers at the ports, and organize medical care and other necessities.[99] While Ord was wrangling with Indian administrators over the exact parameters the latest extension of the overseer-state in the Straits would take, another scandal broke over alleged kidnapping by unscrupulous recruiters, this time in Allahabad in the northwestern region of India.

The case was brought to the attention of the Lieutenant-Governor of the North Western Provinces, and thence to the public, by Reverend Thomas Evans, a Baptist missionary. Evans recounted how his help had been solicited by his shoemaker. Following his information, the missionary had gone to a local recruiting depot where he had found nearly a dozen women, all of whom claimed to have been decoyed there by a recruiter who had promised them employment.[100] The incident, first reported in the *Pioneer* newspaper of Allahabad, was quickly picked up by London papers, appearing most prominently in the *London Evening Standard.* Its story was printed under the byline "An Indian Slave-Trade," and recounted the incident in Dickensian terms.[101] Although reports of kidnapping, deception, and other forms of coerced recruiting began to multiply in the late 1860s and early 1870s as indenture expanded into new regions of Southeast Asia, Allahabad is one of the few instances where the alleged perpetrators were arrested and convicted. Efforts

[98] Enclosure in Ord to Kimberley, No. 39, February 24, 1871, CO 273/45.
[99] *Geoghegan Report*, 59.
[100] Tinker, *A New System of Slavery*, 126.
[101] *The Standard*, April 5, 1871, 3. This was true in the literal sense, since *Oliver Twist* was explicitly referenced in the article.

to apprehend and prosecute those suspected of participating in this trade repeatedly ended in failure, in large part because recruits typically refused to complain or admit, under questioning, that they were destined for work in the Straits.[102]

Nonetheless, the public outcry was enough to prompt another expansion of the overseer-state in order to more closely regulate the recruitment process. As of 1873, recruiters, known as *maistries*, had to be approved and registered by the Immigration Agent and licensed by the Protector of Immigrants.[103] They had to wear an official badge indicating their status in both the local language and English, and a description of each licensed recruiter was to be publicized in the district where they were working.[104] Although, in theory, this gave the Indian government more authority to punish deception or coercion among recruiters, in practice it also provided such recruiters with even more authority via an air of officialdom. Armed with badges and licenses, they could claim to be agents of the local government rather than representatives of private agricultural interests, and could expect to receive the trust and deference of prospective recruits as a result.[105] In trying to bring labor recruitment under tighter official control, the new regulations inadvertently opened the government to accusations of complicity, and gave those recruited under false premises, and opponents of the system more generally, cause to blame the state for their troubles.

As the Indian government responded to the uproar about kidnapping by extending its authority over recruiting, Straits officials were installing their own apparatus of labor governance to deal with Indian indentured workers. With the resumption of legal emigration from India in 1872, increasing numbers of them had begun arriving for service in the colony's burgeoning agricultural sector. The first comprehensive regulatory structure was provided by Straits Settlement Ordinance No. 1 of 1876.[106] In addition to formalizing the appointment of a suite of labor officials – emigration agents, Protectors of Immigrants, inspectors, medical officers – in order to bring the Straits in line with the current practice in other indenture colonies, the ordinance stipulated a rigorous inspection regime. Building on the precedents set in Mauritius and British Guiana, the state was accorded sweeping powers to oversee the contracts, accommodation, work conditions, and health of the Indian labor force. Paternalistic in language, these measures were coercive in character, and the later sections laid out a series of labor regulations as harsh as any seen thus far

102 Chanderbali, *Indian Indenture*, 95–7.

103 *Government of Madras, Emigration Proceedings in the Public Department*, vol. 274, July 1873.

104 Chanderbali, *Indian Indenture*, 107.

105 Ibid., 107–8.

106 Straits Settlement Ordinance No. 1 of 1876, "An Ordinance for Regulating the Immigration of Native Laborers from British India," s. 43.

across the indenture system. Absenteeism prompted a fine of 50 cents a day (four times the typical daily pay of an agricultural worker) in addition to loss of wages, with up to fourteen days' imprisonment for extended absenteeism (i.e. more than seven days) or a second offense.[107] A worker absent without permission from either the estate or the hospital could be arrested, without warrant, by anyone acting on behalf of the employer.[108] Desertion was punishable by one month's imprisonment with hard labor on the first conviction, two months' on the second, and three months' on the third, with any such imprisonment including a forfeiture of wages for that period.[109] In order to ensure that these penalties did not interfere with the work that the laborer had contracted to deliver, any period of imprisonment automatically extended their contract by the same time span.[110] Lastly, any employer who knowingly hired on a worker already contracted elsewhere or attempted to lure workers away from their current employ before their contract's end faced heavy fines.[111]

These laws were strengthened further in 1882. Such measures were driven less by the Straits planters' demand for labor than by their unwillingness to pay market rates for it. Whereas the labor laws in Mauritius were enhanced to prevent workers from seeking better conditions with other planters within the colony, the Straits laws had to take into account an even wider and more competitive field of potential employers. These included work in the neighboring Federated Malay States, where wages were three times higher than they were in the Straits Settlements; across the Straits of Malacca in the Dutch region of Deli; or up the coast in Burma.[112] While planters sought to justify their low wages by pointing to the expenses of transporting workers and the lack of government underwriting, for Indian workers, indenture in the Straits remained unattractive when compared to the other options. Despite the harsh punishments stipulated by the new regulations, desertion rates continued to rise, while local prisons filled up with violators. According to official reports, in 1889 the number of deserters stood at nearly half the number of new recruits that year.[113] By the late-1880s, nearly a third of all prisoners in Penang were workers convicted of labor law violations.[114] While Indian emigration, both

[107] SS Ordinance No. 1 of 1876, s. 45.
[108] Ibid., s. 46.
[109] Ibid., s. 48.
[110] Ibid., s. 53.
[111] Ibid., s. 55.
[112] R. N. Jackson, *Immigrant Labour and the Development of Malaya, 1786–1920* (Singapore: The Government Press, 1961), 67.
[113] Frank Heidemann, *Kanganies in Sri Lanka and Malaysia: Tamil Recruiter-cum-Foreman as a Sociological Category in the Nineteenth and Twentieth Century* (Munich: Anacon, 1992), 49.
[114] Jackson, *Immigrant Labour*, 67.

indentured and free, to Burma, Ceylon, and the Caribbean continued to grow across the 1880s, the number of Indians signing contracts of indenture for work in the Straits remained low, and began to decline significantly after 1887, going from a peak of 4,736 that year to 2,960 in 1890.[115] That same year, by contrast, some 18,301 free Indian immigrants arrived in the Straits.

The situation in the Straits aptly demonstrated that the power of the overseer-state to immobilize workers could be undermined by the very same principles of a free labor market that the supporters of indenture had employed as justification for the system. By the 1880s, indenture and its attendant apparatus of labor laws were unattractive to workers and employers alike in the Straits on a number of grounds. For the former, the wages and conditions compared unfavorably to what could be obtained either as free laborers in the Straits or as contract workers in other locales. Despite this, plantation labor remained a not unattractive option because even though wages were lower than they were in other types of work, such employment included free accommodation, medical care, and land on which they could raise livestock or grow food for consumption or sale.[116] For employers, the additional costs involved (e.g. advances on passage money and recruiters' fees), the poor quality of recruits themselves, the high levels of desertion, and the expanding tangle of regulations with regard to recruitment, transportation, and inspection all made indenture unappealing. Their general preference was nonetheless to retain *some* indentured workers so as not to be caught entirely shorthanded at crucial periods in the agricultural calendar.[117]

Employers' desires aside, much of the changing landscape of Indian labor organization in the Straits was attributable to the adaptation of workers themselves, who successfully introduced a rival system of labor recruitment and management more suited to their needs than the *maistry*-indenture system was. In the 1890s, large-scale coffee cultivation expanded in the Straits, and was followed a decade later by a boom in the rubber-growing industry. Both developments increased the demand for labor in the region, and a new structure of labor organization accompanied the arrival of European coffee planters from Ceylon. Starting in the final decades of the nineteenth century and continuing through the initial years of the twentieth, the *kangani* (alternatively spelled *kangany*) system, first employed in the 1820s and 1830s to facilitate Tamil labor emigration to Ceylon, gained popularity in the

115 *1890 Labour Commission Report*, 42–3.

116 Ibid., 47.

117 Among other issues, indentured Indian immigrants experienced a mortality rate of up to three or four times that of free immigrants. This was attributed by managers and officials to recruiters who, eager to fulfill quotas and obtain higher commissions, were indiscriminate in their selection of workers. Correspondence Relating to Free and Indentured Indian Immigrants, 1897. Records of the Resident General of the Federated Malay States, 1337/98 (NAM). See also *1890 Labour Commission Report*, 47.

movement of workers from India to the Straits and elsewhere on the Malay Peninsula.[118]

The *kangani* (which translates as "overseer") was a figure similar to the *kheh-thau* in Chinese labor organization.[119] Typically drawn from the ranks of veteran emigrant laborers and working in the employ of an estate-owner, the *kangani* worked as both a recruiter and a headman over his cohort. From the worker's perspective, the *kangani* "free labor" system offered a number of advantages over indenture as run through *maistry* recruiting. The *kangani* was usually a familiar figure in the region where he recruited, and often drew his cohort from among friends, relatives, and neighbors in his home village.[120] In this effort, he could offer a key service which *maistries* could not, which was his capacity to discharge local debts or leave money with the recruit's relatives.[121] Whereas *maistries*' responsibilities often ended once workers were delivered to their employers, and they sought only to fulfill their quotas and maximize their returns on the "coolie trade," *kanganies* remained integral to the entire arc of a worker's engagement with the employer. They recruited, negotiated terms of service, and provided transportation, and once the cohort of recruits had arrived at their destination, they remained on as the labor overseer.[122] *Kanganies* were also motivated to recruit workers in good physical condition, since their failure to provide healthy cohorts could cost them their fees or even their position with their employers.[123]

For workers, the *kangani* system and employment on the coffee and rubber plantations incorporated many of the additional resources that accompanied a contract of indenture while avoiding most of its drawbacks. The work paid better, and came with free housing and medical services, but *kangani*-organized laborers were not locked into long-term, written contracts, nor did the various mechanisms of debt-bondage (e.g. monies owed for passage) constrain their mobility. *Kanganies* also recruited women, which *maistries* tended to avoid, a practice that both made the system more attractive to recruits and encouraged long-term settlement in the region.[124] Lastly, from the perspective of coffee and rubber planters, the *kangani* system was

[118] Heidemann, *Kanganies in Sri Lanka and Malaysia*, 12–13.

[119] From the Tamil *kankani*, a combination of *kan* ("eyes") and *kani* ("sees").

[120] Evidence of John Anderson , *Report of the Committee on Emigration from India to the Crown Colonies and Protectorates* (aka "Sanderson Committee") (London: Her Majesty's Stationary Office, 1910), Evidence, 43.

[121] Kernial Singh Sandhu, *Indians in Malaya: Immigration and Settlement, 1786–1957* (Cambridge: Cambridge University Press, 1969), 90.

[122] Chanderbali, *Indian Indenture*, 117.

[123] Ibid., 117.

[124] In 1903, the average pay for an indentured recruit was 25–30 cents a day for an adult man and 20 cents for a woman (Jackson, *Immigrant Labour*, 104). In comparison, that same year, coffee planters in Perak and Kedah were offering 30 cents a day for men, and in Penang as high as 40 cents a day (Chanderbali, *Indian Indenture*, 117).

unburdened by the regulatory and inspection regime that had been draped over indenture to make the institution acceptable for the Indian government and to mollify its opponents in both India and London. *Kanganies* did not need to be officially licensed as they were not imposing written contracts or, indeed, long-term contracts at all. Nor did they need to work through the system of depots and inspectors that provided state supervision over indentured recruitment.

In the waning decade of the nineteenth century and the first decade of the twentieth, the popularity of the *kangani* system and the competition from coffee and rubber planters provoked a strong reaction. The sugar-planters who depended on a subordinated, immobilized labor supply and landowners in India who were concerned that their low-caste workforce might be poached pushed back. They resisted the encroachment of newcomers into a terrain of labor organization that they had once reigned over uncontested with the powerful undergirding of colonial labor regulations. In such opposition, the tools of the overseer-state were employed as weapons against these interlopers. South Indian employers reported *kanganies* to the police and tried to have them arrested on charges of coerced recruiting or "crimping."[125] Sugar-planters, alarmed that the *kanganies*' influence undercut their own authority over the Indian workforce, accused them of providing inferior workers, concealing their faults, and fomenting discontent.[126] They also claimed that *kanganies* could sometimes abscond with the workers they had brought, robbing planters of both their labor force and their financial outlay toward recruitment and transportation.[127] Their objections were reinforced by those of Straits officials who, building on the persistent alarm over alleged kidnapping, painted the *kanganies* as routinely employing deception and coercion.[128] The condemnation of *kanganies* by state officials grew in proportion to their increasing displacement of indenture as the primary means of labor recruitment and emigration from India to the Malay Peninsula.

Such vilification and the efforts by Straits officials, Indian landowners, and *maistries* notwithstanding, by the end of the first decade of the twentieth century, it was clear that Indian workers had decisively rejected indenture in favor of the *kangani* system. The higher wages, mobility, social cohesion, and local familiarity offered by the latter were responsible for a precipitous decline in indentured recruitment via officially regulated channels. Whereas in 1899 25.5 percent of all Indian immigrants to the Straits had arrived as indentured

125 Evidence of Thomas Heslop Hill, Sanderson Committee, December 3, 1909, 429.

126 Evidence of J. M. Vernon, *Emigration (and Coolie Immigration)*, 1895 and January to March 1896, vol. 1, CO 384/191 (War and Colonial Department and Colonial Office: Emigration Original Correspondence, The National Archives).

127 Chanderbili, *Indian Indenture*, 117.

128 Proceedings of the Straits Settlement Legislative Council, Paper No. 11, April 24, 1903, p. C94.

workers, by 1910 that proportion had declined to a mere 3 percent. In contrast, *kangani*-recruited workers rose from 12 percent in 1899 to 43 percent in 1907.[129] Much of the newly arrived labor force was directed toward the ballooning rubber industry, where acreage under cultivation had increased tenfold from 1905 to 1910 alone.[130] By 1907, the dramatic transformation of Indian immigration required the Straits government to reexamine its entire approach to labor governance. The *kangani* system had come to dominate the organization of Indian labor so thoroughly that the overseer-state was compelled to step in lest control of the workforce be lost entirely to the hands of the new middlemen. The accumulation of "affluence and power" by the *kanganies*, according to a 1904 report, was not just a threat to the rightful authority of managers over their workers; it was becoming "a serous menace to the stability of labour forces throughout the country."[131] An Indian Immigration Committee was constituted, and their work culminated in the passage of the Tamil Immigration Fund Ordinance of 1907 and in the amalgamation of the state apparatus that coordinated Indian labor immigration to the Straits Settlements and to the neighboring Federated Malay States. In contrast with the competition for labor that had previously characterized the relationship between the two regions, what emerged was a state-coordinated cartel of employers. This new arrangement provided funds for immigration through collective contributions and government underwriting, while simultaneously discouraging employers from luring workers from one estate to another with the offer of better wages and conditions.

Bringing the system more firmly under state oversight tempered the *kanganies*' influence to a degree, but the power of the colonial administration to regulate Indian immigration and labor had been permanently undermined. *Kanganies* were compelled to obtain official licenses that stipulated the number of laborers each was authorized to recruit (fifty was the standard), their rate of commission (typically $10 per adult), and their allowed period of activity (usually six months).[132] Such licenses had to be validated by officials in both India and the Straits, and confined their enlistment of workers to their friends and family within their native district. Further layers of inspection and oversight mirroring those employed previously for indenture were also implemented.[133] In the first four years after the Immigration Fund began

[129] From Saw Swee Hock, *The Population of Peninsular Malaysia* (Singapore: Singapore University Press, 1989), 24–5. Note the general spike in immigration in 1903–9, corresponding with the rubber boom.

[130] From 127,000 acres to 1,125,000. Jackson, *Immigrant Labour*, 121.

[131] *Indian Immigration Department Annual Report for 1911* excerpted in Jackson, *Immigrant Labour*, 118.

[132] Jackson, *Immigrant Labour*, 122.

[133] These included the inspection of recruits at the port of embarkation and the certification of their voluntary transport.

underwriting emigration in 1910, the number of Indians arriving in the Federated Malay States under the scheme quadrupled,[134] while within one year of its operation the number of indentured workers arriving in Malaya had gone from 2,500 to almost zero.[135] Unable to decisively abrogate the power of the *kangani* system and increasingly dependent on the laborers it supplied for both profit and the resultant colonial tax revenue, planters and government officials instead adopted a path of compromise, much as they had in the case of the Chinese *kongsi* in the tin-mining industry. An integrated system of recruitment, run largely by Indians themselves, was overlaid with a veneer of official oversight. At the same time, the more coercive and tightly regulated system of indenture, unable either to attract sufficient recruits or to maintain the continuing support of employers, was allowed to languish and expire.

The Decline of Chinese Indenture and the Retreat of the Overseer-State in the Malaysian Mining Industry

The increasingly precarious position of the overseer-state at the end of the nineteenth century was also apparent in official efforts to manage Chinese labor on the Malay Peninsula. By the late 1880s, fueled by a boom in both mining and agriculture, Malaysia was witnessing a veritable flood of Indian and Chinese indentured immigration and an increasing number of free laborers arriving as well. The apex was 1887, when 5,046 Indian workers immigrated via the indenture system, representing nearly 30 percent of all Indian arrivals.[136] The number of Chinese indentured immigrants was considerably higher in absolute terms that year, at 42,400, though this was slightly lower as an overall percentage (25.3 percent) of all Chinese immigrants when compared to the figures for Indian arrivals.[137] By 1903, for Indian immigrants, the number of indentured immigrants had dropped to a mere 503 and 2.3 percent, respectively. Chinese immigration remained high by comparison, but the numbers of those arriving under indenture declined. The latter was going strong in 1900, when 7,462 indentured Chinese laborers arrived in the Federated Malay States, representing a little less than a third of the overall Chinese immigration to the Malaysia peninsula (21,121).[138] The numbers arriving via indenture, however, had dropped off considerably during the 1890s. In 1904, only 8.3 percent of Chinese immigrants to the Malaysian peninsula were indentured.[139] By 1910

[134] From 20,288 in 1909 to 91,236 in 1913. Jackson, *Immigrant Labour*, 120.
[135] Ibid.
[136] Annual Reports on Indian Immigration, cited in Saw, *The Population of Peninsular Malaysia*, 24.
[137] Ibid., 14.
[138] Ibid.
[139] Ibid.

this had slowed to the merest trickle of only 864 in the Federated Malay States.[140] Indian indenture by that year had fallen off nearly as quickly, to 9 percent.[141]

As described earlier, for Indian laborers, much of this decrease was due to the attractions of other regions, which offered better pay and shorter journeys to more familiar locales, all without the shackles of long-term contracts of indenture. For the Chinese laborers, the reasons for the declining appeal of indenture were also closely tied to the conditions of labor in the Federal Malay States and the resilience of the Chinese-organized system of mining labor. By 1872, there were roughly 40,000 miners there, the majority being Cantonese and Hakka. Ulu Selangor mining remained largely dominated by the latter throughout the century. They formed one part of a Chinese immigrant cohort that may have numbered as high as 5 million across the nineteenth century and would be followed by an additional 12 million in the first four decades of the twentieth century.[142]

British colonial control expanded to fully encompass the tin-mining regions of the peninsula in 1874, after a period of fierce competition between rival Chinese mining concerns. The relative stability that followed saw the rapid growth of the industry as new immigrants arrived and Chinese mining entrepreneurs aggressively recruited labor and began a limited program of mechanization. By 1883, Malaysia had become the largest tin producer in the world, and by the end of the century it was providing more than half of the global supply.[143] This period also saw the increasing encroachment of the British state into the regulation of the industry. The Rawang region was a crucial locale for these developments, and had risen, by the end of the century, to become the second-largest mining district in Ulu Selangor.[144]

Chinese tin-mining, as described in Chapter 6, was conducted through companies known as *kongsi*, *kongsi kang*, or *ta kong*. The *kongsi* operated largely as a system of labor organization, and any given mining area could have several different *kongsi* represented, working together and living in the same compound. The mines themselves were low-tech, low-cost affairs, and the financing and leasing was done through the mining employer, the *towkay*, who

140 *Report of the Commission Appointed to Enquire into the Conditions of Indentured Labour in the Federated Malay States* (aka "the Parr Commission"), 1910, 7 (National Archives of Malaysia).

141 Saw, *The Population of Peninsular Malaysia*, 24.

142 Robert E. Elson, "International Commerce, the State and Society: Economic and Social Change," in Nicholas Tarling, ed., *The Cambridge History of Southeast Asia Vol. 3: From c. 1800 to the 1930s* (Cambridge: Cambridge University Press, 1992), 144.

143 Ibid., 143.

144 For an overview of the economic dynamics of the Malay interior in this period, see John Gullick, "The Economy of Perak in the mid-1870s," *Journal of the Malaysian Branch of the Royal Asiatic Society* 83, no. 2 (December 2010), 27–46.

operated as the head of a *kongsi*.[145] *Towkays* also managed the local gambling and opium houses, known as "farms," though such concerns were occasionally in the hands of third-party merchants (often Malays, in such instances). The workforce was composed largely of Chinese laborers brought in for renewable contracts of indenture. At the bottom rung of this system were the *nai chang kang*, or "*naichang* coolies." These were the lowest status and most unskilled of the mine-workers, who were paid piece-rates (as opposed to a daily wage) for heavy manual labor such as removing the top levels of soil from a prospective mining area.[146]

For most of the nineteenth century, Chinese immigration hewed to the corporate structure established by the *kongsi*. Standard practice was a three-year term of indenture on a "credit-ticket" system that controlled their mobility, with wages repaying their credited passage while also covering their food, the opium and gambling as provided by the farms, and occasional remittances to relatives in China.[147] Living conditions among those encompassed by the "pig trade," as it was called, were insalubrious in the extreme. Disease (malaria, dysentery, and beri-beri) and industrial accidents prompted an annual mortality rate that could reach 50 percent in some years.[148] The assertion of British control over the tin-mining industry brought tighter regulation of labor conditions, particularly among fresh cohorts of immigrant indentured workers known as *sin-kheh* (translation: "young pigs"). The Labour Code of 1895 fixed indentures at one-year renewable increments and empowered a Protector of Chinese Labour to ensure that the new regulations were being followed. It represented the most determined effort yet to fully subsume the Malaysian tin-mining industry under British colonial authority. In this same period, the combination of regional stability brought by British suzerainty, which had put an end to the more fractious conflicts between rival Chinese *kongsi*, and unfavorable economic and political conditions in China itself fostered an increase in Chinese immigration. This ready labor supply coincided with a strong demand for tin to foster a mining boom in the 1890s and the early years of the twentieth century. This upswing benefited all of those involved in the system, and even the *naichang* coolies saw their pay rise over time and their conditions improve under the expanded protection provided by the 1895

145 On the *kongsi* system, see Yen Chick-Hwang, "Early Chinese Clan Organisations in Singapore and Malaya, 1819–1911," *Journal of Southeast Asian Studies* 12, no. 1 (March 1981), 62–92; Mak Lau-Fung, "The Kongsi and the Triad," *Southeast Asian Journal of Social Science* 3, no. 2 (1975), 47–58; Wang Tai Peng, "The Word 'Kongsi': A Note," *Journal of the Malaysian Branch of the Royal Asiatic Society* 52, no. 1 (1975), 102–5.

146 On the organization of mining in this period, see Nicholas N. Dodge, "Mineral Production on the East Coast of Malaya in the Nineteenth Century," *Journal of the Malaysian Branch of the Royal Asiatic Society* 50, no. 2 (1977), 89–110.

147 Elson, "International Commerce," 144.

148 Ibid.

Labour Code. Although these changes offered some validation of British claims to have reformed tin-mining in Malaysia, they brought new pressures and problems with a rapid expansion of Chinese contract-labor, still largely subsumed to the *kongsi* system.[149]

In the same period, however, the government's oversight of recruiting and organizing Chinese labor was demonstrating its failings. These were made public in compelling fashion through a series of official inquiries in which the preference of workers and employers alike for free labor immigration, organized through Chinese intermediaries, was readily apparent. Forced onto the defensive, colonial officials continued to vilify the Chinese middlemen (*kheh-thaus*) who remained the dominant avenue for labor importation, advocating further expansion of government control. When interviewed in 1890, British administrators catalogued a host of immoral practices endemic to *kheh-thau* management, including crimping (i.e. coerced recruitment), frequent desertions, and heavy opium use. The villainy of Chinese middlemen, when compounded by the continued employment of debt-bondage, one high official insisted, amounted to a "system . . . of disguised slavery."[150] Even critics of the *kheh-thaus*, however, admitted that Chinese workers themselves preferred this arrangement. A particular appeal was that it was conducted by Chinese intermediaries who, like the *kanganies*, were often themselves former workers (*lau-kheh*, which translates as "old hand") recruited from within their localities.[151] Chinese estate-owners, an influential cohort in the Straits and the Federal Malay States, expressed especially strong support for the *kheh-thau* system over indenture or any other forms of employment in which the state played a direct role. Chinese workers, they asserted, preferred the higher wages of free immigration to the alleged safeguards provided by the government-regulated *sin-kheh* system with its written and officially certified contracts, government depots, and frequent inspections. Whereas British officials contended that state intervention prevented abuses, Chinese employers, in contrast, asserted that government inspections undercut their authority and made their workers grow "undisciplined and insubordinate."[152]

Whatever the comparative merits or faults of both the state-regulated *sin-kheh* system and the Chinese-controlled *kheh-thau* arrangement from the perspective of officials and employers, the numbers provided irrefutable evidence that workers themselves preferred the latter. From an apex of 36 percent

149 Ibid.

150 Testimony of W. Cowan, Acting Secretary for Chinese Affairs, *1890 Labour Commission Report*, 126.

151 Testimony of Superintendent of Government Plantations, Perak, *1890 Labour Commission Report*, 132.

152 Testimony of Lee Keng Liat, estate owner, *1890 Labour Commission Report*, 186. Caribbean plantation owners had made the same arguments, initially, about the implementation of the Protector and grievance system under ameliorated slavery.

in 1881, the percentage of Chinese immigrants arriving via the indenture system had dropped steadily over the 1880s, finally stabilizing at between 10 percent and 13 percent during the 1890s before beginning to decline again at the turn of the century.[153] The early 1890s thus represented a high-water mark for the expansion of the overseer-state in Southeast Asia. The attempt to enhance government control over the labor system in the Straits and the Federal Malay States had left the overseer-state in an acutely awkward position. New regulations, officials, and institutions of governance, such as the Chinese Protectorate, the depot system, new labor laws, and inspections of plantation and mines had all been introduced at considerable expense to employers. These had, to some degree, provided a subordinated and stable labor force, at least in the agricultural sector. The system was unpopular with workers, however, both because it required constant interaction with government officials, for whom many Chinese immigrants expressed an innate mistrust, and because the depressed wages offered by employers to offset the additional expense of funding state intervention were unattractive in an environment of high labor demand and opportunity. Even as British officials sought to tighten their control over the Chinese workforce in the name of maintaining a "free labor market," workers themselves, in collusion with the *kheh-thau* and *kongsi*, sought to escape such control and to leverage their position in a seller's market for labor. The combination of rising labor demand from the rubber plantations, the superseding of indentured recruitment by the *kangani* and the *kheh-thau* systems, and laborers' preference for more flexible arrangements of employment based on informal and customary agreements had effectively ended indentured labor on the Malay Peninsula more than a decade before it was officially outlawed.

Conclusion

In the closing decades of the nineteenth century and the initial decade of the twentieth century, the widespread official criticism and public vilification of indenture, the moral panic over kidnapping, and frequent comparisons to slavery had indelibly tarnished the image of the overseer-state in Southeast Asia. In the Caribbean, during the same period, the economic decline of the sugar industry made the capital investment required by indenture increasingly impractical for estate-owners, and discouraged colonial officials from further underwriting a system that was both politically problematic and expensive to maintain. When a royal commission appointed in 1897 to investigate the economic situation in Britain's Caribbean colonies delivered its report on the state of the sugar industry, it expressed particular concern that the moral obligations of colonial labor governance were becoming incompatible with

153 Saw, *The Population of Peninsular Malaysia*, 14.

the economic situation in the region.[154] A series of labor disturbances had thrown further doubt on the claim by colonial governments that the extension of their authority over the laboring population was conducive both to their prosperity and to public order.[155]

As colonial governments' direct intervention in labor recruitment and management was subject to increasing criticism and resistance from a variety of quarters, from dissenting officials to estate-owners to workers themselves, the public and the official perceptions of the overseer-state, and of indenture in particular, had suffered most acutely. Repeated government inquiries and public scandals had painted the picture of a colonial labor apparatus riddled with coercion, corruption, deception, and myriad other forms of injustice. The moral stain left by the state's mismanagement of labor migration in Britain's plantation and mining colonies, from British Guiana and Trinidad to Mauritius and Malaysia, would provide yet another arrow in the quiver of indenture's critics, who would assert that state officials tolerated or even abetted the most coercive aspects of labor recruitment and organization. The overseer-state, its opponents would argue in the decade preceding the First World War, was a fit shepherd neither for the rights nor for the well-being of its Indian and Chinese subjects, and its promises of prosperity, public order, and cultural uplift rang hollow.

Indian and Chinese workers, meanwhile, had experienced firsthand the injustices of the colonial labor apparatus and the tensions between its systems of control and the other structures of labor management across the empire. Their refusal to subordinate themselves to the ever-expanding machinery of labor laws, state-sponsored recruitment, and a colonial judiciary that consistently overlooked abuses and reinforced the authority of employers played a crucial role in the decline of indenture. Just as the practices, agents, institutions, and ideas of the overseer-state linked the Caribbean, Mauritius, and Malaysia, the patterns of grievance, complaint, and contestation it provoked

[154] The commissioners warned that "the necessity of keeping faith with the East Indian immigrants," such as through the provision of return passages, would likely become problematic in the face of declining sugar – and, by extension, tax – revenues. Given the industry's falling fortunes, "it would be impossible to levy the cost from the sugar estates," and the cost of repatriation "must fall upon the public funds" that were themselves already strained." PP 1898, *Report of the West India Royal Commission* (aka the "Norman Commission"), 1897 (C. 8655), 7.

[155] The most prominent of these was the Hosay Massacre, which took place in Trinidad in 1884. For an insightful intervention into the long-running scholarly debate over the event, see Prabhu P. Mohapatra, "'Following Custom'? Representations of Community Among Indian Immigrant Labour in the West Indies, 1880–1920," *International Review of Social History* 51, supp. 14 (2006), 181–2. Overall, at least fifty-two different strikes were conducted by Indian workers in Trinidad between 1870 and 1900. Archana Tewari, "Protests by Indians in Trinidad (1845–1917)," *Proceedings of the Indian History Congress* 70 (2009–10), 910.

followed a similar course. They filtered up, via the overseer-state's own mechanisms of reporting and accountability, from the testimony of those toiling in mines and plantations to reach the ears of the highest officials in the imperial system. They also formed the raw materials for political opposition, sensationalized public commentary, and repeated episodes of official embarrassment. Well before the largest indenture scandal yet broke in South Africa, the state's own processes of recording and reporting criticisms from officials within the system, repeated public associations with slavery, rising labor demand, and workers' concerted resistance had all combined to make indenture an increasingly untenable practice in the empire. In the final two decades of the nineteenth century, they weakened the system both politically and economically, heightening the visibility of its failings and transgressions, and leaving it vulnerable to widespread public criticism and eventual abrogation.

Conclusion

The Persistent Legacies of the Overseer-State

Historians have long recognized that the post-emancipation decades were ones haunted by the legacies of slavery.[1] The overseer-state, in terms of both labor governance and responses to it, was among the most significant of these legacies. The effects of the indenture system that it supported were profound and widespread, most visibly in the social, political, and cultural dynamics of multiracial (but highly unequal) societies in Mauritius, the British Caribbean, and Southeast Asia, and in the establishment of long-range, long-term labor mobility as the norm in a racialized and exploitative global system of agriculture and mining. Through the overseer-state, the lingering impact of slavery and its aftermath were felt acutely even in places such as Malaysia, where plantation slavery had never been a prevalent practice. In the regions where the British imperial state was most powerful, such as the Crown colonies of the southern hemisphere, the dynamics of race, labor, and governance and the history of amelioration and indenture remained entangled well beyond the centenary of the slave trade's abolition. These entanglements persisted for decades after the "second abolition" of indenture as well.

The series of events that led to the formal outlawing of indenture throughout the British Empire has been thoroughly chronicled elsewhere. The efforts by Mohandas K. Gandhi in Natal were crucial to mobilizing Indian opposition to indenture there in the first decade of the twentieth century. Gandhi, through his writings and public speeches, effectively linked attempts to restrict the rights of indentured workers empire-wide to an attack on the rights of all Indians in Britain's southern African colonies.[2] Domestically, in the same period, the Conservative government's introduction of 64,000 indentured Chinese mine-workers to South Africa in the wake of the Second Boer War (1899–1902) turned out to be a political disaster. White union leaders sounded the clarion call of "yellow slavery" as an unconscionable betrayal of the British

[1] See, for example, the various pieces in *The International Journal of African Historical Studies* 48, no. 2 (2015), Special Issue: Exploring Post-Slavery in Contemporary Africa.

[2] Radhika Mongia, "Gender and the Historiography of Gandhian *Satyagraha* in South Africa," *Gender and History* 18, no. 1 (April 2006), 130–49; Hugh Tinker, *A New System of Slavery: The Export of Indian Labour Overseas, 1830–1920* (London: Oxford University Press, 1974), 283.

working class who had borne the brunt of the war's cost in blood and treasure.[3] A Liberal–Labour coalition employed the issue as a moral bludgeon against the long-standing Conservative government and, in 1906, achieved a landslide victory that redefined the landscape of prewar British politics.[4] In the wake of this turmoil, Gandhi's protégé, Manilal Maganlal Doctor, effectively mobilized opposition to indenture in Mauritius. The impartiality of magistrates was a key criticism, and Doctor's intervention in a series of high-profile court cases involving Indian laborers served only to emphasize the degree to which the state was colluding with planters in the denial of rights and justice for its Indian subjects.[5]

Past inquiries conducted by metropolitan and colonial governments had salved the conscience of the state without prompting substantive reform. Now, in the wake of 1906 and growing political and humanitarian opposition, such inquiries accelerated the demise of indenture. The Sanderson Committee, convened by the British government in 1910 as the anti-indenture campaign was ramping up in both Natal and Mauritius, was largely supportive of indenture. But its witnesses provided evidence for indenture's growing chorus of opponents by pointing out many intractable defects of the system that had proven stubbornly resistant to prior efforts at reform.[6] Other reports in the same period were far less equivocal. The Clayton Commission, convened by the Natal government, emphasized the general undesirability of further Indian emigration to the colony, from the perspective of the white population.[7] Negative portrayals of Indian indenture and the abuses endemic continued to proliferate, the most notable being Henry Polak's *The Indians of South Africa: Helots within the Empire and How They Are Treated* (1909).[8] Amidst the growing criticism of the system, the passage of the Indian Emigration (Amendment) Act by the Indian Legislative Council in 1910 provided the legal framework for the permanent outlawing of indenture.[9] Following another

3 Sascha Auerbach, *Race, Law, and "The Chinese Puzzle" in Imperial Britain* (New York: Palgrave Macmillan, 2009), 33–7.

4 As Kevin Grant points out, this tactic was effective not because voters had any real sympathy for Chinese workers but rather because the opposition effectively portrayed them as a threat to the white working class in Britain itself. Kevin Grant, *A Civilised Savagery: Britain and the New Slaveries in Africa, 1884–1926* (New York: Routledge, 2005), 82, 98–105.

5 Tinker, *A New System of Slavery*, 307–8.

6 Among the most dramatic was the admission by Edward Bateson, a stipendiary magistrate, who, when queried as to whether he worked largely for the convenience of the employer, responded, "I was a machine for sending people to prison." Tinker, *A New System of Slavery*, 310.

7 Ibid., 313.

8 Henry Polak, *The Indians of South Africa: Helots within the Empire and How They Are Treated* (Madras: G. A. Natesan, 1909).

9 Ibid.

critical government inquiry, the Parr Commission, indenture was ended in British Malaya.[10]

The political debate over indenture in the first decade of the twentieth century occurred against the backdrop of economic, political, and cultural trends that were increasingly inhospitable to the prospect of large-scale immigration by Indian or Chinese workers to British (or, for that matter, any European) colonies. These included the continued decline of the Caribbean sugar industry, the growing political self-determination of unionized workers in the white-settler colonies, and a marked increase in anti-Chinese xenophobia. This last was becoming prevalent particularly in the US, Australia, and Canada, but was present, to one degree or another, in Britain, Continental Europe, and across the breadth of European colonies.[11] This Sinophobia manifested most concretely in the various exclusion acts passed across the later nineteenth and early twentieth centuries. These anti-immigration laws were accompanied by increasingly vocal rhetoric about "white man's countries" and by incidents of rioting and violent attacks on the persons and property of Asian cohorts from Vancouver to Sydney.[12]

Although Chinese residents were the most common focus of this widespread counterreaction, the political mobilization of a white working-class identity that sought to include a variety of European ethnic and cultural groups was predicated on an equally determined exclusion of *all* groups identified as "non-white," South Asians, Africans, and African-Caribbeans foremost among them.[13] Far from stemming the flow of labor migration, by then too intrinsic to colonial economies to be excised, the new laws and the violent anti-immigrant rhetoric did serve to further marginalize non-white cohorts politically, socially, and economically.[14] With some notable exceptions, it also made the overt government support of labor migration programs politically untenable except in the most extreme circumstances.[15] As Indian and Chinese labor, in public

10 Ibid., 316.

11 The many ways in which anti-Chinese sentiment formed a cultural foundation-stone of "China's unequal position in the world economy" and the multitude of strategies by which Chinese migrants adapted and responded to it are admirably charted in Mae Ngai, *The Chinese Question: The Gold Rushes, Chinese Migration, and Global Politics* (New York: Norton, 2021).

12 Marilyn Lake and Henry Reynolds, *Drawing the Global Colour Line: White Man's Countries and the International Challenge of Racial Equity* (Cambridge: Cambridge University Press, 2008).

13 Ibid., 215; Jonathan Hyslop, "The Imperial Working Class Makes Itself 'White': White Labourism in Britain, Australia, and South Africa before the First World War," *Journal of Historical Sociology* 12, no. 4 (1999), 398–42.

14 Grant, *A Civilised Savagery*, 105–16.

15 The later instances included the British government's concession to the *Het Volk* party in South Africa that Chinese indentured workers already in place on the Rand gold mines could continue until the expiration of the last contracts in 1910, and the employment of

discourse and political rhetoric, shifted from being a crucial resource for burgeoning colonial economies to a potential threat to the social and economic status of white workers, both metropolitan officials and their imperial counterparts were increasingly reluctant to give anything but the most tepid approval to international migration schemes.[16] The wake of the 1906 General Election in Britain assured that any metropolitan politician seen to be openly supportive of "yellow slavery" faced a dire risk to their reputation and career. A resurgent humanitarian movement further discouraged administrators, whether metropolitan or colonial, from advocating continued labor migration between colonies, unless it was to the obvious benefit of the white working population.[17]

The continued, concerted resistance of indentured laborers themselves, from the Caribbean to South Africa to Southeast Asia, lent weight to arguments against the system both on moral grounds and as an alleged threat to public order.[18] By the conclusion of the First World War, the political climate across the empire had turned decisively toward restricting the movement of Indian and Chinese workers to within their delineated regions, redirecting state oversight of non-white labor migration toward exclusion rather than facilitation, and placing the onus of organization and transport almost entirely in private hands.[19] "Free" immigration, with minimal government oversight and regulation, became the norm in those regions that depended

some 140,000 Chinese indentured workers as manual laborers by the Allies in the First World War. Paul J. Bailey, "'An Army of Workers': Chinese Labour in World War I France," in Santanu Das, ed., *Race, Empire and the First World War* (Cambridge: Cambridge University Press, 2011), 35–52. See also Radhika Singha, "The Short Career of the Indian Labour Corps in France, 1917–1919," *International Labor and Working-Class History* 87 (Spring 2015), 27–62. The migration of indentured Indian workers to Fiji also grew steadily across the first decade of the twentieth century, reaching its height in 1911–12 (Sunanda Sen, "Indentured Labour from India in the Age of Empire," *Social Scientist* 44, no. 1/2 [January–February 2016], 67).

16 Lake and Reynolds, *Drawing the Global Colour Line*, 124.

17 Grant, *A Civilised Savagery*, 141–3.

18 Among the most serious of these was the Rose Hall Massacre, which saw sixteen Indian workers shot dead in British Guiana in 1913. The event is described in detail in Gaiutra Bahadur, *Coolie Woman: The Odyssey of Indenture* (Chicago, IL: University of Chicago Press, 2013). That same year, more than 20,000 Indian workers in Natal staged a mass strike that included both agricultural and mine workers. This, event, too, saw several workers killed by police gunfire and dozens more injured. M. Swan, "1913 Natal Indian Strike," *Journal of Southern African Studies* 10, no. 2 (1984), 239–58. See also Rosemarijn Hoefte, "A Passage to Suriname? The Migration of Modes of Resistance by Asian Contract Laborers." *International Labor and Working-Class History*, 54 (1998), 19–39.

19 Lake and Reynolds, *Drawing the Global Colour Line*, 310–18; Tinker, *A New System of Slavery*, 372.

on its influx to meet their labor demands, most notably in Ceylon, Burma, and Malaysia.[20]

As Chapter 7 has shown, however, well before its official termination in 1916, indenture and the colonial state's general management of Indian and Chinese labor migration had been challenged from within and from without, putting officials who supported it in the Caribbean and Southeast Asia on the defensive. Influential administrators and magistrates had condemned the system and its critics had repeatedly associated it with slavery. Multiple government inquiries, while generally supportive, had provided enough damning evidence to undermine officials' claims that the system was conducive to public order and that it was morally, economically, and socially beneficial for the immigrant workforce. Indian and Chinese workers, meanwhile, had challenged the moral legitimacy of indenture and its associated practices. They had held the colonial state primarily responsible for endemic abuses and injustices, and had pursued alternative mechanisms of immigration and employment. These efforts had allowed them to obtain better wages and to take best advantage of their position in a competitive labor market. Indenture's last gasp in South Africa, and the attendant political opposition and public condemnation that emerged from London to Natal to Calcutta, only hastened an end that was already on the horizon.

With this model of decline, then abolition, it would be tempting to equate the "second abolition" of indenture with Eric Williams's pioneering argument about the abolition of slavery in the British Empire a century earlier.[21] But the overseer-state had repeatedly adapted to new circumstances – from its inception with ameliorated slavery, when it merged with established institutions and agents of French, Dutch, and Spanish governance, to its introduction in Malaysia, where it grafted itself onto preexisting structures of *nayang* Chinese labor organization such as the *kongsi*. And it had one last trick up its sleeve. In the waning decades of indenture, colonial labor regulation increasingly fell under the aegis of the ubiquitous "master and servant" laws that had operated as the backbone of non-indentured labor governance in the wake of emancipation. This coordinated, pervasive matrix of regulations often reinforced indenture by providing legal precedents, institutional frameworks, and, in some cases, specific statutes that empowered both magistrates and employers at the cost of workers' rights. English master and servant laws, which dated to the sixteenth century, shared many of the characteristics of

[20] These three regions saw their peak of labor immigration reached in the 1920s, well after the outlawing of indenture and the dismantling of most of the regulatory scaffolding by which the colonial state had maintained it. Rana P. Behal, *One Hundred Years of Servitude: Political Economy of Tea Plantations in Colonial Assam* (New Delhi: Tulika, 2014), 93–4; Tinker, *A New System of Slavery*, 374–5.

[21] Eric Williams, *Capitalism and Slavery* ([1944]; repr. ed. London: Penguin, 2022).

ameliorated slavery, apprenticeship, and indenture.[22] They installed the state, in the form of magistrates, as the primary mediators between employers and their workforce; they prescribed a stern system of punishment for labor offenses; they elevated the contract as an intrinsically fair and moral device for determining the reciprocal obligations between worker and employer; they were justified with a paternalistic discourse; and, though adapted to their specific context, their implementation in different colonies borrowed freely from precedents set elsewhere.[23]

In the final decades of the nineteenth century and the early decades of the twentieth, even as indenture came under concerted political attack both from without and from within, master and servant laws continued to gain strength throughout the empire. Those who advocated their enhancement and expansion often did so with the same justifications of workers' well-being, liberalism the free labor market, and public order that had been at the core of indenture's growth in the first half of the nineteenth century. While indenture became politically untenable, master and servant laws, which constituted the other mode of labor inspection and regulation installed during indenture, along with their attendant apparatus of enforcement, quietly absorbed many of indenture's key features and rose to fill much the same functional role.[24] This came as a shock to some workers, who found that, stripped of even the nominal protections delineated by the regulations governing indenture, they were subjected to even harsher punishments as free laborers.[25] In this manner, even as the direct state management of labor migration waned, the state's authority over a largely non-white labor force remained a prominent feature of colonial governance.

The broader consequences of the state's movement from supporting and organizing non-white labor migration to regulating and immobilizing

22 For a comprehensive assessment of the long history of master and servant laws in Britain and the empire, see Douglas Hay and Paul Craven, eds., *Masters, Servants, and Magistrates in Britain and the Empire, 1592–1955* (Chapel Hill: University of North Carolina Press, 2004).

23 India was a prime example of this, and saw the considerable extension of state control over labor with measures such as the Workman's Breach of Contract Act of 1859. Michael Anderson, "India 1858–1930: The Illusion of Free Labor," in Douglas Hay and Paul Craven, eds., *Masters, Servants, and Magistrates in Britain and the Empire, 1592–1955* (Chapel Hill: University of North Carolina Press, 2004), 430–1.

24 In Assam, for example, prosecutions under the Breach of Contract Act rose considerably in the years succeeding the outlawing of indentured labor. Prahbu P. Mohapatra, "Assam and the West Indies, 1860–1920: Immobilizing Plantation Labor," in Douglas Hay and Paul Craven, eds., *Masters, Servants, and Magistrates in Britain and the Empire, 1592–1955* (Chapel Hill: University of North Carolina Press, 2004), 469.

25 For example, in Natal, corporal punishment was forbidden by the regulations on indenture, but permitted for free workers governed by the Master and Servants' Ordinance of 1850. *Report of the Coolie Commission, Appointed to Inquire into the Condition of the Indian Immigrants in the Colony of Natal* (Pietermartizburg: Keith & Co., 1872), 7.

a multiracial workforce within an ostensible legal and political paradigm of "free labor," however, played out very differently across the various regions where the overseer-state had once formed the anchor of colonial authority. In South Africa, the strengthening of the state's control over non-white labor, in the wake of the violent industrial demonstrations orchestrated by the White Union movement in 1922, helped reconcile the tensions between an increasingly cohesive white working class and the commercial, mercantile, landholding, and industrial elite. Enhanced labor controls served as an engine for the political empowerment of British, Afrikaner, and other European-descendant workers and an aegis for their rights vis-à-vis employers even as they continued to operate as a mechanism for the economic and political suppression of their African counterparts. The year 1924, in which a coalition government of the Nationalists (former *Het Volk*) and a white-interest Labour Party took power, solidified a labor law regime that borrowed the most coercive elements of indenture and master and servant law to control "native" (i.e. black African and "colored") labor. Through adaptation of older legislation such as the Native Labour Regulation Act (1911) and the Mines and Works Regulations Act (1912) and newer measures such as the Industrial Reconciliation Act (1923) and the Mines and Works Amendment Act (1926), black workers were hemmed in by long-term contracts and the heavy criminalization of labor offenses.[26] As with the previous operation of the overseer-state, these measures were implemented under the guise of paternalism and an alleged need to protect the economic conditions of a laboring cohort that was incapable, by dint of its racial inferiority, of protecting itself.[27] The same suite of regulations excluded black workers from unions, collective bargaining, and the industry-wide agreements that safeguarded the pay and conditions of white workers. In succeeding decades, these regulations, combined with the Natives Land Act (1913) and other measures of disfranchisement and forced resettlement, came to form the core of the apartheid system that would persist until the 1990s.

A very different pattern unfolded in Malaysia, where the growing rubber industry kept the demand for labor high. The state's attitude toward labor control was shaped by this need and by the vital strategic importance of both rubber and tin, which rapidly became mainstays of both civilian industry and military logistics.[28] Although the Labour Code of 1912 enhanced the power of

[26] Martin Chanock, "South Africa, 1841–1924: Race, Contract, and Coercion," in Douglas Hay and Paul Craven, eds., *Masters, Servants, and Magistrates in Britain and the Empire, 1592–1955* (Chapel Hill: University of North Carolina Press, 2004), 361.

[27] Ibid.

[28] Rubber was essential for the shielding of electrical, telegraph, and telephone cables, as well as in the nascent automobile industry. Tin, meanwhile, was crucial for food storage, including the tinned provisions carried by soldiers in the First World War, though demand for it had stabilized by 1930 due to more economic use of the resource and

the colonial state to discipline plantation workers there, officials were increasingly reluctant to deploy the heavy-handed measures that had been more commonly employed in the later nineteenth century. Labor codes implemented in 1909 and 1910 established a series of protective measures, such as guaranteeing minimum wage rates and setting maximum work hours.[29] The sanitary concerns that had often been at the heart of the overseer-state's inspectorial regime and its coercive power to address "vagrancy" were reframed in the light of new language about workers' welfare.

While such measures helped maintain the productivity of Malaysia's multiracial workforce, the colonial state colluded with Malay and British elites to keep Indian and Chinese laborers in a subordinated position. By 1931, the majority of the population in the Straits Settlements and the Federated Malay States were Indian and Chinese workers brought in through various schemes of recruitment licensed by the state and underwritten by employers.[30] In the same period, the British colonial government, responding to the global economic downturn and the resulting decline of the rubber and tin markets, passed legislation that restricted immigration and prevented Chinese and Indian residents from buying land.[31] Many of the regulations implemented in the previous two decades in order to assure the health of plantation workers fell into disuse, leading to a rise in disease and mortality rates.[32] Declining economic opportunities prompted a wave of departures by Chinese and Indian workers, with the latter losing a third of their original cohort (243,000) from 1930 to 1933 alone.[33] For those who remained, the colonial state was disinclined to enforce regulations that ensured fair wages, prevented overwork, and safeguarded laborers' health. Indian and Chinese workers, brought over in such large numbers and with considerable state support and management, were largely abandoned to the mercies of the rubber planters. The latter's political power was further bolstered by the global expansion of their industry and the incorporation of former colonial officials into their lobbying and management structures.[34] Tin, meanwhile, the demand for which had stabilized, moved largely into the control of

improved methods of recovery and reuse. Barbara Watson Andaya and Leonard Y. Andaya, *History of Malaysia* (London: Macmillan, 1982), 215.

29 Lynn Hollen Lees, *Planting Empire, Cultivating Subjects: British Malaya, 1789–1941* (Cambridge: Cambridge University Press, 2017), 193.

30 That year, the Malay population stood at 1,864,872, the Chinese population at 1,284,888, and the Indian population at 570,987. Saw Swee-Hock, *The Population of Peninsular Malaysia* (Singapore: Singapore University Press, 1989), 54.

31 Specifically with the Immigration Restriction Ordinance of 1928 (replaced by the Aliens Ordinance 1933) and the Small Holders (Restriction of Sale) Bill 1931.

32 Lees, *Planting Empire*, 197.

33 Ibid., 216.

34 Ibid., 217.

European investors who edged out the Chinese commercial concerns that had dominated the industry for much of its existence.[35]

These were the first steps in a road that would culminate in the relegation of Indian and Chinese cohorts, whose labor had driven the Malayan economy forward for nearly a century prior, to a state of permanent subordination. Ongoing ethnic tensions, especially between Malays and Chinese, continued to prevail in the post–Second World War decades, exacerbated by the postwar civil conflict (i.e. the Emergency) and the political struggles that accompanied independence in 1949.[36] Although a multitude of factors had fostered these circumstances, the state-sponsored systems of labor emigration, the demonization of Chinese culture by British officials, and the stern controls of labor implemented in the name of public order were all essential to the process. Even as British officials in late nineteenth-century Malaysia had espoused the empire's "civilizing mission," moral reform, multiracial harmony, and economic modernization, the legacy of the overseer-state there was the creation of a society that was increasingly diverse, but increasingly segregated, and the establishment of a racial hierarchy, ingrained in both law and culture, that persists to this very day.[37]

In the Caribbean, the legacies of late-stage slavery, amelioration, indenture, and the overseer-state that formed their institutional scaffolding were thoroughly entangled. Although the long-term effects on the social, political, economic, and cultural relationship between the creole population, Indo-Caribbeans, Chinese-Caribbeans, and African-Caribbeans were indeed complex, there can be little doubt that the most negative consequences were borne by the last of these groups.[38] In many instances, the political progress of Indo-Caribbeans in the wake of indenture's abolition came at the cost of the continued marginalization of African-Caribbeans, with tensions between the

35 European ownership of Malaysian mines grew from one-quarter in 1913 to two-thirds by 1937. Andaya and Andaya, *History of Malaysia*, 215.

36 Ibid., 256–300.

37 In modern-day Malaysia, this legacy is epitomized in the *bumiputera* (trans. "son of the soil") system, which ensures the preservation of the privileges of ethnic Malays. These range from their dominance in the financial, commercial, and military sectors to favorable mortgage arrangements and guaranteed places in the higher education system. By contrast, the "glass ceiling" faced by Straits Chinese residents is a perpetual source of frustration for them. Chin Yee Whah and Benny Teh Cheng Guan, "Malaysia's Protracted Affirmative Action Policy and the Evolution of the Bumiputera Commercial and Industrial Community," *Sojourn: Journal of Social Issues in Southeast Asia*, 32, no. 2 (July 2017), 336–73.

38 This was readily apparent, for example, in the treatment of African-Caribbean freedwomen in the criminal justice system. Anne Ulentin, "'She Has Not Been Seen or Heard of Since': Gender, Incarceration, and Punishment in the Bahamas, 1860s–1920s," *New West Indian Guide* 96 (2022), 233–65. For Guyana, see Clare Anderson, Kellie Moss, and Shammane Joseph Jackson, "Coloniality and the Criminal Justice System: Empire and Its Legacies in Guyana," *Slavery & Abolition* 43, no. 4 (2022), 682–704.

two groups exacerbated by their contrasting involvement in the apparatus of the overseer-state. This process had begun in the nineteenth century, when formerly enslaved Africans, freed from bondage but bereft of economic resources or political self-determination, struggled against a system that remained firmly in the control of white plantation-owners.[39] Some (and historians continue to debate how many) were willing to return to the plantations as paid laborers, while others served instead as overseers and drivers there or joined the policing and military contingents, reinforcing the disciplinary regime deployed by the state against Indian, Chinese, and other African-Caribbean workers.[40] The apparatus of laws and institutions that sustained plantation discipline in the Caribbean remained powerful well into the decade preceding the First World War, when the prosecution of indentured Indians for labor offenses in British Guiana and Trinidad remained high, reaching a peak of over a third of the population from 1905 to 1909.[41] The postwar decades witnessed rising tensions among both the African-Caribbean and the Indian workforces across the Caribbean, culminating in a wave of strikes and demonstrations in the 1930s, in some cases violent and in some prompting violent suppression by state authorities. These tensions were particularly high in the colonies where indenture had once operated.[42]

The legacy of indenture and the overseer-state was thus crucial to sustaining a cultural, social, and economic division between the two cohorts. British Guiana and Trinidad effectively operated with two working classes in the first half of the twentieth century. One was African-Caribbean, including an artisanal contingent but working primarily in a variety of relatively low-skill occupations, from dockers to small market farmers and in more high-skill occupations in industry and resource-extraction. The economic progress of this group was hampered by the long legacy of dispossession and disfranchisement that had accompanied emancipation. The other working class was

[39] Walter Rodney, *A History of the Guyanese Working People 1881–1905* (Baltimore, MD: Johns Hopkins University Press, 1981), 42–3.

[40] For a general survey, see William A. Green, *British Slave Emancipation: The Sugar Colonies and the Great Experiment 1830–1865* (Oxford: Clarendon Press, 1976), especially ch. 7, 191–228. On Guyana, see Barbara P. Josiah, "After Emancipation: Aspects of Village Life in Guyana, 1869–1911," *Journal of Negro History* 82, no. 1 (Winter 1997), 105–21. On the historiography of post-emancipation society, see P. Emmer, "Scholarship or Solidarity? The Post-Emancipation Era in the Caribbean Reconsidered," *New West Indian Guide/Nieuwe West-Indische Gids* 69, no. 3/4 (1995), 277–90.

[41] Mohapatra, "Assam," 468.

[42] See O. Nigel Bolland, *On the March: Labour Rebellions in the British Caribbean 1934–39* (Kingston: Ian Randle, 1995). Trinidad saw labor unrest in the capital, Port of Spain, in June 1933 and a series of demonstrations on sugar plantations in July 1934. Guyana witnessed strikes on more than a half-dozen plantations in 1934 and 1935, with one involving some 2,000 workers. Then 1938 saw over 30 disputes involving more than 12,000 workers.

Indian, which still dominated plantation labor, but, by dint of the funds accumulated during the indenture period, the incentives of land that had been offered to those who renewed their contracts, and a generally more favorable (or, at least, less innately violent and rebellious) status in the eyes of the white elite, was able to make inroads into the artisanal and shopkeeping sectors. The economic crisis of 1929 and the subsequent labor unrest had fostered unionization of both the agricultural and the industrial and mining sectors, with Indians leading the way and dominating the former, while African-Caribbeans did so for the latter.[43] This split, which accompanied and reinforced the cultural and religious divisions between the two groups, was reflected in the rise of ethnically based political parties in the 1940s.[44]

This entire landscape of ethnicity-based politics, culture, and society was, in many respects, a historical legacy not just of slavery but also of the overseer-state and its role in amelioration, apprenticeship, indenture, and the vast raft of labor control regulations that had accreted through all of these institutions. These had cemented the legal, economic, and social legacy of dispossession and disfranchisement of African-Caribbeans in the post-emancipation period. In the nineteenth century, the overseer-state had brought Indians to the Caribbean in great numbers and confined them to the plantations. As indenture waned, the collusion of colonial administrators and private landowners facilitated the steady transfer of capital (in the form of wages and post-contract land grants) from the formerly enslaved population to the formerly indentured one, and sometimes installed African-Caribbeans as the overseers and constables who directly enforced plantation labor discipline. This last dynamic replicated itself during the labor unrest of the 1930s, which witnessed a largely African-Caribbean police force deployed against Indian strikers.[45] After some aborted attempts at collective action and reconciliation, ethnic tensions in former indenture colonies were given further institutional solidity by the introduction of universal adult suffrage (1946 in Trinidad and 1951 in British Guiana), and the shifting demographic balance in favor of the Indian population.[46] By the post–Second World War period, Indians were noticeable among the urban middle class and were increasingly assertive in the political sphere. Even as African-Caribbean political and intellectual figures rose to prominence in the 1950s and 1960s, the wider population in Trinidad and elsewhere in the Caribbean continued to suffer from slower economic and social progress than that of their Indo-Caribbean counterparts. De facto

[43] Vishnu Priya, "Ethnicity and Politics: East Indians in the Political Process of Guyana and Trinidad," *India Quarterly* (November 2004), 102–3.

[44] Ibid., 101.

[45] Ibid., 103.

[46] Indians became a clear majority of 51 percent in British Guiana by 1946 and continued to gain ground in Trinidad and Tobago, constituting 34 percent by 1961 and growing to 41 percent by 1981. Ibid.

segregation remained the order of the day in everything from education to politics to the national pastime of cricket.[47]

In Mauritius, where Indians became the overwhelming majority of the population, this equation differed yet again. There, indenture declined and eventually vanished as the Indian population went from workers to small landowners via the *morcellment* process.[48] This was accompanied by the slow transfer of political power from the Anglo-French landowners to an Indian merchant and landholding cohort and the steady growth of Indo-Mauritian enfranchisement. This process accelerated with the establishment of the Mauritian Labour Party in 1936, though the fuller political mobilization of working-class Indo-Mauritians did not occur until a wave of strikes took place across the late 1930s and 1940s.[49] By 1948, the electorate had grown to 71,569, and by 1959, to 208,726, most of whom were direct descendants of indentured laborers.[50]

Across Britain's plantation and resource colonies in the southern hemisphere, the overseer-state and its most concrete manifestation, Indian and Chinese indenture, had helped to construct multicultural societies typified by a multifaceted workforce whose descendants, in the twentieth century, became increasingly prominent in the political and intellectual leadership of these colonies. But the legal, economic, and cultural categorizations that lay at the heart of colonial labor regulation had helped to entrench and sustain ethnic tensions that would persist for generations. Despite significant regional differences in how these dynamics played out, another common legacy was evident in those regions where the collusion of state structures and private interests in support of labor migration and control had served to anchor colonial authority. This legacy stemmed from the continual engagement, negotiation, and resistance that characterized workers' interactions with state agents and institutions across the decades of the overseer state's operation. This ongoing interaction helped foster nascent anti-colonial movements from the Caribbean to South Africa and India. The bitter memory of indenture and the state's collaboration with plantation-owners made it clear to Indian activists in particular that they would never achieve political recognition and racial equality under the British principles of liberalism and the attendant definitions of freedom. For Mohandas K. Gandhi, who dedicated much time and energy to a condemnation of indenture as an "artificial state" that perpetuated an "unnatural relationship" of

[47] Viranjini Munasinghe, *Callaloo or Tossed Salad? East Indians and the Cultural Politics of Identity in Trinidad* (Ithaca, NY: Cornell University Press, 2001) ; C. L. R. James, *Beyond a Boundary* ([1963]; repr. Durham, NC: Duke University Press, 2013).

[48] Richard B. Allen, *Slaves, Freedmen, and Indentured Laborers in Colonial Mauritius* (Cambridge: Cambridge University Press, 1999), 142.

[49] Vijayalakshmi Teelok, *Mauritian History: From Its Beginnings to Modern Times* (Moka: Mahatma Gandhi Institute, 2009), 376.

[50] Ibid., 382, 392.

inequality between white Britons and Indian subjects, the languages of liberalism and paternalism eventually revealed themselves as mere camouflage for coercion, denial of rights, social marginalization, and economic exploitation.[51]

Meanwhile, even as the impetus for international labor rights built up steam, Indian and Chinese workers alike in the British Empire gained next to nothing from the endeavor. The determination of the British government that immigrant workers on plantations were *not* protected under the auspices of the International Labour Organization created in 1919 as an agency of the League of Nations served as an abject lesson that the new rights and safeguards in the offing were not for this cohort to enjoy.[52] More broadly, the rights and the identity of white laborers across the empire continued to be defined and built on the explicit *exclusion* of their African, African-Caribbean, East Asian, and South Asian counterparts. This was apparent in measures such as the "White Australia" policy and in the various exclusion laws that continued to operate there and in Canada and South Africa. White workers and their spokesmen in politics and public culture remained adamantly opposed to "yellow slavery" and saw no common cause with the empire's "coolie" population. This continued marginalization of Chinese and Indian workers, the overt antagonism of white-dominated labor union movements both in Britain and abroad, and the failure of attempts at solidarity with the burgeoning African-Caribbean trade union movement in the early twentieth century help to explain the appeal of more divergent ideologies of liberation such as Gandhi's *Satyagraha*, Nehru's Indian nationalism, and both anarchism and Communism in Malaysia.[53]

For all the ways that its legacies continued to shape societies in the Caribbean, South Africa, and the Indian Ocean World in the aftermath of indenture's abolition, the overseer-state was hardly the sum total of what historians today understand as colonialism in Britain's plantation and mining colonies. Nor can we equate the legacies of colonial rule solely with the state's decisive intervention into labor migration, labor regulation, and mediation between the workforce and those who employed them. Rather, the overseer-state both gave concrete form to the cultural dynamics of race and racialized labor governance even as its processes served as sites for the imposition, modification, and contestation of ideas about race, class, gender, labor, rights,

[51] Mohandas K. Gandhi, "Indentured Labour," in *Mahatma Gandhi: His Life, Writings and Speeches* (Madras: The Cambridge Press, 1917), 91.

[52] Lees, *Planting Empire*, 193.

[53] C. F. Yong, "Origins and Development of the Malayan Communist Movement," *Modern Asian Studies* 25, no. 4 (1991), 633. The Trinidad Workingmen's Association had been formed in 1897 and, despite being deemed illegal by the colonial government, it and other similar organizations (e.g. the British Guiana Labour Union) continued to be active in organizing demonstrations and strikes among the African-Caribbean workforce throughout the early twentieth century.

authority, justice, and a host of other concepts and practices that were central to colonialism. These legacies were felt well beyond the colonies that have constituted the focus of this study, since almost every European empire employed indentured labor to one degree or another.[54] Much as British imperialism's influence was hardly confined to the regions of formal rule, the extent of the overseer-state's influence in the economic, social, legal, and political dynamics of global labor extended well beyond the empire's formal boundaries.[55] It helped establish a system of mobile, contracted, subordinated labor as a global phenomenon. And it firmly entrenched the popular conception in Britain, Europe, and North America that the primary role of Chinese and Indian immigrants was as laborers and that only in this role were they an indispensable adjunct to the expansion of capitalist agriculture, resource-extraction, and manufacture.

The overseer-state also cemented the persistent belief – among government officials, the propertied classes, and the financial, mercantile, agricultural, and industrial elites, both domestic and colonial – that to preserve public order and the ascendency of white workers, these cohorts, much like the emancipated Africans that had set the precedents for their treatment, had to remain thoroughly subordinated. They would be accorded the minimal protection of the state under paternalistic regulations, but would be excluded from formal political participation, denied recognition as integral cohorts to civil society, debarred from mainstream cultural and intellectual activity, and otherwise omitted in a multitude of ways from the national identities and communities that subsequently developed. As coolies they had arrived and, in both official and public perception, coolies they would remain, until their crucial economic and social role in postcolonial societies and their determined efforts in the political and cultural sphere finally, many decades after indenture's abolition, could no longer be denied.

Across the nineteenth century, the coercive methods of the overseer-state, deployed in conjunction with a discourse of paternalistic supervision and justified by the elevation of free labor and the contract as the epitome of just governance and moral colonization, helped demarcate boundaries of racialized labor exploration deemed tolerable in official practice and public perception.[56] Today, the transportation of workers from the Global South across far distances to regions where, locked into long-term, unbreakable contracts enforced by law and coercion, they remain socially and politically marginalized remains commonplace. Some key exemplars of what is today designated as

[54] For the full extent of the global indenture system, see David Northrup, *Indentured Labor in the Age of Imperialism 1834–1922* (Cambridge: Cambridge University Press, 1992).

[55] Hence the alternative title for this volume, *The Imperialism of Free Labor*, a nod to the groundbreaking work of Ronald Robinson and John Gallagher, "The Imperialism of Free Trade," *Economic History Review* 6, no. 1 (1953), 1–15.

[56] My thanks to Dr. Hannah Richter for this particular insight.

"modern slavery" are, in structure and function, closer to modern indenture.[57] This is an insidious development. Slavery, as a concept and practice, has become an anathema to the advocates of human rights and a gross violation of national and international law. The term "indenture," by contrast, has been relegated to historical obscurity, and work conditions that resemble it are often recognized by critics as being exploitative, but rarely designated by national or international law as being illegal.[58] In spirit if not in word, however, wherever men and women, on the false promises of freedom and opportunity, are lured across oceans and forced to work long hours under the meanest conditions, denied any collective voice or any control over the terms of labor, and hemmed in by the collusion of employers and the state, indenture persists. The overseer-state, much like the fox of ancient Latin proverb, has changed its fur, but not its habits.[59]

57 "Modern slavery" embraces a very broad array of exploitative labor practices, the defining feature being loss of freedom and absence of any control over the circumstances of work. Nineteenth-century indenture fitted this definition well and, by extension, one of the most commonly seen exemplars of "modern slavery," debt-bondage or bondage-labor, fits the parameters of nineteenth-century indenture. "What Is Modern Slavery?" *Anti-Slavery International*, n.d., www.antislavery.org/slavery-today/modern-slavery.

58 One recent, egregious example of this was the organization of labor for the construction of the World Cup stadium in Qatar. Annie Kelly, "Ten Years of Hurt: How the Guardian Reported Qatar's World Cup Working Conditions," *Guardian*, November 19, 2022, www.theguardian.com/global-development/2022/nov/19/qatar-working-conditions-world-cup-guardian-reporting.

59 *Vulpes pilum mutat, non mores* ("a fox changes its fur, not its behavior"), attributed to Suetonius.

BIBLIOGRAPHY

National Archives

The National Archives, Malaysia (Kuala Lumpur)

Records of the British Resident General's Office, Selangor
Records of the Chief Magistrate, Kuala Lumpur
Records of the District Commissioner of Police, Kuala Lumpur
Records of the Office of the High Commissioner for the Federated Malay States and Brunei
Records of the Office of the Protector of Labour, Federated Malay States
Records of the Superintendent of the Straits Settlements Emigration Depot, Negapatam

The National Archives, Mauritius (Moka)

Almanac and Civil Service Register, 1862, 1865
Blue Books, 1850–80
Committee of Council Appointed to Inquire into the Subject of Immigrant Labor in Mauritius, 1844 (HA 73)
Letters from Stipendiary Magistrates, 1850–75
Magistrates' Correspondence, 1841–5
Magistrates' Reports on Plantation Visits, 1865
Protector of Immigrants Correspondence, 1893–1902
Records of the Supreme Court, 1850–80

The National Archives, Singapore

Annual Reports of the Chinese Protectorate
Papers of the Legislative Council of the Straits Settlements
Straits Settlements, Acts and Ordinances of the Legislative Council, 1868–98 (3 vols.)
Straits Settlements Annual Reports, 1871–1907
Straits Settlements Blue Books
Straits Settlements Government Gazette, 1859–81

The National Library, Singapore

Report of the Commissioners Appointed under Act XXI of 1867 to Enquire into "The Penang Riots"

The National Archives, Trinidad (Port of Spain)
Minutes of the Legislative Council of Tobago, 1831–8

The School of Oriental and African Studies (London)
Straits Settlements Legislative Council Proceedings

Public Documents

British Government

Acts of British Parliament
Bill of the Abolition of Slavery throughout the British Colonies 1833, s. 15

House of Commons Debates, 1812–1906

House of Lords Debates, 1812–1906

House of Commons

1823–4. *Papers in Explanation of the Measures Adopted by His Majesty's Government for the Melioration of the Condition of the Slave Population in the West Indies, and on the Continent of South America* (London: R.G. Clarke).

1824–5 (010). *Further Papers in Explanation of Measures for Melioration of Condition of Slave Population in W. Indies and S. America, 1825.*

1824–5 (512). *Return of Slave Population at Cape of Good Hope, Mauritius, and West Indies.*

1825 (205). *Papers in Explanation of Measures Adopted by His Majesty's Government for Melioration of Condition of Slave Population in W. Indies and on the Continent of S. America.*

1826. *Copies of the Record of the Proceedings of the Fiscals of Demerara and Berbice in Their Capacity of Guardians and Protectors of Slaves and Their Decisions in All Cases of Complaints of Masters and Slaves.*

1826. *Further Papers Relating to the Proceedings of the Fiscals of Demerara and Berbice in Their Capacity of Guardians and Protectors of Slaves and Their Decisions in All Cases of Complaints of Masters and Slaves.*

1826 (401). *Further Papers Relating to Slaves in the West Indies (Demerara and Berbice).*

1827. *Papers in Explanation of the Measures Adopted by His Majesty's Government for the Melioration of the Condition of the Slave Population in the West Indies, on the Continent of South America, and at the Mauritius.*

1827. *Papers in Explanation of the Measures Adopted by His Majesty's Government for the Melioration of the Condition of the Slave Population in the West Indies and on the Continent of South America, Part I – 1827.*

1827. *Papers in Explanation of the Measures Adopted by His Majesty's Government for the Melioration of the Condition of the Slave Population in the West Indies, on the Continent of South America, and at the Cape of Good Hope, Part II – 1827.*
1827 (465). *Trinidad Slaves: Copy of All Laws and Regulations.*
1827 (551). *Report of His Majesty's Commissioners of Legal Inquiry on the Colony of Trinidad.*
1828. *Papers in Explanation of the Measures Adopted by His Majesty's Government for the Melioration of the Condition of the Slave Population in the West Indies, on the Continent of South America, and at the Mauritius.*
1828 (577). *Second Report of the Commissioners of Enquiry into the Administration of Criminal and Civil Justice in the West Indies and South American Colonies: United Colony of Demerara and Essequebo and Colony of Berbice.*
1829 (335). *Copy of Any Reports Which May Have Been Received from the Protectors of Slaves in the Colonies of Demerara, Berbice, Trinidad, St. Lucia and the Cape of Good Hope.*
1830 (373). *Slaves: An Order of the King in Council for Consolidating the Several Laws Recently Made for Improving the Condition of the Slaves in His Majesty's Colonies of Trinidad, Berbice, Demerara, Saint Lucia, Cape of Good Hope and Mauritius.*
1830 (676). *Papers in Explanation of the Measures Adopted by His Majesty's Government for the Melioration of the Condition of the Slave Population in the West Indies, on the Continent of South America, and at the Mauritius.*
1831. *Order in Council for Consolidating the Several Laws for Improving the Conditions of Slaves in His Majesty's Colonies of Trinidad, Berbice, Demerara, St. Lucia, the Cape of Good Hope, and Mauritius.*
1831. *Papers in Explanation of the Measures Adopted by His Majesty's Government for the Melioration of the Condition of the Slave Population in the West Indies, on the Continent of South America, and at the Cape of Good Hope, and the Mauritius.*
1831 (230). *Papers in Explanation of the Measures Adopted by His Majesty's Government for the Melioration of the Condition of the Slave Population in the West Indies, on the Continent of South America, and at the Cape of Good Hope.*
1831 (262). *Copy of Any Reports Which May Have Been Received from the Protectors of Slaves in the Colonies of Demerara, Berbice, Trinidad, St. Lucia and the Cape of Good Hope.*
1831–2 (009). Colonial Office, *Papers in Explanation of Measures Adopted for Melioration of Condition of Slave Population in H.M. Possessions in W. Indies, S. America, Cape of Good Hope and Mauritius: December 1831.*
1831–2 (561). Assembly of Jamaica, *Report from House of Assembly, Jamaica, on Injury Sustained in Recent Rebellion.*
1832 (285). *West India Colonies: Slave Insurrection.*
1832 (379). *Papers in Explanation of the Measures Adopted by His Majesty's Government for the Melioration of the Condition of the Slave Population in the West Indies, on the Continent of South America.*

1832 (733). *Papers in Explanation of the Measures Adopted by His Majesty's Government for the Melioration of the Condition of the Slave Population in the West Indies, on the Continent of South America, and at the Mauritius.*

1833–5 (177). *Papers in Explanation of the Measures Adopted by His Majesty's Government for Giving Effect to the Act for the Abolition of Slavery Throughout the British Colonies, Part I: Jamaica, 1833–1835.*

1835 (278-I). *Papers in Explanation of the Measures Adopted by His Majesty's Government for Giving Effect to the Act for the Abolition of Slavery Throughout the British Colonies, Part II: Jamaica (continued), Barbados, British Guiana, and Mauritius, 1833–1835.*

1836 (166-I). *Papers in Explanation of the Measures Adopted by His Majesty's Government for Giving Effect to the Act for the Abolition of Slavery Throughout the British Colonies, Part III: Jamaica (continued).*

1836 (560). *Report from the Select Committee on Negro Apprenticeship in the Colonies.*

1837 (522-I). *Papers in Explanation of the Measures Adopted by His Majesty's Government for Giving Effect to the Act for the Abolition of Slavery Throughout the British Colonies, Part IV: Jamaica, Barbados, British Guiana.*

1838 (154-I). *Papers in Explanation of the Measures Adopted by His Majesty's Government for Giving Effect to the Act for the Abolition of Slavery Throughout the British Colonies, Part V: Jamaica.*

1838 (154-II). *Papers in Explanation of the Measures Adopted by His Majesty's Government for Giving Effect to the Act for the Abolition of Slavery Throughout the British Colonies, Part VI: Barbados and British Guiana.*

1839 (463). *Correspondence Relative to the Condition of the Hill Coolies and of the Other Labourers Who Have Been Introduced into British Guiana.*

1840 (77). *Copies of Reports from, or Despatches to, the Governor of British Guiana, Respecting the Hill Coolies Introduced into That Colony.*

1840 (151). *Copies or Extracts of Any Correspondence between the Secretary of State for the Colonies and the Governor of British Guiana, Respecting the Immigration of Labourers into That Colony.*

1840 (331). *Copies of Correspondence Addressed to the Secretary of State for the Colonial Department, Relative to the Introduction of Indian Labourers into the Mauritius; and of the Report of the Commissioner of Inquiry into the Present Condition of Those Already Located in That Colony.*

1841 (307). *British Guiana: Copy of a Despatch from the Governor of British Guiana to Her Majesty's Principal Secretary of State for the Colonies, Dated 16th July, 1851, Transmitting a Report on the State of the Labouring Population of Demerara and Berbice.*

1841 (43). *Hill Coolies. Copies of Papers Respecting the Exportation of Hill Coolies, Received from the Government of India.*

1841 (45). *Hill Coolies. Return to an Order of the Honourable the House of Commons, Dated 29 January 1841; – for, Copies of a Letter from the Secretary to the Government of India to the Committee Appointed to Inquire Respecting the*

Exportation of Hill Coolies, Dated the 1st Day of August 1838: – of the Report Made by That Committee; with the Minutes of Evidence and Appendix: – of Any Minute Recorded on That Report by Any Member of the Committee: – of the Letters from the Government of India to the Court of Directors of the East India Company, Dated the 16th and 19th Days of October 1840, on the Same Subject.
1841 (427). *Hill Coolies. Copies of Papers Respecting the Exportation of Hill Coolies, Received from the Government of India; in Continuation of Those Presented to the House of Commons on the 11th Day of February Last.*
1841 (483). *Hill Coolies and Indian Labourers. Report of the Committee to Enquire into Alleged Abuses in Exporting from Bengal to Other Countries* (referred to in text as *Dickens Report 1*).
1842 (26). *Mauritius. Correspondence Relative to the Introduction of Indian Labourers into the Mauritius.*
1842 (479). *Report from the Select Committee on West India Colonies* (also known as the *Dickens Committee Report*).
1845 (641), *Mauritius. Report of the Committee Appointed to Inquire into the State of the Indian Immigrants.*
1846 (691-I). *Papers Relating to the Labouring Population of the British Colonies – West Indies and Mauritius* (also known as the "Rawson Committee Report").
1847 (325). *Immigration of Labourers into the West India Colonies and the Mauritius.*
1847–8. *Reports from Committees – Sugar and Coffee Planting, Part III.*
1849 (297). *First Report from the Select Committee on Ceylon and British Guiana.*
1852 (1499). *12th General Report of the Colonial Land and Emigration Commission.*
1853 (986). *Chinese Immigrants Recently Introduced into the Colonies of British Guiana and Trinidad.*
1856 (432). *Correspondence between the Governor of British Guiana and the Secretary of State for the Colonies, on the Subject of the Recent Disturbances in That Colony.*
1857. *Immigration to the West Indian Colonies.*
1859 (31). *Condition of the Labouring Population of Such Colonies, Both Native and Immigrant, and the Supply of Labour. Part I. British Guiana, Jamaica, Trinidad.*
1871 (393). *Report of the Commissioners Appointed to Enquire into the Treatment of Immigrants in British Guiana* (with accompanying volumes of evidence, 393-I, 393-II).
1871 (403). *Correspondence Respecting the Emigration of Chinese Coolies from Macao.*
1872 (641). *Further Correspondence on the Subject of the Recommendations of the Commissioners of Enquiry into the Treatment of Immigrants in British Guiana.*
1875 (1115). *Report of the Royal Commissioners Appointed to Enquire into the Treatment of Immigrants in Mauritius.*
1884–5. *Correspondence Respecting the Recent Coolie Disturbances in Trinidad at the Mohurrum Festival.*
1898 (8655). *Report of the West India Royal Commission* (also known as the "Norman Commission") (with accompanying evidence, proceedings, and documents, pt. I – 8656; pts. II, III, IV, and V – 8657; pts. IV–XIII – 8669).

1904 (1989). *Immigration Ordinances of Trinidad and British Guiana.*

1910 (5185). *Report of the Mauritius Royal Commission* (with accompanying proceedings and evidence, pt. II – 5186, and documents, pt. III – 5187).

1910 (5192). *Report of the Committee on Emigration from India to the Crown Colonies and Protectorates* (also known as the "Sanderson Committee") (with accompanying evidence, pt II – 5193, and documents, pt. III – 5194).

PP 1914–16 (7744). *Report on the Condition of Indian Immigrants in the Four British Colonies: Trinidad, British Guiana or Demerara, Jamaica and Fiji, and in the Dutch Colony of Surinam or Dutch Guiana* (also known as "the McNeill-Lal Report"). *Part I – Trinidad and British Guiana.*

PP 1914–16 (7745). *Report on the Condition of Indian Immigrants in the Four British Colonies: Trinidad, British Guiana or Demerara, Jamaica and Fiji, and in the Dutch Colony of Surinam or Dutch Guiana* (also known as "the McNeill-Lal Report"). *Part II – Surinam, Jamaica, Fiji, and General Remarks.*

Government of India

J. Geoghegan, *Report on Coolie Emigration from India* (also known as the Geoghegan Report). Calcutta, 1873.

Report of the Labour Enquiry Commission. Calcutta, 1897.

Government of the Straits Settlements

Report of the Commission Appointed to Enquire into and Report on the Question of the State of Labour in the Strains Settlements and the Protected Native States. Singapore: Government Printing Office, 1891.

Straits Settlement Ordinance no. 1 of 1876, "An Ordinance for Regulating the Immigration of Native Laborers from British India," s. 43.

High Commissioner of the Federated Malay States

Report of the Commission Appointed to Enquire into the Conditions of Indentured Labour in the Federated Malay States (also known as "the Parr Commission"), 1910.

Other Public Documents

Gopal Krishna Gohkale, Resolution in the Imperial Legislative Council, March 4, 1912.

Report of the Coolie Commission, Appointed to Inquire into the Condition of the Indian Immigrants in the Colony of Natal, reprinted in the Third Session, Sixth Council, LC No. 1. Pietermaritzburg: Keith & Co., 1872.

Newspapers and Periodicals

Colonist (Georgetown, British Guiana)
New York Times
Singapore Free Press and Mercantile Advertiser
Standard
Straits Settlement Government Gazette
Straits Times
Times of London
Trinidad Royal Gazette, 1838–79

Printed Primary Sources

African Institution, The. *Reasons for Establishing a Registry of Slaves in the British Colonies*. London: Ellerton and Henderson, 1815.

Anderson, Charles. *Outlines of a Plan Submitted to Her Majesty's Government for the Purpose of Establishing an Authorized Committee to Regulate and Carry on the Introduction of Indian Laborers at Mauritius*. London: Nichols, 1840.

Anon. *Slave Law of Jamaica: With Proceedings and Documents Relative Thereto*. London: James Ridgeway, 1828.

("A Landowner"). *Demerara After Fifteen Years of Freedom*. London: T. Bosworth, 1853.

Anson, Archibald Edward. *About Others and Myself, 1745 to 1920*. London: John Murray, 1920.

Barrett, William Garland. *Immigration to the British West Indies: Is It the Slave-Trade Revived or Not?* London: A. W. Bennett, 1859.

Beaton, Patrick. *Creoles and Coolies; Or, Five Years in Mauritius*. London: James Nisbet, 1859.

Beaumont, Joseph. *The New Slavery: An Account of the Indian and Chinese Immigrants in British Guiana*. [1871]; repr. ed. [online] Caribbean Press, 2011.

Bolingbroke, Henry. *A Voyage to the Demerary*. London: Richard Phillips, 1809.

British Guiana: The Commission of Inquiry into the Treatment of Immigrants. *Report of the Commission*, 4 vols. Georgetown: L. McDermott, "The Colonist" Office, 1870.

Bryant, Joshua. *An Account of an Insurrection of the Negro Slaves in the Colony of Demerara, Which Broke Out on the 18th of August 1823*. Georgetown: Guiana Chronicle Office, 1823.

Buckley, Charles Burton. *An Anecdotal History of Old Times in Singapore, Vol. 2*. Singapore: Fraser & Neave, 1902.

Burns, Peter L., ed. *The Journals of J. W. W. Birch, First British Resident to Perak, 1874–1875*. Kuala Lumpur: Oxford University Press, 1976.

Clarkson, Thomas. *Thoughts on the Necessity of Improving the Condition of Slaves in the British Colonies, with a View to Their Ultimate Emancipation; and on the Practicability, the Safety, and the Advantages of the Latter Measure.* London: Society for the Mitigation and Gradual Abolition of Slavery Throughout the British Dominions, 1823.

Clementi, Cecil, with an introduction by Anne-Marie Lee-Joy. *The Chinese in British Guiana.* [1915]; repr. Georgetown: Caribbean Press, 2010.

Colonist Office. *The Coolie Riots in Essequebo: A Report of the Proceedings and Evidence at the Inquest on the Bodies of Five Rioters, Killed by the Fire of the Police (Carefully Corrected and Collated with the Official Records).* Georgetown: "The Colonist" Office, 1872.

Cooper, Thomas. *Facts Illustrative of the Condition of the Negro Slaves in Jamaica: With Notes and an Appendix by Thomas Cooper.* London: J. Hatchard & Son, 1824.

Crockall, Lawrence. *British Guiana.* London: T. Fisher Unwin, 1898.

Cropper, James, and John Gladstone. *The Correspondence between John Gladstone and James Cropper on the Present State of Slavery in the British West Indies and in the United States of America and on the Importation of Sugar from the British Settlements in India.* Liverpool: West India Association, 1824.

Dalton, Henry G. *The History of British Guiana*, 2 vols. London: Longman, Brown, Green, and Longmans, 1855.

De Joux, C. M. *The Mauritius Almanac and Civil Service Register for 1865.* London: Harrison and Sons, 1865.

Del Tufo, M. B. *Malaya (Federation) Superintendent of Census.* London: Crown Agents for the Colonies, 1949.

Des Voeux, George William. *My Colonial Service in British Guiana, St. Lucia, Trinidad, Fiji, Australia, Newfoundland, and Hong Kong, Vols. 1 & 2.* London: John Murray, 1903.

Experiences of a Demerara Magistrate 1865–1870, ed. Vincent Ruth. Georgetown: Daily Chronicle, 1948.

Gandhi, Mohandas K. *Mahatma Gandhi: His Life, Writings and Speeches.* Madras: Cambridge Press, 1917.

Gordon, Arthur. *Mauritius: Records of Private and Public Life, 1871–1874, Vol. 1.* Edinburgh: R. & R. Clark, 1894.

Grey, George. *The Colonial Policy of Lord John Russell's Administration, Vol. 1.* London: Richard Bentley, 1853.

Hill, Richard. *Lights and Shadows of Jamaica History.* London: Ford and Gall, 1859.

Jenkins, John Edward. *The Coolie: His Rights and Wrongs.* New York: George Routledge & Sons, 1871.

Madden, R. R. *A Twelvemonth's Residence in the West Indies, during the Transition from Slavery to Apprenticeship; with Incidental Notices of the State of Society, Prospects, and Natural Resources of Jamaica and Other Islands*, 2 vols. London: J. Cochrane, 1835.

Maine, Henry. *Ancient Law: Its Connection with the Early History of Society, and Its Relation to Modern Ideas.* London: John Murray 1861.

McDonnell, Alexander. *Considerations on Negro Slavery with Authentic Reports Illustrative of the Actual Condition of the Negroes in Demerara*. London: Longman, Hurst, Rees, Orme, Brown and Green, 1824.

Pickering, W. A. "The Chinese in the Straits of Malacca." *Fraser's Magazine*, October 1876: 438–45.

"Chinese Secret Societies and Their Origin." *Journal of the Straits Branch of the Royal Asiatic Society* 1 (1878): 63–84.

"Chinese Secret Societies and Their Origin, Pt II." *Journal of the Straits Branch of the Royal Asiatic Society* 3 (1879): 1–18.

Polak, Henry. *The Indians of South Africa: Helots within the Empire and How They Are Treated*. Madras: G. A. Natesan, 1909.

Premium, Barton. *Eight Years in British Guiana*. London: Longman, Brown, Green, and Longmans, 1850.

Report of the Indian Immigrants Commission, 1885–7 ("Wragg Commission Report"). Pietermaritzburg: Davis & Sons, 1887.

Rodway, James. *History of British Guiana, from the Year 1668 to the Present Time, Vol. 2: 1782–1833*. Georgetown: J. Thomson, 1894.

Schlegel, Gustav. *Thian Ti Hui – The Hung-League or Heaven and Earth League: A Secret Society with the Chinese in China and India*. Batavia: Lange & Co., 1866.

Scoble, John. *Hill Coolies: A Brief Exposure of the Deplorable Condition of the Hill Coolies in British Guiana and Mauritius and of the Nefarious Means by Which They Were Induced to Resort to These Colonies*. London: Harvey and Darnton, 1840.

Singapore and Straits Directory for the Year 1881. Singapore: Mission Press, 1881.

Smith, Adam. *An Inquiry into the Nature and Causes of the Wealth of Nations, Book IV: Systems of Political Economy*. London: W. Strahan and T. Cadell, 1776.

Stephen, James. *Reasons for Establishing a Registry of Slaves in the British Colonies*. London: Ellerton and Henderson, 1885.

Swettenham, Frank. *The Real Malay*. London: John Lane, 1900.

Theobold, William. *The Legislative Acts of the Governor General of India in Council, from 1834 to the End of 1867, Vol. III, 1859–1861*. Calcutta: Thacker, Spink and Co., 1868.

Trollope, Anthony. *The West Indies and the Spanish Main*. London: Chapman & Hall, 1860.

Williams, James. *A Narrative of Events since the First of August, 1834*. [1837]; repr. Durham, NC: Duke University Press, 2001.

Secondary Sources

Articles and Books

Abbott, Edith. "Federal Immigration Policies, 1864–1924." *University Journal of Business* 2, no. 2 (March 1924): 133–56.

Adamson, Alan H. *Sugar without Slaves: The Political Economy of British Guiana.* New Haven, CT: Yale University Press, 1972.

Ahuja, Ravi. "Review – Making the Empire a Thinkable Whole: Master and Servant Law in Transterritorial Perspective" (review of Douglas Hay and Paul Craven, eds., *Masters, Servants and Magistrates in Britain and the Empire, 1562–1955* [Chapel Hill: University of North Carolina Press, 2004]). *International Review of Social History* 52, no. 2 (2007): 387–99.

Allen, Richard B. *Slaves, Freedmen, and Indentured Laborers in Colonial Mauritius.* Cambridge: Cambridge University Press, 1999.

"Reconceptualizing the 'New System of Slavery.'" *Man in India* 92, no. 2 (April 2012): 225–45.

"Slaves, Convicts, Abolitionism and the Global Origins of the Post-Emancipation Indentured Labor System." *Slavery & Abolition* 35, no. 2 (2014): 328–48.

"Satisfying the 'Want for Labouring People": European Slave Trading in the Indian Ocean, 1500–1850." *Journal of World History* 21, no. 1 (March 2010): 45–73.

Altink, Henrice. "Slavery by Another Name: Apprenticed Women in Jamaican Workhouses in the Period 1834–8." *Social History* 26, no. 1 (2001): 40–59.

Amrith, Sunil. "Indians Overseas? Governing Tamil Migration to Malaya, 1870–1941." *Past & Present* 208 (August 2010): 231–61.

Crossing the Bay of Bengal: The Furies of Nature and the Fortunes of Migrants. Cambridge, MA: Harvard University Press, 2013.

Andaya, Barbara Watson, and Leonard Andaya. *A History of Malaysia*, 2nd ed. Honolulu: University of Hawai'i Press, 2001.

Anderson, Clare. "Convicts and Coolies: Rethinking Indentured Labour in the Nineteenth Century." *Slavery & Abolition* 30, no. 1 (2009): 93–109.

"The Politics of Punishment in Colonial Mauritius, 1766–1887." *Cultural and Social History* 5, no. 4 (2015): 411–22.

"Transnational Histories of Penal Transportation: Punishment, Labour and Governance in the British Imperial World, 1788–1939." *Australian Historical Studies* 47, no. 3 (2016): 381–97.

"The Andaman Islands Penal Colony: Race, Class, Criminality, and the British Empire." *International Review of Social History* 63, special issue 26 (August 2018): 25–43.

Convicts: A Global History. Cambridge: Cambridge University Press, 2022.

Auerbach, Sascha. *Race, Law, and "The Chinese Puzzle" in Imperial Britain.* New York: Palgrave Macmillan, 2009.

"Margaret Tart, Lao She, and the Opium-Master's Wife: Race and Class among Chinese Commercial Immigrants in London and Australia, 1866–1929." *Comparative Studies in Society and History* 55, no. 1 (2013): 43–51.

Armed with Sword and Scales: Law, Culture, and Local Courtrooms in London, 1860–1914. Cambridge: Cambridge University Press, 2021.

"Of Rights and Riots: Indenture and (Mis)Rule in the Late Nineteenth-Century British Caribbean." *English Historical Review* 137, no. 589 (December 2022): 1662–92.

Bahadur, Gaiutra. *Coolie Woman: The Odyssey of Indenture*. Chicago, IL: University of Chicago Press, 2013.

Ballantyne, Tony. "The Changing Shape of the Modern British Empire and Its Historiography." *Historical Journal* 53, no. 2 (June 2010): 429–52.

Banivanua-Mar, Tracey. *Violence and Colonial Dialogue: The Australian-Pacific Indentured Labour Trade*. Honolulu: University of Hawai'i Press, 2007.

Bates, Crispin, and Marina Carter. "Sirdars as Intermediaries in Nineteenth-Century Indian Ocean Indentured Labour Migration." *Modern Asian Studies* 51, no. 2 (2017): 462–84.

Bates, Crispin, and Marina Carter. "Kala Pani Revisited: Indian Labour Migrants and the Sea Crossing." *Journal of Indentureship and Its Legacies* 1, no. 1 (2021): 36–62.

Behal, Rana P. "Coolie Drivers or Benevolent Paternalists? British Tea Planters in Assam and the Indenture Labour System." *Modern Asian Studies* 44, no. 1 (2010): 29–51.

One Hundred Years of Servitude: Political Economy of Tea Plantations in Colonial Assam. Delhi: Tulika Books, 2014.

Bell, Duncan. *Reordering Empire: Essays on Liberalism and Empire*. Princeton, NJ: Princeton University Press, 2019.

Benton, Lauren. "Colonial Law and Cultural Difference: Jurisdictional Politics and the Formation of the Colonial State." *Comparative Studies in Society and History* 41, no. 3 (1999): 563–88.

A Search for Sovereignty: Law and Geography in European Empires. Cambridge: Cambridge University Press, 2010.

Benton, Lauren, and Richard J. Ross, eds. *Legal Pluralism and Empires, 1500–1850*. New York: New York University Press, 2013.

Bischof, Christopher. "Chinese Labourers, Free Blacks, and Social Engineering in the Post-Emancipation British West Indies." *Past & Present* 231, no. 1 (May 2016): 129–68.

Blair, Sandra. "The Felonry and the Free? Divisions in Colonial Society in the Penal Era." *Labour History* 45 (November 1983): 1–16.

Boehme, Kate, Peter Mitchell, and Alan Lester. "Reforming Everywhere and All at Once: Transitioning to Free Labor Across the British Empire." *Comparative Studies in Society and History* 60, no. 3 (2018): 688–718.

Bolland, O. Nigel. "Systems of Domination after Slavery: The Control of Land and Labor in the British West Indies after 1838." *Comparative Studies in Society and History* 23, no. 4 (October 1981): 591–619.

Briggs, Chris. "The Availability of Credit in the English Countryside, 1400–1480." *Agricultural History Review* 56, no. 1 (2008): 1–24.

Brown, David, and Miles Taylor, eds., *The Victorian Empire and Britain's Maritime World, 1837–1901*. London: Palgrave Macmillan, 2013.

Brown, Vincent. "Social Death and Political Life in the Study of Slavery." *American Historical Review* 114, no. 5 (2009): 1231–49.

Browne, Randy. *Surviving Slavery in the British Caribbean*. Philadelphia: University of Pennsylvania Press, 2017.

Burnard, Trevor. *Hearing Slaves Speak*. Georgetown: Caribbean Press, 2010.

"A Voice for Slaves: The Office of the Fiscal in Berbice and the Beginning of Protection in the British Empire, 1819–1834." *Pacific Historical Review* 87, no. 1 (2018): 30–54.

Burnard, Trevor, and Kit Candlin. "Sir John Gladstone and the Debate over the Amelioration of Slavery in the British West Indies in the 1820s." *Journal of British Studies* 57 (October 2018): 760–82.

Burton, Antoinette. *The Trouble with Empire: Challenges to Modern British Imperialism*. Oxford: Oxford University Press, 2015.

Bush-Slimani, Barbara. "Hard Labour: Women, Childbirth and Resistance in British Slave Caribbean Societies." *History Workshop Journal* 36 (Autumn 1983): 83–99.

Cain, P. J., and A. G. Hopkins. "Gentlemanly Capitalism and British Expansion Overseas I: The Old Colonial System, 1688–1850." *Economic History Review*, 2nd ser. 39, no. 4 (1986): 501–25.

"Gentlemanly Capitalism and British Expansion Overseas II: New Imperialism, 1850–1945." *Economic History Review* 40, no. 1 (February 1987): 1–26.

Campbell, Persia Crawford. *Chinese Coolie Emigration to Countries within the British Empire*. London: King & Sons, 1923.

Carter, Henderson. *Labour Pains: Resistance and Protest in Barbados, 1838–1904*. Kingston: Ian Randle, 2012.

Carter, Marina. *Lakshmi's Legacy: The Testimonies of Indian Women in 19th Century Mauritius*. Stanley, Rose Hill, Mauritius: Editions de l'Ocean Indien, distributed by African Books Collective, Oxford, 1994.

Servants, Sirdars, and Settlers: Indians in Mauritius, 1834–1874. Delhi: Oxford University Press, 1995.

Voices from Indenture: Experiences of Indian Migrants in the British Empire. London: Leicester University Press, 1996.

Chambliss, William. "A Sociological Analysis of the Law of Vagrancy." *Social Problems* 12 (1960): 67–77.

Checkland, S. G. "John Gladstone as Trader and Planter." *Economic History Review* 7, no. 2 (1954): 219–29.

Chakrabarty, Dipesh. *Provincializing Europe: Postcolonial Thoughts and Historical Difference*. Princeton, NJ: Princeton University Press, 2000.

Chanderbali, David. *Indian Indenture in British Malaya: Policy and Practice in the Straits Settlements*. Leeds: Peepal Tree, 2008.

Chen, An. "Secret Societies and Organized Crime in Contemporary China." *Modern Asian Studies* 39, no. 1 (2005): 77–107.

Chick-Hwang, Yen. "Early Chinese Clan Organisations in Singapore and Malaya, 1819–1911." *Journal of Southeast Asian Studies* 12, no. 1 (March 1981): 62–92.

Cohen, Stanley. *Folk Devils and Moral Panics*. [1972]; repr. Abingdon: Routledge, 2002.

Colley, Linda. *Britons: Forging the Nation, 1707–1837*. New Haven, CT: Yale University Press, 1992.

Comber, Leon. "Chinese Secret Societies in Malaya: An Introduction." *Journal of the Malayan Branch of the Royal Asiatic Society* 29, no. 1 (May 1956): 146–62.

Condos, Mark, and Reeju Ray, eds., *The Malevolent Engine of Empire: Colonial Violence Across Temporal, Spatial, and Trans-imperial Boundaries* (London: Routledge, forthcoming winter 2025).

Connolly, Jonathan. "Indentured Labour Migration and the Meaning of Emancipation: Free Trade, Race, and Labour in British Public Debate, 1838–1860." *Past & Present* 238, no. 1 (February 2018): 85–119.

"Indenture as Compensation: State Financing for Indentured Labor Migration in the Era of Emancipation." *Slavery & Abolition* 40, no. 3 (2019): 448–71.

Cooper, Frederick, and Ann Laura Stoler, eds. *Tensions of Empire: Colonial Cultures in a Bourgeois World*. Berkeley: University of California Press, 1997.

Cowling, Camillia. *Conceiving Freedom: Women of Color, Gender, and the Abolition of Slavery in Havana and Rio de Janeiro*. Chapel Hill: University of North Carolina Press, 2013.

Cumper, G. E. "Labour Demand and Supply in the Jamaican Sugar Industry, 1830–1950." *Social and Economic Studies* 2, no. 4 (1954): 37–86.

Cumpston, I. M. *Indians Overseas in British Territories, 1834–1854*. Oxford: Oxford University Press, 1953.

Cundall, Frank. "Richard Hill." *Journal of Negro History* 5, no. 1 (January 1920): 37–44.

Da Costa, Emilia Viotti. *Crowns of Glory, Tears of Blood: The Demerara Slave Rebellion of 1823*. Oxford: Oxford University Press, 1997.

Das, Santanu, ed. *Race, Empire and the First World War*. Cambridge: Cambridge University Press, 2011.

Davis, Natalie Zemon. *Fiction in the Archives: Pardon Tales and Their Tellers in Sixteenth-Century France*. Stanford, CA: Stanford University Press, 1987.

De Barros, Juanita. *Order and Place in a Colonial City: Patterns of Struggle and Resistance in Georgetown, British Guiana, 1889–1924*. Montreal: McGill-Queen's University Press, 2002.

"Sanitation and Civilization in Georgetown, British Guiana," *Caribbean Quarterly* 49, no. 4 (December 2003): 65–86.

"The Death of Molly Shultz: Race, Magic, and the Law in the Post-Slavery Caribbean." *Journal of Social History* 55, no. 2 (2021): 345–73.

DeBernardi, Jean Elizabeth. *Rites of Belonging: Memory, Modernity, and Identity in a Malaysian Chinese Community*. Pasadena, CA: Stanford University Press, 2004.

De la Fuente, Alejandro, and Ariela J. Gross. *Becoming Free, Becoming Black: Race, Freedom, and Law in Cuba, Virginia, and Louisiana*. Cambridge: Cambridge University Press, 2020.

De V. Phillips [De Vere Phillips], Anthony. "Emancipation Betrayed? Social Control Legislation in the British Caribbean (with Special Reference to Barbados), 1834–1876." *Chicago-Kent Law Review* 70 (1995): 1349–72.

Dodge, Nicholas N. "Mineral Production on the East Coast of Malaya in the Nineteenth Century." *Journal of the Malaysian Branch of the Royal Asiatic Society* 50, no. 2 (1977): 89–110.

Dooling, Wayne. "Slavery and Amelioration in the Graaff-Reinet District, 1823–1830." *South African Historical Journal* 27, no. 1 (1992): 75–94.

Slavery, Emancipation and Colonial Rule in South Africa. Athens: Ohio University Press, 2007.

Dorsett, Shaunnagh, and Ian Hunter, eds. *Law and Politics in British Colonial Thought*. New York: Palgrave Macmillan, 2010.

Doyle, Mark. *Communal Violence in the British Empire: Disturbing the Pax*. London: Bloomsbury Academic Press, 2016.

Draper, Nicholas. "Rise of a New Planter Class? Some Countercurrents from British Guiana and Trinidad, 1807–33." *Atlantic Studies: Literary, Cultural and Historical Perspectives* 9, no. 1 (2012): 65–83.

Drescher, Seymour. *Econocide: British Slavery in the Ear of Abolition*. [1977]; repr. ed. London and Chapel Hill: University of North Carolina Press.

"Eric Williams: British Capitalism and British Slavery." *History and Theory*, 26, no. 2 (1987): 180–196.

The Mighty Experiment: Free Labor versus Slavery in British Emancipation. Oxford: Oxford University Press, 2004.

"The Shocking Birth of British Abolitionism." *Slavery & Abolition* 33, no. 4 (2012): 571–593.

Echeverri, Marcela. "'Enraged to the Limit of Despair': Infanticide and Slave Judicial Strategies in Barbacoas." *Slavery and Abolition* 30, no. 3 (2009): 403–26.

Elkins, Caroline. *Legacy of Violence: A History of the British Empire*. London: Bodley Head, 2022.

Eltis, David, Stanley L. Engerman, Seymour Drescher, and David Richardson, eds. *The Cambridge World History of Slavery*. Cambridge: Cambridge University Press, 2017.

Emerson, Rupert. *Malaysia: A Study in Direct and Indirect Rule*. Kuala Lumpur: University of Malaya Press, 1964.

Emmer, Pieter. "Scholarship or Solidarity? The Post-Emancipation Era in the Caribbean Reconsidered." *New West Indian Guide/ Nieuwe West-Indische Gids* 69, no. 3/4 (1995): 277–90.

Emsley, Clive. "Policing the Empire, Policing the Metropole: Some Thoughts on Models and Types." *Crime, Histoire & Sociétés/Crime, History & Societies* 18, no. 2 (2014): 5–25.

Epstein, James. "Politics of Colonial Sensation: The Trial of Thomas Picton and the Cause of Louisa Calderon." *American Historical Review* 112, no. 3 (June 2007): 712–41.

Faruqee, Ashrafi. "Conceiving the Coolie Woman: Indentured Labour, Indian Women and Colonial Discourse." *South Asia Research* 16, no. 1 (Spring 1996): 61–76.

Fergus, Claudius. "The *Siete Partidas*: A Framework for Philanthropy and Coercion during the Amelioration Experiment in Trinidad." *Caribbean Studies* 36, no. 1 (January–June 2008): 75–99.

Fisher, Michael. *Indirect Rule in India: Residents and the Residency System 1764–1858*. Delhi: Oxford University Press, 1991.

Foucault, Michel. *The Will to Knowledge: The History of Sexuality Volume 1*. [1976]; trans. R. Hurley. London: Penguin, 2008.

Frederickson, Mary E., and Delores M. Walters. *Gendered Resistance: Women, Slavery, and the Legacy of Margaret Garner*. Urbana: University of Illinois Press, 2017.

Fuentes, Marisa J. *Dispossessed Lives: Enslaved Women, Violence, and the Archive*. Philadelphia: University of Pennsylvania Press, 2016.

Fynn-Paul, Jeff, and Damian Alan Pargas, eds. *Slaving Zones: Cultural Identities, Ideologies, and Institutions in the Evolution of Global Slavery*. Leiden: Brill, 2018.

Galenson, David W. "British Servants and the Colonial Indenture System in the Eighteenth Century." *Journal of Southern History* 44, no. 1 (1978): 41–66.

"White Servitude and the Growth of Black Slavery in Colonial America." *Journal of Economic History* 41, no. 1 (1981): 39–47.

"The Rise and Fall of Indentured Servitude in the Americas: An Economic Analysis." *Journal of Economic History* 44, no. 1 (1984): 1–26.

Gallagher, John, and Ronald Robinson. "The Imperialism of Free Trade." *Economic History Review* 6, no. 1 (1953): 1–15.

Gallagher, John, Gordon Johnson, and Anil Seal, eds. *Locality, Province, and Nation: Essays on Indian Politics, 1870 to 1940*. Cambridge: Cambridge University Press, 1973.

Gash, N. "After Waterloo: British Society and the Legacy of the Napoleonic Wars." *Transactions of the Royal Historical Society* 28 (1978): 145–57.

Gaspar, David Barry. "Working the System: Antigua Slaves and Their Struggle to Live." *Slavery & Abolition* 13, no. 3 (1992): 131–5.

Gehrke, Jules P. "A Radical Endeavor: Joseph Chamberlain and the Emergence of Municipal Socialism in Birmingham." *American Journal of Economics and Sociology* 75, no. 1 (2016): 23–57.

Gillion, Kenneth Lowell. *Fiji's Indian Migrants: A History to the End of Indenture in 1920*. Melbourne: Oxford University Press, 1962.

Gocking, C. V. "Early Constitutional History of Jamaica: (With Special Reference to the Period 1838–1866)." *Caribbean Quarterly* 6, no. 2/3 (1960): 114–33.

Grant, Kevin. *A Civilised Savagery: Britain and the New Slaveries in Africa, 1884–1926*. New York: Routledge, 2005.

Graubart, Karen B. "*Pesa Más La Libertad*: Slavery, Legal Claims, and the History of Afro-Latin American Ideas." *William and Mary Quarterly* 78, no. 3 (2021): 427–58.

Green, William A. *British Slave Emancipation: The Sugar Colonies and the Great Experiment, 1830–1865*. Oxford: Clarendon Press, 1976.

"Emancipation to Indenture: A Question of Imperial Morality." *Journal of British Studies* 22, no. 2 (1983): 98–121.

Gross, Izhak. "Parliament and the Abolition of Negro Apprenticeship." *English Historical Review* 96, no. 3080 (July 1981): 560–76.

Guha, Ranajit, and Gayatri Chakravorty Spivak, eds. *Selected Subaltern Studies*. Oxford: Oxford University Press, 1988.

Guha, Ranajit, ed. *A Subaltern Studies Reader, 1986–1995*. Minneapolis, MN: University of Minneapolis Press, 1997.

Gullick, John. "The Economy of Perak in the Mid-1870s." *Journal of the Malaysian Branch of the Royal Asiatic Society* 83, no. 2 (December 2010): 27–46.

Hall, Catherine. *Civilising Subjects: Metropole and Colony in the English Imagination 1830–1867*. Chicago, IL: University of Chicago Press, 2002.

Hall, Catherine, Keith McClelland, and Jane Rendall. *Defining the Victorian Nation: Class, Race, Gender and the Reform Act of 1867*. Cambridge: Cambridge University Press, 2000.

Hall, Catherine, Nicholas Draper, Keith McClellan, Katie Donington, and Rachel Lang. *Legacies of British Slave-Ownership: Colonial Slavery and the Formation of Victorian Britain*. Cambridge: Cambridge University Press, 2014.

Hall, Douglas. "Flight from the Estates Reconsidered: The British West Indies, 1838–42." *Journal of Caribbean History* 10 (January 1978): 16–23.

Hall, Stuart, Chas Critcher, Tony Jefferson, John Clarke, and Brian Roberts. *Policing the Crisis: Mugging, the State, and Law and Order*. [1978]; repr. London: Macmillan, 1984.

Halpern, Rick. "Solving the 'Labour Problem': Race, Work and the State in the Sugar Industries of Louisiana and Natal, 1870–1910." *Journal of Southern African Studies* 30, no. 1 (March 2004): 19–40.

Harries, Patrick. "Plantations, Passes and Proletarians: Labour and the Colonial State in Nineteenth-Century Natal." *Journal of Southern African Studies* 13, no. 3 (April 1987): 372–99.

Harvey, Mark. "Slavery, Indenture and the Development of British Industrial Capitalism." *History Workshop Journal* 88 (Autumn 2019): 66–88.

Hassankhan, Maurits S., Brij. V. Lal, and Doug Munro. *Resistance and Indian Indenture Experience*. New Delhi: Manohar, 2014.

Hay, Douglas. "Patronage, Paternalism, and Welfare: Masters, Workers, and Magistrates in Eighteenth-Century England." *International Labor and Working-Class History* 53, no. 1 (Spring 1998): 27–47.

Hay, Douglas, and Paul Craven, eds. *Masters, Servants, and Magistrates in Britain and the Empire, 1562–1955*. Chapel Hill: University of North Carolina Press, 2004.

Heidemann, Frank. *Kanganies in Sri Lanka and Malaysia: Tamil Recruiter-cum-Foreman as a Sociological Category in the Nineteenth and Twentieth Century*. Munich: Anacon, 1992.

Heuman, Gad, and David Vincent Trotman, eds., *Contesting Freedom: Control and Resistance in the Post-Emancipation Caribbean*. Oxford: Macmillan Caribbean, 2005.

Higman, B. W. *Slave Populations of the British Caribbean, 1807–1834*. Kingston: University of the West Indies Press, 1984.

Hoefte, Rosemarijn. "A Passage to Suriname? The Migration of Modes of Resistance by Asian Contract Laborers." *International Labor and Working-Class History*, 54 (1998): 19–39.

Holt, Thomas. *The Problem of Freedom: Race, Labor, and Politics in Jamaica and Britain, 1832–1938*. Baltimore, MD: Johns Hopkins University Press, 1992.

Hooker, M. B. "The East India Company and the Crown, 1773–1858." *Malaya Law Review* 11, no. 1 (1969): 1–37.

Hopkins, Benjamin D. *Ruling the Savage Periphery: Frontier Governance and the Making of the Modern State*. Cambridge, MA: Harvard University Press, 2020.

Hossain, Purba. "'A Matter of Doubt and Uncertainty': John Gladstone and Post-Slavery Labour in the British Empire." *Journal of Imperial and Commonwealth History* 50, no. 1 (2022): 52–80.

Hsuan-Chih, Tai, and Ronald Suleski. "Origin of the Heaven and Earth Society." *Modern Asian Studies* 11, no. 3 (1977): 405–25.

Huzzey, Richard. *Freedom Burning: Anti-Slavery and Empire in Victorian Britain*. Ithaca, NY: Cornell University Press, 2012.

Huzzey, Richard, and Henry Miller. "Colonial Petitions, Colonial Petitioners, and the Imperial Parliament, ca. 1780–1918." *Journal of British Studies* 61 (April 2022): 261–89.

Hyslop, Jonathan. "The Imperial Working Class Makes Itself 'White': White Labourism in Britain, Australia, and South Africa before the First World War." *Historical Sociology* 12, no. 4 (December 1999): 398–421.

Jackson, R. N. *Immigrant Labour and the Development of Malaya, 1786–1920*. Singapore: Government Press, 1961.

"Grasping the Nettle: First Successes in the Struggle to Govern the Chinese in Malaya." *Journal of the Malaysian Branch of the Royal Asiatic Society (JMBRAS)* 40, no. 1 (211) (July 1967): 130–9.

Pickering, Protector of Chinese. Kuala Lumpur: Oxford University Press, 1965.

James, C. L. R. *Beyond a Boundary*. [1963]; repr. Durham, NC: Duke University Press, 2013.

Jagan, Cheddi. *Forbidden Freedom: The Story of British Guiana*. [1954]; repr. Georgetown: Hansib, 1994.

John, A. Meredith. *The Plantation Slaves of Trinidad: A Mathematical and Demographic Inquiry*. Cambridge: Cambridge University Press, 1988.

Jones, Wilbur Devereux. "Lord Mulgrave's Administration in Jamaica, 1832–1833." *Journal of Negro History* 48 (1963): 44–56.

Josiah, Barbara P. "After Emancipation: Aspects of Village Life in Guyana, 1869–1911." *Journal of Negro History* 82, no. 1 (Winter 1997): 105–21.

Joyce, Patrick. *The Rule of Freedom: Liberalism and the Modern City*. London: Verso, 2003.

The State of Freedom: A Social History of the British State since 1800. Cambridge: Cambridge University Press, 2013.

Kai, Rajesh. "The 1857 Panic and the Fabrication of an Indian 'Menace' in Singapore." *Modern Asian Studies* 47, no. 2 (2013): 365–405.

Kale, Madhavi. *Fragments of Empire: Capital, Slavery, and Indian Indentured Labor in the British Caribbean*. Philadelphia, PA: University of Philadelphia Press, 1998.

Kerr, Ian. "Labour Control and Labour Legislation in Colonial India: A Tale of Two Mid-Nineteenth Century Acts." *South Asia: Journal of South Asian Studies* 27, no. 1 (2004): 7–25.

Kim, Diana S. *Empires of Vice: The Rise of Opium Prohibition Across Southeast Asia*. Princeton, NJ: Princeton University Press, 2020.

Kim, Khoo Kay. "The Origin of British Administration in Malaya." *Journal of the Malaysian Branch of the Royal Asiatic Society*, 39, no. 1 (1966): 52–91.

Knox, Bruce. "The Queen's Letter of 1865 and British Policy towards Emancipation and Indentured Labour in the West Indies, 1830–65." *Historical Journal* 29, no. 2 (June 1986): 345–67.

Koditshek, Theodore. *Liberalism, Imperialism and the Historical Imagination*. Cambridge: Cambridge University Press, 2011.

Kolsky, Elizabeth. "Codification and the Rule of Colonial Difference: Criminal Procedure in British India." *Law and History Review* 23, no. 3 (Fall 2005): 631–83.

"The Colonial Rule of Law and the Legal Regime of Exception: Frontier 'Fanaticism' and State Violence in British India." *American Historical Review* 120, no. 4 (October 2015): 1218–46.

Kondapi, C. *Indians Overseas, 1838–1949*. New Delhi: Indian Council of World Affairs, 1951.

Kumar, Ashutosh. *Coolies of the Empire: Indentured Indians in the Sugar Colonies, 1830–1920*. Cambridge: Cambridge University Press, 2017.

Laidlaw, Zoë. "'Justice to India – Prosperity to England – Freedom to the Slave!' Humanitarian and Moral Reform Campaigns on India, Aborigines and American Slavery." *Journal of the Royal Asiatic Society* 22, no. 2 (April 2012): 299–324.

Protecting the Empire's Humanity: Thomas Hodgkin and British Colonial Activism 1830–1870. Cambridge: Cambridge University Press, 2021.

Lake, Marilyn, and Henry Reynolds. *Drawing the Global Colour Line: White Men's Countries and the International Challenge of Racial Equality*. Cambridge: Cambridge University Press, 2008.

Lal, Brij V. "Kunti's Cry: Indentured Women on Fiji Plantations." *Indian Economic and Social History Review* 22, no. 1 (1985): 55–71.

"Understanding the Indian Indenture Experience." *South Asia: Journal of South Asian Studies* 21, no. 1 (1998): 215–37.

Lambert, David. "'[A] Mere Cloak for Their Proud Contempt and Antipathy towards the African Race': Imagining Britain's West India Regiments in the Caribbean, 1795–1838." *Journal of Imperial and Commonwealth History* 46, no. 4 (2018): 627–50.

Soldiers of Uncertain Rank: The West India Regiments in British Imperial Culture. Cambridge: Cambridge University Press, 2024.

Lambert, David, and Alan Lester, eds. *Colonial Lives Across the British Empire: Imperial Careering in the Long Nineteenth Century*. Cambridge: Cambridge University Press, 2006.

Lange, Matthew. "Embedding the Colonial State: A Comparative-Historical Analysis of State Building and Broad-Based Development in Mauritius." *Social Science History* 27, no. 3 (Fall 2003): 397–423.

Lau-Fung, Mak. "The Kongsi and the Triad." *Southeast Asian Journal of Social Science* 3, no. 2 (1975): 47–58.

Laurence, K. O. *A Question of Labour: Indentured Immigration into Trinidad and British Guiana, 1875–1917*. London: James Currey, 1994.

Lazarus-Black, Mindie. *Legitimate Acts and Illegal Encounters: Law and Society in Antigua and Barbuda*. Washington, DC: Smithsonian Institution Press, 1994.

Lean, John H., and Trevor Burnard. "Hearing Slave Voices: The Fiscal's Reports of Berbice and Demerara-Essequebo." *Journal of the British Records Association* 27, no. 107 (2002): 120–33.

Lee, Jack Jin Gary. "Plural Society and the Colonial State: English Law and the Making of Crown Colony Government in the Straits Settlements." *Asian Journal of Law and Society* 2 (2015): 229–49.

Lee, Maureen Elgersman. *Unyielding Spirits: Black Women and Slavery in Early Canada and Jamaica*. New York: Garland, 1999.

Lee, R. W. "Romano-Dutch Law in British Guiana." *Journal of the Society of Comparative Legislation* 14, no. 1 (1914): 11–23.

Lees, Lynn Hollen. *Planting Empire, Cultivating Subjects: British Malaya 1786–1941*. Cambridge: Cambridge University Press, 2017.

Legge, John. "The Colonial Office and Governor Ord." *Journal of Southeast Asian Studies* 29, no. 1 (March 1998): 1–7.

Lemke, Thomas, Monica J. Casper, and Lisa Moore, *Biopolitics: An Advanced Introduction*. New York: New York University Press, 2011.

Leong, Nancy. "Racial Capitalism." *Harvard Law Review* 126, no. 8 (June 2013): 2151–226.

Lester, Alan, and Fae Dussart. *Colonization and the Origins of Humanitarian Governance: Protecting Aborigines Across the Nineteenth-Century British Empire*. Cambridge: Cambridge University Press, 2014.

Lester, Alan, Kate Boehme, and Peter Mitchell. *Ruling the World: Freedom, Civilisation and Liberalism in the Nineteenth-Century British Empire*. Cambridge: Cambridge University Press, 2021.

Levine, Philippa, and Susan R. Grayzel, eds. *Gender, Labour, War and Empire*. London: Palgrave Macmillan, 2009.

Lewis, Catherine, and J. Hilary Beckles. *Centering Women: Gender Discourses in Caribbean Slave Society*. Princeton, NJ: M. Wiener, 1999.

Lightfoot, Natasha. *Troubling Freedom: Antigua and the Aftermath of British Emancipation*. Durham, NC: Duke University Press, 2015.

Look Lai, Walton. *Indenture Labor, Caribbean Sugar: Chinese and Indian Migrants to the British West Indies, 1838–1918*. Baltimore, MD: Johns Hopkins University Press, 1993.

Luster, Robert. *The Amelioration of the Slaves in the British Empire, 1790–1833*. New York: Peter Lang, 1995.

Lydon, Jane. "A Secret Longing for a Trade in Human Flesh: The Decline of British Slavery and the Making of the Settler Colonies." *History Workshop Journal* 90 (Autumn 2020): 189–210.

Mahase, Radica. "'Plenty a Dem Run Away': Resistance by Indian Indentured Labourers in Trinidad, 1870–1920." *Labor History* 49, no. 4 (2008): 465–80.

Mahmud, Tayyab. "Cheaper Than a Slave: Indentured Labor, Colonialism and Capitalism." *Whittier Law Review* 34 (2012): 215–43.

Major, Andrea. "'The Slavery of East and West': Abolitionists and 'Unfree' Labour in India, 1820–1833." *Slavery and Abolition*, 31, no. 4 (2010): 501–25.

Slavery, Abolitionism and Empire in India, 1772–1843. Liverpool: Liverpool University Press, 2012.

"'Hill Coolies': Indian Indentured Labour and the Colonial Imagination, 1836–38." *South Asian Studies* 33, no. 1 (2017): 23–36.

Malone, Betty. "Clarke, Sir Andrew (1824–1902)." *Australian Dictionary of Biography, Vol. 3*, 409–11. Manchester: Manchester University Press, 1969.

"The Hincks-Beaumont Imbroglio: Partisan Politics in British Guiana in the 1860s." *Boletín de Estudios Latinoamericanos y del Caribe* 43 (December 1987): 99–114.

Mangru, Basdeo. "Indian Government Policy towards Labor Recruitment for the Sugar Colonies, 1838–1883." *Journal of Third World Studies* 9, no. 1 (Spring 1992): 118–38.

"Indian Militancy on Sugar Estates: The 1869 Leonora Episode." *Guyana Journal* (October 2007): n.p.

Manning, Helen Taft. "Who Ran the British Empire, 1830–1850?" *Journal of British Studies* 5, no. 1 (1965): 88–121.

Mantena, Karuna. *Alibis of Empire: Henry Maine and the Ends of Liberal Imperialism*. Princeton, NJ: Princeton University Press, 2010.

Marshall, Woodville K. "Notes on Peasant Development in the West Indies Since 1838." *Social and Economic Studies* 17, no. 3 (1968): 252–63.

Mason, John Edwin. "Slaves and Their Protectors: Reforming Resistance in a Slave Society, the Cape Colony, 1826–1834." *Journal of Southern African Studies* 17, no. 1 (March 1991): 103–28.

Social Death and Resurrection: Slavery and Emancipation in South Africa. Charlottesville: University of Virginia Press, 2003.

Massaro, Toni M. "Empathy, Legal Storytelling, and the Rule of Law: New Words, Old Wounds?" *Michigan Law Review* 87, no. 8 (August 1989): 2099–127.

Mbembe, Achille. "Necropolitics." Trans. Libby Meintjes. *Public Culture* 15, no. 1 (2003): 11–40.

McKinley, Michelle A. *Fractional Freedoms: Slavery, Intimacy, and Legal Mobilization in Colonial Lima, 1600–1700*. Cambridge: Cambridge University Press, 2016.

Meh née Lum, Choy Chee. "History of the Malaysian Branch of the Royal Asiatic Society." *Journal of the Malaysian Branch of the Royal Asiatic Society* 68, no. 2 (269) (1995): 81–148.

Melamed, Jodi. "Racial Capitalism." *Critical Ethnic Studies* 1, no. 1 (Spring 2015): 76–85.

Merry, Sally Engle. *Getting Justice, Getting Even: Legal Consciousness Among Working-Class Americans*. Chicago, IL: University of Chicago Press, 1990.

Metcalf, Thomas R. "The Impact of the Mutiny on British Attitudes to India." *Proceedings of the Indian History Congress* 23 (1960): 24–31.

Metcalf, Thomas. "The British and the Moneylender in Nineteenth-Century India." *Journal of Modern History* 34, no. 4 (1962): 390–7.

Mohapatra, Prabhu P. "'Following Custom'? Representations of Community Among Indian Immigrant Labour in the West Indies, 1880–1920." *International Review of Social History* 51, supplement 14 (2006): 173–202.

"Eurocentrism, Forced Labour, and Global Migration: A Critical Assessment." *International Review of Social History* 52, no. 1 (2007): 110–15.

Money, Duncan, and Danelle van Zyl-Hermann. "Revisiting White Labourism: New Debates on Working-Class Whiteness in Twentieth-Century Southern Africa." *International Review of Social History* 66, no. 3 (December 2021): 469–91.

Mongia, Radhika. "Gender and the Historiography of Gandhian *Satyagraha* in South Africa." *Gender and History* 18, no. 1 (April 2006): 130–49.

Indian Migration and Empire: A Colonial Genealogy of the Modern State. Durham, NC: Duke University Press, 2018.

Moree, Perry J. *A Concise History of Dutch Mauritius, 1598–1710: A Fruitful and Healthy Land*. London: Routledge, 1998.

Morgan, Jennifer. *Laboring Women: Reproduction and Gender in New World Slavery*. Philadelphia: University of Pennsylvania Press, 2011.

Murray, Hannah-Rose. *Advocates of Freedom: African-American Transatlantic Abolitionism in the British Isles*. Cambridge: Cambridge University Press, 2020.

Musa, Mahani. "Malays and the Red and White Flag Societies in Penang, 1830s–1920s." *Journal of the Malaysian Branch of the Royal Asiatic Society* 72, no. 2 (1999): 151–82.

Myers, J. C. *Indirect Rule in South Africa: Tradition, Modernity, and the Costuming of Political Power*. Rochester, NY: University of Rochester Press, 2009.

Nelson, Cary, and Lawrence Grossberg, eds. *Marxism and the Interpretation of Culture*. London: Macmillan, 1988.

Nettlebeck, Amanda. *Indigenous Rights and Colonial Subjecthood: Protection and Reform in the Nineteenth-Century British Empire*. Cambridge: Cambridge University Press, 2021.

Ngai, Mae. *The Chinese Question: The Gold Rushes, Chinese Migration, and Global Politics*. New York: Norton, 2021.

Northrup, David. *Indentured Labor in the Age of Imperialism, 1834–1922*. Cambridge: Cambridge University Press, 1995.

Nwulia, Moses D. E. "The 'Apprenticeship' System in Mauritius: Its Character and Its Impact on Race Relations in the Immediate Post-Emancipation Period, 1839–1879." *African Studies Review* 21, no. 1 (1978): 89–101.

Ortner, Sherry. "Resistance and the Problem of Ethnographic Refusal." *Comparative Studies in Society and History* 37, no. 1 (January 1995): 173–93.

Ostinidië, G. ed. *Fifty Years Later: Antislavery, Capitalism, and Modernity in the Dutch Orbit*. Pittsburgh, PA: University of Pittsburgh Press, 1996.

Owensby, Brian P. "How Juan and Leonor Won Their Freedom: Litigation and Liberty in Seventeenth-Century Mexico." *Hispanic American Historical Review* 85, no. 1 (February 2005): 39–79.

Ownby, David. "The Heaven and Earth Society as Popular Religion." *Journal of Asian Studies* 54, no. 4 (1995): 1023–46.

Palmer, Bryan D. "Nineteenth-Century Canada and Australia: The Paradoxes of Class Formation." *Labour/Le Travail* 84 (Fall 1996): 16–36.

Pande, Amba, ed. *Indentured and Post-Indentured Experiences of Women in the Indian Diaspora*. Berlin: Springer, 2020.

Parmer, J. Norman. "The British Legacy." *Wilson Quarterly* 11, no. 5 (1987): 54–69.

Paton, Diana. "Punishment, Crime, and the Bodies of Slaves in Eighteenth-Century Jamaica." *Journal of Social History* 34, no. 4 (Summer 2001): 923–54.

No Bond but the Law: Punishment, Race, and Gender in Jamaican State Formation, 1780–1870. Durham, NC: Duke University Press, 2004.

Peng, Wang Tai. "The Word 'Kongsi': A Note." *Journal of the Malaysian Branch of the Royal Asiatic Society* 52, no. 1 (1975): 102–5.

Penson, L. M. "The Making of a Crown Colony: British Guiana, 1803–33." *Transactions of the Royal Historical Society*, 4th series, 9 (1926): 107–34.

Petley, Christer. "Slaveholders and Revolution: The Jamaican Planter Class, British Imperial Politics, and the Ending of the Slave Trade, 1775–1807." *Slavery & Abolition* 39, no. 1 (2017): 53–79.

Pitts, Jennifer. *A Turn to Empire: The Rise of Imperial Liberalism in Britain and France*. Princeton, NJ: Princeton University Press, 2006.

Prakash, Gayan. *Bonded Histories: Genealogies of Labor Servitude in Colonial India*. Cambridge: Cambridge University Press, 1990.

Price, Richard. *Making Empire: Colonial Encounters and the Creation of Imperial Rule in Nineteenth-Century Africa*. Cambridge: Cambridge University Press, 2008.

Priya, Vishnu. "Ethnicity and Politics: East Indians in the Political Process of Guyana and Trinidad." *India Quarterly* (November 2004): 100–41.

Raha, Bipasha. "Moneylenders and Peasants: Credit Relations in Rural Bengal, 1793–1885." *Proceedings of the Indian History Congress* 68 (2007): 640–7.

Ray, Karen A. "Lakshmobai and the 'Ladies': Women's Labour and the Abolition of Indentured Immigration from India." *Labour, Capital and Society/Travail, capital et société* 29, no. 1/2 (April/November 1996): 126–52.

Riviere, W. Manuel. "Labour Shortage in the British West Indies after Emancipation." *Journal of Caribbean History* 4, no. 1 (May, 1972): 1–30.

Rivington, Kate. "The London Emancipation Society and Transatlantic Abolitionism in the Civil War Era, 1859–1865." *Slavery & Abolition* 43, no. 4 (2022): 798–818.

Roberts, Christopher M. "From the State of Emergency to the Rule of Law: The Evolution of Repressive Legality in the Nineteenth-Century British Empire." *Chicago Journal of International Law* 20, no. 1 (January 2019): 1–61.

Rodney, Walter. *A History of the Guyanese Working People, 1881–1905*. Baltimore, MD: Johns Hopkins University Press, 1981.

Rogers, Nicholas. "Policing the Poor in Eighteenth-Century London: The Vagrancy Laws and Their Administration." *Histoire sociale/Social History* 34, no. 47 (May 1991): 127–47.

Saha, Jonathan. *Law, Disorder and the Colonial State: Corruption in Burma c. 1900*. New York: Palgrave Macmillan, 2013.

"Racial Capitalism and Peasant Insurgency in Colonial Myanmar." *History Workshop Journal* 94 (Autumn 2022): 42–60.

Said, Edward. *Orientalism*. New York: Routledge and Kegan & Paul, 1978.

Sain, Pravina Bhim. "A Study of the Problems Faced by Indian Indentured Labour in Mauritius Due to Violation of Contract, 1834–1878." *Proceedings of the Indian History Congress* 41 (1980): 813–22.

Sandhu, Kernial Singh. *Indians in Malaya: Immigration and Settlement, 1786–1957*. Cambridge: Cambridge University Press, 1969.

Sartori, Andrew. *Liberalism in Empire: An Alternative History*. Berkeley: University of California Press, 2014.

Saw, Swee Hock. *The Population of Peninsular Malaysia*. Singapore: National University of Singapore Press, 1988.

Scott, James C. *Domination and the Arts of Resistance: Hidden Transcripts*. New Haven, CT: Yale University Press, 1990.

Scully, Pamela. *Liberating the Family: Gender and British Slave Emancipation in the Rural Western Cape, South Africa, 1823–1853*. Portsmouth, NH: Heinemann, 1997.

Seeley, John Robert. *The Expansion of England*. [1883]; repr. Cambridge: Cambridge University Press, 2010.

Sen, Sunanda. "Indentured Labour from India in the Age of Empire." *Social Scientist* 44, no. 1/2 (January–February 2016): 35–74.

Shaoqing, Cai. "An Overview of the Secret Societies in China during the Late Qing Period." *Cina* 21 (1988): 39–47.

Shephard, C. Y. "The Sugar Industry of the British West Indies and British Guiana with Special Reference to Trinidad." *Economic Geography* 5, no. 2 (April 1929): 149–75.

Shepherd, Verene A. *Maharani's Misery: Narratives of Passage from India to the Caribbean*. Barbados: University of the West Indies Press, 2002.

Simpson, Thomas. *The Frontier in British India: Space, Science, and Power in the Nineteenth Century*. Cambridge: Cambridge University Press, 2021.

Singha, Radhika. "The Short Career of the Indian Labour Corps in France, 1917–1919." *International Labor and Working-Class History* 87 (Spring 2015): 27–62.

Siok-Hwa, Cheng. "Government Legislation for Chinese Secret Societies in the Straits Settlements in the Late 19th Century." *Asian Studies* 10, no. 2 (1972): 262–71.

Sires, Ronald V. "Constitutional Change in Jamaica, 1834–60." *Journal of Comparative Legislation and International Law* 22, no. 4 (1940): 178–90.

Skinner, G. W. *Chinese Society in Thailand: An Analytical History*. Ithaca, NY: Cornell University Press, 1957.

Smith, Kevin D. "A Fragmented Freedom: The Historiography of Emancipation and Its Aftermath in the British West Indies." *Slavery & Abolition* 16, no. 1 (1995): 101–30.

Stanziani, Alessandro. *Labour on the Fringes of Empire: Voice, Exit and the Law*. New York: Palgrave Macmillan, 2018.

Stokes, Eric. *The English Utilitarians and India*. Oxford: Oxford University Press, 1959.

Stoler, Ann Laura. "Colonial Archives and the Arts of Governance." *Archival Science* 2 (2002): 87–109.

Along the Archival Grain: Epistemic Anxieties and Colonial Common Sense. Princeton, NJ: Princeton University Press, 2010.

Swan, M. "1913 Natal Indian Strike." *Journal of Southern African Studies* 10, no. 2 (1984): 239–58.

Tagliacozzo, Eric, and Wen Chin Chang, eds. *Chinese Circulations: Capital, Commodities, and Networks in Southeast Asia*. Durham, NC: Duke University Press, 2011.

Tarling, Nicholas, ed. *The Cambridge History of Southeast Asia, Vol. 3: From c. 1800 to the 1930s*. Cambridge: Cambridge University Press, 1992.

Teelock, Vijaya. *Bitter Sugar: Sugar and Slavery in 19th Century Mauritius*. Moka: Mahatma Gandhi Institute, 1998.

ed. *The Vagrant Depot of Grand River, Its Surroundings and Vagrancy in British Mauritius*. Port Louis: Aapravasi Ghat Trust Fund, 2004.

Mauritian History: From Its Beginnings to Modern Times. Moka: Mahatma Gandhi Institute, 2009.

Tewari, Archana. "Protests by Indians in Trinidad (1845–1917)." *Proceedings of the Indian History Congress* 70 (2009–10): 905–16.

Thomas, Martin. *Violence and Colonial Order: Police, Workers and Protest in the European Colonial Empires, 1918–1940*. Cambridge: Cambridge University Press, 2012.

Thompson, Alvin. *Unprofitable Servants: Crown Slaves in Berbice, Guyana, 1803–1831*. Mona: University of the West Indies Press, 2002.

Thompson, F. M. L., ed. *The Cambridge Social History of Britain 1750–1950, Vol. 3: Social Agencies and Institutions*. Cambridge: Cambridge University Press, 1990.

Tinker, Hugh. *A New System of Slavery: The Export of Indian Labour Overseas, 1830–1920*. London: Oxford University Press, 1974.

Trocki, Carl A. *Opium and Empire: Chinese Society in Colonial Singapore, 1800–1910*. Ithaca, NY: Cornell University Press, 1990.

Trotman, David V. *Crime in Trinidad: Conflict and Control in a Plantation Society, 1838–1900.* Knoxville: University of Tennessee Press, 1986.

Turner, Mary. "The 11 O'Clock Flog: Women, Work, and Labour Law in the British Caribbean." *Slavery & Abolition* 20, no. 1 (1999): 38–58.

Turner, Sasha. *Contested Bodies: Pregnancy, Childrearing, and Slavery in Jamaica.* Philadelphia: University of Pennsylvania Press, 2017.

Twaddle, Michael, ed. *The Wages of Slavery: From Chattel Slavery to Wage Labor in Africa, the Caribbean and England.* London: Routledge, 1993.

Twomey, Christina. "Protecting Slaves and Aborigines: The Legacies of European Colonialism in the British Empire." *Pacific Historical Review* 87, no. 1 (2018): 10-29.

Ulentin, Anne. "'She Has Not Been Seen or Heard of Since': Gender, Incarceration, and Punishment in the Bahamas, 1860s–1920s." *New West Indian Guide* 96 (2022): 233–65.

Vahed, Goolam. "Power and Resistance: Indentured Labour in Colonial Natal, 1860–1911." *Man in India* 92, no. 2 (April 2012): 299–317.

Van Cleve, James. "'*Somerset's Case*' and Its Antecedents in Imperial Perspective." *Law and History Review* 24, no. 3 (Fall 2006): 601–45.

Venezia, Luciano. *Hobbes on Legal Authority and Political Obligation.* London: Palgrave Macmillan, 2015.

Vink, Markus. "'The World's Oldest Trade': Dutch Slavery and the Slave Trade in the Indian Ocean in the Seventeenth Century." *Journal of World History* 14, no. 2 (2003): 131–77.

Wagner, Kim A. "'Treading upon Fires': The 'Mutiny' Motif and Colonial Anxieties in British India." *Past & Present* 218 (February 2013): 159–97.

Walkowitz, Judith R. *City of Dreadful Delight: Narratives of Sexual Danger in Late-Victorian London.* Chicago, IL: University of Chicago Press, 1992.

Walvin, James, ed. *Slavery and British Society.* London: Palgrave Macmillan, 1982.

Ward, J. R. *British West Indian Slavery: The Process of Amelioration.* Oxford: Clarendon Press, 1988.

Wen, Cheng U. "Opium in the Straits Settlements, 1867–1910." *Journal of Southeast Asian History* 2, no. 1 (March 1961): 52–75.

Wenzelhuemer, Roland. "Indian Labour Immigration and British Labour Policy in Nineteenth-Century Ceylon." *Modern Asian Studies* 41, no. 3 (May 2007): 575–602.

Whah, Chin Yee, and Benny Teh Cheng Guan. "Malaysia's Protracted Affirmative Action Policy and the Evolution of the Bumiputera Commercial and Industrial Community." *Sojourn: Journal of Social Issues in Southeast Asia,* 32, no. 2 (July 2017): 336–73.

White, Sophie. *Voices of the Enslaved: Love, Labor and Longing in French Louisiana.* Chapel Hill: University of North Carolina Press, 2019.

Wiener, Martin. *Reconstructing the Criminal: Culture, Law and Policy in England, 1830–1914.* Cambridge: Cambridge University Press, 1990.

An Empire on Trial: Race, Murder, and Justice under British Rule. Cambridge: Cambridge University Press, 2009.
Wiethoff, William E. "The Nature and Limits of Slave Insolence in the American South." *Quarterly Journal of Speech* 87, no. 2 (2001): 197–207.
The Insolent Slave. Columbia: University of South Carolina Press, 2002.
Williams, Eric. *Capitalism and Slavery*. [1944]; repr. ed. London: Penguin, 2022.
"Massa Day Done (Public Lecture at Woodford Square, 22 March 1961)," *Callalloo* 20, no. 4, Eric Williams and the Postcolonial Caribbean: A Special Issue (Autumn 1997): 724–30.
Willis, James. "Transportation versus Imprisonment in Eighteenth- and Nineteenth-Century Britain: Penal Power, Liberty, and the State." *Law & Society Review* 39, no. 1 (2005): 171–210.
Wood, Donald. *Trinidad in Transition: The Years after Slavery*. Oxford: Oxford University Press, 1986,
Wyman-McCarthy, Matthew. "Perceptions of French and Spanish Slave Law in Late Eighteenth-Century Britain." *Journal of British Studies* 57, no. 1 (2018): 29–52.
Yang, Anand A. *The Limited Raj: Agrarian Relations in Colonial India, Saran District, 1793–1920*. Berkeley: University of California Press, 1989.
Yen, Ching Wan. *Ethnic Chinese Business in Asia: History, Culture and Business Enterprise*. London: World Scientific Publishing, 2013.
Yong, C. F. "Origins and Development of the Malayan Communist Movement." *Modern Asian Studies* 25, no. 4 (1991): 625–48.
Yoong, Ng Siew. "The Chinese Protectorate in Singapore, 1877–1900." *Journal of Southeast Asian History* 2, no. 1 (1961): 76–99.

Unpublished Doctoral and Master's Dissertations

Lean, John H. "The Secret Lives of Slaves: Berbice, 1819–1827." Unpublished PhD thesis, University of Canterbury, 2002.
Manton, M. G. "The Rise of the British Managing Societies in North Eastern India 1836–1918." Unpublished MPhil thesis, School of Oriental and African Studies, 2017.
Perry, John Allen. "A History of the East Indian Indentured Plantation Worker in Trinidad, 1845–1917." Unpublished PhD dissertation, Louisiana State University, 1969.
Rajendra, Negandiram. "The Straits Settlements, 1867–1874." Unpublished MA thesis, Australian National University, 1976.
Spence, Caroline Quarrier. "Ameliorating Empire: Slavery and Protection in the British Colonies, 1783–1865." Unpublished PhD dissertation, Harvard University, 2014.

Websites

Anti-Slavery International, www.antislavery.org/slavery-today/modern-slavery.

INDEX

For EU product safety concerns, contact us at Calle de José Abascal, 56–1°,
28003 Madrid, Spain or eugpsr@cambridge.org.

www.ingramcontent.com/pod-product-compliance
Ingram Content Group UK Ltd.
Pitfield, Milton Keynes, MK11 3LW, UK
UKHW021956160325
456344UK00007B/16

* 9 7 8 1 0 0 9 3 1 5 7 9 1 *